HISTORY
OF THE
TOWN OF LEEDS
ANDROSCOGGIN COUNTY MAINE

FROM
ITS SETTLEMENT

JUNE 10, 1780

J. C. Stinchfield, Et Al.
WITH
NEW MATERIAL ADDED BY **David C. Young**

HERITAGE BOOKS
2012

HERITAGE BOOKS
AN IMPRINT OF HERITAGE BOOKS, INC.

Books, CDs, and more—Worldwide

For our listing of thousands of titles see our website
at
www.HeritageBooks.com

A Facsimile Reprint
Published 2012 by
HERITAGE BOOKS, INC.
Publishing Division
100 Railroad Ave. #104
Westminster, Maryland 21157

Originally published c.1901

Copyright © 1996 Heritage Books, Inc.

— Publisher's Notice —
In reprints such as this, it is often not possible to remove blemishes from the original. We feel the contents of this book warrant its reissue despite these blemishes and hope you will agree and read it with pleasure.

International Standard Book Numbers
Paperbound: 978-0-7884-0541-9
Clothbound: 978-0-7884-9470-3

CONTENTS

CHAPTER.		PAGE
	Preface.	
I.	Name—Location—Natural Features, etc,	1
	Petition and Act of Incorporation	6
II.	The Aborigines	9
III.	Early Settlers and Their Families	17
	Stinchfield Family	17
	Millett Family	41
	Lane Family	50
	Francis Family	55
	Bishop Family	63
	Lothrop Family	69
	Gilbert Family	74
	Jennings Family	79
	Turner Family	84
	Foss Family	89
	Leadbetter Family	107
	George Family	109
	Sylvester Family	112
	Fish Family	115
	Cushman Family	117
	Lindsey Family	124
	Knapp Family	133
	Foster Family	140
	Brewster Family	147
	Gould Family	150
	Pettingill Family	153
	Curtis Family	157
	Otis Family	162
	Caswell Family	166
	Howe Family	168
	Wing Family	169
	Additon Family	172

HISTORY OF LEEDS

Chapter		Page
	Howard Family	175
	Deane Family	196
	Mitchell Family	198
	Herrick Family	199
	Boothby Family	205
	Ramsdell Family	218
	Parcher Family	220
	Bates Family	221
	Merrill Family	222
	Hanscom Family	224
	Leadbetter, Horace	226
	True Family	227
	Gordon Family	229
	Other Families	231
IV.	Heads of Families in the Early Part of the 19th Century	244
V.	First Mills and Other Industries	248
VI.	A Condensed Review of the History of the Baptist Churches in Leeds from about A. D. 1800 to 1901	251
VII.	History of the Methodist Episcopal Church of Leeds	254
VIII.	Universalist Church	257
IX.	Churches	261
X.	Schools of Leeds	263
XI.	Professional Men	269
XII.	Excerpts from Town Records	271
XIII.	List of Leeds Town Officers	275
XIV.	Military Record of Leeds	285
XV.	Mail Routes—Post-Offices—Postmasters	297
XVI.	Ladies' Aid Society	300
XVII.	Secret Societies	302
XVIII.	Androscoggin Railroad	306
XIX.	Gleanings	311
XX.	Marriage Intentions with Date of Certificate	323
XXI.	Genealogy	362

ILLUSTRATIONS

The Indian Carry	Frontispiece	
John Clark Stinchfield	Opposite page	17
Hon. Samuel B. Stanchfield	" "	37
Francis Davis Millett	" "	49
Rev. Thomas Davis Francis	" "	55
George T. Bishop	" "	67
Solomon Lothrop and Wife	" "	71
Hon. Davis Francis Lothrop and Mrs. D. F. Lothrop	" "	73
Col. W. L. Lothrop	" "	73
John Turner, M.D.	" "	87
Benjamin Turner	" "	88
Rev. Walter Foss	" "	100
G. W. Foss	" "	104
Laura M. Sylvester	" "	115
Stephen Knapp	" "	137
Charles Knapp	" "	138
Hannah L. Pollard	" "	139
Henry M. Brewster	" "	148
Elisha D. Gould	" "	151
W. E. Gould, M.D.	" "	152
Samuel Pettengill	" "	155
Isaiah B. Additon	" "	172
Fred L. Additon	" "	173
E. E. Additon	" "	174
Stillman L. Howard, Esq.	" "	177
Hon. Seth Howard	" "	180
Mrs. Seth Howard	" "	180
Major-General Oliver Otis Howard	" "	182
Rev. Rowland Bailey Howard	" "	187
Brevet Brigadier-General Charles H. Howard	" "	189
Elder Luther Loomis Howard	" "	192
Otis Hill Monument	" "	195

Coat of Arms	Opposite page	197
Major Israel Herrick	" "	203
Frank H. Herrick	" "	204
Lucy M. Herrick	" "	204
Rev. Samuel Boothby	" "	211
Hon. Thomas H. Boothby	" "	212
Mrs. Thomas H. Boothby	" "	212
Lieutenant-Colonel Stephen Boothby	" "	213
Hon. R. C. Boothby	" "	215
Daniel Parcher	" "	220
D. P. True	" "	228
Mrs. D. P. True	" "	228
Shore of Androscoggin Lake from Lewiston Club House	" "	229
Benjamin Woodman	" "	241
Leeds Center Looking from the Lake	" "	248
Baptist and Universalist Churches, Chapel Hill, Leeds	" "	251
Androscoggin Lake from Meeting-House Hill	" "	252
School-House, West Leeds	" "	263
View Looking Toward Androscoggin Lake	" "	297

PREFACE.

In the preparation and publication of a town history, no inexperienced individual is aware of the innumerable difficulties that are met by the unfortunate who so dearly pays the penalty of the great mistake of a lifetime. Of the many reasons that might be assigned for engaging in the arduous task, one only is presented by the writer—that of necessity,—forced on him because of his family connection with the first settlers, who were concerned in primitive events of the town. On one condition was the responsibility assumed, and that was that a committee elected by the town, consisting of ten or more of its citizens, should furnish the data embodying the material of which the history was to be composed, and do it sufficiently early to enable the writer to have as much of the limited time as possible to prepare the work for publication. How well and fully that condition has been complied with may be imagined but not realized. We offer no apology! The work is submitted, and must fall or stand on its merit.

Special effort has been made to obtain biographies and family records,—a feature of greater value than all else combined. In gathering data, more and more were we impressed that too long, already, has this work been neglected. A few years hence, and much herein contained, had it remained unwritten, would pass with those who hold it in trust, beyond the power of man to reclaim. Even now, in the absence of reliable records, interesting, valuable, and noteworthy matter is entombed with the silent dead. But a few years ago, and the shade and gloom now attaching to ripening years and waning intellects, drawing their shroud over fallen relics of other days, were resplendent lights, shining brightly on the pathways of their cherished ancestors.

Although regrets are in vain, many are those of the writer for the omission of families who should have appeared in their proper places in this work. Those there are to whom appeals have been repeatedly made, to lend their aid in supplying matter pertaining to their own family history, who, in their ease, will criticise the arrangement, sneer at the diction, and curse the other fellow for omissions for which they themselves are censurable. None are omitted by intention or design; but, for want of material information. We do not pose as a public store-house of knowledge, from which may be drawn, in unmeasured quantities, the family affairs of those whose concerns are their own. Much of the given time in which to prepare this work has been consumed in obtaining the material of which it is composed. The hurry in submitting it to writing and preparing it for publication are offered for the imperfections which may appear.

We would not lose sight of the purpose of this feature of the work, and forget our deep obligations to those who so kindly have rendered aid and contributed much of the valuable matter which this volume contains. To Hon. Seth Howard many thanks are due for record matter in the archives of State and town, and valuable data of families; to those who have contributed family biographies and records, of whom special mention should be made, are Hon. Joshua H. Millett, of Boston, Mass.; Hon. R. C. Boothby, of Livermore Falls, Me.; F. C. Howard, of New York; Hon. Z. A. Gilbert, of Greene, Me.; Hon. J. M. Benjamin, of Winthrop, Me.; Hon. G. W. Walton, of Wayne, Me.; Hon. George Parcher; Mr. and Mrs. F. H. Herrick; Mr. W. R. Pettingill; Miss Marion T. Bishop; Miss Abbie Deane; Mr. G. A. Jennings; Mrs. Rose Hanscom; Mr. E. E. Additon; Mr. J. C. Wing; Mrs. Alfred Beals; H. M. Brewster, Esq.; Mr. R. Ramsdell; Mrs. Kittie Russell; Mrs. Orrah M. Jennings, of Farmington; Mr. N. P. Gould.

To Ephraim D. Foss, of Maineville, Ohio, we are indebted for an account of some of the early events.

To the wonderful memory of Mrs. Hannah L. (Knapp) Pollard, a life-long resident of the town and one of its best productions, may be ascribed the fountain from which has been drawn reliable and valuable information which could have been obtained from no other source.

Church Histories were written—Baptist, by William R. Pettingill; Methodist, by Rev. F. A. Hall; Universalist, by F. H. Herrick; Free Baptist, Friends and others by ———

The chapter on schools was prepared and written by Mrs. Lucy M. Herrick, to whom the people of the town are especially indebted.

Secret Societies—Miss Abbie Deane, et als.

Professional Men—W. Gould, M.D.

J. C. STINCHFIELD.

WAYNE, June 10, 1901.

FOREWORD TO THE NEW EDITION.

Over three-quarters of this book is devoted to genealogical records of the early settlers of Leeds, Maine. The main section contains biographical and genealogical information regarding more than forty of the town's leading families. Additional noteworthy chapters include the records of Marriage Intentions from 1801-1901 and the Genealogy section containing Leeds men who were living at the time the book was published (c1901) and listing their children, parentage and paternal and maternal grandparents. The narrative history covers: the founding of the town, its location and natural features; Aborigines; Churches; Schools; Professional Men; some First Things; List of Town Officers 1801-1901; and Military Records for the American Revolution, War of 1812 and Civil War.

Six families have been added to this edition. Three are headed by African-American Revolutionary soldiers. There is also a "Schedule of Settlers on Townships on Pegyscot (Pejepscot) Patent: Littleboro' (Leeds)" between 1781 and 1794, from the original at the Maine Historical Society. Another list of settlers in Leeds dates from around 1800 and is copied from Pejepscot Claim papers in the Androscoggin Historical Society. A lot map for the town of Leeds, drawn by the surveyor for the Pejepscot Land Company in the early 1800s, enhances this edition.

The new master index will give the researcher access to the treasures within this book. This everyname index includes women's maiden and married names, and also contains subjects and towns. Illustrated with fifty portraits and town views.

We found a few questionable statements, i.e., "Water BOOTHBY" on page 330, should read "Walter BOOTHBY"; "Bluefield Maine" on page 332, likely should read "Buckfield; Betsey LEABETTER" on page 108 should read Betsey LEADBETTER; on page 74 line 24 "a yound lady should read a young lady; on page 325, Nathan KEITH married in 1809 "Harry NEBIT" could her name have been "Harriet ?"; and on page 23 Ezekiel Stinchfield who married Tamson Eldridge of Bucksport ME would appear to have settled in both Milo & Wesley ME & died on 17 June 1851 & Lawrence MA in 1852. People only die once.

We do not think a few typographical errors detract from the value of this work to anyone doing research in Androscoggin County. Readers who identify additional errors may write us at: P.O. Box 152, Danville, Maine 04223 or the Androscoggin Historical Society, 2 Turner St., Auburn, Maine 04210. If you have a question, a self-addressed, stamped envelope is neccessary for a reply.

We would like to thank the Androscoggin Historical Society for granting us permission to print Amos Davis' Lot Plan for the Town of Leeds, Maine.

David C. Young
Elizabeth K. Young
1 Apr. 1996

HISTORY OF LEEDS.

CHAPTER I.

NAME—LOCATION—SOIL—NATURAL FEATURES—ACT OF INCORPORATION, ETC.

The town of Leeds, the plantation name of which was Littleborough, took its name from Leeds, England, the birthplace of John Stinchfield, the father of Thomas and Roger, the pioneer settlers. It is located in the Androscoggin valley—meridian 70° 15' west longitude, and 44° 15' north latitude. It is bounded north, by East Livermore; south, by Greene and Wales; east, by Wayne and Monmouth; west, by the Androscoggin River, or Turner and Livermore. Auburn, the county seat, is fifteen miles distant in a south-western direction; and Augusta, the State capital, about twenty miles easterly. As originally surveyed and laid out, in 1780-1, by the proprietors of the "Pejepscot Claim," its northern boundary was the northern boundary of that claim on the east side of the Androscoggin River, and extended from said river to "Androscoggin Great Pond" on a direct line of which, the north line of "Old Elder Thomas D. Francis'" farm was a part. It was given the name of Littleborough, in honor of Col. Moses Little, who was the agent and a prominent owner in that company. Livermore bordered it on the north from river to pond. February 16, 1801, it was incorporated the 128th town in the District of Maine. In 1802, that portion of Livermore south of a line extending from the Androscoggin River to the western boundary of Wayne, of which the north line of the farm of Increase Leadbetter (now the farm of Samuel P. Francis) was a part, was annexed to Leeds. In 1809, taken from Monmouth and annexed to Leeds, was a piece of land 160 rods wide and the length of the line between those towns. In 1810, that part of Leeds known as the Beech Hill section, was annexed to Wayne. In 1852, that portion of Leeds sometimes called New Boston, was set off and annexed to Wales. As now constituted, the town is about twelve miles in length, and its width varies from about one mile in the extreme northern portion, to near five in the central and southern, and has an area of twenty-two thousand acres. Its native forestry was chiefly pine, for which it was long and widely noted. Probably no other township was its equal in the production of gigantic monarchs of the forest. The Androscoggin Valley in which Leeds is situated, has a drainage area of 36,000 square miles—extreme length 110, and 70 in breadth from Randolph, N. H., to Readfield, Me. In the eastern extremity of this area is the water-shed of the "Thirty Mile River." From the highlands, which form the divide from Sandy River, to the great Androscoggin, a chain of fourteen lakes, ponds and their connecting streams clothe the valley in mirrored sunshine and beauty. The last in the course, more beautiful than all the rest,—that which our fathers loved most and best, and around which cluster fond remembrances of childhood's happy days, is our own Androscoggin thrice sung in county, river, and lake. Dead River, the terminal of the "Thirty Mile River," is the natural and only outlet of these waters and receives them in two branches near the mean portion of the lake. Flowing inland they form a junction and thus united, the river continues on its meandering way along the alluvial banks, a distance of nearly two miles where it follows its channels of ages agone to its confluence with the Androscoggin. The land surface of Leeds, not unlike that of many New England towns, is of a diversified character, and along the central and eastern portions hills of considerable magnitude overlook the middle and lowlands which, in some localities, are broken by bogs and meadows. The soil varies from a light, sandy loam, which prevails more extensively, to a strong, heavy loam on the elevations, while in some sections clay predominates. The interval lands along Dead River, and here and there on the shores of the Androscoggin, are rich in alluvial deposits, and have been very productive; yet, like all else, were not made of that material which improves with age and use. The range of hills along the Androscoggin from its source to the receding waters of the sea, is continuous through Leeds. The Fish or Otis and Bates—better known as Quaker Ridge,—together with Bishop and Hedgehog hills, are notable members of that range. These and lesser elevations are mostly free from boulders, while the miles of stone walls are remaining evidence that the ground was once liberally strewn with stones in those sections. Interspersed among the uplands are occasional ledges, outcroppings of granite and trap rock, which especially abound on the northern part of Bishop hill, where it was said of Zadoc Bishop, who came there from Monmouth in 1783, and like the wise man of old, built his house on a rock that, "he made a practice of filing the noses of his sheep, that they might reach the scanty verdure that grew in the close crevices of that rock-bound hill." Be that as it may, labor and industry have been rewarded with prosperity and plenty, and some of the best farms in Leeds are on this eminence. From the several elevations extended and most beautiful views are presented.

It is only a matter of little time when Leeds, with its delightful scenery,—pure air and water,—pleasant drives and lake advantages, will become a favorite summer resort. The most striking geological feature of the town is the alluvial deposit. "The Cape," lying on either side of Dead River from beyond and between the outlet of the lake and its ancient western shore, one mile and more in length, by one-third of a mile in width, is the continual alluvial growth of ages unknown. It is irregularly divided by the river in its tortuous way, gracefully sweeping to the one side in close approach to the lake shore, leaving but a narrow connection of the peninsula. One of these of less width than others, distant from the mainland one-half mile, or more, was utilized by the Indians, and since by palefaces to carry their canoes and wangan from river to lake, and retains the name of "Carrying Place" to this day. The story of a ditch having been dug across it by the Indians, as related in the history of Androscoggin County and other works, is the imagination of some over-zealous mind. It was the work of Col. Leavitt Lothrop, dug for the purpose of stopping cattle, instead of building a fence. The rocky promontories forming the head of the lake were formerly islands of the cluster near the middle of the lake, and their outlines are now as distinct as when surrounded by water.

Leeds is an agricultural town and compares very favorably with the best in the Androscoggin Valley. Development of the west revolutionized no New England industry more than that of agriculture. In earlier years, all the grains common to Maine were extensively cultivated and grown with profit to the hardy tiller of the soil. He supplied his family with flour ground from wheat of his own raising; and to have bought for the consumption of his family, or his stock, a bushel of corn, meal or other feed, would have been to acknowledge his eligibility to the ranks of drones. How changed! Flour of better quality can now be purchased for less money than would be required to pay a laborer to raise the wheat, to say nothing of the use or cost of the land from which it is grown. Stock raising became an important and paying industry. The superior quality of beef produced from the Durham and Hereford families gave to New England, and especially Maine towns, where they were abundantly bred and reared with pride and profit, a great precedence in the big markets, over the inferior stock of the west of Spanish origin. In time, the shrewd stock ranchers of the plains procured bulls in the east, turned them out with their native herds, and soon monopolized the beef markets of the world. Driven from their stronghold, Yankee ingenuity brought out the creameries, butter, cheese, and canning factories and now defy the west, or the world, in competition. The people of Leeds, noted from its settlement to the present for their patriotism, intelligence, industry and thoughtfulness, early established these industries within their borders and have acquired a reputation for the excellency of their products. Orcharding has been attended with favorable results in some sections of the town. The first apple tree set out in Leeds produced a crop in 1900. It is now standing near the buildings of I. S. Carver; and, with five others, was brought from New Gloucester, by Thomas Stinchfield, in the spring of 1781, and planted there.

The saw and grist mills of our fathers, located on Bog Brook that constituted the water-power of the town, where the giant pines were converted into material of which many buildings are composed and the grain products of the farmers were ground and bolted into meal and flour, have yielded up their business,—the former to those of steam and water-powers of larger pretensions, and the latter to the great western concerns. The tanner—the country shoe-maker—the cabinet-maker—the skilled carpenter—the potter—the clock-maker—the tailoress and seamstress—the cloth-maker—the butter- and cheese-maker, all, and many more, have forever disappeared and will live only in history. They have been supplanted by machinery operated by capitalists and combinations of capital, and the business of the country is now being done by one machine more powerful than all the rest—monopoly. "The post-riders" on fleet horseback, with mail-pouches securely strapped on behind them and others in front, containing matter collected and for distribution, making the woods resound with blasts from their long, tin trumpets—a warning of approach that delay be avoided,—who made weekly rounds of the towns in this section,—later giving place to the cheery, bustling mail and passenger coaches, are among the things that were; while steam and electricity in that capacity, constitute the things that are. The blow that killed hundreds of New England towns gave to Leeds a new lease of life. With the disappearance of the stage-coach came the railroad, which extends the entire length of the town. The four stations, and a fifth just outside its limits, viz.: Leeds Crossing, Curtis Corner, Leeds Center, North Leeds, and Strickland's Ferry, afford the people facilities that few municipalities enjoy. Where stood the little saw and grist mills on the brook at West Leeds, ample and convenient, perhaps, for their day, the capacious box and dowel factory of R. E. Swain is doing an extensive business, which offers to the people a good home market for their timber; while at the Center, G. W. Lane has a steam mill, capable of grinding all the corn and grain grown in the town in excess of that used in his trade. Near the Dead River bridges, C. H. White & Son have a plant for the sawing and manufacture of lumber, the product of which would have taxed all the little old mills of former days far beyond their capacity, had they been operated continuously twenty-four hours every day in the year. Nor are these all that have replaced those primitive little conveniences. At Curtis Corner is another steam mill where large quantities of lumber of various kinds are sawed and manufactured; while near the brick school-house, still another establishment is operated. Dairying and the production of sweet corn are chief among the industries now engaging the people. A ready money market for the corn is found each year at the factory in the center of the town, at remunerative prices. The corn fodder is nutritious and of worth in the production of milk and cream, and an important factor of the profit derived from dairying; therefore, the two industries are rendered almost inseparable. The production of cheese has been a paying business for several years; and while many factories have been idle, Leeds has continued hers in operation, showing, conclusively, that skill and good judgment remains with her people. No place in New England possesses greater natural features of interest, or is more inviting to pleasure or rest seekers from the hurry and bustle of city life, than the shores of Androscoggin Lake. Its spacious, mirrored waters, whitecapped now and then by the summer breezes, affords unexcelled boating; and already rowing, sailing, steam, and naphtha launches are every day visible in their graceful meanderings; or, pushing out from shaded beaches to angle for pickerel along the margin of the lily-pads and blossoms of varied hues, in which the shores abound; or to the more rocky bottoms to troll for the gamey black bass; or to the deep waters where white perch furnish rare sport for the unprofessional lady anglers and children. The piny elevations gradually rising in beauty from the lake shore and river banks, are dotted here and there with gurgling springs of pure cold water, where the gay, rambling parties tarry to refresh themselves and linger in their invigorating shades. Such extensive and beautiful landscape scenery as that presented to view from the summits of the surrounding hills, is unsurpassed on this continent. The cottages by the lakeside, of recent construction, with many more in prospect,—the rapid increase in the numbers of summer guests at the public and private residences in the vicinity, evidence the fact that the charms which cluster around our lakes and hills have not escaped the vision of the tourist, nor failed of worthy mention to his associates and more numerous acqaintances. Mingled with the new faces are those of many whose childhood days, never forgotten, were spent in Leeds. Wherever their worldly pursuits may have led them, or whatever they may have been, the fond memories of youth bring them back to greet anew the friends and scenes they love so well. Relatives and friends may have departed, but their graves in the valleys, the river, the lake and the meadow beside it, the hills and the wild-wood, all are here to give silent welcome to their sons and daughters. Let us ever revere their memory and render thanks to heaven, that we are the descendants of a most worthy ancestry, and natives of one of the most beautiful of the picturesque New England towns.

Petition and Act of Incorporation.

To the Honorable the Senate and House of Representatives in General Court Assembled:

We your petitioners inhabitants of the Plantation of Littleborough in the District of Maine HUMBLY SHEWETH

That whereas we are now deprived of many important advantages, from our present situation, which we should otherwise enjoy as a body corporate, and as we are zealous to obtain all the privilidges, which as citizens we are entitled to, and the many inconveniences resulting from transacting business, in our present capacity, must be considered as giving some weight, connected with many other claims,—having the number of one hundred, and four settlers, and from the natural increase the great necessity of Public Grammer Schools, must be apparent, the bad state of roads, can in no way be improved, which is an object of magnitudge to ourselves, as well as the public, the remidy of one, and the important right of the other, we are now debarred of.

From these considerations, we are induced to pray for an act of Incorporation, for your petitioners, with all the privilidges, and immunities, of a body corporate, by the name of Cuba. From the infancy of the Country, and the inability of many of the inhabitants, we likewise pray an exemption of the State Tax for the term of five years. As in duty bound shall ever pray.

Isaac Collier,
Stephen Wellcome,
Josiah Turner,
Morgan Brewster,
Samuel Strong,
John Jennings,
Zoar Samson,
Beriah Samson,
James Samson,
Simon Wood, Juner,
Jacob Bailey,
John Bates,
Levi Bates,
Nathaniel House, jnr.,
Elias Lane,
Bachler Wing,
Nathaniel Owen,
Joseph Mitchell,
Daniel Lane,
Peter Lane,
Oliver Randell,
Abiel Dailey,

Ephraim Andrews,
Amos Beany,
Joshua Barry,
Stephen Foster,
Solomon Millet,
Thomas Additon,
Thomas Francis,
Eleazer Rand,
Thomas Epes,
Oliver Otis,
Jamey Lain,
Andrew Cushman,
James S. Panley,
Cornelius Gilbert,
Jonathan Fish,
Richard Higgins,
Giddins Lane,
Daniel Lane, Jun,
Obadeah Pettingill,
William Turner,
William Pettingill,
Thomas Lindsay,

HISTORY OF LEEDS

(Illegible) Fish,
Daniel Robins,
Thomas Millet,
David Woodman,
Rogers Stenchfield,
Samuel Gilbert,
Benjn. Gilbert,
Micah Samson,
Heircy Gilbert,
William Gilbert,
Edward Bailey,
Beriah Samson, juner,

Joseph Bishop,
Daniel Lothrop, Jur.,
George Turner,
Sulliven Lothrop,
Daniel Lothrop,
George Lothrop,
Jacob Day.

In the House of Represent's, Jan'y 14, 1800.

Read & committed to the standing Committee on applications for Incorporations of towns, &c to consider & report.
Sent up for Concurrence.

EDW'D H. ROBBINS, Spk'r.

In Senate, January 14, 1800. Read and concurred.

SAM'L PHILLIPS, Prsdt.

Endorsed:

PETITION OF THE INHABITANTS OF LITTLESBOROUGH.

Copied dld).
N B Boundries of the within Littelsborrough Beginning N W Corner of Greene running N on Anderscoggin Rivver to Livermore Line thence E to Vane (Wayne) thence S By Monmouth Line to Greene thence N W to the first Mentned Bounds Containing about 16000 Acres of Land including Boggs & warter.

In the House of Representatives, June 6. 1800.

Read & committed to the stand'g Committee on applications for Incorporations of towns & to hear the parties & report.
Sent up for Concurrence.

EDW'D H. ROBBINS, Spkr.

In Senate, June 10, 1800. Read & concurred.

SAM'L PHILLIPS, Presdt.

COMMONWEALTH OF MASSACHUSETTS,
OFFICE OF THE SECRETARY,

Boston, Mass., March 7, 1901.

A true copy.
[L. S.]

Witness the seal of the Commonwealth.
WM. M. OLIN, Secretary of the Commonwealth.

CHAPTER 41, ACTS OF 1800.
COMMONWEALTH OF MASSACHUSETTS.

In the Year of Our Lord One Thousand Eight Hundred and One.

An ACT to incorporate the plantation of Littleborough, in the County of Kennebeck, into a town by the name of Leeds.

Sect. 1.—Be it Enacted by the Senate and House of Representatives, in General Court assembled and by the Authority of the same, That the plantation heretofore called Littleborough, in the County of Kennebeck, as described within the following bounds, vizt.: Beginning at the Northwest corner of Grene, thence runing Northerly on the Great Amariscoggin River, to the line of Livermore, thence Easterly on the Southerly line of said Livermore, till it strikes the line of Wayne, thence southerly by the line of Monmouth to Green, thence Northwest to the bounds first mentioned, together with the Inhabitants thereon, be and hereby are incorporated into a Town by the name of Leeds. And the said Town is hereby vested with all the powers, privileges and immunities, which other towns, do or may enjoy by the Constitution and Laws of this Commonwealth.

Sect. 2.—And be it further Enacted, That John Chandler, Esqr., be & he is hereby empowered to issue his Warrant, directed to some suitable Inhabitant of the said town of Leeds, requiring him to notify and warn the Inhabitants thereof, qualified to vote in town affairs, to meet at such time and place, as shall be expressed in said Warrant, to choose all such Officers as towns are by Law required to choose in the month of March or April annually.

In the House of Representatives, Feb'y 13, 1801.
This Bill having had three several readings passed to be Enacted.
EDW'D H. ROBBINS, Spkr.

In Senate Feb'y 16th, 1801.
This bill having had two several readings passed to be enacted.
SAM'L PHILLIPS, Presdt.

February 16th, 1801.
By the Governor approved.
CALEB STRONG.

COMMONWEALTH OF MASSACHUSETTS,
OFFICE OF THE SECRETARY,

Boston, Mass., March 7, 1901.
A true copy. Witness the seal of the Commonwealth.
[L. S.] WM. M. OLIN, Secretary of the Commonwealth.

CHAPTER II.

THE ABORIGINES.

The origin of the primitive inhabitants of North America is involved in complete obscurity. That they were one of the ancient nations of mankind, no logical or reasonable doubt can be entertained. At what date, or by what means they became inhabitants of the western continent must remain shrouded in mystery and uncertainty,—an unsolved problem,—until further research shall discover the mysteries of "The great unknown."

The earliest books on America contained tales that only the wildest fancy could imagine and picture. Cartier claimed that a people might there be found who neither ate nor drank. And Lafitau believed that a headless race existed there. What a conception of one of the most noble races of men! They were endowed by Nature with propensities befitting their surroundings. The Redman is nowhere at home except in the chase, or gliding along some lake or stream in his bark canoe. Such a race could live only in a country of woods and wild animals. Deprived of these, he pines, languishes and dies broken-hearted. The illimitable hunting-grounds, forest, hill and river, were the Indian's earthly paradise, and the type of his home hereafter. Not unlike the nations of the East, governments existed with them, founded on principles more just and equitable and less barbarous and tyrannical than most others of their time. They were divided into nations and subdivided into tribes, and again, into clans. Their plan of government may have had weight with the founders of our Republic. Their nations like our States had their great sachems or chiefs, and their advisory councils from the smaller chiefs of the tribes corresponding to our counties, while their clans, like our towns, had their chiefs, who were admitted to the councils of the tribes. Without the knowledge of the existence of foreign nations, a union of their nations or States, for self-preservation, was instinctively provided for. Lying south of the land of the Esquimaux, embracing nearly all of Canada and that portion of the United States east of the Mississippi River and north of the thirty-seventh parallel of latitude, spread the great family of the Algonkins. The council-seat of this great confederation of nations was on the Ottawa River. Within this vast domain, like an oasis, the hunting grounds of those powerful nations, the Huron-Iroquois, were situated. Their jurisdiction extended from Georgian Bay and Lake Huron to Lakes Erie and Ontario, south of those lakes to the valley of the Upper Ohio, and eastward to the Sorel River. Two nations of the Algonkin confederacy,—the Etchemins or canoemen, and the Abenakis, occupied Maine and the eastern coast of Canada. The Etchemins dwelt both on the St. John and St. Croix Rivers and the coast as far west as Mount Desert. The Abenakis occupied all the territory from the land of the Etchemins to the eastern boundary line of New Hampshire. The number of tribes into which a nation divided was determined by the number of rivers within its jurisdiction that empties its waters into the sea or large lakes. On these, their wigwam villages were planted, while the tents of their clans, for convenience in hunting, were spread on its tributaries or by the lakeside where corn could conveniently be grown. The names given to the nations, tribes, and clans were those suggested by the prominence of some natural feature of the place of their location. The Indians had an undying love for running water, which has even been a favorite highway to no people more than they—a means of immigration best suited to the genius of savage life; and even civilized man has no path so free as the lake, the river, and the sea. Thus the four principal rivers of Maine were the hunting grounds for the four tribes into which the Abenakis Nation was divided, viz.: Wawenocks on the Penobscot; Canibas on the Kennebec; Anasagunticooks on the Androscoggin; and Sokokis on the Saco. The Wawenocks were later called Penobscots, and the Anasagunticooks Androscoggins.

To the everlasting credit of the Indian may the fact be stated, that, to the early English voyagers, their advances were friendly, and their many acts of kindness and faithfulness can never be blotted from the books of the nations. Had the colonies reciprocated their kindness and the nation ever treated them with a degree of fairness, thousands of innocent lives of people, both white and red, would have escaped the sacrifice. In 1676, three hundred and fifty innocent, confiding Indians, on the Maine coast, were enticed on board of vessels, made captives, shipped to Boston, and sold into foreign slavery. For thirteen years like cruelties were perpetrated and endured by them, with no retaliation save repeated, sorrowing protests. They were the recipients of every indignity the magistrates could conceive of and execute. No redress was left to the noble and pure-hearted Indian but brute force, to which he was cruelly forced to resort. Friendship turned to hatred seeks the most cruel means of revenge. The memory of treachery is indelibly stamped on the whole human race. In June, 1689, a council-fire was lighted around which gathered the Abenakis chiefs, which resulted in the declaration of war on the settlers along the coast of Maine. At Cocheco, where, thirteen years before, their kindred had been kidnapped and sold into slavery, the blood of the white man was first spilled in the east. In a descent on that place the settlers' huts were fired, twenty-three people were killed, and twenty-nine taken to their lodges in the forests. In August of that year a band of one hundred warriors from the Canibas tribe on the Kennebec attacked the stockade at Pemaquid, which at the end of two days capitulated, the defenders and their families were made prisoners and long held for exchange for those sold into slavery. The settlements east of Falmouth (Portland) were thus broken up and deserted. Blood once spilled was beyond recall. When the white man invaded the country of the Abenakis he did so at the risk of his scalp; yet those there were who did it. In July, 1722, the government of Massachusetts, by resolution, declared the eastern Indians traitors and robbers, and private parties offered one hundred pounds each for Indian scalps. In March, 1723, Westbrook headed an expedition to the Penobscot to scalp the Wawenocks. On the 9th of that month they came upon the Indian settlement at Oldtown. Under the cover of darkness they set fire to the stockade, and ere the rising of the sun every camp was in ashes. Fancy, if we must, the perpetrators of this crime in their second act—slaughtering and scalping men, women, and children by the light of their own burning wigwams. This act alone, under public auspices, was one of the most atrocious crimes ever conceived by man. Not content with the murder of these helpless squaws and pappooses for the tempting money value of their scalps, these representatives of a people who came to this country that they might enjoy religious freedom and worship according to the dictates of their conscience, committed other like atrocities. View these as we may, it was a crushing blow to the Wawenocks, and the few remaining joined their kindred in other tribes.

The previous year Westbrook had twice attempted the extermination of the Canibas tribe of the Kennebec, whose principal village was on the east side of that river in Norridgewock,— nearly opposite the mouth of the Sandy River,—and although unattended with success, was effected in 1724 by a body of men under Harmon and Moulton sent from Fort Richmond. For want of space, an extended account of this butchery is omitted. Included in the list of slain was Father Sebastian Rasle, a French Jesuit priest who had for many years been the spiritual adviser and teacher of this tribe. The story of his death is poetically told in Whittier's "Mogg Magone," but of the awful butchery and destruction of the men, women, and children of this village it is silent. In 1833, with the lapse of a century and more, Bishop Benedict Fenwick, of Boston, purchased an acre of land embracing the site of that fated chapel where fell the Jesuit priest and most of his people, and on the 23d day of August, the 109th anniversary of the massacre, erected thereon an obelisk of granite, surmounted with a cross, first of iron, since of granite, to the height of eighteen feet—a perpetual memorial of the tragic end of Father Rasles and his band of red men of the Kennebec. With the death of Father Rasles, the last Catholic missionary in New England was removed. The influence of the French had thus been overthrown with their missions, and the Indians with whom they had been allied, encouraged though unaided, were left to fight their own battles.

The warriors of the Sokokis tribe on the Saco, having been badly reduced by continued warfare, and driven from the coast farther inland, were vigorously attacked by John Lovewell and a party by him organized. Twice they returned laden with Indian scalps. In his third expedition, which was to destroy their encampment in the town of Fryeburg, he was overpowered by a superior force and his blood emptied on the soil of that town near a sheet of water which has taken his name, and the little stream that empties into it is still known as Battle Brook. The small remnant of that tribe abandoned the graves of their fathers and placed themselves under the protection of the French, in Canada.

With misgivings of the conduct of many of the early settlers of New England, we trace the history of the fourth and last of the tribes of the Abenakis nation,—the Anasagunticooks of the Androscoggin. From Merrymeeting Bay, where the majestic waters of the Kennebec and Androscoggin, so long separated on their missions of irrigation kiss anew their greetings, to the Rangeleys, and even to the source of the winding river, Androscoggin, and the many tributary lakes and streams along its course,—the most beautiful and picturesque water system in nature, their wigwam villages were spread. From these waters, stretching back to the hills and more majestic mountains, their loved hunting grounds were laid. In these chaste waters wild geese squawked their unmelodious songs, ducks quacked their more discordant notes of accompaniment, finny tribes gorged and gamboled in the shades of morn and twilight, forest animals laved and slacked their thirst.

In the earliest history of the Indians, this was the most numerous of the tribes of New England, the most favorably located. The great length of the Androscoggin,—formerly Aumoughcawgen,—in its flexuous meanders of more than one hundred and sixty miles, skirted along its course by numerous and beautiful lakes around which towered the evergreen hills,—nothing was wanting to make it the Indians' earthly paradise. In 1615, a deadly plague visited this tribe and cut them down like grain before the reaper.

When freed from this scourge but fifteen hundred warriors remained. From 1689 to August 6, 1726, at which time a treaty with the eastern tribes was effected by the colonies of Massachusetts, the warriors of this tribe, by continual warfare and other causes were nearly annihilated,—but five remaining above sixteen years of age. In 1750 their number had increased to one hundred and sixty; while in 1780, when Leeds was first settled, they could boast of five hundred. Centuries unknown had come and gone since the council-seats of the four tribes of the Abenakis nation had been planted on the rivers, a short distance up their banks from the sea, the evident purpose of which was to facilitate easy communication by boat along the coast of Maine. With the advent of the white men that of the Anasagunticooks was at Brunswick Falls. After hostilities were instituted, it was removed to the junction of the Little Androscoggin with the main river, adjacent to the upper Pejepscot Falls. A little distance up this tributary their fleet of canoes were tethered, their tents of skins, with holes in the top for smoke to escape, their inclosure of stakes firmly driven obliquely and sharpened with their stone tomahawks, or made pointed by fire, presented them in their true aspect of home. This historic fort and home was captured in 1689, by Major Benjamin Church, and later selected by Edward Little, Esq., for his last resting place, and there he was first buried. Again was the main encampment, or principal village of the tribe, driven farther from the coast into the wilds of the forest, a demonstration of their treatment from our earliest history to the present! The natural advantages for defense presented by the broken flow of water, the hills along the river banks, the abrupt windings of the river from Livermore Falls to Canton, to which they gave the name of Roccomeco, together with the utility of the soil in the upper portion, for corn culture, were the inducements that caused them to plant their depleted village of wigwams there. As in the past, the clans of the tribe were beside the lakes and streams throughout the entire Androscoggin valley. From the time of the capture of their fort at the upper Pejepscot Falls (Auburn) they improved every opportunity to engage their enemies in mortal combat. They contested the encroachments of the white settlers with all the vigor and strategy peculiar to their race. Those familiar with Indian history will recall the incident of the company of Caghnawga Indians,—a name given to a portion of the Anasagunticooks,—from "Phipps Canada" (then the name of Jay and Canton), who, joining with a party of French under D'Aillebout, DeMantel, and LeMoyne, destroyed the village of Schenectady on the Mohawk, above Albany, N. Y., on the night of the eighth of February, 1690. Continuing in their work of death and destruction their war-whoops grew more fierce and bloodcurdling than the howling of wild beasts in the forests about them.

But many a whoop, echoed by the sound of a rifle, was silenced forever by the white man's bullets. When the treaty was effected there remained scarce enough warriors in this tribe to swear by. Recuperated from the boy-ranks, they gradually spread their tents anew on the hunting grounds of their fathers. Not forgetful of the past, though their numbers were comparatively few, they feebly aided the French in their war, from 1754 to 1760, by their incursions on the settlers near the coast who had come in during the time of peace. With the close of this war open hostilities ceased and an era of peace and safety dawned. Again they returned to their wigwam fastnesses in the forest, receding with the advance of the white settlers, until—where are they? The red man's sun has nearly set, far away o'er the western hills, and his glory is "a thing of the past."

No place in the Algonkin country afforded better facilities for Indian life than the banks of the Androscoggin in Leeds and the shores of its tributary waters of the "Thirty-Mile River" (the name early given to the chain of lakes and ponds extending from the mouth of Dead River to the water-shed of the Sandy River).

Nor was there another locality so thickly studded with wigwams. Not only were the best hunting grounds and fisheries found here, but the light, productive soil was better adapted to their methods of cultivation and the crude implements (shells and dried shoulder-blades of moose and bear) used for the growing of corn and interment of their dead. The natural water-ways constituted an easy and convenient means of transportation to and from the chase.

Do we forget that those there are now living who well remember the first settlers of Leeds? Many there are who can recall the interesting conversations with the first white child born in the town and the eventful tales of adventure related by her. Do we realize that we are daily walking in the paths, stepping in the foot-prints scarcely grown cold, made in common by the white and red children of the forest? Should we make mention of the one and purposely forget the other? Who will question the fact that a work of this kind would thus be rendered incomplete? How oft, when a child, did I draw near, or, perched on my grandfather's knee, attentively listen to the tales of his childhood, many of which I vividly recall as of yesterday. With brains less fertile and more accurate, many tales laid at the Indian's door would never have found a place in print. In 1780 Indians were quite plentiful in Leeds. One encampment was by the river near the place now owned by the Deane Brothers. Another was on the farm owned by Reuben Campbell, near the mouth of Dead River. Still another was on the east side of the road northerly of the old Francis George house, now owned by D. P. True. At the south end of the *Androscoggin Lake, on the place now occupied by Herbert Parker, was an encampment; while Stinchfield's Point was another place occupied by them. These were small villages—those of families, or clans. Others of a few tents were scattered along the shores of the Thirty-Mile River and in such other places as afforded good facilities for hunting and fishing. To say that on the Norris, or White-Oak Island, was an Indian cemetery is only to repeat the story familiar to every householder, not only in Leeds, but nearly all in the surrounding towns. This was only one of many in the vicinity.

Not unlike the white people of this country from colonial times to the present, they buried their dead in family cemeteries. They consecrated a place apart from others for the final resting place of their families, but none were placed therein until they had been before buried in a single lot, where they remained apart and alone. When an Indian died he was placed beside his wigwam in a sitting posture and so was he buried. This was the universal custom of all Indian nations. The narrow house in which he sat was often hedged round with a palisade, and for many moons the women would repair to it thrice daily, to weep.

In no way could they be induced to believe that the body would be raised up; yet they believed in immortality, in the continuance of life. No civilized nation paid so great regard to the remains of their ancestors. They were carefully wrapped in the choicest furs and preserved with affectionate veneration. Once every few years the bones of their scattered dead were collected and with great solemnities cleaned from every remainder of flesh and deposited in the common grave of their fathers,—the wigwam of their dead. These were guarded and cherished as their holy family relics. The deepest sorrow of the Indian was that of being driven from the sacred grounds where his heroic ancestors sleep. With the advance of settlers, the Indians gradually disappeared from place to place along the Androscoggin valley, and subsequently occupied the upper waters of both the Androscoggin and Kennebec. Twice each year, in the seasons of sea-fowl, they descended the river to the coast, stopping along the way to visit the graves of their dead and consecrate them anew. Their course lay along the main river to the mouth of Dead River, up which they paddled to the opening of "Father Thomas," where they always halted and sold their fur. A stay of a few days was here made—a time for those to come in who had scattered along the route on holy missions. Here they divided into two parties, one returning to the Androscoggin River, down which their halting course was made to the sea; while the other crossed the cape and lake, over their old portage to Wilson; thence along its waters to Anabessa-

*Sometimes designated as Stinchfield Pond, Androscoggin Great Pond.

cook; thence to Cobbosseecontee, following its outlet to the Kennebec; thence to the coast. There large quantities of sea-fish and fowl—important adjuncts to the Indian's larder—were taken and carried back to their forest fastnesses. In the absence of salt, fish and meat were preserved by the use of smoke, and later dried by the sun. On these occasions all but those too aged and infirm to endure the journey were taken along, the squaws to spread the tents, gather the wood, bring the water, dress and cure the flesh and fish, and perform such other duties as the warrior's dignity forbade him. These journeys were made in birch-bark canoes and attended with an array of paint and feathers—a sight worth seeing! Their last tribal trip to the sea was in the spring of 1796, on which occasion they bade a last sad farewell to their few white friends on the lower Androscoggin waters, abandoned the graves of their fathers to the watchful care of here and there a lone Indian in solitude, and followed the broken fragments of their kinfolks of the Abinakis nation to Canada. Where are they? To an island in the Penobscot River came such of them, in later years, as lacked the ambition and endurance to journey to the far west, and diluted by the blood of French Canadians while in their country, since, freshly infused, but a lingering spark of the red man's blood remains where once their mighty nations dwelt. Not one pure blood is left—the last having passed to the happy hunting grounds thirty and more years ago.

> Far away 'neath the sunset hill,
> Lingering there in the dismal shade
> The red man's grave, in which to fill,
> His tottering form will soon be laid.

JOHN CLARK STINCHFIELD.

CHAPTER III.

EARLY SETTLERS AND THEIR FAMILIES.

STINCHFIELD FAMILY.

The pioneer settlers of Leeds were Thomas[2] and Rogers[2] Stinchfield. They were hardy sons of John Stinchfield[1], who was born in Leeds, England, October 12, 1715, and Elizabeth Burns[1], born in the north of Ireland, of Scotch parentage, December 21, 1713. John[1] and Elizabeth[1] formed an acquaintance on shipboard during their passage to this country in 1735, and two years later were united in marriage in Gloucester, Mass., at which port they landed and continued their residence until 1755, when they moved, with their family of six children, to New Gloucester, District of Maine, a tract of land granted by general court in 1735, to inhabitants of Gloucester, Mass., from which it derived its name. The block house to which John[1] moved his family had been built and prepared by him, as were a few others by his fellow-pioneers the year previous, and was located at the base of the northerly portion of Stinchfield Hill, south-easterly and adjacent to the old cemetery, southerly from Gloucester Lower Corner. A stockade was also built just north of the cemetery in which resort could be taken in defending the families against attack by Indians. Still another similar building was erected in which to corral the cows and goats that fed by day on the vast meadows of natural grasses that furnished them winter food as well. For a complete account, which includes the heroic defence of this little colony from Indian attacks, from 1754 to 1760, the reader is referred to the "Maine Historical Society," which is contemplating the erection of a granite memorial on the same site,—a *fac simile* of the original building, to the memory of John Stinchfield[1], two of his sons, and the nine others whose names appear in the list of heroes of those years. The parents of Thomas[2] and Rogers[2] Stinchfield passed the remainder of their lives in New Gloucester. The father died January 3, 1783, and the mother August 19, 1785. They were buried in the old cemetery near where they had lived.

Their children were all born in Gloucester, Mass., to wit: John[2], born October 23, 1738; William[2], b. January 9, 1741; Elizabeth², b. May 18, 1743; James², b. July 13, 1745; Thomas², b. December 29, 1747; and Rogers² M. W., b. October 13, 1752.

John² married Mehitable Windship. This was the first marriage solemnized in New Gloucester. They resided and died in Danville. William² married Mary Bodge, of Windham, and lived and died in New Gloucester. Elizabeth² married Deacon John Walker, of Gray, and settled there. James² married Sarah Parsons, and resided on the old homestead. Thomas² married Sarah Paul, *nee* True, a daughter of Deacon Benjamin True, one of the very early settlers of the town of Turner, who went there from New Gloucester. She was a widow and the mother of one son (Marshfield Paul), at the age of twenty-one years. Thomas² and Sarah were married in New Gloucester December 17, 1765. Rogers² M. W. married Sarah Babson, in New Gloucester, in 1773.

If not from choice, necessity required the people of those times to devote much of their time to the use of the gun in the extermination of the ferocious wild beasts of the forest; and to provide their families with meat, moose, deer, caribou, and other favorite animals were pursued and taken. Thus led on, fur-bearing animals were sought for their money value, and all, combined with a natural fondness of adventure, brought out many a full-fledged hunter and trapper who, under other circumstances, with different surroundings, would have acquired a like prominenece in the higher pursuits of life. To them we owe much for what we are and what we enjoy. None but the bravest, intelligent, independent, ambitious, hardy, and strong, could have come out to a new, wild country of such magnitude, with a fixed purpose of subduing and civilizing it, and effected the establishment of a government, the equal of which the sun has never warmed and lighted.

May it be remembered that the children of the early settlers of this country were reared under Scriptural teachings, Christian influences, and moral training. Education was by no means neglected, schools for the youth being a close second to churches, where the parents assembled for mutual instruction. Neither was physical culture omitted. The gun, the axe, the spade, and hoe, the scythe, rake, and fork, and the ever-remaining walls of stone are all evidence of their efficiency in that important branch of education.

As a boy, Thomas², with others whose parents composed the little colony of New Gloucester and did their field work in common, was often posted beside a rock or stump, to watch and give warning of the approach of Indians; while the parents and elder boys, with their guns stacked a few rods in advance of them, did the planting, hoeing, and harvesting. This became distasteful to him, and as he grew in years, he often remonstrated with his people, presenting his earnest, honest conviction that man, whether civilized or savage, could best be conquered and won by kindness, but never by the prevailing and practiced belief that "there are no good Indians but dead ones." So firmly was he established in his faith of Indian manhood, that honesty and kindness would be met with reciprocity, not wanting in courage or bravery, with gun in hand and hunting-knife in his belt as a defense against the forest animals, tinder-box and flints in his pockets, he frequently was absent from home for days in the trackless woods. His first meeting with Indians was on the west bank of the Androscoggin River, at the mouth of the "Twenty-Mile Stream." He approached the little encampment unobserved until he stepped into the small open with the muzzle of his gun pointing downward, an indication of peace. His youth, too, may have been an element in his unmolested admission to their wigwams. The piercing eye of Sabattis, the chief, detected no purpose in the youthful Thomas but an open and honest one, and a friendship was there created that in future years extended to all the Indian tribes in the northern part of Maine. Probably no other white man every enjoyed the full confidence, which he never betrayed, of so many Indians as he. To him they gave the name of "Father Thomas," and his name was known to them throughout the whole land. His services were sought in all disputes or quarrels of theirs, and his decisions were invariably received as the highest order of unwritten law. Exceptions were never taken nor appeals made, but silent submission as of right. To this friendship is the town of Leeds indebted for its first settlers. Easterly from the railroad crossing, near where the railroad bridge spans Dead River, distant about twenty-five rods, formerly the wigwams of Pocasset and his clan were spread. To this clearing were they moved from the north-easterly shore of Pocasset Lake, northerly of where Jennings stream empties its waters. How long that land had been under Indian cultivation is unknown, but the fact that it was a permanent, fixed village, might indicate that many crops had been there harvested. It was a favorite place of the red men but as an inducement to Thomas[2] to settle in their midst, Sabattis presented it to him and removed his village to a spot about twenty rods north of that now occupied by the Francis George house, owned by D. P. True.

In the spring of 1779 Thomas[2] and his younger brother, Rogers[2], came up the Androscoggin and Dead Rivers in a dugout loaded with farm implements, camp utensils and stores to found homes with none but Indian friends and neighbors. After spading the ground and planting the seeds their attention and labor was given to the building of a log or block house, which they located where the wigwam of Sabattis had stood and many times been shared by Thomas while on hunting expeditions.

This was the first permanent structure planted on the forest lands now included within the boundary lines of the town of Leeds. On the opposite bank of Dead River, westerly from the county road, they then built a second block-house, for Rogers[2]. This completed they returned, as they had come, to their families in New Gloucester. In the time of harvest they came again, erected hovels, secured their crops, buried their potatoes in the ground and were gone. Another visit was made on the March crust, and this time a goat was led in, followed by three others, and constituted the primitive domestic animals of the town. The stock of camp utensils was also replenished by means of loaded sleds drawn by these men, whose strength and endurance were unbounded. A goodly amount of venison was secured and dried, and quantities of maple sugar and molasses made and stored for future consumption. These homes prepared—humble and unpretentious though they were—early in June, these brothers returned to New Gloucester for their wives and children. On the tenth day of that month, one of warmth and sunshine, a party composed of two ladies, five men, two young men, and nine children, with five horses on which were packed the ladies, five children, and their belongings, started out from New Gloucester. They followed a narrow, bushed-out path to the Androscoggin River. Here their course turned to the north along its west bank to the Little Androscoggin, which they forded. On a small plat of grass, the only cleared spot that marked their pathway, just below Lewiston Falls, long since utilized for building lots in the city of Auburn, they halted to lunch. On the opposite side of the river three or four houses were seen, probably those of Paul Hildreth, David Pettengill, Lawrence J. Harris, Asa Varnum, or others of the early settlers of Lewiston. Remounted, they proceeded up the river, on a trail made by families who had recently settled in Turner, to the mouth of the Twenty-Mile Stream, where they arrived at mid-afternoon. Here Thomas[2] and Rogers[2] had each left a dug-out canoe while *en route* to New Gloucester.

From the backs of the horses the ladies and children were transferred to the canoes and landed on the opposite bank of the river. Under the care and guidance of Rogers[2] they made the remainder of the distance, about four forest miles, on foot; arriving at the log-house on the south bank of Dead River ere the sunset. The three men and five horses, whose services were of great aid in making the journey of the ladies and children less fatiguing, returned to New Gloucester that night. The baggage was transferred to the canoes, one manned by Thomas[2] and Thomas[3], Jr., a lad of twelve years, and the other by his step-son, Marshfield Paul, and the other young man, and conveyed up the Androscoggin and down Dead River to their destination, where they arrived the following day. Thus runs the narrative of the primitive settlement of Leeds. These homes were hospitable resting places for other pioneer settlers in this section of the District of Maine, and without regard to color or race, none went away hungry or cold.

For the convenience of the Indians, who were then very numerous, and subsequently for the early settlers, Thomas[2] established a trading post and did a large business in the fur trade. From the lake regions, even to the head waters of the Androscoggin, the Indians made semi-annual excursions to the coast and always brought their season's catch of fur to "Father Thomas." His was the first store in town. Only necessary articles were kept on sale, and those were purchased in Portland, packed on horses, brought to Turner and boated down Dead River; or, by winter roads, crossing the Androscoggin on ice. In the fall of 1780, with the assistance of settlers in Lewiston and New Gloucester, a winter road was bushed out through Greene to Lewiston, and in December three cows were gotten through to Leeds. From the natural grass meadows by the lake, that specie known as bluejoint, then growing there in abundance, had been gathered and garnered for winter food for the goats then on the premises and the cows that were to be.

On account of navigation of the river, settlements were made earlier in the Kennebec valley than in the Androscoggin. Winthrop (Pond Town) was first settled in 1765, by Timothy Foster. The fourth family to settle in that town was that of John Chandler, who came there from New Ipswich, N. H., in 1767. He was a man of means and in 1768 erected a saw- and grist-mill on the site where the mills now stand in Winthrop village. This was a great convenience to the early settlers, not only of Winthrop, but the neighboring towns as well. In 1774, the proprietors of Livermore Township induced the people of Winthrop to open a cart-road from the mills to the westerly line of Winthrop, near the dwelling of Job Fuller, the first settler of Wayne, and to erect a bridge across the stream connecting the two small bodies of water, now known as Berry and Dexter Ponds. The bridge was built by Mr. James Craig and still bears the name of Craig Bridge. In 1775 Job Fuller, Reuben Besse, Ebenezer Handy, and William Raymond, representing the only families then in Wayne, assisted by Ichabod Howe and son, of Winthrop, opened the road as formerly surveyed from Winthrop line, near Craig Bridge, through Wayne village to Livermore line, at the extreme northern boundary of the Androscoggin Great Pond, Bear Brook. In the fall of 1780 Thomas[2] and Rogers[2] bushed out a foot-path from the east shore of the Great Pond, intersecting this road near the house of Job Fuller. This completed, their way lay across the pond on ice, or in boats, a distance of three miles; thence over land to the mills twice that distance, where they obtained their first meal ground from corn grown on Leeds soil.

This path was utilized by other early settlers along the banks of Dead River, until 1786, when Thomas Wing built a grist-mill on the Thirty-Mile River, in Wayne, on a dam built by Jonathan Howe, of Winthrop, in 1783, and on which the same year he had erected a saw-mill. With the building of this mill the tow-path was forever abandoned for that purpose for which it was made and that mill received the patronage of Leeds farmers.

In the spring of 1781 two pairs of steers, three years old, and a bull, two years old, were driven and led from New Gloucester over the route the families came the year previous, and swimming the Androscoggin at West Leeds, were installed in their homes in the forest, where later they became important factors in clearing and subduing it. A crooked yoke was made for the bull and he did such work as was subsequently done by horses. In winter, hitched to a sled in like manner as horses are, loaded with boys and bags of corn, he was a frequent visitor at the mill; and of evenings, in like manner harnessed, made merry the boys and girls in their neighborly calls on the young people of the other early families, who settled in the vicinity.

The seasons of 1781 were busy ones for these pioneers. A communication was opened with settlers in Turner, on True's hill, westerly from Turner Center Bridge which spans the Androscoggin River. This path lay from near the house of Rogers[2] across Dead Hole, over the southerly end of Otis Hill near the churches at Leeds Center, to the river, nearly opposite the mouth of Twenty-Mile Stream, closely following that spotted out by which the families were piloted in. By a preconcerted agreement, the Turner settlers cut a path to the west branch of the river, which, together with a dug-out furnished by each little colony, completed the connection of the neighboring settlements.

In the year 1790, Thomas[2] built the first frame house in Leeds. It was located on the same site now occupied by the dwelling-house of Isaac S. Carver.

The carpenter work was done by Robert Erskine, who later settled on Beech Hill in Wayne. The bricks used in the cellar and in the construction of the chimney were made by hand on the south bank of Dead River, between the county road and the railroad and burned in a kiln near by. These were the first bricks made in Leeds.

Of the family of Roger[2] Stinchfield, three children were born in New Gloucester, viz.: Betsey[3], b. April 14, 1774; Abigail[3], b. March 18, 1776; Susanna[3], b. Sept. 2, 1778; and eight born in Leeds, viz.: Rogers[3], b. Feb. 9, 1781, the first white male child born in the town; Zebulon[3], b. July 2, 1783; Sarah[3], b. May 27, 1785; William[3], b. Nov. 14, 1787; Ezra[3], b. Feb. 22, 1790; Solomon[3], b. March 13, 1792; Ezekiel[3], b. April 17, 1795; and Benjamin[3], b. June 29, 1798.

HISTORY OF LEEDS 23

Betsey[3] married Oliver Otis and settled on that part of her father's original farm in Leeds known afterward as the Otis Hill. She died where she had lived, and was buried in Leeds.

Abigail[3] married Shubel Davis, located on Stinchfield ridge, in the town of Milo, and died there March 27, 1852.

Susanna[3] married Stephen Freeman and settled in Greene.

Capt. Rogers[3] married Mary Lindsey and settled in Wayne. He later moved to Milo; thence to Robbinston; thence to Marion, Iowa, where his wife died. He subsequently married Fannie Allen. He returned to Robbinston, Me., and there died May 31, 1862.

Zebulon[3] married Sarah Stewart and settled in Milo. His second wife was Keziah Freeman. Zebulon died in Milo, March 25, 1836.

Sarah[3] married John Rowe and settled in Danville.

William[3] married Sarah Canwell, of Fayette. They settled in Milo, but subsequently moved to Minnesota, where he died October 25, 1850, and his widow July 1, 1868.

Ezekiel[3] married Tamson Eldridge, of Bucksport; settled in Wesley, Me., and died there June 17, 1851.

Solomon[3] married Jerusha Keene, of Turner; settled in Milo, where his wife died September 20, 1867; and he August 14, 1869.

Ezekiel[3] married Tamson Eldridge, of Bucksport; settled in Milo; subsequently moved to Lawrence, Mass., where he died in 1852.

Benjamin[3] married Mary A. Herrick, settled in Milo, and subsequently moved to the Province of New Brunswick and further of him not known.

Rogers[2], Sen., continued his residence in Leeds until his wife's death, February 10, 1822, and burial in the cemetery near Lothrop's Corner, and soon followed his children to Milo, where most of them settled, dying in that town May 2, 1827. Of his eleven children and ninety-one grandchildren, none of his descendants are remaining in Leeds.

Nothing is more commendable in a historian than accuracy. In the Atlas of Androscoggin County, published in the year 1873, among the items of history of the town of Leeds, mention is made of two young men who accompanied the families of Thomas and Rogers Stinchfield from New Gloucester to their primitive homes in Littleborough (Leeds). Who were they? While Thomas and his son, Thomas, Jr., came in one canoe, the two young men came in the other. One of them was Marshfield Paul, a son of the wife of Thomas, by a former husband. Of the other, we come in conflict with the above named publication. It is due the public and of sufficient moment to one of the prominent families of the town to justify the writer in using sufficient space in this work to present the facts and correct a long standing error. We refer

to the account given in that work of the life of Rev. Thomas
Davis Francis—a man who did more in shaping the early course
of the town and is nearer the hearts of the people, perhaps, than
any one who has ever lived within its borders. The substance of
that narrative, as there given, is: *"He came to America and
landed here in May, 1778; in the succeeding fall was at Bangor,
went to New Gloucester, fell in with a man by the name of Stinchfield, who, having sons in Leeds, hither he came to teach school.
But four families were then residing in the town, to wit: Thomas
and Rogers Stinchfield, Jirah Fish, and Daniel Lane." These
events are all therein said to have transpired in the year 1778.
These facts follow in contrast with the above. There is no question
with that part of the narrative relating to the place and date of
his birth, his early boyhood, the manner and date of his arrival in
America, his subsequent service at Castine, his journey through
the wilderness and the hardships he encountered; or the time and
manner of his arrival in New Gloucester; but from that date
impossibilities mark its course. Thomas and Rogers Stinchfield
were the pioneer settlers of Littleborough and the date on which
their families came to the plantation was June 10, 1780. Did
Thomas Davis Francis come here in the fall of 1778, to teach the
children? The order of settlement by families was: Thomas and
Rogers Stinchfield in June, 1780; Jirah Fish, in the fall of 1780;
Thomas Millett, in the fall of 1781; Daniel Lane, in the fall of
1782; Zadock Bishop, in the spring of 1783, etc. Were the
Stinchfields, Fishes, and Lanes the only families living here in
1778? In speaking further of the early settlers the account says:
"In 1783, or the year following, William Gilbert and Daniel
Lothrop, Jr., came in. About the time they came, or soon after,
perhaps about 1785, Daniel Lane and Thomas Millett came. Then
came Increase Leadbetter and many Revolutionary soldiers followed, some of whose names were: James and William Lindsey,
William and Obadiah Pettingill, William and Josiah Turner,
Morgan Brewster, Francis George, Andrew Cushman, and Daniel
Robbins. Then there were young men who came in from 1783 to
1790, who soon married and had families, to wit: Thomas Francis,
Uriah and Phineas Foss, John, Samuel, and Nathaniel Jennings,
and others whose surnames were: Collier, Bailey, Otis, Dunham, Sampson, Berry, Caswell, Carver, Knapp, Paul, Drake,
Woodman, Whiting, Gould, Pratt, Daily, and subsequently Lamb,
Herrick, Howard, and others." If Thomas Millett came about
1785, and Thomas D. Francis from 1783 to 1790, how is the fact
that Thomas D. Francis married in July, 1784, Eunice, the eldest
daughter of Thomas Millett, and was obliged to go from Little-

*Correct narrative given in the account of the Francis family in this
work.

borough to New Gloucester to have the marriage service performed, to be explained? If Marshfield Paul came to Littleborough from 1783 to 1790, it could not have been he who came with his mother in 1780. If Thomas D. Francis went to New Gloucester in the fall of 1778, as borne out in the historical account of the engagement at Castine in which he participated, where was he from that time until he came to Leeds? The facts are that when he and his comrades, one of whom was Francis George, went to New Gloucester, in 1778, after that memorable journey from Bangor, he was taken into the family of Thomas Stinchfield, with whom he continued to live, and when the family of which Marshfield Paul was a member came to Littleborough, they came as members of it and were the two *young* men mentioned in the foregoing narrative. He lived in the family of Thomas Stinchfield until his marriage in July, 1784, when he lived in the family of his wife's father until the spring of 1785. at which time he and his wife and son moved into his log house on the farm where he spent the remaining years of his useful life.

The foregoing in relation to Thomas D. Francis and Thomas Millett is here inserted for the purpose of correcting the error that crept into the narrative by S. L. Howard, Esq., through the faulty memory of his informant.

The children of Thomas[2] Stinchfield and his wife, Sarah Paul, *nee* True, were, all but one, born in New Gloucester, viz.: Thomas[3], Jr., b. Sept. 8, 1768, who remained single and died at his father's house in 1798, and buried in the family lot on his father's farm; Sarah[3], called Sally, b. July 10, 1770, married in 1789 Zephaniah Hicks and settled in Leeds. She had a family of twelve children, viz.: Abigail[4], b. Feb. 3. 1790; Sarah[4], b. Aug. 19. 1793; Thomas[4] S., b. July 19. 1795; Abraham[4], b. July 6, 1798; Sullivan[4] and Franklin[4], b. March 17, 1799; Samuel[4], born Aug. 20. 1801; Hannah[4], b. Feb. 19, 1804; Zephaniah[4], b. Aug. 19. 1806; Elbridge[4], b. Dec. 6, 1807 (died young); Annie[4], b. March 14, 1809, and Elbridge[4], b. Nov. 15, 1811.

Zephaniah Hicks, Sen., died in Leeds, Oct. 6, 1812. Sarah Stinchfield[3], his widow, died in Greene, in 1848, was buried in Leeds.

James[3], the third child of Thomas[2] Stinchfield, born Aug. 10, 1773, came to Leeds with his parents; married by Rev. Thomas D. Francis June 29, 1802, Hannah, a daughter of William Pettingill and his wife, Lydia Cobb, who came to Leeds from Bridgewater, Mass., in 1790, and settled on the farm now occupied by William R. Pettingill, a grandson. James[3] settled on that part of his father's original claim bordering on the most western portion of Androscoggin Lake, then bearing the name of "Androscoggin Great Pond" (in some documents and records "Stinchfield Pond") which included within its limits nearly all that portion called

Hedgehog Hill. On a small, level plat of ground on the easterly side of that hill and near its southern extremity, at an altitude of fifty feet above the lake, in the year 1801, co-existent with the incorporation of the town, he erected a large frame house and barn. There his children were born and reared, viz.: John[4], b. Dec. 6, 1802; Isaac[4], b. May 5, 1804; Mary[4] (called Polly), b. Dec. 9, 1805; James[4], b. Sept. 9, 1807; Elvira[4], b. June 29, 1809; Joel[4], b. March 4, 1811; Thomas[4], b. Dec. 6, 1812; Hannah[4], b. Dec. 25, 1814; Abigail[4], b. Oct. 16, 1817; Aramantha P.[4] (called Armenta), b. Aug. 24, 1819; Sewall[4], b. March 29, 1822; Allen[4], b. April 8, 1825; Eliza[4], b. Nov. 24, 1830.

James[3] Stinchfield, Sen., died July 28, 1857, and his widow, Hannah Pettingill, who was born in Bridgewater, Mass., Feb. 14, 1786, died June 19, 1874. They were buried in a cemetery about two miles northerly of their former home, on the road to Beech Hill, in the town of Wayne.

Martha[3] (called Patty), the fourth child of Thomas, b. Nov. 28, 1774, married Isaac Freeman Aug. 7, 1794, and settled in Leeds, on the farm which he cleared, that now owned and occupied by Truman Deane. Their children were: Allen[4], b. March 1, 1795; Isaac[4], b. Oct. 9, 1796; Martha[4], b. Aug. 13, 1799; Elizabeth[4], b. Aug. 20, 1801; Keziah[4], b. May 24, 1803; Fannie[4], b. Jan. 9, 1805; Isaac[4], b. May 2, 1807; Ezra[4], b. Sept. 13, 1809; Lydia[4], b. Oct. 7, 1811; Lois L.[4], b. Nov. 1, 1813; Sarah True[4], b. July 12, 1816; Samuel[4], b. Sept. 24, 1818; Barzilla[4], b. Sept. 24, 1820; and Rosilla[4], b. Aug. 22, 1822. Martha[3] Freeman, *nee* Stinchfield, died in Greene in 1850, and was buried in Leeds. Her husband, Isaac Freeman, was born June 7, 1771. (The date of death unknown to writer.)

Capt. Samuel[3] Stinchfield, the fifth child of Thomas[2], was born Nov. 6, 1777. He built the house in which Davis P. True now lives, in the year 1805, and in the same year married, in New York City, Mary King, who was born there Dec. 9, 1780. His early life was devoted to the study of navigation and at the early age of twenty-four, he was master of a vessel. At the age of twenty-eight he married, and the year following brought his wife and son from New York and occupied his new house in Leeds. There his other children were born: George K.[4], b. in New York, April 2, 1806; James K.[4], born in Leeds, July 9, 1808; Mary Ann[4], b. May 15, 1810; Samuel[4], b. Feb. 1, 1812; Thomas B.[4], b. Jan. 19, 1814; Adelia[4], b. Jan. 6, 1816; John K.[4], b. July 6, 1818; Stephen D.[4], b. May 15, 1820, and Anson G.[4], b. Sept. 7, 1822.

May 20, 1826, Capt. Samuel[3] was thrown from his team, his neck broken, causing instant death. He was buried in the Lothrop cemetery at Leeds Center. His widow died at the home of her eldest son, in Fond-du-lac, Wis., Jan. 21, 1858, and buried in that state.

HISTORY OF LEEDS

John[3], the sixth child of Thomas[2], was born Sept. 13, 1779. He, too, was a sea-faring man and was buried in a sailor's grave; but there is no available date of when. He was young and unmarried.

Rebecca[3], the seventh child of Thomas[2], was born in Leeds, Dec. 11, 1780. She was "The babe in the woods"—the first white child born in Leeds. Her name must have been selected with the full knowledge of its significance—she was truly an enchanting beauty! In 1799 she married Capt. Phineus Foss, who was born in Saco, Feb. 10, 1772, and settled near the Foss corner, at North Leeds. They had issue, John[4], b. Oct. 10, 1800; Harriet[4], b. Aug. 14, 1802; Allura[4], b. Feb. 5, 1805; Alvin[4], b. Apr. 6, 1807; Eliza[4], b. June 13, 1809; Loring[4], b. June 18, 1812, and Phineus[4], b. Jan. 8, 1814.

Capt. Phineus Foss died April 14, 1814, and Rebecca[3], his widow, Mar. 3, 1869. Their place of burial is in the cemetery beside Dead River, near where the middle bridge formerly crossed it, but long since removed and gone.

Nov. 18, 1791, Sarah Paul, *nee* True, wife of Thomas[2] Stinchfield, died, and was buried on the top of a small hill, about thirty rods westerly from the buildings now occupied by Isaac S. Carver. That site was selected for its seclusion and beauty. From its summit, in the foreground, is spread the placid, charming waters of the lake—the gracefully encircling meadow land of Stinchfield cove; in the distance, rising high above the eastern shore, towers Morrison's Heights, wrapped, near and far, in endless, unbroken chains, from which Nature's most beautiful pictures are suspended; while the background, gently sloping to the smooth, winding waters of Dead River, around which so many fond remembrances cluster, is lost in the wooded, abruptly rising ridge of land from a narrow intervale extending along the opposite shore. A beautiful spot, selected with an artistic eye as a fitting resting-place of the dead! The second wife of Thomas[2] Stinchfield was Hannah, a daughter of Thomas Lindsey, who came to Leeds in 1797, settled on Bishop Hill, and was drowned in Androscoggin Great Pond, Dec. 25, 1802. She was born in 1752. The fruit of this marriage was one child, Hannah, b. Dec. 4, 1793. She married Elezer Carver, April 7, 1816, and settled near Dead River, about one mile northerly from the home of her youth. They had issue Betsey[4], b. Nov. 8, 1816; Jason[4], b. April 13, 1818; Mary Ann[4], b. Aug. 27, 1819; Thomas S.[4], b. Mar. 29, 1821; Arvilla A.[4], b. July 17, 1822; Hannah[4], b. Dec. 12, 1824, Mary[4], b. Dec. 12, 1824, (twins); Nancy[4] b. Dec. 12, 1825; Alice[4], b. Mar. 19, 1827; Isaac S.[4], b. May 20, 1829; John[4], b. June 22, 1830, and James[4], b. Mar. 15, 1834.

Elezer Carver died Dec. 4, 1856, and Hannah[3], his widow, Jan. 18, 1872. They were buried in the cemetery at North Leeds, sometimes denominated "The Robert Gould cemetery."

The Stinchfields were a people of fine physique, of medium stature, full, round chests, broad shoulders, excessive muscular powers, and nerves of the spring-tempered-steel kind. They were a hardy, healthy people, endowed with longevity. Yet the hardships and feats of endurance they experienced, incident to the settlement of a new country, bore its fruits in succeeding generations and in some of the branches, early decay and death has been the sad result. Asking the indulgence of the reader we here digress for the purpose of relating an incident that occurred in the life of Thomas[2] Stinchfield—which to the incredulous may mean little—showing the wonderful nerve-power and decision he possessed,—a feature common in the family, and probably in other early families, as well. In the late fall of 1825, when the employment of horse-power in threshing grain was in its infancy, a machine was being operated in his barn. Although Thomas[2] was then seventy-eight years old, he was the motive-power of all parties of workmen of which he was a member. He stood before the beater of the machine and fed it with unthreshed grain. By some means, a hand was caught by the teeth of the rapidly revolving beater and drawn into the meshes, literally tearing it in shreds, and tenaciously seeking more to devour. But for an active brain, quick thought and Herculean strength, the whole arm would have been drawn in and masticated. Messengers were dispatched to Leeds Centre and Wayne village for Doctors Thomas Bridgham and Thomas Brigham. As was his custom, Dr. Brigham had imbibed freely of the ardent, and when, if ever, uninfluenced by it, made little pretension in surgery. Neither of them possessed surgical instrument more than a knife and dull, rusty saw. Thus equipped, they stripped for business. A table and ropes were ordered, on, and with which to bind the unfortunate patient. Opiates, in such cases, were then unheard of, but stimulants were freely given. Many of the sympathetic relatives, friends and neighbors had gathered to render any possible aid, among them a young man of twenty-one years—a favorite grandson, Isaac[4] Stinchfield. When the order of the doctors was given for brandy, table and ropes to be brought in, it was promptly countermanded by the patient with unmistakable emphasis. "I will neither be bound nor drunken! It is essential for someone to know what is being done." Turning to the grandson, who stood beside him, he said, "Isaac, you may stand here and if I can't hold my arm steadily, you can take hold and support it." He extended it and told the doctors to begin. Neither protest, persuasion nor threat availed anything—all knew he said what he meant and he meant what he said. It was a long, tedious operation, but not a muscle was seen to move, nor a word uttered by him, while carefully watching the bungling performance, until the old saw entered the marrow, then, casting his eyes aside, he said,

"Isaac[4], that is a little tough." Such fortitude is seldom displayed!

In after years he wielded with agility the axe and hoe, single-handed, and did much that another—a younger man—should have done. He died Oct. 25, 1837, where he had lived fifty-seven years, at the advanced age of ninety. His final resting-place, beside the wife of his youth, remains unmarked, his epitaph unwritten. That he, whose moral and financial duty it was to erect a fitting memorial at the grave of Leeds' first adopted son, should have failed that honor, is inexcusable. His second wife died Jan. 12, 1839, and was placed beside him. This memorable spot, where the remains of the pioneer are reposing, is seldom visited. It is the few, even, of the present generation, who have the knowledge of its location. With the passing of future generations it will be forgotten and lost to man; but ever fresh in the memory of Him "Who knoweth all things."

Of the family of James Stinchfield[3] and his wife, Hannah Pettengill, John[4], their eldest son, remained single. He and his brother Isaac[4], settled on a portion of the land taken up by their grandfather, Thomas[2]. Their buildings were erected on the east side of the first wrought road in the town,—that from Portland to Farmington,—about one and one-half miles northerly from the railroad and county-road bridges which span Dead River. After the death of his father, he returned to his parent home and cared for his aged mother. He was a man of unquestionable character, respected by all his acquaintances, and beloved by the children for whom he always had a kindly greeting and a feast of sweetmeats. He died Nov. 2, 1871, and his remains were laid beside those of his parents. His memory will live on until this generation shall have passed to the "Great unknown."

Isaac[4], the second child of James[3] married, Sept. 18, 1833, Abigail L., the eldest daughter of Charles Knapp and his wife, Catherine Lindsay. The place of their settlement has been described in the preceding Art. To this farm he subsequently added the entire cape north of Dead River. As a boy in school, he led his classes and obtained a very liberal common school education.* When he reached the age of manhood he went to Massachusetts, and for seven years was in the employ of Oliver Ames, of shovel fame, whose plant was on the Taunton River at a place which bore the Indian name of Squaw-Betty. After his return he married, reared a family of nine children and devoted

---

*School-books were then very few and grammar but little taught. He obtained the loan of one for three days. In the afternoon of the third day the teacher deputed an older scholar to hear his recitation. In the course of time the teacher became much interested and his attention was divided, and at the close asked: "How far did he go?" "From one cover to the other." The book was Murray's Grammar.

the remainder of his life to farming. He was a man of ability and his word or veracity was never in question. The records of Androscoggin County Court of Probate are evidence of his efficiency in the settlement of estates. A prominent feature of his life was, as that of his wife, the education and training of the children, that they might make useful and respectable citizens, wherever their lot might. fall. Their eldest child, Isaac[5], was born in Leeds, Oct. 29, 1836. At the age of seventeen he was a teacher in the schools of the neighboring town of Wayne. Subsequently he was an omnibus driver in Boston. Like many of the earlier members of the family, he fancied the sea, and returning from a voyage to the West Indies he made a voyage of the world. In the early summer of 1858 he went to California, and Sept. 8, 1860, he died in Oakland, in that state, of black diphtheria. There his remains were buried. At the time of his death he was less than twenty-four years of age and unmarried.

Thomas Jefferson[5], their second child, was born in Leeds April 6, 1838. He taught several terms of schools and later engaged in the grocery business on Washington Street, Boston. By close application and honest dealing he acquired a competency, but too close confinement and overwork had its destroying effect, and a long-neglected cold terminated in consumption, of which he died, at his boyhood home in Leeds, May 24, 1867. He, too, was unmarried.

Charles Knapp[5], the third child of Isaac[4], was born in Leeds February 26, 1840. His boyhood days were spent on the farm, which was a portion of the first land owned by a white resident of the town, and until recently has been occupied by members of the Stinchfield family. He began his education in the old schoolhouse that formerly stood in the sands of Beech Hill, near the dwelling of the late H. J. Ridley, in Wayne. From this schoolhouse many teachers and several persons of more or less eminence have been sent out. From there he went to Towle Academy, in the town of Winthrop, where he was first in his classes, under the tuition of Professor C. K. Hutchins, who was reared and educated by Charles Knapp, of Leeds. He next went to "Maine State Seminary," in Lewiston, where he completed his preparatory course. During this time the winter months found him imparting to others his attainments in the capacity of teacher, from which source he derived the necessary funds to enable him to continue his studies. He graduated from the Medical Department of Bowdoin College in the Class of 1865, from which he received the degree of M.D. From there he went to New York City where he availed himself of the advantages in the clinics at Bellevue Hospital Medical College. He established himself in an extensive and lucrative practice in the city. While there he had a severe attack of pneumonia, which resulted in the entire loss of the use of his right lung. He returned to his old home where, after a hard fight with the effects of this malady, he partially recuperated. Having the use of but one lung, the city air with its impurities was avoided. By earnest request of his many friends to locate near home, he was induced to make his residence, if but temporary, in Wayne. He went there in 1870, and practiced when his health would admit. He was always deeply interested in the cause of education. He was supervisor of schools in that town in 1872 and 1873, the duties of which office he discharged with credit to himself and to the satisfaction of the townsmen. His ambition merited a much stronger physique. He was often restrained from carrying into effect many things that would have been of interest and benefit to the people had he not been handicappd by this malady, which was a source of great sorrow and suffering. In the winter of 1874-5, he contracted a severe cold, terminating in the consumption of the remaining lung, and he died at his parents' home, April 1, 1875. He was buried in the family lot in the cemetery which he passed and re-passed in going to and from the old school-house, in and around which cluster many fond remembrances of the boyhood school days of the writer. He, like his older brothers, was never married.

John Clark[5], the fourth child of Isaac[4], was born in Leeds November 3, 1843. From the district and high schools of Wayne he took a course at Towle Academy. Impaired health, which has changed the life course and blighted the ambition of many a school-boy, is here assigned as a reason for retiring from the school-room to the more active and out-of-door labors of life. During his school days he was a teacher in the schools of his native and neighboring towns, initiated at the age of sixteen in the little white school-house in the Additon district in Leeds. July 4, 1863, he married Catherine H., the youngest daughter of Charles Graves and his wife, Paulina Ridley, of Wayne, born November 19, 1844. He became a resident of Wayne July 5, 1863. They had issue Minnie Etta[6], born in Wayne, January 1, 1868, and Roger[6], born in Wayne, January 2, 1876. They became residents of Wayne village, May 8, 1868. Ten years later, January 7, 1878, his wife died. June 13, 1886, he married Henrietta, the youngest daughter of Stillman L. Howard, Esq. She was born in Leeds, December 7, 1853. They have one son, Allen Howard[6], born May 8, 1888. Minnie Etta[6] married H. S. Sleeper, M.D., of Lewiston, Dec. 15, 1897, and resides in that city. From 1868 to March 20, 1890, he was engaged in buying and selling cattle, horses, and sheep; at the same time shipping to the Boston market and retailing meats, etc., since which time he has been engaged in hotel business at Wayne village, making a specialty of entertaining summer guests. He is the present proprietor of the Pocasset House in that town. His name in the list of civil officers of Wayne is of frequent occurrence. In the discharge of public duties he is conscientious and systematic. He is interested in the cause of education, the advancement of young people to positions of responsibility and trust, the progress and improvement of the town, the development of its industries and natural resources, prominent in the societies and corporations with which he is connected, and careful and particular in the discharge of the duties imposed on him.

Rose Ellen[5], the fifth child of Isaac[4], was born in Leeds, December 6, 1845. She married Joseph G., the only son of William Gott and his wife, Ruth Gould, January 3, 1862. They settled at North Leeds. Subsequently they purchased the first farm taken up in the town, that of her great-grandfather, Thomas[2]. Mr. Gott's name is familiar to the people of Leeds, who repeatedly placed him on their list of civil officers and selected him to represent them in the State Legislature. Their present residence is Monmouth. They have two children (lost a son of great promise), viz.: Ida Lorena[6], born in Leeds Feb. 24, 1863, and Winifred A.[6], born in Monmouth July 17, 1880. Ida L.[6] married Harry H. Cochrane June 9, 1887, who was born in Augusta April 6, 1860. Mr. and Mrs. Cochrane have a daughter, Lorena[7], born in Monmouth March 2, 1888, who is the only descendant of Isaac Stinchfield[4] in her generation.

Abbie Lovina[5], the sixth child of Isaac[4], was born in Leeds January 3, 1848. She was a teacher in the schools of Wayne. In that town she married Jason M. Ridley March 16, 1865. A few years they resided in Leeds in the employ of her parents. December 15, 1867, to them was born a son, Charles Adelbert[6]. On May 8, 1868, they settled in Wayne village, where they resided for years, when they removed to Oakland where he engaged in the manufacture of shovel handles. After years of lingering disease she died in that town. Her remains were carried to Wayne and buried in the village cemetery. Her husband and son continue their residence in Oakland, and in connection with their former business the son is a successful dry and fancy goods merchant in that town and commands the respect and esteem of a large circle of acquaintances.

Sewall Wallace[5], the seventh child of Isaac[4], was born in Leeds May 10, 1850. Educated in the district school, he learned the trade of masonry. He became skilled in his work and several fine structures in the cities of New England have been erected under his supervision. In later years he was a contractor and builder in Massachusetts, Rhode Island, and Connecticut. Overexertion and care caused decline, and returning to Maine he died in Monmouth February 22, 1899. His remains were buried in the village cemetery in Wayne. His widow, Jennie S. (Teague) Stinchfield, born in Mt. Vernon, July 4, 1854, is a proprietor and resident in Wayne village. They had a son, Guy C., born in Leeds November 29, 1873.

George Swain[5], the youngest son of Isaac[4], was born in Leeds November 25, 1852. He was educated and a teacher of great promise. His was the exemplary life of a young man beloved by every one within his circle of acquaintances. Conscientious, strictly honest, ambitious, cordial, and moderately dignified, he was a born leader, and his memory is widely and lovingly cherished. Nov. 14, 1877, by the accidental discharge of a gun in the hands of a workman he was mortally wounded, from the effects of which he lived but a few hours. This, the fourth death of sons grown to manhood, he on whom they depended to care for them in their declining years, was a sad blow to his parents, one of whom, the father, survived but a few weeks. Accompanied to his last resting place by a large concourse of relatives and sympathetic friends, his remains were deposited in a flower-decked grave in the family lot in the cemetery where many of his people are reposing.

Ella Frances[5], the youngest child of Isaac[4], was born in Leeds Nov. 1, 1856. She was well educated and fitted herself for a teacher. Not unlike others she changed her mind, and Sept. 29, 1878, married Charles K. Leadbetter. Her married life was not so desirable and pleasant as that of her childhood, and with tear-drops of pity we note her death, which occurred in Wayne village, June, 1889. She was buried in her parents' lot, beside her brothers. She left two beautiful daughters and a son, Rena May[6], born in Leeds Oct. 10, 1879, whose home has been with Mr. and Mrs. Harry H. Cochrane; Shirley Francis[6], born in Leeds Oct. 27, 1881, who has been with his great-aunt, Mrs. Hannah L. Pollard; and Verner Fay, born in Leeds July 19, 1884.

Isaac Stinchfield[4] died in Leeds Jan. 9, 1878, and his widow, born in Leeds March 3, 1814, died in Wayne village, October 6, 1884.

Polly[4], the third child of James[3], married in Leeds, Dec. 11, 1823, Elijah Gott, born in Greene Feb. 1, 1797. They settled on the Lake road in Wayne, near the line which divides that town from Leeds. She was a kind neighbor, model housekeeper, indulgent mother and beloved by all with whom she associated. They had issue Elvira S.[5], born in Wayne April 22, 1825, and Mary Ann[5], born Feb. 16, 1827, both of whom were teachers in the schools of their native town. Elvira S. married John P. Snow Oct. 3, 1852, who was born Nov. 22, 1814. To them were born, in Winthrop, Murietta Edora[6], April 8, 1855, and Elbert[6], Aug. 28, 1858. John P. Snow died Nov. 19, 1861, and Elvira S. died March 19, 1886. They were buried in Wayne.

Mary Ann[5] married, in Boston, Lucius Clark Leadbetter, March 5, 1852, who was born in Wayne Dec. 30, 1825. They settled in Wayne on the farm formerly owned by her father, and subsequently on the Asa Foss farm where they now reside. To them were born four children, viz.: Freddie Clark[6], March 14, 1854, died Sept. 17, 1857; Nellie Ann[6], b. June 19, 1858, married Ulmer P. Francis April 27, 1882; Arthur Clark[6], b. Aug. 17, 1860, married Grace Turner in September, 1892; and Charles Frederic, b. Nov 14, 1866.

Elijah Gott died in Wayne June 22, 1875, and Polly[4], his widow, May 25, 1890. They were buried in Wayne in the cemetery near the dwelling of the late Jared Knapp.

James[4], the fourth child of James[3], married Clarissa, a daughter of Rufus Gould, Feb. 1, 1839, who was born in Livermore April 30, 1819. He built the brick house now standing on the lake road, in Leeds, northerly from Dead River bridges, in 1838, and settled there at the time of his marriage. To them, in this town, were born Eliza Ann[5], Dec. 2, 1839; Levi G., Dec. 4, 1841; James H., April 28, 1845, died June 1, 1846; Dora M., b. in Wayne July 25, 1847; Henry W., Jan. 18, 1852; and Evelyn P., March 25, 1857. In 1846 he sold his place in Leeds, erected a house in Wayne village, to which he removed his family. His children were all educated, some of whom were succssful teachers. Eliza Ann[5], married A. R. Dickinson, a teacher of notoriety, Aug. 10, 1859. At a later date they settled in South Braintree, Mass., where she died July 17, 1892, and Mr. Dickinson Aug. 29, 1899.

Levi G.[5], the second child of James[4], went to California when twenty-one years of age, where he married and reared a large family.

Dora M.[5] remained at home, kept her father's house and cared for him in his declining years. After his decease she went to her sister in Massachusetts and continued her family obligations in caring for her during the time of her sickness; since which, she resides with a younger sister. She is a maiden lady closely endeared to her relatives and friends.

Henry W.[5], the fifth child of James[4], left home early and was engaged in mill business. He returned later to aid in the care of his father and farm duties, where he remained until his father's death. He married Lizzie ———, had one daughter, and subsequently removed to California where he now resides.

Evelyn P.[5], the youngest child of James[4], was a beautiful child, an accomplished young lady, and is a model housewife. Feb. 5, 1891, she married George L. Duckworth, who was born in Bridgewater, Mass., Aug. 23, 1856. Theirs is a pleasant and happy home in South Braintree, Mass.

Clarissa, the wife of James Stinchfield[4], died in Wayne Oct. 10, 1874, and he Dec. 21, 1887. They were buried with their kinfolks in the western part of Wayne.

Elvira[4], the fourth child of James[3], has already received mention.

Joel[4], the fifth child, married Frances Dolly, March 8, 1847, who was born in Jay April 21, 1833, in which town they settled. To them were born Elmira[5], June 19, 1849; Eliza J., March 4, 1852; Lucinda, Jan. 17, 1854; Alluva H., Nov. 24, 1858; John Allen, Sept. 18, 1862; F. Carabelle, Feb. 9, 1867; Fred E., Feb. 7, 1870, and Charles A., June 5, 1872.

Joel[4] died in Jay Sept. 12, 1888. His widow resides at Livermore Falls.

Thomas[4], the next in the list of children of James[3], married Elizabeth Gray, a descendant of one of the first setlers of Monmouth, who was born in that town Oct. 31,1817. They settled in East Livermore where they spent most of their married life. To them were born ten children, many of whom died in childhood (one only remaining), viz.: John Allen[5], July 8, 1840; Almira C. Jan. 3, 1844; Ann Eliza, Oct. 31, 1845; Ann Eliza, Nov. 17, 1848; Emma J., Oct. 10, 1850; Christiana B., Sept. 18, 1852; Florence E., Jan. 7, 1855; Hannah E., July 15, 1857; John Allen, June 15, 1859; Thomas S., Aug. 17, 1852.

Thomas[4] died in East Livermore Sept. 1, 1863, and his widow in Wayne Dec. 20, 1878. They were buried in Wayne, with their people.

Hannah[4], the eighth child of James[3], married Greenwood C. Gordon, Oct. 4, 1840, who was born Feb. 7, 1815, and settled first in East Livermore, later in Wayne, and finally in Leeds where they now reside—an aged and much respected couple. Their children are Hezekiah S.[5], born in East Livermore Dec. 21, 1842; John Allen[5], b. in Wayne June 12, 1846; Henry G.[5], b. in Wayne April 19, 1848, and Viola H.[5], b. in Leeds Oct. 16, 1851.

Hezekiah S.[5] married Phebe Jane, a daughter of Charles Gordon. They have issue Costello D.[6], b. in Leeds Oct. 25, 1868; Josephine E., b. in Leeds Sept. 11, 1870, and Irving, b. in Monmouth Jan. 23, 1874.

John Allen[5] married May 22, 1890, Adelia C. Hartt, born May 16, 1860, and resides on the parental home farm. They have one son, John H. Gordon, b. July 21, 1894.

Henry G.[5] married Carrie E. Peaslee, b. June 8, 1861, and resides in Wayne. They have issue Ira D., b. in Wayne, Aug. 22, 1885; Ellery W., b. March 8, 1889, and Leland H., b. Nov. 6, 1894.

Viola H.[5] married William R. Millett, who was born Dec. 3, 1845. They had one son, William A., born in Leeds July 27, 1874. William R. Millett died Aug. 5, 1875, and Viola H. died Feb. 26, 1896.

Abigail C.[4], the next in the list of children of James[3], married John W. Vose Oct. 22, 1846, who was born in Kingfield

March 7, 1822. They settled first in Wayne, and later in Winthrop, and had issue John W.[5], Jr., b. in Wayne Aug. 15, 1847; Abbie E., b. in Winthrop Aug. 29, 1849; Charles Allen and James Sewall, b. April 1, 1854, and Miney E., b. Jan. 25, 1858.

Abigail C.[4] died in Winthrop Nov. 27, 1897, and her husband a few weeks later.

Aramantha P.[4], the next in the list of children of James[3], married Simon P. Gray, who was born in Monmouth and settled first in East Livermore and later on the old Herrick place, at Barker's Mills, Lewiston, where she died Aug. 9, 1862. She had two daughters, Augusta Ann[5], who died in Lewiston; and Mary[5], who married Luville, a son of Harrison Gould and his wife, Sarah Stinchfield. Mary has issue two or more children.

Sewall[4], the eleventh child of James[3], was engaged in whale fishery. After retiring he spent a few years at home on the farm and married Hannah Raymond, by whom he had a son, Sewall Warren, and a daughter, Nancy Maria. He subsequently went to California, where later his family were removed and now reside. There he has been successfully engaged in mining.

Allen[4], the youngest son of James[3], was engaged in whale fishery, and later went to California where he accumulated wealth. He was a prominent factor in building and equipping the Street Railway in Portland, Ore. He disappeared several years ago and his people have no further knowledge of him. He was a single man and one much respected by all his acquaintances. He was unlike many, being the only individual who knew his business and attended strictly to it, leaving that of others entirely alone.

FAMILY OF CAPT. SAMUEL AND MARY (KING) STINCHFIELD.

George K., their eldest son, married Jan. 1, 1834, Jane, born Jan. 13, 1810, eldest daughter of Eben and Sarah (Foster) Libby, who was born in Saco, Sept. 6, 1788, and settled in Leeds in 1807. When George was twenty years old his father died and much of the care of the family devolved on him. He was a man of good executive ability which was recognized by his townsmen whose services they sought on their municipal board of selectmen. In 1855 he removed to Fond-du-Lac, Wis., where he died Dec. 4, 1881. His wife died there Oct. 22, 1878, and his mother Jan. 21, 1858. To them were born in Leeds, Me., two children, Sarah Jane and Samuel B. Sarah Jane, b. Nov. 6, 1834, was a young lady of great promise. At the age of eighteen she went into decline. Hoping that a change of location and climate might benefit her, in 1855 her father disposed of his property in Leeds to Samuel P. True and removed to Wisconsin. There she died Sept. 30, 1855.

HON. SAMUEL B. STANCHFIELD.

Samuel B., b. March 17, 1836, received a liberal education in his native State, and accompanied his parents to Wisconsin, where they located on a farm on an eminence just outside the business center of Fond-du-Lac. It is a beautiful location overlooking the town. Mr. Stanchfield is an able, progressive, influential man, appreciated by the people in his section of the State. In public life his services have been in constant demand. In 1874 he was elected town clerk, which office he held for a term of years; is now entered on his eighteenth year as chairman of town board of Fond-du-Lac; was five years chairman of county board of supervisors; serving on his seventeenth year as secretary and treasurer, and six years as president of the Empire and Friendship Insurance Co.; president of the Fond-du-Lac County Agricultural Society two years; president of the Wisconsin Central Stock Growers and Industrial Association three years; was elected to Assembly in 1885 and '86, and in 1888 elected State Senator for four years.

March 18, 1863, he married Ophelia Edgerton, born in Rome, N. Y., Nov. 6, 1837. They have issue three sons, namely: Gancello S., George H., and Bartley K.

Gancello S., b. May 31, 1864, is a farmer; married and has a son and daughter.

George H., b. July 3, 1868, graduated as a civil engineer from the State University, is city engineer of Watertown, Wis. He is married and has two daughters.

Bartley K., b. Oct. 2, 1872, is a graduate of the State University as a mechanical engineer in which profession he is actively engaged.

James K.[5], the second son of Capt. Samuel, a young man of ability and beloved by everybody, by multiplied trouble of deaths and anxiety for the living, suicided March 28, 1838.

Mary Ann[5], the eldest daughter of Capt. Samuel, Sept. 28, 1839, married Stephen, a life-long resident of Leeds, a son of the before mentioned Eben and Sarah (Foster) Libby, who was born in that town May 24, 1814. They settled on the farm where Mrs. Libby now resides—a remarkably smart lady, approaching the last decade of a century. They had issue Ebenezer A., born Nov. 23, 1840, died in New Orleans May 25, 1862; Helen H., b. Aug. 4, 1842 (who married Rev. Aaron Hartt); Charles F., b. Dec. 20, 1843 (married Clara Hartt); Henrietta B., b. March 10, 1846 (married Clark S. Brewster); and Mary Jane[5], b. May 6, 1845 (married George S. Buck), died Feb. 13, 1887.

Stephen Libby died in Leeds April 23, 1890.

Samuel[4], the fourth child of Capt. Samuel[3], was a very promising young man. His death, which occurred July 7, 1834, was a heavy blow to his people. He was held in high esteem by his associates.

Thomas Bartley[4], M.D., the fifth child of Capt. Samuel[3], was a graduate of Bowdoin Medical College. He went to Egypt, Wharton County, Texas, where he had a successful and lucrative practice. July 4, 1848, he there married Susan Ann, a daughter of Capt. W. J. E. Heard, who commanded a company under General Houston, in April, 1836, at the battle of San Jacinto, which gained the independence of Texas. She was born in Egypt, Texas, Feb. 15, 1832, on the first plantation opened on the Colorado River, in that state. This plantation with its wealth of slaves and stock had a money value of more than two hundred thousand dollars. Here were born to them three children, viz.: Gancello Bartley[5], May 6, 1850; Mary V., June 15, 1852: and Olivia Morton, Sept. 5, 1854. In 1858 he took his family to Chapel Hill to educate his children. He was a firm believer in state rights. When the Civil War was instituted he espoused the cause of the South and entered the service in the capacity of surgeon. He died at Chapel Hill, Jan. 9, 1862. By the emancipation proclamation their wealth in slaves was lost, and in October, 1867, yellow fever broke out at Chapel Hill, with which his daughter, Mary V., died on the fifth, the son on the seventh, and his widow and an infant grandchild on the tenth of that month. But one child recovered, Olivia M., who married, Oct. 19, 1870, Richard E. Carter, a prominent lawyer of that state. They had five children, all of whom, together with their mother, have since died, and the family thereby became extinct.

Adelia[4], the sixth child of Capt. Samuel[3], is a maiden lady, and for a term of years superintended the home of her youngest brother in Massachusetts. She is spending a season with a nephew in Wisconsin.

John K.[4], M.D., the seventh in the list, graduated from the Medical Department of Bowdoin College in the Class of 1848. In 1852 he went to Elmira, N. Y., where he continued in active practice until the time of his death. In St. Peter's Church, in the city of New York, June 3, 1852, he and Glovina, a daughter of George Smith, Esq., one of the most prominent citizens of Wayne, Me., were married. His wife was born in Readfield, Me., June 16, 1822. To them were born two sons, John Barry[5], March 30, 1855, and George Barclay, May 18, 1859. John Barry was a graduate of Amherst College in the Class of 1876. He is a lawyer and for several years was a law partner of Governor Hill. He is a resident of Elmira, N. Y. He is an able man and has held several important offices in that state. Two terms he served his county in the capacity of district attorney. In 1900 he was the democratic nominee for the office of Governor of New York. His brother, George B., was a student of Princeton College. When near graduation he was attacked with malarial fever and died June 9, 1880. In January, 1883, the parents visited the

Pacific coast. In returning they made a stop in Denver, Col., to visit the doctor's brother. There the doctor sickened and died, July 11, 1883. His remains were brought to Elmira, N. Y., for interment.

Stephen Decateur[4], the eighth child of Capt. Samuel[3], after completing his education, went South, where he was engaged for a term of years in teaching. In 1846, he was elected to a Professorship in Rutherville College, in Texas. On account of illness he was obliged to return to his native State. Recuperated, he studied law and was admitted to the bar at Portland, in 1849. He practiced law one year with Hon. Abram Sanborn, in Bangor. In 1850, he removed to Fond-du-Lac, Wis., where he resided fourteen years in practice, there holding the office of Clerk of Courts, and at the same time edited the "Democratic Press." In 1864 he removed to Elmira, N. Y.; thence to Baltimore, Md., in 1867, and to Boston in 1879. These places proving not congenial to his health in April, 1881, he removed to Denver, Col. There he was engaged for a short time on the State Business Directory. In 1882 he was appointed postmaster, and in November of that year was chosen one of the judges of the city court, both of which offices he held at the time of his death.

In 1856 he married Miss Eveline B. Rice, of Geneva, N. Y. To them were born a son and three daughters, two of whom died in infancy. The son, Edward Everett[5], was born October, 1857, and Mary K., ———, 1869. Edward Everett is a successful merchant of that city, and has held important offices in its government.

Anson Gancello[4], the youngest child of Capt. Samuel[3], prepared for college at the "Maine Wesleyan Seminary," and Monmouth Academy, and graduated at Bowdoin College in the Class of 1847. He studied law with Hon. Henry W. Paine at Hallowell, Me.; was admitted to the Maine bar April 2, 1850, and later to the Circuit and Supreme Courts of the United States. While in Maine, where he was in practice twenty and more years, he was a heavy owner in the Hallowell Granite Quarries. In 1871 he removed to Newton and engaged in practice in Boston, principally in the United States courts, continuing therein until the present time. Single.

EBEN STINCHFIELD[4], (JOHN[3], WILLIAM[2], JOHN[1]).

Eben Stinchfield of the fourth generation was born in Pejepscot February 7, 1787. In 1809 he married Mary Woodbury, who was born in Pejepscot Sept. 25, 1786. They came to Leeds in 1809 and settled on the lake road, northerly from the dwelling of James[3] Stinchfield. They had issue Susan[5], born Sept. 2, 1810; Seth, b. Aug. 30, 1812; Sarah, b. May 12, 1815; Woodbury A., b. July 2, 1817, and Eben, b. Nov. 22, 1820. Susan married Samuel P. True, settled where D. P. True now resides, had no issue, and died Jan. 23, 1879.

Seth[5], the second child, when he became of age, went into the eastern part of the State where he engaged in lumbering business. He was one of five of the first settlers of the town of Danforth, Washington County, Me. He owned the water power and land where the village has been built. He was a prominent factor in building it up; and later was instrumental in giving it railroad connection with the outside world. He married Hannah Harding, by whom he had seventeen children, viz.: Seth[6], died in infancy; Keziah H.[6], b. in Danforth Aug. 6, 1837, married Melville S. Springer Nov. 14, 1856, has four children; Eurania T., b. Nov. 28, 1839, married Edward Russel, of Athens, had six children, second, married Nathan Walls of Lewiston, had one child; Mary Augusta, b. April 24, 1841, married Edwin W. Vosmus, of Lewiston, Sept. 13, 1871, has no issue; Rufus B., b. March 18, 1843, married Lydia Kelley, of Bancroft, has four children; Betsey R., b. March 3, 1845, married D. P. True, of Leeds, has no issue; Llewellyn A., b. March 27, 1847, married Sept. 29, 1874, Almira Russell, of Athens, had no children; Eben P., b. Nov. 17, 1848, married Allie Marston May 1, 1887, had two chidren; Eben P., died in Lewiston; Amaziah P., b. Oct. 2, 1850, married Rose Foss, has four children; Annette, b. April 30, 1852, died Sept. 3, 1860; Willington, b. March 24, 1854, married Estella Scribner, has no issue; Sarah, b. June 21, 1855, married James M. Moulton, of Wayne, May 3, 1879, has four children; Frederic W., b. Aug. 19, 1856; Orilla D., b. Oct. 9, 1858, married Charles S. Merrill, of Auburn, Sept. 29, 1883, has two children; Thirza M., b. Oct. 21, 1860, died Dec. 20, 1864; Estella M., b. March 27, 1862, married Thomas H. Boothby of Leeds, November, 1892, has no issue; Horace W., b. Oct. 3, 1866, died Sept. 3, 1867. The life of Seth Stinchfield has been one of industry and usefulness. Though his sight and hearing are much impaired, he is a hale and strong old gentleman.

Sarah[5], the third child of Eben[4], spent several years in Lowell, Mass. She married Harrison, a son of Robert Gould, of Leeds. To them was born a son, Luville, a conductor on the Maine Central Railroad, with whom she resided in Portland after the decease of her husband. She died in that city Jan. 10, 1901.

Woodbury A.[5], the fourth child of Eben[4], was a natural mechanic, a man of trades, a valuable and industrious gentleman. He settled in Wayne village where he built several houses. He married Frances Fuller, an estimable lady of that town, Aug. 9, 1851. To them were born Edith Helen[6], Nov. 24, 1852, and Florence Mabel[6], Jan. 14, 1856. Edith H. studied law and also married a lawyer, Charles E. Conant. They are both in practice and life-long members of the firm. They are in the west. Florence Mabel is also a lawyer of prominence. Woodbury A.[5] died in Leeds, in 1881, and was buried in the village cemetery in Wayne.

Eben[5], the youngest child of Eben[4], married Hannah Lincoln, who was born in Leeds Nov. 5, 1819. To them were born two sons, Lewis D., born in Leeds April 11, 1845, married in North Bridgewater, Mass., April 28, 1874, Harriet M. Chessman, b. in South Weymouth, Mar. 10, 1855, resides at Campello, Mass.; and Eben A. W., b. in Turner March 30, 1848, who married, Jan. 28, 1879, Abbie A. Atwood, b. in Rochester, Mass., Aug. 26, 1861. His residence was at Plymouth, Mass., and his business that of baggage master on the Old Colony Railroad, where he accidentally lost his life.

Eben[5] died in Wayne Jan. 22, 1849. His father, Eben[4], died in Leeds Jan. 23, 1877, and his mother, Mary (Woodbury), Oct. 1, 1852. They were buried in Wayne where many of the Stinchfield family repose. Eben[4] Stinchfield had four wives, viz.: Mary Woodbury, of Pejepscot; Diadama Larrabee, of Leeds; Clara Judkins, of East Livermore; Almira Berry, of Leeds. He was a grandson of John, the first born Stinchfield in America, the first man married in the town of New Gloucester, and the eldest brother of Thomas and Rogers Stinchfield, the first settlers of the town of Leeds.

THOMAS MILLET AND FAMILY.

The fourth family to settle in Leeds was that of Thomas Millet. The Millet family is one that is very largely identified with Maine and Massachusetts, and it is now numerously represented in various other portions of the United States. It is notable, however, that the Boston directory records only 34 persons of the name in its two forms—that of Millett being in more common usage—in comparison with the very much greater proportion of various other names apparently no less common in the country at large.

The name is an old one in England and is still older in France. In the English record it is variously spelled. Mylet, Mylett,

Myllais, Millet, Millett are among the early forms. The name appears in the English records early in the fifteenth century. The differences in spelling do not in the least signify any differences in origin. In England there always has been, and there still is, the greatest freedom as to the spelling of one's name. A person is at liberty to write it as he chooses. Near relatives often have very different forms. All genealogical authorities agree that the name, whatever its existing orthography, was originally the same. In Middlesex there are Mylletts and Millets; in Hereford there are Myllets; in Cornwall there are Milletts, and on the Island of Jersey the name is spelled Millais. These families are all of common origin. The two artists, the late Sir John Everett Millais of London, and Mr. Francis Davis Millet, the American painter, are from the same stock. And in all likelihood it would be found that their lines run back to the same French ancestry as that of the famous painter of peasant life, Jean Francois Millet. It has been supposed that the first of the name in England came with William the Conqueror, and that this is indicated by the mural crown in the crest of the arms allowed to John Millet of Hayes Court, Middlesex, in 1616. The first publicly recorded instance of the name in England is that of John Mylet, who came in 1432 as an ambassador from the regent of France, the Duke of Bedford, eldest uncle of Henry Sixth. It is thought that he never returned to his native country. In 1513 one of the secretaries of Henry Eighth was named John Millet. In 1516 the same name appears as that of a clerk of the signet and also as a Letter of Exchequer, probably all the same person. Among the earliest mentioned of the family are the Millets of Perivale, Middlesex. Henry Millet is recorded as dying on Feb. 5, 1500. In 1575 another Henry Millet of that place was Lord of the Manor of Cornhill. Though the name is so variously spelled it is noted that there seems to have been endeavored to keep the original spelling on the monuments, in records of pedigrees and of visitations in the Heralds College. The various branches of the family seem to have radiated from Middlesex, Buckinghamshire, and Surrey. John Millet of Hayes, Middlesex, was Lord of the Manor there in 1613. In 1616 the "Armes Argent a fess gules between three dragons heads erased vert" was exemplified, that is allowed, to him, with the crest of an arm armed, the hand grasping a dragon's head. Arms of that description are held to represent military distinction in opposition to tyranny, while the crest with the mural crown is something granted for the taking of a walled city.

In Cornwall the Milletts were a prominent family. William Millett was sheriff of Cornwall in 1566. In Marazion and Penzance the Milletts were leading people. The mother of Sir Humphrey Davy, whose monument stands in Penzance, was

Grace Millett. At Rosavern a branch of the family lived in one house from 1627 to the present time.

The immigrant ancestor of the American Millets, or at least of that branch of the family which immediately concerns this work, was Mr. Thomas Millet, who was born in England in 1605 and who, before emigrating to New England in 1635, married Mary Greenaway, who was born in England in 1606.

Thomas Millet belonged to the Herefordshire branch of the family, his great-grandfather being John Myllet, gentleman, of Redwood, near Leominster. His grandfather, also a John Myllet, lived in Chertsey, Surreyshire, and here his father, Henry Myllet, was born. Henry Myllet was attorney-at-law in Staples Inn, Holborn, and married Joyce, daughter of John Chapman, of Chertsey. Thomas was one of six children and their third son. The immigrant pair came to Dorchester, Mass., bringing with them a son, Thomas, born in England, in 1635. The fact that his wife's father, John Greenaway, had come to Dorchester in the ship Mary and John two years before with his wife and four daughters, was probably the fact that induced Thomas Millet to make his home in the new Bay Colony. With them also came Ursula Greenaway, his wife's sister, and the ship that brought them was the Elizabeth of London. The place where Mr. Thomas Millet was born does not appear. But he brought a certificate of his conformity from the rector of the Church of St. Saviour's in Southworth and was a teacher in the church. He was straightway made a freeman in Dorchester, where he lived until 1655, when he moved to Gloucester, having purchased there all the possessions of William Perkins, a teaching elder of that town. He succeeded Mr. Perkins in his religious office, the exercise of which gave him the right to the rare title of Mr. Though not an ordained minister, he received a salary "not always voluntarily bestowed" we are told. It was probably his function as teaching-elder that carried him to Gloucester and afterwards to Brookfield, for when an ordained minister was settled in the Cape Ann town Mr. Millet went to Brookfield to succeed Mr. Younglove in ministerial duties, though neither was ever ordained. He owned much real estate in Gloucester. When he died does not appear, but his wife entered his estate for probate in 1676. Beside the son born in England they had six other children, all born in Dorchester. It is notable that one of the first of the Bay colonists to visit Maine was John Millet, second son of Mr. Thomas Millet. The York records, August 8, 1661, show that Thomas Booth agrees with Adolphus Maverick to provide sufficient house room for John Millet and his family. But his stay appears to have been short, for in the Gloucester records are mentions of his marriage by Governor Endicott and the birth of seven children.

The eldest son, Lieut. Thomas Millet, as he was called, married Mary Evelith on May 21, 1655, Governor Endicott officiating. This was about the time his father moved to Gloucester. Their wedded life was passed in that town, lasting thirty-two years, the wife dying in June, 1687, leaving no children. The next year he married Abigail Evelith, widow of his wife's brother, Isaac, and daughter of John Cait. She was his junior by twenty-six years. They were blessed with three sons, Thomas, John, and Nathaniel; the latter dying in infancy. Lieutenant or Ensign Millet had land from his father, and in 1707 he purchased the Blynman farm at Kettle Cove. He was a respected citizen and successful farmer, leaving a large estate to his wife and two sons. Thomas Millet sold to his younger brother, John, his share in the farm. He had taken to the sea and was then styled "Captain and mariner." Giving up his seafaring in 1720 he removed to Durham, N. H., where he married Love Bunker and settled on Dover Neck. He was known as the Hon. Thomas Millet and was one of the most distinguished of the family in America. He was a ship-builder, and made several voyages to England and France in his own ships, as master. From those countries he brought fruit trees and originated the once celebrated "Millet apple," supposed to be a variety of the Normandy pippin. He also visited relatives bearing the family name in both England and France. He held prominent local and state offices and for twenty years was Judge of the New Hampshire Supreme Court.

John Millet, the younger brother, who was born April 19, 1692, remained in Gloucester all his life. He married Eunice Babson Dec. 24, 1723. They had nine children. He was an active man, but over-venturesome in his disposition, so that his proneness to speculation proved of much damage to his estate. Much of his property was lost in the Land Bank, and he died poor in 1747. It was with him that the Millet connections with Maine began. In the year 1737 he, with two other Gloucester men, were appointed a committee to lay out lots in the township of New Gloucester, and the next year, in the first distribution of lots, he drew No. 22. In the same year he was chosen to cut and make a good way, twelve feet wide, from North Yarmouth to New Gloucester through the town to the spot selected for a meeting-house.

It is an interesting coincidence that, in the year that the Maine connection originated, Thomas Millet, the seventh child and fourth son, was born Oct. 2, 1737. He lived in Gloucester until after the Revolution, marrying Eunice Parsons on May 29, 1763. Here also four of their six children were born, the other two first seeing the light in New Gloucester, Me. His adventures in the Revolutionary War were of an exceptionally interesting and varied character. It seems a pity that they were never fully chronicled. Apparently he lived quietly at home up to the time of his enlistment in the Continental Army on May 3, 1775. He was then nearly 38 years old.

The company to which he belonged was in the battle of Bunker Hill. On the way to the battle the company was divided, one part marching under the captain, and the other under the lieutenant. He was with the lieutenant, and when they reached the scene of battle the Americans had begun the retreat from the rail fence. The siege of Boston over, he went with the army of Washington and remained until after the battle of Trenton as one of the soldiers who remained after the time of their enlistment had expired.

He then returned to Gloucester, and in April he shipped for a year on board the Hancock, a Continental ship of 32 guns under the command of Capt. John Manley. Sailing from Boston in May, 1777, they cruised off Newfoundland and there they captured two prizes, a merchant vessel and the sloop of war Fox. But in August he was captured by the British war ship Rainbow, and was impressed into service with her crew. At Halifax, however, on Christmas day, he, with two companions, managed to escape; they jumped overboard and swam three miles to shore. He then made his way to Liverpool, N. S. Here he shipped on the sloop Bermuda, for Antigua, and from that island to. St Eustasia.

In May, 1778, he shipped on a Dutch schooner for North Carolina, but in the same month was captured by a British ship and taken to New York. Here he was held a prisoner until the next September, when he was taken to Elizabethtown, N. J., to be exchanged.

Sixteen months had passed since his family had heard from him. In the meantime his wife and four children had gone to New Gloucester, Me., to live with her brother, William Parsons. Thither he went to join them, and it is said that afterwards for a short time he again served in the patriot army.

Thomas Millet never returned to Massachusetts to live, and when the war was over he settled in Leeds, then in the heart of the wilderness, inhabited by only three other families when he went to live there. Here in 1781 he built a log house and lived for the rest of his life. He was 81 years old when, in 1813, he applied for a pension. This was granted and he enjoyed it through the remainder of his long life. The youngest son, Benjamin, always lived at the homestead, but as the other children grew up they all settled on places near by, in clearings from the wilderness. In 1820 he was living with Benjamin and had a lease of 75 acres of land. But he was then too feeble to do any work, or even to dress himself without assistance. Three years later, in 1823, he died, about 91 years old. His wife, Eunice, was the twelfth child of Thomas Parsons, Jr., of Gloucester. In the absence of a family record the dates of their death are unknown.

That Thomas Millet had a high sense of patriotic duty is evident not only from the fact of his enlistment, leaving a wife and four children at home, but from his remaining to fight at Trenton after his term of service had expired, followed by his shipping to serve at sea. His courage and his physical vigor are also attested by his plunge for liberty into the icy December waters of Halifax harbor to swim three miles to shore.

Following is a list of their children:

Born in Gloucester, Mass.

Eunice, b. Sept. 23, 1764, d. Dec. 24, 1852.
Thomas, b. 1769, d. Aug. 26, 1834.
Zebulon Parsons, b. Oct. 9, 1773, d. Oct. 1, 1856.
John, b. Feb. 2, 1776, d. Dec. 21, 1862.

Born in New Gloucester, Me.

Benjamin, b. 1780, d.
Betsey, b. 1783, d. Nov. 2, 1853.

From these children of Thomas Millet came the Millets of Leeds. All of them lived well into the nineteenth century, and their numerous descendants are now widely scattered throughout the United States. Eunice married the Rev. Thomas Francis, the first minister of Leeds, a man of remarkable character, whose story is told elsewhere in this volume.

Thomas Millet married Matilda Knapp of Leeds, a sister of Joseph Knapp. Who their father was does not appear, his name not having been recorded. Having no children of their own, they adopted two of the nephews of Thomas, John and Samuel Francis, sons of the minister, and left them their property.

Zebulon Parsons Millet, the third child, married Deliverance Rich of Sandwich, Mass., on April 6, 1797. The Cape Cod town was the parent of New Sandwich, now Wayne, Me., and the relations between the two sections thus established doubtless led to this union. Zebulon and his brother John were in the Leeds militia, called out for coast guard duty in the War of 1812, and it is recorded that for this service they each received a land warrant in later days. The children of Zebulon and Deliverance were Solomon (1798), Parsons (1798), Thomas (1801), Lydia (1803), Obadiah (1805), Isabella (1807), Aaron (1809), Francis Davis (1811), Asa (1813), Polly Francis (1815), Lydia

(1818), Adelia (1822). Of these children Solomon married Phœbe Gould, of Wayne, and lived the greater part of his life in Leeds. Their ten children were born there, but later the family moved to East Bridgewater, Mass., Solomon dying there in 1880. Thomas married Almira A. Day, of Baring, Me., where the first of their twelve children was born; the next two were born in Leeds, and the others in Palmyra, where the mother died. The father then married Fannie Gordon, of St. Albans, Me., who became the mother of six children. Thomas died in Palmyra in 1874. Obadiah Millet remained in Leeds, marrying Eliza Safford, of Turner. They had two children, Lydia and Charles Holmes.

Isabella married Eben Cobb, of Livermore, where their four children were born. Aaron moved to West Bridgewater, Mass., where he married Myra Holmes. They had nine children. Francis Davis remained in Leeds. In 1835 he married Elathear True, who died in 1841. In 1852 he married Lucina Phillips. Their only child was Elathear True, who in 1880 became the wife of Lot Howard. Francis Davis Millet, or Davis, as he was commonly called, was of a genial, upright nature, and was universally respected through his long and useful life. The ties between him and his younger brother were uncommonly strong. This brother, Asa, moved to Plymouth County, Mass., and there became eminent as a physician. In the Civil War he was a surgeon with the Union army and was a member of Governor Andrew's council. He devoted years of research to the preparation of a Millet genealogy, which was nearly completed at the time of his death in 1893. To the manuscript of this interesting and important work the writer of this chapter is mainly indebted for his facts. His eldest son, Francis Davis Millet, who was born at Mattapoisett, Mass., after serving with the Union army as drummer boy in the Civil War, was graduated at Harvard University. He then devoted himself to art, studying in Europe and becoming celebrated as a painter. At the Columbian World's Fair at Chicago, in 1893, he had charge of the decorative features and was director of festivities, originating the scheme of treatment that gave rise to the name "The White City." He devised also the scheme of mural decoration for the exhibition buildings that gave such an impetus to the art of mural painting for public buildings of this country. In literature and journalism he also became celebrated; he has written several books and numerous magazine articles—fiction, travel, etc.—and was a notable war correspondent with the Russian army in the Russo-Turkish war, and twenty years afterwards with the American army in the Manila campaign. The second son of Dr. Millet, Josiah Byram, is a prominent Boston publisher. The youngest son, Charles Sumner, following his father's footsteps as a physician, has gained a name for his successful treatment of consumption, and has recently converted the family homestead at East Bridgewater, Mass., into a model sanitorium for the treatment of tuberculous patients, naming it "The Asa Millet Sanitorium," in honor of his father.

John Millet, the last of the Gloucester-born children of Thomas, married Sally George, whose father, Francis George, of Taunton, Mass., probably moved to Maine soon after the Revolution, in which he served with the Continental army. They were married in 1799. Their ten children were all born in Leeds. The oldest of these children, Joshua, born in 1803, was a prominent Maine divine. He entered Waterville College, and later went to the Newton Theological Institute, Mass., where he was graduated in 1835. The next year he became pastor of the Baptist church at Charlestown, Me.; in 1838 he took charge of the Baptist Society at Cherryfield, and in 1844 was called to Wayne, where he lived until his death on March 10, 1848. While at Wayne he wrote the notable contribution to Maine history, "A History of the Baptists in Maine." His grave is at his birthplace in Leeds. He married Sophronia Howard of West Bridgewater, Mass. They had several children. Sophronia, the eldest, died in 1859. Their son, Joshua Howard, was educated at Waterville College and is a lawyer in Boston, Mass. George Lewis, their youngest child, served in the Civil War and died of typhoid fever in January, 1865, while in the service.

The other children of John Millet were Seth (1805), John (1807), Ozias (1809), Catherine (1811), Polly (1813), Francis G. (1816), Betsey (1818), Sarah (1821), Amanda M. (1824). Not any of these are now living. Of the children, all except Seth left their native town and found homes elsewhere, many of them in Massachusetts. Seth, who remained in Leeds, lived the greater part of his life on a farm near the railroad on the road leading to Wayne, not far from his father's. There he reared a large family of children, Elmira, Matilda, Warren L., Joseph C., John R., William R., Lucy A., Eliza A., and Ella C. Those now living are widely separated and only one remains in Leeds.

Seth Millet was an industrious and respected citizen. He often held offices of trust, both in the town and in the church, of which he was a devoted member. He died in 1879.

John went to West Bridgewater, Mass., where he married Elizabeth Holmes and afterwards lived, except a short time when he resided at Leeds on his father's farm. They had three children one of whom, the youngest, was born in Leeds.

Ozias was a graduate of Waterville College and for several years thereafter was the principal of Hebron Academy. Resigning his position he returned to Leeds and took up his residence on his father's farm in which he became interested. While there he

FRANCIS DAVIS MILLETT.

became one of the projectors of the railroad from Bath to Farmington, now a part of the Maine Central Railroad, and becoming a civil engineer was active in promoting and building it. While thus engaged he removed from Leeds and did not return to live. Later he became interested in mining and with his family went to Colorado, where he died, leaving a widow, a daughter, and a son. The latter, James O., was born in Leeds.

Catherine married Rev. Wilson C. Ryder, A.M., then pastor of the Baptist Church in Leeds. In 1840-1 on account of ill health he resigned his pastorate and moved to Middleboro, Mass., his native town. They had four children of whom Wilson Clarkson, the eldest, was born in Leeds.

Francis G. married Sarah Noyes, of South Abington, Mass., where he lived. They had two children, one of whom, a son, is now living.

Betsey married Atwood B. Bumpus, of Hebron. Their only child is now the wife of Rev. Fred Hovey Allen, of Boston. Sarah married Nehemiah B. Bicknell, of Boston. They had one child. Amanda M. married Hiram Curtis, of Boston. There were no children.

Benjamin Millet, the youngest son of Thomas, and the first child of his parents born in Maine, married Cynthia Dyer, of West Bridgewater, Mass. Their four children were all born in Leeds.

Betsey Millet, the other Maine-born child of Thomas, married Levi Foss, to whom she bore ten children.

All told, the grandchildren of Thomas Millet numbered 52. Only a few descendants bearing the family name now live in Leeds. One of these, Herbert Millet, has his home on the old farm.

Francis Davis Millett[6] (Zebulon P.[5], Thomas[4], John[3], Thomas[2], Thomas[1]) was born in Leeds, Oct. 1, 1811. He was one of nine children of Zebulon P. and his wife, Deliverance (Rich) Millett. He was a life-long resident on the farm taken up by his father over a century ago. He was educated in the common schools of Leeds, to which he added a life of study and practical knowledge. He succeeded to the homestead and devoted himself to its cultivation and improvement. He erected thereon a modern, convenient, and imposing set of buildings nearly opposite those of his childhood. Mr. Millett was twice married. His first wife was Elethea, a daughter of Benjamin True, to whom he was married in December, 1835. She died in June, 1841. In 1852 he married Lucina, born in Turner Jan. 9, 1819, a daughter of Otis and Lydia (Staples) Phillips, of Auburn. Their daughter and only child, Ella T., born in Leeds Aug. 6, 1853, married Lot, a son of Luther L. Howard[3], of Leeds, May

10, 1880. They have a son, an only child, Francis Davis Millett Howard, born Feb. 13, 1891. Mr. and Mrs. Howard succeeded to the home of Mr. Millett where they continue their residence. Mr. Millett joined the Free Will Baptist Church in 1864, and from 1866 to the time of his death was one of its deacons. He was a liberal and generous contributor to various religious and educational interests of the town. His worth was recognized by his townsmen, whose services they sought on their board of municipal officers, which position he filled with ability. He was unassuming, genial, kind in his manner, and had the esteem and respect of his townsmen. He died December 28, 1893, and his widow Oct. 31, 1900.

DANIEL LANE AND FAMILY.

The Lane family is among the oldest in town, being fifth in the order of settlement. The head of the first family who bore the name was Daniel. He is introduced as a resident of Gloucester, Mass., where he married Mary ——— about 1764, and where several of his children were born. Many of the early settlers of Leeds were natives of that old town which has ever been noted for the intelligence of its inhabitants, who sprang from noble English families. They first moved to New Gloucester, which was ceded to that colony in 1735, thence to Littleborough. Most of them had been in active service in the Revolutionary War. Daniel Lane was one of them. He was taken prisoner and detained in Dartmoor Prison nearly two years. In his absence, his wife and children with relatives, removed to New Gloucester, and after his release he joined them there, and in 1782 came to Leeds and settled near the center of the town. They had six sons and three daughters, to wit: Daniel, James, Giddings, Elias, Peter, Samuel, Mary, Judith, and Lydia. The sons all settled on adjoining farms west of the south end of Androscoggin Lake except one, Elias, who in 1790, located on the place now occupied by his grandson, Davis F. Lothrop.

1. Daniel, married Eunice Verrill and had six children, to wit: Joshua, Daniel, Eunice, Nancy, Lois, Mary. His wife died and he married Ruth Pratt, by whom he had [1]Eliphalet Gilman, [2]Olive, [3]Lorinda.

2. James, born in Gloucester, Mass., Sept. 26, 1767; married in Leeds in 1793, Abigail, a daughter of Increase Leadbetter, born Oct. 29, 1774. They had issue:

    1. Phebe, b. July 23, 1793; m. John S. Cary and had issue John L., Orman and others, all of whom died in infancy.

2. Joanna, b. Oct. 18, 1794, m. Perez S. Jennings, and had issue Orville, Gustavus A., Gessius F., Eliza A., Roscoe G., Rollin F.
3. John, b. in Leeds Aug. 31, 1796, a farmer living most of his life in that town, m. April 20, 1823, Vesta Phillips, b. in Greene, Aug. 20, 1800. Their children were: Charles Cary, George Bailey and Abigail Rackley.
   1. Charles Cary, b. Nov. 7, 1832; m. Mary Jane, a daughter of Hon. Leavitt and Elizabeth (Lane) Lothrop, Dec. 25, 1855. To them one child was born,—1 Neva C., Dec. 7, 1856, who is a successful teacher in Oregon. Charles C. died, Oct. 25, 1857.
   2. George Bailey, b. in Fayette, Feb. 16. 1833; m. Viola Ann, a daughter of Luther and Achsah (Pratt) Ramsdell, Oct. 24, 1858. To them three children were born, to wit: John, Justin Palmer and Kittie.
      1. John, b. Sept. 5, 1859, was a graduate of Waterville Classical Institute. He m. Emma Foss, by whom he had a son, John Frank. He was engaged in teaching at Collegeville, Cal., and died there on his birthday, Sept. 5, 1883.
      2. Justin Palmer, b. Dec. 12, 1866; d. Feb. 16, 1885.
      3. Kittie, b. Feb. 27, 1875, was and is a successful teacher in the schools of her native and neighboring towns. She m. Ernest A. Russell Mar. 24, 1894. They have one child, Eula, b. Feb. 3, 1896.
   3. Abigail Rackley married John O. Palmer June 3, 1860, and had issue Irving O., b. May 17, 1862; Justin A., b. Dec. 10, 1863; d. Aug. 20, 1865; Lottie L., b. April 10, 1869, d. young; George L., b. Aug. 9, 1871; Rosie E., b. Aug. 12, 1874, not living. Prof. Irving O. is a graduate of Colby and a successful teacher in Newtonville, Mass. He married Mary Cushing, of Skowhegan, and has issue Marie I., b. Sept. 13, 1892; Marjorie C., b. Nov. 30, 1898.
4. Abigail, b. May 13, 1798; m. Stephen Rackley, had three children, all died in infancy.
5. Aseneth, b. March 24, 1800; m. Dr. David Hale and had three children, Mary, Fessenden, and Flora.
6. Eliza. b. May 1, 1802; m. Nathaniel Perley. They had issue Peleg, John, Samuel F., and Eliza A.

7. Hannah, b. Nov. 15, 1804; m. Ammi Woodman. Their children were: Ellen, Clark, Abbie, Charles Aubry, Laura, and Hannah.
8. Eunice, b. April 20, 1807; never married.
9. Columbus, b. March 23, 1809; m. first, Rachel Billings, by whom he had one child,—Rosabel. Second, m. Abbie Perkins. No issue. He was a merchant in New Hampshire.
10. Alden, b. March 29, 1812; m. Mary Rackley and had issue Ellen, Eliza, Benjamin, and Josephine. He was several years proprietor of the Roccomeco House, at Livermore Falls.
11. James, b. June 2, 1816; m. Louisa Wyman and had three daughters,—Francina, Ella, and Avis.

James, the father of the above 11 children, d. in Fayette, in January, 1862.

Abigail, his wife, d. in Fayette, March 28, 1848.

3. Giddings, m. Jemima Norris, of Wayne, and had 12 children, to wit: Polly, Alpheus, Lydia, Jemima, Dorcas, Fannie, Giddings, Samuel, Susannah, Esther, Calvin, and Nancy.
4. Elias, m. Mary Lawrence, and had issue Elizabeth, David, Warren and Alvin.
5. Peter, m. first, Lois Verrill, and their children were: Eliphalet, Issachar, David, Jesse, Judith and Lois; m. second, Grace Turner, to whom was born Semyntha, Peter, Joanna, Eunice, Benjamin Franklin, Charles and Harriet,
6. Samuel, m. first, Judith Verrill, who had no children. After her decease he m. Sarah Nye, who bore him Henry K., Samuel and Harriet.
7. Mary, m. Stephen Rowe, of Danville, had several children, but the number and names are unknown to the writer.
8. Judith, m. Capt. Daniel Jones, a Revolutionary soldier, who became a Leeds farmer. They had nine children.
9. Lydia, m. Nathaniel Norcross, of Hallowell, and was the mother of nine children.

Of the sons of Daniel Lane, Jr., the eldest son of Daniel, the pioneer.

Joshua, the eldest, m. Mehitable Brett, by whom he had one son, who was a graduate of Bowdoin College. He was a Congregationalist minister, and located in Iowa;

Eliphalet Gillman, second son, and only one by his second wife, m. a Miss Berry and settled on a ranch in Illinois. He died several years ago and little is known of his family.

Of the children of James, the second son of Daniel, Sen., mention has been made. Of the sons of Giddings, third son of Daniel, Sen., Alpheus, the eldest, m. first, Sarah Foss, and settled in Wayne, on the farm now occupied by Charles O. Graves. He subsequently was proprietor of the Pocasset House in the village, and finally removed to Milo, where he died. By his first wife he had two children, Sewall and Sarah. Sewall settled in Baltimore, married a lady from Virginia, and was a railroad conductor. Now dead. Alpheus married second, Betsey, a daughter of Capt. Roger Stinchfield, by whom he had five children, Roscoe, Waldo, Otis, Virginia and Helen. Roscoe was a merchant in California, died there; Waldo was a captain and lost his life in the Civil War; Otis was a farmer in the town of Milo;

Giddings, Jr., second son of Giddings and brother of Alpheus, m. Cassandra, a daughter of Dr. Cyrus Benson, of Bridgewater, Mass. He was a valuable business man and took a deep interest in all public enterprises of benefit to the people generally, and particularly to those of his native town. He filled many positions of honor and trust and discharged the duties ably and satisfactorily. To them were b. two sons, Cyrus Benson and Gustavus W. Cyrus B. was several years a merchant at North Monmouth. After returning to the home farm in Leeds, where he has since resided, he has officiated in several positions of trust in his municipality. He m. Lydia A., a daughter of Solomon L. and Hannah (Turner) Lothrop, by whom he had a daughter, Cassandra B. (Mrs. C. C. Farmer.)

Gustavus W., when a young man, was engaged in the manufacture of boots and shoes in Brockton, Mass. He m. Helen M. Snow, of that city, who died, leaving no issue. He later returned to Leeds and engaged in an extensive trade in groceries, grain and feed at the railroad station in the center of the town. He has held municipal and other important offices, and is interested in various industries tending to the improvement of the people in their several vocations. His second wife was Susan E., a daughter of Willard and Emeline L. (Boothby) Lothrop. They have no issue.

Samuel, a brother of Giddings, Jr., was a mechanic. He m. Catharine Pingray and had one son, Alonzo.

Calvin, also a brother of Giddings, Jr., m. Dulcina Lothrop and settled in Carrol, Me. They had issue Erastus, Daniel, Esther, Francis and Clara.

David, eldest son of Elias, m. Lydia Brewster, and had four children. He was a farmer.

Warren, a brother of David, died at the age of 21 years.

Alvin, the only other brother of David, m. Lucy Mitchell, by whom he had one son, Orsan, who m. first, Susannah, and second, Viora, daughters of Rev. Samuel Boothby. Alvin m. second, Mrs. Hannah Dunham, and by her had one daughter, Susan Scott.

Eliphalet, eldest son of Peter, fifth son of Daniel the pioneer, m. Lydia Trask, by whom he had three sons and several daughters. The sons' names were: Eliphalet, Ebenezer and Franklin.

Issachar, second son of Peter and brother of Eliphalet, m. Dorcas, a daughter of Giddings, Sen., and Jemima (Norris) Lane, and by her had three children, Rosamond (Mrs. Davis Francis), Adoniram Judson, who m. Ann H., a daughter of Rev. Walter Foss, and Esther (Mrs. Eli N. Berry). Issachar was frequently one of the officers of his town and represented his district in the State Legislature. His son, A. J., is a farmer in Leeds and the father of seven children, Ada A., Freemont, Willie E., Sadie E., Scott W., Allie and Issa.

Davis, third son of Peter, was a clothier, which trade he followed in early life, but later settled on a farm about one mile easterly of Wayne village. He m. first, a Miss Hayward, who died without issue; second, Mrs. Almira Spear, by whom he had three children, Almira, Olive and Davis. Davis is a dentist and resides in Huntington, L. I.

Jesse, fourth son of Peter, m. Charlotte Jones, by whom he had two children, Emery and Davis He was a merchant in Leeds and died here several years ago. His sons both died when young, unmarried men.

REV. THOMAS DAVIS FRANCIS.

Peter, fifth son of Peter and first son by his second wife, Grace Turner, was thirty-one years in the mercantile business in Portland, fifteen years of which he was a wholesale dealer in dry goods. He retired from business several years ago, and returned to Leeds, where he erected a fine set of buildings on the farm formerly owned by his uncle, Daniel Lane, which he designated "Chapel Farm." He continues his residence there in affluence. He is far advanced in years, and in poor health, but retains an active interest in the business and political spheres of life. He married first, Lucretia P., a daughter of Hon. Stillman and Lydia (Lothrop) Howard. She died without issue. His second wife was Mary J., a daughter of Capt. James Palmer, of Brighton. To them was born a daughter who died in childhood.

Benjamin F., sixth son of Peter, Sen., m. a Miss Hammon, of Brunswick. He was a mechanic, and his residence, Lowell, Mass.

Charles H., seventh son of Peter, Sen., m. first, Sarah Turner. He spent some time in Colorado where he accumulated an amount of property, much of which he lost through a bogus banking house, buying a draft in that state payable in New York. Since his return to Leeds, he has been engaged in trade at the center, but chiefly in farming. About 1890 or '91 his wife died without issue. In 1893, he erected a set of buildings on the Crummett place at Leeds Center, and in October, 1894, m. Mrs. Millie M. Wright, of Greene. They have no issue.

It is a matter of regret that so little interest has been taken in this work by so many of the members of the Lane family, which accounts for the absence of important details so valuable in works of biography.

FRANCIS FAMILY.

The founder of this family was Thomas Davis Francis[1], born in Hay, Breconshire County, South Wales, Nov. 23, 1764. When a lad of seven years of age he was sent to London to be educated in the schools of that city, and at the same time apprenticed to Doctor Williams, an apothecary and surgeon. At the age of ten years he ran away from the doctor and traveled on foot to his home in Hay, a distance of nearly one hundred miles He was at once returned by his mother and again placed under the doctor's charge, where he continued for three years more, when he again ran away and hired as cabin boy on board a vessel bound to the Southern Ocean to make an observation on the transit of Venus. On returning to England, he enlisted on board the King's ship bound to the Island of Jamaica with a cargo of military stores. This voyage completed, he again enlisted on an English man-of-war vessel, and, with that vessel, was captured by the American ship Black Prince, commanded by Richard Crowninshield. He and his shipmates were confined in irons and nearly devoured by lice. On application to the commodore, who was moved with sympathy for the youth, his shackles were removed and permission given him to mingle and labor with the sailors of the Black Prince who manned the captured man-of-war vessel and took her into an American port (presumably Boston), where they landed in May, 1778. The succeeding fall, this vessel was impressed into the American service, sent to the Maine coast to aid in driving the British from the Penobscot, and young Francis, having sworn allegiance to the cause of America, acted in the capacity of "captain of the top" in the engagement at Castine that soon followed, in which this vessel was an active participant. Soon after this engagement, having proceeded up the Penobscot River to near where the city of Bangor is now situated, and being hemmed in and pursued by a superior force of Red Coats, the vessel was abandoned, blown up and sunk in that river.

The crew escaped in the woods and set out through the wilderness for Falmouth (Portland) *via* the Kennebec and Androscoggin valleys. For the first three days they were piloted by Indians and then abandoned to find their way as best they could. At the end of fourteen days of toilsome wandering, they came to a settlement where the city of Augusta is now located. From there their course lay through Winthrop, Greene and Lewiston to New Gloucester, where they at last arrived—tired, foot-sore and nearly famished. In describing this journey Mr. Francis said, "We were so destitute and hungry that, on one occasion, I stole a *Bible* and gave it to a Dutchman for a dinner, and then stole it from him to barter again when hunger should press." In New Gloucester the crew rested and were refreshed at the home of Thomas Stinchfield, the pioneer settler of Leeds, whose sympathy for the fatigued and foot-sore soldier boy without home or relatives, moved him to tender the lad a place in his family. This proposition he rejected and accompanied the crew to Gray. Destitute of shoes and other necessities, with no prospect of an immediate supply or betterment of his condition, he decided to return to Stinchfield's, and when installed in his family gave up his roving propensity and decided to settle down to quiet life.

He attended the school of New Gloucester in the winters of 1778-9 and 1779-80, and when the families of Thomas and Rogers Stinchfield came to Leeds he accompanied them, being one of the *young* men mentioned in the account given in another place in this work of the journey of the first settlers to their homes in the wilderness. He it was who came in the boat with Marshfield Paul from the mouth of the twenty-mile stream up the Androscoggin to the mouth of Dead River, and down that to the lone cabins of the previous day, now enlivened by the songs of the ladies and merry chatter of the children, echoed along the river banks—a memorable welcome to the new home. Outside the members of the families of Thomas and Rogers Stinchfield, Francis was the third white person to dwell in Littleborough; while Jirah Fish, who came in the fall of 1780, and whose log house was built near where White's mill now stands, was the head of the third family to settle therein. Thomas Millett came the same fall, built a log house on the farm where Herbert Millett now lives, made a cut-down, and in the spring of 1781 came again to make a burn, plant corn and potatoes, and brought his family in the time of harvest. These four families were sufficiently numerous to constitute a school of a goodly number of children, and Francis was established the first tutor in the plantation of Littleborough. He thus continued as the instructor of these children during term time, being employed the remainder of the year in the clearing of land taken up by Stinchfield in whose family he lived. Extending from the Lake to the Androscoggin River, and 160 rods in width, adjoining the south line of Livermore, constituted the land claim of Thomas Stinchfield. This he divided into four lots, retaining the easterly portion for himself, the second to his wife's son, Marshfield Paul, the third to Thomas D. Francis, and the fourth, adjoining the Androscoggin River, to Isaac Freeman, a son-in-law, who married his daughter, Martha (called Patty).

The lot that went to Marshfield Paul, who made extensive clearings and later built a frame house thereon, was subsequently purchased by Barnabas Howard, and is now the property of W. Henry Francis. When opportunity offered during the year 1783, Stinchfield and his older boys aided young Francis in clearing land on his lot and in building a house and hovel on the premises. In July, 1784, he married Eunice, born in New Gloucester Sept. 23, 1764, the eldest child of Thomas and Eunice (Parsons) Millett. To have the marriage service performed they were obliged to go to New Gloucester, the bride-elect on horseback, the groom on foot, tracing their way by spotted trees. Teaching school the following winter, in the spring of 1785 he removed his wife and son, Thomas, Jr., to the log house on the farm where he continued his residence the remainder of his long and useful life, dying May 9, 1836; and his widow, Eunice, Dec. 24, 1852.

As a noted theologian, his church record is portrayed in this work in a chapter devoted to churches. In this connection and as a local statesman he exerted a salutary and powerful effect in molding the institutions and giving character to the town. For a long series of years he was clerk and chairman of the municipal board of officers of Leeds, and its first representative (in 1804) to the General Court. For a time he was in the State Senate and stood the peer of the ablest in that body. In the War of 1812 he was appointed chaplain of a regiment and was a strong supporter of the government cause. During his long pastorate connection with the church, it is said that he never had a salary. His influence was exerted for the benefit of the early settlers of the town, and their differences were satisfactorily adjusted by him. During life, he was much loved and respected, and his memory is revered by the town in which he lived so long and well. To them were born fourteen children, who, with one exception, grew to man and womanhood. They made useful, respectable and respected citizens, and many of them have been prominent in public life, which duties they discharged ably and conscientiously. They were, viz.:

Thomas[2], Jr., born Jan. 26, 1785; died Jan. 27, 1869;
John[2], born Dec. 2, 1787; died Sept. 23, 1864;
Mark[2], born Oct. 7, 1789; died Oct. 2, 1864;
Davis[2], born April 9, 1791; died March 19, 1830;
Esther[2], born June 6, 1793; died Dec. 22, 1813;
Eunice[2] and Lois, twins, born Dec. 9, 1794; Eunice died Dec. 18, 1862; Lois, Dec. 12, 1794;
Matilda[2], born Oct. 9, 1796; died ———;
Betsey[2], born Oct. 10, 1798; died Aug. 24, 1816;
Polly[2], born July 28, 1800; died March 15, 1813;
Susanna C.[2], born Aug. 9, 1892; died ———;
Benjamin[2], born Oct. 31, 1804; died June 3, 1884;
Samuel[2], born Aug. 23, 1806; died Feb. 11, 1889;
Lorania[2], born June 13, 1808; died Sept. 30, 1831:

The eldest child, Thomas, Jr.[2], was a man of letters and of sterling worth to the town, filling many offices of trust. He married Alice, born April 4, 1795, a daughter of Daniel and Dolly (Whiting) Lothrop, one of the very early settlers of Littleborough, whose place of location was near where the buildings of Greenwood C. Gordon now stand. He brought his wife to the home of his father where they continued their residence during the remainder of their lives. He was a member of the First Baptist Church in Leeds over which his father so long exercised a fostering care. He was a kind and accommodating neighbor, a pleasant and indulgent husband and father, and much respected by the citizens. They had but two children, a son and daughter, viz.: Davis[3], born Nov. 2, 1823; and Mary[3], born April 1, 1833.

Davis[3], the son, married first, Rosamond, born March 28, 1827, a daughter of Isaacher and Dorcas Lane. He in turn, brought his wife to the paternal homestead where, for years, three generations of the Francis family lived in peace and happiness. Here Davis[3] was born and passed his life on the place cleared by his grandfather, tilled by his father and highly prized by himself. In early manhood he was a teacher in the schools of his native and neighboring towns. In the time of the Civil War an act requiring the organization of the State militia was passed, and, in conformity therewith, a meeting of the three towns of Monmouth, Leeds, and Greene was called and held in the church yard near Greene Corner. At that meeting organization was made and the two most important officers were elected from the ranks of the Leeds boys—Davis Francis[3] to the office of Captain, and the writer to the office of Lieutenant. From this organization a selected company was subject to government call. He held offices of trust in his town successively as clerk and one of the board of selectmen. December 24, 1863, his wife died, leaving a family of six small children. In 1865 he married Julia Ann Fernald, whose maiden name was True. She was born Jan. 12, 1835. He died August 29, 1883, at the age of sixty years, and was mourned by a large and sympathetic circle of friends. His wife, who bore him one son, died in the fall of 1876. The children of Davis[3] and Rosamond Francis were:

Wallace L.[4], born May 12, 1850;
Frederick D.[4], born May 11, 1852; died Sept. 23, 1859;
B. Franklin[4], born Dec. 9, 1854; died April 12, 1880;
Thomas Edwin[4], born March 18, 1857; died Sept. 18, 1874;
Rosa Lena[4], born April 14, 1861; died Nov. 30, 1891;
Fremont Davis[4], born Aug. 23, 1863; died Feb. 16, 1864.

Of Davis and Julia Ann:
Fred E.[4], born Oct. 7, 1874.

Wallace L.[4], the only remaining child of Davis[3] and Rosamond Francis, married in 1879, Georgia A., born in Concord, N. H., June 8, 1859, a daughter of John G. and Hester A. (Haskell) Francis. They have issue two daughters, viz.:

Gard Rosamond, born Feb. 29, 1880;
Gladys Hester, born Jan. 5, 1883.

He passed his boyhood days on the old Francis farm in Leeds, that on which his great-grandfather settled. When he arrived at manhood he engaged in the hotel business in Auburn, continuing therein several years. He was later a merchant at East Livermore Mills where he did an extensive and prosperous business. After the decease of his step-mother and the failing health of his father, duty called him back to the old homestead where he remained until the decease of his father, which occurred in 1883, when he exchanged the farm with Charles Lane for a store and stock of goods at Leeds Center (formerly called Lothrop's Corner), where by his kindly, genial ways and honest dealings he built up and still holds a very large and lucrative trade. Through the changes of administration he has held the office of postmaster and discharged the duties of that office to the satisfaction of its patrons. He is a prominent member of the orders of F. A. M., O. F., and J. O. A. M.

His half-brother, Fred E. Francis, was a lad of eight years at the time of his father's decease, and the care of his education, home instruction and guidance, was assumed by the elder brother. In the store and business connected therewith he obtained a good practical knowledge of trade, fitting him for mercantile life. In August, 1900, he married Alice Foster and resides in East Boston, Mass.

Mary H.[3], the only daughter of Thomas, Jr., and Alice (Lothop) Francis, never married, and remained at home with her parents and brother Davis until his death, when she made her home with her nephew, Wallace L., where she died July 25, 1893.

John[2], the second child of Rev. Thomas and Eunice (Millett) Francis, and his brother Samuel, were both adopted by their uncle, Thomas Millett, who had no children of his own, and heired his property, the real estate being that (now owned by Herbert Millett) later owned by Rev. Samuel Boothby. In November, 1809, he married Patience Parcher, by whom he had three children, a son and two daughters, viz.: Sewall, born Sept. 18, 1811; died Aug. 22, 1814; Esther, born June 26, 1815, and Orissa Helen, born May 20, 1828. Esther married in Kentucky a gentleman whose surname was Francis. Orissa never married and remained at home.

During the time of his residence therein few people who have lived in the town of Leeds were in public service more than Capt. John Francis. He was a man of commanding appearance and rare executive ability. As a military officer he was particular and exacting, yet highly respected by his men. His general knowledge and practical common sense made him a desirable associate on the board of education, and of sterling worth in the discharge of the municipal affairs of the town. In 1836 he went west and settled in Minnesota. At the close of a useful life, twenty-eight years of which were spent in that state, he died Sept. 23, 1864.

Mark[2], the third child of Thomas[1], was never married and spent his single life on the parental farm. To him is due the honor and praise of always being on the premises and attending to the routine labors of farm life. He died in the harness Oct. 2, 1864. He was much respected by friends and neighbors.

Davis[2], the fourth child, remained at home and never married. But little has been learned of his life. He died when comparatively young, March 19, 1830.

Esther[2], the next in the list, died Dec. 22, 1813, at the age of 20 years.

Eunice[2] and Lois[2] were twins, but the latter lived but three days. Eunice was a maiden lady and spent her life on the farm where she was born, dying Dec. 18, 1862.

Matilda, the eighth child of Thomas, married Ansel Turner in August, 1832, and settled in Leeds on the place now occupied by Henry Pettingill. She was his second wife, the first being her sister, Lorania. To her was born one son, Thomas Francis Turner, April 26, 1833. He became an M.D. in a neighboring state and acquired some notoriety. After his father's decease he returned to Leeds, and disposing of the farm, purchased that now owned by W. Henry Francis and constructed a fine house thereon.

The inducement to procure that place was an ambiguous one—first, to gratify his mother's desire to spend the remainder of her days beside the home of her childhood she loved so well, and the beautiful site and valuable soil of which that elevation of land is composed. He died Dec. 26, 1876. The date of his mother's death has not been obtained.

Betsey[2], the next child of Thomas D.[1] died Aug. 24, 1816, when near 18 years of age.

Mary[2], called Polly, tenth child of Thomas D., died March 15, 1813, at the early age of 12 years.

Susanna C.[2], whose numerical position was eleven, married Cyrus Knapp, M.D., in January, 1829. Doctor Knapp was a son of Ziba Knapp[2], a brother of Joseph[2], sons of Joseph[1], early settlers of Leeds. He graduated from the medical department of Bowdoin College in the class of 1825. In 1827 he located in practice in Winthrop, where he acquired a high reputation as a physician. In 1838, he changed his location to Augusta, and was subsequently appointed to the office of Superintendent of the Insane Asylum. From thence he went to Rochester, N. Y., and there made for himself a name amongst those of the most eminent physicians in the nation. Unfortunately, further details of Susanna's family have not been obtained.

Benjamin[2], whose name follows that of Susanna C., was endowed by nature with both physical and mental structures of a superior order, which, ever exercised in the farm labors on the old homestead, secured to him a long lease of life and one that the citizens of Leeds can point to with a good degree of pride and honor. A single man—unburdened by family cares—books occupied much of his attention that otherwise would have been bestowed. His native ability, superior judgment, high sense of right and unquestionable veracity, to which he added a general and practical education—those qualities so essential in the faithful, impartial and successful discharge of the duties of municipal offices and many other public positions of trust, were early recognized by his townsmen, and his long and varied terms of service in the several municipal departments of his native town bespeak his sterling worth. He died in his 80th year June 3, 1884.

Samuel L.[2], the youngest son of Thomas D. Francis[1], was adopted by his Uncle Thomas and Matilda (Knapp) Millett, who had no children of their own. In 1833, he married first, Sarah S., born Jan. 25, 1806, a daughter of Joshua M. and Lucy (Page) True. His life work was that of a farmer. Some time subsequent to the death of his uncle, whose adopted son he was, which occurred in 1834, he changed his location and for many years resided on a farm near North Turner bridge. Thence he removed to the present residence of his son, William Henry, where he died Feb. 11, 1889. His first wife died Feb. 3, 1837, leaving a small child—having buried another but a few weeks previous. He later married her sister, Naomi P. True, born Feb. 11, 1815; who died Oct. 12, 1881.

To Samuel L. and Sarah S. Francis were born:

Susan Maria, March 5, 1834; died Jan. 29, 1837; and William Henry, born Jan. 12, 1836.

To Samuel L. and Naomi P. Francis were born:

Page True, Feb. 12, 1843, and John Adams, Jan. 10, 1850. On, or about, Jan. 1, 1859, William Henry married Zipporah L., born Sept. 8, 1835, a daughter of Esquire Ulmer and Louise H. (Merrill) Perly, of Livermore. Their residence was the same as that of his father. Not unlike the earlier members of the family, he was not wanting in native wit nor shrewd business capacity; yet, never swerving from an honorable position in his dealings, or departing from the course of truth and veracity, he sustains the confidence and esteem of his townspeople whom he has served in an official capacity. He is one of the neat and tidy farmers of Leeds, aided by a worthy and estimable helpmeet. They have issue Samuel P. and Ulmer P., twins, born Oct. 23, 1859; Augustus S., born Nov. 17, 1864; Louise H., born Nov. 15, 1874, and Millie B., born June 7, 1880.

Samuel P. married Lucy, a daughter of Capt. Fernando Foss; settled and now resides at North Leeds on the farm taken up by Increase Leadbetter. (Their children are omitted for want of information which was earnestly sought.)

Ulmer P. married Nellie, a daughter of L. Clark and Mary Ann (Gott) Leadbetter, of Wayne; settled and now resides on the farm of his Grandfather Perly in Livermore. They have no issue.

Augustus S. married Ida A. Sarner, born in Stockholm,

Sweden. Their children are Franklin, born July 22, 1893; Roy P., born July 9, 1896; Percy W., born Aug. 2, 1897; died Aug. 10, 1898; Herbert Henry, born April 17, 1900. Reside in St. Paul, Minn.

Louise H. married John Knowlton, of East Livermore. They have issue Harry Hale, born Dec. 30, 1893; Carrie Denning, born Sept. 9, 1897.

Millie Bursely married Nathan Merrill, of Turner. To them was born Perley L., July 2, 1900.

Page True[3], the eldest son of Samuel L.[2] and Naomi P. (True) Francis, profited by the advice of "Horace Greeley" 'and went west. He subsequently settled in Graford, Nebraska, and in 1882 married Betty Johnson. Their children are: Frank, Grace, Louise, and Ruth, whose respective ages are 18, 14, 10, and 8 years. (1901.)

John Adams[3], the other child of Samuel L.[2] and Noami[1] P., resides in Montana. It is said of him that he married there, but of his family the writer is not informed.

Lorania[2], the youngest child of Thomas D.[1] and Eunice (Millett) Francis, married Ansel Turner in November, 1829. They settled in Leeds. Sept. 30, 1831, she died, leaving no issue.

The foregoing sketch of one of the earliest and perhaps as prominent as any of the families in the discharge of official duties in the town, although produced under certain difficulties, has not been colored or blazoned by vain imagination, and such errors as have appeared in former accounts have been carefully corrected or eliminated.

BISHOP FAMILY.

The earliest ancestors in this country of the Bishop families in Winthrop, Monmouth, Wayne, Leeds, and other New England towns of whom we have knowledge was Edward, who resided in Salem, Mass., as early as 1639. The church records of that city show that he was a member thereof in 1645; and the city records are evidence that he was constable in 1660. He died in that place in 1695. His son, Edward second, married Hannah ———. lived in Beverly, but subsequently moved to Salem where he died in the year 1705. Among the historic events in Salem are recorded the drastic crimes committed by that unholy man of God, Cotton Mather, and his associate rulers, in their false accusations of the poor, innocent victims of their hatred who dared to assert diametrical religious views. Imprisonment and various inhuman methods of punishment were instituted for witch-craft, or casting out devils, and finally death upon the gallows was the penalty they suffered for the freedom of their faith. A blot will ever remain on the pages of history of that municipality. The first victim of that tyrant power was Bridget Bishop, the second wife of Edward second, which occurred June 10, 1692.

Edward third was born in Salem in 1648. He married Sarah Wildes; was a farmer, a native of Salem, in which place he lived. He was present at the hearing in April, 1692, given Sarah Cloyce accused of witch-craft; and hearing John, an Indian servant in the family of Samuel Parris, the minister, who was her accuser, give false testimony against her, cured that servant by a good flogging and declared his belief that he could likewise cure the whole company thus afflicted. For this both he and his wife were imprisoned. With the overthrow of that tyrant, priestly power, they were released, and in 1693 moved to Rehoboth, Mass., where he died May 11, 1711. In his will mention is made of Jonathan fourth, born in the year 1686. He married Abigail Avery. The date of his death is unknown to the writer but his will was probated April 7, 1725. Gould Bishop, son of Jonathan fourth, was born in Rehoboth, Mass., March 25, 1712. He married Mary ———, March 15, 1732. Two of the sons of Gould and Mary Bishop, Squire and Zadock, settled in the District of Maine, the former in Winthrop and the latter at New Meadows, a part of Brunswick. Squire was born in Rehoboth Nov. 4, 1733. He married Patience Titus and settled in Winthrop, Me., obtaining the grant of lot of land No. 17 in the Pond town plantation, June 11, 1766. His family, consisting of wife and six children, came the following spring and his was the second family to settle in that town. He was the first inn-keeper in Winthrop, and for several years the town meetings, beginning with that of organization, were held in his home. He held several offices of responsibility and trust in that town and there died Sept. 6, 1801, and his wife April 21, 1802, where they were both buried.

Zadock was born in Rehoboth April 24, 1749, and married Mary Rawson Feb. 28, 1770. Soon after his marriage Zadock went to New Meadows and, according to the history of Monmouth, he came to Monmouth from that town. While he was at New Meadows a son, Jonathan, was born. Zadock did not see him until years afterward, when he lived in Leeds, and then did not know him until informed of his identity.

Soon after the birth of the son, Mary died. A few years after his wife's death Zadock returned to Rehoboth and from there moved to Swansea, where he married Elizabeth, a sister to Nathan Hale. After their marriage, Zadock with his wife, returned to New Meadows, thence to Monmouth in the year 1781-82; and to quote from the history of that town, "Zadock Bishop built his cabin near the Moody Stream in North Monmouth about twenty rods south-east of the south wing of the mill dam. When Gen. Dearborn built his mill at East Monmouth he backed the water up until it covered Bishop's farm almost to his door-step. 'Hey,' said the old man, 'they've flowed me out as they would a musquash,' and gathering his household effects he made a bee-line to the highest elevation in the town of Leeds. . . . One thing is certain, he was not driven from his strong-hold by the backing up of a mill stream." Another thing may be said, although it was a high elevation it is not the highest in Leeds. The place of his location in Leeds is that where his grandson, George Bishop, now resides, and the year of his removal there was 1783. How long he lived at Swansea or New Meadows we have not as yet learned, but only ten years at most could have elapsed from the time he left Rehoboth until we find him by the stream in North Monmouth. To Zadock and Elizabeth Bishop nine children were born, viz.: Joseph, Welcome, Jesse, Squier, Mary, Lydia, Zadock, James, and Cyrus. Welcome, their second son, was born June 21, 1774. He married Betsey Lindsey and they had one son, James. James was a preacher and he confined himself so closely to his holy work he was called to leave it at an early age.

Jesse, the third son of Zadock and Elizabeth, was born June 12, 1776. He moved to Wayne and married Patience Titus; his wife died March 3, 1863, and Jesse followed June 23, 1864. The children of Jesse were Demas, Mary H., Squire, Jesse, Naaman, Savilla Ann, Jonathan G., Nathan, and Samuel T. Demas born April 7, 1801; married Isabelle Farnham in February, 1823; lived and died in West Peru. Mary H., born March 27, 1802; married Benjamin Lovejoy December, 1827; lived and died in Peru. Squire, born April 10, 1806; married Hannah Morey, November, 1827; lived and died in Wayne; Jesse, born April 29, 1808; married Lucy Maxim June, 1834; lived and died in Wayne on the place settled by his father, Jesse, in 1805. Naaman, born Jan. 1, 1811; married Mary Ridlon August, 1823; lived and died in Leeds. Savilla Ann, born Jan. 25, 1813; married John Burgess January, 1834; lived and died in Peru. Jonathan G., born Feb. 29, 1816; married Margaret W. Clark July 4, 1846; died in Sangerville. Nathan, born Aug. 18, 1818; married Harriet E. Tobin, July, 1845. His second wife was Mrs. Lucy Chisolm. He lived and died in South Boston, 358 Dorchester Street. Samuel T., born May 18, 1821; married Julia True May, 1845. He lived and died in Wayne.

Squier, son of Zadock and Elizabeth, was born Sept. 8, 1780. We have not learned much concerning him. Mary was born April 24, 1783. She did not marry. Lydia, born in Leeds Oct. 12, 1785; married Thomas Graffam, of Leeds, and was the grandmother of George T. Howe, of Leeds Junction—the veteran brick-maker. Zadock was born July 19, 1788. James was born Aug. 5, 1793, and Cyrus March 5, 1797.

Joseph, the eldest son of Zadock and Elizabeth Bishop, was born Sept. 24, 1772. He married Jane Turner and lived on the old homestead in Leeds. They lived to a good old age; Jane died March 15, 1857, and Joseph followed her Feb. 11, 1863. They had nine children: Phebe, Abial, Elizabeth, Joseph, Amos, Walter, Zadock, Nathan and George. Phebe, born Jan. 6, 1798; married Jarius Manuel and lived and died in North Monmouth. Abial D. was born Dec. 31, 1799. He married Dorcas Lindsey and lived on a farm adjoining that of his father. Seven children were born to them: Luvernia, who was born Nov. 3, 1826; married Arza Gilmore Sept. 15, 1846; married Solomon Brewster Aug. 15, 1858. Charles, born Jan. 6, 1829; died unmarried Dec. 14, 1869. Sylvia, born April, 1832; died July 27, 1854; unmarried. Mary, born May 5, 1835; married David Trask; married Charles Lindsey; lived in Leeds and died there April 4, 1890. Harriet, born in 1836, died an infant. Aluria and Angelia, born Sept. 8, 1838. Aluria married William Canwell and lives in North Monmouth; Angelia married H. M. Brewster, of Leeds. Elizabeth, daughter of Joseph and Jane Bishop, born Sept. 17, 1802; married Steve Foy; lived in Canton and died there in 1853. Joseph, son of Joseph and Jane Bishop, born Sept. 17, 1802; married Jemima Norris, of Wayne, in March, 1825; their children were Julia, born June 13, 1825; married Loring Roberts and now lives in Greenwood, Me. Nathan N., born 1827; died in infancy. Adeline, born Oct. 5, 1822; died 1847. Lendall, born Jan. 29, 1833; married and resides in St. Johnsbury, Vt. Mahala, born April 14, 1834; married Wm. C. Lincoln and now lives in Wayne. Has six children. Octavia J., born Jan. 11, 1839; died Sept 12, 1890; married Jacob Davis, of New Gloucester, had two daughters. Francina J., born Jan. 11, 1839; now Mrs. Emmons; lives in West Paris, Me. Amos H., son of Joseph and Jane, born July 13, 1811; married Eliza Burgess May 9, 1836. Nine children were born. Eliza died Dec. 14, 1871.

Amos married Mary Thompson; he died Oct. 11, 1873. The children of Amos and Eliza were: Amos Bradford, born Nov. 3, 1837; married Elmina Wheeler and lives in Winthrop. They have six children living. Erastus, son of Amos and Eliza, born May 5, 1839. He enlisted in Company I, Second Maine Cavalry, at the breaking out of the Civil War, was Sergeant of his company and was stationed at Barrancos, Fla. He contracted a fever and returned home only to stay three weeks; the fever proved fatal and he died on his birthday, 1865. Roxanna L., their only daughter, born Feb. 9, 1841; married Aleck Mank; lived in Fayette and died there Nov. 1, 1892. George T. was born May 4, 1843. Henry H., born April 7, 1845; married Julia Jackson Dec. 21, 1872; occupation, farmer in Winthrop, Me.; they have one daughter, Bertha, born Dec. 25, 1873.

GEORGE T. BISHOP.

Winfield Scott, born June 22, 1847; married Elvira Rackley May 11, 1869. Their children are: Clifton D., born May 15, 1873; married Ella Smith and lives in Columbia Falls. Glen C., born June 9, 1876; married Melvin Libby and lives at Leeds Junction; Nedd R., born Dec. 30, 1879; married Myrtle Grant; have one child, Reginald S., born Feb. 21, 1901. Laura E., born Jan. 27, 1886. Horace W., son of Amos and Eliza, born Sept. 1, 1849; died unmarried May 13, 1884.

Zadock, son of Joseph and Jane Bishop, born May 14, 1815; married Emily Lothrop, of Leeds, and his occupation was that of a farmer in Carroll, Me.; he died Dec. 22, 1893. They had eight children: Frank P., born Feb. 23, 1860; occupation, lumberman in Minnesota. George R., born Sept. 8, 1863; lumberman in Carroll, Me. Ellen W., born Aug. 24, 1848; died Dec. 27, 1853. Emma L., born Dec. 26, 1854; married W. H. Brown, Carroll, Me. Ellouisa, born May 13, 1857; married R. H. Staples; died June 21, 1900. Clara I., born March 31, 1867; married James Grant, farmer in Montreal, Quebec. Jennie W., born Dec. 19, 1869; married B. B. Lindsey, of Carroll, Me.

Nathan, son of Joseph and Jane Bishop, born Nov. 10, 1818; married Lucy Skillings March 6, 1860, and lived in North Monmouth at the time of his death in 1893. The greater part of his life was spent in North Monmouth. Six children were born to them: Ellen W., born Feb. 10, 1862; Alice M., born Oct. 6, 1865; Emily E., born July 25, 1867; married George McKenney Feb. 17, 1896; lives in Gardiner. Emery N., born March 24, 1874; farmer on the homestead in North Monmouth. Twin sons born March 21, 1877, died in infancy.

George, youngest son of Joseph and Jane, born March 4, 1821; married Susan Lowell Feb. 27, 1827, and lives on the place cleared and made habitable by his grandfather, Zadock Bishop. It was at this place the first house was built on "Bishop Hill." The six children of George and Susan Bishop were Joseph P., born Nov. 25, 1852; he has been and is an energetic, successful business man; his home is in Winthrop. Walter, born Jan. 6, 1855; occupation, farmer in Monmouth. Rosilla, born Sept. 6, 1857; married Cyrus Howe, a farmer in Leeds; died August, 1898. Anna L., born May 22, 1862; married Fred Pinkham, a blind and sash manufacturer in Augusta. Emery B., born Nov. 6, 1858; died in infancy. Georgia L., born Sept. 4, 1869; married Morris Shapeiro, a traveling salesman; died Nov. 16, 1899.

BIOGRAPHY OF GEORGE T. BISHOP.

G. T. Bishop, the subject of this sketch, was born in Leeds May 4, 1843. He remained on the farm with his father until eighteen years of age and had the advantages of a common school education. When the Civil War broke out he yielded to the patriotic spirit which took possession of so many men of our country and enlisted in Company I of the 23d Maine Volunteers. For nine months he underwent all the privations and hardships of war; he was made Corporal of his company only a little while before his term of enlistment expired. At the expiration of his term he enlisted again, but yielding to the entreaties of his mother, he got his discharge on the ground that he was still under age. He then returned home but remained only a short time before he went to Lewiston where he worked at several trades. It was here he met Miss Julia Byron, whom he afterward married in the year 1869. He remained in that city about a year and then obtained employment on what was then the Androscoggin Railroad between Lewiston and Brunswick, and afterward he went from Lewiston to Farmington; served as either engineer, fireman or conductor until the fall of 1873, when he was called home by the death of his father. At the settlement of his father's estate he bought out the several heirs and the homestead was his own. Since then he has labored diligently and has added to it nearly all the farm that formerly belonged to Abial Bishop. For a time he was engaged quite extensively in the cattle business and his was the first carload of cattle that was shipped over the Sandy River Railroad. In later years he engaged in lumbering and as in all other business he has undertaken, was successful in this.

His interest has always been closely connected with that of his native town and for eight successive years served as one of the selectmen, and for three of those years was chairman of the board. He worked continually for the good of the town and after making several much needed repairs and with its business in a flourishing condition, resigned his office.

Three children were born to Mr. and Mrs. Bishop: Weston H., born July 18, 1873; remains with his father on the farm and has been closely allied with the schools of the town, part of the time as a teacher and afterward as Superintendent and a member of the School Committee; Florrie M., born July 8, 1876; is a graduate of Maine Wesleyan Seminary and Farmington Normal School. She is a successful teacher, having taught in her native and neighboring towns; Marion T., born July 19, 1883; is a student at Kent's Hill and a teacher in the schools of Leeds.

Mr. Bishop has always been a man of untiring industry and temperate habits, decided and firm in his convictions; in business exacting but always honorable, to his town he has been of incalculable worth; his career has been an honorable one, a credit to himself, his family and his friends.

LOTHROP FAMILY.

The founder of the Lothrop family in Littleborough was Mark—the second Lothrop pioneer in this country. He came from England in 1643 and settled in Bridgewater, Mass. He was a proprietor in that town in 1656 and in 1657 took the "Oath of Fidelity." In 1658 he was elected a constable and for twenty-five years was a man of prominence in public life. His sons were Samuel[2] and Mark[2]. Samuel settled and continued his residence in Bridgewater. His son, Samuel[3], Jr., was born in that town May 17, 1685, and died in January, 1772. His son, Daniel[4], was born in West Bridgewater, May 2, 1721. In 1744 he married Rhoda, a daughter of Thomas Willis. He was Major in Col. Crafts' Regiment, Dorchester Heights, when Washington took command of the army. He was one of the original members of the First Baptist Church of Bridgewater. In 1811, when 90 years of age, he came from Bridgewater on horseback to visit his son, Daniel,[5] Jr., and being so well pleased with the site, remained until his death, which occurred in 1818, at the advanced age of 97.

Col. Daniel Lothrop[5], Jr., was born in Bridgewater, Dec. 10, 1745. He married first, Hannah Howard, Aug. 23, 1764, who died in 1771; second, Lydia Willis, Sept. 5, 1775; third, Mary Turner, Sept. 1, 1785, a sister of William and Josiah who came from Bridgewater and were among the early settlers of Littleborough Plantation. He was a soldier in the War of the Revolution and rose to the rank of Colonel; yet, to him, it was a sacrifice of wealth for honor. He sold his real estate at the time of his enlistment, for which payment was to be made on a later date, and was made, but in Continental money, which was worthless. This financial loss and the death of his second wife, with a family of children to provide and care for, in the fall of 1784 he came to Littleborough, took up the farm now owned by Greenwood C. Gordon and a portion by Wallace Gordon at the south end of Androscoggin Lake, made a cut-down, built a log house and hovel and returned to Bridgewater. In the spring of 1785 he came again, made his burn, planted corn and potatoes, spent the remainder of the season in felling trees and clearing land, in August returned for his family and in September, after marrying Mary Turner, brought them to the wilderness of Leeds, leaving behind one daughter, Hannah, who married Joshua Gilmore and whose son, Col. John Gilmore, came to Leeds and was many years a prominent resident. When the town was organized Col. Daniel Lothrop was elected on the Board of Selectmen and subsequently filled many offices of trust. His children, born in Bridgewater, were: George[6], June 13, 1765; Daniel[6], March 28, 1767; Thomas[6], 1769; Hannah[6], 1771; Samuel[6], 1777; and Sullivan[6], 1778.

His children by his last wife were born in Leeds, to wit: Polly[6], Oct. 29, 1787; Lydia[6], May 5, 1789; Alson[6], Feb. 7, 1792; Jonah[6], July 23, 1795 (died Aug. 23, 1795); Rhoda[6], April 29, 1799. He died in 1837. His many descendants have proven themselves worthy of their name and noted ancestry. In both civil and military offices they have been prominent, and especially in the legislative halls of the State.

George[6], his eldest son, married in 1783 Polly Thayer. Eventually he located in Leeds, where his wife died Oct. 25, 1831, and he March 4, 1839. Their children were: Solomon[7], born Feb. 26, 1788; Leavitt[7], born May 19, 1793; Hannah[7], born March 19, 1800; Jeremiah[7], born Oct. 29, 1802; and Polly[7], born Dec. 17, 1802. The only persons now living in Leeds by the name of Lothrop are descendants of George Lothrop, Esq.

Solomon[7], eldest son of George[6], married July 15, 1810, Sarah W., a daughter of Capt. Daniel and Sally (Whiting) Lothrop, his cousin. He was an active business man for many years at Lothrop's Corner, which by his energy and efforts, became a smart business center. He was the first postmaster in town and was in trade many years at that place. He acquired wealth and became owner of a large acreage. His home, where his youngest son, Willard, now lives, was purchased of Abial Daily, M.D., the first resident physician in the town. He held numerous offices and was active in social and religious circles. They had issue George Daniel[7], born Aug. 24, 1811; Betsey[7], born Dec. 13, 1813; Solomon Leavitt[7], born June 10, 1817; Orissa[7], born Dec. 30, 1819; and Willard, born June 18, 1828.

George D.[7] married Hulda Gilmore. They had issue Mary Francis[8], born Dec. 3, 1837; Helen Augusta, born July 15, 1841. The latter married W. W. Noyes.

Betsey[7] married Joshua S. Turner and has three children: Ermina J., born Aug. 6, 1834 (Mrs. E. D. Hamilton); Emma born Jan. 13, 1837 (Mrs. James Norris); Francis A., born April 16, 1839.

Solomon L.[7] married April 20, 1840, Hannah, born Oct. 11, 1818, a daughter of George and Betsey (Gilbert) Turner. They had issue Lewis Leavitt[8], born Oct. 21, 1840, died Feb. 4, 1842; William Henry[8], born May 17, 1842, and Lydia Albina, born Aug. 3, 1844. William Henry[8] married Dec. 12, 1866, Georgia F., a daughter of W. S. Noyes, of Boston, and died, leaving a widow and four boys residing in Portland.

Lydia Albina married Cyrus B. Lane. She died, leaving one daughter, Mrs. Cassie B. Farmer, who has three children.

Orissa[7] married Alson Lothrop, Jr., and located at Jay Bridge.

Willard[7], the youngest child of Solomon Lothrop[6], married Jan. 10, 1860, Emma L., a daughter of Rev. Samuel and Sarah (Leadbetter) Boothby. They have issue Susie E. (Mrs. G. W.

SOLOMON LOTHROP AND WIFE.

Lane), born Jan. 11, 1861; Frank B., born July, 1863, and Sarah Clyde, born Aug. 6, 1879. Mr. Lothrop resides on the old homestead—a valuable and well cultivated farm. He has contributed much to the advancement of the town by securing the establishment of various industries therein. He has represented his district in the State Legislature and is especially interested in the Universalist church, of which he is Superintendent of the Sabbath School.

Hon. Leavitt[7], the second son of George[6] and Polly (Thayer) Lothrop, was born in Vassalborough, Me., May 19, 1793. In 1816 he married Betsey, a daughter of Elias and Mary (Lawrence) Lane. He settled in Leeds and in 1826 moved to the farm now occupied by his son, Davis Francis Lothrop, and there resided until his death, which occurred April 17, 1849. His widow died in Auburn, Jan. 12, 1878. Mr. Lothrop was an energetic man of business, and in all activities of the community worked diligently and well. He was nominally a farmer and carried on agriculture extensively and profitably, owning, at the time of his death, 800 acres of land in Leeds, 200 in Canton, 100 in Greene and 50 in Hallowell. He was deeply interested in all enterprises that gave promise of benefit to the people, and his personal services were freely given to their development and improvement. He took an active part in the establishment of the Androscoggin and Kennebec Railroad and assisted in procuring the charter of the Leeds and Farmington Railroad, subscribing $1000 to its stock. In both civil and political life, his good common sense, sound judgment and honesty of purpose, rendered his presence in public positions valuable to his constituents and the community. He represented the classed towns of which Leeds was one, in the State Legislature. In 1841 he commenced a three-years' term on the board of county commissioners of Kennebec county, and in 1846-7 was a Senator from that county. He was also prominent in the State militia, serving in successive grades to that of Colonel, by which title he was generally known. In the war of 1812 he was for a time engaged on the lower Kennebec in the construction of fortifications, etc. In these and numerous other places of responsibility, such was his wise sagacity, pleasing urbanity and thoughtful consideration, that his associates in councils and labors became lasting friends. He was a Baptist in religion and liberal in sustaining Christian institutions. In the home circle he was kind and affectionate. His children were: Elias Lane, b. Nov. 19, 1817; Davis Francis, b. Sept. 11, 1820; Warren Lane, b. July 5, 1823; Caroline Elizabeth, b. Oct. 17, 1825, and Mary Jane, b. July 12, 1833.

Elias L.[8] and Davis F. in their early manhood were successful school teachers. Elias L. married in 1847 Jane Morse, of Lisbon, and had issue Leavitt, b. June 10, 1848, and Mary Morse, b. Dec.

3, 1849. In the spring of 1849 he and his brother, Davis F., sailed from Boston, Mass., to San Francisco, Cal., in the ship Capitol, arriving there July 6. On Sept. 30, 1852, he died in that state. The son was a graduate of Bowdoin College, went to New Orleans and was accidentally shot and died. The daughter married.

Hon. Davis Francis⁸, was educated in the town schools and Monmouth Academy. He inherited many of the characteristics of his father. He has been active and valuable in many public positions of trust, discharging the duties of such offices as selectman, county commissioner and representative to the State Legislature, to his credit and the satisfaction of his constituents. In 1846 he married Caroline S., a daughter of Jonathan and Jane (Libby) Morse. They had issue Flora Louvisa, b. Sept. 1, 1847; Adonia, b. March 26, 1849; d. Sept. 9, 1852; Eugene, b. Oct. 6, 1851; d. Aug. 30, 1852; Elias, b. July 7, 1853; Serville, b. Jan. 10, 1853; d. Jan. 16, 1856; Irvin Scott, b. Feb. 22, 1856; Olive Morse, b. May 5, 1858, and Ralph, b. Nov. 24, 1860.

Flora L., married Hon. Frank Higgins, of Limerick, Me. Ruggles Higgins, of Livermore Falls, is her son.

Elias and Irvin S. reside in Louisiana, where they own adjoining plantations on the Mississippi, 24 miles below New Orleans. Elias married Lucile Piazia, a daughter of the Swiss consul at New Orleans at the time of the Civil war. They have a large family of children.

Irvin S. is unmarried.

Olive M. married Doctor John M. Turner Sept. 26, 1888, who was born in Leeds Aug. 12, 1856, and settled in Bangor, but subsequently located in Gardiner, where the Doctor had a large and lucrative practice. They had one daughter, Flora E., born June 11, 1891. Mrs. Turner is now a widow lady, her husband having died Dec. 24, 1899. Ralph is unmarried and remains on the old homestead, which has been given into his care. He is an active, energetic man of business, and many kindly acts of assistance to those needing financial aid attest his worth in the community in which he resides and moves.

Hon. Davis Francis Lothrop, as stated of his brother Elias, went to California in 1849, where he remained nearly three years, returning to Maine once during the time. He was one of "The Old Forty-Niners." He was financially successful but his energy or ambition was not blunted thereby and his later life, devoted to farming, has been one of success and profit. He is a member of the Baptist church, a liberal supporter of all enterprises tending to the betterment of the community, and a highly respected citizen. At the age of 80 years few men are so well preserved, so active, so interested in public affairs, so well

HON. DAVIS FRANCIS LOTHROP.

MRS. D. F. LOTHROP.

COL. W. L. LOTHROP.

informed. February 16, 1901, his wife died, mourned by her family and fondly cherished by her many friends.

Col. Warren[8], the third child, enlisted in the United States army in 1845 and was stationed at West Point. On the breaking out of the Mexican War his company was ordered to the front and joined General Scott at Vera Cruz. He was in every battle fought from there to the capture of the City of Mexico. For "meritorious conduct," at the close of the war, he received a lieutenant's commission, and was assigned to the Fourth Artillery, stationed at Fort Kearney and Randall on the Western frontier. In April, 1861, he was stationed at St. Louis and was commissioned Major of the First Missouri Light Artillery, under Col. Frank Blair, who was elected to Congress, and Maj. Lothrop promoted to Colonel. At the close of the war he was made chief quartermaster of the Department of the Gulf, with headquarters at Tallahassee, Florida, where he died in 1866.

Caroline[8] E., the fourth child of Col. Leavitt[7], married Augustus Foss. Her residence has been in California, where five of her seven children are located, the other two residing in Manchester, N. H., with whom she is now living.

Mary Jane[8], the youngest child of Col. Leavitt[7], married Charles Lane, who died in 1858. She resides in Pendleton, Oregon, where her daughter and only child, Neva, is a teacher.

Hannah[7], the third child of George Lothrop[6], Esq., married George Gould and settled on the west side of the highway running southerly from North Leeds Railroad Station and about one-third of a mile distant therefrom. About 1850, Mr. Gould erected, at the north end of his farm, the buildings now occupied by Frank Foss, in which he lived several years. They had one son, Orville.

Jeremiah[7], fourth child—no data except died Sept. 25, 1874.

Polly[7], the youngest child of George[6], married Ruel Foss in June, 1827, and settled at Foss Corner, on the farm now owned by N. P. Gould. To them were born three children, Orinthia (Mrs. Dana Goff), Rodney, and Florida (Mrs. B. J. Hill). They moved to Auburn, Me., about 1866, where they both died.

Capt. Daniel[6], the second son of Col. Daniel Lothrop[5], the pioneer of Leeds, married first, Sarah (Sally) Whiting, in 1787. They had issue ten children. His second wife was Lucy Gilbert, who also bore him ten children. He was an able man and much in public service. Ten years was he a representative in the State Legislature. About 1835 he moved to Carroll, Me., and died in Lee. His was a very prominent family and many of his sons and grandsons have distinguished themselves in public places of honor.

Of the other sons of Col. Daniel[3], Thomas, Samuel, and Sullivan, they married and reared large families, none of whom are now residing in town, save Mrs. Rowland Gilmore, a granddaughter of Thomas, and her son, John. The name of Lothrop in Leeds is now borne by the descendants of George[5] only, and those who bear it are: Hon. Davis Francis[8], Hon. Willard[8], and their respective families, and Mrs. Solomon L. Lothrop, the widow of a brother of Willard.

Of the children of Col. Daniel[5] and his third wife, Mary Turner, all of whom were born in Leeds, Polly[6] married Luther Cary and died in Bradford, Me., in 1881.

Lydia[6], married Hon. Stillman Howard and spent her whole long life in the town of her birth. They had issue six children, of whom mention is made in the Howard family, in another part of this work. The only one of her children now living is Hon. Seth Howard,—a life-long resident of Leeds. She died April 6, 1872.

Alson[6], married Huldah Richmond and settled in the town of Jay, near Jay Bridge. They reared a large family of children in that town, and when advanced in years, moved to Carroll, leaving the farm to Alson, Jr., who married Orrissa, a daughter of Solomon Lothrop, of Leeds.

Rhoda[6], the youngest child of Col. Daniel[5], married Nathan Richmond. They had one child, Mary Reliance, born in 1824, who married Odlin Watson and had issue Flora, who died when a yound lady; Fred Odlin, who has long been and now is Register of Probate in Androscoggin county; Henry, Thomas and John.

To Hon. Seth Howard is due much of the credit in the production of this sketch.

GILBERT FAMILY.

The Gilberts, in their name and in their connection by marriage, were a numerous family in the southern part of the town of Leeds in the earlier years of its settlement. A singular fact is, that at this centennial anniversary of its incorporation, only a single person bearing the name remains a citizen of the town.

Capt. William Gilbert, the first settler of the name to locate in Leeds, came from Scituate, Mass., in the year 1783, just after the close of the Revolutionary War. He had served in the army of the revolution, in which service he was honored with a lieutenant's commission. His title of Captain, by which he was distinguished through life, is supposed to have been gained from his connection with the militia affairs of his early time, in which he took an active part. He was induced to come to the locality by the proprietor, Col. Moses Little, to aid by his example and influence in colonizing the town. He married Betsey Bailey, of Hanover, Mass., to whom two children were born before moving to Maine. Capt. Gilbert was given the privilege of selecting four hundred acres of land from any lots in town not already taken up. His choice was on the height of land in the south-west part of the town, long known as "Welcome Hill," in what is now known as the Additon neighborhood, together with another near-by lot for many years designated as the "Phillips Turner place." The selection of the first-named lot was made on account of the fine growth of oak timber characterizing that locality, indicating the superiority of soil on which it stood. That his selection was wisely made, everyone who knows the land in that locality will readily admit. This land was conveyed to Mr. Gilbert through a warrantee deed given by Moses Little, it being the first warrantee deed given to a settler of the town up to that time. The house and other buildings erected on this farm were located on the north side of the road, just opposite the buildings now occupied by F. L. Additon, and torn down many years ago.

Capt. Gilbert was an active, influential man, a leader in all public affairs and an extensive and successful farmer. His home was headquarters for new comers to the town, and every one always found a warm welcome at his house. His influence was widespread and was successful in drawing many other settlers to the town, both his own connections as well as others, many of whom he employed in clearing his lands and in his extensive farming. In 1796, Rev. Paul Coffin was a guest at this farm and thus wrote of its crops: "This man raises, annually, about five hundred bushels of breadstuff and fourteen hundred weight of flax, etc. His hay and breadstuff will this year exceed two tons of hay, and more, by the acre on uplands." It is not out of place to state in this connection that the proprietor of this farm secured the immigration of Jabez Daggett, an expert flax dresser, who located on land adjoining his farm, that he might have the benefit of his labors in his extensive flax business.

Capt. William Gilbert died May 25, 1816, aged 60 years. He was buried in the South Leeds cemetery, where a humble slate headstone hands down this tribute, "He was a kind husband, a tender father and a good neighbor and citizen."

His wife, Betsey, died August 11, 1834, aged 74 years.

Capt. Gilbert, when he came to Maine, was accompanied by his brothers—Elijah, who took up a large tract of land in Turner, near where the Center Bridge now spans the river, and which now is divided into the several farms of that locality; Levi, who located in Buckfield; Nathaniel, who also located in Turner but later moved to Kingfield and to Anson, where he made the first clearing in town; Hersey, who located on a section of his brother William's home farm, next west, later known as the "Joshua Turner place." These buildings, also, as with the first Gilbert homestead in the town, have been torn down; thus leaving, as with the families who occupied them, no other memorial of their existence than the silent monuments in the near-by burial ground on which their names are chiseled.

Capt. William Gilbert's children were Betsey, who married George Turner, Esq., and had thirteen children, of whom one died young, and the others were, Josiah, Lydia, Betsey, William, Washington, Cynthia, Hannah, Sobrina, Sarah, John, Benjamin and Martha; Lucy, who married Daniel Lothrop; Sally, who married Codding Drake; Jane, who married Daniel Lindsey; Julia, who married Warren Mitchell, had children, Henry, Clara and Ellen; William, Jr., who never married, and Henry A., who married Christina, daughter of Benjamin Alden, of Greene. These families all settled in town; but Lothrop, Drake and Lindsey and other families later, finding the titles of their farms unsound, accepted the offer of the State of the gift of a lot of wild land, and moved to what was then designated "Number 6," now the town of Carroll, in upper Penobscot county, where they began pioneer life over again and made permanent homes.

William Gilbert, Jr., located on that part of his father's original purchase before designated as "Phillips Turner place," where he lived during his stay in town, but finally went to Carroll, and spent his last days with his sisters.

Henry A. Gilbert first located on his father's home farm but later lived at several different places in Leeds, and finally moved to Turner and made a home with his son, Alden, where he died in 1881, aged 77 years. His wife, Christina (Alden) Gilbert, died in 1889, aged 86. Their children were Annie, who married Joseph Kilbreth, of Manchester, and died in 1851, at the age of 22; Betsey Alden, who married Alfred Jewell, of Winthrop, and died in 1891, aged 62 years; Christina died in 1850, aged 18; Julia married first, Ruel Phillips, and second, Hiram Phillips, both of whom she still survives; Alden, died in 1865, aged 31; Tertia, Otis Hayford and James Henry, all of whom died young.

Hersey Gilbert was a cabinet maker, a fine workman, and made much of the furniture used by the people of the town, many pieces of which are to be found at the present time among the descendants of those early families. His labors thus supplied an important want of the people among whom he lived. He married in Massachusetts, before coming to Maine, a lady by the name of Randall, and a large family was the result of their union. They were:

Cornelius, born in 1778, who lived in Leeds for a time but moved with his family to Canada and never returned. A daughter, Susan, came back to town to visit friends, and while here, formed an alliance with Ira Sampson, whom she married. They settled on the bank of the Androscoggin river—near the recent ferry. Four children were born to her, Laura, Julia, William and Ira.

In a delicate state of health, in rescuing a child from drowning, she took cold and died therefrom.

Levi, who settled in Leeds for a time, later moved to the town of Parkman, where he died.

Charles G., who married Martha Day in 1809, located on the farm near Keen's Corner recently occupied by their son, the late J. Ransom, where he died. Their children were Charles, Nathaniel, James C., Judith, who married a Bishop, Huldah, Nancy, who married a Crossman, Rhoda, Spirren, Caleb S., James Nelson, and Joseph Ransom.

Ruth, born in 1776, who married Joseph Day.

Rebecca, born in 1780, who married Jacob, brother to Joseph Day.

Olive, born in 1782, who married Alvira Gilbert.

Hersey, Jr., born in 1784, who married Mehitable Morse.

Priscilla, born in 1787, who married John Foster.

Polly, born in 1790, who married Richard Crockett, and Sally, Lucinda, and Wealthy, whose descendants, if any, cannot now be traced.

Hersey Gilbert, Jr., married Mehitable Morse and located in the east part of the town. Their children were: Dennis, born in 1811; Irvilla, who married Warren Foster; Caleb S., who married Louisa Torsey; Levi J., Jerome B., Joseph R., Drusilla, who married Holman H. Torsey; Alfred and Chandler. None of this family are now living in Leeds.

James Nelson Gilbert married ——— Keen, daughter of John Keen, and lived on the place now owned by George Howe, at Leeds Junction. Their children were Marcellus, now a resident of Boston, and Addison.

Joseph Ransom Gilbert married Mary A. Crummett and lived on the homestead farm near Keen's Corner, where he died in 1898. Their children were: Martha Almedia, Erastus Everett, George Elliot, Elvetta Delilah, Emma Amelia, and Lewis Irvin. None of them are now residents of Leeds.

Caleb S. Gilbert married Louisa Torsey, and had children: Lucilla Alice, who married Alonzo D. Morton; Lovinia Josephine, who married Joseph H. Day, late of Lewiston; Joseph R., who married Ann Whitney, now a resident of Lewiston, and Jedson D.

Near the close of the century, or about the year 1800, the exact date of which cannot now be fixed, several nephews of Captain William Gilbert came to Leeds to labor on the farm of their uncle, and were soon followed by their widowed mother, bringing with her the remaining members of a family of nine children. These children were Marcus, Ahira, Benjamin, William S., Jedson, and one other son whose name is not now recalled, and three daughters, Deborah, Joanna, and, probably, Huldah.

Deborah Gilbert married Joseph Turner in 1802 as a first wife. They located on a farm on Quaker Ridge, and six children were born to this union: Phillips, Eunice, Julia A., Joseph, Joanna, and William G.

Joanna Gilbert was the first wife of Caleb Wing. They were married in 1809 and had one son, Adna.

The record of marriages in town shows that Elijah Gilbert, Jr., of Turner, and Huldah Gilbert, of Leeds, were married July 3, 1806. The bride here named is supposed to have been sister to Joanna and Deborah named above.

Marcus Gilbert was a maker of carpenter's bench tools and was considered a fine workman. His bench plane-stocks were widely celebrated for their workmanship and were in demand wherever known. He located on the "Welcome Hill" before mentioned, where, with several removals, he lived during his life. He married first, Jane Sampson, and two children were born to this union, Aranda and Jane. His second wife was Marian Coburn, by whom he had two children, Marian and Lafayette. Marcus was called out in the War of 1812, went into camp, and about fifty years afterwards drew 160 acres of land which he sold at two dollars an acre. He died in 1876, aged 85.

Aranda married Diana T. Wing and located in the same neighborhood with his father, following a carpenter's trade. They had four children, Rollin, Abbie, Lois, and Rosa, all of whom are now living. Aranda lived in Leeds during his active life, and died in Poland at his son Rollin's in 1876, at the age of 58 years. His widow died in Leeds in 1899, aged 81 years. Their son, Rollin, married in Lewiston Carrie L. Sweeny in 1870. They had three children, Walter Guy, Earle S. and Mabel. Abbie married Charles Bowers, a civil engineer in Lewiston. Lois married Fred A. Parker, of Leeds, in 1879, and has always lived in town. Their children are Lindley, Percy, Sylvie, Gladys, and Stanley. Rosa married Mellen J. Hanscom, of Leeds, in 1877, and they are now located on a farm in Leeds near Leeds Junction. Jane married William Cushing and is now living in East Abington, Mass. Marian married Abram Toothaker and now lives in Brunswick. Lafayette married Elizabeth Getchell and lives in South Framingham. They had six children, three of whom are living.

William T. Gilbert located on the farm situated between the South Leeds cemetery and the Friends burial ground, where Frank Austin now lives, and later moved to Hallowell. He married Annie Sampson, sister to Jane, wife of Marcus, and they had three children—Proctor, who moved to Norfolk, Va., where he still lives; Earl and Jane, neither of whom are living.

Jedson Gilbert went to New York, where he remained during life.

Ahira Gilbert married Olive Gilbert before mentioned. He was a house carpenter and called a first-class workman. In their earlier years of married life they fluctuated between the Gilbert neighborhood in Leeds and the adjoining neighborhood across the line in Greene. Finally they located permanently in the town of Greene near the Center Bridge, where they died at a ripe old age. Their children were Cornelius, Jedson, Leonard, Ransellear, Deborah, Caroline, Mary Ann, and Albion, who is still living in Abington, Mass.

Benjamin Gilbert, familiarly known as "Ben Gilbert," settled in the same neighborhood of those who preceded him on what was long designated the "Day place," and near where the old brick "Powder House," belonging to the town, was located. The landmarks of this home, like its occupants, have long since disappeared, while what was once a productive farm is now a desert of drifting sand. He married Lydia Jones, and they raised up a large family of children: Sanford, married Adaline Day; Nelson, married Rebecca Sampson; Edward, married Deborah Turner and lived in Vassalboro; Wilson, married Catherine Day; Jedson, married and located in New York; Gustavus, married Hannah Ballou and lived at Keen's Mills, Turner; Benjamin, married several times and lived mostly in New York.

The daughters: Joanna never married; Lydia married a Hammond, is now a widow and still living; Judith married a Hall.

Sanford, Wilson and Nelson located on Quaker Ridge and lived there during life. Of the two first named none of their descendants remain in town. Nelson had two sons and one daughter—Oliver, Philo, and Hannah. Oliver married Lucia Turner and they had two daughters—Ella and Rozilla, the latter of whom married Ralph Buckley and they now live in town. Philo had no family, and is the only descendant of the once numerous Gilbert families bearing the name at the present time living in town. Hannah married and moved to Massachusetts.

JENNINGS FAMILY.

The Jennings family traces its origin to the early part of the sixteenth century, and legend states it is in direct connection with Sir William Jennings, of England.

But, owing to inaccuracy of the records at that early time, it cannot be fully traced; yet English records inform us that Sir William had a brother, and that he emigrated to America during the sixteenth century. We first find our name on this side of the water, in the persons of John Jennings and his wife, Ruhama, from whom we have perfect, unbroken records to the present time. In all probability, if not the brother of Sir William alluded to, he was a son of that brother. They lived and died in Sandwich, on Cape Cod, Mass. Their issue was one son, Samuel, born Feb. 9, 1684. According to English naval practices at that time, he was impressed on board the frigate Milford, but freed himself by swimming ashore; was caught in the attempt by a shark, from which he wonderfully delivered himself, but not without the loss of one hand and foot. From these injuries he recovered and betook himself, for a livelihood, to trade. Being a man of much natural force, he was called to occupy places of much importance in the town where he resided. He was town clerk some twenty-five years, and died in 1764, at the advanced age of 80. He had two wives—first, Remember Fessenden, by whom he had two children; and second, Deborah Newcomb, who bore him the following named children: Samuel, born Sept. 9, 1727; Esther, born April 29, 1731; and John, born Sept. 3, 1734. The Leeds branch trace their descent from John, the last named, who migrated from Sandwich, Mass., to New Sandwich, now Wayne, about 1780. The Hon. Judge May, late of Lewiston, was a lineal descendant of Esther, the elder sister of John. The issue of John Jennings and his wife were: Deborah, born Dec. 7, 1760; Samuel, born Nov. 15, 1762; John, born Feb. 9, 1765; Hannah, born Aug. 12, 1766; Bathsheba, born Aug. 27, 1768; Sarah, born April 2, 1770; Polly, born June 16, 1773; and Nathaniel, born May 26, 1775. All born in Sandwich, Mass. Samuel and John, of the above named family, removed to Littleborough, now Leeds, in 1783, or '84, using the small lakes, streams, and rivers as thoroughfares *en route* to their new homes, transported thither in their birch-bark canoe.

Nathaniel, the youngest, also came to Leeds, but shortly after went to reside with his father upon the old homestead in that part of an adjoining town now known as North Wayne. His descendants still live there. Samuel and John chose some fine, alluvial land upon the banks of the Androscoggin, from which they cleared the primitive forest and made for themselves and families excellent homes. Samuel married Olive Tupper and had children as follows: Samuel, Jr., born in Sandwich, Mass., Feb. 7, 1787; Perez S., born in Leeds March 2, 1792, who was among the early children born in the town. Of these children Samuel settled in Wayne, but Perez S. remained with his father on the homestead. Samuel raised a large family of children and died in Wayne, at the advanced age of 89 years. Perez S. married Joanna, daughter of James Lane, one of the early settlers of the town, and had the following named children: Orville, born Jan. 14, 1825; died Oct. 3, 1866, at Little Rock, Arkansas; Gustavus A., born June 13, 1827; Gessius F., born Jan. 28, 1829; Eliza

GESSIUS F. JENNINGS.

Ann, born Oct. 9, 1831; Roscoe G., born June 11, 1833; Rollin F., born June 16, 1837. Orville was a graduate of Bowdoin, in the Class of 1849, and that year he removed to Jackson, Tenn., where he studied law, and after admission to the bar opened an office for practice at Washington, Ark., remaining there till the breaking out of the Rebellion in 1861. By close application to business in the place of his adoption, he became distinguished, first as prosecuting attorney, then judge of the circuit court. Elected representative to the Legislature, he opposed the secession of the state from the Union. At the close of the war he removed to Little Rock and was appointed United States District Attorney, which office he held to the date of his death. He married Juliet P. Black, of Washington, Ark., by whom he had four children, all of whom are now dead except the youngest son, Chester, who is an enterprising physician at Little Rock.

Gustavus A. Jennings was born in Leeds June 13, 1827. October 6, 1850, he married Elvira A., a daughter of Columbus and Mary H. (Sumner) Jennings. She was born in Leeds Feb. 19, 1831. They settled at West Leeds on the old homestead of his father, where they have continued their residence since. They have no issue to care for, nor to care for them in their years of decline; yet they reared and educated a daughter by adoption, who was a teacher in the schools of that town. The life of Mr. Jennings has been devoted to agriculture and his name is prominent among the many thrifty, enterprising and successful farmers of his native town. Among the public positions of trust to which his services have been called may be enumerated those of selectman and town treasurer, the duties of which he ably and faithfully performed, and that of postmaster for a term of years, conducting the office to the satisfaction of its patrons and the department, (J. C. S.)

Gessius F. Jennings was born Jan. 28, 1829. He married Orrah M., daughter of Uriah and Mary (Leadbetter) Foss, of North Leeds, May 24, 1860. He resided in town about ten years, and received tokens of trust from his fellow-townsmen, serving them as selectman, town clerk, and superintending school committee. He then removed to Farmington, where he now resides. While in Farmington he has served the Maine Central Railroad Company twenty-five years as station agent. He has two children, Elmer E. Jennings, who married Mary Jacobs, of Farmington; Flora M. Jennings, who married J. Eugene Brown, of Farmington.

Eliza Ann Jennings was born in Leeds Oct. 9, 1831. She married Isaiah B., son of Thomas and Ann Additon, of Leeds, May 5, 1852. They had five children, three girls and two boys. The girls are all dead. The boys are Orville I., who now resides in the state of Georgia, and is in business there; Fred L., who lives in Leeds on the homestead farm, and is, at the present writing, chairman of the Board of Selectmen.

Roscoe G. Jennings was born in Leeds June 11, 1833. After studying medicine with Dr. Garcelon, of Lewiston, he graduated from Bowdoin Medical College. He first established himself at Laper, Mich., where he secured a fine practice, but deeming it more for his interest, he went south and settled in Washington, Hempstead County, Arkansas. Here he successfully practiced his profession till the breaking out of the Rebellion. When that state seceded, he felt compelled, for his own safety, to enter the rebel army as surgeon. When opportunity offered he left the rebel cause, and flying across to the Union lines, went to Little Rock, where he was appointed surgeon of the United States Hospital at that place, in which position he continued until the termination of the war. He was in both the Confederate and United States service during the whole war.

He was married to Miss Gertrude E. Elliott of Camden, Ark., in April, 1869. They had three children, namely: Octavia, Orville, and Cresos. Dr. Roscoe G. Jennings died of penumonia at Little Rock, Ark., April 5, 1899, and in accord with his oft-expressed wish, his remains were taken to St. Louis and cremated.

Rollin F. Jennings, born June 15, 1837; married, in 1857, Harriet, a daughter of Oliver P. Frost, late of Leeds. They had one son, Roscoe W. Jennings, born the twenty-second of March, 1860, who settled in the state of Iowa. The second wife of Rollin F. was a Miss Temple, of Wisconsin, by whom he had one son, David Jennings, who is now living at Mason City, Iowa.

After the war broke out Rollin F. enlisted, in 1862, for three years, in the First Maine Light Artillery, and in one of the terrible battles in which his battery engaged it was so cut to pieces as to lose its organized identity and afterwards merged into Hall's Second Maine Battery, in which he served until the close of the war, participating in all of the hard-fought battles of the Potomac, Fredericksburg, The Wilderness, Gettysburg, and many others, winning a record for valor and unflinching bravery of which his sons and this generation may be proud. He died April 18, 1896, in Mason City, Iowa.

The other branch of the Jennings family who first settled in Leeds was John Jennings, who married Sarah Morton, and their issue was: Alexander, born in Winthrop Dec. 18, 1787; John, Jr., born June 11, 1789; Sarah, born Nov. 25, 1790; Betsey, born Aug. 18, 1792; Franklin N., born June 5, 1794; Phebe W., born May 22, 1796; Robert, born June 24, 1798; Deborah C., born Dec. 21, 1799; Esther M., born Feb. 21, 1802; Columbus, born Dec. 14, 1803, and Sturges N., born Dec. 21, 1806. Alexander, oldest son of John Jennings, was a resident of Leeds,

HISTORY OF LEEDS

to which place he came with his parents when a small boy and remained through life, leaving a large family. His wife was Mary Lindsey. Their children were: Mary, born Dec. 11, 1811; Thomas L., born Dec. 25, 1813; Sarah, born Dec. 31, 1815; Frank N., born April 17, 1818; Pamelia, born June 8, 1820; Howard L., born Feb. 26, 1823; Alexander, Jr., born Nov. 30, 1827, and Sturges N., born Aug. 7, 1831. All of the above named children of Alexander Jennings are now dead. Howard L. Jennings married Julia E. Maine, of Bolton, Conn., in 1858. They had issue Thomas L., born Jan. 12, 1861; Daniel M., born Oct. 29, 1867; and William A., born July 3, 1869, who married Hannah M., a daughter of Samuel Adams, of Greene, and had issue Howard S., Fred M., and Harold W. These Jennings brothers, Thomas L., Daniel M., and William A., are now living on a large farm at Leeds Center. They are very enterprising and successful farmers. John Jennings, Jr., married Hannah Carlton, of Winthrop, and removed to Livermore. Columbus, the youngest son of John, Sr., married Mary H., daughter of Houghton Sumner, one of the early settlers of Leeds. Their children were as follows: Rodolphus, born Jan. 19, 1830; Elvira A., born Feb. 19, 1831; John F., born Oct. 23, 1832; Lavinia, born Nov. 8, 1834, died Feb. 19, 1837; Mary L., born Feb. 13, 1836, died Aug. 1, 1858; Augusta E., born Nov. 13, 1841, died Sept. 22, 1862. Columbus lived on the old homestead; died July 26, 1877. Mary H., his wife, died Jan. 21, 1887. Rodolphus removed to Minneapolis, Minn., where he now resides,—is in business there. He married Leonora M. Hasley and had two children—Frank N., born Feb. 28, 1858; Leonora L., born July 7, 1865, who also reside at Minneapolis, Minn.

John F. married twice; his first wife, Eliza A., a daughter of Thomas Additon, died March 15, 1862. Sept. 19, 1863, he married Emeline, a daughter of Timothy Foster, a life-long resident of Leeds. They have but one child now living, viz.: Gertrude M., an estimable young lady.

John F. is an extensive farmer, whose name is of frequent occurrence in the list of civil officers of the town. As a breeder of cattle and horses he has acquired a reputation. His is a familiar name to many of the people of Androscoggin and adjoining counties.

NOTE.—In the absence of records, remote incidents and dates, and especially the latter, are liable to meet with changes when handed down from generation to generation only from memory. As stated in the foregoing biography of the Jennings family, the date of settlement in Littleborough—1783 or '84—may be correct and probably is; but the place and date of birth of Samuel, Jr., eldest child of Samuel one of the two pioneer brothers, which was Sandwich, Mass., Feb. 7, 1787; and the place and date of birth of

Alexander, eldest child of John the other pioneer brother, which was Winthrop, Me., Dec. 18, 1787, would indicate that the two brothers settled there and lived four or five years the lives of bachelors, or settled there with their families about the year 1790.

TURNER FAMILY.

The earliest available records of the progenitor of the Turner family in this country from whom descended the settlers of Leeds, make mention of George[1], who settled early in West Bridgewater, Mass., and died there about 1696, at which date John Turner[2], son of George[1], settled his father's estate. It is also record matter that in 1668 George[1] was to maintain his brother, John Robbins Turner. In 1678 Thomas Turner was a town officer in West Bridgewater, showing conclusively that at that date there were, at least, three Turners, and presumably George[1] and two brothers. John[2], a son of George[1] and his wife Hannah ———, had issue John[3], born in 1686; William[3], born in 1687, and Hannah, born in 1689. Both John[2] and his wife Hannah, died in 1728. The son, William[3], married in 1714 Eleanor, a daughter of Abiah Whitman, of Weymouth. She was born in that town in 1688. Their children were: Mary, born in 1715; Eleanor[4], in 1717; Hannah[4], in 1719; Margaret[4] and Elizabeth[4], in 1722; Joanna[4], in 1725, and George[4], in 1728. William[3] died in 1747. Of his children, Eleanor married in 1740, Jacob Macomber; Hannah married James Lindsey in 1744; Margaret married Joseph Crossman, of Easton, in 1756; Elizabeth married Thomas Lindsey in 1745, and Joanna married David Manley in 1752. The only son, George[4], and his wife, Desire ———, had issue Josiah[5], born in 1754, Mary[5], born in 1755. His wife, Desire, died in 1756, and in 1759 he married Jane ———, who bore him William[5], in 1760; Desire[5], in 1761; George[5], in 1763; Isaiah[5], in 1764; Jenny[5], in 1766; George[5] and Isaiah[5], in 1769, and Alpheus[5], in 1779. Josiah[5], the eldest son of George[4], married in Bridgewater, Lydia Pettingill in 1778. To them were born in that town five children, and in Leeds five children, to wit: Cynthia, Feb. 15, 1779; Joseph, March 19, 1781; George, Jan. 2, 1783; Lewis, Nov. 15, 1784; Lydia, Oct. 16, 1786; in Leeds, Josiah, Jr., Jan. 1, 1789; Desire, March 31, 1791; Benjamin, April 6, 1793; Hannah, July 10, 1797, and Diana, Oct. 18, 1799.

In 1787 Josiah[5] and his half-brother, William[5], moved with their families to Leeds, the former settling on the west side of Quaker Ridge where Josiah[7], his grandson, now lives, and the latter in the east part of the town. Of the children of Josiah[5] and Lydia Pettingill, Cynthia[6] married Stephen Welcome and settled in the extreme south-western part of the town near the

Center Bridge, where he was many years in trade. They had no issue but brought up several children of their relatives.

Joseph[6] married first, Deborah Gilbert, and remained on the homestead of his father. To them were born six children, to wit: Eunice, July 25, 1803; Phillips, Aug. 8, 1805; Joseph, Jr., Nov. 5, 1807; Julia Ann, Oct. 13, 1809; Joanna, Feb. 26, 1812; and William G., April 21, 1814.

Joseph[6] married second, Hannah Pettingill, to whom was born John, Oct. 14, 1816, died March 1, 1817; Deborah, February, 1818; Lydia, November, 1820; Cynthia, 1822, died in 1826; Jane R., Aug. 7, 1824; Cynthia W., Sept. 15, 1826, and Josiah, Oct. 11, 1829.

Joseph[6] married third, Mrs. Esther Scammon. No issue. He died April 30, 1860; his first wife April 24, 1814; his second wife, ———, and his third wife, Sept. 29, 1855.

George[6], third child of Josiah[5] and Lydia Pettingill, married Betsey Gilbert and settled on the farm now owned by E. V. Daly. They had issue Cynthia, b. Dec. 10, 1801; d. July 19, 1803; Betsey Palmer, b. Oct. 2, 1803; Cynthia, b. March 31, 1805; Sobrina, b. Oct. 3, 1807; George Washington, b. March 6, 1810; Lydia, b. Jan. 21, 1812; Deborah, b. May 2, 1814; d. Sept. 3, 1815; Josiah, b. May 25, 1816; Hannah, b. Oct. 11, 1818; William, b. Feb. 27, 1821; John, b. Aug. 10, 1823; Sarah, b. Nov. 13, 1826; Benjamin, b. July 8, 1828, and Martha Ann, b. March 25, 1832.

George Turner[6], Esq., died Oct. 2, 1862, and his wife April 8, 1854.

Lewis[6], the fourth child of Josiah[5], married Hannah Collier and lived on the north end of Quaker Ridge. Their children were Oscar Dunreath[7], b. May 29, 1809; Joshua Shaw[7], b. July 13, 1811; Francis Orman, b. March 24, 1813; d. July 30, 1818; Lucius Clark, b. Dec. 15, 1816; Amanda Fitzelen, b. Oct. 20, 1822, and Charles Osburn, b. Jan. 25, 1826.

Lewis Turner[6] died Aug. 19, 1866.

Lydia[6], the fifth child of Josiah[5], married Masey Sylvester.

Josiah[6], Jr., sixth child, married Almira Smith.

Desire[6], seventh child, married Caleb Wing.

Benjamin[6], eighth child, was never married.

Hannah[6], ninth child of Josiah[5], married Moses Collier.

Diana[6], the youngest child, married Almond Smith.

Of the children of Joseph[6], the eldest son of Josiah[5], one of the pioneer settlers of Leeds, Eunice[7], his eldest child, married Abiatha Briggs and settled in Parkman.

Phillips[7] married Mary L., a daughter of Hon. Stillman and Lydia (Lothrop) Howard and resided on the farm now owned by Mr. Seymour. They had issue two children: Victoria Helen, b. March 3, 1838, and Herbert Phillips, b. Nov. 3, 1842; d. Feb. 2, 1846. Victoria H. married Stephen R. Deane April 3, 1859, and is the mother of four children, three of whom are now living, of which further mention is made in an article on the Deane family.

Phillips[7] died March 3, 1844, and his widow Aug. 17, 1856.

Joseph[7] married Ann Coburn. They had no issue. The care of a near relative of the wife, who had a cancer, was assumed by them and they both died of cancer when comparatively young, with only a few months intervening.

Julia Ann[7] married Stillman L. Howard, Esq. They had issue nine children, of whom mention is made in the Howard family. She died March 7, 1901, at the advanced age of 91 years. Although an invalid for several years, her mental faculties were unimpaired. To her wonderful memory the writer is indebted for much of the data embodied in this article.

Joanna[7], died March 8, 1835, at the age of 23 years, unmarried.

William G[7]. was but three days old when his mother died. He was reared by his uncle and aunt, Stephen Welcome. Anna Clark Robb, his first wife, to whom he was married in November, 1835, lived less than one year thereafter, dying without issue. His second wife was Mary S. Loring. Their place of residence was that where he was reared, near that of the late I. B. Additon. Their children were Stephen Welcome, b. Dec. 6, 1838; Anna Clark, b. Jan. 24, 1840; Henry Sewall, b. Feb. 13, 1841; Cynthia Welcome, b. Dec. 16, 1842; Samuel Loring, b. July 19, 1844; Mary Thomas, b. Feb. 6, 1847; d. March 5, 1850, and William P., Hannah E. and Jacabina—small children—who died of diphtheria in March, 1862. William G[7]. was a soldier in the Civil War. He removed from Leeds to Bedford, Mass. He died in Plymouth, in 1897.

John[7], the eldest child of Joseph[6] and his second wife, Hannah Pettingill, died March 1, 1817, when a few months old.

Deborah[7], their second child, married in April, 1838, Edward Gilbert, and settled in Leeds, but subsequently in Vassalboro. They had three sons,—Wallace, Vantile and Ellerson, all of whom were in the Civil War. Deborah died in 1899.

Lydia[7], their third child, married John S. Loring. Had issue.

Cynthia, their next child, died at the age of two years, in 1826.

Jane R.[7], their fifth child, died when a young lady.

Cynthia[7], their next child, married Isaiah Gifford and settled in Vassalboro. They had two children, a son and daughter, the latter dying at the age of eleven years. Many years Mr. Gifford was a deputy sheriff in Kennebec County.

Josiah[7], the youngest child of Joseph[6] and Hannah Pettingill, married Hannah E. Donham in March, 1856. They settled on the home farm of his father and grandfather. They had issue

JOHN TURNER, M.D.

Lizzie Donham, b. July 10, 1857; Ernest Linwood, b. Jan. 22, 1865; Alice Gertrude, b. May 4, 1869, d. June 25, 1884.

Of the children of George Turner[6], Esq., second son of Josiah[5], the pioneer, Cynthia[7], the eldest, died when a little child—less than two years old.

Betsey P.[7], his second child, married Hazel Rose, of Greene. They first settled in that town, but subsequently lived in Leeds. They reared a family of several children, some of whom now reside in the latter town.

Cynthia[7], the third child, married Harrison Piper, of Portland.

Sobrina[7], his fourth child, remained single.

George W., the next child, was a physician. He married Miss Smith and settled in Dixfield. They had no issue. He later married and resided in Sumner. They had one daughter, Lucia A. She was a graduate of the Farmington Normal School and a successful teacher in the schools of Lewiston many years. She later married C. C. Bailey of that city. Doctor Turner died in Sumner when the daughter was a small child.

Lydia[7], the next child—no record.

Deborah[7], the seventh child, died in 1815.

Josiah[7], the next child—no record.

Hannah[7], the next one in the list, married Solomon L. Lothrop and is now living at Leeds Center. Her family is made mention of in the Lothrop family record.

William[7], the tenth child of George Turner, Esq., married Sarah ——— and lived in Leeds, later removed to Lewiston but subsequently returned to Leeds where he died. They had three children, to wit: Kate Ina, b. May 15, 1859; Fred Otis, b. May 13, 1861; Charles Clark, b. Nov. 8, 1865.

John[7], the next child, married in November, 1854, Elizabeth B. Manwell, and settled on the homestead of his father, George Turner, Esq. He assumed the care of his parents in their declining years and made *his* the home of his father's family. He was an active, able, and industrious man. He did much business outside of farming and held office in the town many years. After the decease of his parents, he changed his place of residence and occupied the farm where Hon. Seth Howard now resides. Several seasons he was in New York State, engaged in patent roofing business. His wife died Aug. 31, 1886, since which time he has been in Gardiner and is now residing in that city. They had issue John Manwell[8], b. Aug. 12, 1856; d. Dec. 24, 1899; Marion Elizabeth[8], b. Oct. 28, 1860; Benjamin Manwell[8], b. March 14, 1864; Lelia Annah[8], b. Aug. 12, 1866; d. in 1899.

Doctor John M. married in September, 1888, Olive M., the youngest daughter of Hon. Davis F. Lothrop. After a short residence in Bangor, they permanently settled in Gardiner, where the doctor established an extensive and lucrative practice. His standing as a physician, was among the best and his death was a heavy blow to his people and his patrons. His widow and only child, Florence E., born June 11, 1891, are now residing in Leeds.

Marion Elizabeth, second child of John, was a successful teacher in the schools of Gardiner, and later married, in that city, William L. Powers, of Brownville. They have one child, John E.

Doctor Benjamin M. Turner[8], his third child, also located in Gardiner, where he married Carrie Dingley, of that city. He, too, died young (October, 1900), at the age of 36 years, leaving a widow but no children.

Lelia Annah, the youngest child of John, was a teacher in the Gardiner schools. She was a maiden lady and died in 1899, at the age of 33 years.

Sarah[7], the twelfth child of George Turner[6], Esq., married Charles Lane and lived most of her years in Leeds. They had no issue.

Benjamin[7], whose numerical position was thirteen in the list, married in June, 1852, Harriet H., a daughter of Peter Lane. They settled on the farm of her father, now the property of their son, Peter L. Turner, and continued their life-long residence there. In connection with the farm work, for a long term of years he was engaged in the business of buying wool, but more especially in purchasing sheep, lambs, calves, hogs, beeves, etc., and shipping the slaughtered goods to the Boston market. He was a successful business man and accumulated a goodly competency. He erected a fine and commodious set of buildings on the highly enriched farm but lived only a few years to enjoy them. His good judgment and business tact was recognized by the townsmen, who elected him to positions of responsibility and trust. He was widely known and highly respected. His wife died Jan. 7, 1892. His death occurred Oct. 18, 1896. They had three children, two sons and a daughter. Their eldest son, George Henry[8], b. June 2, 1855, was liberally educated and went from school to Portland, where he was employed in mercantile life. He married in that city Annie Hunter by whom he has one child, George Henry, Jr. He for a long time has been a commercial traveler, commanding a heavy salary. His natural business tact and experience has placed him among the best salesmen of that city.

Peter L.[8], the second son of Benjamin[7], was born Sept. 15, 1857. He was educated in the schools of his native town and has, thus far, spent most of his life here. He assumed the farm cares some years previous to the death of his parents and has since been one of Leeds' most successful citizens. In July, 1891, he married Adelaide C., a daughter of Albert Abbott and Har-

BENJAMIN TURNER.

riet Harrington, of Medway, Mass. They have issue Harriet Grace, born Sept. 22, 1895; Benjamin Abbott, b. March 14, 1898, and Roy Stanley, b. April 3, 1900. Mr. Turner is a member of the school board and has an active interest in education and other public matters pertaining to the advancement of the people.

Grace Haywood[8], the third and youngest child of Benjamin[7], born March 10, 1863, married Arthur C., a son of Lucius Clark Leadbetter, of Wayne, in September, 1892. They reside in Portland, where Mr. Leadbetter has been engaged for several years in the milk business. They have no issue.

Martha Ann[7], the youngest child of George Turner, Esq., married in September, 1856, Sturges N., a son of Alexander Jennings, and was taken to the home of his father,— the farm adjoining that of Peter Lane on the east, and continued their residence there during the life of the husband. They had issue.

FOSS FAMILY.

The earliest ancestor in this branch of the Foss family to whom the attention of the writer has been cited was Walter Foss, of Biddeford, Massachusetts, which was incorporated the fourth town in November, 1718. In 1762, it was divided and that portion of it lying on the east side of the Saco River was incorporated under the name of Peperellboro, and later, in 1805, changed to Saco. Thus in what is now Saco, Me., we locate the progenitor of the Fosses who settled in Leeds. Walter Foss and his wife, Sarah, were living in Biddeford as early as 1730. The tax-list of 1755 shows that his home was on the east side of the river, and his name is given as the eleventh in a list of twelve who paid the highest rates. The first paid £4 0s. 5d., and the last paid £1 10s. 2d. Walter took part in King George's war— he and Thomas—probably a brother—being enlisted in Capt. George Berry's company which belonged to Col. Waldo's regiment, and took part in the campaign for the capture of Louisburg,—the French stronghold in America. The fort was taken June 17, 1745. The old veteran died in Peperellboro, Dec. 9, 1791. From the family record of his children we copy:

I. Walter, Jr., m. Sept. 29, 1748, Hannah Carll.
II. Levi—.
III. James, bapt. at First Church, Scarborough, Aug. 16, 1730; m. 1751, Abigail Hill.
IV. Pelatiah, bapt. Scarborough, Nov. 5, 1732; in Revolutionary war, killed at Ticonderoga.
V. Joseph, bapt. June 22, 1735; m. Dec. 22, 1757; buried Feb. 15, 1773.

- VI. Lemuel, bapt. April 16, 1738; m. first, Elizabeth, second, Olive Smith.
- VII. Sarah, bapt. April (?) 29, 1741.
- VIII. Mary, bapt. Oct. 16, 1743.
- IX. John, bapt. Feb. 15, 1746; m. May 4, 1768, Rachel Milliken.
- X. Nathaniel, bapt. Jan. 7, 1749.
- XI. Benjamin, bapt. Jan. 14, 1753; m. Mary ———.

Of the above named children of Walter, the second son, Levi was the father of the three pioneers of Leeds, to wit: Uriah, Phineas, and Hannah. Little is known regarding him except his Revolutionary War record. His name appears on the muster roll of Capt. Jeremiah Hill's Company in Col. Edmund Phinney's Battalion of Forces, raised in the State of Massachusetts Bay, dated in garrison at Fort George, Dec. 8, 1776. He enlisted Aug. 1, 1776. From Jan. 10, 1777, to Jan. 1, 1778, he was corporal in Capt. Hancock's Company, Col. Vose's Regiment. At the end of the record he was put down as dead. His children, so far as known, are:

- I. Uriah, b. in Peperellboro, March 6, 1760; d. in Leeds June 16, 1824.
- II. Samuel, had children, George, Asa, Eliakim, Samuel, and Levi. George, Asa, and Eliakim settled in Wayne.
- III. Hannah, m. Isaac Boothby, Sr., who came from Peperellboro to Leeds and receives mention with her family.
- IV. James, had a daughter, Sarah, who m. Benjamin Edgecomb.
- V. Capt. Phineas, b. in Peperellboro, Feb. 10, 1772; m. in 1799 Rebecca, the youngest child of Thomas and Sarah (Paul, *nee* True) Stinchfield, the first white child born in what is now the town of Leeds, and the date was Dec. 11, 1780. He d. in Leeds April 13, 1814, and his widow March 3, 1869.

Uriah^3 (Levi^2, Walter^1,), the eldest son of Levi^1, married Dec. 16, 1779, Sarah Goodrich, who was born Aug. 24, 1759. They resided in Peperellboro, where to them were born three sons,—Levi, Cyrus, and Daniel, the last two being twins. Sept. 7, 1782, he and his son, Levi, were baptised in the First Church in Scarborough, and on the same day both he and his wife joined the church. In the spring of 1786, with his little family, he left Peperellboro—now Saco—and came to the plantation of Littleborough—now Leeds—where he had bought a tract of land, said to contain 400 acres, on which was a heavy growth of pine. It was situated on the east bank of Dead River and at that time was within the limits of the "Livermore Grant," but subsequently was included within the boundary lines of Leeds. On this vast tract of wilderness land he built a log house and hovel where later he erected a fine set of more modern biuldings, being the same now owned and occupied by a grandson, Walter Payson Foss. In the fall of 1785 he had visited this spot, effected the purchase and made a cut-down. When he came with his family the following spring, not unlike many of the early settlers, a temporary stay was made at the home of "Father Thomas," whose latch-string was always out and whose aid in preparing the first clearings for the harvest and constructing the new homes in the wilderness, was generally sought and freely given. Mr. Foss proved to be a valuable citizen and in later years, as may be learned by consulting the list of town and church officers, was a man who commanded the confidence and esteem of the people. He was a ship-carpenter. After having built his log house on this lot and made arrangements for the comfort of his young wife and children, he went to Bath, where he worked at his trade until he earned money enough to pay for his land. It may be remembered, at that time there were no well-kept highways—all about was wilderness. This sturdy young man walked to and from his work, making monthly visits to his home forty miles distant, guided in his travels only by spotted trees. He left his wife in care of Thomas Stinchfield, his nearest neighbor—*three miles away.* It was a brave woman who staid alone in that cabin home. The forests were alive with wild beasts, and Indians were often seen, but never molested this lone woman, who always treated them kindly whenever they came to the cabin. Both Mr. and Mrs. Foss were very benevolent, kind-hearted people, ever ready to do a kindness and lend a helping hand to new settlers as they came. They were staunch Baptists of the strict old school. At that time five counties only constituted the Province of Maine, and Kennebec extended nearly fifty miles north of its present boundaries, including the town of Phillips within its limits. The fine pine lumber on his farm proved a small fortune to this man, who selected it with judgment and foresight. Dead River served him well as a means of transporting it to the mill and market. This remarkable river is seven miles in length and forms the connection between the Androscoggin Lake and Androscoggin River. Its current varies, sometimes flowing into the lake and at other times into the river. Along the western banks farms were later taken up by David Berry, Daniel Parcher, Shephard Cary, Peletiah and John Gould, Samuel Leadbetter, Isaac Pratt, Gilman Moulton, and others, most of whom had large families. A brother and sister of Mr. Foss, Capt. Phineas and Hannah, came to Leeds early, married, settled and spent their remaining years there. Hannah married Isaac Boothby and further mention of her may be found in the family of Mr. Boothby. Capt. Phineas lived near his brother, on the opposite side of where the highway was later built, so near that they could converse with each other while standing on their individual door-steps.

With the elapse of time it was deemed necessary that a road be opened to connect this region and up-country settlements with the sea-port town of Falmouth (Portland). The route was a much agitated question. The county was divided in regard to the matter, the eastern settlers favoring one route, while those in the western portion desired another. While the controversy waxed furious, Augusta men took the opportunity to push the matter of opening a road which should connect this region with the head of navigation on the Kennebec. In this scheme were they aided by Deacon Elijah Livermore and Capt. Fish, who represented the proprietors of the Livermore Grant, and succeeded in procuring the laying out and constructing of a road, beginning at the terminal point of a road from Augusta to the eastern boundary of Wayne, near the Craig Bridge; thence through Wayne over Beech Hill to the Androscoggin River to a point a short distance northerly of Strickland's Ferry. Thus the settlers of this section of Leeds were left out in the cold. "Uncle Uriah," though busy working on his farm, had no idea of being side-tracked in that way. When the new road was completed, he thought it time to be in evidence. He drew up a petition to which he obtained the signatures of his two neighbors, Thomas Stinchfield and Robert Gould, presented it to the County Commissioners and obtained a road about six miles in length, beginning at Dead River, near the house of Stinchfield, and terminating at the Augusta Road near Strickland's Ferry. This, together with the road that had been built from Farmington to Greene, entering the town at Beech Hill, passing along the western shore of the lake and so along by Lothrop's Corner and over Quaker Ridge, gave them extra accommodation of travel and pleased the Portland faction. The Augusta men railed long and loudly, but "Uncle Uriah" calmly enjoyed his victory. New settlers took advantage of these facilities for travel. Brothers Stinchfield, Gould and Foss had a great many guests, and especially in spring and fall when the people in the back country were laying in supplies and hauling their products to market. For, strange to relate, most of the new comers and old were *"Good Baptist Brethren."* In 1820 Mr. Foss was instrumental in having another road laid which crossed his farm. This was a county road leading from the Androscoggin River north of North Turner Bridge, by the house of Benjamin Woodman, through North Leeds to Wayne.

After years of prosperity, the old family mansion was built—still standing with its yellow coating of paint, as were all those built in that region in "ye olden time."

While working on the road in June, 1824, Mr. Foss dropped dead near his home. His widow survived him seven years, dying in 1831. Previous to his death he had settled two of his sons, Levi and Cyrus, on the northerly portion of his large domain, and after his decease the remainder was divided equally between two younger sons, Walter and Ruel.

Uriah Foss was born in Peperelboro, March 6, 1760, and died of heart disease in Leeds, June 16, 1824. He was of English descent. Sarah Goodridge, his wife, was born Ibid (?) Aug. 24, 1759, and died in Leeds Jan. 28, 1831. She was of Scotch ancestry. They were married Ibid. Dec. 16, 1779. The Robert Gould cemetery at North Leeds is their resting-place.

Their children were:

1. Levi, b. April 10, 1782, in Peperellboro; d. Nov. 23, 1831.
2-3. Cyrus and Daniel, twins, b. Jan. 21, 1785, in Peperellboro; Cyrus d. Oct. 16, 1836; Daniel d. Sept. 14, 1824.
4. Rachel, b. March 19, 1788, in Leeds; d. July 8, 1819.
5. Ephraim W., b. Sept. 6, 1791, in Leeds; d. Aug. 15, 1877.
6. Thaddeus, b. July 13, 1793, in Leeds; d. May 10, 1819.
7. Simeon, b. July 5, 1795, in Leeds; d. July 12, 1868.
8. Sarah, b. March 25, 1797, in Leeds; d. Aug. 25, 1826.
9. Walter, b. May 18, 1799, in Leeds; d. April 13, 1875.
10. Ruel, b. Feb. 24, 1802; d. Jan. 21, 1877.

Levi, the eldest son, married in September, 1802, Betsey, a daughter of Thomas Millett, the fourth pioneer at the head of a family to settle in the Plantation. They settled on the farm now owned by A. Dascomb and there spent their lives. He was a man of prominence in his town and county, and held many offices in both. As a Justice of the Peace it was said of him, "He united more people in marriage than any man in the county." He was of worth to the people in the capacity of civil engineer and did an extensive business in running and establishing lines. He died of typhoid fever at the age of 49 years. They had issue:

1 Almira,   4 Rachael,   7 Eunice,
2 Esther,   5 Levi, Jr.,   8 Jedidah,
3 Uriah,   6 Sarah,   9 Augustus L.

Of these children of Levi and Betsey (Millett) Foss, Almira, the eldest, married John Drout and had issue one daughter, Elizabeth. The mother went into decline and soon died of consumption. The daughter was reared in the family of her Grandfather Foss.

Esther, the second child of Levi, married Stillman Moulton and settled in Leeds—removed to Veazie, Me. To them were born three sons and a daughter who grew to man and womanhood. The family subsequently moved to California, where the parents and two of the children died. One of the two remaining sons, Levi F., who resides in Colusa, is reputed to be a millionaire. The other son, Stillman, lives in San Jose.

Uriah, third child and eldest son of Levi, is a familiar name in Leeds, and associated with it are municipal and other important offices and public positions. He married Mary Leadbetter and brought her to his parental home, where they assumed the care of his mother and continued to reside until a few years prior to his death, when, after a lingering illness, he died in Farmington, at the age of 75 years. His mother died in 1853 and his widow, whose home was with her only daughter, Mrs. Jennings, of Farmington, died in December, 1899, at the advanced age of 92 years. They had issue seven children:

1. Adeline, who died when young.

2. Fernando C., who married and settled in Oldtown, in the time of the Civil War received, on May 13, 1861, a Captain's commission of Co. K, 2d Maine Infantry Regiment, and continued in the service until Dec. 29, 1862, when he was discharged on account of wounds. In the first Bull Run battle his regiment was engaged and terribly cut to pieces. After the retreat, at the peril of his life, he went back to search for a brother-in-law; and here we introduce a clipping from a newspaper printed at that time, which speaks of him as follows: "The report of the brave action and terrible execution among the rebels by Capt. Foss, of Oldtown, is undoubtedly true. In his search, after the retreat was commenced, for a relative, left dead on the field, he found him, decently composed his limbs, spread the soldier's blanket over him and performed the same office for another comrade. While doing this he came upon a rebel officer, lying wounded on the ground, whom he placed in an easier position, gave him drink from his canteen, and emptied some into the officer's canteen. The officer thanked him and said he should never be able to repay him for the kindness. Capt. Foss told him that he would be well cared for by his own friends, and asked him to see that his (Capt. Foss') dead comrades had decent burial. It was just after this that he was set upon by three, one or more of them cavalry, whom he dispatched as we mentioned yesterday. The third rebel he shot from his horse and just missed catching the animal. Capt. Foss came to the determination that he would not be taken a prisoner." He had a son and two daughters. The son, Arthur C., who is well known on the M. C. R. R., is Station Agent at Danville Junction. One of the daughters is Mrs. Samuel P. Francis, of North Leeds; and the other daughter resides in Waltham, Mass.

3. Gidding L. was twice married and resides in Farmington. By his first wife, Cordelia, a daughter of Harrison Gould, he had

two children, Uriah and Anna. The former is a railroad employee in Syracuse, N. Y. Anna is the wife of a Mr. Donally, a conductor on the B. & A. R. R. By his second wife he also had a son and daughter. Howard C., the son, is an electrician and Miss Ethel, the daughter, is a student in the Farmington High School.

Mr. Foss has spent much of his life in the employ of the M. C. R. R. Co., and later held a position on the Sandy River Railroad. He has now retired from active life—in poor health.

4. Orrah M. married G. F. Jennings and resided for a time in West Leeds. To them were born a son, Elmer E., and a daughter, Flora M.; after which time they removed to Farmington where Mr. Jennings was in the employ of the Maine Central Railroad twenty-five years, when he retired from active business life by reason of the infirmities of age. The son, Elmer E., married Mary Virginia, a daughter of I. S. Jacobs, of Farmington; and the daughter, Flora M., married J. Eugene Brown, who is a printer in that town. They have two children, Zilda J., and Leo J., aged 10 and 6 years, respectively.

5. Cordellus, after a course at Colby College, studied medicine with Doctor Edgecomb, in Auburn. When his studies had been nearly completed, he sickened with fever and died at the Elm House, in that city.

[An old adage in the family is, "A Foss was never known to live who had a fever."]

6. Volney H., when 18 years old, enlisted in the 1st Maine Cavalry,—was in the service during the remainder of the Civil War. He experienced many hardships, sickness and wounds, but unflinchingly and heroically stood at his post until his Regiment received its discharge. On returning to Maine and recuperating, he entered the employ of the M. C. R. R., where he remained nearly forty years. He married a Miss Heath, of Farmington, and his present residence is in Bangor, where he has a fine home. They have issue two daughters and a son. The daughters are both married, the eldest residing in Everett, Mass., and the younger in Bangor. The son is a graduate of Tufts College, and a civil engineer in Boston.

7. Hartland, the youngest of the seven children of Uriah and Mary (Leadbetter) Foss, on arriving to manhood, obtained a position as fireman on a locomotive on the Farmington Branch of the M. C. R. R. In a remarkably short time he was placed in charge of an engine, and later, was retained at headquarters in Portland, under advanced pay as a special runner, and when quick runs were to be made, and especially when the officers' train passed over the road, Harty was at the lever and throttle. He was fearless, always ready to undertake the most difficult feats, and the faster he drove the better he seemed to enjoy it.

Later, he removed to Water Valley, Miss., where the country was better adapted to making fast time, and where he is still in the enjoyment of his chosen vocation. He married Clara Woodford, of North Leeds, and had issue one son and two daughters. Leroy, the son, is a locomotive engineer on the M. C. R. R., and lives in Lewiston. He married Fannie Rafter and has two sons, William and Charles, aged 10 and 7 years respectively: Rena May, the eldest daughter, married F. A. Chaplin and resides in Portland, Me.; Georgie Baker, the other daughter, is with her parents in their home in Mississippi.

Rachael, fourth child of Levi, married John Higgins, of Starks, Me., in which town their five children were born, all of whom lived and grew to man and womanhood. The family later moved to Hutchinson, Minn., where the parents died. Their eldest child, Almira, married and died young of consumption, leaving two children. Two sons reside in that place and the other two, Holmes B. and Wilbur T., in San Jose, Cal. Levi, Jr., fifth child of Levi, married Emeline Leadbetter and settled in Wayne village, where he built a dwelling house which is still known as the Levi Foss house. In 1849, when gold was first discovered in California, he was among the first to seek a fortune there. At the close of a successful year, he sent for his wife and son who joined him there. The parents are now dead. The son survives and continues his residence in that State. Sarah, better known as Sally, sixth child of Levi, married Beniah Taylor and their place of residence was Weeks Mills, in the town of New Sharon, Me. They had one daughter and three sons. Sarah Jane, the daughter, married John Jerry, and died of consumption in Farmington, leaving one daughter, who is now Mrs. Burns, of Nashua, N. H., to which place the family had moved, and in which city Sarah died at the ripe age of 80 years. Mr. Taylor, the husband and father survives in the home of his only remaining son, Hon. James M. Taylor of that city.

Eunice, the 7th child of Levi, married Amos Woodward. Their home was in Nashua, N. H., and there Eunice died, without issue, at the age of 77 years. Her husband survives and resides in that city.

Jedidah, the youngest daughter of Levi, married George Harmon and settled in Livermore,—near the "Norlands,"—where they reared a large family. In 1859 they emigrated to what was then called "The Far West"—Colorado—and lived to see that State grow up in population, thrift and wealth. The father died some years since, and the mother in May, 1900. They left four children, all of whom reside in Watson, Pitkin County, Col.

Augustus L., the youngest child of Levi, married Caroline, a daughter of Col. Leavitt Lothrop, of Leeds, in which town they spent most of their married life. He was a successful farmer.

They had a family of eight children. Frank, a young man of great promise, sickened with fever and died in 1869, at the age of 20 years; Lizzie died in Chicago; Emma resides in Valejo, Cal.; Levi lives in Collegeville, Cal., and Carrie F. Barker, his sister, a graduate of the Farmington Normal School, resides with him; Mrs. Jennie F. Kenniston, another sister, lives in Auburn, N. H.; Warren L., the youngest child, is in the hardware business in Fort Wayne, Ind.

Augustus L., the father, died of heart failure at North Leeds, March 21, 1882, at the age of 67 years. His widow has a home with their daughter, Jennie, in New Hampshire.

1. Capt. Cyrus[4], (Uriah[3], Levi[2], Walter[1]) second son of Uriah and Sarah (Goodridge) Foss, born in Peperellboro, June 21, 1785, married Mary—called Polly—a daughter of Giddings and Jemima (Norris) Lane, July 10, 1808, who was born in Leeds, Feb. 6, 1790.

He served as a private in Capt. Nathaniel Pettingill's company of drafted militia, in Lieut.-Col. Ellis Sweet's Reg't, on duty at Bath and vicinity in 1814. He was later commissioned Captain of a militia company. He was constable and collector of taxes in Leeds from 1823 to 1831, and a Justice of the Peace many years. He settled on the farm and built the house now owned and occupied by Mr. A. Barker, where he afterward lived and died. He was a kind-hearted and benevolent man, a good neighbor, valuable friend, and a helper of the poor. He died in Leeds, Oct. 16, 1836, and his widow, in Livermore, Sept. 6, 1871. They are resting in the cemetery near the river at North Leeds.

To them were born in Leeds, 11 children, to wit: Christopher Gore, Giddings Lane, Jemima Lane, Daniel, Cyrus Wilson, Thaddeus Warsaw, Alpheus Lane, Anourille Coolidge, Rosalinda Lane, Mary Jane, Josephine Bonaparte.

    I. Christopher G., b. May 22, 1809; m. Jan. 7, 1835, Olive Lothrop, b. June 14, 1806. Their last place or residence was Milo, Me. Mr. Foss was postmaster in that town from 1837 to 1843, and a Justice of the Peace many years. He died there Nov. 21, 1843, and his widow Feb. 15, 1889. No issue.

    II. Giddings L., b. Sept. 23, 1810; d. in Leeds Dec. 18, 1837; unmarried.

    III. Jemima L., b. Sept. 5, 1812; m. in Leeds, Aug. 27, 1835, Lewis Page True, son of Daniel and Sally (West) True, of Litchfield, who was born in that town May 18, 1811. They had seven children, of whom three are now living in Portland. One only was b. in Leeds—Emma Sarah, June 8, 1840.

IV. Daniel, b. July 25, 1814; m. July 10, 1841, Nancy, an only daughter of James and Mary (McKenny) Moulton, of Wayne. She was born April 1, 1812. Mr. Foss was an Inn-keeper in Wayne several years, dying there Sept. 21, 1858, and his widow, who later m. Hiram Hinds, d. April 22, 1892. No issue.

V. Cyrus W., b. Aug. 15, 1816; m. first, Aug. 21, 1839, Charlotte Towle, of Bangor. She was b. there Sept. 5, 1817. To them were born in that city four children. Mrs. Foss d. in Bangor, July 29, 1849. He m. second, Jan. 22, 1850, Catherine B., a daughter of Andre and Catherine M. (Murphy) Swanson, of Philadelphia, Pa. She was b. in that city Jan. 8, 1828. They had issue two children, one of whom, Mrs. Aubrey Edgecomb, is now residing at North Leeds. Of the children of Cyrus W., four are now living. Mrs. Foss d. in Philadelphia, Dec. 15, 1883, and Mr. Foss d. in North Leeds, Feb. 23, 1890.

VI. Thaddeus W., b. June 12, 1818; m. Aug. 17, 1841, Martha Jane Shaw. They had two sons, both of whom, with their mother, are residents of Augusta, Me. Mr. Foss d. in that city April 27, 1885.

VII. Alpheus L., b. June 8, 1820; m. in Lowell, Mass., Feb. 18, 1843, Abigail Jane Hall, who was b. in Paris, Me. They had two daughters, one of whom is living. Both Mr. and Mrs. Foss d. in Des Plaines, Ill.

VIII. Anourille C., b. Oct. 29, 1822; d. in Leeds, Feb. 20, 1842; unmarried.

IX. Rosalinda L., b. in Leeds, June 3, 1825; m. in that town, Jan. 4, 1848, Benjamin, Jr., a son of Capt. Benjamin and Sarah (Foss) Edgecomb, who was b. in Livermore, Me., Jan. 17, 1824. They settled in Livermore, where they continued their residence many years but subsequently purchased the old farm at North Leeds, cleared and settled by Robert Gould, who came early to the town. Here they lived together until the death of Mr. Edgecomb, which occurred Aug. 5, 1900, and here the widow continues to reside. They had issue two sons and a daughter, to wit: Aubrey Wilson, Sarah Etta and Eli.

   I. Aubrey Wilson, b. in Livermore March 19, 1849; m. in Philadelphia, Pa., April 7, 1879, Annie W., a daughter of Cyrus W. and Catherine B. Foss. She was b. in Philadelphia Nov. 4, 1850. Their residence is at North Leeds. He is a farmer on the place left him by his father. Their children are Mary Cardiff, b. in Leeds Aug. 15, 1881; m. Dec. 15, 1900, James B. Neal, of Leeds, who is a successful farmer; Sarah Etta, b. in Leeds March 31, 1886, who is a student in the "Leavitt Institute."

II. Sarah Etta, b. in Augusta, Me., March 2, 1836; d. in Livermore Jan. 27, 1861.

III. Eli, b. in Livermore Sept. 13, 1863; m. in Auburn, May 1, 1892, Eva Mae, a daughter of Loring Curtis and Martha (Bragdon) Fickett. She was b. in Auburn Oct. 29, 1871; is a graduate of Edward Little High School and an assistant teacher with her husband. He graduated from Bates College in the Class of 1890; is Principal of Leland and Gray Seminary in Townsend, Vt.

X. Mary Jane, b. Aug. 4, 1827; d. in Lincoln, Me., Nov. 20, 1841—unmarried.

XI. Josephine B., b. Sept. 8, 1830; m. in Wayne, April 2, 1850, John Wesley, a son of Rev. Daniel and Mary (Knight) Clark, who was b. in Minot, Me., March 29, 1826. Their place of residence is Hallowell, Me. They had two children, both of whom are dead

Daniel[4] (Uriah[3], Levi[2], Walter,[1]), third son of Uriah, the pioneer of Leeds and the twin brother of Cyrus, born in Peperellboro, June 21, 1785; m. first, Eunice Lane, in February, 1807; and second, a Widow Scammon, whose maiden name was Turner. His place of residence was Leeds Center, and it is said that what was known by the name of "Dwinold house" was his home. He was a carpenter by trade and built many of the residences in Leeds and adjoining towns. He died at the age of 36 years Jan. 14, 1821. We are not informed of his having left any issue.

Rachael, fourth child of Uriah, b. March 19, 1788—his first child born in what is now Leeds; in July, 1804, m. John Leadbetter, by whom she had five children, to wit: Alva, Aseph, Eliza, Warren, and Rachael. For a good reason she returned to her parental roof with her children, where they were brought up in the family of their grandparents. She d. July 3, 1819, at the early age of 32 years.

Ephraim W., fifth child of Uriah, b. Sept. 6, 1791; m. first, Mehitable S. Church, of Phillips, in December, 1826, in which town they resided several years, where their two sons, one of whom d. in infancy, were born. The other son, Ephraim D., now a gentleman of 83 or more years, residing in Maineville, Ohio, is the father of seven children, five of whom are living in that state. He m. second, Harriet Townsend, of

Auburn, Me., by whom he had three daughters, Marcena, Almira, and Orissa. For more than thirty years Marcena was a sucessful milliner in Wayne village, where she is now retired from business and spending the remainder of her single life.

Almira m. J. D. Martin, of Everett, Mass. They have one daughter, Hattie, who is the wife of E. Clarence Colby of Everett, by whom she has a son,—Fred.

Orissa m. George D. Plimpton, of Litchfield. They had issue Fannie, who m. W. A. Braley, of Lewiston, and has a son George; and George Elias, who m. Alice Bradstreet, of Augusta, and now resides in Bath, Me.

Mr. Foss was a farmer, jeweler, and for many years a Justice of the Peace. From Phillips he came to Leeds where he resided several years on the farm occupied by Everett Carver; thence he moved to Beech Hill, in Wayne, and years later to Wayne village, where he died at the home of his daughter Aug. 15, 1877.

Thaddeus, sixth child of Uriah, b. June 13, 1793; m. Jerusha Hanes, by whom he had one daughter, Columbia. Thaddeus was a Methodist preacher and acquired a reputation as an interesting and efficient speaker. He died May 10, 1819, at the early age of about 26 years. His widow m. Job Haskell, of East Livermore.

Simeon, seventh child of Uriah, b. July 5, 1795; studied medicine and became an eminent physician in Belfast, Me., where he settled. He m. first, Sarah Norris, by whom he had two daughters—twins—Frances and Florilla. He later moved to Lisbon, Me., where his wife died. He married second, a lady who bore the name of Cousens, and whose residence was Portland. He died July 12, 1868.

Sarah (Sally), eighth child of Uriah, b. March 25, 1797; m. Alpheus Lane, had two children, Sarah and Sewall, both of whom died young; and the mother died in Wayne, Aug. 25, 1826, at the age of 29 years.

Walter, ninth child of Uriah, b. May 18, 1799, was a man of prominence in his native town. His name is in evidence with most of the enterprises and industries intended to improve the condition of the people financially, morally or spiritually. He was a Baptist minister, ordained as early as 1826, and his untiring labors in connection with his pastorate at Keene's Corner are portrayed in the history of that church. Nearly fifty years he was a preacher of the gospel. Few there are who realize the interest he felt and the work he did in connection with the "Union Chapel" near his home, that it might be preserved in cleanliness and remain

REV. WALTER FOSS.

a lasting structure in which children and children's children could assemble for Divine worship. Since his death this work has cheerfully been taken up and faithfully performed by his son, Walter Payson, who is deserving of much credit for the same. He solemnized nearly 500 marriages, and his funeral services exceeded that number. In 1826 he was appointed postmaster, which office he held many years. In 1823 he became a Mason and at the time of his death was chaplain of Oriental Star Lodge.

Immediately near the chapel Mr. Foss selected a beautiful spot and laid out a cemetery where he should rest from his labors and gather around him his children and grandchildren, who are many. He m. Dorcas S. Morrison, of Wayne, in 1826, who was b. Aug. 10, 1806. He died April 12, 1875, and his widow April 29, 1882. To them were born, on the "old Foss homestead," at North Leeds, 15 children, all of whom were living when the youngest was four years of age. They were namely:

1. Lucy M., b. Jan. 14, 1827; m. Jonathan Moulton, of Wayne, Dec. 5, 1852, by whom she had two sons.
    1. Sumner C., b. Oct. 1, 1853; d. Oct. 1, 1876.
    2. James M., b. Sept. 26, 1859; m. Sarah, a daughter of Seth Stinchfield; resides in Wayne; has four children, Jonathan E., Nancy L., James W., and Estella A.

    Jonathan Moulton d. Nov. 7, 1887; Lucy, his widow, d. Jan. 3, 1894.
2. John M., b. Dec. 29, 1827; d. in Leeds Jan. 3, 1875.
3. Thomas C., b. March 18, 1829; m. Dec. 12, 1854, Elizabeth Cobb, of Leeds, b. July 13, 1835. About the time of his marriage and the construction of the railroad from Leeds Junction to Livermore Falls, he built a house, stable and store at North Leeds, where he engaged in trade, in which business and place he continued during the remainder of his life, making a specialty of wool buying. When his store was in readiness to receive goods, he invited his brother-in-law, Jonathan Moulton, who was a merchant in Wayne village (a man who was fond of practical jokes), to accompany him to Portland, introduce and recommend him to the wholesale dealers with whom he might open an account; which invitation was cheerfully accepted. It was necessary at that time, for Mr. Foss to ask for some credit, and feeling, naturally, a little delicate, gave Mr. Moulton an opportunity which he improved. Entering a place of business he thus presented Mr. Foss: "Let me introduce a young man from the country who wishes to do business with you. I will

recommend him to be good for all he pays for. Mr. Foss—Mr. Milliken." They had issue:

1. V. Richardson, b. June 3, 1857; d. in Portland March 3, 1896.
2. Isabella, b. Aug. 1, 1862.
3. Preston W., b. Sept. 1, 1865; d. in Leeds Aug. 23, 1869.
4. Grace, b. May 21, 1871.
5. Catherine, b. Oct. 5, 1874.
6. Thomas C., b. May 26, 1878.

Elizabeth, wife of T. C. Foss, d. Aug. 6, 1882. He m. second, Abby J. Cox, of Gardiner, who d. Oct. 25, 1891, leaving no issue. Mr. Foss d. Nov. 22, 1891.

4. Sarah E., b. Sept. 19, 1830; m. Emery, only son of Asa Foss, of Wayne, March 7, 1852, who was born in Wayne April 10, 1823. Her children were:

1. John M., b. in Wayne Jan. 20, 1854. He spent several years in Wisconsin.
2. Walter E., b. July 29, 1860; m. Cora, a daughter of E. B. Chandler, formerly of Wayne. Residence, Norway, Me.

Sarah E. d. in Wayne Feb. 4, 1864. Emery Foss d. in Wayne Sept. 11, 1872.

5. Adoniram Judson, b. Jan. 30, 1832; m. Theresa, b. May 24, 1835, a daughter of Franklin Howard, of Leeds, Jan. 30, 1859, and now resides on the farm which was taken up by his wife's grandfather, Capt. Seth Howard, and the same on which Gen. O. O. Howard and brothers were born. In early manhood Mr. Foss was in trade with Wellington Hunton, at Livermore Falls; from which place he went to California, where he remained several years, later returning to his native town, where he has since lived. He is an industrious and intelligent farmer. His executive ability and business capacity, recognized by his townsmen, have been exercised in the offices within their gift. To them were born two daughters:

1. Lena H., b. in Leeds March 1, 1867.
2. Lucy M., b. in Leeds Sept. 15, 1878.

Theresa, his wife, d. in Leeds Jan. 18, 1897.

6. Ann H., b. Aug. 18, 1833; m. Adoniram Judson Lane Sept. 18, 1853, who was b. in Leeds July 18, 1830. They reside on the farm which was taken up and settled by Oliver Otis. Their children were:

1. Ada A., b. May 23, 1855; d. Nov. 8, 1873.
2. Fremont, b. Jan. 21, 1857; d. June 30, 1863.

3. Willie E., b. Aug. 11, 1860; d. May 29, 1899.
4. Sarah E., b. May 28, 1864.
5. Scott W., b. Sept. 13, 1865.
6. Allie, b. July 4, 1873; d. Sept. 6, 1874.
7. Issacher, b. Sept. 7, 1877.

7. James M., b. Aug. 4, 1835; died at McDougal Hospital, New York, Nov. 4, 1864, from wounds received while in action at Newbern, N. C. He enlisted in the 44th Regiment Massachusetts Volunteers, and later in Co. I, 59th Regiment, in which he was a Sergeant.

8. Dorcas E., b. Dec. 14, 1836; m. Nov. 4, 1857, Russell S. Linscott, b. in Nashua, N. H., Jan. 22, 1835. They had issue:

   1. Walter, who died in infancy or when a small boy.
   2. Hattie E., b. in Boston Dec. 14, 1859.

   Dorcas E. d. in Boston Dec. 21, 1859; Mr. Linscott d. in Oakland, Cal., Aug. 30, 1887.

9. Laura M., b. May 22, 1839; d. Feb. 25, 1852.
10. Rachael E., b. Dec. 6, 1840; d. Jan. 28, 1853.
11. Catharine M., b. June 6, 1842; m. April 6, 1871, Melvin Berry, b. in Leeds in 1815. They had no issue. She d. in Leeds Sept. 10, 1874. He d. in Leeds May 10, 1888.
12. Walter Payson, b. Jan. 6, 1844; m. Dec. 25, 1874, Hattie F. Cox, who was b. in Gardiner, Nov. 9, 1841. They reside on the homestead of his father and grandfather who redeemed it from the forest. The house in which they live is the handiwork of the pioneer, Uriah. Mr. Foss is a neat and careful farmer, and for a time made a specialty of sheep-raising. He has been a buyer of wool and still continues in the business, but the scarcity of sheep limits purchases to small and scattered lots. He has been a member of the Board of Selectmen and officiated in various other positions of trust. The care of his parents was entrusted to him, which duty he faithfully and tenderly performed. Nor did his labors cease when they were laid at rest in that place which had been so carefully and beautifully prepared by the father. The trust accepted of perpetuating the result of the father's labors will cease when he, too, shall sleep the sleep of the just. One child only is the fruit of his marriage, George M., b. Feb. 16, 1881.
13. Vesta P., b. Jan. 18, 1846; m. Jan. 31, 1869, Frank G. Foss, b. in Leeds Jan. 3, 1842. They reside at North Leeds, in the house built by George Gould in the year 1852. Mr. Foss is a mason by trade, in which business he is engaged

when his time is unemployed on the farm. Mrs. Foss succeeded her son, Guy W., in the post-office, and holds a commission at the present time. They had issue:

1. Alvin Wilson, b. June 3, 1871; d. Dec. 3, 1872.
2. Guy Wilson, son of Frank G. and Vesta P. Foss, b. June 12, 1874; d. Jan. 3, 1901. He was a young man of sterling character, respected and beloved by a large circle of friends. At the age of 21 years he was appointed postmaster at North Leeds, the duties of which office he ably and faithfully performed until a short time prior to his decease. His early death was occasioned by consumption.
3. Annie Howard, b. Oct. 3, 1876; m. Frank G. Davis Sept. 23, 1897. To them one child was born, Muriel, March 29, 1898; d. May 28, 1900.
4. Oliver Johnson, b. Oct. 13, 1882.
5. Frank Maynard, b. June 29, 1890.

14. Charles Wilson, b. Oct. 11, 1847; went to California in 1868, where he engaged in the lumbering business. From an injury received by a rolling log, he died in Nevada City, Aug. 31, 1868.
15. Varnum R., b. April 10, 1850; d. Aug. 19, 1854.

Of the foregoing fifteen children of Rev. Walter and Dorcas S. (Morrison) Foss, four only are now living, namely: 5, Adoniram Judson; 6, Ann H. (Mrs. A. J. Lane); 12, Walter Payson; 13, Vesta P. (Mrs. Frank G. Foss).

Ruel, tenth and youngest child of Uriah, the pioneer, b. Feb. 24, 1802, m. in June, 1827, Polly Lothrop. They settled on a portion of his father's original homestead at North Leeds. He was a man whom his and the neighboring children and young people enjoyed very much. His cheerful nature, cordial greetings and funny sayings made him a welcome member in the society of people of all ages alike. His memory is cherished and associated with many pleasant events in the lives of those, his friends, who are yet in time. For a term of years he was postmaster, prior to the moving of the office from Foss' Corner to the store near the Railroad Station. To them were born, in Leeds, two daughters and one son, namely:

1. Orintha, m. Dana Goff, of Auburn; issue, one son.
2. Rodney, m. Miss Merrow. Their residence was Auburn. They had issue two sons.
3. Florida, m. Capt. Benjamin J. Hill and resides in Auburn. They have issue one daughter.

About 1865 Mr. Foss sold his farm at North Leeds and removed to Auburn, where he lived with his son, Rodney, and

G. W. FOSS.

died there Jan. 21, 1877. The forgoing comprises the descendants of Uriah[4] and Sarah (Goodridge) Foss. The descendants of his brother follow:

Capt. Phineas Foss[3] (Levi[2], Walter[1],), the youngest son of Levi, was born in Peperellboro Feb. 10, 1772. His father was a Revolutionary soldier and died in the service. When his brother, Uriah, came to Littleborough in 1786, Phineas was a lad of 14 years and living at home with his mother. After her decease, about 1790, he came with his sister Hannah, to Littleborough, where they both lived in the family of their brother until they had homes of their own. Phineas worked on the land purchased by Uriah while he was at Bath, earning money to finish paying for the same; after which, he was rewarded for his labors by sharing a portion of it, and on which he erected buildings, where he resided the remainder of his comparatively short life. In September, 1799, he married Rebecca, the youngest child of Thomas and Sarah (Paul, *nee* True,) Stinchfield—the first white child born in the Plantation, the date of her birth being Dec. 11, 1780. To them were born seven children, yet few are their descendants. Their children were:

1. John, b. Oct. 10, 1800.
2. Harriet, b. Aug. 14, 1802.
3. Allura, b. Feb. 5, 1805.
4. Alvin, b. ———, 1807.
5. Eliza W., b. June 13, 1809.
6. Loring, b. June 18, 1812.
7. Phineas, b. Jan. 8, 1814.

   I. John, married Laura Rowe and for a time was engaged in the boot and shoe business with his brother, Loring, in Winthrop, Me. They made a specialty of manufacturing boots for river drivers and had a large trade in the eastern part of the State and in the Province of New Brunswick. While on a business trip to that locality he disappeared and his folks were never able to learn more of him. He left no known issue.

   II. Harriet was a maiden lady. When the buildings of Eben Stinchfield were burned, about 1875, in attempting to remove some of her effects, she was cut off by the flames and thus met her death.

   III. Allura married John Stanley, of Winthrop, in which town they resided. They had issue four children— three daughters and a son, neither of whom married.

   IV. Alvin was drowned when a small boy.

V. Eliza W. married in 1831 Wingate Linscott, born in Chesterville, Me., June 27, 1809. Most of their married life was spent in New York and Boston, where Mr. Linscott was in business. In later years they purchased the old homestead of Mrs. Linscott's father at North Leeds, where they constructed a fine set of buildings—the same now owned and occupied by Charles Lovell. To them were born four sons and four daughters, viz.:

1. Frances Ellen, born in Utica, N. Y., Jan. 12, 1832; married Henry A. Choate, of Boston, in November, 1856. They had issue Alice Frances, Arthur Henry, and Harry Wingate. Mrs. Choate died in New York Nov. 30, 1901.
2. Russell Streeter, born in Nashua, N. H., Jan. 22, 1835; m. Nov. 4, 1857, Dorcas E., b. in Leeds, Dec. 4, 1836, a daughter of Rev. Walter Foss. They had issue a son and daughter, Walter E., who died in infancy, and Hattie E., born in Boston, Dec. 14, 1859.

Mrs. Linscott died in Boston Dec. 21, 1859; and Mr. Linscott died in Oakland, Cal., Aug. 30, 1887.

3-4. Samuel C. and Calvin W., both died in infancy.
5. Edwin Wingate, b. in Nashua, N. H., Feb. 28, 1842; married in 1865 Elizabeth Razin, at Dorchester, Mass. Issue, two children, Elizabeth and Edwin W., Jr.; Mr. Linscott died in Brooklyn, N. Y., in October, 1900.
6. Harriet Eliza, born in Boston Nov. 14, 1844; died September, 1855.
7. Jennie Augusta, born in Boston, Dec. 14, 1847; married William D. Pennell at Lewiston, June 22, 1869. They have three children, Dwight Richard, Frances Cornelia, and Maude Robie.
8. Caroline Wilhelmina, born in Boston Oct. 4, 1850; married first, in Portland in 1884, Frank W. Patterson, of Belfast, Me.; second, married Henry D. Clark, of Belfast, Me. No issue by either marriage.

Eliza W. (Foss) Linscott died in Lewiston, Me., June 27, 1870; Wingate Linscott died in Brooklyn, N. Y., October, 1883. Both were buried in the family lot Forest Hill Cemetery, Forest Hill, Mass.

VI. Loring married Jane, a daughter of William and Rhoda (Knapp) Gott, July 15, 1838. She was born in Wayne, May 2, 1815. They resided for a time in

Leeds, but later lived many years in Winthrop, where he was in business. He returned to Leeds, beside the lake, where he died in 1895, and his widow the following year in Lewiston. No issue.

VII. Phineas married a Miss Bradford, and after living some years in Winthrop, profited by the advice of Horace Greeley and went west. They reared a small family of smart children, to the sons of whom is entrusted the perpetuation of the name in this branch of the Foss family.

LEADBETTER FAMILY.

Among the names of the early settlers is that of Leadbetter, in 1785. In that year Increase Leadbetter, who had been a soldier in the Revolutionary War, with a large family came from Camden and settled in the extreme north end of the town—then a part of Livermore. The farm by him taken up, cleared and subdued, is the same now owned and occupied by Samuel P. Francis. His wife, who was a Miss Calderwood, with her parents, resided in Camden at the time of her marriage. In that town children were born to them to the number of seven or eight, and the balance of the number of thirteen were born in Leeds, viz.: Thomas, Benjamin, John, Samuel, James, Luther, Jabez, Ezra, Abigail, Betsey, Hannah, Sally, and Joanna. While in the war he left his wife with small children, on a farm stocked with cattle and sheep, all of which she cared for during his absence. With her own hands she sheared the sheep, carded, spun, wove, colored cloth, cut and made clothing for her children, and at the same time attended to raising crops of breadstuff, thereby making them comfortable while awaiting the uncertain return of the father. After their removal to Leeds for a time their only means of conveyance was by boat to and from his farm along Dead River and across Androscoggin Lake to Wayne Mills. Like most of the early settlers he was a strong, hardy man, of good physique. Most of his children married and settled in Leeds. Thomas married Miss Clark; Benjamin m. Miss Collier; John m. Rachael Foss; Samuel, born in 1774; m. Betsey Parcher, of Saco, d. September, 1859, and his wife April, 1854; James, m. Fannie Otis, of Leeds; Luther m. Jemima Lane, of Leeds; Jabez m. Lucretia Howard, of Leeds; Ezra, m. Sally Woodman, of Leeds; Abigail, m. James Lane, of Leeds; Betsey, m. Simeon Gould, of Leeds; Joanna, m. Benjamin Woodman, of Leeds; Hannah was drowned at the age of sixteen years, caused by the falling of a foot bridge across Dead River, near her father's house; and Sally died of fever, the same year.

Of the children of Thomas and Benjamin, sons of Increase Leadbetter, the writer is not informed, but of the others, mention is here made.

John's children were, Alvah, Asaph, Eliza, Warren and Rachael.

Alvah moved to the Province of New Brunswick, married a Miss Durkeshire, who bore him six children.

Asaph was killed by Indians in the far West.

Eliza married Seth Millett, of North Leeds, and had a family of children.

Warren died of fever when in youth.

Rachael married John Fletcher, and settled in Nashua, N. H.

Samuel's children were, Mary, b. Oct. 20, 1807; m. Uriah Foss, lived with him fifty-five years in their home in North Leeds; had a family of seven children, four of whom are living, and died in Farmington, at the home of her daughter, Mrs. Orrah M. Jennings, at the advanced age of about 92 years.

Lorenzo, b. March, 1809; was engaged in lumbering in the eastern part of the State several years, and subsequently in Michigan, where he died; Sally, b. Sept. 9, 1811; Horace, b. Nov. 18, 1813, spent most of his life on a farm at North Leeds, where he raised a family, though subsequently he went to California, where he died at the home of his son, Wallace; Samuel, Jr., b. August, 1816, married Colista, a daughter of Charles Knapp, settled in Glenburn, Me., raised a family of six children and died in that town; Emerline, b. June, 1822; Charles H., b. July, 1826, drowned July, 1840.

Ezra's children were: Pamelia, Orson and Orisa.

Jabez's children were: Nelson H., b. 1821; Rosa, b. 1823; Lucius Clark, b. 1825; Laura M., b. 1827; Aurelia B., b. 1829; Rhodephus H. and Delphina, b. 1832; Lucia J., b. 1836, and Henry B., b. 1844.

Joanna Leadbetter and Benjamin Woodman's children were: Henry, Jason, Emily, Julia, Charles, Benjamin, Edward, Sewall, and John.

Betsey Leabetter and Simeon Gould's children were: Lloyd, Elizabeth and Frank.

Abigail Leadbetter and James Lane's children were: Joanna, m. Perez Jennings; Pheba, m. Shepherd Cary; John, m. Vesta Phillips; Abigail, m. Stephen Rackley; Asenath, m. Doctor Hale; Eliza, m. Nathaniel Perley; Hannah, m. Ammi Woodman; Columbus, m. Miss Perkins; Alden, m. Mary Rackley; James, m. Lovisa Wyman.

GEORGE FAMILY.

Around this man cluster many and varied tales relating to his birth, life, and death. He was an Englishman and is said to have been a member of the royal family. It is further said that, on account of the established laws of descent in the families of nobility, he, having an older brother and thus being deprived of equal position and honor, resolved to make his own course in life, and quietly leaving his home shipped on a man-of-war vessel, left England in the spring of 1778, and came out to America to fight in his country's cause. This was the same vessel on which Rev. Thomas D. Francis came, and the story of his experience tells the story of Francis George until they separate in Gray,—the former returning to New Gloucester, to the house of Thomas Stinchfield, where he afterward remained; and the latter, with his comrades, after recuperating and receiving a supply of clothing, proceeded to Falmouth and reported for further orders. It is said of him further, that the inequality of birth of brothers and other matters in his family and nation were so distasteful to him that he espoused the cause of independence with more vigor and endured the hardships of a soldier's life with less murmur, than any of his associates. After the war closed in 1783 he was in Taunton, Mass., where he married a young widow, Charity Chubbock, who had a daughter, Charity. They settled, as did many of his comrades, in Saco; but a little later— about 1785—came to Littleborough and took up a piece of land on Fish Street, the house having stood on the east side and near that road, northerly and distant from the buildings now occupied by Seth Fish, about 20 rods. The old George well on that place is still utilized by Mr. Fish. Later, he dwelt on the side of the hill on the north side of the road, between the Foss bridge and the corners near the house of Freedom Gould. Later, the buildings were occupied by his grandson, Seth Millett. "A rolling stone gathers no moss." For a time he lived at the corners where the old road from the bridge across Dead River and the Otis Hill road intersected. In the year 1830 he purchased the buildings formerly occupied by William Carver, which stood near the east bank of the river, nearly opposite the buildings on the town farm. These he removed to the place where the old George house now stands, on the North Leeds road, northerly of the dwelling of Davis P. True. There he spent the remainder of his long life, dying in March, 1852. It was said, at the time of his death, that his age was 112 years. In the absence of a family record, or other data at hand, the writer cannot vouch for the years, but the saying. Elezer Carver was the authority and claimed to have verified the statement by the military record of his age when he entered the Revolutionary Army. At the time of his death one of the longest and most severe snow storms prevailed and ten days the roads were impassable for teams. His remains were kept at the house six days and finally placed on a horse-sled and drawn by men to the Robert Gould cemetery, a distance of nearly two miles, and buried.

His children were:

Sally, Priscilla, Francis, Jr., Lucinda, Malinda, and George Washington.

Sally married John Millett in 1799 and spent her life in Leeds. Her children have received mention in the sketch of the Millett family in this work.

Priscilla married Thomas Drinkwater, of Livermore, in July, 1809. They settled in Palmyra, Me.

Francis, Jr., was a minister of the gospel and became quite noted as a preacher. He married Nancy Fish, of Leeds, in August, 1818. Of his, or his sister Priscilla's family, we have no reliable information.

Lucinda married Samuel Wing, of Livermore, in June, 1824. Their family has not been traced.

Malinda married James Campbell, of Livermore, in March, 1824. They settled in that town and raised a family of children, one of whom, John, is, or was, a resident of Fayette Mills.

George Washington, the youngest child, married first, Mary Ann Gilbert, of Leeds, in March, 1832, but they lived together less than twenty-four hours. He married second, Clarissa Leighton, of Hartford, in December, 1839, and brought her to his father's house where they spent their lives. Assuming the care of his father and step-mother, and having a large family of children of his own, his energies and efforts were heavily taxed to provide for their every want; but his honesty and integrity at all times and under all circumstances were so well appreciated, that he met with success, where many would have failed. They had issue:

Francis, born in 1842.
Loren, born in 1844.
Otis B., born in 1846.
Augustus S., born April 3, 1848.
Eliza Jane, born in 1850.
Charles L., born in 1852.
Henry, born in 1854.
Volney, born in 1856.
Cyrus, born in 1858.

Francis, the eldest child, was a soldier in the Civil War. He enlisted in the "Third Maine Infantry Regiment," and re-enlisting when his first term ended, he went through the war. On his return he was some time an employe in the Elm House, in

Auburn. He was later in Lewiston, where he married Ida Ray. They had one child, Mira, who married Rev. Mr. Starbird, a Free Will Baptist minister, whose residence is Farmington. Mr. George, later, entered the employ of the Maine Central Railroad, and at Farmington was jammed between two cars and so badly injured that he never fully recovered and died in Togus, at the Soldiers' Home. His remains were taken to Brunswick for interment.

Loren, the second child, has never married. He has lived in several families in Leeds and Wayne, and at present is residing in Wayne.

Otis B., the third child, went out in the "Eleventh Maine Infantry Regiment," a substitute for Llewellyn Gould. On his return went to Lewiston, where he learned painting. He there married Amanda Hundon, of North Auburn. From there he removed to Brunswick. The hospital practice he received while in the army he here turned to good account, and as a professional nurse his services were in constant demand. Later, he took a course in Boston, learning the massage treatment which he afterwards practiced successfully until his death.

He was buried in Brunswick. He left his widow a fine residence in that town, tenements in other villages in the State, and a bank account of several thousands of dollars. He had one son, Ernest, who is a locomotive driver on the Mountain Division of the Maine Central Railroad.

Augustus S., fourth child of George W., was also in the Civil War. He went out in the "Eleventh Maine Infantry Regiment," a substitute for Ezra Ramsdell, of Leeds. After returning from the army he was an employe of the Elm House, Auburn. He married July 3, 1869, Hulda J. Sprague, of Greene. After living in Greene a few years he returned to his native town, where he engaged in farming. Later he removed to Wayne village and for eleven years was owner and driver of the mail stage from that town, first to Winthrop, and afterward to North Leeds. During the time he purchased a farm, about a mile from town, where he now resides. He is past commander of Lewis H. Wing G. A. R. Post, and a good working officer in the Methodist Episcopal Church.* He is a good and respected citizen. They have issue Lewis W., b. April 29, 1870, and Annie A., b. March 26, 1874. From school Lewis W. learned telegraphy and entered the employ of the Maine Central Railroad. He was an operator at Oakland, and later made station agent at that office. His business ability, morality, punctuality, honesty and accuracy

---

*He is a member of the Norland Grange, Pomona Grange, and will become a member of the National Grange ere this work is issued.

were recognized by the higher officials and he was given full charge of the station at Belfast, Me., where the receipts amount to more than $100,000 annually. He married Georgie Todd, of Freeport, Me.

They have no issue—lost one child, Donald D., b. May, 1897; d. Nov. 19, 1897.

Annie A. married June 1, 1895, Fred Walker, of Sabattus, Me. They have one child, Owen McKinley, b. Nov. 3, 1896.

Eliza Jane, fifth child of George W., married Almond Ray, of Lewiston. They had four children. She died at the age of 25 years.

Charles L., the next child, is single. He has lived in many families in Leeds and Wayne and now resides in the family of I. D. Lincoln in the latter town.

Henry, next in the list, has always lived in the family of R. S. Loring, M.D. He is a farmer and takes special pride in the care of the cattle and horse stock in his charge.

Volney and Cyrus both died young.

George Washington was a member of Capt. Giddings Lane's military company that went through the Aroostook War with no fatalities.

It will be noticed that the George family has been loyal and patriotic through its several generations. The father, son, and grandsons have, in turn, rallied to their country's call.

SYLVESTER FAMILY.

From the time of the first settlement of Leeds until a few years ago the Sylvester family has lived in the western part of the town upon the River Road.

Here, upon the eastern bank of the Androscoggin, Harvey Sylvester built his cabin and settled in the wilderness, near where A. P. Russell now lives. He came from Greene where he had married his wife, Hannah Brown, and where his two eldest children were born.

After living in his new home a short time, he sold part of the tract of land he had bought and his house to one Ramsdell and went farther up the river. Here he built again near the river and in this home lived until he built the old-fashioned house that still stands upon the old Sylvester place where W. C. Dunton now lives. This house was built about 1826. On this place grew to manhood and womanhood his eleven children of whom one only, Hannah, is still living at an advanced age.

The family is of English descent. Harvey's grandfather came to the Massachusetts Colony from England and settled in Scituate, the tradition being that he ran away from his home while a young lad, and came to the new country to better his prospects in life.

Harvey's father, Elisha Sylvester, was one of the first settlers of Greene, and the second teacher in that town. He was a successful teacher, a man of ability but with many peculiarities. He had more education than was common to those times and a talent for writing poetry, but he lacked ability to meet the realities of life.

He came to Greene from Scituate, Mass., where he was born Nov. 28, 1752. He died Jan. 1, 1836, at the age of 83 and was buried in Scituate, Mass. He married Abigail Palmer, of Scituate, who died July, 1814, aged 66, and was buried at Leeds in the neighborhood burying ground upon the River Road.

Harvey Sylvester was born in Greene June 12, 1779, and died Nov. 12, 1864. He married Hannah Brown, of Greene, who was born Sept. 17, 1783, and died Aug. 3, 1870.

The children of Harvey and Hannah Sylvester were as follows:

Sophronia, born Nov. 28, 1801; died March 16, 1884. She married Cyrus Leavitt, of Turner, and lived and died in that town.

Lorenzo, born Aug. 23, 1803; died Nov. 24, 1883. He married Sarah Leavitt, of Turner, sister of Cyrus Leavitt, mentioned above, and died in Leeds on the home place.

Harvey, Jr., born Aug. 23, 1805; died Jan. 29, 1868. Married Iva Taylor and died in Buckfield.

Rosalinda, born Jan. 9, 1808; died Nov. 24, 1896. Married Amos Thomes and lived in Leeds with the exception of the last few years of her life, which she spent in Turner, where she died.

Orilla, born Nov. 11, 1809; died July 4, 1873. She married first, Josiah Skillings; second, G. W. Jones. She died in Greene.

Alonzo, born Oct. 8, 1811; died Aug. 30, 1838. Married Rhoda Caswell. He was killed by a stroke of lightning. Died in Livermore.

Ruggles, born Nov. 25, 1813; died Dec. 24, 1851. He married Harriet Howard and died in Leeds.

Bradbury, born Nov. 19, 1815; died Aug. 31, 1889. He married for his first wife Lydia Bean, for second, Caroline M. Morse. He died in Wayne.

Sewall, born Nov. 5, 1817; died May 16, 1876. Married Jane Foster, of Leeds. He died in Lawrence, Mass., where he had been a book-keeper for many years.

Hannah, born Oct. 30, 1819; living. Married Charles Sylvester and lives upon the old Sylvester place in Greene.

Jeremiah, born March 12, 1822; died March 13, 1890. Married Rachel Brown, of Greene, and died in Chicago.

Lorenzo, second child of Harvey and Hannah, came to the old home place to care for his father and mother in their declining years. He had lived previously in Livermore and Lewiston. In the latter place he managed successfully a boarding-house for mill hands when Lewiston was a small village. He was also well known in his own and surrounding towns as a successful school teacher, having taught many winters in difficult schools. He was a cooper by trade and some of the tubs which he made are still in use in Leeds.

In politics he was a stanch Republican and a Baptist in religion.

Lorenzo and Sarah Leavitt Sylvester had three children:

Delora, born Dec. 30, 1827. Married Harrison G. O. Mower, of Turner, Jan. 18, 1852.

Sophronia, born June 6, 1831. Married Sumner Bailey, of Turner, June 6, 1854.

Lorenzo Mellen, born Oct. 1, 1834. Married Saphila C. Metcalf, of Hope, Knox County, Me., Aug. 20, 1861.

He was born in Livermore. He attended the common schools and Lewiston Academy. When a young man he worked in the mills of Lawrence, Mass., as also did his wife before her marriage. This was at a time when the operatives in the cotton mills of the Massachusetts cities were composed largely of energetic young men and women from the farms of Maine, New Hampshire, and Vermont.

He, with his wife, came to the old place to care for his parents. They lived there till the fall of 1893, when they moved to Turner and have since made their home with their son, Arthur M.

He was always a great reader and well informed on the topics of the day. In politics it was ever principles rather than party with him. He was one of the first to enter the Republican party at its formation and was a pioneer in the Greenback movement.

Lorenzo Melen and Saphila C. (Metcalf) Sylvester had four children:

Arthur Mellen, born Nov. 30, 1865.
Lucy Metcalf, born April 26, 1867.
Laura Metcalf, born April 26, 1867.
Henry Cole, b. March 26, 1874; died Dec. 4, 1896.

Arthur M. Sylvester is a successful farmer in Turner, where he has a large farm upon the River Road, six miles from Auburn. He keeps a large herd of cows, selling the milk in Lewiston and Auburn.

Lucy M. began teaching at the age of sixteen; graduated from Farmington Normal School in 1888. Taught in the ungraded schools of the State and Grammar Schools at Bowdoinham, Andover and Skowhegan. From 1892 to 1894 taught a Grammar School in Stockbridge, Mass. Since her marriage

LAURA M. SYLVESTER.

to Frank H. Herrick, of Leeds, she has taught in the schools of that town, Wayne, and Greene.

Laura M. began teaching at an early age. Graduated from Farmington Normal School in 1888. Taught in ungraded schools in Leeds, Monmouth, Vassalboro; Free High School at Fayette and Grammar School in Bowdoinham.

She served her town during the years of 1890 and 1891 as supervisor of schools, being the only woman who has ever held that office in the town of Leeds.

For the past nine years she has taught in Massachusetts, having taught five years in the Grammar Schools of Pittsfield, Great Barrington, and Stockbridge, and four years in the ninth grade, High School, Arlington, Mass., where she is teaching at present.

SKETCH OF WILLIAM FISH AND SOME OF HIS DESCENDANTS.

William Fish was among the early settlers of the territory that is now the town of Leeds. He came here from Sandwich, Mass., previous to the year 1790. He was a man of great strength and physical endurance. He had been a sea-faring man and tradition says he was impressed into the service of the British navy, and that he cleared himself by swimming several miles to the shore. It is said that he afterwards joined the Revolutionary Army. His hearing was considerably impaired, occasioned by a fall from the yard-arm to the quarter-deck of a vessel. A good story is told of him as follows: The wives of two of his neighbors, John and Samuel Jennings, were visiting at his house one winter's day. A great storm came up suddenly and the ladies could not get home on foot. Mr. Fish kindly offered to take them home with his ox-team. The women were comfortably seated on the sled and he trudged along beside the oxen. When about half way on their journey the sled tongue came out. At the top of their voices the ladies called, but not hearing them in the blinding storm he kept right on till he reached the home of one of them, when, looking back, in great astonishment, he exclaimed, "*Where in the world are Sam's wife and John's wife?*"

William Fish settled on the farm now owned by the Deane Brothers, on the Androscoggin River, about half a mile north of West Leeds village. The buildings were near the south line of the lot. He cleared his farm and few men could do as much work in a day and still fewer could work as many days in succession. He was converted and baptised during the great revival in Leeds. He lived to an advanced age and sleeps in the soil of his native town.

His wife was Mehitable Tupper, of Sandwich, Mass. She had a sister, Olive, who married Samuel Jennings; another sister,

Grace, married James Stanley, of Leeds; and still another sister, Esther, married Col. John May and was the mother of Judge Seth May, who died in Auburn, Me., Sept. 20, 1881.

Mrs. Fish was a person of superior intellectual attainments for the times in which she lived and was a teacher. She died while on a visit to her daughter in Wayne, Me., Jan. 10, 1838.

The children of William and Mehitable Fish were William, Jr., Grace, Mary, Olive, Seth, Caroline, Patience, Desire, Enoch, and Warren. All were born in the town of Leeds and all lived to mature age.

William, Jr., born July 25, 1790, married Lydia Reed in 1826; lived in Leeds where he died in 1866. No children.

Grace, born Oct. 15, 1792; married Abel Stevens in 1815. Mr. Stevens was a prosperous farmer of Fayette, Me. Their children were Hiram, Abel, Jr., Harriet, John and Emily. Mrs. Grace Stevens died in Fayette Jan. 1, 1832, and was buried in the Lovejoy cemetery in that town.

Mary, born March 9, 1795; never married. She died in Leeds in 1884.

Olive, born Dec. 10, 1797; married Lewis Pettingill in 1824. They had a family of several children. She died Dec. 21, 1843.

Seth, born Nov. 14, 1800; married Rosilla Leadbetter. They had a family of five children. Capt. Seth Fish's buildings were on the north half of his father's lot, where the Deane Bros.' fine set of buildings now stand. He removed to Solon, Me., about 1837.

Caroline, born May 22, 1803; married in 1824 Nathaniel Walton, of Wayne. She died Dec. 30, 1886. She was a woman of great industry and energy, and possessed the physical endurance of her father and the mental vigor of her mother. Skilful with wheel and loom, spinning the yarn and weaving the cloth, not only for her own household, but was relied on to do the same for many other families. She was a kind mother, a devoted wife and faithful friend. Their children were Lucy A., Jeremiah D., Martha M., and George W. Jeremiah D. carried on the Foster place at Leeds Center for a term of eight years. He is a thorough and successful farmer. He now owns and occupies the William Wing farm, in Wayne. He married Beulah P. Norris, by whom he has three sons, Fred W., of Montana, Charles H., of California, and Herbert N., living with his parents.

George W., who has been a life-long resident of his native town, is an enterprising citizen and successful farmer. His connection with the schools of Wayne and many other Maine towns in the capacity of teacher, and his long and efficient service on the school board and as supervisor, together with his record in the legislative halls of Maine, are sufficient evidence of his standing in the community in which he lives. In 1866 he married Sarah

E., a daughter of Deacon Francis Dexter, of Wayne. They had issue Carrie May, born in 1867; graduated from Hebron Academy in June, 1891, was a teacher, died in 1895; and Winfred W., graduated from Kent's Hill in 1894; is a teacher and the present superintendent of schools in Wayne.

Patience, born April 3, 1806; married Ira Sampson in 1835. They had one son, Leonard G., whose widow and her daughter, Ada, and son, John, now reside in Leeds.

Desire, born March 10, 1808; married Nathaniel Daggett in 1828. They had two sons, Warren and Lloyd. Warren was for many years a successful scythe-maker at North Wayne. He married Pamelia Wing. Their son, Fred, graduated from Bates College and is now a lawyer in Boston, Mass. Lloyd served in the navy during the Civil War. By a second husband, Eben Hodgdon, Desire had three children, Charles, who died in childhood, Martha Jane, and Matilda.

Enoch, born Sept. 10, 1810; married Eliza Kimball in 1837. Their children were Enoch, Jr., Eliza M., William H., Olive R., Sarah J., Caroline W., and Elmira A. William H. was a soldier in the War of the Rebellion and lost his life in the service. Enoch Fish removed to Lexington, Me., where he died March 15, 1888.

Warren, the tenth child of William and Mehitable Fish, born Jan. 10, 1812; married Irena Andrews in 1837. Their children were Austin A., Arvilla, Octavia, and one son whose name is unknown to the writer. Warren Fish was a blacksmith by trade. He died Dec. 4, 1849.

LIFE OF ANDREW CUSHMAN, BY HIMSELF.

Andrew Cushman was born in Plympton, Mass., Jan. 6, 1761, and died in Leeds Feb. 6, 1844, aged 83 years. His wife, Bathsheba Cushman, was born in Sandwich, Mass., Aug. 12, 1768, and died in Leeds May 12, 1843, aged 75. Her name before marriage was Bathsheba Jennings. Isaac Cushman, the father of the writer, was born in Plympton, Mass., Feb. 22, 1732, and died at Niagara, New York, Jan. 11, 1819. The wife of Isaac died at the age of 78, but what year is not remembered. A record of the family is now in the hands of Levi Cushman, of Sumner, Me., which will furnish the family with any desired information.

I enlisted in the War of the American Revolution May 8, 1777, and went first from Plympton to Boston, where I tarried about two weeks, when I proceeded to Ticonderoga, New York, and remained there about a fortnight. General Burgoyne came upon us from Quebec with ten thousand men. The American soldiers at that time were under the command of General St.

Clair whose number was said to be not more than five hundred men. While in the fort at Ticonderoga they made three successive attempts to rout us, but without success till they drew up some cannon to the top of a high hill called Mount Defiance, which was directly opposite to our fort, from which lofty elevation they could pour down into our fort the fire of cannon. Perceiving the danger and peril to which we were exposed, our men concluded that it would be prudent to retire from our fort in the morning, accordingly we retreated the next morning, and traveled thirty-two miles, to the nearest house, and arrived about dark at Habbleton. Our baggage was conveyed down Lake Champlain in two schooners. During the night the British General sent down some of his men and cut off our rear guard. I was all the preceding day with this guard, but at evening wishing to be with those with whom I was best acquainted, I managed to join the main body of the army in their march. On the day after this rear guard was cut off we started for Bennington, Vt., and continued our course three days towards Bennington, but learning that General Burgoyne was directing his course towards North River, we immediately changed our course and proceded directly towards Fort Mella at which we arrived three days after we had changed our course, having been nearly destitute of food for six days at Fort Mella. General Burgoyne came upon us; our men had cut down trees to prevent the British artillery from proceeding. Before, however, we arrived at Fort Mella, about twenty of us were compelled to camp out in the woods over night, having no protection from the rain which fell upon us during the night. In the morning we found that we had missed our way, but finding ourselves not a great way from Fort Mella, we repaired thither and recruited ourselves from the store of provisions. We remained perhaps one week at this fort; some of our company died from long abstinence from food and from fatigue. Finding the British coming upon us, we proceeded as was supposed with about five hundred soldiers. This was in the spring of the year. We marched to Saratoga where we tarried two days. Then we retreated down within ten miles of Albany. General Burgoyne heard that three brigades were coming to the assistance of General Gates from New York. General Burgoyne, therefore, made a halt at Saratoga, and did not immediately proceed. General Gates moved on to Stillwater and three miles beyond is a place called Beeman's Height, where we engaged in action during one whole day. At night the British hoisted their flag, and then we hoisted ours, when the engagement ceased for that day. The British agreed to meet us the next day, but the next day came and they did not appear. About ten days after we had another engagement with Burgoyne's remaining troops which amounted to about two thousand. This action lasted about half a day. Our men rushed on with all their force and were at one end of their cannon at the same time they were at the other and bravely drove the enemy back leaving two of their cannon loaded in their retreat. Our men raised a general shout at which the British made a halt, when we killed Fraizer, their General. We rushed on and took possession of their line. They buried their General that day. On the following day they hauled up stakes and retreated eight miles as far as Saratoga; having started late in the afternoon they did not arrive that night at Saratoga. The following day it rained and our men remained in the camp, but the day following being fair weather, we marched towards Saratoga, and arrived there in the afternoon. On our arrival there the same night, General Burgoyne, finding himself in close quarters, sent to General Gates proposals of adjustment, to which General Gates would not agree. Hearing by one of General Washington's aids that a large number of soldiers were coming from New York to his assistance, we tarried in a waiting posture at Saratoga about three days, at the end of these days, about sunsetting, General Gates sent to Burgoyne that unless he would surrender before eight o'clock the next morning he should engage with him in hot battle. To this Burgoyne replied that he would surrender the next morning at the rising of the sun, at the time appointed by himself. He came and rode through two brigades of our army which were paraded on both sides of the way. General Gates received them on the right at the end of the parade, and he delivered his sword into the hands of General Gates. Having achieved this victory without fighting, our men then immediately marched to Albany, where we tarried about ten days, after which we proceeded down the North River to Querman's Overslough, so called, which is on the west side of the river. General Washington sent orders to us to march to Valley Forge, at Philadelphia, but some of our members had a permit to go to Boston and be vaccinated for the small pox. I was among that number, but instead of going to Sewall's Point near Boston, where the other soldiers went, I proceeded to Plympton, and arrived from Philadelphia to Plympton in the month of March, 1778, where I remained two months till recovered of the small pox.

    I then went in company with about thirty soldiers to Delaware. While there we learned that the British were marching through New Jersey, wherefore we tacked about and marched to Monmouth, New Jersey, where we engaged in battle with the enemy on the plat of ground which had been selected by General Washington. On the morning before this battle General Washington rode through our ranks and addressed us; encouraged us to be courageous to fight valiantly for our country's cause, telling us that the country's liberty depended upon that day's battle.

We were greatly animated by the General's moving address. It infused new courage into our hearts. The action continued till the sun was about one hour high, when we compelled them to retreat. This battle was very warm, some of our cannon balls melted at the cannon's mouth and stuck fast beneath the mouth of the cannon. Having traveled during the night previous to the battle, we were unable through fatigue and weariness to pursue the British troops, so we let them go. After this action, Washington commended our men for their bravery in fighting. About one o'clock in the morning those who survived the battle set out from the field of action, and after three days' march going at the rate of only ten miles a day we crossed, I believe, Passaic River in New Jersey and proceeded to King's Ferry, crossed over and went to White Plains, New York. In passing over the Passaic River we crossed on a bridge, at which our company stopped one day, which was the Fourth of July, and celebrated the National Independence. We tarried at White Plains until August, when hearing that the British were invading Rhode Island, Gen. Washington sent orders for two brigades to go to the assistance of Gen. Sullivan, who then commanded a part of the United States troops in that quarter. We were among the number who had orders to march thither. We therefore immediately proceeded and arrived at Hartford, Conn., and tarried there about ten days, but in the meantime hearing that the British had left Rhode Island, we changed our course and went to West Point, where we wintered. The close of which completes my two years' service in the army.

This spring, about the first of April, about 1,000 of the most robust young men at West Point were selected and thoroughly trained, daily, in military tactics, for what future purpose we were not then informed. This military exercise lasted till the last part of June. Orders then came to us from Gen. Washington to march in our regimental coats, or if not, in our regimental shirts, but to what place none except the officers knew! All the orders we had were to march. We accordingly took up our line of march, and halted within two miles of Stony Point, which is eighteen miles from West Point, and when we halted it was about sunset. We were then drawn up under the command of Gen. Wayne, and the most severe orders were read to us of what we were to do that night. We were informed that we must take the enemy's fort by storm, and the question was proposed directly who would go first and with the point of the bayonet. All stood in profound silence. When our captain, Isaiah Stetson, said "I will go," then said Gen. Wayne, "go." Capt. Stetson answered, "I will choose my own men, I know what they are." The platoon I belonged to was in the middle, and consisted of about sixteen or eighteen soldiers. At eleven o'clock that night we were to start. Being myself near Gen. Wayne, I saw him with his watch, while he held it up by the starlight, and heard him say to us, "it is time to move." When we got up to start all the officers shook hands with our captain, and bid him farewell, never expecting to see him again in time. The orders were if any man was afraid to go with the company and storm the fort to stand aside. We were further ordered that if any man flinched back, he should be instantly put to death by his right-hand man, or his officer. As soon as we had entered the fort, the whole company cried out at the top of their voices, "We command you in the name of Gen. Washington to deliver up the fort." The shout was so loud that it could be heard at some distance. I entered the fort in the front platoon, a ball whizzed close by my ears. My right-hand man was wounded and my left-hand man killed. One of the enemy was about to kill the French Colonel who piloted us into the fort. My right-hand man, at the moment he was wounded, knocked off my hat, which I caught in falling. This wounded man cried out, "For God's sake, Cushman, don't leave me." But I made no reply, knowing my orders. The French Colonel previously surveyed this fort with a spy-glass, and when we entered the fort he was at my right hand, and rushed forward and took hold of the colors and pulled them down, which the British colonel, Johnson, seeing, ordered the men to lay down their arms. We lost of our men that night about twenty-eight, and the British lost about thirty men to my knowledge. This was a very strongly fortified fort; Colonel Johnson had said he would defy all the American army to take it. I counted thirteen brass mortars to throw bombs.

After taking the fort, I returned to West Point, and served my time out for which I enlisted, which was the eighth of next May following, when I got my discharge and came home to Plympton, being then nineteen years of age. In January of that year, at the age of twenty-seven, I went from Plympton to North Yarmouth, where I remained about five years, after which I went to Winthrop, and married Bathsheba Jennings, remained in that town one winter and came to Leeds, Maine, where I have lived during the past fifty-five years. When I first came to Leeds the place was almost a wilderness, there being no grist mill in the town at that time. I went to mill in the town of Winthrop, and often carried my grain on my shoulders, and my way was marked out by spotted trees. About five years after I came to Leeds the house in which I lived took fire, accidentally, and was burned to the ground. I saved nothing of my furniture, except a great silver spoon, a quart basin, and my money, amounting to about seventy dollars. I have been wonderfully carried through many imminent dangers, for which I desire to thank the Lord.

CUSHMAN FAMILY.

Isaac Cushman, a son of Andrew, succeeded his father on the old homestead, where he cared for his parents in their late lives, who had rendered him a like service in his youth. Very appropriately the family record of the old soldier and pioneer might here be introduced, and its absence is not attributable to the writer. In after years regrets for neglect may find their own reward.

Isaac, born in Leeds July 17, 1801; married first, Dorcas H. Loring, of North Yarmouth, Me. Their children were:
1. Corrilla F., b. April 16, 1841; d. Aug. 22, 1843.
2. Marcellus F., b. Aug. 9, 1842.
3. Corrilla F., b. Nov. 6, 1843.
4. Thirza S., b. Aug. 28, 1845.

Isaac married, second, Angeline Harvey, of Winthrop, Me. The fruits of the marriage were:
1. Flavilla A., b. April 15, 1854.
2. Angie D., b. March 27, 1856.
3. Emogene, b. Nov. 4, 1857.
4. John B., b. June 16, 1860; died Sept. 9, 1881.

Isaac Cushman was born, brought up and died on the old Cushman homestead at West Leeds. His age was 81 years, 6 months. His entire life was devoted to farming. His neighbors speak of him thus: "He was an honest man, and his word as good as gold. He was a hard-working man, always up and at it in the morning. He usually kept one or more hired men and knew when he got a good one." He manifested great interest in the education of his children, did what he could to aid them and lived to see the happy results. He lived an honest Christian life and died a triumphant death.

2. Marcellus F., his only son who grew to manhood, enlisted in the old store of Solomon Lothrop at Leeds Center, April 30, 1861. With him John Q. Robbins and Wansbrow Turner affixed their names to the roll of recruits to the Federal Army. They went to Monmouth, where they were drilled in military tactics, and in August mustered into United States service at Augusta, Me. Their regiment was at once sent to the front and continued to hold a front position all the time. When the advance on Richmond was in progress the Seventh Maine Regiment to which he belonged, was sent up the James River where it did skirmish duty. They met the Confederates at Warwick Creek and later at Williamsburg, Mechanicsville, Golden Farm, Savage Station, Malvern Hill, second Bull Run, and Antietam; after which the regiment came home to recruit. Feb. 14, 1863, he was discharged on account of disability. After spending a

few years at home on the farm, in 1868, he married Matilda, a daughter of Deacon Jason and Lydia (Gordon) Pettingill, of Leeds. His present residence is Waterville, Me., to which place he removed his family in 1886, and has since built himself a house in that city.

Their children were four in number, two of whom died in infancy, and another in childhood.

Rolinston F., the remaining child, was graduated from Coburn Classical Institute in 1891.

4. Corilla F. married Silas Harvey and occupies the homestead of her father and grandfather. Her husband being the only representative of his people, in Leeds, no place is more fitting in this work to present him than in the family of which his wife is a member. He was a native of Winthrop, Me., and a brother of Mrs. Cushman, second wife of Isaac Cushman. When a young man he followed the life of a sailor, first a coaster and later a whaler. In the latter service voyages of three or four years were made and numerous foreign countries visited. The life of a whaler is attended with hardships and dangers, to which he, like many another, was subjected. While absent on his last voyage he learned of the Civil War at home. On landing on his native soil he repaired to a recruiting office in Saco, Me., and in September, 1862, enlisted in the military service of his country. He went to the front as a recruit to the Fifth Maine Regiment, then in active service on picket line in front of Fredericksburg, and took part in the battle that followed. He was one of the men from the Fifth Maine Regiment who volunteered to cross the river in boats, under a hail-storm of rebel bullets which were being fired to prevent the laying of pontoon bridges. Many who started were killed or wounded, but enough there were who reached the shore to put the enemy to flight, and the bridges were laid without further hindrance. History enumerates the battles in which the regiment was engaged. After the battle of Gettysburg he was transferred to navy—ship Ino, where he was later made captain of a gun and remained until the close of the war. Returning to his native town, on a visit to his sister in Leeds, he became acquainted with and married Miss Cushman. They reside on the Cushman farm where peace and good-will abound, and where all the kin-folks and many friends are cordially received and shown the old landmarks. They have issue:

1. Ray L., b. in Leeds, Dec. 13, 1869;
2. Wilbert N., b. in Leeds, Jan. 18, 1872.

4. Thirza S., third child of Isaac, early manifested a desire to obtain an education and improved her time and talent in the schools of her native town. To obtain means to defray the expense of furthering her design, she entered the cotton mills in

Lewiston. After remaining there for a time, she was heard to say, "There is something higher for me." This motto characterized her after life financially, morally and spiritually. By her own efforts as a teacher, she obtained the money to pay expenses while in the State Normal School in Farmington, from which she was graduated with a high rank. As a teacher she was of the best. Although years have come and gone since she was a teacher in her native and other Maine towns, words of praise remain on the lips of her pupils, and her memory is dear to many of those who knew her best. In 1871 she went to Nebraska where she continued in her school work. In 1873 she married Professor J. W. Love, of Omaha, and as assistant to him, entered the Institute of which he was Principal. Both Mr. and Mrs. Love recently died—but a few months intervening—leaving two daughters whose residence is in Fremont, Neb.

5. Flavilla A. was graduated from the State Normal School at Farmington and became a successful teacher. She, like her sister, went to Nebraska, where she was several years engaged in school work, and later married Robert O. Fink—a real estate dealer in Omaha. They have three children.

6. Angie D., a graduate of the same school as the older sisters, followed the same vocation; first, in Maine, and later in Nebraska. She, too, was a young lady highly prized by her many friends whom she left in her native State. She married Franklin Tym, of Omaha, in which city they now reside. They have a son whose age is 7 years.

7. Emogene, the youngest daughter of Isaac Cushman, received a good common school education. She remained at home with her mother, to whom she was strongly attached, and ministered to her every want. She married E. Brown, of Wales, Me., where they now reside. The mother is a member of the family in which she has so long received tender care.

8. John B. died at the age of 21 years.

LINDSEY FAMILY.

In the early part of the 18th century, there lived in the North part of Ireland a Scotch family, consisting of a widow and two fatherless sons, whose names were James[1] and Thomas[1] Lindsey. In the year 1725, the family came out to America and settled in Bridgewater, Mass., where the mother had relatives. The sons were but 4 and 2 years old respectively, and although of foreign birth, lived more years in the New World than most native-born inhabitants. When reared to manhood in their forest homes, they married and devoted their energies to subduing the wild lands in the home of their adoption. In 1744, James married

Hannah, born in 1719, a daughter of William and Eleanor (Whitman) Turner, who were also the parents of George Turner, a pioneer of Leeds.

No fruit was born of this marriage. Thus the common progenitor of the Lindsey family, if not in this country, in this section of it, was Thomas.

I. Thomas, b. in the North of Ireland, in 1723; m. in Bridgewater, Mass., in 1745, Elizabeth, b. in 1722, a sister of his brother James' wife. To them were born in that town four children, to wit:

1. William^2, b. June 16, 1747.
2. James^2, b.
3. Thomas^2, Jr., b. 1756.
4. Hannah^2, b.

William and James were soldiers in the Revolutionary War, and soon after their discharge, in 1785, came to Littleborough where they settled, the former on the farm now occupied by one of his granddaughters, Catherine L. Knapp; and the latter near the buildings now owned and occupied by Greenwood C. Gordon—between them and the lake. Thomas, Jr., their younger brother, remained at home with his parents, for whom he cared until their decease, when in 1797 he, too, came to Littleborough and settled on Bishop Hill, where he took up the farm later occupied by his son, Howard, and now owned by one of his grandsons, Lewis L. Lindsey. On Dec. 25, 1802, returning on the ice from Wayne village on horseback, when nearing the home shore at the south end of Androscoggin Lake, both he and his horse broke through and were drowned. Hannah, their only sister, came to Littleborough in 1788, and made her home with James. In 1790, she was employed in the family of Thomas Stinchfield, whose wife died in 1791, leaving a family of children. In 1792 she married Mr. Stinchfield by whom she had one daughter, Hannah, who married Elizer Carver, Jr., and became the mother of a large family.

I. William^2, the eldest son of Thomas^1 and Elizabeth (Turner) Lindsey, m. in Bridgewater, in 1774, Hannah, a daughter of Increase and Catherine (Babcock) Leadbetter, who settled about 1786-7 on the farm now occupied by Samuel P. Francis at the extreme north end of the town. She was b. in Bridgewater Nov. 6, 1752. They had a family of eleven children, namely:

1. John[3], b. March 19, 1775; d. Feb. 1, 1834.
2. Polly[3], b. March 21, 1777; d. June 9, 1819.
3. Abigail[3], b. Jan. 26, 1779; d. July 23, 1813.
4. Azel[3], b. Jan. 6, 1781; d. July 23, 1802.
5. Hannah[3], b. June 17, 1783; d. April 13, 1874.
6. Lucy[3], b. Aug. 30, 1785; d. April 8, 1816.
7. Catherine[3], b. in Leeds April 15, 1787; d. March 27, 1823.
8. James[3], b. May 20, 1789; d. Feb. 28, 1870.
9. William[3], b. Aug. 26, 1791; d. March 31, 1810.
10. Betsey[3], b. July 24, 1793; d. July 30, 1796.
11. Archibald[3], b. May 22, 1795; d. Nov. 15, 1870.

Of the children of William and Hannah (Leadbetter) Lindsey,

1. John[3] went to Missouri when a young man where he married and died.
2. Mary (Polly), m. June 5, 1799, Capt. Roger Stinchfield (the first white male child born in Leeds—date, Feb. 9, 1781). She was the mother of nine children. She died in Marion, Iowa, June 10, 1819. Their children were Elizabeth (Mrs. Alpheus Lane); Azel (d. young); Alice S. (Mrs. Barnabus Davee); Sarah B. (Mrs. Herbert Libby); Ezra (who m. Abigail S. Johnson); Catherine (who d. young); Azel (d. young); John R. (who m. Maria L. Foster), and William (who d. in childhood).
3. Abigail was a maiden lady.
4. Azel died in Martinique.
5. Hannah was the second wife of Charles Knapp, a son of Joseph, a pioneer of Leeds. She will receive further mention with her family.
6. Lucy m. Simeon Knapp, another son of Joseph. She had a family of children, and two of her grandsons, Charles K. Hutchins and Charles B. Knapp, were captains in the late Civil War.
7. Catherine was the first wife of the aforesaid Charles Knapp and further mention will be made of her with her family.
8. James m. Lydia Lane in 1813, and some years later removed to Milo, Me., where he died. He raised a family of smart children, one of whom, John, was a captain in the Civil War.

9. William d. at the age of 19 years.
10. Betsey was a maiden lady.
11. Archibald m. first, Susanna Turner; second, a Mrs. Davis, by whom he had a daughter. He was a prominent man, a colonel in the militia, a thirty-second degree F. A. M. He d. in Milo, Me. His father, William, d. in Leeds March 31, 1831; and his mother, Elizabeth Turner, May 7, 1831.

II. James, second son of Thomas and Elizabeth (Turner) Lindsey, was born in Bridgewater, Mass., July 22, 1755. He m. Phebe, a sister to William and Obadiah Pettingill, early settlers of Leeds. She was born in Bridgewater Oct. 25, 1755. James d. Jan. 9, 1849, and Phebe, his wife, Oct. 13, 1843. They had eight children, namely:

1. Betsey, b. March 18, 1780; m. Welcome Bishop; settled in Lagrange, Me.; issue, James, Welcome, Thomas, Persia, Phebe and Job. d.———
2. Ann, a maiden lady; b. July 29, 1781; d. April 12, 1864.
3. Mary, b. Feb. 9, 1783; d. young.
4. Daniel, b. Feb. 11, 1784; m. in October, 1808, Jane Gilbert, and settled on the farm now owned by Rev. G. C. Gordon, where he remained until February, 1835, when, on account of poor titles to the real estate in that section of the town, with several others who had once paid for their farms, removed to Carroll, Me., where most of his family settled, and where he d. May 27, 1863. Issue:

   1. William Henry, b. Feb. 1, 1809; d. Oct. 18, 1850.
   2. Caroline, b. May 1, 1810; d. Dec. 15, 1895.
   3. James Greenleaf, b. Oct. 19, 1811; d. March 7, 1894.
   4. Charles Frederic, b. Dec. 13, 1813; d. in Minnesota.
   5. Julia Ann, b. Aug. 25, 1815; d. Nov. 28, 1858.
   6. Silas Augustus, b. Dec. 30, 1817; d. Oct. 9, 1845.
   7. Betsey, b. Oct. 16, 1819; d. ———.
   8. Alvin H., b. Nov. 13, 1821; d. April 20, 1896.
   9. Josephine B., b. Aug. 14, 1823; d. March 18, 1901.
   10. Clarinda F., b. July 19, 1825; d.———.
   11. Everett Howard, b. Sept. 3, 1827; d. ———, 1830.
   12. Wallace B., b. May 2, 1830; d. March 27, 1861.
   13. Daniel Webster, b. Aug. 5, 1832.
      The above named children of Daniel were b. in Leeds. It is said by some that the youngest

child was b. in Carroll. The date of his birth compared with the date of his father's removal from Leeds to that town is strong evidence against it.

William H. m. Sophronia Stevens; settled in Carroll; no issue.

Caroline m. Howard Lindsey; settled in Leeds; had issue; receives further mention in family of Howard.

James G. m. Ann Graffam, of Leeds, Sept. 13, 1842; settled in Carroll; had issue Charles F., b. Nov. 13, 1845; George S. and Silas (twins) b. Feb. 28, 1850; Rose Jane, b. March 3, 1855; James W., b. Feb. 13, 1857; Anna Ann, b. Oct. 28, 1859.

Charles F. m. Mary Bishop, of Leeds, had one son, Ernest, who came to Leeds, lived with his grandfather, Abial Bishop, and died when a young man. His father was two years in the Mexican War, participated in nearly every battle and witnessed the surrender of the city. He died in Minnesota.

Julia Ann was a maiden lady.

Silas D. m. Matilda Dunham; no issue.

Betsey m. John Douglass, of Lee; had issue Charles, Olive J., Frank, Herbert, Julia A., and Daniel W.

Alvin H. m. first, Eliza Muzzy, of Carroll; issue, Lorinda B. and Ernest; m. second, Augusta E. Gates, of Lincoln; issue, Daniel and Jennie.

Josephine B. m. Henry Douglass of Lee, Me.; issue, William, John L., Ellen, Isabelle, James, Wallace B., Abbie A., Carrie, Jefferson, and Forest.

Clarinda F., m. Ransom B. Austin, of Upper Stillwater; no issue.

Everett H. died in early boyhood.

Wallace B. m. Martha Brown, of Carroll; no issue.

Daniel Webster m. Abbie Gilpatrick, of Weston, Me.; issue Thomas, b. July 21, 1854; Elisha G., b. April 27, 1856; Mary E., b. Jan. 15. 1858; Martha E., b. Jan. 3, 1851; Josephine B., b. Nov. 18, 1867; Wallace B., b. Oct. 30, 1869.

5. Persis, fifth child of James and Phebe (Pettingill) Lindsey, b. March 10, 1786; m. in 1830, Elezer Carver; no issue.

6. Thomas, sixth child of James, b. in Easton, Sept. 1, 1789; m. in Leeds March 30, 1816, Olive

Creach, b. in Barnstable Aug. 9, 1784; settled in Leeds where Wallace Gordon now lives; later, in 1834, moved with his family to Carroll; issue, Elvira, Emeline, Orrin L., Nancy, Celia, Naomi, Ruth, Miranda, and Edward. Seven of the above children of Thomas were born in Leeds. Elvira, Oct. 14, 1817; m. July 14, 1836, Moses Larrabee, of Carroll; issue, seven children, namely: Henry, Melvin, Elvira, Lovina, Lucia, Everett B. and Freeman H. Eveline, b. Feb. 17, 1821; m. July 2, 1837, John A. Larrabee, of Carroll; issue, 1 daughter, Eveline. Orrin L., b. July 26, 1822; m. April 11, 1837, Abbie Lewis, of Lee; issue, five children, namely: Viola C., Evelyn F., Orrin H., Berton B., and Daisy. Nancy, b. Dec. 4, 1824; m. July 6, 1851, Eli H. Lamb, of Carroll; issue, Leonie, Frederic, Leonie. Celia, b. Aug. 16, 1826; m. Sept. 20, 1846, Joseph W. Staples; issue, Willis T., Rose E., Alma, Charles, Frank B., Myra B., and Roland H. Naomi, b. April 17, 1829; m. Nov. 17, 1850, William A. Farrar, of Carroll; issue, Olive B. and Daniel S. Ruth, b. Oct. 2, 1830; m. March 29, 1854, Elisha Rome, of Oldtown, Me.; issue, Minnie and Tena. Marinda, b. in Carroll Feb. 1, 1836; m. Nov. 21, 1858, Stillman H. Lothrop; issue, Elmina, Frederic and Harry. Edward, b. in Carroll Jan. 27, 1838; d. in Carroll July 22, 1838.

Thomas, parent and grandparent of the above, d. in Carroll April 21, 1864.

7. Alvin, b. Aug. 29, 1792; single; d. in New Brunswick.
8. James, the youngest child of James and Phebe Pettingill, b. June 12, 1795; d. July 8, 1795.

The foregoing comprises the children and most of the grandchildren of James Lindsey, one of the three pioneer brothers of Leeds.

III. Thomas, third and youngest son of Thomas[1], who came to this country in 1725, m. in Bridgewater, Mass., Thankful, a daughter of Jonathan Bailey. She was a sister to Desire Bailey, the wife of Capt. Seth Howard, who was an early settler of Leeds. Their children were:

1. Mary, m. in 1811, Alexander Jennings, of Leeds, and settled near the center of the town where they reared a large family and lived the remain-

der of their years. Her children receive mention in a sketch of the Jennings family.

2. Ira, m. Joanna Merrill, of Turner, by whom he had a daughter and son, Silvia, who married Lewis J. Pollard, and Levi, who was brought up in the family of his Uncle Howard, and later went west.

3. Roland went west with his brother, Ira, where he married and reared a family of which the writer knows little.

4. Hannah, m. Charles Bates, and settled on the Bates Hill, another name of which is Quaker Ridge. She was the mother of several children, whom we hope to present in a sketch of the Bates family.

5. Robert, b. Oct. 5, 1798; m. Vesta Merrill, of Turner in 1821, who was b. in that town in December, 1802; and d. Jan. 1, 1853. He d. Jan. 3, 1876. Both were taken to Massachusetts, where they were buried. They had issue:

1. Forest[4], b. Jan. 16, 1822; d. in Illinois.
2. Tiley Merrill[4], b. Oct. 24, 1823; m. Oren S. Bates in August, 1857; settled in Leeds; d. Aug. 1, 1889.
3. Ira L.[4], b. July 29, 1825; killed at Battle of Cold Harbor.
4. Maria Theresa[4], b. March 17, 1827; d. in Worcester, Mass.
5. Franklin Jennings[4], b. April 16, 1837; m. Hulda L. Richmond in April, 1871; now living in Turner, Me.
6. Converse Lowell[4], b. Aug. 21, 1842; disappeared from his hotel in New York several years ago and nothing of him has been learned since.

6. Howard, b. in Leeds Jan. 25, 1800, was the youngest son of Thomas and Thankful (Bailey) Lindsey. After attaining to manhood he assumed the care of his mother, and the farm on which his parents settled passed into his hands. There he spent his life. In October, 1829, he married Caroline, the eldest daughter of Daniel and Jane (Gilbert) Lindsey, who was born in Leeds May 1, 1810. They had issue ten children: Roland, Everett, Roscoe Greene, Rossa Jane, Frederick Shaw, Julia Ann, Thomas Jennings, George Albert, Lewis Leavitt, and Robert.

1. Roland, b. April 6, 1830; d. Aug. 6, 1855.
2. Everett, b. May 20, 1831, was a soldier in the Civil War. On the eleventh of November he enlisted in the Sixth Maine Battery to serve three years, or during the war; was injured in the battle of Cedar Mountain, and by reason of disability was discharged Feb. 18, 1863. On the 7th of September, 1864, he re-enlisted in the navy and attached to the United States war vessel Monadnock, took part in the capture of Fort Fisher. He was discharged June 26, 1865. March 11, 1866, he married Mary Jane, a daughter of Deacon Warren Howard, by whom he had one child who died at birth. Soon after, the mother died, in 1868. October 31, 1869, he married his brother's widow, Mrs. Eliza Ann (Berry) Lindsey. They had issue:

1. Mary Howard, b. Sept. 30, 1870.
2. Josephine A., b. Oct. 15, 1872.
3. Roscoe E., b. July 31, 1874.
4. Charles Frederic, b. Dec. 30, 1876; d. May 9, 1883.
5. George Albert, b. June 23, 1880.
Mr. Lindsey and family reside in North Monmouth.

3. Roscoe Greene, b. Feb. 5, 1833; m. in Leeds Jan. 17, 1856, Eliza Ann Berry. Their children were:

1. Clara J., b. in Leeds Nov. 29, 1856.
2. Howard E., b. March 2, 1858; m. Alice A. Crockett Nov. 6, 1880; is a merchant at North Monmouth.
3. Roland B., b. in Monmouth June 22, 1860; m. Maria L. Nutting, of Norridgewock, June 10, 1884. Residence, Lawrence, Mass.
4. Roscoe, Jr., b. in Presque Isle, March 20, 1862; d. in Leeds July 23, 1864. Roscoe G. enlisted in the Second Maine Cavalry Regiment, Co. I; d. at Barrancas, Fla., Sept. 9, 1864.

4. Rossa Jane, b. Sept. 8, 1834; m. Charles Warren Foster Nov. 2, 1854; have one son; reside in Lawrence.
5. Frederic Shaw, b. Sept. 29, 1837; enlisted with his brother, Everett, on the 11th of November, 1861, in the 6th Maine Battery. After a few months' service was discharged on account of disability. He died in Bangor Nov. 6, 1874.

6. Julia Ann, b. Oct 6, 1839; m. William Benson Sumner Jan. 24, 1864. They had issue three children—Caroline Howard, Sophia Benson and Robert Lindsey.
7. Thomas Jennings, b. March 12, 1844; enlisted in Co. I, 23d Me. Vol. Reg't service three months. Nov. 26, 1869, he m. in Lawrence, Mass., Grace Adelia Ladd, by whom he had one daughter. His residence is Lawrence, Mass.
8. George Albert, b. Dec. 17, 1845; m. Nov. 14, 1871, Mary Elizabeth Culver, of Groton, Mass. Their residence was Lawrence, Mass. He was a man of prominence in that city and none were held in higher esteem. His popularity was the reward of merit. He was in the city government, a member of the board of Aldermen. The several orders in which he held membership were Tuscan Lodge of F. A. M.; B. P. O. Elks, No. 65; Mt. Sinai R. A. C.; May-Flower Colony; Pilgrim Fathers. He was beloved, and when his death occurred, Feb. 9, 1893, the floral tributes, so bountifully bestowed, and the multitude of people who assembled to pay their last respects to the honored dead, best bespoke his true worth. He left no issue.
9. Lewis Leavitt, b. Dec. 8, 1847, when a young man, like most of his brothers, spent several years in Massachusetts. Later, he returned to the farm where he was born—where his father was born and on which his grandfather settled. He married in November, 1872, Flora E., a daughter of Abner and Mary H. Curtis, who was born in Leeds, June 2, 1852. They assumed the care of his parents, and when their last duty to them in life had been done, tenderly laid them to rest in the cemetery in the valley, westerly of where they died; the father, Jan. 21, 1880; the mother, Dec. 15, 1895. No words of the writer are necessary to present Mr. Lindsey and his family to the readers, and especially to the people of their native town, who know them best. Theirs is, and ever has been, a pleasant and hospitable home for all relatives and friends, who are many. They have two sons and three daughters:

1. Arthur L., b. July 15, 1874.

    2. Bertha M., b. Nov. 30, 1875.
    3. Alice B., b. June 3, 1880.
    4. Annie L., b. April 10, 1885.
    5. Harry C., b. Nov. 6, 1892.
10. Robert, b. Nov. 27, 1851; m. Annie Etta Smallidge, of Mt. Desert, in Lawrence, Mass., May 31, 1882. Their residence is Lawrence; have no issue. Robert was the youngest child of Howard and Caroline Lindsey, and went to Lawrence when a very young man. He is said to be a man of means and held in high esteem in that city.

7. Dorcas, who m. Abial Bishop in 1826, settled near her parental home and reared a family which is further mentioned in a sketch of the Bishop family.

KNAPP FAMILY.

The Knapp family trace their origin to Saxony, a province in Germany. Their early history in England leads many of the descendants to fix their nationality as Anglo-Saxon or English. The name is derived from a Saxon word, the root of which is spelled Cnoep; signifying a hill-top or summit. Of several of the same name who lived on the same hill, John occupied the top or knob, and thus was called John of the cnoep or knob. Subsequently, the preposition was eliminated, for convenience, and he was called John Cnoep; the German formation being Knopp, and the English Knapp.

The family Arms, together with a full description, may be found in the Herald's College, in London. They were granted to Roger de Knapp by Henry VIII, to commemorate his skill and success at a tournament held at Norfolk, England, in 1540, in which he is said to have unseated three knights of great skill and bravery. By the descendants of his son John, these Arms are still preserved as a precious memento of worthy ancestry. The Arms of a family are what a trade mark is to a merchant—his own private property. It is generally expressive of some important principle. The origin of the Arms of the Knapp family is given in English Heraldry. It describes them as used by John Knapp and his son John in 1600. They are expressive and full of meaning. The Shield and Helmet, clad in mail, denotes a preparation for war. The Shield on which the Arms are displayed is of gold, expressive of worth and dignity; the Arms in sable or black, denote authority; the three helmets on the shield are acknowledgments from high authorities for victories gained.

The helmet, which is placed between the shield and the crest and rests upon the former, is an esquire in profile of steel, with visor closed and turned to the right side of the shield. The wreath borne away by the victor, as represented on the sword, is positive proof of laurels won and honors bestowed. The Lion passant, on the shield, denotes courage, or consciousness of strength, and yet, walking quietly when not provoked or forced to defence. The Arm that bears the broken sword, indicates the character of the family. Though having fought in defence until the sword was broken, his courage does not fail; his arm is still uplifted; grasping the broken sword, and in the heat of battle he exclaims, "In God we Trust," which is the family motto. In the 15th century, the Knapp family was one of wealth and position in Sussex County, England.

In 1630, a large colony of well-to-do farmers left England under the command of Winthrop and Salstansall and landed on the coast of Massachusetts. Of the number were three brothers, namely: William, Nicholas and Roger Knapp.

William, who was born in England, in 1570, settled in Watertown, Mass. His children were William, Mary, Elizabeth, Ann, Judith, John and James. They and their children settled later in Taunton, Roxbury, Newton, Boston and Spencer, Mass.

Nicholas settled in Watertown, and his children by his first wife, Eleanor, were Jonathan, Timothy, Joshua, Caleb, Sarah, Ruth and Hannah. In 1648, he removed to Stamford, Conn., where by his second wife, Unity, his children were Moses and Lydia. His children settled in Norwalk, Greenwich, Rye, Peekskill, Danbury and other neighboring towns.

Roger settled in New Haven, and later in Fairfield, where by his will he mentions his wife, Elizabeth, and children, Jonathan, Josiah, Lydia, Roger, John, Nathan, Eliza and Mary. They settled in the towns of Fairfield County. In that century, and even as late as 1800 many spelled the name with one p, thus: Knap. One of the original proprietors of the town of Turner, Me., was Joseph Knap; to whom, with other Revolutionary soldiers, the grant was made for meritorious services rendered in that war. Although a proprietor, he was not a settler in that town. He was born in Scituate, Mass., and when a child, his mother moved to Bridgewater, where he was reared to manhood, and where he married Susan Packard. They had issue Joseph, Matilda, Elijah, Ziba and Rhoda. The father, and son Joseph, espoused the cause of liberty and independence, and although the son was but a mere boy, he accompanied the father and fought by his side through the war. This son,

Joseph Jr., was born in Easton, Mass., in 1763. Soon after his return from the army, in 1784, he married Eunice Carver and settled in Bridgewater. To them were born in that town, Bashaby, 1784; Simeon, 1786; Charles, July 2, 1788; Joseph, Sept. 14, 1790. In 1791, the parents and these children came to Littleborough, built their log house and hovel where the buildings on the town farm now stand, and there their other children were born, namely: John, in 1792; Elijah, 1794; Eunice, 1796; Polly, 1798; Stephen, Sept. 16, 1800; Ruth, 1802; Asa, 1804; Matilda, 1806; Betsey, 1808; Lucretia, 1810.

In the spring of 1792, Joseph, Sen., and his other children, followed from Bridgewater to Leeds, and settled a short distance northerly of Joseph, Jr., on the site where Barnabas Howard, Jr., later lived. This place, too, is now owned by the town.

Matilda, second child of Joseph, Sr., and Susan Packard, married Thomas Millet, a son of one of the earliest settlers of Leeds. They had no issue.

Elijah, third child of Joseph, Sr., married Patience Gould and settled in the Stinchfield neighborhood, near the town line. They had issue Pelatiah, Abial, Jane, Rhoda, Jared, Dorothea and Ward. Pelatiah married Abigail, the widow of Noah Wing, whose maiden name was Abigail Norris. To them two sons were born, namely: Abial D., whose second wife was Ella Millett; and Woodbury S., who married Rachael Greenwood, and who erected the buildings at North Leeds now owned by their only child, Willis Knapp. Pelatiah married a second time, and the issue was George Henry, who was many years conductor of a passenger train on the Farmington branch of the Maine Central Railroad; and Mary Ann, who now resides in East Livermore, his only remaining child.

Neither Jane, Rhoda nor Dorothea married; all dead.

Abial left home when a young man, and died without issue; Jared married Susan Gott; settled in Wayne, where he resided until death, which occurred in 1898. Their children were Elijah, who is a resident of that town, Miranda Ellen and Anson G. Ward married and settled in Saco, where he was many years an overseer in a cotton mill.

Ziba, fourth child of Joseph, Sr., settled where B. F. Trask resides: married Betsey Baisy, of Falmouth, Me., by whom he had three sons and two daughters, namely: William, Ziba, Cyrus, Betsey and Susan. William and Ziba went to sea and died of yellow fever; Betsey married a Mr. Redding, who was lost at sea; later married a Mr. Morse, of Gray, but of their issue we are not informed; Susan married a Mr. Knight, and her husband was also lost at sea. She, later, married a Mr. Johnson, of whom we are no further informed.

Cyrus graduated from the medical department of Bowdoin College in the class of 1825. He married Susan, a daughter of Rev. Thomas D. Francis, of Leeds. They settled in Winthrop in 1827, where he acquired a reputation as a physician. In 1838 he removed to Augusta, and after several years' practice there was appointed superintendent of the Insane Hospital. From there he went to Rochester, N. Y., and his fame became worldwide. Of his children, we know little more than the fact that one son became a skillful and widely noted physician.

Rhoda, fifth and youngest child of Joseph Knapp, Sr., married William Gott, of Greene, whose residence was near the line between that town and Leeds, and who in 1807, removed to Wayne and settled on the lake road near the town line, where they afterward lived and died, Rhoda, Dec. 21, 1850, and her husband, Jan. 10, 1860. To them eight children were born in Greene and six in Wayne, namely: William, Jr., b. Oct 6, 1795; m. Ruth Gould, of Livermore; settled in Livermore; later in Leeds; had issue Eliza, Malinda, Louisa and Joseph. Elijah, b. Feb. 1, 1797; m. Polly Stinchfield, of Leeds; settled on a portion of his father's farm; had issue Elvira and Mary Ann. Sarah, b. Oct. 5, 1798; m. Stephen Knapp, of Leeds, her cousin; settled in Leeds; reared a large family of children. Mehitable, b. Sept. 12, 1800; m. a Mr. Harrison; had issue. Jared, b. 1802; died young. Anson and Matilda, twins, b. May 27, 1804; former settled in Turner; latter m. Roland Maxim; settled in Wayne; had issue several daughters and one son, Martin V. Charles, b. July 1, 1806; m. Jane Foss; settled in Wayne; issue Gardiner G., Charles S., Elijah, William and Howard C.; later m. Annie Wood, of Mercer; issue John W., George H., John M. and Jennie M. Susan, b. in Wayne, July 21, 1808; m. Jared Knapp, her cousin. Mary, b. Oct. 31, 1810; m. Thomas Wing, of Fayette; issue Charles Wing, M.D.; Harrison, b. 1813, d. young; Jane, b. May 2, 1815; m. Loring Foss, of Leeds, no issue; Alfrida, b. July 12, 1817; m. Otis Howard, no issue. Aurelia, b. Jan. 15, 1821; m. Nathan Coffin, now of Leeds, issue Manley and Edith. The above children and grandchildren of Rhoda are given, for the reason that many of them are connected with other Leeds families.

Joseph Knapp, Sen., was a lineal descendant of William, the eldest of the three brothers who came to this country in 1630.

Returning to the family of Joseph, Jr., and Eunice (Carver) Knapp, Bashaby, their eldest child, never married.

Simeon, second child, m. Lucy Lindsey in 1806; settled in Kingfield, Me.; issue John, Levi, Louvisa, William, Irena and Statira. Simeon m. second, Jane Spear; issue Charles, Owen, Simeon, Rachael, Mary and Jane.

Charles, third child, will be mentioned farther on.

Joseph, fourth child, m. Deborah Cushman, of Leeds; settled in Kingfield; issue four sons and six daughters; one of whom is Judge Cyrus B. Knapp, of Livermore Falls; another is Mrs. Lemuel Sumner, who is an aged and much respected resident of Leeds.

STEPHEN KNAPP.

John, fifth child, m. Martha Wing; settled in Freeman, Me.; issue, seven or eight sons and three daughters.

Elijah, sixth child, m. Celia Pullen, of Kingfield, Me.; settled in Freeman; issue six sons and four daughters.

Eunice, seventh child, m. Zenas Vaughn, of Kingfield, Me.; issue nine children.

Polly, eighth child, m. Noah Blanchard, of Kingfield; issue Catharine, Elizabeth, Mary Ann, Lucretia and Joseph K.

Stephen, eighth child, b. in Leeds Sept. 16, 1800; m. Sarah, daughter of William and Rhoda (Knapp) Gott, of Wayne, in 1820. She was b. in Greene Oct. 6, 1798. They first settled in the town of Anson, Me., where they resided about three years, when he came back to Leeds and lived on the farm of his brother Charles, which is the same now owned by the town, until the spring of 1831, at which time he removed to the place now owned and occupied by his son, Steven D., where he spent his remaining years, which were many. He d. April 5, 1892, and his wife April 18, 1870. He was an honest, upright and truthful man. They had issue:

William G., b. in Anson, Dec. 27, 1821; m. Cynthia Ripley; lived first in Turner and later in Hartford; issue, Alma A., Susan Ellen, Mary, Henry, Delphinia, William, Lillian and Stella. He d. May 3, 1901, and his wife March 15, 1894.

Asa, b. in Anson Dec. 29, 1822; m. Sarah Thompson; settled in Turner; removed to Canton and subsequently to Livermore, where he d. Dec. 5, 1896, and his widow December, 1899. He was a farmer. Their children were: Isabelle, Ella, Hattie and Mary J. Mary J., b. in Leeds Aug. 12, 1825; m. Jacob Shaw, of Lowell, Mass. Issue, one child, Ada.

Rossa, b. March 2, 1827; d. Oct. 5, 1891; single.

Elizabeth, b. May 8, 1828; m. first, David Kenney; issue, Charles P.; m. second, Caleb Battles; issue Abbie and Winfield. She d. Sept. 16, 1893.

Charles, b. July 17, 1829; d. in California, Aug. 2, 1883.

Earl, b. Feb. 10, 1831; m. Eliza Berry. Both living; residence, Wilton, Me.; issue, Almira, Richard, Herbert, Isabella, Edward, Ina and Margie.

Lucinda, b. June 17, 1833; m. T. A. Dascom; residence, Leeds; issue, Anna A., Alice and George W.

Sarah F., b. April 2, 1836; m. first, Henry Dexter, of Wayne; m. second, John Fairbanks; no issue; d. March 19, 1898.

Stephen D., b. Nov. 22, 1839; m. Lizzie B. Moore, of Livermore, Nov. 1, 1867. She was b. March 23, 1850. They reside on the homestead of his father at North Leeds. Issue, Frank M., Willie B., Charles R. and Rollie D. The two oldest are married.

Ann R., b. Sept. 22, 1841; m. David Berry and settled at North Leeds on the old Berry farm, now owned by Russell S.

Gould; subsequently removed to California, where she died May 9, 1895. Their children were: Willis R., Charlie E., Fannie S. and Edith.

Ruth, ninth child of Joseph, Jr., m. Hon. Rufus J. H. Porter, of Kingfield; issue Matherine, Elizabeth, Mary Ann and Lucretia.

Asa, tenth child, d. when 8 years old.

Matilda, eleventh child, m. Stephen Pullen, of Kingfield; issue two sons and four daughters.

Betsey, twelfth child, m. Nathan Peabody, of Freeman; issue four sons and one daughter.

Lucretia, thirteenth child, m. John Thompson, of New Portland; issue two sons and two daughters.

Charles, third child of Joseph, Jr., b. in Bridgewater, Mass., July 2, 1788; came to Leeds with his parents when 3 years old— 1791. In 1810 he married Catherine, a daughter of William Lindsey, one of three brothers who settled in Leeds. He remained on the homestead and carried his wife there. Later he removed to the home of his wife's father, which is the farm now owned and occupied by Catherine L. Knapp. They assumed the care of her parents. There he erected buildings and spent the remainder of his life. To them were born:

Azel, May 20, 1811; Abigail L., March 3, 1814; Colista, May 15, 1816; Hannah L., March 17, 1818; Archibald L., Aug. 7, 1819; Charles Sewall and Catherine, Aug. 15, 1821. His second wife was Hannah, his first wife's sister. To them was born a daughter, Catherine L., Aug. 31, 1825.

Uncle Charles Knapp, as he was familiarly known both near and far, was an industrious, enterprising and honest farmer. As a boy he was always busy, never allowing an hour to pass without something to show for it. He commenced working out for a peck of corn per day in compensation for his labor. When he was grown and for many years after his marriage, his winters were spent in the woods in the northern part of the State, where he commanded better pay than any of his fellows, for the good reason that he earned it. Not only was his own team fed by four o'clock in the morning, but the others were gotten ready by him, while their drivers were sleeping. Such was his course through life,—always driving his work before him. By his labor and economy he acquired a goodly amount of property—such as honest toil merits. His was a home of hospitality, and seldom free from some of the many of his relatives who made it a haven if sickness or misfortune came upon them. Seconded by two of the most patient and sympathetic women Leeds ever raised, he always made them welcome and tenderly cared for them until restored to health. But no drones could long inhabit his hive; a place for them was at once found in the field or woodland, which

CHARLES KNAPP.

HANNAH L. POLLARD.

they accepted or hunted their honey in other bowers. Work was his nature, but never was he so busy if his neighbors, near or remote, were sick, that he could not find time to do theirs. Seemingly severe on lazy people, he was tender and kind to the needy and sick, and always ready to aid those who would try to help themselves. In the cause of education was he likewise interested. His children and others whom he assisted in that most noble enterprise, were urged and required to do earnest work. His eldest son, Azel, was liberally educated and went to Missouri, where he successfully engaged in teaching in the schools of that state. He was subsequently a preacher of the gospel and died at the age of 33 years, Aug. 10, 1844.

His second child, Simeon, died when 11 years old, July 27, 1823.

Abigail L., the next child, m. Isaac Stinchfield Sept. 8, 1834. Her children are mentioned in the sketch of the Stinchfield family.

Colista, fourth child, m. Samuel Leadbetter May 16, 1838; settled in Glenburn, Me.; issue Mary, Lucius, Herbert, Roscoe, Charles and Horace. She died in Bangor Jan. 23, 1872.

Hannah L., next in the list, was liberally educated, and especially fitted herself for a teacher, in which work she was many years engaged in her native town and various others in the State. We recall no one who had a greater or more successful experience than she. Feb. 16, 1859, she married Barnabas Davee, and located where she now resides. He was a man of prominence in Leeds, as per records of the town, having ably discharged the duties of the various offices to which he was, from time to time, elected. He is pleasantly remembered as a teacher of vocal music, in which position he was a long time engaged. After his decease she married, Nov. 17, 1878, Lewis J. Pollard, who shared her home, ever made pleasant and enjoyable by her kind and genial disposition, witty sayings and fostering care. Although her faculties are wonderfully good, she is not so young as she used to be; yet by no means old at eighty-three. No issue.

Arch L., sixth child of Charles, married in February, 1844, Jane White; settled in Leeds; later removed to Dixfield and subsequently to East Livermore. They had issue Flavilla, Rose Emma, Charles, Bradford and Jennie.

Flavilla, married; resides in Farmington and has a family;
Rose Emma, married; resides in Dakota and has issue;
Charles, married; resides in East Livermore and has a family;
Bradford, married; wife died; no issue;
Jennie, married, resides in the west.

Arch L. was an honest, industrious man—a worthy son of noble parents, a kind and indulgent husband and father. He died at the home of his son, Bradford, in New Sharon, Me., May 8, 1897. His place of burial is in East Livermore.

Charles Sewall, seventh child, had a twin sister who died in infancy or early childhood. He married Vesta A. Soule Oct. 12, 1854. He remained on the homestead of his father where he worked from the cradle to the grave. He was a man of honesty, integrity and uprightness, and commanded the respect of all who knew him. He died Jan. 5, 1892. They had issue Mary, Bartley and Ralph. Mary is dead; Bartley is a locomotive engineer in Wisconsin; married; Ralph is on the old homestead; twice married; widower; has issue.

Catherine L., youngest child of Charles Knapp, was highly educated and a very able teacher in many of the schools in the State. Her early years gave promise of a very successful and useful life. Possessed of a liberal endowment of executive ability, a pure, powerful and progressive mind, none were better qualified or fitted for the higher pursuits of life than she. That the misfortune of others should mar or pervert a life of such promise is a matter of the greatest regret. Her family ties, her sense of duty has made hers the life of a benefactress, yes, more, a living martyr. She has grown prematurely old in the service; yet, her great sacrifice is too little appreciated by those for whom it has been made. She is a maiden lady of 75 years.

Charles Knapp died Sept. 26, 1875. His place of burial is in the Robert Gould cemetery, at North Leeds, where many of his people are reposing.

STEPHEN FOSTER.

One of the early settlers of Littleborough was Stephen Foster, a native of Winthrop. He came from that town with his family in 1786. He was the youngest of eleven children, sons and daughters of Capt. Timothy Foster, who was born in Attleborough, Mass., May 14, 1720. The wife of Capt. Timothy was Sibler Freeman, born Oct. 29, 1723. They removed from Attleborough to what is now Winthrop, Me., in 1765. The spot selected for his home was on the westerly shore of Cobbosseecontee Lake and about two miles from its northerly end, an extensive meadow, and brook running through it, close by.

His dwelling was at the southerly end of a lateral moraine, about ten rods from the Lake shore and well protected from prevailing winds. Here, in the wilderness, with fish and game all around him, Stephen Foster, best known as "Old Hunter Foster," was born, Feb. 28, 1766,—the clerk quaintly adding to the records these words: "The first Christian Child born in this Plantation." At the date of his birth, this was the only family in the vicinity. They were on the extreme verge of civilization. West to Lake Champlain, north to Canada line, there was no echo from the settler's axe, or smoke from his fires seen curling through the foliage. Born and reared under these circumstances, it is no wonder that he loved the woods and the excitement of the hunt and chase. His boyhood days thus spent, so hardened and toughened his muscles and matured his instincts, that he was accepted in his father's company of militia at the age of fourteen, and took part as soldier therein in the disastrous campaign against Bagaduce in 1779.

In 1785 Capt. Timothy Foster died from the effect of a blow on his head from a falling tree.

Winthrop was now getting so dense in population, its game either captured or driven back—that less hunted fields were to be sought, if "Old Hunter" was to succeed in his chosen calling. In his rovings through and about the country he could not have failed to see that in and around the waters of "The Great Androscoggin Lake" and particularly of Dead River, the game would thrive in abundance, and so, with a hunter's instinct, he selected this place for his future home. In previous years, when on these hunting expeditions, his camp was a hollow, giant maple tree standing on the Stinchfield cape on the northerly side of Dead River between its bends, nearly opposite the "Carrying Place." Stones and a few bricks which constituted his fire-place remain there to this day, and the spot is called "Old Foster's Camp." The log house to which he moved his wife and two sons, Stephen and John, was located on the southerly side of Foster Brook, a few rods easterly of where the railroad crosses it, at the extreme southeastern border of Androscoggin Lake. The farm he redeemed from the wilderness has since remained the property of his descendants, and is now occupied by a great-granddaughter, Mrs. Orrie A. (Foster) Davis. Farming, however, with him was incidental. Hunting and trapping in their seasons were his chief pursuits in which he was an expert and became widely known. His wife was Sally Streeter, by whom he had seven children. She died, and in 1835 he married Diadama, widow of William Johnson, of Monmouth, and for a time lived with her in her home in that town. The union did not prove harmonious, separation soon followed and he returned to his old home in Leeds.

Mr. Foster was for a time a member of the Society of Friends and conformed to their habits and dress. It is related that on one occasion he became so highly exasperated at his treatment by one of his neighbors, that his temper got the better of the peaceful tenets of the order, and divesting himself of his coat, throwing it on the ground exclaimed, "Lay there, old Quaker, till I've licked this fellow," which having executed satisfactorily, resumed his garb.

His death was the result of an unfortunate mistake. He left his home on one of the last days of March for Augusta, to collect his pension. The route was over Bishop Hill and past the residence of Zadoc Bishop, one of Leeds' earliest settlers. Meeting Mr. Bishop by the wayside he must stop and have a talk. While so engaged Mr. Bishop casually remarked, "You have lived all your life in the woods and know everything that grows there, tell me what is that bush growing up out of the wall there, I've thought it might be Dogwood and would like to know." Mr. Foster replied, "I don't know what it is, bring me some. I can tell if it is Dogwood—I know Dogwood." A twig bearing red berries and dried leaves was brought. Looking it over carefully Mr. Foster says, "No, it isn't Dogwood. I don't know what it is, but I know Dogwood and it isn't that, I am not afraid to eat it," and taking leaves and berries into his mouth, chewed them vigorously and soon drove on.

It was not long before he felt a soreness in his mouth and a sickness coming upon him, and by the time he reached the home of Enos Fairbanks in Winthrop, about four miles distant, he was violently sick. Mr. Fairbanks was an old acquaintance, born in the same neighborhood. They had always known each other and Mr. Foster was accustomed in his trips to Winthrop to call on his old friend.

He now stopped from necessity, and his condition was found so serious that medical aid was at once summoned from the village three miles distant. Nothing could avail, and after a day or two of intense suffering, the old pioneer, the adventurous and skilful hunter and youthful soldier closed his eventful life, April 2, 1842.

The funeral service was held in the Universalist Meeting-House in Winthrop village, conducted by Rev. Giles Bailey, the pastor. The services being closed, a grandson of the deceased tendered the minister the usual fee. A person who had assisted in the musical exercises standing near by, said to the minister after the grandson had retired, "Mr. Bailey, you've preached the old hunter into Heaven, with all his horses, his dogs, his guns and his traps, and you've only got ten dollars for it; Parson Thurston wouldn't have done it short of twenty-five."

The burial was in the "Fairbanks Cemetery" in Winthrop. On this elevated spot, overlooking the home of his boyhood, the Lake now widely noted for its beauty and as a place of public resort, the hills and meadows where his youthful muscles were trained and hardened for his chosen calling, his remains were quietly laid at rest beside his kin-folks.

Years came and sped by, another generation had lived and passed away, the place unmarked and forgotten, when, after a prolonged and diligent search, it was at last discovered, a plain slab of marble erected, marking the spot and recording the fact, that here rests the remains of "A Soldier of the Revolution" and of "The First Christian Child born in this Plantation."

[It has been known to the author several years, that diligent search for the grave of Winthrop's first-born white child and Leeds' early adopted son had, at last, been rewarded, and a memorial with a fitting inscription thereon erected thereat. Without the knowledge or consent of Winthrop's most highly esteemed historian and philanthropist, to whose favor and kindness the people of both towns, and especially the family are indebted for the foregoing interesting story of the adventurous life and tragic death of the "Old Hunter," and the properly inscribed memorial where his remains are reposing, I present the name of the Hon. John M. Benjamin.]

For the benefit of the descendants of Stephen Foster and others who may be interested in preserving and perpetuating a genealogical record, the following is subjoined: Capt. Timothy Foster, the pioneer of Winthrop, was b. in Attleborough, Mass., May 14, 1720, and his wife, Sibler Freeman, Oct. 29, 1723. They were m. in 1744, and to them were b. in that town ten children, and another in the year following their settlement in Winthrop in 1765. He was a member of the first board of selectmen of Winthrop and frequently re-elected to that and various other public offices in his town. He died April 3, 1785, and his widow Dec. 8, 1813.

Their children were:

1. Timothy, Jr., b. March 21, 1745;
2. Billy, b. Sept. 24, 1747;
3. Eliphalet, b. July 27, 1749;
4. Susan, b. April 15, 1751;
5. David, b. May 26, 1753;
6. Thomas, b. May 23, 1755;
7. Stuart, b. April 8, 1757;
8. John, b. April 20, 1759;
9. Oliver, b. March 5, 1761;
10. Sibler, b. April 27, 1763;
11. Stephen, b. Feb. 28, 1766.

Soon after the battle of Lexington was fought, April 19, 1775, four of the sons of Capt. Timothy Foster, to wit: Capt. [2]Billy, [3]Eliphalet, [6]Thomas and [8]John, repaired to the headquarters of the Provincial Army, at Cambridge, Mass., enlisted in the privateering service, and never returned to their home fireside. Another of his sons, [9]Oliver, we are unable to account for.

1. Timothy, Jr., married Abigail Allen and had issue:
Otis, b. May 8, 1773;
Daniel, b. June 3, 1775;
Elizabeth, b. Aug. 29, 1777;
Molly, b. Feb. 24, 1783;
Hannah, b. Nov. 17, 1786.

Timothy, Jr., died Aug. 1, 1825.

4. Susan, married Micajah Dudley (not traced);

5. David, married Jan. 13, 1783, Millicent Howe, born April 25, 1762, and d. Jan. 3, 1820. They had issue:

Ann, b. Dec. 11, 1783;
Ichabod, b. June 9, 1785;
Preston, b. April 30, 1788;
Clarissa, b. Aug. 6, 1790;
Lavina, b. July 8, 1792;
Freeman, b. Dec. 30, 1793;
David, Jr., b. July 4, 1795;
Nathan, b. March 2, 1798;
John Winthrop, b. Feb. 12, 1800.

7. Stuart, married Jerusha Wadsworth. Their children were:

Wadsworth, b. Jan. 7, 1788;
Oliver, b. Aug. 29, 1789;
Sibyl, b. July 21, 171;
Moses, b. Nov. 10, 1793;
Eunice, b. Jan. 4, 1796;
Isaac, b. April 22, 1798;
Stuart, Jr., b. June 7, 1800.

10. Sibler, married Ephraim Stevens, b. June 29, 1758; and had issue:

Hannah, b. Jan. 6, 1783;
Thomas, b. May 29, 1784;
Aran, b. Feb. 26, 1786;
Ephraim, Jr., b. March 17, 1788;
Eliphalet, b. April 11, 1790;
Sybil, b. March 15, 1792;
Joshua, b. March 21, 1794;
Anna, b. Jan. 20, 1796.

11. Stephen married Sally Streeter and had issue Stephen, Jr., b. in Winthrop, in 1784-5; m. Adeline Drake and settled in West Leeds, where they lived a long time; later removing to Lagrange, Me., where he died. They had issue nine children, viz.:

Adaline and Stephen (twins), Amanda, James, Columbus, Orra A., Phœbe, Melissa and Harriet. These were born in Leeds; yet most of the descendants of Stephen, Jr., reside in Lagrange.

John, second child of Stephen, b. in Winthrop, in 1786; m. Priscilla Gilbert in 1801. They settled and lived in Leeds, where he d. Oct. 16, 1853; and his widow Feb. 6, 1861. Our data says they had nine children.

Timothy, third child of Stephen, b. in Leeds Dec. 3, 1787; m. Nancy Morse in 1806. They lived on the homestead of his father. Mr. Foster, by his industry and close attention to farming accumulated property. When the Androscoggin Railroad was built, he subscribed heavily to the stock, induced by the promise that a railroad station should be built near his house and the agency given to one of his sons. It was built there; but, a little later removed to its present site at Leeds Center. Mr. Foster retained an antipathy against the company who fraudulently obtained his money, rendering him or his little equivalent therefor. He d. in Leeds July 27, 1867, and his widow Oct. 2, 1871. They had issue eleven children, namely: Alonzo, Amelia, William Henry, Leonard, Amanda, Ward L., Charles Robert, Martha R., Lydia, Emeline and Everett.

Alonzo, first child of Timothy and Nancy (Morse) Foster, went away from Leeds when young, and no further data is at hand;

Amelia, second child of Timothy, no data;

Rev. William Henry, third child of Timothy, b. in Leeds, March 12, 1812; m. in May, 1840, Harriet L. Curtis, and settled in Leeds. In 1844 he was assigned to the Fayette circuit in the Maine Methodist Conference, and for a period of 46 years, he continued a Methodist minister; since which time he has held a superannuated relationship with the conference.

His present residence is Livermore Falls.

To them were born:

Orrie A., in Leeds May 20, 1841; m. Alonzo Davis. They reside on the Foster homestead in Leeds; no issue; Timothy H., in East Livermore; d. in New Portland when a small boy;

Charles Henry, in East Livermore, Oct. 4, 1845; d. in Leeds, May 9, 1900, where he had held the office of Railroad Station Agent several years; single;

Hattie A., in New Portland July 11, 1847; m. Lorenzo Leadbetter; lives in California; no issue;

Alice I., in East Readfield in 1855; m. Lyman Kempton; residence Rangeley; no issue;

N. Emma, in New Sharon Feb. 3, 1858; m. Albert Simpson; residence California; three children.

Leonard, fourth child of Timothy, died.

Amanda, fifth child, m., but her family is broken and she is dead.

Capt. Ward L., the 6th child, settled in Massachusetts; no record of his family. He was 3 years in the Civil War and Captain of a Massachusetts company.

Martha R., seventh child of Timothy, m. a Mr. Russell and settled in Waterville, Me., where she died. Lydia, the next child; account wanting. Emeline, m. John Frank Jennings, of Leeds, is now living. They have a daughter, Gertrude.

Charles Robert, another child of Timothy and Nancy Foster,

b. in Leeds Feb. 14, 1825; m. Sarah Stevens. They had issue two children, Charles Freemont and Henry Ward. Their residence is Lowell, Mass. Mr. Foster was a farmer and shoemaker. He spent his early life on a farm. He was in the late Civil War and died at the Soldiers' Home, in Chelsea, Mass., April 1, 1901.

Everett, the youngest child of Timothy, was born in Leeds Nov. 20, 1837. As a boy and young man he followed the pursuits of farmer and shoemaker. When opportunity offered, his gun and traps were in evidence, which he much enjoyed. Early in manhood he entered the railroad machine shops at West Farmington, where he learned the machinists' trade. After four years' service he went out on the road as engineer of a freight locomotive, which he run ten years, when, in 1879, he was given the passenger train out of Farmington, where he remained until his death, March 12, 1901. In 1858, he married Mary J. Morse. They had issue five children, one of whom only is remaining, the others dying in childhood. Frank L., their only child now living, b. Aug. 14, 1865, graduated from Wendell Institute, Farmington, in 1880. From school, commenced firing his father's engine, and in due time became an engineer. April 12, 1890, he married Sadie E. Pratt, of New Vineyard, Me. His residence and that of his mother is Farmington, Me.

Sally, fourth child of Stephen, the pioneer, was b. in Leeds in 1790. In June, 1809, she m. Ebenezer Libby and settled in Leeds, where they remained through life and where their five children were born, viz.: John, Ebenezer, Tillotson, Stephen and Jane.

Abigail, their fifth child, sometimes called Tabbie, was born in 1800. Jan. 1, 1818, she m. Lewis Jennings, who later died, and she m., second, Sullivan Lothrop, in February, 1831. She was the mother of nine children.

Hannah, the next child of Stephen, b. in Leeds Jan. 8, 1804; m. Nov. 14, 1831, Daniel Irish, by whom she had several children. He died and she m. second, Charles Crummett and bore him children. She d. Sept. 27, 1888.

Ann, the youngest child of Stephen, the pioneer and hunter, was b. in Leeds, Aug. 28, 1807. Dec. 22, 1822, she m. Robert Crummett, of Leeds, and settled at Leeds Center, where they kept an inn many years. They had five children.

An unusual effort has been made to obtain a more complete sketch of this family, and especially dates; but little interest has been awakened, and we submit it with many thanks to those who have contributed a portion of what is contained therein.

BREWSTER FAMILY.

Morgan Brewster, the sixth in regular descent from Elder William Brewster, of the Mayflower, was born in Lebanon, Conn., Aug. 26, 1762.

His parents were William Brewster, born Aug. 13, 1741, and Olive (Morgan) Brewster, born May 8, 1737. His boyhood was spent on his father's farm in Lebanon, Conn., and Rome, N. Y. His school privileges were limited, but by perseverance he obtained a fair education.

He served three years in the Revolutionary War and was once taken prisoner by a British sailing vessel.

After the close of the war he went to Hanover, Mass., and worked at shipbuilding. He married Martha Stetson, at Hanover, March 31, 1785.

In the spring of 1786, he moved his family to Freeport, Me., and during the summer he walked through the wilderness, by spotted trees, to Littleborough and bought a one-hundred-acre lot, where Job Young had a small opening and had built a log house.

In the spring of 1787 he moved his family to their new home in the wilderness, and planted a small piece of corn where Job Young had burned off the wood. That season he commenced clearing away the sturdy forests, and the next season he planted several acres of corn and potatoes.

He built a barn in 1790. Previous to 1794 he had built a framed house and moved into it, having lived in the old log house seven years.

Many were the hardships he had to encounter during the first years of his abode in Littleborough.

There was no grist mill nearer than Turner. With a bag on his back, containing 5 pecks of corn, he tramped through the woods, guided by spotted trees, to Turner village and back, a distance of twelve miles. He used to work in a ship yard at Hallowell with Levi Bates, one of his neighbors. In figure Morgan was short, stout and robust and very quick. Levi was tall and slim. They would work until Saturday noon and then walk home, a distance of twenty miles. The writer has heard Grandfather Morgan say, that he was obliged to take five steps to Mr. Bates' three, but had no trouble in keeping up. They worked all one winter for (two and six) 42 cents per day with board.

He died Feb. 13, 1856, aged 93 years, 5 months, 17 days.

He raised a family of seven children. William, the eldest, married Christina Briggs, of Greene, and unto them were born sixteen children, several of whom are now living. He was one of the early settlers of Parkman, Me., was a prosperous farmer and held many offices of trust; was chairman of the Board of Selectmen many years; religious preference, Baptist.

Mary, their second child, married Aaron Morse.

Lydia, next in the list, married David Lane and settled in Leeds. They had issue four children, one of whom, Louisa, is now living, aged 70 years.

Oliver, their fourth child, married first, Arvida Briggs; and second, Lyman Wheeler. She was the mother of seven children, one of whom is now living, Orin Wheeler, of Lisbon.

Martha married William Sprague, of Greene. She was the mother of five children of whom only one, Mrs. Lorania Ray, of Webster, is now living.

Morgan, Jr., married Hannah Robinson and settled on the lot next south of his father. He had a family of four children, two of whom are now living,—Mrs. Hannah Steven, of Island Pond, Vt., and Bryant M. In his declining years he gave his property to Orin Sprague to take care of himself and wife during their natural lives, which duty Mr. Sprague performed with tenderness and care, to the entire satisfaction of all concerned. He died Feb. 8, 1881.

Salmon, the youngest son, was born Sept. 4, 1802. Nov. 23, 1823, he married Betsey, daughter of Zebedee Shaw, of Greene. They settled on the homestead farm with his father. His occupation was farming, carpenter, painter and sleigh manufacturer.

In 1847, he opened a general store on Quaker Ridge and continued there until 1855. When the Androscoggin Railroad commenced operations in Leeds, in 1852, he built a store at Curtis Corner and did a successful business until 1863, when he sold out to his son, Henry M.

He was a prominent Methodist and the first class leader in Leeds. Through his efforts and liberality, the church on Quaker Ridge was built. In 1856, he sold his old homestead farm on Quaker Ridge and bought a farm at Curtis Corner, where he built a large and commodious house which he occupied during the remainder of his days. His wife died Feb. 28, 1857. In September, 1857, he married Laverna C., widow of Arza Gilmore. She bore him two children.

He was postmaster at Curtis Corner from 1853 to the time of his death, which was Dec. 9, 1887.

His children were Octavia Ann, born March 4, 1824; married Ormand T. Wing and has two sons now living, O. D. and F. B. Wing, merchants at Keen's Mills. She died Oct. 4, 1898.

His second daughter, Martha, born June 26, 1826; married Job C. Dennen and died in April, 1857.

His eldest son, Henry M., born Nov. 3, 1831, was educated in the common and high schools, and spent his boyhood working on the farm. After reaching the age of sixteen, he was occupied on the farm and driving a team to haul goods from Hallowell to Quaker Ridge, and in the store. At the age of twenty-one, he

HENRY M. BREWSTER.

took charge of his father's store at Curtis Corner; was appointed assistant postmaster and has had continuous charge of the office as assistant and postmaster up to the present time.

Jan. 1, 1853, he was appointed railroad station agent at Curtis Corner, which position he held forty years and one month. In 1857, he purchased one-half interest in the store and the business was conducted under the firm name of S. Brewster & Son until 1863, when he purchased his father's share and continued to do a successful business for many years. In 1898, he rented one-half of his store to R. D. Rand & Co.; since that time has kept a stock of tobacco, cigars, confectionery, stationery and small wares.

He has held a commission as justice of the peace and trial justice for the past thirty-eight years; solemnized thirty-three marriages; conducted fifty-seven funerals, and has also done considerable business as administrator. Has attended forty-seven annual town elections, and every state and national election since 1853. His political and religious preferences have always been decidedly republican and Methodist. He has always been an earnest advocate of temperance, a total abstainer from intoxicating liquors and tobacco, and is a member of the Subordinate Lodge of Good Templars; of Maine Grand Lodge, and the Supreme International Grand Lodge of the World.

In 1859, he married Angela, daughter of Abial D. and Dorcas (Lindsey) Bishop. She bore him four children, Hattie M., born Oct. 16, 1863; married Albion H. Hodsdon; lives in Watertown, Mass., and is the mother of two children: Maria B., born April 30, 1867; unmarried; Charles B., born Nov. 23, 1871; married Lizzie, daughter of Hon. Thomas H. Boothby; is a successful farmer, living on the Isaac Boothby farm. They have one child, Carrol H., born July 4, 1882; living with his parents.

Salmon C., son of Salmon, was born Jan. 21, 1844. He entered the Union Army in 1863, and served until the close of the war. He married Henrietta, daughter of Stephen Libby. She is the mother of two sons, Charles H. and George, both living. He died June 20, 1888.

Jennie M., eldest child by his second wife, was born in September, 1858. She married Frank A. Tinkham, merchant and postmaster at South Monmouth. She is the mother of seven children, all living.

Albion, born in July, 1860; married Lilla, daughter of Moses G. Beal; died June 11, 1895.

GOULD FAMILY.

The name Gould, from whom the families of Leeds and other New England towns have descended, is first found in what is now Saco, Me. In 1725, three English brothers, Pelatiah, William and Simeon came out to the wilds of America. Soon after their arrival in this country Simeon died; William went to Ohio, where he settled and reared a family; Pelatiah settled in Saco, and from him the Goulds of Leeds trace their line of ancestors. A son, Samuel, born in that town in 1750; died at the age of 42 years. He was the father of eleven children, namely: Isaac, Robert, Joseph, Simeon, Samuel, Pelatiah, John, Eunice, Patience, Dorcas and Sally; all of whom except Eunice and Sally, came to Leeds. In 1808, Isaac and Robert came to North Leeds for the purpose of shaving shingles. So well were they impressed with the place, the following spring found the other members of the family there. They constituted a colony of their own and settled near each other; Isaac, about one-quarter mile southerly of the railroad station; Robert, where Aubry Edgecome now resides; Joseph, where J. F. Burnham is living; Simeon, on the place now occupied by Welcome B. Gould; Samuel, on the hill northerly of the buildings of the late William Boothby; Pelatiah, where now Freedom Gould resides, and John, where Fred H. Knight now lives. The children of Isaac were George, Rufus and William.

Robert, who d. in 1868, reached a greater age than any other resident, 99 years; m. Annie Parcher, and had issue Jeremiah, Oren, Asa, Robert, Harrison, Olive, Philena, Sally, Eunice and Cordelia.

Joseph, m. ——— Hanes; issue William, Annie, Ruth, Betsey and Joseph.

Simeon, m. first, Stewart; issue Calvin, Stewart and Ingraham. Simeon m. second, Betsey Leadbetter. She was said to be, like some other step-mothers, unpleasant at times and cruel at other times. In retaliation, on a certain occasion, Ingraham used a chair in self-defense and floored the old lady. This, in one way, was a profitable feature in the life of the boy. His father gave him the remaining time of his minority after digging and removing the stumps on a certain piece of land. So great was the sympathy for the boy, all the young men and boys in the neighborhood turned out and helped perform the work. Thus resulted his fight for liberty and freedom.

The children of Simeon by his second wife were: Samuel, Eli, Lloyd, Caroline, Elizabeth, Frank and Russell.

Samuel m. Ruth Besse and settled in that portion of Leeds which was annexed to Wayne. They had issue Samuel, Phœbe, Hamilton, John and Pelatiah (twins), Patience, Jabez, Pelatiah,

ELISHA D. GOULD.

Abigail, Theodore, Cyrus, Ruth, Hepsibeth, Luther, Ruth, Granville and Elias. Of this family, two or more are now living; Cyrus, who resides in Wayne and whose age is 85 years, and Hamilton, whose residence is in Wilton, who is nearing the century mark.

Pelatiah, b. in Saco, Me., in 1783; m. Mary Chamberlain and had issue Morris, Ivory, Miriam, Pelatiah, Levi, Gustavus, Simeon, Freedom, Fannie who d. in youth, and Fannie, who m. Benjamin Franklin Howard. The land deeded to Pelatiah Gould by James Sands in 1809, was the home of this family, and is now occupied by Freedom W. Gould, whose wife was Adelia Perley, of Livermore. Their children were Fannie H., who d. at the age of 20 years, and Nathaniel P., who resides at North Leeds. Mrs. Adelia Gould d. in February, 1882.

John, m. Ruth Elden and had issue William, Leonard, Chessman, Joseph, Charles, Irenia, Octavia, Susan and Effie.

Susan m. Elisha D. Gould, of Lisbon, Me., of whom further mention will be made at the close of this sketch.

Eunice, m. Eld. George Parcher, of Saco. Their son, George, residing in Saco, has officiated in many positions of honor and trust: has been collector of customs of that port, etc.

Patience, m. Elijah Knapp, of North Leeds. They had a family of seven children, namely: Pelatiah, Abial, Jane, Rhoda, Jared, Dorothea and Ward.

Dorcas m. Nathaniel Durrill, of Kingfield, Me.

Sally, m. David Dennett, of Saco, Me.

Elisha D. Gould, who was born in Lisbon, Me., in October, 1812, was not known to have been a relative of the Goulds who early settled in Leeds. Joseph Gould, born about 1746, was an English ship owner who settled in what is now Bath, Me., previous to the Revolutionary War. He was the father of three sons, Moses, Jacob and John, all of whom settled in Lisbon, Me., about 1790. One of these, Moses, born about 1776, married Ann, a daughter of Capt. Adams, of Bowdoin, who, with two sons, were killed at sea by pirates in 1795. The children of Moses and Ann Gould were: Thomas, Charlotte, Moses, Sarah, Elisha, Samuel and Joseph. Of these, Elisha, whose father was killed in 1815, and who at the age of 12 years was turned adrift in the world, never knowing what a home was until he married in 1838, Susan, a daughter of John and Ruth (Elden) Gould, of Leeds, and made one of his own in that town. On a farm located on the west side of Dead River in the extreme northern portion of the town they settled, reared a large family and died. In a family lot on the farm of Russell L., a son, are they resting from their labors. Mr. Gould was a charter member of Asylum Lodge, F. A. M., located at Wayne. They had issue Chessman D., Loring B., Russell L., Welcome B., Frank E., George B. and Elisha T.

Chessman D. m. Lizzie Gardner, of Weymouth, Mass.; settled on the old Carver homestead, in Leeds; issue Loring, Harry, Samuel and Gertrude. He is a Mason and farmer. In early life worked at his trade in Massachusetts. Residence, Leeds.

Rev. Loring P., a Free Baptist minister; m. Mary E. Brown, of East Livermore, Me.; issue Charles, Merritt, Ernest and Susan; residence, East Livermore.

Russell L., a farmer, Mason and soldier; m. S. Ada Greenwood, of North Leeds; issue Willis E., John C., Alice May and Moses G. By his own efforts and labor, Mr. Gould has succeeded in a manner such as honesty and industry merit. He can well be classed among the most thriving and intellectual farmers in the town. His is the Ezra Berry farm revised and built anew; address, North Leeds.

Welcome B., a carpenter and farmer; m. Betsey A. Brown, of East Livermore, Me.; issue Georgina, graduate of Bates College; m. Walter A. French, lawyer; residence, Leeds; and Blanche. Mr. Gould spent many years in Lewiston; returned to Leeds; purchased the Simeon Gould farm; built a new house thereon and is now giving new life to soil so long dormant.

Frank E., a painter and farmer; m. Sarah L. Peare, of Leeds; issue Frank, Maud and Carl. Mr. Gould, after some years of absence, occupied in work at his trade, returned to the home farm where he cared for his parents in their years of decline.

George B., remained at home until he was several years advanced in manhood when he went to California where he has since remained. He is a single man.

Elisha T., a graduate of the medical department of Bowdoin College, is in the practice of medicine in Sonora, California. He was married in that state, but of his family we are not informed.

Willis E. Gould, M.D., a son of Russell L. and S. Ada (Greenwood) Gould, was graduated from the medical department of Bowdoin College. He located at the home of his childhood where he was best known, and where he has made for himself a name and acquired fame. He has taken an active part in the school work of the town and officiated in the capacity of superintendent. Other responsible positions have been and are being filled by him; among which are those of clerk and auditor of the Androscoggin and Kennebec Telephone Company.

Capt. Chessman, a son of John and Ruth (Elden) Gould, born in Leeds; removed to Wisconsin; was with Gen. Sherman in his march to the sea, acting Colonel of the 4th Wisconsin Regiment; present at the surrender of Gen. Lee.

Joseph F. Gould, his brother, born in Leeds; settled in South Boston; was a doctor and the father of two doctors, Lawrence and Clark.

W. E. GOULD, M.D.

PETTINGILL FAMILY.

The first to come to this country of those who bear the name of Pettengill or perhaps, as originally spelled, Pettingell, was Richard, who came from England about 1635, and settled in Salem, Mass. In 1643, Richard Pettengill m. Joanna, daughter of Richard Ingersoll. They moved to Newbury, Mass., in 1650. They had three sons and one daughter who reached the years of maturity. Their son, Samuel, born at Salem, Mass., in 1645; m. in Newbury in 1673, Sarah Poor. To them were born twelve children. Of these, Daniel was b. in Newbury in 1678. He was twice married; first, to Mary Stickley, in 1694; second, to Esther French, in 1707. By both wives he had thirteen children—seven b. in Newbury and six in Abington, Mass.

Of the latter was born Joseph, in 1717. He m. first, Mary Edson at Bridgewater, in 1745; and second, Lydia Phillips at North Bridgewater in 1746. He had eleven children, ten of them by his second wife. Among these were William and Obadiah, who were also among the early settlers of Leeds.

William was b. in Bridgewater, Mass., in 1759; died in Leeds Nov. 16, 1846. He was a Revolutionary soldier, as were nearly a hundred more of the descendants of Richard Pettengill. In 1784, at Bridgewater, Mass., he m. Lydia Cobb, who died in Leeds, Dec. 3, 1853, at the advanced age of more than 92 years; having moved to this town in 1790 or 1791. To them were born eleven children, viz.:

1. Joseph, b. in Bridgewater, Mass., Aug. 4, 1785; came with his parents to Leeds when five or six years of age. He m. Alice Allen, of Greene. Later he removed to Monmouth, where he resided mainly until his death, Jan. 25, 1869. He followed the carpenter's trade and was accounted a capable and faithful workman in the pioneer settlement. Many rural homes, even at this day, stand as monuments of his handiwork.

2. Hannah, b. in Bridgewater Feb. 14, 1786; removed to Leeds with her parents, and in June, 1802, m. James Stinchfield. She died in Leeds June 19, 1871.

3. Lydia, b. in Bridgewater, Nov. 3, 1787; m. George Gordon, of Wayne, Jan. 30, 1811; d. Feb. 27, 1819.

4. Sarah, b. in Bridgewater, May 8, 1789; m. Jonathan Gordon, of Wayne, 1809; d. December, 1879.

5. Reuel, b. in Leeds Sept. 17, 1792; d. Oct. 23, 1862. March 24, 1813, he m. Lydia Briggs, who d. Dec. 21, 1873. Their children were:

Lydia, b. Dec. 14, 1813; m. Calvin Briggs; removed to Stillwater, Minn. (They had three children b. in Leeds, Cordelia, Prudence A. and Francis V.)

2. Reuel, Jr., b. Feb. 18, 1816; remained a bachelor; d. Jan. 26, 1899.

Arvida B., b. June 27, 1818; m. Elvira A. Sumner Jan. 1, 1843; d. Nov. 16, 1899. Their children were:

Elvira J., b. Oct. 26, 1843; m. E. K. Prescott, of Monmouth, Feb. 16, 1879;

Mary R., b. Aug. 17, 1849; d. July 23, 1866;

Augusta W., b. Oct. 27, 1851; m. Frank Niles, of Auburn, March 6, 1881;

Frank E., b. July 5, 1861; m. first, Edith M. Coffin, May 1, 1881; had two children, Lena M., b. April 21, 1882; and Aubrey E., b. May 18, 1885; m. second, Georgia Beal, of Leeds, March 8, 1891.

3. Cyrenius, third son of Reuel, b. March 27, 1820; m. Amy A. Bates Jan. 15, 1845. They had four children, Henry F., b. April 20, 1846; has been an efficient officer in the affairs of his town and county; m. Addie M. Gordon, of Vienna, Nov. 30, 1871. To them have been born five children: Winifred, b. Feb. 26, 1874; is a graduate of State Normal School, Farmington, and a teacher of large experience and of marked success; m. Jan. 1, 1900, Alton G. Millett. Carl S., b. May 14, 1876, and Irving H., b. July 3, 1880, are engaged in mercantile business in Wilmington, Mass. Ethel G., b. Aug. 29, 1878. Clarence B., b. Jan. 13, 1884. Emily A., second child of Cyrenius, b. Sept. 14, 1850; d. Nov. 27, 1855. Emily A., third child of Cyrenius, b. Aug. 28, 1860; m. Manley M. Coffin June 19, 1881. Ermina E., fourth child of Cyrenius, b. Nov. 18, 1862; m. O. E. Curtis Dec. 23, 1883. Coming into this family in her infancy and brought up as one of their own children, was a niece of Cyrenius and Amy Pettengill, Mary Emma Hammond, b. Oct. 21, 1859; m. Junius C. Wing May 6, 1883.

4. Irison B., fourth son of Reuel, born Oct. 10, 1839; entered the Federal Army, Co. I, 23d Regiment, Maine Volunteers, Sept. 29, 1862; d. in Maryland at Lock 21, on the Potomac, near Geogetown, D. C., March 21, 1863, of small pox.

6. Jeannette, fourth daughter of William, b. in Leeds Jan. 31, 1795; m. Ebenezer Hammond, of East Livermore, Dec. 29, 1814; d. Jan. 14, 1883. They had issue three sons and two or more daughters.

7. Isaac, third son of William, born in Leeds April 10, 1797; m. Hannah Norris in 1819, and moved to East Livermore about 1832. His occupation was farming and blacksmithing, in which trade he was a skilled workman. He died Sept. 15, 1872. Of his nine children, six were born in Leeds, but during childhood moved with their parents to other towns.

At this date, his only surviving son, Sewall, is a resident of Wayne and for many years has held positions of public trust in his native town and county.

8. Ruth, fifth daughter of William, b. May 18, 1799; m. George Gordon, of Wayne, Nov. 2, 1819; d. Dec. 9, 1862.

SAMUEL PETTENGILL.

HISTORY OF LEEDS 155

9. William, Jr., fourth son of William, b. Dec. 10, 1801; m. Eunice Day May, 1827. He died April 11, 1881. She died Sept. 3, 1896. To them were born eleven children, five of whom lived to maturity, viz.:

Ruth, b. Feb. 26, 1828; m. Lewis Churchill, of Leeds; died April 13, 1890;

Samuel W. was b. March 1, 1842. At twenty years of age he enlisted in Co. E, 16th Regiment Maine Volunteers, Aug. 14, 1862. He endured the rigors of the autumn campaign of that year, and participated in the battle of Fredericksburg on that fatal 13th of December, 1862. Although he went through the battle unscathed, by various causes, among which was the exertion of rescuing a wounded comrade from capture by the enemy, he sustained injuries from which he never fully recovered. From this time on to the expiration of his term of enlistment, he was obliged to serve in the Veteran Reserve Corps, from which he received his discharge in 1865. He continued in failing health for several years, dying of pulmonary disease June 11, 1868;

On Oct. 23, 1845, there were born to William and Eunice Pettengill twin daughters,—Lucetta and Lydia. Lydia m. William E. Elder, of Lewiston, in 1864; Lucetta m. William H. Erskine, of Wayne, in 1865; died Oct. 15, 1884;

William R., second son of William, Jr., b. Oct. 19, 1847; married Fannie P. Libby Aug. 22, 1868. To them were born eleven children, viz.: Grace Vernon, b. June 30, 1869; m. John Plaisted, of Chicago March 10, 1900;

Samuel Henry, b. Aug. 31, 1870; a locomotive engineer on Maine Central Railroad; m. Jessie Robinson, of Bartlett, N. H., Dec. 25, 1899;

Emma Gertrude, b. April 18, 1871; m. Sanford Adams, Station Agent at Poland Spring, Portland & Rumford Falls Railroad, Sept. 15, 1893;

William Tillotson, b. Oct. 6, 1873; at present a student in Theological Institute at Saratoga Springs, N. Y.;

Clara Eunice, b. July 23, 1875; d. Dec. 3, 1877;

Ruth Eugenia, b. Dec. 23, 1876; in her Senior year at Bates College;

Clara May, b. March 24, 1879; employed in publishing house at Waterville, Me.;

James Garfield, b. Dec. 6, 1880; in business in Lewiston;

Fannie Lovisa, b. July 3, 1882;

Sarah Ruby, b. Feb. 23, 1884;

Fred Russell, b. Sept. 23, 1886.

10. Mary, sixth daughter of William, Sen., b. Jan. 20, 1805; m. Orlando Blake, of Monmouth; d. Jan. 6, 1895.

11. Araminta, seventh daughter of William, b. Nov. 22,

1807; m. Joshua Elder, of Lewiston, Feb. 24, 1850; d. May 5, 1888.

Obadiah, younger brother of William, Sen., b. in Brockton, Feb. 9, 1761; m. Eleanor Cobb (sister of Lydia, wife of William, Sen.), March 8, 1792. He died March 29, 1845. Their children were:

1. Arcadius, b. in Brockton, Mass., Jan. 19, 1793; m. Polly H. Tribou Dec. 19, 1814; d. Oct. 31, 1883. To Arcadius and Polly were born Ann P., Dec. 9, 1815; m. Alpheus Tribou April 17, 1842; d. Feb. 27, 1899; Joel, b. March 20, 1817; d. Oct. 8, 1883; William H., b. June 21, 1819; m. Nov. 27, 1845; d. June 11, 1882; Arcadius, Jr., b. Dec. 11, 1822; m. first, Ann Merrill, Oct. 1, 1843; d. June 7, 1898. Contracted later marriages with Jane Norris, Mrs. Theresa Morse and Mrs. Florenda Moore.

2. Obadiah, Jr., second son of Obadiah, b. in Brockton, Sept. 26, 1795; d. Feb. 12, 1880.

3. John, third son of Obadiah, b. Oct. 29, 1798; m. Maria Arno July 2, 1843; d. Dec. 7, 1858. These were a line of remarkable mechanics, especially as workers of wood. Of John, it was said, "he could even *grow* wood together." His children were Benjamin, b. May 17, 1844; m. Evelyn H. Outhouse, of Wrentham, Mass., March 7, 1900; and Maria, b. May 31, 1845; d. June 13, 1845.

The mechanical abilities of the father seem to have been transmitted to the son, as, from his early boyhood, Benjamin has been actively occupied in mechanical arts. For quite a number of years he has been extensively engaged in the construction and re-construction of carriages at his factory in Wayne.

4. Phebe, eldest daughter of Obadiah, b. Aug. 20, 1801; d. Oct. 31, 1896.

5. Phillips, fourth son of Obadiah, b. June 21, 1804; m. Joanna Harris, June 2, 1844; d. May 14, 1884. To them were born Eleanor C., May 16, 1845; m. Francis E. Herve of Greene, Me., Jan. 1, 1868; d. Aug. 31, 1896; J. Elizabeth, b. April 22, 1847; m. Wallace W. Mower, of Greene, March 23, 1875.

6. Irena, second daughter of Obadiah, b. Feb. 9, 1806; m. James Clark; d. Aug. 20, 1866.

7. Jason, fifth son of Obadiah, b. Feb. 23, 1808; m. Lucetta Gordon April 9, 1845; d. April 4, 1862. She d. May 13, 1901. They had five children, George B., b. Jan. 27, 1846; d. May 4, 1869; Melintha G., b. Dec. 28, 1847; m. Asa G. Gordon Jan. 1, 1885; Lois A., b. March 3, 1849; m. Rocellus C. Norris, May 1, 1876; Matilda F., b. Aug. 16, 1850; m. Marcellus F. Cushman, Aug. 30, 1868; Wilbert H., b. Sept. 2, 1856; d. Aug. 24, 1874.

8. Sarah C., third daughter of Obadiah, b. July 22, 1814; d. April 4, 1892.

CURTIS FAMILY.

The Curtis family County of Kent Arms, Arg. a ches sa between three Bull heads cabossed gun crest; a Unicorn pass or between four trees ppr.—Curtis, Cortis, etc., are ancient English families; settled in the counties of Kent and Sussex.

Stephen Curtis was a resident of Apledore, Kent, in 1450, and several of his descendants were mayors. Tenterden, a town from which some of the first settlers of Scituate came. The earlier descendants of those people are taken from an original record of their pedigree in possession of the family under the hand and seal of office of Sir William Segar, Garter King of Arms; transcribed by John Philpot, Blanch Lion, and entitled this descent of the Ancient familee Curtises in the County of Kent; faithfully collected out of the office of Arms; the public records of the Kingdom; private evidence of the families and other memorable monuments of antiquities, in which pedigree, and also in several old MSS. in the Harleian Musiam, the Arms of the family are given as annexed without reference to any particular grant, but as borne by them in virtue of ancient usage. William Curtis came to New England, in the Lion, in 1632; was a resident of Boston that same year, and later of Roxbury, where his descendants still reside. He was the ancestor of George T. and Berry R., Esquires, of Boston.

Richard, William and John Curtis were residents of Scituate in 1643; and Thomas in 1649, who was of York, Me., and who returned there. John left no issue of whom there is record. Thomas left issue, a few of his descendants still living in Scituate and elsewhere, and more of the descendants of Richard, and those of William are numerous in that town, Hanover and other towns in Massachusetts. Those of William, among whom are the Curtises of Leeds, are here given. Of his wife, or the dates of their births or deaths we have no record, but he was a farmer and his farm was on the North River. He was a member of the second church. His children were: Joseph, b. in May, 1664; Benjamin, b. in January, 1667; William, Jr., b. in January, 1669.

William, Jr., whose wife's name does not appear on our data, was the father of three children, viz.: Mary, who m. Joseph Benson, of Hull, March 17, 1727; Rachael, who m. Nehemiah White, April 25, 1737, and William third who was b. about 1696, and m. Margaret Pratt, Jan. 20, 1718. His residence was on Curtis Street, Hanover, where he d. March 4, 1737. His children were born: Abel, Nov. 24, 1719; Joel, Aug. 14, 1721; William fourth Aug. 27, 1724; who m. Martha Mane Nov. 13, 1747; d. June 11, 1759, leaving children, one of whom, William fifth, b. Dec. 4, 1752; married Deborah Curtis, Jan. 5, 1775. In 1786, he was a member of the Board of Selectmen. He continued his residence in Hanover and there d. Jan. 26, 1793. He had issue eight children who came to Maine, viz.: Ebenezer, William, Abner, Josiah, Libbeus, Lincoln, Charity and Deborah.

Ebenezer, b. in Hanover, Mass., in 1775; m. first, Cynthia Stetson, by whom he had Roa, b. 1805; Jeremiah, b. 1806; Mary, b. 1808; Cynthia, b. 1810. His second wife was Esther Randall, by whom he had three children, Hannah, b. 1816; William B., b. 1818; Betsey, b. 1821. He d. Aug. 22, 1868. Roa, his eldest daughter, m. Seth Dunbar, of Hingham, Mass.; Jeremiah, his eldest son, m. Christina Berry and settled in Leeds, in which town his uncles, William and Abner, had settled A. D. 1800. Jeremiah's children were Mary H., b. July 31, 1832; Ebenezer, b. April 21, 1836; Amanda T., b. Oct. 3, 1842; Amy A., b. Nov. 1, 1844. Jeremiah d. Aug. 11, 1880; Christina, his wife, d. Jan. 5, 1848. Of these children of Jeremiah, Mary H. m. Abner Curtis, Jr., and lived in Leeds; Ebenezer m. Cordelia Briggs; resides in Leeds; no issue. He was a soldier in the Civil War, in which service he continued until its close—a term of three or more years; Amanda T. m. Levi Owen; issue one child; and Amy A. is omitted in the data. Mary, the second daughter and third child of Ebenezer, m. Benj. Monroe, of Hanover, Mass.; Cynthia, his next child, m. William Whiting, of Hanover; Hannah, the next in the list of Ebenezer's children, m. John Damon of Scituate, Mass.; William B., whose numerical position was sixth in the list, married Augusta Sumner, of Leeds, where he spent his life. They had issue William H. and Henry; both of whom reside in Leeds, and neither of whom are m.; Betsey, the youngest child, m., as per data, John Damon, of Massachusetts.

William, second child of William and Deborah Curtis, settled in Leeds in the year 1800. He located in that part of the Plantation now called Curtis Corner. His old home is still standing on the Brewster farm. He m. Olive Stubbs, to whom was b. twelve children, nine of whom grew to man and womanhood, namely: Charles, Joseph R., Washington, George, Mary, Sophia, Olive, Ann and Harriet.

Of Charles, no data; Joseph R. was a sea captain of experience and note. He m. Louisa Sumner; reared a family and d. in a foreign port; Washington and George, no data; Mary m. Amos Berry and lived in Leeds; Sophia, m. Caleb Sumner, whose residence was Leeds; Olive and Ann, no data; Harriet, m. Rev. W. H. Foster, a son of Timothy, whose residence was Leeds. Most of these children of William Curtis had large families, of whom some receive mention in another place in this work.

Abner, third child of William and Deborah Curtis, was b. in Hanover, Mass., March 4, 1782. He came to Leeds in 1800; settled at what is now called Curtis Corner, near the house of his brother, William. He m. Lydia, a daughter of William Turner, of Leeds, by whom he had twelve children, namely:

Joanna, b. Feb. 20, 1804;
William, b. April 6, 1806;
Louisa, b. May 29, 1808;
Almon, b. Jan. 2, 1810;
James, b. April 6, 1813;
Obed, b. Oct. 15, 1815;
Gracia, b. Feb. 3, 1817;
Ansel, b. Feb. 20, 1819;
Lydia J., b. May 10, 1821;
Adeline, b. July 7, 1823;
Abner, b. Dec. 28, 1825;
Oren, b. Feb. 3, 1827.
Abner Curtis, Sen., d. Dec. 13, 1867.
Lydia, wife of Abner, Sen., d. March 6, 1872.
Of their children, Louisa, James and Obed d. in infancy.
Abner, Jr., d. Feb. 11, 1876, in Leeds; and Oren J. in California, date ———.

Joanna, eldest daughter of Abner, Sen., m. Martin Bates, of Leeds, by whom she had twelve children, namely: James, Orlando, Silas, Charles H., John O., Roswell, Francis, Helen, Adeline, Mary and Joanna, and another who died in infancy.

William, second child of Abner, Sen., m. Lucretia Smith; issue two children, Lydia F. and William H. Lydia F. married Mr. Anthony and had three children; and William H. married Eliza A. Bryant, of Turner, and has two sons, Edward B. and Walter P., both of whom are m. and the former has one child.

Almon, fourth child of Abner and Lydia (Turner) Curtis, m. Charlotte Mitchell, of Vienna, Me., Jan. 1, 1834. To them were born five children, viz.:

Sarah A., March 10, 1835;
Reuben D., Nov. 22, 1840;
William D., May 10, 1842;
Ervin H., Aug. 17, 1846;
Ledru R., Aug. 19, 1850.

Two of these children d. in infancy, Reuben D. and Ledru R.; Ervin H. d. April 12, 1861; aged 16 years.

Sarah A., the only daughter of Almon, m. Alfred Beals, of Greene, Aug. 15, 1859. They resided at North Leeds, and were charter members of Leeds Grange, of which he was treasurer several years. They had one son, Horace P., who m. and lives in Lowell, Mass., and in turn has a son, E. Alfred. Mr. and Mrs. Beals later removed to Lewiston, where he died March 6, 1900, and in which city Mrs. Beals now resides.

William D., is not accounted in the data of this family.
Almon Curtis, the father of these children, was twice commis-

sioned, by the Governors of Maine, Captain of Leeds Rifle Co., and received his discharge from the same. His wife d. Dec. 14, 1894; aged 84 years, 9 months; he d. July 13, 1897; aged 87 years, six months.

Gracia, seventh child of Abner and Lydia (Turner) Curtis, m. A. G. Day, of Leeds, Sept. 6, 1835. They had issue eight children, viz.:

William S., b. April 6, 1837; d. July 4, 1837;
Almon C., b. July 3, 1838;
Lydia J., b. July 21, 1840;
Henry F., b. March 29, 1843; d———;
Charles A., b. Feb. 22, 1846;
Hester A., b. March 20, 1848; d. March 9, 1852;
Wallace O., b. Jan. 13, 1852; d ———;
Clara A., b. Oct. 11, 1854.
Mr. A. G. Day d. May 18, 1880.

There being no separate account of the Day family obtained for this work, we here include such data as we have of the children of Gracia Curtis and her husband, A. G. Day.

Almon Curtis Day, b. in Leeds, July 18, 1838; m. Clara Bradford, of Turner, July 5, 1862. They settled in Buckfield and continued their residence there until 1885, when they removed to Turner, where they now reside. They have four children, viz.: Elsie A., b. April 15, 1864; m. Robert Haskell, of Auburn, Jan. 1, 1889; have two children, Weston B., b. Feb. 27, 1893; and Ada Louise, b. Dec. 11, 1897; Nellie A., b. Nov. 22, 1865; m. Walter Lawrence, of Sumner, April 21, 1894; have one son, Almon D., b. May 8, 1896; Wallace E., b. March 4, 1867; m. Winifred G. Francis, of Livermore, Jan. 1, 1900, and Clara Addie, b. July 26, 1871; who m. a music teacher whose name is not given. Mr. Day, Sen., was a farmer and for twenty years was engaged in the sale of nursery stock. Mr. Almon Curtis Day was a member of the municipal and school boards in both Buckfield and Turner, and represented his district in the House of Representatives of Maine.

Lydia J. Day m. Martin K. Bumpus, of Hebron, Me., Sept. 15, 1859, and had issue:

Raleigh M., b. May 1, 1861;
Hester A., b. May 19, 1866;
Nora B., b. Dec. 31, 1871.
Martin K., the husband and father, d. Aug. 10, 1900.

Raleigh M., m. Mabel L. Perham, of Bryant's Pond, Feb. 19, 1890; had issue Clare, Harold and A. Francis. Raleigh M. is a farmer and resides on the old homestead in Turner.

Hester A., m. Fred B. Marston, of Farmington, N. H., Dec. 21, 1894. She was a successful teacher in the schools of Maine and New Hampshire.

Nora B., m. H. I. Mason, of Sumner, April 9, 1889. She is a music teacher and artist. Her husband is superintendent of the butter factory in Augusta, Me.

Clara A., m. Daniel Cary, Nov. 5, 1878. They have one son, Ralph, b. Sept. 19, 1881.

Ansel, eighth child of Abner and Lydia (Turner) Curtis, m. Minerva White, by whom he had six children, namely: Willard M., Clementine, Millard, Florentine, Irven and Estella. He removed from Leeds to Waltham, Iowa, in 1868, and later to Iroquois, South Dakota. His son, Willard M., d. July, 1900. His daughter, Florentine, is m. and lives in California. The others are single.

Lydia J., ninth child of Abner and Lydia (Turner) Curtis, m. Nathaniel Harris, of Greene, Aug. 18, 1855; had one child, Minnie A., b. Nov. 7, 1857. Mrs. Harris m. second, Samuel Blake, of Monmouth, Sept. 18, 1868; no issue. Her daughter, Minnie A., m. James B. Packard, of Monmouth, Sept. 12, 1880. They have issue Winfield Forest, b. Aug. 27, 1881; Harold Winwood, b. Jan. 15, 1886; Florence Grace, b. Dec. 21, 1889; and James Roy, b. Aug. 26, 1892.

Adeline, tenth child of Abner and Lydia, m. James D. Gilbert, of Sumner. They had issue Emma F., Ann C. and Roswell C.

Abner, Jr., eleventh child of Abner and Lydia, m. Mary H. Curtis, of Leeds, in June, 1851. To them were born in Leeds, three children, to wit: Flora E., Albina L. and Oren E. Flora E. m. Lewis L. Lindsey of Leeds, Jan. 8, 1873. They have issue:

Arthur L., b. July 15, 1874;
Bertha M., b. Nov. 31, 1875;
Alice B., b. June 3, 1880;
Annie L., b. April 10, 1885;
Harry C., b. Nov. 6, 1892.

L. Albina, second child of Abner and Mary Curtis is a maiden lady.

Oren E., their youngest child, m. Mina Pettingill and lives on the old homestead farm of his parents and grandparents. He is one of the successful farmers of Leeds. Their children are:

Ada C., b. May 5, 1885;
Walter, b. Jan. 2, 1887;
Archie, b. Dec. 25, 1894.

Oren J., twelfth child of Abner and Lydia (Turner) Curtis, m. Sarah Bosworth, of Abington, Mass., in 1853. To them was b. a daughter, Marion, Oct. 27, 1854. She m. Henry H. Farr, April 6, 1873. They have a daughter, Bertha Estella, b. July 26, 1874. She m. Arthur S. Green in 1897. Their residence is in Milton, Mass. Mr. Farr d. in Littleton, N. H., several years ago, in which place his widow now resides.

In 1854 Oren J. went to California, and in the winter of 1855, lost his life in a snow and land-slide while mining in Butte County, in that state.

Josiah, fourth child of William and Deborah Curtis, came from Hanover, Mass., to Leeds, in 1800, and settled near Curtis Corner. He m. Hannah Billington. They had four children, viz.: Deborah, Adeline, Chesman and Laura.

Deborah and Adeline never married. Chesman m. Prudence Goch. They had three children, Letitia, Sarah and Abbie.

Laura m. John P. Hodsdon who resides in Wayne.

Lebbeus and Lincoln, fifth and sixth children of William and Deborah, moved to Searsport, Me., with their families. Several of their children were sailors and became masters of vessels.

Charity, seventh child of William and Deborah Curtis, m. Sylvanus Hammond, of Wayne, and lived in that town. They had several children.

Deborah, the youngest child of William and Deborah, m. Robert Curtis, of Greene; no issue.

OTIS FAMILY.

In Massachusetts the name of Otis is a common one, and many of its representatives are among the families of prominence. When such names as James and Harrison Gray Otis are mentioned to people of Boston, a spirit of pride is at once awakened and a golden chord attaches to their memory. In Leeds, the name first appears in the year 1792, in the personage of Oliver, who was born in Scituate, Mass., Nov. 8, 1768. He was a relative of the said James and Harrison G., but in what degree our data is wanting. At the age of twenty-three, hearing of the cheap and rich farming lands in the District of Maine, and especially in the Androscoggin valley, hither he came and purchased with money he had saved from mackerel fishing, a section of land in Turner. He made his temporary home in the family of Doctor Childs, who had a very extensive practice. On horseback he frequently rode through the neighboring settlements of Greene, Leeds, Livermore, etc., collecting bills for the doctor. On one occasion, he came to the house of Rogers Stinchfield on the south bank of Dead River. Betsey, the eldest child of Rogers was then a young lady of eighteen. She was born in New Gloucester, April 14, 1774. As young Otis rode up to the door, she glanced through the window and there sat the handsomest young man she had ever seen. (Her notion!) That picture, for an instant at the window, and the hospitable reception and entertainment of the young collector on that trip, and subsequently on soliciting trips, resulted in a "proposal" and "acceptance," and on Oct. 11, 1792, they were married. Some time before their marriage, young Otis disposed of his land in Turner, and made his stay in Lewiston. On the 26th day of June, 1792, Adams Royal conveyed Lot No. 64 in Littleborough, to Oliver Otis, of Lewiston. On this lot a log house had been built and a clearing made. The house stood westerly and near the present residence of A. J. Lane. When they were married he said to his wife: "If we have good luck, in six years we will be able to have a frame house." They moved into the log house and proceeded with the clearing, fencing, orcharding and stocking of the farm.

In less than six years, in 1797, although there were several open-mouthed young Otises to feed, they moved into their new house, which is the same now occupied by Mr. Lane and is nearly opposite the school-house which has since been erected on the same site where the former school building stood. They had issue:

Fannie, b. May 11, 1793;
Ensign, b. April 11, 1795;
Sarah B., b. April 28, 1797;
Lydia P., b. June 24, 1799;
John, b. Aug. 3, 1801;
Oliver, b. July 26, 1803;
Eliza, b. Dec. 10, 1804;
Ann F., b. Sept. 8, 1806;
Oliver, b. Sept. 29, 1809;
Harrison G., b. March 13, 1812;
Amos, b. Sept. 19, 1813;
Martha J., b. Sept. 30, 1821.

Three of the children died young, Oliver April 24, 1807; Oliver May 6, and Harrison G. May 7, 1814. Of those remaining,

1. Fannie, married first, James Leadbetter, July 3, 1814; second, Jonathan Bartlett in January, 1826. By her first husband she had two children, one of whom died young. The other, Laura Ann, married a Mr. Wingate of Houlton, Me. By her second husband she had two sons and a daughter, James, Jonathan and Mary. The former resides in California and the others in Montville, Me.

2. Ensign, married first, Martha Davis, of Montville, Me., Jan. 14, 1822. She died August 18, 1858, leaving one son, John, whose residence is Auburn, Me. He has three children, or more. One son, Oliver, is a noted editor, and resides in Belfast, Me.

His second wife was Laura Howard, by whom he had one son, Ensign, who died young. The dates of the deaths of Ensign and his widow are not known to writer. He was an earnest promoter of the Androscoggin Railroad and several years on the board of directors. To his efforts and those of Giddings Lane is largely due the establishing of that enterprise.

3. Sarah B., the third child of Oliver Otis, married Ephraim Woodman, of Wilton, Me., July 19, 1812. He was born in Buxton, Me., April 25, 1787. They had issue:

Olive B., born in Wilton, Me., Nov. 27, 1814; married Samuel L. Hazard, of Boston, Feb. 9, 1840; Oliver Otis, born in Wilton Oct. 7, 1816; married Carrie Thomas, of Raymond, Miss. He was the first mayor of Vicksburg. He subsequently removed to New Orleans, and died in Virginia Aug. 30, 1869, on his way north for his health; was brought to Massachusetts and buried at Mt. Auburn; left no issue; Ivey F., fourth child, married Frances Strickland, of Livermore, in 1842, and died on a plantation in Mississippi, April 25, 1872; leaving one daughter; Ephraim W., the youngest child of Sarah B. (Otis) Woodman, married in Wilton, in June, 1847, Elizabeth Fenderson. She died in 1852; no issue. He then went to California, returning in 1859; in 1860, married Sarah Hiscock of Wilton. He was in the Civil War and received his commission as Captain of Co. A, 8th Maine Infantry Regiment, Sept. 7, 1861; promoted to Major October 8; further promoted to Lieutenant-Colonel of that regiment Dec. 23; to Col. of the 28th Regiment Nov. 3, 1862; mustered out Aug. 31, 1863. Dec. 18, 1863, he was commissioned Colonel of the 2d Maine Cavalry, its only Colonel; mustered out Dec. 6, 1865. He died in Vernon, Madison County, Miss., March 17, 1869, leaving a widow and three sons; the youngest, two months old and the eldest seven years. The widow died. No date.

4. Lydia P., married Addison Martin, her second cousin, July 10, 1826. She was killed instantly by lightning July 5, 1842. She left four children. Addison Martin, Jr., born in Guilford Nov. 9, 1826; married Louisa Brooks of Portland, in 1855; reside in San Francisco, Cal.; issue two children, Oliver and Lydia.

2. Lydia Martin, born in Guilford, Mach 19, 1828; married David S. Parker, of Corinth, Dec. 23, 1847; died in Milford, Aug. 17, 1868; had eight children; two of whom died young; those remaining, Elsie F., Lizzie O., David C., Flora M., Lillie L. and Mabel H.

3. Emily F. Martin, born in Guilford May 13, 1831; married Henry Hudson March 30, 1850; had six children, three of whom died young: the others, Henry, b. in Guilford, March 19, 1851; a lawyer; Micajah, b. Ibid., Nov. 23, 1854; James, b. Ibid., Oct. 22, 1857.

4. Martha Martin, born in Guilford Aug. 28, 1836, is a maiden lady. Hers has been a life devoted to the cause of education, and largely spent in teaching in the schools of Maine and Massachusetts.

5. John, fifth child of Oliver and Betsey (Stinchfield) Otis, married Frances Vaughn, of Hallowell, Me., Jan. 12, 1831. They had issue seven children, two of whom died in infancy. Of the others, Welleon O. was a lawyer; living in Texas; Maria, married a Mr. Merrick, of Philadelphia, Pa.; and died, leaving three children; Vaughn, died at home in Hallowell, when 20 years old; John, who resides on a plantation in Mississippi, and Frances, who died at home at the age of 18 years.

The first wife of Hon. John Otis died July 25, 1846. In August, 1848, he married Ellen Grant, of Hallowell. The fruit of this marriage was three children, to wit: Samuel, Mary and Elizabeth. Their home is in Hallowell, Me.

Hon. John Otis was a lawyer and held many public positions. He was a member of both branches of the State Legislature and representative in the thirty-first Congress. Hon. Elihu Washburn and several other prominent Maine lawyers studied law with him. He died Oct. 29, 1856.

6. Eliza, married Roland Bailey Feb. 29, 1828, a son of Hon. Seth Howard, whose residence was where A. J. Foss now lives. She accompanied him to this place where they continued to reside until his death, which occurred April 30, 1840. They had issue General Oliver Otis Howard, whose biography appears in another place in this work; Rev. Roland Bailey, and General Charles H., of whom further mention will be made elsewhere.

In June, 1841, she married Col. John Gilmore, of Leeds, by whom she had one son, Rodelphus H., who is a lawyer in Denver, Col. He married first, Rose Ellen Deane, of Leeds, Aug. 8, 1866. He will receive further mention in connection with the family of Eliza, his mother.

7. Ann F., married Jonas P. Lee, of Leeds, July 17, 1828, by whom she had three children: Sarah, Silas and Samuel Perry.

Sarah married first, a Mr. Sargent, by whom she had five children, three of whom died young. Mr. Sargent died in 1842, and she married J. F. Talbot, of Machias, Me., but later moved to Malden, Mass.

Silas was a surgeon in the western division of the army in the Civil War, and died in St. Louis.

Samuel Perry was a sea captain, and in the Civil War was, for a time, in the Navy, but Sept. 7, 1861, received a Lieutenant's commission in Co. E, 3d Maine Infantry Regiment; promoted to Captain Oct. 1, 1862; promoted to Major of the 3d Regiment, Nov. 28, 1862; transferred to invalid corps

July 2, 1863. He was fearfully wounded at Fredericksburg, and at Gettysburg he was so badly wounded that his arm was removed at the shoulder. He was subsequently placed on the retired list and made his home in Vineyard Haven, Mass.

8. Amos, the next child, married Laura D. Woodbury, of Minot, Me., March 31, 1842. He died Aug. 3, 1844; and his widow on the 12th day of the following October; without issue. He was a physician and in active practice.

9. Martha Jane, the youngest child of Oliver and Betsey (Stinchfield) Otis, married in Hallowell, C. H. Strickland, of Wilton, Me., Dec. 21, 1841. He died in Richmond, Ind., in 1876. They had issue one son and three daughters. The son died several years ago. One, or more, of the daughters married, but further knowledge of them has not been obtained by the writer.

Oliver Otis and his wife, Betsey, accumulated a large amount of wealth and enjoyed the reputation of being the richest family in the town. When advanced in years, more than 70, he removed to Hallowell, assigning as a reason that his taxes in Leeds were too high. When he died in that city, Sept. 28, 1844, his remains were brought to Leeds and buried in the cemetery northerly of Lothrop's Corner. His widow died in Hallowell in 1855, and was buried beside him, near her childhood home.

CASWELL FAMILY.

From the town of Hanover, Massachusetts, came Levi Caswell to Littleborough Plantation in the year 1795. He settled near the southern boundary in the eastern portion, on a tract of land which he redeemed from wilderness to cultivation, the same having been known by the name of Caswell farm since. In 1796, he married Alice Clark, of Scituate, Mass., by whom he had eleven children, to wit:

    I. Levi, Jr., b. April 20, 1797; d. in Lubec, Me., leaving a widow and four sons, one of whom is now residing in Melrose, Mass.; is a policeman.

    II. Alice, b. April 27, 1798; m. Hannibal Farewell, of Vassalboro, Me. She is the mother of twelve children, two of whom, Chandler and Alanson, accumulated great wealth.

    III. Druzilla, b. May 12, 1799; d. Feb. 15, 1801.

    IV. Job, b. Dec. 20, 1800; m. Elvira Sprague, of Greene, by whom he had two sons, Augustus B., who died in Auburn; and Cyrus M., who is a merchant in Portland.

V. Alanson B., b. Nov. 4, 1802; was in the Railway Mail Service several years; m. Elmina, a daughter of Jeremiah and Desire (Butterfield) Stinchfield, of Farmington, Me., Nov. 12, 1835. His wife died June 29, 1844, and he died later in Washington, D. C. They had issue two daughters, both of whom died young.

VI. Chandler, b. July 27, 1804; drowned June 17, 1818.

VII. Jason, b. March 23, 1806; had an unwritten history; died in Greene.

VIII. Lendall, b. Sept. 10, 1807; d. in Farmington, Nov. 23, 1845.

IX. Druzilla, b. Feb. 2, 1809; m. Silas Coburn, of Greene, by whom she had five children; none of whom are living.

X. Peleg B., b. Aug. 19, 1811; m. Mary Q. Robbins, of Greene. They had nine children, namely:

1. Earl, b. Sept. 25, 1837; m. Augusta M. Young, of Belgrade, Me., by whom he had five children; three of whom are living. He has been in trade at North Leeds and in Chesterville, and has recently returned to North Leeds;
2. Mary A., b. Feb. 5, 1839; d. Feb. 24, 1859;
3. Sarah J., b. Sept. 24, 1840; d. Feb. 1, 1859;
4. Lloyd B., b. Aug. 5, 1842; resides in Minneapolis, Minn.;
5. Levi G., b. Nov. 13, 1844; m. Annie L. Richards, of Boston, by whom he had six children, two of whom are living, Frederick L., who is a conductor on the Boston Elevated Railway, and Harry R., a student in Boston English High School;
6. Lendell S., b. May 9, 1846; m. Theresa H. Parsons, of New York. They reside in Minneapolis;
7. Clark R., b. March 21, 1848; m. Elvira F. Emerton, of Bingham, Me., by whom he had two children, W. Benson, a graduate of Maine State College; now a civil engineer in Philadelphia; and Mary H., who is taking a course in Colby. Mr. Caswell was a fine machinist. His residence was Waterville, where he died Jan. 5, 1898;
8. John Q., b. Feb. 11, 1850; d. Feb. 15, 1859.
9. Nancy E., b. Nov. 24, 1853; m. Leander Patten, of Greene, and had issue Lorey, b. April 4, 1888.

XI. Juliette, b. Sept. 10, 1813; d. March 18, 1815.

Mr. Levi Caswell, the subject of this sketch, was born in Hanover, Mass., and died in Leeds, but the dates are, unfortunately, unknown to the writer.

HOWE FAMILY.

Prominent among the early settlers of the town of Winthrop is the name of Icabod Howe. To him was granted in that town Aug. 22, 1770, Lot No. 70. The first meeting, that called for the purpose of municipal organization, May 20, 1771, was presided over by Mr. Howe. He was also elected a member of the Board of Selectmen. His name frequently occurs in the list of officers in that town's early history, and in 1775, the earliest date given that Winthrop sent a representative to the Provincial Congress, held at Cambridge Feb. 5, he was elected to that office. By direction of the Provincial Congress to discipline the inhabitants in military tactics, Mr. Howe was elected Captain. The place of Mr. Howe's nativity was Marlboro, Mass. He was a son of Jonathan and Sarah (Hapsgood) Howe. He married Sarah ————, and resided for a few years in New Ipswich, New Hampshire, from which place he moved his wife and three children to Winthrop in 1768. Their children were: Jonathan, b. July 31, 1760; Millicent, b. April 25, 1762; Sarah, b. March 15, 1766; Stephen, b. Dec. 9, 1768; David, b. Sept. 1, 1771; Susanna, b. April 13, 1774; Eunice, b. Feb. 22, 1776.

To his eldest son, Jonathan, were the people of Wayne indebted for their first mill and mill-dam, he being the first man to obstruct the free course of the waters of the "Thirty-Mile River," on their way to the sea. Not to this mill alone were the energies of Mr. Howe confined. In 1801, he started to erect a mill at the south end of Androscoggin Lake, on the site where the mills of George Gordon were subsequently built. At his mill in Wayne village his lumber was sawed and prepared, put in the water, rafted and started on its course, but before reaching its destination Mr. Howe was accidentally drowned.

Stephen, the second son of Ichabod Howe, was his first child born in Winthrop. He married Eleanor Turner and settled in Leeds, about 1790. His children were: Lewis, Christina, Lovina, Jane, Stephen, Jonathan, Cyprian and George.

One of these sons, Cyprian, married Mary, a daughter of Thomas and Lydia (Bishop) Graffam, of Leeds. They had issue George T., Jane, Charles, Frances, Lydia, Marcellus, Cyrus and Moses. George T., born June 26, 1836, was educated in the town schools and in the high schools in Winthrop and Lewiston. In June, 1853, he started in to learn the trade of brick-maker. From 1857 to 1860, he carried on a successful business in Lewiston. From there he went to Brunswick, and after the great fire in Boston in December, 1872, he furnished large quantities of brick used in the reconstruction of buildings in that city. January 1, 1879, he married Edith, a daughter of James and Edith (Walton) Hutchins. They have issue one daughter, Edith, born

March 11, 1880. In May, 1880, he opened the extensive and celebrated brick plant which he has operated 21 years at Leeds Junction, and supplies the local trade in addition to the immense business of the Maine Central Railroad, which, in connection with the quantities sold for public and private buildings, amount to an annual output of more than 1,200,000. Aside from this business, he is engaged in the wood and lumber trade and extensively in agriculture. At the present time he owns more than 500 acres of land in the vicinity of Leeds Junction, and holds 27 deeds of real estate there and in other places. Few farmers in Maine cut the quantity of hay harvested by Mr. Howe,—160 tons in a single year. Mr. A. G. Bates has been in his employ most of the time since 1867, alone preparing the clay and sand to make more than twenty millions of bricks; and when ready for shipment, has loaded them on the cars. Although Mr. Howe has never joined any church, he is a liberal contributor to the support of all the different societies in his section, and in that (he says) makes no mistake. If we should fail to say that he is a "Jeffersonian, Tilden, Cleveland Democrat," we might merit his displeasure.

It is a matter of regret that a more complete sketch of the Howe family of Leeds, has not been furnished for this work.

WING FAMILY.

The Wing family is one of the oldest in Leeds.

Bachelder Wing and family came from the town of Sandwich on Cape Cod, Barnstable County, Mass., in 1793, and settled in Leeds on the river road on the farm now owned by Augustine V. Deane. But wishing to avail himself of the society of the Quaker settlement, then established at the south end of the town on and near what is now known as Quaker Ridge, he exchanged places with a Mr. Deane on Richmond Hill, so called, securing a rugged, but fertile farm, where he reared his family of twelve children, viz.: Nabby, Hannah, Caleb, James, Experience, Allen, Mary, Mehitable, Sands, Phebe, Almira and William. Of these, Nabby married Cyrus Sampson and settled in South Leeds at the corner where Mr. Sampson was in trade at the time, and remained here for several years, later removing to East Winthrop;

Hannah married Benjamin Dunham; settled on the farm where George Beckler and son now live, remaining there through life;

Caleb settled on the south half of the homestead lot, building a new set of buildings thereon and remained there;

James married and went to Somersworth, N. H.; was engaged

in a cotton mill for several years, when he returned to Quaker Ridge and purchased the farm where A. S. Tuck now lives, this being at present one of the oldest houses in Leeds;

Experience, married a Dudley and moved to China, Me.;

Allen, married and moved to Chandlersville;

Mary, married Hazel Sampson, settled in South Leeds, where Thomas Packard now lives;

Mehitable, married Howard Sylvester and settled in North Greene;

Sands, lived on the home place for several years when he moved to Monmouth, and later, to Manchester; where he remained till death on the place where his son, Willis, now lives;

Phebe, married Cyrus Estes and located at East Winthrop;

Of these, the only remaining line of descendants now in Leeds are those of Caleb, who was twice married. His first wife, Joanna Gilbert, bore one son, Adna, who died at the age of 54 years, unmarried.

By his second wife, Desire Turner, he had seven children, Salmon A., Joanna, Diana, Ormand T., Hiram C., Stephen D. and William. Of these, Salmon A., born in 1813, after reaching his majority, went to Hallowell, then called "Forks of the Road," where he learned the oil cloth business in the employ of Pope & Sampson, who sent him to Prattsville, N. Y., to superintend the building of a factory and establish the manufacture of oil cloths, or rubber cloths, so called at that time, which were made in one piece to fit a room, and all of hand labor.

The journey from Maine to New York required one week at that time.

While there, he married Ardelia Coffin, of Livermore, Me., and through the ill effects of a confined life in the factory, and with a strong and natural love for his native place and farm life, he returned to "Quaker Ridge," Leeds, and purchased the farm where he remained till the time of his death. Through this marriage five children were born: Duane Snyder, Vesta Coffin, Elsie Howard, Junius Carlos and Stephen Arland. Of them we will say that when the War of the Rebellion broke out, Duane was ready to volunteer and enlisting in the navy on board the Monadnock, he sailed for Cuba. Was in the battle of Fort Fisher and many other engagements. After three years' service he was discharged and returned home, where he married Clara Howard, by whom two children were born, Elsie H. and Alfred S.; lived for a few years, but having a natural liking for railroad work, he chose this for his life vocation and is, at this writing, making his daily run from Portland to Boston and return as Pullman conductor. He has a pleasant home in Portland;

Vesta Coffin, has been twice married. By her first husband,

Augustus Jones, three children were born: John B., Louis A. and Ralph D. Is now living on Quaker Ridge on the farm before mentioned—the wife of A. S. Tuck;

Elsie Howard, married Cyrus H. Farley, of Portland, Me. To them five children have been born: Philip H., Elizabeth, Charles H., Henry G. and Florence;

Junius C., still living on the homestead, has been twce married, having one son, Harold, by his first wife, Mary E. Hammond. By the second marriage, with Dora L. Howard, three children have been born: Beulah A., Arland J. and Stella A.;

Stephen A., after a few years of farm life in Leeds, married Carrie Boothby, of Leeds, and moved to Nashua, N. H. and engaged in a cotton mill; from which place, after a few years of success and advancement, he was called to the position of overseer in Putnam, Conn.

Of the remaining children of Caleb Wing, Joanna married John Loring and located in Leeds, near where Fred Additon now lives, but moved to Lewiston, and later to Billerica, Mass.;

Diana, who was well known in earlier life as a successful teacher in town, married Aranda Gilbert, settled at South Leeds where E. E. Additon now lives. Through this union four children were born: Rollin, Abbie, Lois and Rosa. Mr. and Mrs. Gilbert being of an ambitious and enterprising nature, made several successful changes in location, being at Lewiston for some time, successful in business and securing the advantage of an opportunity for the children to acquire an education, which was not to be obtained in the country. Those who knew her best could but feel that her efforts and ambition were rewarded by the peace and comforts with which her declining years were surrounded in the home of her daughter, Mrs. Rosa V. Hanscom, of Leeds;

Ormand T. married Octavia Brewster. To them were born four children; Orville D., Clara A., Ellen M. and Fred B. They located first at North Greene, then moved to the Ridge and engaged in trade, which he followed in different locations till the time of his death, which occurred in Turner, Me., where he left two sons, as successors to his business. Hiram C. died in youth.

Stephen D., a carpenter by trade, built the houses now owned by E. V. Daly and A. J. Foss, besides assisting on several others; died at the age of 24 years; unmarried.

William married Frances A. Bates. To them were born two children—Roswell S. and Alena M., located at South Leeds, where they remained the greater part of their married life, with the exception of a few years in trade in Lewiston, returning to the farm for the declining years of life, and served the public as postmaster at that place.

ADDITON FAMILY.

From Plymouth, Duxbury, and other towns of the Old Colony of Massachusetts the descendants of the early Pilgrims have gone in various directions, carrying with them that unflinching adherence to duty, that regard for law and order, and that faithful attention to imposed trusts which were so strong elements in the Pilgrim character, and where they settled they and their descendents have been most useful citizens and formative influences in producing the best civilization. Among the early families of Duxbury, Mass., was that of Arddaton (now Additon), which probably came from England prior to 1640. All through the residence in Duxbury the original spelling of the name continued, as Thomas of the Revolution (father of the Thomas born March 2, 1763, who became an early settler of Leeds) used this orthography.

Thomas Additon, the pioneer of the Leeds family, with his wife, Bethiah, born March 17, 1764, made their home on Quaker Ridge between 1785 and 1790, and on this place, long since forsaken, they reared 9 children, namely: Ruby (named from a Duxbury aunt), born in 1786; John, 1788; Otis, 1790; Joseph, 1792; Thomas, 1794; Phebe, 1796; David, 1799; Chloe, 1802; Hulda, 1804.

Thomas Additon, Jr., born June 7, 1794, married Anna daughter of Isaiah Beals. Their children were Isaiah B.; Lovisa (Mrs. Dr. S. A. Allen); Amanda (Mrs. Seth Howard); Thomas J.; Loren J.; Everett; Eliza A. (Mrs. J. F. Jennings). Mr. Additon was a farmer, a quiet, unostentatious man of strict probity, valued for his good qualities. He died Feb. 4, 1869, and his wife April 30, 1871, on the place now owned by Elwin E. Additon. Isaiah Beals Additon, son of Thomas and Anna (Beals) Additon, was born Nov. 10, 1823. He was educated in town, taught 26 terms of district school, and won a deserved reputation. He was a farmer on the place settled by his Grandfather Beals, purchased by his father in 1827; consisting of 125 acres of land, and made a specialty of cheese-making. He married May 5, 1852, Eliza A., daughter of Perez S. and Joanna (Lane) Jennings. Children: Flora L. (died Feb. 15, 1862, aged 9 years; Juliette J. (died Feb. 15, 1862, aged 7 years); Orville I.; Lorette (died March 10, 1862, aged 7 months); and Fred L. Isaiah B. Additon was always a Democrat, of the minority party in politics; and yet he was elected one of the selectmen 18 years, and in 1859, 1860, 1861, 1870, 1871, 1872, 1873, 1874, 1875, 1876, 1877, 1878, 1879, 1880, 1881, 1882 and 1883 was chairman of the board. He had an extended acquaintance in the county and has been the nominee of his party for representative, in one campaign coming close to an election in a strong

FRED L. ADDITON.

Isaiah B. Additon

Republican district. He was several times candidate for county commissioner, receiving flattering votes. He was United States census agent for Leeds and Greene in 1860; has often been selected for important trusts, and has performed delicate offices with acknowledged ability. He was firm and decided in his opinions, cautious and conservative in thought, tenacious in his convictions, and frank, sincere and honest in declaring them. He was always a Universalist and a liberal supporter of the cause. Genial, hospitable and kind-hearted, he had many friends, among his warmest ones those of opposing politics. He was a very useful citizen. A firm and conscientious official, and opposed anything like extravagance in the administration of town affairs, and by a long and faithful service acquired the esteem and confidence of his townsmen. He died July 31, 1894. His three daughters died when quite young. His oldest son, Orville I., born Aug. 31, 1855; graduated at Westbrook Seminary, in 1880. He married Lucy A. Benner. Children: Forest O., Henrietta S. and Flora L. He went to Illinois and was for some time principal of the High School at Cardova; also taught in other places. At the present time he is doing an extensive and profitable business manufacturing house furnishings in the state of Georgia. His youngest son, Fred L., born Jan. 28, 1864; married Lenora I., daughter of Francis E. and Eleanor (Pettengill) Howe, and has seven children, as follows: Orville J., Ernest F., Leslie F., Ivan B., Clayton E., Edna, Florus J. He is a Democrat and a Universalist, and lives on the farm left him by his father, but has added largely to the number of acres, until he now has one of the largest and best farms in town; has at present time twenty cows in milk and sends cream to the factory. Mr. Additon is a progressive farmer and adds each year to his herd of cows. Like his father he is interested in public affairs, especially the welfare of his town. In 1898, he was elected on the Board of Selectmen. In 1899, was re-elected to the same position, and in 1900, was elected chairman of the board, which office he now holds. He has won the confidence and esteem of his fellow-townsmen by the interest he has taken in town affairs, and the impartial manner in which he has discharged the duties of his office. He is a Patron of Husbandry and was lecturer of Leeds Grange two years, filling the office to the satisfaction of his brothers and sisters, but declined to serve longer on account of other duties.

Thomas Jefferson Additon, brother of Isaiah B., was born August 20, 1832. He was always a farmer and occupied the homestead of his father. He married Razzilla Smart, born in Parkman, March 13, 1832. Their children are Luetta M. (Mrs. Dr. W. H. Thomas, of Lewiston), Chester J. (deceased), Elwin E., Annie S. (Mrs. T. M. Shaw of Readfield).

Thomas J. Additon was a kind-hearted man, strictly honest in all his dealings, attending to his own business and doing everything in a thorough manner, as his farm and stock would show at any time. He was always interested in the welfare of his town and his fellow-citizens, and at his death, which occurred March 20, 1897, left many warm friends.

Elwin E. Additon, b. in Leeds, Aug. 24, 1864; a great-great-grandson of Thomas, of Duxbury, Mass., and great-grandson of Thomas, the pioneer of Leeds; resides on the farm where his grandfather lived and died. At the early age of 17, he was a teacher in his native town, and at 22, was a member of the school board. The following year he was elected Supervisor of Schools which office he held two years; and later, officiated three years in the capacity of Superintendent. Under his supervision the district system was abolished, adding new and arduous labors which were satisfactorily accomplished. The deep and lasting interest he feels and manifests in the cause of education is worthy of perpetuation. Since 1893, with the exception of one year, he has officiated as moderator in the annual meetings of the town; is now serving his fourth term in the office of constable and collector of taxes; said to be an efficient man in that capacity, collecting more and having less remaining on his books at the close of each year than any of his recent predecessors. As a member of the Order of Patrons of Husbandry, he has given time and attention to the duties of the various offices to which he has been elected therein, scarcely missing a meeting during the three years he held the office of Overseer, and the three years he officiated as Master of the Leeds Grange. He also holds prominent membership in Pomona Grange; ably discharging the duties of the office of Lecturer, and is the present overseer of that organization.

In politics, he is a member of the Republican party.

To the homestead of his father and grandfather on which he lives, he has added other land, enabling him to keep a large dairy; making those famous *Additon Cheese* for which the family has so long been noted.

For several generations, the Additons have been successful tillers of the soil and good representatives of New England's intelligent farmers.

Feb. 9, 1886, Mr. Additon married Mary A., a daughter of Charles L. and Hannah (Maxwell) Thomas, of Greene. They have issue Louise M., Marion L., Orland H. and Vina A.

E. E. ADDITON.

HOWARD FAMILY.

The name Howard first appeared in Leeds in the year of its incorporation, 1801. It was personified by Capt. Seth Howard[5] a lineal descendant of John Howard, who came from England in boyhood, lived in the family of Plymouth Colony's military man Capt. Miles Standish, and in 1651, became one of the proprietors and original settlers of West Bridgewater, Mass. Under the tuition of Capt. Standish, his military education and native ability carried him to the front as the first officer in the new plantation. He received the oath of fidelity in 1657. He married Martha, a daughter of Thomas Hayward. They had issue John, James, Jonathan[2], Elizabeth, Sarah, Pelatiah and Ephraim. His third child, Jonathan[2], who became a major; married Sarah Dean, and to them were born, Jonathan, in 1692; Joshua, in 1696; Susanna, in 1698; Ebenezer, in 1700; Seth[3], in 1702; Abigail, in 1704; Sarah, in 1707; Henry, in 1710 and Kezia, in 1712.

Seth[3] married Mary, a daughter of Thomas Ames, in 1735. They had issue Mary, in 1738; Jesse[4], in 1740; Susanna, in 1742; Betty, in 1749, and Ebenezer, in 1752.

Capt. Jesse[4] married Melatiah, a daughter of Samuel Dunbar, in 1761. Their children were Seth[5], b. in 1762; Perez, 1765; Calvin, 1768; Barnabas, 1770; Jesse, 1776 and Lloyd, 1778.

Capt. Seth Howard[5] was born in Bridgewater, Mass., Nov. 21, 1762. Desire, a daughter of Jonathan Bailey, was born Jan. 23, 1762. Capt. Seth Howard[5] and Desire Bailey were married Nov. 21, 1782. The fruits of this marriage, born in West Bridgewater, were Stillman[6], May 20, 1785; Everett, Nov. 22, 1787; Ward, Dec. 18, 1789; Seth, Aug. 9, 1792; Roland Bailey, July 29, 1795; Aurelia, June 28, 1797 and Lucretia Feb. 2, 1800. Subsequent to their removal to Leeds, District of Maine, in 1801, the list was increased by the birth of Valentine Rathburn, April 11, 1803, and Benjamin Franklin, June 4, 1806.

He was a man of executive ability and discharged the duties of presiding officer of the many assemblies to which he was chosen with a degree of dignity becoming one in that capacity. In 1806, he represented his district at the General Court, in Boston. When his family came to Leeds in 1801, his eldest son, Stillman, a lad of sixteen, drove the pair of horses attached to the carriage that bore seven members of the family to their new home where A. J. Foss now resides; while the other member, Roland Bailey, then a little fellow of six summers, rode on the back of another horse much of the distance.

Stillman[6], who, in 1814, was Captain of a military company, married Lydia, a daughter of Daniel Lothrop, an officer of Revolutionary fame, Sept. 27, 1807. She was born May 5, 1789. He was a man of ability which was well appreciated, not only by his fellow-townsmen, who elected him repeatedly to the offices within their gift, while the people of Kennebec County called him to the office of commissioner, and subsequently to a position on the Governor's Council. He represented his district when Maine became a State. For a long term of years he held commissions by the Governors, of Justice of the Peace and Quorum. After his marriage, he settled on the place now occupied by John F. Jennings, where he continued his residence until March, 1834, when he purchased the Captain Dwinal place, at Leeds Center, to which he removed his family. During the time there, he held the office of postmaster two years. He subsequently removed to the western part of the town, to the place now occupied by Mr. House, where he died in 1861. He was buried in the cemetery at Leeds Center. His widow died April 6, 1872. To him and his wife had been born Stillman L.[7], March 3, 1810; Rozilia A., Jan. 30, 1812; Mary L., May 14, 1816; Lydia A., March 25, 1818; Lucretia P., Sept. 19, 1820; and Seth, June 6, 1828.

Everett, the second child of Capt. Seth, died in Georgia.

Ward, the next in the list, settled in New York. Four years he was collector of customs in that city. He was also State Marshal. He died in Omaha, Neb., in 1855.

Seth, the fourth son of Capt. Seth, died in Mississippi in 1847.

Valentine R., another son, was a physician, and died in Alabama in 1828.

Roland B., fifth in the order, after living several years in New York, returned to Leeds and died on the old homestead April 30, 1840. Receives further mention with his sons, Gen. O. O., Rev. R. B. and Gen. C. H. Howard.

Benjamin Franklin, the youngest son, married Philena Gould, by whom he had two sons and two daughters, viz.: Theresa, b. ———————; Marcellus, b. ———————; Coridon, b. ———————; and Cordelia, b. ———————. The only remaining member of the family is Coridon, who resides in Bridgewater, Mass.

Benjamin F., died Dec. 30, 1882, on the old Capt. Seth Howard farm, then the home of his daughter, Mrs. A. J. Foss, who has since died.

Aurelia, the eldest daughter of Capt. Seth, married Thomas W. Bridgham, M.D., the second physician who was located in Leeds. After his decease, she married Samuel Leadbetter, a son of Increase, an early settler. After the decease of Mr. Leadbetter, she made her home with a son, Thomas W. Bridgham, whose residence was in China, Me., where she died. Her remains were brought to Leeds and buried beside those of her first husband.

Lucretia, the second and last daughter, married Jabez Leadbetter and settled in Wayne village, on the place now owned by

STILLMAN L. HOWARD, ESQ.

Mr. A. S. Wright. They had issue four sons and five daughters, of whom further mention will be made in an article devoted to the family of Mr. Leadbetter. The death of Lucretia occurred at the home of her son, Rodelphus, in the town of Winthrop, Dec. 28, 1884. Of the family of Hon. Stillman Howard, eldest son of Capt. Seth, whose names and births already have been given, first occurs that of Stillman Lothrop Howard[7]. April 14, 1833, he married Julia Ann, a daughter of Joseph Turner, of Leeds. She was born Oct. 13, 1809. They settled in West Leeds on the farm now owned by his brother Seth, where he erected a fine set of buildings, the same burned by lightning Aug. 11, 1891. They had issue Ward Benton, b. Jan. 8, 1834; Howland, b. Aug. 3, 1837; Daniel H., b. Jan. 19, 1840; Lucius, b. March 9, 1842; Julia, b. Dec. 14, 1849 and Henrietta, b. Dec. 7, 1853. His eldest child, Ward B., was educated in the schools of Leeds, in which town, in early life, he engaged in farming. From the effects of an injury received when a boy, he was never strong, yet seldom sick. Like several of his ancestors he was fond of a good horse and enjoyed using them. Jan. 5, 1862, he married Hannah L., a daughter of Warren Howard, of whom mention will be made in this work. For several years Ward B. was collector of taxes in Leeds. His cordial greeting and genial, though decided manner of business well fitted him for that work. He accompanied his parents to Wayne in 1875, where he was engaged in the hotel and livery business. He has one daughter, Lizzie, b. Dec. 10, 1874.

Howland went to Lebanon, Ky., when a young man; married there Miss Lizzie Kirtz, Oct. 17, 1861. To them were born Katie Julia, in 1862, and Minnie Stillman, in 1864. He was taken prisoner by Morgan's army in one of its raids through that country, but was soon parolled. Unfortunately for him, his business, that of shoe merchant, was one that suffered the ravages first of the Confederate, and later, the Union soldiers without money or price. In poor health he started on a visit to Maine, but died in Albany, N. Y., May 11, 1864. His remains were carried back to Kentucky for burial, where his widow and daughters now reside.

Daniel H.[8], third child of Stillman L., settled in Lebanon, Ky., where he married Miss Emma Maxwell, Oct. 23, 1866. He is a man who commands the respect and confidence of the people with whom he is associated. His life has been largely devoted to public service, and not without adventure. While holding the office of Internal Revenue Collector for twenty consecutive years, in a section of the State where moonshiners are engaged in the manufacture of whiskey, on which they try to avoid the government tax, he was a target for their posted guards. Horses were shot under him, yet he never turned back without accomplishing his purpose. In the settlement of estates his services are extensively employed. Fire has been an effective element in depriving him of property, yet he has never faltered by the wayside, nor neglected the education and development of his children in business pursuits. He has three sons and two daughters, viz.: Howland Maxwell, born in 1867; Lucius Stillman, in 1871; Ward Ray, in 1872; Emma Dunton, in 1875, and Julia Etta in 1877. Howland Maxwell married, Feb. 19, 1895, Miss Lillian daughter of H. H. Hoffman, of Cincinnati, Ohio. They have two children. The remaining children of Daniel H.[8] are single.

Lucius[8], the fourth child of Stillman L.[7], married Miss Melinda L. Brooks, of Auburn, Me., Sept. 7, 1864; in which city he settled, and engaged in the furniture business in Lewiston. He subsequently moved to Portland, and later, to West Medford, Mass., and for years engaged in the carpet business in Boston. Poor health caused him to retire from active life and he now resides in that city. He has one son, Barker Brooks[9], born in Auburn, April 21, 1867, who is the eldest male of the Howard family in the ninth generation. Fresh from school where he was liberally educated, he entered the employ of the Boston Tow-Boat Co. He is a young man of good executive ability, prominent in the various societies with which he is connected, and although not of the party faith which prevails in his city, he has been in the city government much of the time since its institution. He commands the esteem and respect of the people within the circle of his acquaintance. He is a dutiful son of respected parents, both of whom have long been in poor health.

Julia, the eldest daughter of Stillman L., was educated and fitted for the life of a teacher. From the schools of her native town, she was a student in Monmouth Academy, Edward Little Institute, and later, in the State Normal School, in Farmington. At the close of a successful series of terms taught in Leeds, she was called to the house of sickness of her brother, Lucius, where her care has since been constantly required.

Henrietta[8], the youngest of the family, was graduated from the State Normal School, at Farmington. She taught in the schools in Leeds, and subsequently was a teacher in the city of Lewiston, where, for several years, her time was devoted to that work. June 13, 1886, she married J. C. Stinchfield and became a companion in his home in Wayne village. March 20, 1890, at the earnest solicitation of her parents, coupled with a child's duty, she and her husband abandoned their home, and assumed their care. May 8, 1888, a son was born, Allen Howard Stinchfield.

After the death of Stillman Lothrop Howard, Esq., which occurred Nov. 9, 1890, the following appeared in the "Lewiston Evening Journal" of Nov. 17: "Stillman Lothrop Howard, Esq., whose death occurred at his home in Wayne village on Sunday, the ninth inst., from the effects of an injury caused by the kick of a horse on the previous Wednesday, was born in Leeds, March 3, 1810. He was the eldest son of Hon. Stillman Howard and Lydia Lothrop, whose birthplace was Bridgewater, Mass. He received an academic education at Monmouth and Kent's Hill. For several years a portion of his time was devoted to the assistance of his father in his extensive business, and the remainder to teaching in Maine and Massachusetts, in which his efficiency earned for him a wide reputation. He specially prepared himself in navigation with a view of instructing the sea-going youth on our coast. April 14, 1833, he married Julia Ann, a daughter of Joseph Turner and Deborah Gilbert, of Leeds. With the exception of a few months in Auburn, he resided in Leeds sixty-five consecutive years. His integrity and fidelity, with a good degree of business capacity carried him to the front in the respect and esteem of his townsmen and a wide circle of acquaintances. More than forty years was he continually active in public life, having filled for a series of years the offices of school committee, selectman, treasurer, etc. Forty-two years he held a commission as Justice of the Peace; being the first justice appointed and commissioned in Androscoggin County. Thirty years he was a member of the board of trustees of Monmouth Academy. The history of Leeds was written by him for the Atlas of Androscoggin County. Not unlike his long line of military ancestry, he held a Captain's commission in the State militia. In May, 1875. he purchased the hotel at Wayne village at which place he has since resided. In this town, as in Leeds, although advanced in years, he held the office of selectman and treasurer. His extensive public business in legal affairs, and especially in the courts of probate, enabled him to be a valuable and wise counsellor and instructor. To his efforts and influence may be ascribed many public changes and improvements. His was a busy, profitable and pleasant life. The many deeds of charity and kindness, the assistance he rendered the poor and needy bespeak his worth. To the faults of others he was charitable, and slow to censure. As a husband and father, he was always cheerful, pleasant, kind, and indulgent. With feelings of pride, respect and love will they cherish his memory while they deeply mourn his loss. He was buried from the house on Thursday, at which place a large concourse of relatives and friends performed the last sad rites. He was interred in the cemetery at West Leeds, near his former home." His widow survived him, and at the advanced age of 92 died March 7, 1901.

Rozilia Augusta[7], the eldest daughter of Hon. Stillman, married Oscar D. Turner, Jan. 1, 1832. To them were born two daughters, Lucia and Florence. Lucia, married Oliver Gilbert;

settled in Leeds and had two children. Florence, married Albert Additon, of Greene; moved to New Hampshire; had four children, and since the death of her husband, has made her home there with them.

Mary Louisa[7], married Phillips Turner, and settled in Leeds. To them were born Herbert, who died in childhood, and Victoria Helen[8], who married the late, respected citizen, Steven R. Deane. Phillips Turner died about 1842, and his widow, Mary L., Aug. 17, 1856. In the biography of the Deane family, further mention will be made of Victory.

Lydia Arvilla[7], married Lloyd Gould, Nov. 13, 1839. To them was born a daughter, Columbia Arvilla, May 12, 1843. She was a maiden lady and died in Lewiston, April 5, 1876. Lydia A., her mother, died Nov. 9, 1848; Mr. Gould died in 1880.

Lucretia Phillips[7], married Peter Lane, Feb. 16, 1840; had no issue and died in Brighton, Me., Dec. 23, 1844.

Hon. Seth[7], the youngest child of Hon. Stillman Howard[6] and Lydia Lothrop, received a liberal academic education in a college preparatory course of three years at Monmouth. On account of failing health he was obliged to sacrifice the fruits of his ambition, although he has added the study and practical education of a life-time, a feature of no less value. Freed from confinement, returned to open air and farm exercise, his health, the most essential feature in life, was restored and has been retained by the same remedy.

During the farm vacations, in winter, his love for the schoolroom caused him to engage in teaching, in which capacity several seasons were spent with a good degree of success. His ability has been recognized by his townsmen who have frequently called him to services on the Boards of Selectmen, Superintending School Committee and the office of treasurer. The district composed of East Livermore, Greene and Leeds was represented by him in the State Legislature. He is a Deacon of the Baptist Church in Leeds, a position he has held for more than twenty years. "He is one of the best types of the intelligent and well read farmers of Maine, liberal of his time and means in religious and educational causes." Oct. 31, 1849, he married Amanda, a daughter of Thomas Additon, Jr. and his wife, Anna Beals. They had issue Elsie Amanda[8], b. May 17, 1851; Fletcher and Florilla (twins), b. Oct .5, 1853; Lydia Ann., b. June 18, 1857; Seth Adelbert, b. June 6, 1859; Dora Lovisa, July 29, 1863, and Lucretia Lane, b. Aug. 22, 1866.

Elsie A.[8], married Herbert W. Lincoln, April 11, 1869. They reside in West Leeds. To them were born two daughters and a son, viz.: Annie E.[9], b. July 21, 1870; Howard Elliot, b. Dec. 16, 1877, and Mabel Dora, b. Nov. 12, 1879. Annie E. married Alton L. Thomas, May 10, 1890; has a son, Fletcher A.[10], born

HON. SETH HOWARD.

MRS. SETH HOWARD.

April 17, 1896, who is the first great-grandchild of Hon. Seth Howard[7]. Howard E.[9] married Gertrude E. Howie, Dec. 1, 1896.

Fletcher[8] was a graduate of Bates College in the Class of 1879. In 1880, he went to Onawa, Iowa, where he studied medicine with Doctor Allen and with whom he was several years associated in the drug business. July 21, 1883, he married Nancy P., a daughter of Hon. Peleg F. Pike, of Wayne, Me. He is a man of character and ability. He has held the position of chairman of the state committee of the political party of which he is a member. He is Commissioner of Pharmacy, to which office, in terms of three years each, he has received his third appointment. Not actively engaged in agriculture, he owns and has operated an extensive wheat ranch. His residence is Des Moines, Iowa. They have no issue.

Florilla[8], married James C. Pike, a brother of Mrs. Fletcher Howard, Nov. 18, 1877. He is extensively engaged in farm and stock business, in Onawa, Iowa. They have three children, viz.: Frank Howard[9] Pike, b. Jan. 4, 1879; Cora May, b. Oct. 15, 1881, and Edna Amanda, b. Dec. 19, 1883.

Lydia Ann[8], married Charles S. Pike, a brother of James C., Sept. 13, 1882. They have no children. Their residence is in Onawa.

Seth Adelbert[8] went to Onawa, Iowa, in 1879 and engaged in the mercantile business, continuing therein since, with a good degree of success. Sept. 27, 1883, he married Stella Tyron, of Galesburg, Ill. They have two sons, George[9], b. July 28, 1884; and Seth, b. Feb. 15, 1886. The name Seth has been one of prominence in the Howard family for more than two hundred years.

Dora Lovisa[8] was graduated from the Normal School in Framingham, Mass. She was an efficient and successful teacher in the schools of her native State and also in Iowa. Nov. 24, 1891, she married Junius C. Wing and made her home in the town which gave her birth. She is the mother of three children, viz.: Beulah A.[9], b. March 4, 1893; Arland J., b. March 3, 1897, and Stella A., b. Aug. 21, 1900.

Lucretia L.[8] is a maiden lady, who, much of the time since her mother's death, which occurred Jan. 20, 1892, has been the efficient housekeeper in her father's home.

On the evening of Aug. 11, 1891, the large and commodious farm buildings of Mr. Howard, in West Leeds, the same built by his brother Stillman were burned by lightning, together with much of their contents, comprising a larger part of the house furnishings, all the contents of the stable and barns, forty tons of hay, farming tools, carriages, two horses, cows, etc. Thus deprived of a home, he soon purchased the Rackley farm, opposite the residence of R. S. Loring, M.D., near the center of the town, where he now resides. The house in which he lives was built in the year 1804, by James Lane, who, three years later, set the giant elm now more than four feet in diameter in the front yard, where it stands a living, growing memorial of the planter. Among the relics of his esteemed ancestors, Mr. Howard has his grandfather's brass clock, made by Frederic Wingate, of Hallowell, in 1806; which is well preserved and continues to enumerate the passing time with accuracy. He also has a mirror and arm-chair brought from Bridgewater by Capt. Seth Howard[5] when he moved his family to Leeds.

MILITARY CAREER OF O. O. HOWARD, MAJOR-GENERAL, U. S. ARMY, RETIRED.

Entered West Point as cadet, 1850; graduated 1854, fourth in general standing; promoted 2nd lieutenant ordnance department; stationed first at Watervliet arsenal, New York; in 1855, for about a year, in command of Kennebec Arsenal, Maine, returning to Watervliet early in 1856; sent thence to Florida, reporting to General Harney for duty as his chief of ordnance in the field against the Seminole Indians; in the fall of 1857 ordered to West Point, became instructor of cadets in mathematics; remained there the four years preceding the War of Rebellion; resigned in May, 1861, and took colonelcy by election of the 3d Maine Vols.; organized regiment and moved it immediately to Washington shortly after arrival directed by McDowell, commanding in Virginia, to select three other regiments and take command of brigade thus formed; he took the 4th and 5th Maine and 2nd Vermont besides his own; this brigade he commanded in the first battle of Bull Run; promoted to a brigadier-general of volunteers, September 3d, 1861; during winter of '61-2, had a new brigade, 81st Pennsylvania, 61st and 64th New York, 5th New Hampshire, 4th Rhode Island, and 45th New York, in camp on front line in Virginia; latter two regiments soon detached, leaving first four. He commanded this brigade in all operations in the spring [1862] having his first independent expedition to Rappahannock under General Sumner, receiving much credit; then with McClellan's army, back to Alexandria, and by water to Peninsula, in battles, Yorktown, Williamsburg and Fair Oaks with same brigade; at Fair Oaks was twice wounded in right arm and had two horses shot under him; for this, receiving medal of honor; while on leave for couple of months, arm then recently amputated, he spent his time of convalescence in raising volunteers, filling the quota of his state, Maine; returned to the field two months and twenty days after Fair Oaks; was assigned to 2d brigade, 2d division (Baker's brigade), some-

MAJOR-GENERAL OLIVER OTIS HOWARD,
United States Army (Retired).

times called California brigade; this he commanded in second battle of Bull Run, where he received credit for successfully commanding the rear guard in the retreat; same brigade in the battle of Antietam. At Antietam, Sedgwick, his division commander being wounded, he succeeded to command of the division, 2d division 2d corps; commanding same division in completion of this battle, and also in the battle of Fredericksburg, with other divisions charging Marye Heights; continuing in command same division, sometimes temporarily in charge of the 2d corps, during that succeeding winter, 1862-3. Was promoted to Major-General of Volunteers, Nov. 29, 1862. In April, 1863, assigned by President to command of the 11th army corps; had this corps in the battle of Chancellorsville; where the corps met with a repulse from Stonewall Jackson's attack; also same corps at Gettysburg where he received marked credit, especially for his work the first day, from Gen. Meade and from Congress for selecting the famous field of battle, and holding it with his reserve troops, while keeping superior force in check all day from the time of Gen. Reynold's death till near night; participating also creditably in the remainder of the battle, till its triumph and close; after Gettysburg one division taken from him and sent to South Carolina; the 11th corps, thus diminished, and the 12th corps, were detached and sent to the Army of the Cumberland; with this corps Gen. Howard engaged in the battle of Wauhatchie, 28th October, receiving commendation in orders of his army commander, Gen. Thomas; engaged also in the battle of Missionary Ridge, 24th and 25th Dec., '63. Here his activity was so pronounced that Sherman asked to have his corps move with his own, the 15th, northward to the relief of Knoxville; this work being successfully accomplished, the 11th corps went back into winter quarters in Lookout Valley. The next spring, April, 1864, Gen. Howard was assigned to the command of the fourth army corps, Army of the Cumberland, while his own 11th was consolidated with the 12th, forming the new 20th corps, under Gen. Hooker. Howard began the spring campaign in the battle of Tunnel Hill, and participated satisfactorily to Sherman and Thomas, in all the operations of that campaign in the following battles: Dalton, Resaca, Adairsville, Kingston and Cassville, New Hope Church, Pickett's Mills, Muddy Creek, Kenesaw Mountain, Smyrna Camp Ground, Peachtree Creek, Ezra Church, Jonesboro and Lovejoy Station. After the engagement of "the Battle of Atlanta," 22d July, in which Gen. McPherson was slain, Gen. Howard was assigned by the President to command the Army of the Tennessee. In the battle of Ezra Church, 28th July, he commanded the field that day in which the 15th corps was the one mainly engaged, the 16th and 17th and the artillery supporting the 15th and furnishing re-enforcement; for this action especially,

Gen. Howard received the brevet of major-general in the regular army, conferred 13th of March, 1865. His march on Lovejoy Station was so rapid as to secure for the enemy a divided force; the enemy, so divided, attacked Howard there and was defeated, and Howard's and Thomas' commands completed the victory. It was a division of his army under Gen. Corse that fought the brilliant action of Allatoona Pass. In the march to the sea Sherman gave Howard his right wing, Slocum his left. Howard marched *via* Gordon, leaving Macon to his right. A division of his, Charles R. Woods' under his supervision fought the successful battle of Griswoldville; Walcutt's brigade doing most of the fighting. He moved on successfully on that route towards Savannah, while Slocum passed through Milledgeville, northward. Howard successfully marched three columns to the vicinity of Savannah, sending his scouts down the Ogeechee River to successfully communicate with the fleet; he chose and sent the division of Hazen to attack Fort McAllister, and was with Sherman observing that brilliant operation. Gen. Howard was made a brigadier-general in the regular army Dec. 21, 1865. After the taking of Savannah, about the 23d of December, 1864, Sherman chose Howard's command to begin Jan. 1, 1865, and move by water from Savannah, Ga., to Beaufort Island, S. C., to cross to the main land and sweep northward through Garden's Corner, Pocotaligo, across the branches of the Salkehatchie and the Edisto, *via* Orangeburg, up the Congaree, across the Saluda and the Broad, and into Columbia; while Slocum's left wing crossed the Savannah, and so kept abreast further northward. After Columbia had fallen, and Charleston, with the forts along the coast, Howard's wing passed across the Carolinas, joining with Slocum to finish very successfully the battle of Bentonville, March 19, 20 and 21, 1865; a little later, after Joseph E. Johnston's surrender, April 26, 1865, Howard marched his command from 20 to 25 miles a day from Raleigh to Washington, *via* Petersburg and Richmond; he himself being ordered, while his officers continued the march from Richmond, to proceed from Richmond to Washington by water in accordance with a request which Mr. Lincoln had left with his secretary, Mr. Stanton. Gen. Howard was assigned to duty in the War Department, the 12th of May, 1865, as Commissioner of the Bureau of Refugees, Freedmen and Abandoned Lands; he had charge of this bureau for the next seven years, and though it was much complained of at times, he was abundantly successful in its administration, particularly in its industrial and its educational features, having founded many permanent institutions of learning—such as Howard University, Hampton Institute, Atlanta University, Lincoln, Fiske, Straight and others.

In 1872, he was chosen by Gen. Grant, then the President, and sent to make peace with the only Indian tribe then at war with the government namely the Chiricaua Apaches; and also to settle numerous difficulties with other tribes in Arizona and New Mexico; all this Gen. Howard thoroughly accomplished without arms. On complaints about his administration of the Freedmen's Bureau there were two investigations; one in 1870 by a committee of Congress, which ended in a vote of thanks to him by the House of Representatives; the other was by a court of inquiry composed of seven general officers of the army; this ended in complete acquittal of all the charges preferred against him, and in unrestricted commendation. He had hardly completed this Bureau work when he was assigned to command the Department of the Columbia, August, 1874. During the next six years he, in command, passed through two Indian wars—one called the Nez Perce war, 1877; the other the Piute and Bannock, 1878. He brought these wars, after many battles and long, fatiguing campaigns, to a successful termination. In the spring of 1879, another Indian tribe called the "Sheepeaters" becoming rebellious in points near the Salmon River, he sent out and captured them *en masse*, brought them in as prisoners, put them at work at Vancouver and their children at school. From the Department of the Columbia, in the winter of 1880-81 he was assigned to the command of the West Point Military Academy, which he held for two years. July 13, 1882, he was assigned to command the Department of the Platte, to which he gave successful administration until his promotion to a major-general in the regular army, 19th of March, '86. He then passed to the military division of the Pacific, which included the Department of the Columbia, of California and Arizona. This division he administered to the satisfaction of the War Department and the President till November, 1888, when he was transferred to command the military division of the Atlantic. This division he held till the divisions were broken up: after that he commanded the Department of the East, which was substantially the same as the division of the Atlantic, until his retirement by law, Nov. 8, 1894. Removed to Burlington, Vt., where he has since resided. From 1897 to 1901 he was managing director of Lincoln Memorial University, an industrial school for whites at Cumberland Gap, Tenn.

For his work at Gettysburg he received the thanks of Congress dated Jan. 28, 1864; received the decoration of the Legion of Honor from the President of the French Republic, when on temporary duty he was attending the French manouvers during an absence from his Department of the Platte, in 1884; elected honorary member of the Society of Army and Navy of Spain December, 1883; received the degree of A.M. from Bowdoin College, Me., and LL.D. from Bowdoin, Waterville College, Me., 1865, Shurtliffe College, Indiana, 1865, and Gettysburg Thelogical Seminary, Pa., 1866. Howard is the author of the following books; Donald's School Days, Nez Perce Joseph, or the Nez Perces in Peace and in War; published by Lee and Shepard, Boston; Agenor de Garparin, a Biographical Sketch, partly a translation, by Putnam Sons, New York; "Gen. Taylor," in the Great Commander series, D. Appleton & Co., N. Y.; "Fighting for Humanity," Neely Co., N. Y.; in preparation, Personal Experiences Among the American Indians; Worthington & Co., Hartford, 1901; Isabella of Castile, a Biography, Funk & Wagnalls, N. Y.; a series of monographs published extensively in the "National Tribune," Washington, D. C.; military articles in the United States Military Service Journal, Governor's Island; and numerous articles, a part of them of a military character, but the most on subjects of current interest, published in syndicates, monthlies and dailies, appearing at all times from 1865 to the present day. Gen. Howard has prepared lectures upon the lives of Grant, Sherman, Thomas and Slocum, also upon war subjects and others of public interest, and delivered them with acceptance before large audiences; in fact his lectures seem to be in greater demand than his writings, though the latter find ready publishers.

During the Spanish-American War, he served on the Y. M. C. A. Christian Commission, speaking in all the camps and visiting Santiago, Cuba.

(Addenda to Gen. O. O. Howard.)

A leaf in the history of General Howard is here turned backward to a more domestic part of life.

General Oliver Otis Howard was born in Leeds, Kennebec (now Androscoggin) County, Me., Nov. 8, 1830, on a portion of that vast section of land taken up by his great-grandfather, Roger Stinchfield, one of the two pioneer brothers—settled by his grandfather, Capt. Seth Howard, and now owned by A. J. Foss. He was the eldest of three brothers, viz.: Oliver Otis, Roland Bailey, Jr. and Charles H. His parents were Roland Bailey Howard, born in Bridgewater, Mass., July 29, 1795 and his wife, Eliza Otis, born in Leeds, Dec. 10, 1804. His paternal grandparents were Capt. Seth Howard, born in Bridgewater, Mass., Nov. 21, 1762 and his wife, Desire Bailey, born Ibid. Jan. 23, 1762. His maternal grandparents were Oliver Otis, born in Scituate, Mass., Nov. 8, 1768 and his wife, Betsey Stinchfield, born in New Gloucester, April 14, 1774.

His early boyhood days were spent on the farm, and his education was actively begun in the district school from which he attended Monmouth Academy, where he took a college preparatory course. At the age of sixteen, he was enrolled at Bowdoin College. At the age of nineteen he graduated. Unsolicited, he received an appointment from Maine, as a cadet in the Military

REV. ROWLAND BAILEY HOWARD,
Secretary American Peace Society.

Born 1834. Died 1891.

Academy at West Point, which he entered Sept. 1, 1850, and from which he graduated, No. 4 in rank, in June, 1854.

Feb. 14, 1855, he married Elizabeth Ann Waite, born in Bangor, Me., in 1832. On the following day he was commissioned 2d Lieutenant of Ordnance and assigned to the Kennebec Arsenal, Me., to which place he removed his helpmeet. To them seven children were born, namely:

1. Guy, b. in Kennebec Arsenal, Augusta, Me., Dec. 16, 1855;
2. Grace E., b. in Leeds, Me., June 22, 1857;
3. James Waite, b. in West Point, N. Y., Dec. 1, 1860;
4. Chauncey Otis, b. in Augusta, Me., May 3, 1863; (second day's battle at Chancellorsville.)
5. John, b. in Washington, D. C., June 15, 1867;
6. Harry Stinson, b. in Washington, D. C., July 25, 1869;
7. Bessie, b. in Washington, D. C., Sept. 19, 1871.

Of his children, Col. Guy Howard met his death while gallantly serving his country on the firing line in the Philippines in 1900. He was one of the ablest officers in the regular army and was greatly honored by all who knew him. His widow and two children survive him.

Grace Howard, eldest daughter of the General, married Capt. Gray, of Portland, Oregon, and has five children.

James W. Howard, second son of the General, is a civil engineer in New York. He is married and has one daughter.

Chauncey O. Howard, third son, is in the government service in Washington, D. C., is married, and has four boys.

John Howard, fourth son, is a major in the United States Army and is in service in the Philippines. He is married, but has no children.

Harry S. Howard, fifth son, and Bessie Howard, the General's youngest daughter, live with their parents in Burlington, Vt.

LIFE OF ROLAND BAILEY HOWARD.

Roland Bailey Howard was born in Leeds, Me., in 1834; died in Rome, Italy, in 1891. He prepared for college at Yarmouth Academy and was graduated from Bowdoin in the Class of 1856. After this he studied law in Troy, N. Y., then gave up the law for the ministry, for which he prepared in the Bangor, Me., Seminary. He married in 1860 Ella Patten, daughter of Capt. David Patten of Bath, Me., a large ship owner in his time. His first parish was the Old South Congregational Church, Farmington, Me., where he remained ten years, and where his first three children were born, after which he was pastor of the Congregational Church in Princeton, Ill., and later of the Grove

Street Congregational Church, East Orange, N. J. His last pastorate was in Rockport, Mass.

During and later his East Orange pastorate he was Eastern Editor of the "Chicago Advance" of which his brother Charles was Editor-in-Chief.

While in Rockport he became deeply interested in the cause of international arbitration and finally gave up all other work to become Secretary of the American Peace Society of Boston, the oldest society of this type in America, which position he held during the remaining years of his life. He found the Society in a disorganized condition, and through untiring effort placed it upon a solid basis for practical work in the advocacy of its great cause. He enlisted the sympathies of the leading public men in America and Europe in international arbitration, gaining their personal allegiance in a permanent manner. He attended three World Conferences in this interest in Europe and advocated an International Court to decide the differences existing between nations. For these services he was greatly honored by the friends of peace, especially in England and the United States, and he met his death through over-taxing his strength while at the International Peace Congress in Rome, his last address being an eloquent appeal for the establishments of international justice through a High Court of Appeal in place of the historic methods of war.

All through his ministerial experience he was greatly beloved from the fact of his large-hearted personality and broad sympathies with all people. He often said that he would rather minister humbly to the needs of his parishioners than to be a great preacher. He combined, however, the personal charm with his public service and was a man of great eloquence when occasion demanded it.

He was present with his brother, General O. O. Howard, through the battle of Gettysburg and gained an impression at that time which resulted later in his strong stand against war.

He was a clear and forceful writer, contributing often to magazines and various publications, a great lover of books with a large library, and a deep student of all questions touching mankind.

His first wife died in Princeton, Ill., in 1872. He was married to Miss Helen G. Graves of Farmington, Me., in 1874.

He had three children by his first marriage, the eldest, David Patten Howard, born in 1861, a lawyer in Cripple Creek, Colorado, served nearly two years as Captain in the 1st Colorado Regiment in the Philippines during the Spanish War. His second son, Oliver Otis Howard, Jr., born in 1865, is a business man in San Francisco, Cal. The third, Francis Gilman Howard, born in 1869, is an artist in New York.

BREVET BRIG.-GENERAL CHARLES H. HOWARD.

All three of above sons are married.

He had two children by his second wife, Rowland S. and Ella who live with their mother in Farmington, Me.

Mr. David Howard has one daughter, Dorothy.

LIFE OF GEN. CHARLES H. HOWARD.

Charles H. Howard was born in Leeds, Me., in August, 1838; was fitted for college at Yarmouth Academy and Kent's Hill, Me., also at Topsham Academy. Graduated from Bowdoin in 1859, spent a year with his brother, then Lieut. O. O. Howard, at West Point, studying the various phases of army service. Then went to Bangor, Me., where he taught in the High School. Entered Bangor Seminary for preparation for the ministry but left in 1861 to assist his brother, then Col. O. O. Howard, to organize the 3d Maine Regiment of Volunteers. Enlisted himself in the regiment and was detailed as secretary to his brother, and then as aide-de-camp, in which capacity he served in the Battle of Bull Run. He filled the posts of Adjutant-General and Corps Inspector-General at subsequent times. His first commission was as a Lieutenant, and while serving on the brigade staff at the Battle of Fair Oaks, he was wounded in the thigh and carried from the field at the same time that his brother, then General O. O. Howard, was being removed from the fight after having his right arm shot away by the enemy's fire.

Charles H. Howard was in active service in the battles of Antietam, Fredericksburg, Chancellorsville and Gettysburg. He was again wounded by a bursting shell at Fredericksburg. In 1863 he was promoted to Major and was commissioned by Abraham Lincoln as aide-de-camp on the staff of the 11th Corps. After this he was in the battle of Lookout Valley and Missionary Ridge, receiving his orders direct from Gen. Grant and reporting direct to him.

During the Atlanta campaign he was Inspector-General of the 4th Army Corps of the Army of the Cumberland.

When Gen. O. O. Howard became commander of the Army of the Tennessee, Charles H. Howard became his senior aide, went with his army through to Savannah, and was the first officer to see Abraham Lincoln and report after the march of Sherman's army to the sea.

He was promoted to Lieutenant-Colonel for gallantry at Gettysburg, and was breveted Colonel for gallantry in the battle of Ezra Church. He was Inspector-General on the staff of Gen. Saxton and established freedmen's schools in South Carolina, Georgia and Florida. Became Assistant Commissioner of the Freedmen's Bureau until 1868. Then was appointed western secretary of American Missionary Association, with headquarters in Chicago. Bought the land for Toogaloo University in Mississippi; erected the first buildings of Straight University, New Orleans.

In 1873, he became editor and proprietor of the Chicago Advance, a Congregational newspaper, and continued in this position till 1882.

President Garfield appointed him Inspector of Indian Agencies in 1882, and in 1884 he edited the National Tribune for one year, since which he has purchased the "Farm, Field and Stockman," changing its name recently to the "Farm, Field and Fireside," a monthly publication issued in Chicago, of which he is now editor.

Gen. Charles H. Howard has five sons and two daughters, none of whom are at present married.

Otis McGaw Howard, born 1868; is a lawyer and is president of the Howard Publishing Co., Chicago.

Burt Foster Howard, born 1871; is a physician in Bangor, Me.

Nina Foster Howard, born 1873; is assistant editor of "Farm, Field and Fireside."

Arthur Day Howard, born 1874; is instructor in Northwestern University.

Lawrence Riggs Howard, born 1875; is a clergyman in Providence, R. I.

Donald Charles Howard, born 1879; is steward of the Dakota Mission for the Indians.

Katherine Howard, born 1889; lives with her parents in Glencoe, Ill., near Chicago.

BARNABUS HOWARD FAMILY.

Barnabus Howard[5], a brother of Capt. Seth Howard, was born in Bridgewater, Mass., Aug. 22, 1770. He married Mary Hayward (later spelled Howard), who was born Jan. 14, 1778. They settled in that town and subsequently in Scituate. In these towns nine of their family of twelve children were born. In 1815, he removed with his family to Leeds, where he purchased of Marshfield Paul the place now owned and occupied by W. Henry Francis. This place, as well as that settled by his brother, Capt. Seth, which is that now owned by A. J. Foss, were parts of the original claims of Thomas and Rogers Stinchfield, which extended from the Lake to the Androscoggin River, and south to the south line of the farm of Oliver Otis, of which his land was a part. The house to which Barnabus moved his family was a frame house of the pattern of most of the colonial dwellings, and stood on a spot westerly and near his family cemetery. The season of 1816 was that known in history, with its sorrowful experiences of hunger and sufferings of the people, as the "Cold season." Raising few, if any crops, a large family, with a long winter before them, Barnabus, like all wise men, hied himself back to old Massachusetts where there was bread in plenty. But the following spring, with renewed courage, found them all back to Leeds again where they afterward remained and became important factors in the building of educational and religious structures, and their genial, pleasant manners and kindly greetings, won for them the esteem and friendship of their neighbors and many acquaintances. Barnabus Howard died Dec. 14, 1859, and his widow March 12, 1862. Their children were:

Luther Loomis, born April 29, 1796; Daniel, b. May 7, 1798; Jason, b. July 6, 1800; Anna, b. Dec. 28, 1802; Warren, b. Aug. 1, 1805; Barnabus, Jr., b. March 7, 1808; Melvin, b. April 19, 1810; Mary Dunbar, b. April 25, 1812; Harriett Newall, b. March 19, 1815; Sewall, b. in Leeds, Aug. 2, 1817; Cornelia, Bradford, b. March 30, 1820; Laura Jane, b. April 14, 1822.

Luther Loomis married, March 30, 1823, Rhoda B. Mitchell, the fruit of which union was a son, Luther Loomis, second, born October 18, 1825. March 28, 1826, the husband and father died. (Mention of the widow and son will be made farther on.)

Daniel married, on June 1, 1840, Mary F. Crosby; settled in Belfast, Me., where he extensively engaged in the manufacture and sale of furniture. Having early learned the trade of cabinet maker, and possessed of native and acquired business ability, he became very successful and sustained a thriving business in the town where he so long lived, and later died.

Jason, the third child of Barnabus[5], married Caroline A. Howard, and settled in West Bridgewater, Mass. Of his family little has been learned, but his early death, which occurred Aug. 10, 1827, is reasonable proof that if he was a father, but few children were legitimately entitled to the right of calling him by that name.

Anna, the fourth child, who died July 8, 1824, at the age of 21 years, was unmarried.

Warren, the fourth son and fifth child of Barnabus[5], was born in Scituate, Mass. He married, Feb. 28, 1828, Rhoda B. (Mitchell) Howard, the widow of his eldest brother, Luther Loomis, whose only child, Luther Loomis second, was tenderly cared for by him, never lacking for a father's love or parental guidance. Mrs. Howard was a faithful helpmeet and a kind and indulgent wife and mother. It was the lot of this couple to care for and administer to the wants of his parents in the years of their decline, and to tenderly lay them away in the family burying place on the farm where their children were reared and from whence they had gone forth to participate in the various walks of life. Deacon Warren Howard was a man of sterling worth;

his kindly nature and earnest piety won for him the respect and esteem of his townsmen. His large family of children were "reared in the fear and admonition of the Lord." He died March 12, 1876.

Their children were: Melvin Clark, born Aug. 28, 1828; Lucy Mitchell, b. Oct. 24, 1830; Marilla Mark, b. Nov. 19, 1832; Almina Augusta, b. Sept. 27, 1834; Mary Jane, b. June 6, 1838; Dexter Waterman, b. July 23, 1840; Hannah Lane, b. Jan. 23, 1843; Clara Cornelia, b. Aug. 17, 1845.

Barnabus, Jr., the sixth child of Barnabus[5], married Eunice Gould April 9, 1834, and settled near Dead River, on the farm taken up and cleared by Joseph Knapp, Sen., the buildings on which stood about 60 rods northerly of those on the present town-farm. After selling this farm to the town of Leeds, he resided, for a term of years, on Quaker Ridge, and subsequently removed to Brockton, Mass., where both he and his wife died.

Their children, who grew to manhood, were Oren G., b. Aug. 21, 1835; Sewall P., b. Aug. 9, 1836, and Henry Harrison, b. Feb. 1, 1842.

Melvin, the next son of Barnabus[5], and his sister, Mary D., both died young, the former, March 19, 1820; and the latter, July 8, 1830. Harriett Newall, his next child, married Ruggles Sylvester on the 19th day of March, 1840. Mr. Sylvester died Dec. 24, 1852, leaving a widow and one daughter.

Sewall, the tenth child of Barnabus[5], died April 26, 1832.

Cornelia B., whose numerical position was eleven, married Alvin Foss, July 30, 1837, who was born Nov. 12, 1816. She has been a resident of Leeds much of her long and useful life. Although for many years a widow since Oct. 22, 1869, she has lived to see her children and grandchildren grow up about her and to them has ever been a faithful and loving parent. Their children were:

Ann, born Nov. 6, 1838; Francis G., b. Jan. 3, 1842; Warren Howard, b. Nov. 3, 1847; Fred C., b. June 25, 1849; Minnie A., b. June 6, 1859, and Preston E., b. Jan. 12, 1862.

Laura Jane, the youngest child of Barnabus[5], died Sept. 26, 1839, at the age of 17 years.

Luther Loomis second, the only child of Luther Loomis[6] and Rhoda B. Mitchell, married Sarah P. Hussey of Mount Vernon, Me., who was born in that town Jan. 28, 1822. She had a twin sister, both of whose pictures recently appeared in the State and Massachusetts papers, together with their biographies. Her death, which occurred in Hallowell, Dec. 14, 1900, was deeply mourned by all who knew her.

Elder Howard (as he is called by his Leeds neighbors and friends), early espoused the cause of religion, and has made the Bible a life-long study. He is a worshiper of "The true and living

ELDER LUTHER LOOMIS HOWARD.

God," and has, for many years, been a teacher and a preacher of the gospel. He is a firm believer and advocate of the faith of the second coming of Christ and the setting up of His kingdom on earth. Mr. Howard has spent many of his useful years in the town that gave him birth, and has a warm place in the hearts of the people. On account of declining health, he removed to the home of a daughter, in Hallowell, in 1899, where he now resides. The loss of his companion he deeply feels, yet silently endures his sorrow, and has a cheerful word for those who are likewise sorrowing. They had issue nine children, viz.: Melissa Almira, born in Hallowell, Me., Jan. 28, 1847; Melvin Clark, second, b. Ibid. Dec. 1, 1848; Luther Loomis, third, b. in Chelsea, Me., Nov. 24, 1850; Ella Marilla, b. in Augusta, April 3, 1853; Lizzie T., b. in West Poland, May 15, 1855; Sarah Florence, b. in West Poland, Aug. 5, 1857; Lot, b. Ibid. Feb. 24, 1861; Leander M., b. in Rome, Me., March 19, 1863, and Fred N., b. in Rome, April 6, 1866.

Of the children of Deacon Warren Howard", Melvin Clark died at the age of 24 years, Jan. 15, 1853.

Lucy Mitchell married, Nov. 3, 1852, Ezra B. Ramsdell, who was born June 3, 1828. They settled in Leeds. To them were born four children, viz.: Luther, March 10, 1855; Mildred, June 23, 1858; Marilla, March 28, 1864, and Howard, Oct. 12, 1866. Left a widow July 24, 1874, Mrs. Ramsdell later removed to California where she has since made a home with her children.

Marilla Mark and Almina Augusta, the third and fourth children of Deacon Warren, both died when young ladies, the former Sept. 21, 1850, and the latter Jan. 25, 1853, aged 17 and 18 years, respectively.

Mary Jane, the fifth child, married Everett Lindsy and spent her short life in Leeds, dying April 28, 1868, aged 29 years; had no issue.

Dexter Waterman, the sixth child, on the breaking out of the Civil War in 1861, enlisted into the 3d Maine Infantry Regiment, Co. K, which went into camp at Augusta, May 28, and was organized June 4, 1861. From a private he was promoted to Sergeant and transferred to the 17th Maine Regiment, Co. C; and later promoted to 2d Lieutenant, Co. E.; and still later promoted to Lieutenant. Step by step he advanced to the position of Captain, with a bright military prospect before him; but from wounds received in the many hard-fought battles in which he participated, he died June 20, 1866, after a lingering sickness at his parental home, among his many friends and loving relatives, who tenderly cared for his every want and made his last days as endurable as the nature of his wounds and their effects would admit. He was a beautiful young man, a favorite with associates and his death was mourned by a large concourse of friends and relatives.

Hannah Lane, the seventh child, married, Jan. 5, 1862, Ward B., a son of Stillman L. and Julia A. (Turner) Howard. He was born in Leeds, Jan. 8, 1834. They settled in Leeds where they continued their residence until May, 1875, when they removed to the adjoining town of Wayne, where they have since continued their residence. She is a prominent member of the Baptist Church in which she exerts a manifest interest and influence. They have one daughter, Lizzie Emma, born in Leeds, Dec. 10, 1874. She married George E. McAllister, June 26, 1892. To them were born Irene H., May 5, 1893; Florence O., July 27, 1894, and Henrietta W., Nov. 4, 1897. Their residence is Wayne.

Clara Cornelia, the youngest child of Deacon Warren, married Duane S. Wing, in January, 1866, who was born in Leeds, Nov. 18, 1842. To them was born a daughter, Elsie, who died when a young lady; and a son, Alfred, who resides with his parents, in Portland, Me.

The three children of Barnabus, Jr., viz.: Oren G., Sewall P. and Henry H., the dates of whose birth have been given, all settled in Brockton, Mass., where they married. Oren G. has one daughter (Mrs. Clark Lane). Sewall P. has a daughter, and Henry H. has no children.

Of the children of Cornelia B. whose husband was Alvin Foss, the eldest, Ann, died Jan. 4, 1867.

Francis G., married Vesta P., the youngest daughter of Rev. Walter Foss, Jan. 31, 1869. Like his father, he is a mason by trade, and in connection with his farm at North Leeds, where he resides, his time and services are in good demand. He has a family of children of whom mention will be made in sketch of Foss family. Her third child, Warren Howard Foss, was many years a locomotive engineer on the Old Colony Railroad, and later, and now is, an officer in the Custom House, in Boston. He married Maria Deane, Oct. 20, 1872, and settled in South Braintree, Mass., where he is an extensive owner of real estate. They have two daughters. The fourth child of Cornelia B. is Fred C. He married Eugenia E. Jennings of West Leeds, and resides at Livermore Falls. They have issue one daughter. He is a master mason by trade, and many fine and extensive structures of masonry in Massachusetts and Maine are living monuments of his handiwork. Her fifth child, Minnie A., married, July 9, 1879, O. A. Johnson and settled in Wayne. She has one son, Owen, born April 29, 1887. Her husband died April 2, 1894; since which time her residence has not been permanently established. The son is being educated in the schools of Wayne. The youngest child of Cornelia B. is Preston E. He has been

in the employ of the Old Colony Railroad a long time, and for a term of years a locomotive engineer on that road. He married Edith Chandler in 1891, in South Braintree, Mass., where he has a fine home.

Cornelia B. resides at North Leeds, in the family of her son, Frank G., and on this thirtieth day of March, 1901, is 81 years old. Among the mothers of which Leeds may well be proud, she holds a prominent place.

Of the children of Luther Loomis second, and Sarah P. (Hussey) Howard, Melissa Almira, the eldest, married C. L. Belden, of Westfield, Mass., in which place they reside. Three sons have been born to them, all of whom died in early manhood.

Melvin Clark second, died in Cartagena, South America, in August, 1888.

Luther Loomis third, the third child, married Hattie F. Davis by whom he had a son, Vivian Luther, born Nov. 1, 1874. In May, 1898, his wife, Hattie F., died; since which time he has made his home with the son, Vivian L., in Battle Creek, Mich. This son married, June 1, 1896, Matilda Ostland, and they have two children, viz.: Melvin David, born May 10, 1898; and Esther Sophie, born May 31, 1900.

Ella Marilla, the fourth child of Luther Loomis second, married Eugene L. Howe, of Hallowell, Me., Nov. 11, 1873. To them were born two children, Willard O., Oct. 19, 1874, and Mina I., Feb. 3, 1887. Mr. Howe died, Aug. 25, 1900. It is with this daughter that the Rev. L. L. Howard makes his home.

Lizzie T., the fifth child, died Aug. 25, 1855; and Sarah F., the next child, died March 30, 1873.

Lot, the seventh child, married Ella True, born Aug. 6, 1853, the only child of Francis D. Millett, May 10, 1880. Their residence is the old Millett homestead, at North Leeds. They have one son, Francis Davis Millett Howard, born Feb. 15, 1891. Mr. Howard is one of Leeds' most industrious, enterprising and successful young farmers. Of good physique and high intellect, a great reader with retentive memory, to which may well be added his bright and active business capacity, bespeaks a life of usefulness and worth to himself, his family and the community in which he moves. He is a cheerful and active worker, contributor and promoter of any and all public enterprises of benefit to his native town, and much interested in the cause of education and the up-building of moral principles of the people. His kindly nature, cordial greetings and genial hospitality endear him to his neighbors and many friends.

Leander M., the eighth child in the list, married Clara, a daughter of Bradford Boothby. They reside in Jamaica Plains, Mass. They have no issue.

Fred N., the youngest of the children of Rev. L. L. Howard

married Alma Abbott. Their residence is in Portland, Me. They have two sons, Homer and Roland.

The Howard family has been one of prominence in Leeds, and composed of many members. It occupies a large amount of space in this work as do several other of the early families of the town whose prolificness has been of vital importance in its growth and development. Let us hope that in coming years, the example of our early parents may be closely imitated in this direction, and our sparsely settled districts again sound and resound with the merry chatter and songs of the little ones as they go to and come from the newly dressed houses of education now going down in decay. On this the life of the town,—yea, the life and prosperity of the nation depends. Study and reason as we may to devise means of remedy, we are at once confronted with the naked facts and brought back to the only feasible standpoint that can be successfully maintained.

THE DEANE FAMILY

Descended from John Deane, who, with his brother Walter, came to this country from Chard, England, about 1637 and settled in Taunton, Mass.

Zebulon Deane, born June 12, 1773, of the fourth generation from John Deane and the seventh son of Abial Deane and Zebiah Field, his wife, came to Maine from Taunton, Mass., in 1792 to visit his brother Cyrus, then living in Greene. Later he took up land at South Leeds. In 1796, when 23 years of age, he married Mary Rackley, of Greene, and in 1797 they moved to West Leeds, to the place now owned by his grandson, Volney A. Deane.

Their children were: Zopher, Anna, Susan, Wealthy, Abial, Zebulon, Zebiah and Benjamin Rackley.

In 1814, Mary, the wife of Zebulon died, and in 1815, he married a second wife, Esther Millett, of Turner. Their children were: Stephen Rackley Deane, born Sept. 4, 1816; and Elvira J. Deane, born March 10, 1819. The latter married Nathaniel P. Moulton, of New Bedford, Mass., March 25, 1843.

Stephen R. Deane married Elvira Pratt, of Leeds, May 1, 1844. Their children were Rose Ellen, Henry Homer and Abbie E. Rose Ellen married Hon. R. H. Gilmore, son of Col. John Gilmore, of Leeds, Aug. 8, 1866. They moved to Iowa where she died Sept. 25, 1876.

Henry Homer died Sept. 5, 1851.

Elvira, wife of S. R. Deane, died Oct. 12, 1855. April 3, 1859, he married, second, Victoria H. Turner, daughter of Phillips Turner and Mary L. Howard, his wife, who was the daughter

COAT OF ARMS.

of Hon. Stillman Howard. The children of Stephen R. and Victoria are Stephen Homer, Stillman Howard, Phillips Herbert and Percy Harold. The last named died Aug. 23, 1877.

Stephen R. Deane was educated in Maine and Massachusetts. He taught school at Kent's Hill, Leeds and other towns in Maine, and in 1844-5 taught commercial and writing school in New Bedford, Mass.; after which he went to Lowell, Mass., where he was a member of, and clerk and paymaster for the Merrimac River Lumber Co. for 12 years. He was in trade in Leeds several years; postmaster at West Leeds 15 years; on the school committee 13 years.

He belonged to the Rifle Company of Leeds when 18 years of age. In 1852, he bought of Mr. Joslyn the second farm south of the one owned by his father, Zebulon, the first farm on the south being owned by his brother, Benjamin R. and now owned by Truman Deane, son of Benjamin R. and brother to Volney A.

Stephen R. spent the most of his life after 1859, on this farm. He was of a poetical temperament and always very much interested in the cause of education. He much enjoyed gardening and fruit culture. In 1894, he and his sons S. Homer and Phillips H. built a house on the farm. On Oct. 19, 1898, Stephen R. died, and the place is now owned by Deane Brothers, S. Homer and Phillips H. and known as Sunny Shore Farm. In 1899, they built a barn connected with the house. They now have a good set of buildings. They keep a stock of dairy cows, their cream going to the Turner Center Factory. S. Homer taught school several years; has been on the board of selectmen five years; was overseer of the Grange two years and master three years. He has also been a member of the Republican Town Committee.

Phillips H. Deane has been Deputy Sheriff five years; overseer of the Grange three years and is the present master of the Grange, this being his third year. He has been a member of the Republican Town Committee, and is now a member of the School Committee.

S. Howard Deane, the second son of Stephen R. and Victoria, taught several terms of school, and when 20 years of age, went to Turner to take charge of the farm of J. H. Hooper, where he remained several years. In 1890, he went into the butter factory at Turner Center, where he learned the business; after which, he first took charge of the factory at Brettun's Mills, and subsequently was employed by the firm of Eli Jepson & Son, of Lynn, Mass., and took charge successively of the factories at Livermore Falls, Monmouth and Winthrop. He is now in the employ of the Turner Center Dairying Association, with headquarters at Auburn, Maine. He has had charge of wholesale and retail stores at Worcester, Mass., Bath, Me., the factory at Milo and at present, is running a large wholesale and retail butter and cream store at Providence, R. I., a branch store of the T. C. D. Association. He married on Oct. 20, 1896, Carrie May, daughter of H. S. Blue, of Monmouth, Me.

MITCHELL FAMILY.

The name Mitchell first appears on the records of Leeds in the year 1800. Joseph Mitchell, who, with his parents was a resident of Bath, came to Littleborough in that year and settled on the north end of Quaker Ridge. He took up the farm subsequently owned by Col. John Gilmore. At that time, he had a brother Thomas, who was a boot- and shoe-maker in Bath, and in connection therewith was a merchant, dealing in West India goods. The need of a saw-mill was badly felt in that section of Leeds, and Thomas Mitchell was persuaded by his brother to sell his business in Bath and move his family to the new town and embark in that enterprise. As it is of Thomas and his descendants that we shall make mention (having little data of him and none further of Joseph), it is noted that he was born (presumably in Bath) in the year 1771. He married Mary Lamont who was born in 1778. They removed to Leeds in 1802, and at that time had two children, William and James Warren Lamont, better known in Leeds as Warren Mitchell. He was six years old in 1802. Before moving his family to their future home, Thomas purchased the land and water-power since known as Coffin's Mills, erected buildings where Henry Mitchell, his grandson now resides, built the dam on the stream and a mill, which was the first erected in that locality. Both his house and mill were burned. In company with Elias Lane he built another mill which was run successfully until 1812, when the war so affected and prostrated the lumber business that little work was then done, and the mill was idle for a time. In that year he built a new house near the mill.

They had a family of ten children. William, the eldest, born in Bath, married Abigail Morse, of Turner, in April, 1818. They settled in West Leeds and had issue three or more children.

J. Warren L., their second child, was also born in Bath, in 1795. He married Julia Gilbert, of Leeds, in November, 1820, where he spent most of his years, although he died in Turner. He had issue Clara M., Ellen and Henry,—more?

Clara M. is a widow; married Charles B. Collier in November, 1845, and later a Mr. Crockett; resides at Keen's Mills.

Ellen married Rev. Joseph Crekore, resides in Peabody, Mass., and Henry lives in Leeds, on the old family homestead.

He is the only member of the family of Warren now remaining in town.

Betsey L., a daughter of Thomas, married in May, 1826, Joshua P. Lamont, of Bath, and settled in that town.

Thomas, Jr., settled in Oldtown, Me.

Benjamin, another son of Thomas, married Mary Mitchell, of Brunswick, and settled there. He spent much of his life at sea.

Jesse, the last son of Thomas to be accounted for, married Elvira Knapp, in September, 1840, and settled in Leeds, near the place now occupied by the Jennings Bros. He, later, removed his family to Madrid, Me.

Mary, another daughter of Thomas, married a Mr. Carr, and settled in New Hampshire.

The other three children died in childhood.

HERRICK (ENGLISH FAMILY).

Eirikr, Eric, Erik, Erick, Irik, Eyryk, Erryk, Herik, Hireck, Heryck, Hericke, Hearick, Heyricke, Heyrick, Herrick.

This very ancient and much cherished Scandinavian cognomen has passed through numerous variations and mutations in England, some of which may have been idiomatic, but generally they are referable to the prevailing fancy of the early ages of English literature, and the absence of anything like an established orthography. Recurring to the English orthography of our own name, in all its variety and mutability for many centuries, we perceive something like a progressive transition, from the original Scandinavian Eirikr, down to the settled and permanent English Heyrick and Herrick of the seventeenth century. The earliest English forms were Ericke, Eric and Erik with occasional variations in the final letter, and some few instances of the substitution of I instead of E as the initial. In the twelfth century, Henry of Great Strettan spelled his name Eyryk.

A. D. 1450 Robert of Houghton wrote Eyrick, and about the year 1500 his son Thomas, spelled his name Eyricke and Eyrick, and his son, John of Leicester, merely indulged in a great variety, as; Eyrik, Eyrek, Eyricke, to which last, the engraver of his epitaph, for the first time on record, prefixed the H. unless, indeed, it may have been previously assumed by his son Nicholas of London, who had early chosen the name Heryk, which his sons again changed to Herrick about the middle of the seventeenth century; at this time, or a few years earlier, the sons of John of Leicester had fixed the orthography of the names Herrick and Heyrick which have remained permanent and unchanged to this day; Robert the eldest son, having assumed the latter, and the other sons of John, the former.

The traditions of this very ancient family, claim their descent from Ericke, a Danish chief, who invaded Britain during the reign of Alfred, and having been vanquished by that Prince, was compelled, with his followers, to repeople the wasted districts of East Anglia, the government of which he held as a fief of the English crown. He is recognized in history as Ericke, King of those Danes, who hold the Countrie of East Angle. In an attempt to unite the Danish power in Britain against the Englishmen, Ericke was defeated by Edward, the son and successor of Alfred; and was subsequently slain by his own subjects for alleged severities in his government.

The Norman invasion found this name represented by Eric the Forester, who resided in Leicestershire, and possessed extensive domains along the sources of the Severn and on the borders of Wales. Eric raised an army to repel the invaders and in the subsequent efforts of the English Earls and Princes, to dispossess the Normans of their recent conquest, and to drive them out of the country, he bore a prominent and conspicuous part. But he shared also, in the unfortunate issue of all these patriotic efforts. His followers and allies were stripped of their estates, and the sources of his own power were dried up; and being no longer in a condition formidable to new government, Eric was taken into favor by William—entrusted with important offices about his person, and in the command of his armies; and in his old age was permitted to retire to his house in Leicestershire, where he closed a stormy and eventful life, as became the representative of an ancient and distinguished race.

With this hasty glance at our earliest family remembrances, remote and obscure as they may be, we proceed to deduce the pedigrees of the English and American races through the branch of the posterity of Eric the Forester, which is still respectably known in England, and whence we derive our lineage.

Henry Eyryk, a lineal descendant from Eric the Forester, was seated at Great Strettan in the County of Leicester, England, at a very remote period. His grandson, Robert Evryk of Strettan, by his wife Joanna had Sir William, Robert and John. Sir William Eyryk, Knight of Strettan, was commissioned to attend the Prince of Wales on his expedition into Gascony in the year 1355.

From Sir William, descended Robert Eyrick of Houghton on the Hill, living 1450, who left by his wife Agnes, Robert (who died without issue), and Thomas Eyrick of Houghton, who settled in Leicester. He died in 1517 leaving Nicholas, John and Elizabeth. John Eyrick or Heyrick of Leicester, born 1513; died April 2, 1589; twice mayor of that corporation, 1559 and

1572; married Mary, daughter of John Bond, Esq., of Ward End in Warwickshire, who was born in 1514 and died Dec. 8, 1611.

The following epitaph on the tombstone of John Heyrick, Esq., and Mary Bond, his wife, is found in St. Martin's Church, Leicester, at the last end of the north aisle, in a part thereof called "Heyrick's Chancel," being appropriated as a burying place for that family: "Here lieth the body of John Heyrick late of this Parish, who departed this life ye 2d of April, 1589, being about the age of 76. He did marry Marie, ye daughter of John Bond of Wardende, in the County of Warwicke, Esquire, and did live with said Mary, in one house, full fifty-two yeares; and in all that tyme, never buried, man, woman, or child, though they were sometimes twenty in household. He had yssue by ye said Marie five sonnes and seven daughters. The said John was mayor of this towne in anno 1559, and again in anno 1572. The said Marie departed this life ye 8th of December, 1611, being of the age of 97 years. She did see before her departure, of her children, and children's children, and their children, to the number of 142."

Sir William Herrick, of Leicester, London and Beaumauar Park, son of John and Mary Bond Eyrik or Heyrick, was born 1557. Member Parlement 1601 to 1630. Knighted 1605. Ambassador from Queen Elizabeth to the Sublime Porte; held various lucrative offices in the Treasury; married 1596 Joan, daughter of Richard May, Esq., of London; died March 2, 1652-3, aged 96.

(American Family.) Henerie Hireck—Héricke—Herrick, the Anglo-American ancestor of a numerous race in this country, son of Sir William and Joan May Herrick, of Leicester, London and Beaumauar Park, was born 1604; came over from Leicester, England, to Naumkeag, then first named Salem, June 24, 1629. He married Editha, daughter of Mr. Hugh Laskin, of Salem (who was born 1614 and living in 1674) and settled at Cape-Ann-Syde over against Massies. Died in 1671. Out of a very numerous family (our traditions say twelve sons and several daughters) seven sons and a daughter, whose names are given below, survived their father and are named in his will. Children of Henry and Editha Herrick who survived infancy: Thomas, Zacharie, Ephraim, Henry, Joseph, Elizabeth, John, Benjamin.

Henry Herrick settled on Cape-Ann-Syde of Bass River (now Beverly) on which his farm was bounded. He purchased several farms at Birch Plains and Cherry Hill, on which he settled his sons Zacharie, Ephraim, Joseph and John. Joseph resided on Cherry Hill, where he acquired a good estate. Zacharie, Ephraim and John, at Birch Plains. Henry inherited the homestead at Lower Beverly, Mass.

Henry Herrick was a husbandman, in easy circumstances,

but undistinguished by wealth, or civil rank and influence in the colony. He was a very good and honest dissenter from the established church, and the friend of Higginson, who had been a dissenting minister in Leicester. Mr. Herrick and his wife Editha, were among the thirty, who founded the first church in Salem, in 1629 and on the organization of a new Parish, on Ryal-Syde 1667, they, with their sons and their sons' wives, were among the founders of the first church in Beverly, also. But there are reasons to suspect that neither Henry, nor his sons were, at all times, and in all things, quite as submissive to the spiritual powers of their day, as they should have been. On the Court records of Essex County is an entry like this: "Henerie Hericke, and Edith his wife, are fined 10s. and 11s. for cost of Coort, for aiding and comforting an excommunicated person, contrary to order."

Joseph Herrick of Cherry Hill, Salem, son of Henry and Edith (Laskin) Herrick, died Feb. 4, 1717 or 1718; married first, Sarah Leach, daughter of Richard Leach of Salem, Feb. 7, 1666-7, who died about 1674. Married second, Mary Endicott, of Salem, about 1677-8, who died Sept. 14, 1706. Married third, Mary, widow of Capt. George March of Newbury, June 28, 1707, who survived him.

Joseph Herrick, son of Joseph and Sarah (Leach) Herrick, born April 2, 1667; settled on a farm given him by his father, in the northwest corner of Beverly, near Wenham line; thence he removed to Marblehead, where he kept a tavern; thence to a farm on Mine Hill, Topsfield, gave a lot for burying ground, about half a mile south of Agawam River, March 13, 1739, which is still occupied as such. He died Sept. 11, 1749. His wife died Sept. 30, 1748. (I have no record of his wife's name.)

Benjamin Herrick, son of Joseph Herrick, born April 14, 1700; settled on the farm in Beverly, and Wenham, given him by his father, whence he moved to Gage's Ferry, Methuen, where he died in 1773. He married Lydia Hayward Nov. 27, 1720.

Israel Herrick, son of Benjamin and Lydia (Hayward) Herrick, born Dec. 3, 1721; lived in Topsfield, Methuen, Boxford and Lewiston, Maine. Entered the army as a Lieutenant, 1745; served in nineteen campaigns; left the army 1763, a brevet Major. Fought at Bunker Hill; resigned his commission as Major when the army removed from Cambridge. He died at Lewiston, Sept. 14, 1782. Married first, Mary, daughter of John Bragg, who died June 24, 1748. Married second, Abigail Kilham of Boxford, Mass., who was born Nov. 3, 1725, and died Feb. 8, 1817. Israel and his second wife, Abigail Kilham Herrick, were buried in the cemetery at Barker's Mills, Lewiston, near the old Herrick house which was built by his son, John Herrick. They lived at one time in the Davis house in Lewiston,

MAJ. ISRAEL HERRICK.

but how long is not known to the writer. Children of Israel and Abigail Kilham Herrick: Joseph, John, Elizabeth, Mary, Eli and Samuel (twins) and Abigail.

Samuel Herrick, son of Israel and Abigail (Kilham) Herrick, born in Boxford, Mass., Sept. 5, 1759, married Abigail House, born in Hanover, Mass., April 18, 1761. Children:

Israel, born Jan. 17, 1791;
Eli, born May 26, 1793;
Polly, b. Jan. 4, 1796;
Abigail, born July 5, 1799;
Betsey, born Oct. 5, 1801;
All born in Greene, Maine.

He moved to Leeds in May, 1802, and settled the farm or lot, which his brother Eli bought one year before of Isaac Freeman, and which has ever since been held in possession by the Herrick family. Samuel died Sept. 5, 1834. His wife Abigail died Jan. 22, 1846. They were buried at West Leeds.

Israel Herrick, son of Samuel and Abigail (House) Herrick, born in Greene, Jan. 17, 1791; married Abigail Lamb, of Leeds, born in Charlestown, Mass., Aug. 21, 1794.

Children,—Margaret, born Nov. 6, 1822; still living; Harriet and Horace, born Dec. 1, 1826; Harriet d. Aug. 1, 1829; Horace d. Nov. 9, 1890; Harriet, b. July 7, 1830; d. Sept. 20, 1850; Clarissa, b. Dec. 7, 1834; d. Sept. 4, 1837.

At the death of his father, Israel came into possession of the homestead farm, on which he lived during his life. When a young man he became interested in the manufacture of silk. He obtained a small quantity of mulberry seed and planted it. When the plants were large enough to transplant, he set a mulberry orchard. In 1837, he obtained four hundred silk worms of Macy Sylvester, of Greene, and commenced the manufacture of silk on a small scale. He continued to increase the business from year to year, and in 1844, he built a cocoonery 50 feet in length, by 19 feet in width. This business in connection with the farm afforded quite a means of revenue. The silk business was carried on till about the year 1850, when it was dropped altogether. In politics he was always a Whig until the dissolution of that party, when he became a Democrat. He served on the Board of Selectmen a number of years, and represented the town of Leeds in the State Legislature in 1835 and 1836. In religion he was a staunch Universalist, and always took an active part in church affairs. He died Feb. 27, 1862. His wife died Aug. 17, 1849. They were both buried at West Leeds.

Eli Herrick, son of Samuel and Abigail Herrick, born in Greene, May 26, 1793; died a prisoner of war at Quebec in 1814;

Mary Herrick, daughter of Samuel and Abigail Herrick, born in Greene, Jan. 4, 1796; married Ira Lamb, of Leeds; died in Carroll, Me., Dec. 16, 1875; Abigail K. Herrick, daughter of Samuel and Abigail Herrick, born in Greene, July 5, 1799; died in Leeds, Sept. 13, 1845. She was never married;

Betsey R. Herrick, daughter of Samuel and Abigail Herrick, born in Greene, Oct. 5, 1801; died in Leeds, Aug. 14, 1850. She was never married;

Horace Herrick, son of Israel and Abigail (Lamb) Herrick, was born in Leeds, Dec. 1, 1826. He married Sophronia Lyford Palmer, June 27, 1852. Children:

Frank E. Herrick, b. Sept. 2, 1853; d. April 8, 1855;
Frank H. Herrick, b. Aug. 22, 1856;
Hattie A. Herrick, b. Nov. 15, 1862; d. Aug. 6, 1866;
Loring Herrick, b. June 10, 1866;
Lottie A. Herrick, b. Sept. 3, 1868;
Israel H. Herrick, b. Jan. 5, 1871;

Horace, being the only son, settled on the home place, the same as his father had done. He was the third generation to occupy this farm. During the earlier part of his life he was sick a great deal. At one time he was out of health for five years, and at another, three years. But for thirty years before he died he enjoyed good health, and worked hard nearly all the time on his farm. In politics he was a Democrat. He never aspired to hold office, although he took quite an interest in matters relating to his town. He always attended the Universalist Church when there were Universalist meetings in town. As a neighbor he tried to practice the Golden Rule and not knowingly did he do any one an injury. I think I shall not be questioned if I say that he was an *Honest Man*. He died Nov. 9, 1890. His wife, Sophronia, died March 26, 1901.

Margaret M. Herrick, born in Leeds Nov. 6, 1822, has always made her home with her brother Horace. A large part of her life has been spent in caring for the sick. Probably there are but few persons in town who have been of so much help and comfort to so many families in Leeds in time of sickness as she. Since the death of her brother, she has continued to live on the old place in the family of Frank H. Herrick.

Frank H. Herrick, son of Horace and Sophronia (Palmer) Herrick, was born in Leeds Aug. 22, 1856. He remained at home working on his father's farm during the summer season, and teaching in fall and winter till he was twenty-four. In the spring of 1880, he went to Massachusetts and remained there till the death of his father. During this time he was in the employ of the West End Railroad Company. In the spring of 1891, he returned to Leeds and settled on the home place occupied by three generations of the Herrick family before him. In 1892, he was elected Supervisor of Schools, and re-elected the next spring. He married Lucy M. Sylvester, of Leeds, Aug. 22, 1894. In

FRANK H. HERRICK.

LUCY M. HERRICK.

1899, he was again elected Superintendent of Schools and was twice re-elected. In politics he has followed his father and grandfather, voting with the Democrats. He is a Universalist and always attends the Universalist Church when possible to do so. Laura Margaret Herrick, only child of Frank H. and Lucy (Sylvester) Herrick, was born in Leeds, April 15, 1899. She is the fifth generation of Herricks to reside in Leeds on the same place.

Loring Herrick, son of Horace and Sophronia Herrick, was born in Leeds, June 10, 1866. He attended the common and Free High Schools of Leeds; and fitted for college at the Coburn Classical Institute, Waterville. He entered Colby University in 1888 and graduated in the class of '92. He belongs to the Delta Upsilon Fraternity. Since he left college he has taught most of the time. He has been Principal of a private school in Bradford, Mass., Principal of the High School in Collinsville, Conn., Principal of the High School in Berlin, N. H., and Principal of the High School in Winthrop, Me. He married Linnie E. Clifford of Winthrop, Me., Aug. 17, 1898. At the present time, he and his wife are in Los Angeles, Cal.

Lottie A. Herrick, only living daughter of Horace and Sophronia Herrick was born in Leeds, Sept. 3, 1868. She attended the Normal School at Farmington and taught several terms. Since the death of her father she has made her home with her brother Frank. She is a member of the Main Street Free Baptist Church, of Lewiston, where she has resided considerable of the time during the past few years.

Israel H. Herrick, the youngest of the family of Horace and Sophronia Herrick, was born in Leeds, Jan. 5, 1871. He went to Biddeford when about twenty-one years of age, learned the butter-maker's trade and was in the employ of a company having a butter factory at Biddeford until the company dissolved. He married Alice G. Hanson, of Biddeford, Jan. 29, 1896. He has been in the employ of different railroad companies as fireman enough so that the Grand Trunk Railroad Company offered him a position as engineer on their road. For the past two years he has been in the employ of the Armour Company. He works in one of their stores at Biddeford, where he resides.

BOOTHBY FAMILY.

English Ancestry.

The name and family of Boothby are of great antiquity, and may be traced backward for the long period of a thousand years. A distinguished antiquarian writer states, that about the year 800

A. D., King Egbert divided the nation into counties, hundreds and wapentakes, and that one of the later sections in Lincolnshire was named Boothby. In the same county was a market town named Boothby-Payell; also a manor house of the same designation.

Cambden says: "These places received their names from the Boothby family, then resident there"; and the ancient historian, Leland, makes a like statement. Some modern writers have taken exception to this view from the fact that few surnames existed at so remote a period, but the family tradition is, that the name in its rudimentary form was derived from a Danish tribe named "Bobi" who settled early in Britain, and that the family of Boothby is descended from the chiefs of this tribe, who held lands in Lincolnshire.

Charles E. Boothby, Esq., a distinguished representative of the family in England, says: "Judging from the termination of the name, ethnologists have been of opinion that the name is of undoubted Danish origin. Certainly it is not Roman, nor is it Saxon." In Norman times, the "de" was added. Two parishes in Lincolnshire still bear the name of Boothby; one in Wapentake of Boothby-Graffo, a few miles south of Lincoln; and Boothby-Paynell, a few miles southeast of Grantham. If in King Egbert's reign the Boothbys owned the intervening territory, their possessions must have been very considerable. The ancient manor house which belonged to them is still standing in the last named parish. The name of Paynell came in only when the Boothbys lost their Lincolnshire estates by the marriage of the only child of the owner of them to a Paynell of Devonshire. But the male line of the family was preserved, descending from an uncle of the heiress, in unbroken succession; and the male line has continued unbroken through all the centuries since their first settlement in Lincolnshire in the ninth century. The pedigree of the family was compiled by Dr. Sanderson, who subsequently became bishop of Lincoln, and the manuscripts are preserved in the British museum."

The lineal descent of a family so ancient cannot be traced with certainty through the earlier generations; there are, however, in ancient documents, evidences to prove the existence of the family and name until the regular successsion is established, and these following down the line of descent we have a connected genealogical history, down to the

American Branches.

The history of the early generations of the Boothbys of New England is somewhat obscure, and the traditions and published accounts cannot be harmonized with the vital public records.

Judge Bourne, who was an excellent authority, made the statement that, "Thomas and Henry Boothby came with families from Magwater, Ireland, to Wells in 1720." This may have been true, but I find no evidence that Henry was ever in Wells, and am not sure that one of that name came over at the time stated. Thomas and Richard Boothby were inhabitants of Wells as early as 1726, and I suppose the former was father of the latter, and of the first John Boothby in that town and of Henry Boothby, whose name appears in Scarborough, in 1727, as a church member, but who returned to Wells and died, leaving descendants there who are accounted for in the following pages. Southgate has written of the early settlers of this name in Scarborough as follows: "Joseph and Samuel Boothby emigrated from the north of Ireland to Kittery early in the last century, whence they came to Scarborough." This statement is in part true; in some respects untrue. Thomas Boothby, born in Ireland, came with his parents to Kittery, where he married Lydia Came in 1724, and had sons, Jonathan, Samuel and Joseph. He came to Scarborough with the Deering family with whom his daughters intermarried about 1730-6. The first Samuel Boothby settled in Scarborough was a brother of Thomas, and had children baptized in that town in 1736.

Rev. Samuel Boothby, who traveled as a missionary extensively in Maine, and who was much interested in the family history, left, with other data relating to his ancestry, the following written statement: "Two brothers, so far as known, went from England into Ireland, married and had families. They afterwards came to Nova Scotia, then to what is now the State of Maine. One settled in Wells near the sea; the other in Kittery. The one who settled in Kittery had a son Thomas who came to Scarborough." This statement was doubtless correct, so far as it went, but he makes no mention of Samuel, the brother of Thomas, who also settled in Scarborough, and from whom a large number of the families who bear the name in Saco are descendants.

In consequence of the imperfections in the extant records of Kittery and Wells, and from the absence of an early book of records once belonging to the former town, we cannot make up a complete record of the first two generations.

I have not even found the name of the first Henry Boothby, said to have settled in Kittery, on any document there, but the presence of sons in that place supports the tradition that such a person was at one time an inhabitant of the town. The absence of his name from the existing records is no proof that he was not a resident. From a careful examination of the early records, printed statements, and traditions handed down in various branches of the family, I have come to the conclusion which follows, namely; that Thomas and Henry Boothby, natives of England, settled in the Province of Ulster along with the other English planters in that province; that they married and had sons born there, who had grown to man's estate when they came to seek homes in the New World; that the parents were well advanced in life before coming to New England and soon after deceased. The McLellans came with the Boothbys, and were connected by marriage after settlement here. At this point I must correct another published misstatement. In the history of Parsonsfield (1888) the following may be found: "Brice Boothby came to this country from Scotland and settled in Scarborough, and from him all of the name have descended." This is unwarranted tradition and without a shadow of foundation. The fact is, that Joseph Boothby of the third generation married Susanna, daughter of Brice McLellan, and a son, who settled in Buxton and became the progenitor of the families now living in Parsonsfield, was named for his grandfather.

GENEALOGY.

Thomas Boothby[1], born in England, settled in Ireland, married and had children born there; came by way of Halifax, Nova Scotia, to Wells in the District of Maine, with his sons, where he made his home the remainder of his days. No record of his death.

Henry Boothby[1], born in England, settled in Ireland with his brother Thomas, married there and came with his children to Kittery now in Maine, about 1720, where he settled. It is possible that he removed to Scarborough with his sons, and was the Henry Boothby whose name appeared as a charter member of the Black Point Church; if so, all of that name in town and vicinity, are his descendants, and following down the line of descent from Henry we come to the fifth generation and to the

CHILDREN OF JOHN OF SACO.

Isaac[5], born October 10, 1774; married Hannah Foss, (who died December 27, 1838), and settled in Leeds, Me. With resolute will and strong arms, he swung the shining axe, adding clearing to clearing and field to field until he had one of the largest and best farms in town. From him "Boothby's Hill," north of Leeds Center, took its name. He also engaged largely in the live stock business and carried many a drove of sleek bullocks to Brighton market. With few advantages for education in the schools, he trained his mind to solve the most complicated problems with figures, and there was not an example in Kenney's Arithmetic that he could not perform mentally with more facility than most men with the slate and pencil. He was a man of solid build and constitutionally robust. Positive and uncompromising, shrewd and cautious in business, industrious and frugal, he proved a success. He died May 20, 1835, aged 61. Six children, of whom hereafter.

Lydia, born Jan. 25, 1777; married Hamilton Jenkins, of Wayne, Me.; died December 16, 1833, aged 56 years, 10 months, 21 days. They had one child, Eliza, who married Capt. Benj. Ridley. She died August 15, 1825, aged 20 years, 6 months and 26 days.

Stephen[5], born in Saco, Nov. 7, 1779; first married Susan Buzzell, of Winthrop, (who died May 17, 1817;) settled in Leeds, Me., as a farmer, and had three children: Samuel, William and Abigail. He was an extensive owner of lands in Leeds and Wayne, which he sold to many natives of the Saco Valley, who were induced to settle there. He next married Hepsabeth Tibbetts, of Wells, County of York, who died Sept. 1, 1838; no issue. He next married Mrs. Hannah Page of Belgrade, formerly Hannah Churchill, of Plymouth, Mass., who was buried in Belgrade. He was an industrious and successful farmer and a kind-hearted Christian man. About 1814, he built a large, two-story, square house and other buildings on the old farm in Leeds, Me., which still remain practically as first built. He died June 5, 1871, aged 91 years and 6 months.

Susan[5], born Dec. 1, 1781.

Rev. John[5], born Sept. 30, 1787; married Anna Foss, Nov. 20, 1811, by whom issue, seven children. He died in Saco, April 4, 1878, aged 91. I think he spent some early years in Leeds, but returned to Saco in 1815, and made his permanent home on a large farm where the brick mansion was erected. He was converted during the "Grove Reformation," in Saco, in 1808; was ordained by Elders Henry Frost and Moses Rollins in the town of Wayne, Oct. 12, 1812, the services being conducted out of doors in an ox-cart. He spent the early years of his ministry traveling as an evangelist, preaching in six states; saw his first revival in Eastport, Me., where a Christian church was organized. He served in the Legislature of Maine in 1851-52, and voted for the "Maine Law," framed by Neal Dow. He was engaged in the ministry more than sixty years; one of the most extended terms of service in the sacred office of which we find record. At his funeral twelve elders took part in the services. Elder Boothby was a sturdy pillar of the church, uncompromising and undismayed, and his death was a denominational loss widely felt. He was not an eloquent preacher estimated by the popular standards, but was sound, logical, and at times profound and masterly; his voice was deep, mellow, and of great compass, and was used by way of emphasis upon his hearers with powerful effect. As a counsellor in conventional assemblies he was cautious, discreet and magnanimous. Being venerated by the younger ministers, they vied with each other to do the patriarch servant of the Most High honor. His stately presence at the conference, during his old age, was a benediction. As a farmer he was quite successful, and acquired a comfortable support. His frame was massive and his tall, erect form gave him a commanding and dignified personality. His visage was of elongated mould and his complexion swarthy. In his eye there was an expression of meekness and kindly light that was noticeable. He had his failings, but was a good and eminently godly man. It is related that his wife once expressed grave fears that he would be lost; that having preached to others, he would himself be a "castaway." He asked the reason for her anxiety and was answered in this wise: "John, you know a 'woe' is pronounced against those of whom all men speak well, and you certainly belong to that class." On his return from his appointment soon after this conversation, he gravely informed his good wife that he saw some chance for him, for, as he was passing a crowd of men while entering church, he overheard one say: "There goes that d—d old black John Boothby."

CHILDREN OF ISAAC, SEN., OF LEEDS.

Walter[6], born in 1798; married Betsey Ayer, of Standish, Me., in 1821, and died in Leeds, June 20, 1827; leaving issue, of whom hereafter.

Hannah[6], born in 1800 (twin); died June 20, 1821, in Leeds.

Betsey[6], born in 1800 (twin); died Sept. 21, 1821, in Leeds.

Isaac[6], born Nov. 20, 1809; married first, Jane Graves, of Wayne, who died December 16, 1848, aged 42, by whom thirteen children. He married second, in 1850, Mary Jennings, of Leeds, by whom three children. Mr. Boothby inherited the homestead and always lived there. He was the cultivator of an extensive farm, comprising about 250 acres, and for several years engaged in live stock trade; an owner of valuable timber lands in town; one of original stockholders in the Androscoggin Railroad; liberal in religious views; in politics Whig and Republican; not an aspirant for office, but a man of public spirit, who kept abreast of the current issues of the day; was selectman for nine years; was positive of temperament, perceptive and quick to grasp a situation. In business transactions he was cautious and shrewd; believed in being governed by first impressions; was attached to his fireside, where, when not attending to his business affairs, he employed his time in reading. He was a useful citizen, who manifested an interest in the town's progress and held the respect of those who knew him.

John[6], died young.

REV. SAMUEL BOOTHBY.

Cyrus[6], born August 22, 1791, in Saco; married Charity Chubbuck, of Wareham, Mass., Sept. 28, 1811. She was born Nov. 22, 1791. He settled in Embden, Somerset County, Me. in the spring of 1814, and cleared his farm from the wilderness. Here he spent his days; dying May 10, 1847; his wife died ———. They had eight children, three of whom died in infancy. He was in the War of 1812; many years in the live stock trade; represented his town in the Legislature of 1837 and 1839; a man of sterling integrity, whose word was law; as a man of business, full of energy and enterprise.

CHILDREN OF STEPHEN, OF LEEDS.

Rev. Samuel[6], born April 17, 1808; married May 1, 1831, Sally, daughter of Samuel and Betsey Leadbetter, of Leeds, born Sept. 27, 1811; by whom eight children. He died in Lewiston, Me., July 9, 1884; aged 76 years. His widow died in same city June 12, 1887; aged 76 years. Samuel Leadbetter died Sept. 11, 1859; aged 76 years. Betsey, his wife, died April 25, 1854; aged 68 years.

Elder Boothby was baptized and united with the Baptist Church in Wayne, and in 1840 was ordained. He served as pastor at Turner Bridge four years, and subsequently in Wayne for five years; these were his only pastoral charges. He afterwards labored for a year as a missionary, employed by the Maine Baptist Convention, in Aroostook County, Me. He then entered the service of the American Foreign Bible Society, where he continued until 1883. Since 1857, he resided in Lewiston, Me., where he acted as a local missionary. Shortly before his death, he was asked how the promises of God appeared to him then, and he answered: "Yea and Amen." Being asked if the gospel was his support during his illness, he responded: "The words of the wise are as swords and as nails fastened by the Masters of Assemblies, which are given from one shepherd." He lived for the truth and the truth did not forsake him. He was a good man, a good husband and father, a good citizen, a good church member, a good minister of the New Testament.

It was said of his companion: "Her devoted and self-sacrificing life will ever be fragrant in the memory of her four surviving children, and many others who knew and loved her."

William[6], born Aug. 1, 1810; died Feb. 2, 1901, aged 91 years. He married Caroline Pinkham, of Saco, daughter of Isaac Pinkham; she is still living. They had three children. He spent his whole life on the old farm, and was a very industrious and successful farmer.

Abigail[6], died March 8, 1814; aged 8 months.

CHILDREN OF WALTER, OF LEEDS.

Isaac T.[7], born Sept. 13, 1822; married Louisa M. Spear, of Standish, Me., Oct. 14, 1848, and lived in that town. Children as follows:

    I. Cyrus H.[8], born March 19, 1852, in Leeds, Me.; married Mabel Wilds, of Biddeford, Nov. 21, 1885.

    II. Sarah S.[8], born May 10, 1855; married Nov. 1, 1874.

    III. Frank M.[8], born Nov. 10, 1857; lives in Boston, single.

Hannah[7], born July 19, 1827; married Henry A. Brown, of Lowell, Mass., by whom three sons. She died in 1861, in Lowell.

CHILDREN OF ISAAC, OF LEEDS.

Betsey[7], born May 26, 1831; married Horatio Williams, of Leeds; no children; died in July, 1862;

Lydia J.[7], born Jan. 20, 1833; died May 15, 1849;

Augusta R.[7], born August, 1835;

Rafina A.[7], born July 1, 1837; died Dec. 11, 1842;

Walter W.[7], born June 28, 1838; was sergeant in Company K, Third Maine Infantry, and killed at Fredericksburg, Dec. 13, 1862;

Cyrus[7], born June, 1840; died Dec. 20, 1846;

Charles D.[7], born July 10, 1842; died Dec. 27, 1862;

Thomas Henry[7], son of Isaac and Jane (Graves) Boothby, was born April 24, 1845. He was educated at district school and at Monmouth Academy; married December 28, 1867, Sarah, daughter of Tillotson and Mary (Hart) Libby, a descendant of Eben Libby, an early settler. Mrs. Boothby died Oct. 28, 1888. He married second, Nov. 24, 1892, Estella S., daughter of Seth Stinchfield, of Danforth, Me. Mr. Boothby inherited the property of his ancestors at "Boothby Hill," in Leeds, Me., and is a farmer; also a member of Leeds Grange; Deacon of the Baptist Church; was town treasurer from 1896 to 1901, and a member of the 70th Legislature; has children:

    I. Bessie M.[8], born Nov. 16, 1868; died July 14, 1879.

    II. Lizzie L.[8], born Aug. 28, 1870; married March 2, 1895, Charles B., son of H. M. Brewster, of Leeds.

    III. Charles R.[8], born Sept. 25, 1873; died April 12, 1874.

    IV. Horatio R.[8], born Sept. 25, 1875; died April 1, 1895.

HON. THOMAS H. BOOTHBY.

MRS. THOMAS H. BOOTHBY.

LIEUT. COL. STEPHEN BOOTHBY.

CHILDREN OF REV. SAMUEL.

Susan E.[7], born May 2, 1832, in Leeds; married Orson, son of Alvin and Lucy (Mitchell) Lane, of Leeds, in March, 1852. She died May 14, 1858, leaving no issue. She was a young woman of good natural ability; lived a noble, Christian example and was beloved by all who knew her.

Col. Stephen[7], born Oct. 23, 1833; died June 5, 1864, aged 31 years, unmarried. In his early years he worked at home on his father's farm, and attended the common school at North Leeds. He then took a preparatory course at Litchfield Seminary; entered Waterville College in 1853, and graduated in 1857. He afterwards taught school; also served as instructor and lecturer for teachers institute, under the State superintendent of education. In the spring of 1861, he formed a co-partnership with Mark H. Dunnell afterwards a member of Congress, and engaged in the practice of law in Portland, with flattering prospects of success. This business relation was not long continued, for both members of the firm responded to the call for men to defend the flag. Stephen Boothby entered the First Maine Cavalry as First Lieutenant of Company F, and was promoted to a captaincy after entering the field the next year. He was on duty with his company until appointed Major in March or April, 1863, with the exception of a few months in the autumn of 1862, while aide-de-camp to the military governor of Frederick, Md., during the campaign in that state. In July, 1864, he was promoted to Lieutenant-Colonel, which rank he held until his death. While skirmishing at Shepardstown, he was badly wounded in the back, but remained some time in the saddle. He was allowed to return home for a short time to recuperate. He led a charge in the battle at Beaver Dam Station, Va., May 10, 1864, and was shot through the right breast and right shoulder, necessitating the operation of exsection, the right arm being removed at the shoulder joint. After a wearying ride over the rough roads in an ambulance around Richmond for five days, he was placed on a hospital boat, and his splendid constitution, indomitable courage and unyielding will, kept him up so well that he could help himself considerably. But he died in a hospital at Point Lookout, Md., June 5, 1864, at the age of 30 years, 7 months, and 12 days. His body was taken to his father's home in Lewiston, and received a military burial. Almost the entire Cumberland bar, of which he was a member was present, and a large military escort followed the body to the grave and fired the last salute. The horse he rode in the field was led in the procession. We cannot more appropriately supplement the foregoing than by quoting from an address by Col. C. H. Smith, at a reunion of the First Maine Cavalry at Lewiston, on Sept. 2, 1879:

"Lieut.-Col. Boothby died. And as his noble soul went out,

there came to take its place the spirit of a deeper devotion of duty, a higher love of country, a nobler disregard of danger in the cause of right and justice, that hovered over the regiment until its muster-out, and that still lingers around and guides the comrades who were so fortunate as to serve in the light of his example. Lieut.-Col. Boothby died. And shall we here to-day mourn his loss? Shall we drop a tear, or breathe a word of pity that he died so young, while so bright a future was before him? No! Lieut.-Col. Boothby died. Let us here, standing by his grave, remembering his noble life and glorious death, each one pledge ourselves to emulate his example. Let us each one pledge ourselves anew to keep his memory, and the memory of our comrades, and the memory of the cause for which they died, ever bright, and to practice ourselves, and teach our children lessons of patriotism, of fidelity to duty and to God, of love of liberty, and of reverence for the dear old, grand old Stars and Stripes, the lessons which we read as we stand here by the grave of one who gave his life for them. Then shall Lieut.-Col. Boothby not have lived in vain. Then shall our sacrifices and hardships not have been in vain. Then shall the War of the Rebellion not have been fought in vain. Then shall we be found worthy at the last grand roll-call, to stand by the side of Lieut.-Col. Boothby, in the awful presence of the Great Commander of all, and joyously answer 'HERE!' "

Col. Boothby was one of those noble men whom the military service could not corrupt. Strictly temperate, eschewing the use of either stimulants or narcotics, upright in morals, addicted to no vice or evil habit, inflexibly honest, inaccessible to a temptation to fraud or meanness, he was the very soul of soldierly honor, and commanded the highest respect of his fellows in arms. He deemed no oaths necessary to establish his character for soldierly independence and manliness, or to uphold his authority; he indulged in no boasting to call attention to his bravery or deeds of valor; he assumed no haughtiness of manner to give men to understand that he was one in command; he made no display to bring before the minds of observers the position he held, or to invite from them homage to his rank. But in all those qualities which could render him worthy of honor and deference as a man, a soldier, and an officer, he stood pre-eminent. The following lines were written in memory of Col. Boothby:

They have welcomed home our soldier, but no shouts have rent
    the air,
And no tones of joyous greeting for the gallant sleeper there;
But the strong men bow their faces, and fair woman's tear-drops
    fall
As they yield another treasure at their bleeding country's call.

HON. R. C. BOOTHBY.

They have welcomed home our soldier, but he came not as of
  old—
In the flush of life and gladness—but so pale, and still, and cold;
And with muffled steps they bear him—they who loved the hero
  well,
While with cadence soft and mournful, tolls the solemn minster
  bell.

Ay! 'tis well that they have wrapped him—him the young, the
  brave, the true,
Wrapped him in his own loved banner, of the red, the white, the
  blue,
For that flag he fought so bravely, for that flag his life-blood
  gave,
And 'tis meet that it be waving o'er his honored, cherished grave.

They have welcomed home our soldier, but a welcome strangely
  sad;
Eyes are dim and lips are trembling; tones are hushed erewhile
  so glad.
Ah! we deemed not when he left us, firm of step and strong of
  will,
That that step so soon would falter, that brave heart so soon be
  still.

. . . .

Young he died, the gallant-hearted, but full many a gray-haired
  one
Sinks to rest at close of evening with his race less nobly run.
Life was sweet, but duty sweeter, and he bravely, bravely fell,
For the green vales of our country, for the land he loved so well!

Then raise high the costly marble! place upon the book of Fame,
'Mid our band of valiant martyrs, Boothby's honored, cherished
  name.
In our heart of hearts we'll wear it, grateful that our Father gave
Souls so noble, patriot heroes, our bleeding land to save.

Elias P.[7], born Sept. 22, 1835; died Oct. 31, 1840.
Viora G.[7], born July 8, 1838; married to Orson Lane, of Leeds, Dec. 17, 1859. Three children.
Hon. Roswell C.[7], born Jan. 16, 1840; first, married Julia A., April 27, 1861, daughter of Warren and Betsey Coffin, of Lewiston. She died at East Livermore, Me., March 31, 1868, aged 26 years. Two children of whom hereafter.
He married second, Dec. 6, 1870, Clara A., of Portland, daughter of Hezekiah and Nancy Atwood, of Livermore, Me.,

and by her has two children. His early life was passed upon his father's farm and attending the common schools. In 1857, he moved to Lewiston, Me. with his parents, and there attended High School and the Maine State Seminary (now Bates College), and at the age of seventeen commenced teaching, in which capacity he was very successful. In 1864, he purchased a farm at East Livermore, and two years later he sold this and purchased the grist-mill at Livermore Falls, which he operated in connection with the "feed business," for twenty years; since which time he has been in the wood and coal business.

He was a member of the Board of School Committee 1866-69; Supervisor of Schools, 1871-74; on the Board of Selectmen 1875-87 and 1891-94, and chairman of this board for the last twelve years of his service; County Commissioner from 1883 to 1893; Justice of the Peace and Trial Justice for many years, in which last capacity he has sat as judge in all the cases that could come before that court for at least fifteen years. He was the member of the Executive Council from Androscoggin County during the two years 1897-98, and on the 16th day of March, 1899, was appointed Judge of the Livermore Falls Municipal Court, which position he now holds.

He is a member of the Baptist Church, of which he has been deacon and leader of the choir for a long time.

He has given much attention to vocal music. For many years he has been prominent in Masonic bodies, having held the offices of Master High Priest and D. D. Grand Master.

Emma L.[7], born Feb. 9, 1842, in Leeds; was married to Willard Lothrop, of Leeds, son of Solomon and Sally Lothrop, June 11, 1860, and has three children.

Sarah H.[7], born March 19, 1851; married July 25, 1873, Frederick B. Stanford, of Lewiston, by whom two children. They afterwards went to Brooklyn, N. Y., where they still reside.

Marietta[7], born July 12, 1853; died September 22, 1872.

CHILDREN OF WILLIAM.

Orissa[7], born Jan. 11, 1835; died Feb. 2, 1837.

Lewis P.[7], born June 16, 1839; married Lois A. Hersey, daughter of Samuel and Harriet Hersey, of Fayette, Me. He died Oct. 10, 1890. They had one child, Carrie H., who was born July 4, 1868; married Stephen Wing, son of Salmon and Ardelia Wing, of Leeds. They now reside in Putnam, Conn.

Orrah A.[7], born Feb. 20, 1844; married John L. B. Farrington, son of Rev. James and Melinda F. Farrington, of Wilton, Feb. 20, 1867. They have one daughter, Susan F., born Jan. 3, 1871.

CHILDREN OF SUSAN E. AND ORSON LANE.

Melvin Clark Lane[8], born at Leeds in 1852; married Lizzie Howard, daughter of Orren Howard, of Brockton, Mass., formerly of Leeds. Mr. Lane went to Brockton, Mass., when a young man and for 23 years was engaged in the meat business; was widely known throughout the city, and was highly respected by all who knew him; was an honorable, upright man, a firm and generous friend; was a member of the Porter Congregational Church, and for many years very active in its work. He died June 16, 1898, aged 46.

CHILDREN OF VIORA G. AND ORSON LANE.

Lucy M.[8], born in Leeds, Sept. 16, 1861; educated in the public schools of Lewiston, Me.; resides there with her mother, and is now teaching in said city.

Stephen B.[8], born Sept. 1, 1865, is unmarried; is in the meat business in Brockton, Mass.

CHILDREN OF ROSWELL C. BOOTHBY.

Eugene Humphrey[8], born in Lewiston, Me., Oct. 19, 1863; married Miss Ida K. Simons, of Washington, D. C., Dec. 24, 1890. They have two children, born in Boston, Roswell Eugene, born Jan. 18, 1893, and Marietta, born Feb. 4, 1894. He is connected with a large clothing house in Baltimore, Md.

Vesta Julia[8], born at East Livermore, Nov. 2, 1865; died Nov. 8, 1887.

Samuel Drydon[8], born Oct. 9, 1874; died Aug. 9, 1895.

Heloise Helena[8], born May 5, 1883.

CHILDREN OF EMMA L. AND WILLARD LOTHROP.

Susan E.[8], born Jan. 10, 1861; married Gustavus W., son of Giddings and Cassandra Benson Lane, of Leeds, Sept. 23, 1883; no children.

Frank B.[8], born July 12, 1862, is unmarried; is connected with a dry goods house in Philadelphia and has an office in Boston, Mass., where he resides.

Sarah Clyde[8], born Aug. 6, 1879; is a graduate of Farmington, Maine, Normal School, and a teacher in Massachusetts.

CHILDREN OF SARAH AND FRED STANFORD.

Harold B.[8], born Nov. 17, 1875; resides in Brooklyn, N. Y., with his parents, and connected with a large importing house in New York City.

Louise A.[8], born Oct. 17, 1883.

RAMSDELL FAMILY.

From Edward[1] Ramsdell, who came from England in 1761, the Ramsdells of Leeds and many another municipality trace their line of ancestry. In 1763, he married and settled in Hanson, Plymouth County, Mass. To them were born in that town, six children, four of whom married and settled there, each raising a family in keeping, numerically, with "ye olden time." He was a Revolutionary soldier with four years' service, and held the rank of Lieutenant during that time. In 1804, his son, Gersham[2], moved from Hanson to Leeds, and with him six of his eight children, viz.: William[3], Joshua[3], Luther[3], Rufus[3], Polly[3] and Sarah[3] and settled near the Androscoggin River on the farm now occupied by A. P. Russell. Of the two children remaining in Hanson, viz.: John[3] and Gersham[3], Jr., the former settled in New York, and the latter in New Hampshire. Ex-Gov. E. A. Ramsdell is a grandson of Gersham,[3] Jr. Of the six that came to Leeds, the eldest, William[3], served an apprenticeship and learned the trade of carpenter. He was in the service of the United States Army in the War of 1812, and returning therefrom in 1814, he married Anna Deane and settled on a farm adjoining that of his father, where four children were born to them, viz.: Zophar D.[4], Augustus[4], Roswell[4], and Melvina[4] J. Zopher D. married Almeda Alden, of Turner, and settled in Abington, Mass., in 1840. In 1848, he engaged in the manufacture of boots and shoes, and in 1858, moved to Cereda, Va. (now West Virginia), where he established a manufactory which he operated until the breaking out of the Civil War, when he entered the Union service and with his company, of which he was Captain, joined the 5th Virginia Regiment, and was assigned to the commissionary department, where he completed a service of four years and seven months. He was in many battles, among them Guyandot—the first fought in Virginia—Winchester, Franklin, etc., and final battle of Petersburg. In civil life, he twice was elected to the Senate of West Virginia, and for seven years was a special agent of the government in the Post Office Department. He died at the age of 70 years, leaving a widow and four children.

Augustus[4], the second child of William[3], went to Massachusetts in 1848 and for a year, was a teacher in the schools of that state; at the end of which time, he engaged in business with his brother, Z. D. In 1856, he married Mary A. Alden, a lineal descendant in the fifth generation from John and Priscilla (Mullen) Alden. The succeeding year he returned to Leeds and settled on the home farm. To them were born a daughter, who died in infancy, and a son, B. Roswell, who married Susie G. Wood, of Massachusetts, and now resides on the old homestead in Leeds, where he has two children, Mary M., and Irena W. Mary A. (Alden) Ramsdell, wife of Augustus[4], died in 1891.

Roswell, the third child of William[3], died in childhood.

Melvina J., his fourth child, married R. E. Wood; settled in Westport, Mass., and is the mother of ten children, six of whom are living.

Joshua[3], the fourth child of Gersham[2] and the second who came with him to Leeds, married and settled in Cincinnati, Ohio. He was a physician and master of his profession. They had issue five children.

Luther[3], fifth child of Gersham[2], married Achsa Pratt and remained on the home farm. They had issue five children, viz.: Ezra[4] B., Elisha[4] P., Martha[4] J., Viola[4] A. and A. Ella[4].

Ezra[4] B. married Lucy M., a daughter of Deacon Warren Howard, in 1852, and settled at North Leeds. He died in 1874, leaving a widow and four children; three of whom are now living and with the widow reside in California.

Elisha[4] P. was in the "Civil War" and died in the service.

Martha[4] J., married A. G. Lothrop; settled in Leeds; later in Monmouth and subsequently in St. Paul, Minn., where she died, leaving two sons, both of whom were college graduates, and now reside in the West.

Viola A., married George B. Lane; settled in Leeds, and had issue John,—college graduate, Justin and Kittie. Both sons died in early manhood; Kittie married E. A. Russell and resides on the homestead of her father and grandfather. She has a daughter, Eula.

A. Ella[4], married B. King, and resides in Monmouth, Me.

Rufus[3], the sixth child of Gersham[2], married Hannah Draper; settled in Livermore; raised a family of five children, three of whom are living in this county.

Polly[3], the seventh child of Gersham, married John Thompson and had eight children, all of whom are dead.

Sarah[3], the youngest child of Gersham[2], married John Berry, of Greene. They had issue three children, one of whom only is living.

Of the descendants of Gersham[2], 19 are living in Maine, 14 in Massachusetts, 11 in New Hampshire, 6 in New York, 7 in West Virginia, 1 in Florida, 4 in Ohio, 3 in California, 5 in Washington and 3 in Wisconsin (73).

PARCHER FAMILY.

Though only one Parcher family has lived in Leeds, no name is better known or held in higher esteem. Daniel Parcher was born in Saco, Maine, March 25, 1784. His ancestors came from England to Massachusetts in the seventeenth century. His father, Elias Parcher, who married a Seavy, moved to Saco from Gloucester, Mass. Daniel Parcher went to sea several years in his early life, mostly in the West India trade. In 1808, he came to Leeds and with his brother-in-law, Robert Gould, bought the 400-acre Stone lot upon which he settled. The country was all a wilderness then, the only roads being by spotted trees.

In religion, Mr. Parcher was an active Free Will Baptist; in politics a Whig until the formation of the Republican party. He held various town offices and was a prominent and respected man in the community.

Daniel Parcher was twice married; his first wife being Sally Andrews, and his second, Clara Berry, and had a large family of children.

The eldest daughter, Miranda, married Samuel Elden and lived in Saco; Sewall F. studied medicine and practiced in Turner and East Boston; Martha married John A. True and lived in Livermore; Olive married Eben True and lived in Turner. These four are all dead. Loring married Hannah Huntoon and settled on a farm in Livermore; Aurelia married David L. Page, of Belgrade, in which town she still lives. By his second wife Mr. Parcher had five children, Loraine, Mira, Miranda, George and Effie C., of whom four are living. Loraine married Eliab Sturtevant and died in Charlestown, Mass.; Mira married Ward H. Jennings and settled in Lapeer, Michigan; Miranda married Charles W. Stuart, of Belgrade; Effie C. married George E. Minot, of Belgrade.

George is the only one of these eleven children left in Leeds, and he owns the farm which his father cleared. He married Carrie W. Norton, of Blandford, Mass., Nov. 17, 1869. She died March 8, 1881, leaving a daughter, Clara May, and a son, Fred N. Mr. Parcher in early life, taught school in Maine and Michigan. He has served the people of his native town as a member of the School Committee, as Superintendent of Schools and as selectman; has been a member of the House of Representatives; has twice represented Androscoggin County in the State Senate; has long been a justice of the peace, and is now serving his ninth year as a member of board of county commissioners. He has been an earnest worker in the Grange, and his influence is always felt in whatever will advance the best interests of his town and county. In politics he is an active Republican.

DANIEL PARCHER.

BATES FAMILY.

Solomon Bates moved his family from Scituate, Mass. to Maine, in the year 1787. Three of his sons afterwards settled in Leeds.

Doubty, son of Solomon, was out with his father in the Revolution. He was an iron-smith by trade and a man of excellent character. He married Polly Perry and had five children: Charles, Polly, William, Jane and Huldah, all of whom lived in Leeds and were unmarried except Charles. The father died Jan. 1, 1835.

Charles settled on a farm near his father. He married first, a Miss Merrill and had one son, Lloyd, who resides in Canton, Mass.

His second wife was Hannah Lindsey. They had four children, Orren, George, Silas and Betsey. All married except George, who still occupies the old homestead.

Orren, married Tylia Lindsey and lived and died on a farm near his brother. He had one son, George, who is a dentist, and resides in Winthrop, Me.

Silas moved to Massachusetts, where he died a few years since.

Betsey resides in Detroit, Michigan.

Levi, a ship-carpenter, settled on a farm adjoining his brother Doubty, on Quaker Ridge, Leeds, in 1790. He married Lydia Sylvester, Dec. 30, 1784. They had six children, Amy, Harvey, Levi, Ezekiel, Betsey and Lydia; all of whom married and resided in Leeds, except Amy, who died when quite young.

Harvey, married Nancy G. Rand, of Monmouth, in 1824, and settled on a farm near Curtis Corner. He was a farmer and wheelwright by trade, and an esteemed citizen. He held the office of chairman of the Board of Selectmen for nearly twenty years; was also Justice of the Peace. They had four children, Amy A., born Jan. 15, 1826; married Cyrenius Pettengill Jan. 15, 1845. Cyrenius H., born June 19, 1828; married Mary A. Sturtevant in 1856; died Feb. 25, 1866. His widow and two sons who still survive him, reside in Monmouth; James E., born Jan. 20, 1832; married Augusta L. Wheeler, Feb. 9, 1864; Mary E., born June 28, 1834; married John Hammond, of East Livermore, and died Nov. 20, 1859. His wife died Dec. 12, 1856, and he spent his declining years with his son, James, who still occupies the old homestead.

Levi, born Oct. 14, 1793, a mason by trade, settled on a farm in the south part of Leeds. He married Hannah Bailey who died July 15, 1866. He was considered to be an honest, Christian man and died Dec. 6, 1885, at the advanced age of 92 years.

Ezekiel, born Oct. 25, 1796; settled on his father's farm, where he spent the most of his life. He married Sabrina, daughter of John Bates and had twelve children; six of whom are still living. A few years before his death, which occurred April 24, 1873, he went to live with his son, John Henry, who still resides in the south part of Leeds. His wife died in Greene, Me., April 3, 1897.

Betsey, born April 5, 1800; married Thomas Owen, a farmer, who lived in the south part of Leeds. They had four children, two of whom are still living in Monmouth. Her death occurred Feb. 27, 1877. Her husband survived her but few months, dying Aug. 31, 1877.

Lydia, born June 19, 1803; died Nov. 13, 1832.

John, son of Solomon Bates, settled on a farm near Curtis Corner. He married Deborah Stetson and had five children, Wheaton, Jason, Sibyl, Sabrina and Martin. His death occurred about 1840.

Wheaton, a farmer, spent the most of his life in Leeds. He married first, Lydia, daughter of Levi Bates, and had one daughter, who now resides in Sidney.

His second wife was Eleanor Elms, who had three children, all of whom are dead. His second wife died Feb. 12, 1861. His death occurred Jan. 20, 1880.

Martin, married Joan Curtis and lived in Leeds a number of years, and later, removed to Bath, where he lived until his death. Two of his children came back and settled in Leeds.

Fannie, married William Wing and resides on Quaker Ridge.

Orlando, settled on a farm near the Methodist Church, where he lived until his death in the spring of 1900. He left a widow and a large family of children.

MERRILL FAMILY.

The Merrills of Leeds trace their ancestry from Joseph[1], who moved from Salisbury, Mass., to New Gloucester, District of Maine, about 1756. He married a sister of Deacon Benjamin True, an account of whom may be found in the sketch of the True family in this work. One of their sons, Joseph, Jr., b. in New Gloucester, Feb. 13, 1773, m. Jane Young in 1793, who was b. in Hanover, Mass. They settled in Turner, where to them were born:

   1. Joseph, June 15, 1794; d. Sept. 20, 1796;
   2. Bethia, May 13, 1796; d. ———, 1859;
*3. Charles, April 14, 1798; d. June 1, 1837;
   4. Betsey, March 11, 1800;

5. Ruth, Feb. 5, 1802; d. Aug. 6, 1881;
6. Fanny, Aug. 25, 1804; d. Sept. 20, 1805;
7. John, Aug. 5, 1807; d. April 13, 1808;
8. Cynthia, Jan. 14, 1809;
9. Job, May 29, 1811;
10. Stella, Sept. 30, 1814; d. Aug. 20, 1818.

Dec. 24, 1803, a petition to the House of Representatives was drawn and signed by Jabez, Seriah, Levi, Jabez, Jr., Joseph, Jabez T. Merrill and many more of the citizens, asking to be incorporated by an act of General Court as a distinct religious parish by the name of "The First Universalist Gospel Parish in Turner." Joseph d. in Turner, in 1839.

Of his children, Charles, m. in 1819, Elizabeth W., a daughter of Isaac and Martha (Stinchfield) Freeman, b. in Leeds, Aug. 20, 1801. They settled in Turner, but later, in 1826, removed to Leeds, where they spent the remainder of their lives. He was a sickly man several years prior to his death, which occurred, in Leeds, July 7, 1846. His wife was a woman of executive ability, and to her efforts and labor in her motherly care of the children were they indebted for many of the privileges they enjoyed. Their children were:

Louise Elizabeth, b. in Turner, Aug. 17, 1820; d. July 22, 1892;

Allen Freeman, b. in Turner, Jan. 5, 1822; d. Oct. 1, 1841;

John Young, b. in Turner Oct. 19, 1823; d. Nov. 1, 1898;

Olive Whitman, b. in Turner, May 22, 1825; d. Dec. 24, 1856;

George Bates and Sylvanus Cobb, twins, b. in Leeds, Oct. 30, 1826; living.

Isaac Joseph, b. in Leeds, Oct. 12, 1830.

Of these children,

John Young Merrill, m. Oct. 28, 1855, Nancy S. Manwell, who was b. in Wayne, Jan. 22, 1827. They settled in Leeds where their remaining years were spent. Mr. Merrill was an exceedingly active and industrious man, which marked his entire life; even during his failing health a short time prior to his death, he could not be persuaded to give up work. He was an honest, conscientious man who commanded the confidence and esteem of his townsmen. When the "Prohibitory Laws" were first enacted, he was repeatedly elected Constable of Leeds, and many were the precepts he served and quantities the liquors he spilled. He regarded his oath of office sacred and binding, and never swerved from duty for the sake of friendship, nor accepted hush-money. His wife d. June 19, 1860. They had but two children, viz.:

Freeman, b. Sept. 4, 1857; d. Oct. 26, 1857;

Edwin K., b. Nov. 20, 1859. With the exception of a few years spent in Massachusetts, Edwin K. has lived in Leeds and devoted his time to farming and mill work, owning and operating a saw-mill on the stream near his home. From his father he inherits qualities of industry and drives his work before him, being a busy and enterprising man.

Dec. 24, 1881, he m. Carrie W. Thomas, b. in Hanover, Mass., Feb. 12, 1861. They have issue:

Carl S., b. June 4, 1883;
Belva L., b. Sept. 25, 1884;
Percy W., b. April 5, 1886;
Lester M., b. April 18, 1894.

Sylvanus Cobb Merrill, for many years, was a resident of Leeds and lived near his brother, John Y. Oct. 14, 1855, he m. Rosina Manwell, a sister to his brother's wife. She was born in Wayne, March 4, 1834; d. in Leeds, Oct. 15, 1865. Their children were:

Louisa Elizabeth, b. Jan. 27, 1857; d. Aug. 15, 1882;
Zelinda Ann., b. June 10, 1862;
Burt, b. April 2, 1864; m. Clara Richardson Cary, Nov. 26, 1884, who was b. in Turner, June 17, 1869. They reside in Auburn, Me., and have had two children: Cora Evelyn, b. Dec. 9, 1885; and John Maurice, b. Nov. 26, 1884; d. May 22, 1897.

Sylvanus C., m. second, Eliza Adelaide Rose, of Leeds, June 21, 1873. Their children are:

Rosina, b. March 22, 1874;
Freeman, b. Nov. 27, 1875;
Irving, b. June 22, 1879;
Nellie, b. April 26, 1884.

Their residence is North Abington, Mass.

Zelinda Ann, a daughter of Sylvanus C., m. Feb. 18, 1883, Arthur W. Studley, b. in Hanover, Mass., July 14, 1861. Their children are: Arthur Irving, b. Aug. 15, 1884; Ethel Louise, b. Dec. 2, 1888. Their residence is Hanover, Mass.

Isaac Joseph, m. May 18, 1864, Lydia White, b. in Hanover, Dec. 26, 1812. No issue. Residence, Hanover, Mass.

HANSCOM FAMILY.

Matthias Hanscom was born in Scarborough, Me., in the year 1812. When a small child his parents moved from that town to Monmouth, and settled in that portion of it now included in the limits of Wales. In 1837, he purchased land near Keen's Corner, in Leeds, and a few years later erected a set of buildings thereon, where he continued his residence until his decease. About the year 1839, he married Florence Keen. He was a carpenter by trade, and followed that occupation during the major part of his life; being able to work until a few years preceding his death, which occurred Feb. 14, 1887, aged 75 years. His wife's death was in 1872. They had one child, Mellen J., born in November, 1853. He, too, was a farmer and carpenter, and has always lived on the home place. It is enough to say of his skill, that he was the master-workman, made all the marks by which the other workmen cut the material in the construction of the finest structure in Maine—"Cumston Hall," built in 1899. He received the commendation of the great young artist and architect, Harry Cochrane, to whose fame this structure has added another bright luminary. In Leeds and neighboring towns, many buildings are now standing which are in evidence of his handiwork. He has recently completed the Baptist Church, in Greene. Nov. 27, 1877, he married Rosa V., of Poland, a daughter of Aranda and Diana T. (Wing) Gilbert, born in Leeds, in February, 1855; in which town her parents were also born, the father in February, 1818, and the mother in August, 1818. She graduated from the "Lewiston High School" in 1874; after which time, previous to her marriage, she was a teacher in the schools of Poland, and later, taught nine terms of district school at Keen's Corner, Leeds. Her religious faith is Universalism, and to her efforts in establishing meetings of that denomination at Keen's Corner each summer, and the building of "The Union Chapel" in which they are held, are the people in that place indebted. Nor are these her only acquirements; her example and beneficence have been felt in many ways, all tending toward a higher and brighter order of manhood.

Mr. and Mrs. Hanscom had issue six children, three sons and three daughters, namely:

    I.   Arthur S., b. in August, 1880; graduated from "Edward Little High School," a carpenter and associated with his father in business;

    II. Selden L., b. in November, 1881; a graduate of Edward Little High School," a student in architecture in the office of Calvin Stevens, in Portland;

    III. Henry B., b. in April, 1884; a student at Westbrook Seminary;

    IV. Florence L., b. in December, 1888, and

    V. Eva M., b. in January, 1893, are with their parents and attend the schools in Leeds;

    VI. Ora L., b. in October, 1895; d. in March, 1896.

HORACE LEADBETTER AND FAMILY.

Horace Leadbetter, the youngest son of Samuel and Betsey (Parcher) Leadbetter, and a grandson of Increase Leadbetter, who settled in Leeds in 1785, was born in Leeds, Nov. 28, 1813. He married Eliza Shaw, of Augusta, Me., and settled on the west side of Dead River about one-half mile from its mouth. Their children were: Wallace R., Charles H., Valencia, Lorenzo, Arthur and Jesse. The two daughters died in their youth and were buried at North Leeds, as were their paternal grand and great-grandparents. Wallace R. was educated in the common and high schools of Leeds and at Monmouth Academy. He was a teacher in the schools of his native and neighboring towns, and occupied a place on the school board of Leeds. He married Irene Nichols, of East Monmouth, and settled in Stockton, California, where he has been a successful teacher, school supervisor and held many positions of responsibility and trust. He has a beautiful home in town, and eight miles out, a large ranch. To them has been born two daughters and a son. The latter died in Colorado; and the daughters, Flora and Anita, are both successful teachers in Stockton.

Charles H., the second son of Horace, married Annie Cummings, of Macon, Ga. Their residence is in the state of Washington, where he is engaged in the publication of books. They have five children.

Lorenzo, the third son, married Hattie, a daughter of Rev. W. H. Foster, a native of Leeds, now residing at Livermore Falls. For a time, after their marriage, they remained in this town, on the old Foster farm, but subsequently removed to California where he has been connected in the ranching business. They have no children.

Arthur, the youngest son of Horace, died in Stockton when a young man. His death was a great blow to his aged parents who had left their old home in Leeds, to make one with him on the Pacific coast. From a paper printed in 1886, we quote: "Mrs. Eliza D., wife of Mr. Horace Leadbetter, formerly of Leeds, died in Stockton, California, at the residence of her son, Hon. W. R. Leadbetter, Jan. 6, 1886, aged 70 years. She was in the yard, when she fell, and died soon after being carried into the house. She had been in failing health since the death of her son Arthur, which occurred a few months ago." June 12, 1891, Horace Leadbetter died in Stockton, at the residence of his eldest son, Hon. W. R. Leadbetter, aged 77 years.

Mr. Leadbetter was long a resident of Leeds, and although much attached to his California home, he had a great love for his native State, to which he and his wife made frequent visits and were heartily welcomed by their many friends.

TRUE FAMILY.

Few have been the people in Leeds who bore the name True; yet, in neighboring towns the name is a common one. He from whom the True families in Maine trace their line of ancestry was Henry[1], who came to this country early in the sixteenth century. The generations in a direct line to the parent who came to Maine are Henry[1], Henry[2], Jabez[3], Jabez[4]. The last named lived in Salisbury, Mass., where he married and where part of his children were born. (His father was b. in Salisbury, Feb. 19, 1683.) He removed to New Gloucester, District of Maine, about 1756, and settled near Gloucester Lower Corner. His son, Benjamin, was born in Salisbury, Mass., Jan. 10, 1742. He came to Maine with the family, and at North Yarmouth, Me., Dec. 15, 1762, married Rhoda, a daughter of Deacon Daniel Merrill. Sarah, a daughter, and sister of Benjamin, was b. in Salisbury in 1744. She married in New Gloucester, ―――― Paul, and at the age of 21 years was a widow and the mother of a son, Marshfield Paul. Dec. 17, 1768, she m. Thomas Stinchfield in New Gloucester, who was b. in Gloucester, Mass., Dec. 29, 1747. To them were b. in that town, Thomas, Sarah, James, Martha, Samuel, John. June 10, 1780, Thomas Stinchfield removed to what is now Leeds, and Sarah, his wife, was the first white woman known to have made a foot-print on the soil of Leeds. Dec. 11, of that year, a daughter, Rebecca, was born who was the first white child b. in Leeds. Sarah d. Nov. 18, 1791, and rests on the farm to which she came eleven years before. In May, 1780, among whom were Deacon Daniel Merrill and Deacon Benjamin True, as he was then called, moved from New Gloucester, and settled in Sylvester township (Turner). Turner was incorporated the forty-seventh town July 7, 1786. The first meeting was held March 6, 1787, in which Deacon Benjamin True was elected to the offices of clerk and selectman, in which positions he officiated for a term of years. In 1789, in company with others, he procured land in Auburn, made improvements thereon and later sold to parties in New Gloucester and removed to Livermore, where he died in 1814. "Deacon Benjamin True was a man of genuine ostentatious piety, gentleness and humility. His candor and liberality upon all subjects of religious controversy, softened the asperities and commanded the respect of all who came within the influence of his example."

The children of Deacon Benjamin and Rhoda (Merrill) True were:

1. Elizabeth, b. Aug. 10, 1764; m. in Turner, Oct. 11, 1790, Nathaniel Daily, who was b. in Easton, Mass., Feb. 3, 1765. They settled in Wayne, Me. Nine children;

2. Mary, b. 1773; m. Feb. 19, 1794, Major Joseph Mills; moved to Livermore about 1783; later to Farmersville, N. Y., and d. in Hudson, N. Y., in 1860. Seven children;
3. Sarah (birth not given), m. Capt. Samuel Pompilly, of Turner, Oct. 18, 1792, and resided in that town. She d. in Wayne, Me. (date not given). Eleven children;
4. Giles, b. 1776; m. first, April 18, 1802, Xoa, a daughter of Doctor Daniel Childs, of Turner. He m. second, in New York, Betsey ———, who d. Nov. 26, 1852. His residence was Villenora, N. Y. Nine children;
5. Martha, b. 1777; m. Simeon, a son of Wait Bradford, of Turner. He was b. 1770; was a carpenter; his residence, Farmersville, N. Y. She d. in Wayne, Me., May 21, 1831. Seven children;
6. Jabez, b. 1778; m. 1807, Eliza Shepherdson Allen, of Leeds, Me. He was of the U. S. Marine; d. March 27, 1813. Four children;
7. Benjamin, Jr., b. in Livermore, Me., Jan. 13, 1784; m. July 31, 1806, Abigail Staples, who was b. in Turner, Me., Dec. 3, 1785; d. in Leeds, Me., Feb. 4, 1843. He d. in Leeds, Feb. 19, 1849. Three children;
8. Rhoda, b. June 6, 1788; m. 1805; Alpheus, a son of Obed Wing, and settled in Wayne, Me.; d. in Turner, Feb. 23, 1817. Five children;
9. Jane, b. Dec. 22, 1792; m. 1813, Obed, a son of Obed Wing, of Wayne, where she spent her remaining years on the Wing homestead in that town; dying May 15, 1863. Five children.

Benjamin True, Jr., whose numerical place in the list of children of Deacon Benjamin is seven, came to West Leeds in 1824 and purchased the water-power, or a part of it, and erected a carding mill thereon, which, in company with his son, they operated thirty years. His residence was on the westerly side of the main street of the little village of West Leeds, where he and his wife both died.

Their children were a son and two daughters, viz.:

Samuel Parsons, b. March 17, 1807; Lavania, b. March 30, 1808; Elethea, b. Feb. 17, 1813.

Samuel Parsons True as a boy, had only a common school education, which he obtained with very limited opportunities; but later, entered school anew and fitted himself for teaching, in which capacity each winter, he was engaged twenty or more years. His official service on the school board of Leeds was continuous nine years. Other public positions were held and their duties discharged by him. He was a neat, busy farmer, and when his time was not occupied in the school room or mill, he was delving from early morn. In 1855, he disposed

D. P. TRUE.

MRS. D. P. TRUE.

SHORE OF ANDROSCOGGIN LAKE, FROM LEWISTON CLUB-HOUSE.

of his property in West Leeds and purchased the Capt. Samuel Stinchfield farm where he spent the remainder of his life. Nov. 21, 1841, he m. Ruth, a daughter of Major John Carver, of Leeds. To them was b. a son, Davis P., in West Leeds, May 12, 1845. The wife and mother d. March 7, 1852. June 29, 1853, he m. Susanna W., a daughter of Ebenezer and Mary (Woodbury) Stinchfield, who were both b. in Danville, Me., and came to Leeds in 1809. They had no issue. Mr. True d. Jan. 8, 1865, and his widow Jan. 23, 1878. Their place of burial is in Wayne, on the road from Leeds Center to Beech Hill.

Davis P., the only child of S. P. and Ruth (Carver) True is also said to be the only male member to represent and perpetuate the name in the descendants of Deacon Benjamin True, his great-grandfather. June 10, 1874, he m. Bessie R., a daughter of Seth Stinchfield. She was b. in Danforth, Me., March 1, 1845. They have no issue, and with the death of Mr. True the name may become extinct. They reside on the home place where he has given much time and attention to fruit culture. To this farm he has added the James Stinchfield place—a very desirable location for summer cottages, several of which he has erected and more have been built by other parties.

Lavinia, the eldest daughter of Benjamin, Jr., m. David H. Millett, of Turner. She d. June 21, 1843. They had no issue.

Elethea, the other daughter of Benjamin True, Jr., m. in December, 1835, Davis F. Millett, of Leeds. She d. Jan. 25, 1841. They had issue a son who d. when less than two years old.

GORDON FAMILY.

Alexander Gorden was born in Scotland and was a royalist soldier at the battle of Worcester, England, Sept. 3, 1651. He came to Boston in 1652, and died in Exeter, N. H., in 1697. His wife, Mary Lyssom, was born in Marblehead, Mass. Their son Thomas, born 1678; died 1761, married Elizabeth Harriman, born 1675; died 1720. Their son Daniel born 1704; died 1786. His wife, Susanna, was born in 1706; died 1786. Their son Ithiel died in 1828, and his wife, Mary Glidden, died in 1819. Their son Josiah, born 1755; died 1841, married Elizabeth Smith, who was born in 1765; died in 1840.

Their son Jonathan was born in Deerfield, N. H., Feb. 20, 1786, and died in Wayne, Jan. 18, 1876. In 1808 he married Sarah Pettingill, of Leeds, who was born in Bridgewater, Mass., May 8, 1790; died in Gorham, Me., Dec. 22, 1881. Their children:

William Crosby, born in Chesterville, May 26, 1810, came to Wayne with his parents in 1823, and Jan. 1, 1837, he married

Diana Smith and settled in Leeds, where he died Sept. 27, 1884. They had three children, James C., born Oct. 30, 1840; married Sarah E. Swift, July 5, 1893. He lived in Leeds until June 1, 1897, when he moved to Wayne where he now resides.

Asa G., born Aug. 4, 1843; married Melintha G. Pettingill, of East Livermore, formerly of Leeds. He died Oct. 19, 1886.

Mary Ella, born July 6, 1852; married Chandler F. Cobb, of Leeds, Jan. 1, 1875. They now reside in Vassalboro.

Charles Smith Gorden, born in Chesterville, July 21, 1812; came to Wayne with his parents in 1823; married Florinda Churchill, settled in Leeds, where he died July 8, 1883. They had three children: Phebe Jane, born July 2, 1845; married Hezekiah S. Gardner, of Leeds, Jan. 1, 1868. They now reside in Massachusetts.

Charles Wallace, born Jan. 15, 1849; married Annie Burrill, of Milford, Mass., Jan. 1, 1885; reside in Leeds, where he was born.

Lydia Ann, born Nov. 11, 1850; married Herbert L. Millett, of Leeds, in 1871, where they now reside.

Greenwood C. Gorden, born in Chesterville, Feb. 7, 1815; came to Wayne in 1823; married Hannah Stinchfield, of Leeds, in 1840; settled in East Livermore, where he lived some years, then moved to Wayne, and in 1852 moved to Leeds, where they now reside, at the good old age of 86 years. They had four children, Hezekiah S., born in East Leeds, Dec. 21, 1842; John Allen, born in Wayne, June 12, 1846; married Adelia C. Hartt, of New Brunswick, in 1890; now resides with his father, in Leeds.

Henry G., born in Wayne, April 19, 1848; married Carrie Peaslee, of New Hampshire, Jan. 1, 1885; reside in Wayne. Hannah Viola, born in Wayne, October, 1851; married Rev. William R. Millett, in May, 1871. He died in 1875. She died in February, 1896.

Joseph Pettingill Gordon, born Oct. 20, 1819; died March 27, 1876;

Jonathan Glidden Gordon, born June 22, 1822; died Jan. 10, 1901:

Oliver Cobb Gordon, born Feb. 21, 1825;

Jeremiah Gordon, born Aug. 18, 1827;

Sarah Ann Gordon, born Feb. 7, 1830;

Mary Jane Gordon, born Sept. 22, 1822; died Feb. 21, 1868.

OTHER FAMILIES.

It is a matter of regret that many of the early families have failed to furnish data and thus far received no special mention. Want of interest or other causes, possibly, reflections on some members of the committee whose duty it was to furnish the data for this work is the only legitimate reason that can be assigned. None within the knowledge of the writer have failed of an invitation to contribute family matter. Incomplete as must appear the partial list of families of whom the writer has only a meager, oral knowledge or tradition-follow; better so than omitted!

FISH FAMILY.

In the order of settlement of Littleborough by families, second to those of Thomas and Rogers Stinchfield was that of Jirah Fish. From New Gloucester he came in the fall of 1780. His log house was built on the southern bank of Dead River very near—a few rods southeasterly of where the mill of C. H. White & Son now stands. He had a family of several children when he came to the Plantation, and one more born therein. Seth, his son, was the second white male child born in what is now Leeds. Later he built a frame house on the east side of what is now a highway—on the hill a little distant and northerly from the cemetery which has ever borne the name of Fish-burying-ground. Several of his sons were carpenters, and many of the early buildings in Leeds were built by them. Most of them married, settled in town and reared families, some of whose descendants remain here still. Two of them settled on the westerly side of the hill that was early designated Fish Hill.

Hirah, the youngest son, remained on the homestead where he was living about fifty years ago, and is remembered as a slaughterer of hogs. This brings to mind an incident which occurred in the very early boyhood of the writer. About 1847, to procure the services of Mr. Fish to slaughter the winter store of meats, permitted to accompany his father on this errand, it was necessary to cross Dead River. This was accomplished by passing over a float-bridge composed of logs and poles and between which the water gushed up and wet the horse as he stepped on them. Farther on, very nearly where the buildings of George Burnham are now situated, we came to a barn with large doorways on either side and minus floors. Directly through this the road ran and through it went we also. A gentleman from Farmington, who, about that time, had occasion to pass that way, on arriving at Lothrop's Corner a little farther on, where he visited a shop which had black, board, window-blinds and otherwise peculiarly painted, after imbibing freely therein of Mr. Graffam's noted ardent with porwigles (Polliwogs) from the little pond just back of it, spoke thus: "I have just seen the three great wonders of the world!—a bridge under water,—a road through a barn and a grogery in a pall-house."

BURNHAM FAMILY.

Among the early settlers was Abner Burnham. Little has been learned of his ancestry or nationality. He had two or more sons, Daniel and John. They were hardy and prolific, and many are their descendants. Azel and Abner Burnham, Jr., may have been sons of Abner, Sen., but, be that as it may, they contributed liberally to the numerous family who have since resided in Leeds and other Maine towns. In the late Civil War the Burnham family was represented as fully, perhaps, as any in the town. They first settled in that part of the Plantation called Pine Plains, and there many of them have continued their residence since. Of names and dates we are ignorant, and incomplete as this sketch is, here it is left for want of data.

FROST FAMILY.

Early in the century, among the names of heads of families occur those of Oliver P. and Joseph Frost. They lived in the west part of the town many years where they reared families. Few, if any of the name, are now remaining. Very early Oliver P. had a blacksmith shop at West Leeds, which was the second one located in the town.

GRANT FAMILY.

Effort has been made to obtain a detailed account of this family who is now well represented in the town. No other legitimate reason can be assigned for its absence, than indifference or want of interest. Benjamin was the first to bear the name in Leeds, where he spent most of his years and reared a family of children. He was a soldier in the War of 1812; was a hardy, robust, industrious farmer. We have no knowledge of the place of his nativity nor the time of coming to Leeds. His place of settlement and residence was on the west side of Fish Bogg, where the buildings of his son, Amos, were recently burned. Among his children were Benjamin, Stephen, Sarah, Josiah, Martha, Perry, Amos and, perhaps, others. Benjamin m. a Miss

Phillps; settled on the Phillips place, easterly from North Turner Bridge; no issue;

Stephen m. Columbia, a daughter of Seth and Abigail (Carver) Fish; settled near his father, where he has since erected a new set of buildings and now resides. They had issue three children, Joshua, Flora and Charles. Mr. Grant m. later, a Mrs. Smith whose maiden name was Fish—a niece of his first wife. They have no issue. Mr. Grant has been an industrious farmer. He was also a stone mason, and in former years worked much of his unemployed time on the farm at that business. Josiah m. Rebecca Rose and settled on the opposite side of the road from his present residence. They have one child, Herbert, who married Addie Smith, a daughter of the present Mrs. Stephen Grant. They have two children, Fred and Myrtle. They, in turn, are married and have issue. Sarah m. a Mr. Ludden. Martha m. Charles Peare and lived at West Leeds. They had two daughters. Perry m. Caroline, a daughter of John Dyer Millett. They had issue. Later his wife died, and he again married and resides at West Leeds, where he has several years been in trade, in the meantime holding the office of postmaster until a recent date.

Amos m. ———— Libby (?) and lived on the homestead of his father. The care of his parents fell to his lot, which service was kindly and faithfully rendered. His mother lived nearly a century of years, and for a long time prior to her death was a blind and helpless invalid. A few years since, the buildings were consumed by fire. Sickness and other misfortunes have been of frequent occurrence; yet, Mr. Grant and his family have endured them with patience and fortitude.

LINCOLN FAMILY.

Rufus Lincoln came from Bridgewater to Leeds and settled north of Lothrop's Corner, on the Ridge Road. He is said to have been a distant relative of Abraham, whose early occupation was rail-splitting, and who later became better known as President of the United States. In one particular did they resemble each other—in witty sayings. He was a moulder by trade, at which he worked in early life in Bridgewater. He came to Leeds later than many families and knew less about farming until he learned it in this town. In later years he removed to the northeastern part of Leeds to a little hill easterly of North Leeds railroad station, which still bears the name of Lincoln Hill. He reared a family there, most of whom went to Massachusetts, while one, Salome, m. Micajah Dunham; settled in Vassalboro; no issue; another, Hannah, m. Ebenezer Stinchfield; settled in

Leeds; had issue Lewis Delmar and Ebenezer; m. second, Benjamin Swain; settled in Wayne; removed to Brockton, where they both died; still another, William C., m. Mahala Bishop, of Leeds; settled on the home place; had issue three sons, Ellis L., Norris K. and Charles D.; and later, moved to Wayne where they had Gertrude, Harry and Irving D., and where they all reside and all but one have families.

SUMNER FAMILY.

Houghton Sumner, born in Plymouth, Vermont, March 30, 1783, moved to Scituate, Mass., where he married in June, 1805, Mary Rogers. Born to them in that town, were Mary H., Sept. 22, 1806; Hannah T., May 4, 1807; after which, in the spring of 1808, they removed to Leeds, Me., and settled on the east side of Quaker Ridge where Houghton B. Sumner now resides. Born to them in Leeds, were Albert W., March 31, 1810; Caleb R., Oct. 15, 1813; Rachael D., Feb. 14, 1815; Ruth C., Oct. 18, 1817; Elvira A., Oct. 11, 1819; Louisa J., Aug. 18, 1821; Augusta W., July 6, 1826; Levi C., May 27, 1829; (Houghton B.) (?)

Houghton Sumner died in Leeds, Aug. 28, 1862;

Mary (Rogers) Sumner, died in Leeds, May 10, 1865;

Caleb R. Sumner, died in Leeds, June 9, 1858.

An unsuccessful effort has been made to obtain an extended account of this family.

GREENWOOD FAMILY.

Moses Greenwood, of Keene, N. H., whose wife Asenath Hill, had six children; one of whom, a son, Moses, came to Leeds in 1831. He m. Serena Deane Willis, of Newton, Mass. Their children were: George B., Lovice Jane, Rachael B., Clara C. and S. Ada. Moses Greenwood's wife died in 1851 and in 1853, he married Mehitable Chute, of Wilton, Me. His son, George Bradford, married Sarah Gould, of Leeds; issue one child, Nellie;

Lovice J. married first, Oberon Coolidge; issue one son, Willis; m. second, Rutellius Coolidge; issue George, Clara, Lillie and Tillie;

Rachael B. married W. S. Knapp; issue one son, Willis;

Clara C. married Charles A. Lovojey; issue two children, Arthur and Minnie;

S. Ada married Russel L. Gould; issue Willis E., John C., Alice May and Moses G.

CARVER FAMILY.

In 1779, two families, those of Deacon Elijah Livermore and Major Fish, settled near the central part of what is now the town of Livermore, Me. The next year, Mrs. William Carver and two other families, whose names were Josiah Wyer and Elisha Smith, settled near them. A claim has been made, that this Carver family is the same from whom the Leeds Carvers trace their descent. This may arise from the fact that nearly one-third part of the land now contained within the boundary lines of Leeds was formerly a portion of Livermore; and further, that the old Carver homestead of the Leeds family, the farm now occupied by Chessman D. Gould is in that part of the town that formerly was a portion of Livermore. In Bridgewater, Mass., a family who bore the name resided in the year 1774; a member of whom, Eunice, married in that year, Joseph Knapp, Jr., who removed to what is now Leeds in the year 1791, and settled on the farm now owned by the town. Other known members of that family were, the mother, whose maiden name was Edison, a daughter Ursola, who spent a single life, and a son, Elezer, who was a Baptist minister. Tradition says, that the daughter and son, with their mother, removed to Woodstock, Vt. The son having m. Nancy Jones Sept. 16, 1787, to whom several children were born, in the year 1800, they all removed to Leeds, where they settled on the aforementioned farm of C. D. Gould, and thus became neighbors of Eunice and her family. Few of the early settlers were burdened with wealth, and this family was of the many. From Hallowell, to which place they came in a packet, their entire belongings were conveyed to Leeds in a hand cart. The children of Elezer and Nancy (Jones) Carver were William, b. Dec. 16, 1787; Elezer, b. April 26, 1790; Nancy, b. July 31, 1791; John, b. March 26, 1794; Betsey, b. Aug. 3, 1796; Caleb, b. June 7, 1800; Abigail, b. Aug. 18, 1802; Ursula, b. Feb. 27, 1805; Mary, b. Feb. 13, 1808.

1. William, m. Jane Smith; settled on the east bank of Dead River in Leeds, nearly opposite the town farm buildings; had a family of children, namely: Chandler, Annie, Allura, William; m. second, ———; and had one child, Elezer; later removed to Milo, Me., where he died;
2. Elezer, m. Hannah Stinchfield April 7, 1816, who was b. in Leeds, Dec. 4, 1793. They settled a short distance northerly of his brother William, where they afterward lived and died. Elezer Dec. 4, 1856, and his widow, Jan. 18, 1872. Their place of burial is in the Robert Gould Cemetery at North Leeds. They had issue Betsey, b. Nov. 8, 1816; Jason, b. April 13, 1818; Mary A., b. Aug. 27, 1819; Thomas S., b. March 29, 1821;

Arvilla A., b. July 17, 1822; Hannah and another, twins, b. Dec. 12, 1824; Nancy, b. Dec. 12, 1825; Alice, b. March 19, 1827; Isaac S., b. May 20, 1829; John, b. June 22, 1830; James, b. March 15, 1834.

Of the above children of Elezer, Betsey m. Pelatiah Libby; settled near Curtis Corner, Leeds, where she reared a large family and died.

Jason m. Mary Libby, a sister of Pelatiah; settled on the old Stinchfield homestead, in Leeds; reared a family of three daughters and a son, namely: Hannah (Mrs. Charles Martin, of California,); Thirza A. (Mrs. Seth Fish); Ruphina (Mrs. Edgecom), and John E. After the death of his wife, having then been in the Civil War, he spent some years in California. He later returned; m. Mrs. Wm. Curtis, and died in Leeds.

Mary Ann m. Elbridge Knowlton, of Damariscotta, Me.; spent some years in that town and in Leeds, later lived in Philadelphia, but subsequently returned to Leeds. Mr. Knowlton went to California and never returned. They had a daughter, Clara (Mrs. Jerome Ridley, of Wayne).

Thomas S. m. Elizabeth Nichols, and after a time purchased the farm where he was born and raised. To this place he added a portion of the George Gould estate and also the Eben Libby farm, together constituting one of the most extensive in town. After a term of years his wife died, and leaving his son to care for the farm, he m. Nora Parsons, and lived the remainder of his life at Leeds Center. His children were Viora, Henry and Warren;

Arvilla, m. Phineus Neal, and lived in Livermore. They had a family, but their names are not familiar to the writer.

Of Hannah, Nancy and Alice we have no knowledge —think they died young.

Isaac S., when a young man, went to California where he lived many years, and later, spent some time in South America. There he m. ——————, whom he brought to his native town, and settled where he now resides. They have a son and daughter;

John, m. Mary Taylor; lived for a time on the home farm; later removed to Wayne, where his widow and several of his large family of children reside;

James, m. Mary Fish, of Leeds, in which town they have resided most of their lives; at present, living near North Turner Bridge. James was a soldier in the late Civil War. They have a large family of children, whose names we are unable to recall.

HISTORY OF LEEDS 237

3. Nancy, m. Joshua Campbell; settled in Livermore; had issue Horatio, Calvin and Rosina, and perhaps others.
4. John, m. Jennett Treat b. in Woodstock, Vt., in Sept. 1796, who d. in Leeds June 1, 1842. He d. in Hallowell, Me., Nov. 26, 1876. They settled in Leeds near his older brothers, where a large family of children were b. 'to them. He later m. Mrs. Martha Smith, by whom he had three children. A few years subsequent to his last marriage he purchased the James Stinchfield, Jr., place, near the lake, which he occupied several years; later removing to the western part of the town, in the Deane neighborhood. He was a major in the State militia. The children of his first wife were:
   1. Ruth, b.————; m. Samuel P. True; one child, D. P. True;
   2. Elezer, b. ————; m. ————; 10 children;
   3. Melvin, b. ————; m. ————; 8 children; Elezer and Melvin settled in Canton, Me. Among their many sons, most were professional or active business men.
   4. Bethiah, b. ————; m. ————; 2 children;
   5. Jane, b. May 14, 1823; m. Calvin Campbell; 8 children, namely: Horace L., b. May 2, 1849; John L., b. July 15, 1850; Rose, b. Mar. 8, 1853; Nancy J., b. Oct. 26, 1856; Eldon R., b. June 10, 1858; Callie P., b. July 16, 1861; Emma J., b. Dec. 10, 1864; Bellie, b. Sept. 11, 1868. Nancy J., Eldon R., Callie P. and Bellie are dead.
   6. John, d. in boyhood;
   7. Eliza, b. ————; m. Charles Towle; 6 children;
   8. Jennett, b. ————; m. Thos. Harlow; 6 children;
   9. Emily, b. ————; d. when a young lady;
   10. Abigail, b. ————; m. ————; 2 children;
   11. Mary, b. ————; m. ————; 4 children;
   12. Alice, b. ————; m. ————; 6 children.
   13. Esther A., b. ————; m. ————; no issue.
   Children by his second wife:
   1. George, b. ————; m. ————;
   2. B. Franklin, b. ————; m. ————;
   3. Harriet B., b. ————; m. ————.
5. Betsey, m.
6. Caleb, m. 1st, Bertha Harvey, Apr. 31, 1819; no issue; m. 2d, Augusta Copeland, Nov. 26, 1820. They settled first on the old Carver homestead, but later on the place now occupied by a grandson, Everett L. Carver. Mr.

Carver was colonel of a regiment of State Militia, by which title he was best known. Their children were:

1. Everett, b. July 14, 1821; m. Julia A. Baldwin, Jan. 1, 1846; issue Julia Augusta, b. July 4, 1850; Everett Lowell, b. Dec. 23, 1852; Wallace Elwood, b. June 24, 1863;
2. Augusta, b. Aug. 6, 1822;
3. Louisa, b. Jan. 20, 1824;
4. Russell, b. Oct. 15, 1825;
5. Lloyd, b. Sept. 1, 1827;
6. Lowell; 7, Aurora; 8, Granville; 9, Cordelia; 10, Nancy, and 11, Copeland.

7. Abigail, m. Seth Fish, and settled on the west side of the Fish Bog, in Leeds, where they spent their remaining years. By a former wife, Mr. Fish had issue Lyllis, Samuel, Sally and Hira; and the fruit of his marriage with Abigail: Silas, Lovina, Columbia, Abigail, Mary, Seth and Willard. Of these latter children, Silas had his name changed to Morris; m. Susan Millett, and reared a large family of children;

Lovina, m. Hartley Gray; no issue; Mary, m. James Carver; resides in Leeds; a large family of children; Seth, m. Thirza A. Carver; resides on the homestead of his father; has issue one son, Charles, who m. Hannah Ridley, of Wayne, in which town they reside; Willard went west when a young man and nothing further of him is known to the writer.

8. Ursula; no knowledge of;
9. Mary, m. Joseph Frost; settled in West Leeds. They had issue several children; but for want of information we are unable to further mention them.

WOODMAN FAMILY.

The progenitor of the Leeds branch of the Woodman family was Edward[1], who, it is said, came from Southampton in the ship James, of London, in the year 1635, and settled in the town of Newbury, Mass., or at least, such is the account of his brother Archelaus, who came at same time and settled in the same place. (Mass. Historical Society, Vol. VII., page 319.) His wife, Joanna, accompanied him to the New World. He is said to have been born in Corsham, a village in Wiltshire, within a few miles of Christian Malford. Of the 91 grantees who settled Newbury, Mass., 15 were entitled to appellation of "Mr." One of these 15 was Edward Woodman. He was a man of influence, decision and energy, and had the zeal and courage to defend his own conviction in both Church and State. Mr. Woodman early entered the official arena soon after his arrival in Newbury, for in 1636, '37, '39 and '43 he was a deputy to the General Court, and in 1638, '41, '45 and '46 he was one of three commissioners to end small causes in Newbury, and at various times held other offices of profit and trust in the town and State. Both he and his wife were living in 1687, but his death occurred prior to 1694, at which date his will was entered for probate. The date of his birth is unknown to the writer.

His children were:

1. Edward^2, b. —, 1628; m. Mary Goodridge, Dec. 20, 1653.
2. John^2, b. —, 1630; m. Mary Field, July 15, 1656; both b. previous to coming to this country;
3. Joshua^2, b. —, 1636; m. Elizabeth Stevens, Jan. 23, 1666; d. 1714;
4. Mary^2, b.—; m. John Brown, Feb. 20, 1660;
5. Sarah^2, b. Jan. 12, 1642; m. John Kent, Mar. 12, 1666;
6. Jonathan^2, b. Nov. 8, 1643; m. Hannah Hilton, July 2, 1668;
7. Ruth^2, b. Mar. 28, 1646; m. Benjamin Lowle, Oct. 17, 1666.

Joshua^2, the third child of Edward^1, was, as per his gravestone inscription, the first man child born in Newbury. He took the oath of allegiance in 1678. He married Elizabeth, daughter of Capt. John Stevens, one of the first settlers of Andover, Mass., Jan. 23, 1665. He lived first in Andover and later in Newbury. The inscription on his tombstone is as follows: "Here lies ye body of Mr. Joshua Woodman, who died May ye 3th 1703, aged 67 years; first man child borne in Newbury, & second inturid in this place."

Their children were:

1. Elizabeth^3, b. Feb. 6, 1667; m. Daniel Tenney, of Rowley, June 5, 1712;
2. Dorothy^3, b. Nov. 13, 1669; m. John Thurston, May 17, 1732;
3. Joshua^3, b. Apr. 12, 1672; m. Mehetable Wicomb, Dec. 15, 1703;
4. Jonathan^3, b. Apr. 1, 1674; m. Sarah Mighill, June 24, 1700;
5. A son^3, b. June 30, 1676; d. in infancy;
6. Mehetable^3, b. Sept. 20, 1677; Phillip Goodridge, Apr. 16, 1700;
7. David^3, b. July 30, 1680; m. Dorothy Moody, Nov. 30, 1710;
8. Benjamin^3, b. July 27, 1683; was the father of three brothers who settled in Buxton, Me., who will be further mentioned.

9. Sarah³, b. July 27, 1683; d. Apr. 11, 1712, unmarried;
10. Mary³, b. Apr. 9, 1690; m. James Wheeler, May 7, 1709.

Of the above, Benjamin was born in Andover, July 27, 1683. He married, March 1, 1711, Elizabeth Longfellow, who was born July 3, 1688. Her father was William Longfellow, the only one of the name who came to America, and who was born in Hampshire, Eng., in 1651. "He was a man of talents and education, wrote an elegant hand, but was not so much of a Puritan as some others. He married Annie Sewall, sister of Judge Samuel Sewall and dau. of old Henry Sewall. He enlisted as an Ensign in the ill-fated expedition to Canada, and was drowned at Anticosti in Oct., 1690, when his dau., Elizabeth was a little over two years old." The poet Longfellow is a descendant of Stephen, a brother of Elizabeth, the wife of Benj. Woodman. Mr. Woodman was a tanner at Newbury Falls. The children of Benj. Woodman were:

1. Ann⁴, b. Mar. 1, 1712; m. Benj. Pettingill, May 20, 1742;
2. Sarah⁴, b. Sept. 22, 1713; m. Benj. Plummer, Feb. 17, 1736-7;
3. Joseph⁴, b. May 31, 1715; m. Catherine Smith in 1739; settled in Buxton, Me.;
4. Benj.⁴, b. Dec. 19, 1718; marriage uncertain.
5. Joshua⁴, b. Jan. 22, 1720; m. in Biddeford, May 25, 1749; settled in Buxton, Me.
6. David⁴ and Jonathan⁴, b. Feb. 24, 1722, were twins. David m. Mary Adams, Jan. 22, 1749; settled in Portland, Me.
7. Jonathan⁴ is not known to have married.
8. Nathan⁴, b. June 26, 1726; settled in Buxton, Me.; receives further mention.
9. Stephen⁴, b. Feb. 23, 1728; m. Esther Weeks, Sept. 20, 1752; settled in Portland, Me.

Of the above children of Benj. and Elizabeth (Longfellow) Woodman, Nathan⁴, b. in Newbury, June 26, 1726; m. Olive Gray of Biddeford, Dec. 28, 1749. She was b. Feb. 6, 1730-1. Her parents were John Cary, Esq., who was the commander of Fort Mary, 1720, and his wife, Mrs. Elizabeth Tarbox of Winter Harbor. Nathan enlisted in the Revolutionary Army, May 3, 1775, in the company commanded by Capt. Jeremiah Hill. He afterwards served as corporal in the company of Capt. Daniel Lane, from Jan. 1, 1777, to Jan. 2, 1780, upon the quota of Topsfield. To them were b. in Newbury, Mass., four children, and the others in Buxton, who were:

1. John⁵, b. Oct. 4, 1750; bapt. Dec. 23, 1750;
2. Elizabeth⁵, bapt. Feb. 23, 1752; m. Jonathan Gilman, Oct. 12, 1780; m. 2d, Clement Meservey.

BENJAMIN WOODMAN.

3. Benjamin[5], bapt. Feb. 17, 1754; further mentioned.
4. Olive[5], bapt. Feb. 1, 1756; m. Joseph Chase, of Saco, Sept. 5, 1776; m. 2d. Josiah Black, of Limington;
5. Sewall[5], bapt. Aug. 20, 1758; d. 1774;
6. Susan[5], d. young, 1774;
7. Amos[5], lived to grow up; d. when a young man;
8. Moses[5], bapt. Mar. 2, 1776;
9. Nathan[5], was a Revolutionary soldier; was a sailor;
10. Shuball[5], the youngest child, was b. Sept. 1, 1772.

Of the above children of Nathan[4], Benjamin[5], the third child, m. Sally Bryant, Sept. 27, 1781. She was a cousin of Olive Bryant, who m. Ephraim[3], son of Joshua Woodman. Mr. Woodman was a Revolutionary soldier and pensioner. He settled and reared his family in Saco, Me., near the residence of his cousin Ephraim in Buxton. In 1812, he removed from Saco to Leeds, where he settled in the northwestern part of the town on the old county road leading from Wayne to the old ferry across the Androscoggin about ½ mile up that river from North Turner Bridge. The place by him taken up and on which he settled is the same that has since been occupied by some one of his descendants bearing the name, and is now occupied by his grandson, John. He died on this farm, Aug. 14, 1834, when nearly 82 years old, and his wife, Nov. 6, 1826, aged 69 years. Their children were:

1. Mary[6], b. in Saco, Feb. 13, 1783; m. Shirley W. McDaniel, a sea captain; 9 children;
2. Sewall[6], no date of birth; went to sea when young and was pressed into the English service;
3. Amos[6], b. in Saco, Nov. 21, 1788;
4. Benjamin[6], Jr., b. in Saco, Nov. 21, 1788; further mention;
5. Rosanna[6], b. in Saco, Mar. 1, 1796; m. Elder William Woodsum, of Buxton. She d. in Peru, Me., leaving issue;
6. Sally[6], b. Sept. 17, 1798; m. Ezra Leadbetter, and d. in Livermore, Me.;
7. Olive[6], b. in Saco, Aug. 1, 1801; m. Levi Morrill; issue one son; d. soon after his birth.
8. Pamelia[6], b. in Saco, May 8, 1807; d. unmarried September, 1850;
9. Samuel[6], record uncertain.

Of the children of Benjamin and his wife, Sally Bryant, Benjamin, Jr.[6], (Benjamin[5], Nathan[4], Benjamin[3], Joshua[2], Edward[1]) their fourth child, m. Joanna, daughter of Increase

Leadbetter an early settler of Leeds. She was b. Nov. 1, 1799. They settled on the place to which he came with his parents when a young man, and where he spent his remaining years and died Sept. 4, 1864. He was a military man—Captain of a militia company. Those who remember Capt. Benjamin Woodman knew him as an honest, industrious and energetic farmer. Their children were:

Henry Frost[7], b. in Leeds, Oct. 11, 1821; m. first, Frank E. Whittemore, of East Livermore, in July, 1876, who died Nov. 15, 1877; m. second, Martha Deane, Sept. 23, 1883, who died, July 15, 1885. The fruit of his last marriage was one child, Deane, b. March 24, 1885; d. July 15, 1886.

In early life Mr. Woodman was a teacher. He later officiated on the municipal and school boards of his native town, in which capacity he did honest, able and conscientious work. He held the positions of railroad station and express agent at North Leeds for a term of years. His connection with his brother in mercantile life at North Leeds was of long duration; after which, he returned to the old homestead farm where he has since made his residence until a very recent date, when he sold the place to a younger brother, and now is with his nieces at North Leeds, where he spent so many years in business.

Charles[7], b. Sept. 28, 1828; m. Jerusha A. Haden, Jan. 3, 1864. He was a farmer on the homestead place at North Leeds for a term of years. They had issue three children, one of whom only is living, namely; Almarilla, who is married.

Jason[7], b. Jan. 5, 1830; m. Louisa M., a daughter of William and Ruth (Gould) Gott, July 6, 1854. Their children were: Adda Florence, b. in Leeds, Oct. 15, 1860, a graduate of the State Normal School, of Farmington, in the Class of 1888, and a teacher of experience in the schools of Leeds and other towns; and Mary Louisa, b. Feb. 25, 1867; married Charles A. Whitehouse Sept. 29, 1887, who resides at North Leeds, and is engaged in mercantile business where her father was a long time in trade. They have two daughters, Ruth Louisa, b. Jan. 31, 1889. and Ruby, b. July 2, 1890.

When a young man, Mr. Woodman spent several years in Boston, where he was employed in omnibus work. He was married in that city and soon returned to his native town where he and his brother Henry built and opened a store. They also bought a tract of land near there, built a house, stable and barn, and combined farming with trade. The post-office at that place was later added to their business, and in connection with occasional purchases and sales of fine horses of which they were good judges, they gained a goodly amount of property.

Jason[7] died Dec. 1, 1880, and his widow July 23, 1888.

Emily[7], b. July 27, 1831; m. Thornton Lyford. Feb. 22, 1858, and settled in Bangor. She had a daughter, Marion. Emily d. in Bangor in November, 1878.

Julia Ann, b. Jan. 16, 1833; m. Abial Deane, in 1884; resides in Leeds.

Benjamin, Jr.[7], b. Jan. 25, 1837, was in the Civil War; d. in Alexandria, Va., Nov. 11, 1861.

Edward Kent[7], b. July 28, 1838, was in the Civil War; m. first, Luella Whitney, July 27, 1873, who d. July 19, 1892. He m. second, Nellie M. Swift, Oct. 22, 1895, in Farmington, in which village they live. They have no issue. Mr. Woodman has devoted much of his life to buying and selling a high class of horses, in which business he has been very successful.

Sewall[7], b. Feb. 17, 1841; d. in Nebraska.

John Elmore, b. July 21, 1842, was in the Civil War; m. Laura Ann Whittemore, Jan. 22, 1865. They have issue Frank N., b. April 29, 1878, and Gladys, b. July 27, 1886. Frank Newell was graduated from the College Course of the Maine Wesleyan Seminary and Female College, Kent's Hill, Me., in the Class of 1898. He m. Aug. 29, 1898, Helen Welch, of South Harpswell, Me. They reside in Boston, Mass. Issue Kenneth Elmore, b. April, 1901.

CHAPTER IV.

HEADS OF FAMILIES IN THE EARLY PART OF THE 19TH CENTURY.

Additon, Thos.
Additon, David
Andrews, Ephraim
Bates, Ezekiel
Bates, Charles
Bates, Hervey
Beals, John
Beals, John, Jr.
Berry, Ezra
Berry, Amos
Berry, Joshua
Berry, Amos, Jr.
Berry, Jesse
Bishop, Zadock
Bishop, Joseph
Bishop, Cyrus
Bishop, James
Bishop, Welcome
Boothby, Isaac
Boothby, Stephen
Brewster, Morgan
Brewster, Salmon
Bridgham, Thos. W.
Bridgham, George
Brown, Samuel
Brown, Samuel, 2d.
Brown, Abner, Jr.
Bumpus, Ephraim
Burnham, Abner
Burnham, John
Burnham, Daniel
Carver, Elezer
Carver, Elezer, Jr.,
Carver, John
Carver, William
Carver, Caleb
Carll, Benjamin
Cary, Zachariah
Cary, John S.
Cary, Luther
Cary, Seth
Caswell, Levi
Chambers, Thaddeus
Collier, Moses
Collier, Moses, Jr.
Collier, Isaac
Crummit, Robert
Curtis, Abner
Curtis, William B.
Curtis, Libbeus
Cushman, Andrew
Cushman, Andrew, Jr.
Cushman, Oliver
Daily, Abial
Day, Samuel
Day, Joseph
Day, William
Day, William A.
Deane, Zebulon
Daggett, Nathaniel
Daggett, Jabez
Drake, Oliver
Draper, Hazenan
Drinkwater, Thomas
Dunham, Benjamin
Elder, Joshua
Elms, Robert
Felch, Samuel
Fish, Jirah, Jr.
Fish, Ansel
Fish, Hira
Fish, Joseph
Fish, Benjamin
Fish, William
Fish, John C.
Fish, Seth

Fish, Seth, Jr.
Ford, Daniel
Foss, Capt. Phineus
Foss, Uriah
Foss, Levi
Foss, Walter
Foss, Ruel
Foss, Cyrus
Foss, Ephraim
Foss, Thaddeus
Foss, Simeon
Foster, Stephen
Foster, Timothy
Foster, John
Francis, Thomas
Francis, Thomas, Jr.
Francis, John
Freeman, Isaac
Freeman, Joseph
Freeman, Stephen
Freeman, Joseph, Jr.
Frost, Oliver P.
Frost, Joseph
Gilbert, Capt. Wm.
Gilbert, Cornelius
Gilbert, Ahirah
Gilbert, Samuel
Gilbert, William T.
Gilbert, Marcus
Gilbert, Benjamin
Gilbert, Levi
Gilbert, Nelson
Gilbert, Nathaniel, Jr.
Gilbert, Hira
Gould, Pelatiah
Gould, Isaac
Gould, Samuel
Gould, Robert
Gould, Simeon
Gould, Joseph
Gould, John
Gould, William
Gould, Levi
Graffam, Thomas
Grant, Benjamin
Graves, Samuel
George, Francis

Haines, William
Harmon, Dodavah
Herrick, Israel
Hicks, Zephaniah
House, Nathaniel
House, Nathaniel, Jr.,
Howe, David
Howard, Hon. Seth
Howard, Capt. Stillman
Howard, Barnabas
Howard, Roland B.
Howard, Benjamin F.
Howard, Barnabas, Jr.
Howard, Luther L.
Howard, Warren
Howard, Jason
Jenkins, Hamilton
Jennings, Lewis
Jennings, Samuel
Jennings, John
Jennings, Isaac
Jennings, Perez S.
Jennings, Nathaniel
Jennings, Henry
Jennings, Alexander
Jennings, John, Jr.
Jones, Edward
Kimball, Herbert
Knapp, Joseph
Knapp, Joseph, Jr.
Knapp, Elijah
Knapp, Ziba
Knapp, Simeon
Knapp, Charles
Knapp, Stephen
Knapp, Pelatiah
Lamb, Merrick
Lamb, James
Lamb, James, Jr.
Lamb, Ira
Lane, Daniel
Lane, Daniel, Jr.
Lane, Giddings
Lane, Elias
Lane, Peter
Lane, James
Lane, Issachar

Lane, John L.
Leadbetter, Increase
Leadbetter, Benj.
Leadbetter, Samuel
Libby, Phillip
Libby, Thomas
Libby, Zebulon
Libby, Ebenezer
Lincoln, Rufus
Lindsey, Ira
Lindsey, Thomas
Lindsey, Archibald
Lindsey, William
Lindsey, James
Lindsey, James, Jr.
Lindsey, Daniel
Lindsey, Thomas, 2d.
Lothrop, Daniel
Lothrop, Daniel, Jr.
Lothrop, George
Lothrop, Sullivan
Lothrop, Samuel
Lothrop, Thomas
Lothrop, Leavitt
Lothrop, Sullivan, Jr.
Lothrop, Solomon
Lothrop, Alson
Lothrop, Ira
Magown, Isaac
Magown, Gilbert
Mason, Naphtali
Mason, Ebenezer
Mason, Phillip C.
Millett, Thomas
Millett, Thomas, Jr.
Millett, Benjamin
Millett, John
Millett, Zebulon P.
Millett, Solomon
Millett, Solomon, Jr.
Millett, John D.
Mitchell, Joseph
Mitchell, Thomas
Mitchell, William
Moulton, Stillman
Moulton, William
Murray, Amos

Newton, Emery
Otis, Oliver
Owing, Nathaniel
Owen, Gideon
Parcher, Zachariah
Parcher, John
Parcher, Daniel
Paul, Marshfield
Paul, True
Perry, John
Pettingill, William
Pettingill, Obadiah
Pettingill, Joseph
Pettingill, Ruel
Pettingill, Arcadus
Pettingill, Isaac
Phillips, Amos
Piper, Thomas
Pratt, Othniel
Pratt, Isaac
Pratt, Elisha
Rackley., Stephen
Ramsdell, Luther
Ramsdell, William
Randall, Oliver
Randall, Nathaniel
Randall, John
Richards, Daniel
Richmond, Nathan
Robbins, Daniel
Robbins, William
Robbins, Daniel, Jr.
Rose, Hervey
Rose, Seth
Rose, Asa
Rose, Asa Jr.
Rowe, John
Sampson, Beriah
Sampson, Zoah
Sampson, Hazael
Sampson, Michael
Sampson, Cyrus
Sampson, Ira
Southard, Thomas
Stanley, Jones
Stetson, Nathan
Stinchfield, Thomas

Stinchfield, James
Stinchfield, Samuel
Stinchfield, Ebenezer
Stubbs, Samuel
Sturtevant, John
Sumner, Houghton
Sumner, Caleb R.
Swift, Charles
Swift, Samuel
Sylvester, Hervey
Sylvester, Howard
Thayer, Zachariah
Thompson, John
Trask, Spencer
Turner, William
Turner, Josiah
Turner, Joseph
Turner, Alpheus
Turner, Obadiah
Turner, George
Turner, Lewis
Turner, Joshua
Turner, Ansel
Turner, Oscar D.
Tupper, Enoch
Tupper, Joshua
Webster, Stephen
Welcome, Stephen
Wendall, James B.
Wing, Bachelder
Wing, Caleb
Wing, Caleb, Jr.
Wing, James
Witham, Daniel
Wood, Samuel
Wood, Simeon
Woodman, David
Woodman, Ammi

CHAPTER V.

FIRST MILLS AND OTHER INDUSTRIES.

About the year 1790, John Jennings built the first saw-mill, a small affair at West Leeds for the use of himself and his three sons near him, but accommodated his neighbors by sawing for them. This was located near where Zachary Cary subsequently built a fulling-mill. The second saw-mill was built in 1804, by Thomas Mitchell and Elias and Peter Lane. Andrew Cushman who married Bathsheba Jennings in 1789, and settled in Leeds, built the first grist-mill, in 1814, on the privilege at West Leeds now occupied by R. E. Swain. In 1817, he built a saw-mill on the same power. At his death in 1844, Daniel Hinkley became the proprietor and built a new mill. Stillman and Seth Howard later owned this property. Orrin B. Taylor was the next owner; was succeeded in turn by E. E. Wheeler, Rodolphus Jennings and R. E. Swain. Mr. Swain is the present proprietor of this water-power and has a manufactory of box boards and dowels, which furnishes employment to several persons. Eben Mason built the second grist-mill in town in 1816, on the same stream, deriving power from an overshot wheel 16 feet in diameter, Like most of the early mills this had a short existence. This Eben Mason was the first blacksmith in Leeds. His shop was at the corner near where R. S. Loring, M.D. now resides. Oliver P. Frost was an early blacksmith in the town and had his shop at West Leeds. Charles Bates was another early engaged in that business, and was located on Quaker Ridge, or Bates Hill, which takes its name from him. At Leeds Center, Robert Crumett was the first blacksmith. Stephen Welcome and Cyrus Sampson had "asheries," where they made potash. The trades of tanning and shoemaking were early combined. Samuel More, who served in the Navy in the War of 1812 and was made prisoner, came to Leeds in 1814, put up a small tannery at Leeds Center and was the town's first tanner. He continued to tan leather and make shoes until 1849. In 1881 he died. Other tanners were James and Ira Lamb and Seth Cary.

MERCHANTS.

The first merchant in town was Thomas Stinchfield, who had an extensive Indian trade. Some of the early, wealthier settlers kept large stocks of necessities for their own use, and frequently

LEEDS CENTER, LOOKING FROM THE LAKE.

accommodated their neighbors by sales or barter. The first regular storekeepers, as we now use the term, were Solomon Lothrop, at the Center; Stephen Welcome, in the southwest part; William Turner, in the south part and Cyrus Sampson at South Leeds; while later, Stephen Day (1839), and Joshua Lane (at Dr. Lorings's Corner) had good stores. Solomon Lothrop established at Leeds Center in 1820, and was in trade many years. He was succeeded by Noah Sturtevant, of Winthrop, who continued in trade until the store was burned. It was rebuilt by Mr. Lothrop who again engaged in trade. He was succeeded by Barnabas Davee, who conducted in connection therewith a furniture shop, and for several years did a thriving business. About 1822, Simeon Foss was in trade on the southeast corner at Leeds Center, and Nathan Randall near the town-house. Mr. Davee's successor was a Mr. Fogg, who was in business but a short time when the store remained closed for several years. It was again utilized by Mr. Lothrop and his son, Solomon L., but in 1846, they sold out to Thaddeus More, who in turn, sold in 1847 to Josiah Day. From 1849 to 1853, the railroad contractors run a store at the Center. In 1861, G. C. More, a brother of Thaddeus was in trade in the Lothrop store. After him came Cyrus B. Lane. In 1872, Charles H. Lane was there engaged in business. His successor was W. L. Francis, who has made extensive repairs and annexes and since continued in trade at the old stand, carrying a large general stock of goods and doing a thriving and prosperous business. He has long been postmaster and discharged the duties of the office to the satisfaction of the patrons. At Keen's Corner a store was quite early established. In 1824, John Keene, who then and for many years after run this store, was licensed to sell spirituous liquors. With the coming of the railroad, stores were established at Curtis Corner and North Leeds. With the improved advantages at West Leeds, a store was opened there in 1828, by Jonas P. Lee. His successor was Zachary Cary who continued in business from 1830 to 1837, when he sold to Silas Morse, and in 1840 the store was converted into a blacksmith shop. On the site where the buildings of H. W. Lincoln were recently burned, a store was built by Benjamin Millett, who, after a few years, sold to the late Stephen R. Deane. He was engaged in trade there several years, fifteen of which, he held the office of postmaster. His successors were Rhodolphus Jennings, R. E. Swain and C. H. Foster. In a new store, Perry Grant has been several years in trade where he is now engaged.

In 1852, T. Clarkson Foss built and opened a store at North Leeds. He was an extensive buyer of wool, in which business he was successful and acquired a good property. Since his decease, Robert Scott, Messrs. Chamberlain Bros., and W. C. Tribou have, in turn, done business there. At present, the property is in the hands of A. W. Manter and his wife, who are engaged in trade. A few years subsequent to the building of this store, Henry and Jason Woodman, brothers, erected a store a few rods westerly of the buildings of Mr. Foss and opened a general stock of goods. They were a long time in business. After the decease of Jason, Henry returned to the farm on which he was born and reared and continues his residence there still. C. H. Whitehouse, a son-in-law of Jason is the present occupant of that store and does quite an extensive business in grain and feed. Mr. Guy Foss, in another place at North Leeds was engaged in trade, who was succeeded by his mother, present occupant. About 1850, Salmon and his son, Henry M. Brewster, erected and opened a general store at Curtis Corner. Much of the time since it has been open, and until a recent date has been occupied by a member of the Brewster family. Gustavus W. Lane established himself in mercantile business at the Center in 1883, and has been a heavy dealer in groceries, flour, grain, feed, etc. In connection with his mercantile business, in 1889, he erected a steam grist-mill near his store and the railroad station, the capacity of which was 200 bushels per day. His business was thereby increased from $5,000 to $50,000 annually. He has also been station and express agent, all in all making his a busy life.

Previous to removing from Quaker Ridge to Curtis Corner, Salmon Brewster had been in trade there. He was succeeded in 1851 by O. T. Wing, who was a short time engaged in business, but soon retired. In 1898, W. H. Brewster leased a part of his store at Curtis Corner to R. D. Rand & Co., dealers in groceries, grain and feed. The present staff of merchants in town are: W. L. Francis, G. W. Lane, at Leeds Center; C. H. Whitehouse, Mrs. A. W. Manter and Mrs. Vesta P. Foss, at North Leeds; R. D. Rand & Co., and H. M. Brewster, at Curtis Corner; Perry Grant, at West Leeds.

CHAPTER VI.

A CONDENSED REVIEW OF THE HISTORY OF THE BAPTIST CHURCHES IN LEEDS FROM ABOUT A. D. 1800 TO 1901.

The first religious meeting in the limits of the present town of Leeds of which we have any record, was held in the autumn of 1794.

It was called by Thomas D. Francis, one of the first settlers of Leeds and afterward the first pastor of the First Baptist Church in town. In his old age Rev. Thomas Francis communicated the facts connected with this meeting to younger members of his church.

Mr. Francis read the 51st psalm and a versification of the same psalm was sung in the meeting. He had called the people together under a strong and solemn conviction of duty, and he proceeded forthwith to relate his own religious experience which had been such that he longed for others to have the same.

The spiritual interest in this service became so strong that they resolved then and there that under the leadership of Mr. Francis they would allow no Sabbath to pass without a meeting.

Hearing of the religious awakening in Leeds, Jesse Lee and others commenced regular services on Thursday evenings of each week, and during that fall and following winter 40 persons were converted.

In June, 1795, Elder Potter baptized a few persons and soon after, Isaac Case baptized several more who joined the Baptist Church in Wayne.

Meetings in Leeds at this time, were held in the barn of Giddings Lane.

In 1799, Mr. Francis was ordained as an evangelist.

"On Wednesday, July 2, 1800, certain Baptist brethren of Littleborough, apprehending it would be for the glory of God and their own spiritual interest, having been granted dismission from the Baptist Church in Wayne, were organized into an essential Christian Church." Elder Thomas Francis and fifteen others whose names are as follows subscribed to the Articles of Faith presented at that time:

Thomas D. Francis, Eleazer Carver, Daniel Lothrop, Giddings Lane, Eunice Knapp, Jemima Lane, Daniel Robbins, Matilda Millett, Joanna Turner, Isaac Freeman, James Sampson,

Sarah Foster, Joseph Gould, Thomas Millett, Zebulon Millett, Elizabeth Otis.

The first officer of this church was Giddings Lane, who was elected deacon at its organization.

October 16, 1800, Elder Francis was called to the pastorate of this church—a position which he filled continuously and honorably for 35 years, and excepting the first six years of his ministry, during which Isaac Freeman was clerk of the church, Elder Francis made and kept its records.

Since its organization 447 persons have had membership with this church. Somewhat more than a score of preachers have served as pastors or stated supplies. During the century of our existence 15 of our members have served the church as deacons, and about the same number as clerks—including four pastors.

In 1806, the meeting-house at Leeds Center was completed. In 1836, such repairs and remodeling as were thought best were made. In 1872, a considerable change was made in the interior of the meeting-house and extensive repairs were made upon the outside, at a cost of several hundred dollars. March 12, 1891, it was voted to make thorough repairs on the meeting-house, also a general modernizing of the interior which, in due time, was accomplished at a cost of about $1,200.

Since then the house has remained in a comparatively sound and serviceable condition.

The successors of Thomas D. Francis as pastors and stated supplies were as follows:

Allen Barrows from 1835 to 1837; Wilson C. Rider, 1838; Daniel Hutchinson, 1839; Robert Starr, 1840; Daniel Hutchinson, 1841; S. S. Leighton, 1842 to 1845; J. W. Lawton, 1846 to 1848; Elders Sargent and Tilton, 1849; Allen Barrows, 1850 to 1855; Abram Snyder, 1856; Elder Gurney, 1857; Elder Fulton, 1858; Joel P. Chapin, 1859 to 1863; O. Richardson, 1863; William E. Noyes, 1864 to 1868; Joel Wheeler, 1868; Henry A. Libby, 1869; S. S. Brownson, 1870 to 1873; Abram Snyder, 1876 to 1886; J. R. Herrick, 1888 to 1892; Robert Scott, 1892 to 1895; J. B. Bryant, 1896; E. H. Doane, 1899 to 1900.

The Second Baptist Church and Society was organized at South Leeds June 19, 1843, with a constituent membership of 29, to which additions were made from time to time until they numbered 52.

John Beals was their first church clerk, and Simon Maloon their first deacon.

Sept. 16, 1843, Elder Walter Foss was called to serve this church as pastor—a relation which he sustained with honor until it lost its visibility as an organization about 1870.

For many years this church was a center of religious influence in that part of the town. The devotion of its only pastor

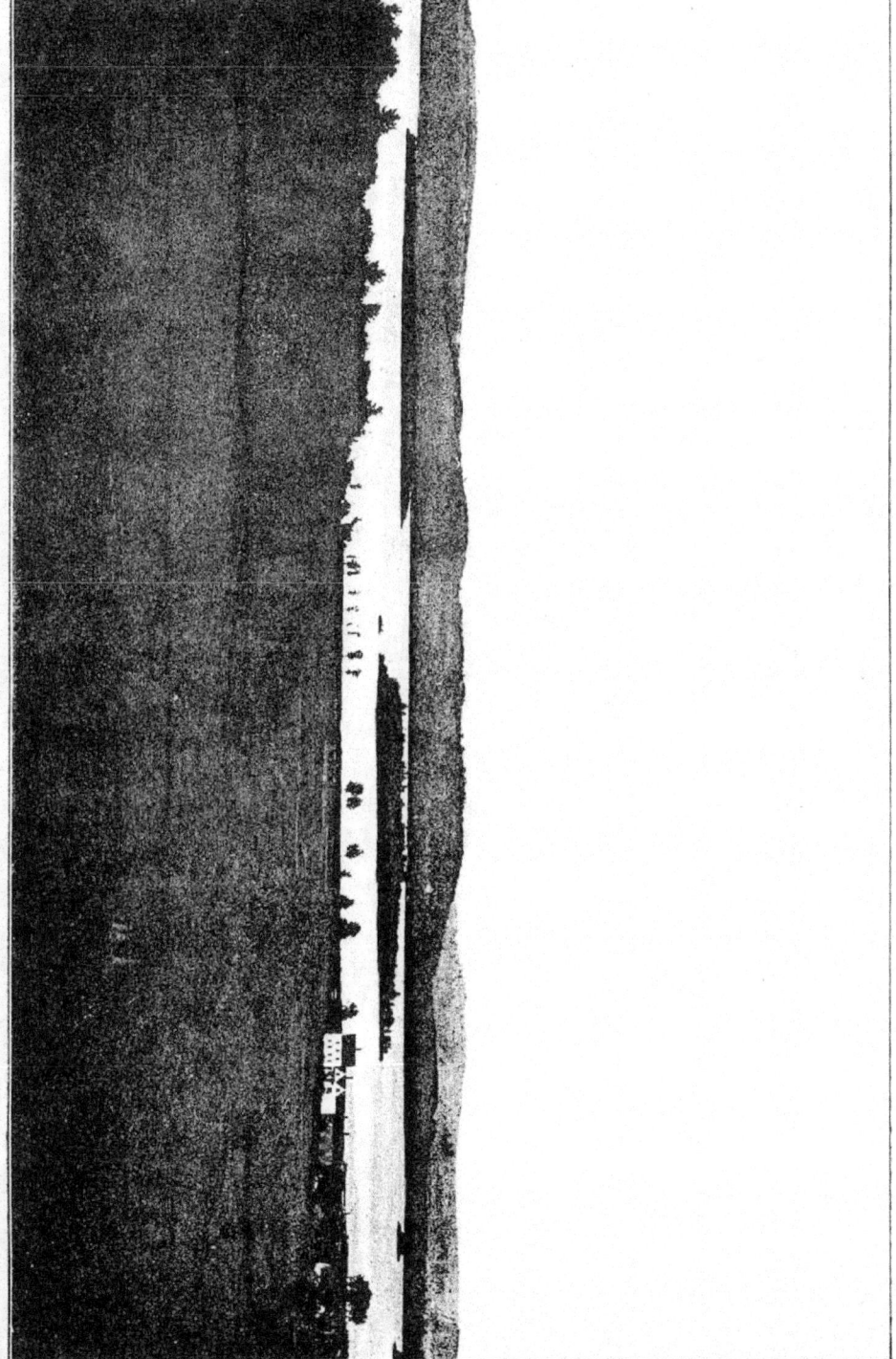

may well serve as an example to Christian workers of a later time. At a mere pittance as a salary, and under the necessity of a journey of not less than fifteen miles at each pastoral visit to this field, he maintained the oversight of this little flock through summer's heat and winter's cold for nearly 30 years.

But words of praise are not needed from us to embellish the character of those whose history we briefly here review. Their record is in heaven. It is but just, however, that we acknowledge our indebtedness to them because of that moral worth and sterling integrity which constituted the very warp and woof of that godly influence which they transmitted unto us.

It is not denied that worthy men and women lived and died outside the churches of their day. It is not denied that *some* at least of those within the church were justly chargeable with fault and foible and possible insincerity, but yet, as we look back at them *collectively* through the vista of the years encircled in the halo of a sainted recollection, the picture takes a charm of form and coloring superior to any likeness of those who are merely sons of earth.

Their calling is from above—their citizenship in heaven. But visions of heavenly character and "peace on earth" are not the only features of interest to us in this scene.

As we contemplate them more closely, they take definite shape before us as a section of that mighty army of the living God which is waging war against the powers of darkness and of death.

But who is this who has marshalled and is leading them?

He appears a mighty man of war. With unwavering courage, with well nigh unerring wisdom and with a zeal which knew no abatement, this man Thomas D. Francis, *born* a leader of men, continues in command of this band of Christ's disciples for more than a third of a century; moulding their belief, giving vitality and suitable form to character and life among them, making them inflexible and staunch in their advocacy of what to them was right, invincible in their conflict with the evils of their time, and little less than really divine in the manner and purpose of their lives.

What this community might have been without the pastors and their churches which have stood, as the century has passed, each in its time and place, as exponents and examples of righteousness and truth, we do not wish to know.

But of this we are assured: Divinely salutary indeed their influence has been. Their illustrious example, however, adds weight to the responsibility which rests on us as their successors.

May this, our obligation, be duly recognized and faithfully discharged. And may the virtues of those whom we commemorate this day be so effectually perpetuated in our lives, that further and more lasting honor shall be added to their names.

CHAPTER VII.

HISTORY OF THE METHODIST EPISCOPAL CHURCH OF LEEDS.

Rev. Jesse Lee, through whose efforts Methodism was established in New England, preached in Littleborough, now the town of Leeds, Dec. 23, 1794. The service of that date was held in a private house, the home of a Mr. Lane. The house was crowded and the power of God was clearly felt in their midst.

The town of Leeds was placed upon the Readfield circuit as early as 1795; later it was made a part of Monmouth circuit and was regularly visited by the preachers.

A class was formed about 1795. The progress of Methodism from this early period until 1838 is not known as no records are preserved, if there were any kept, to give its history during these years.

In 1838, Rev. John Allen held a series of meetings in the school-house on Quaker Ridge, a number of persons were converted and a class of more than twelve members was formed with Salmon Brewster as leader. It is stated that the society increased and the religious services continued to be held at the school-house until January, 1852. In 1849, Joseph Hawkes was sent to the Leeds circuit as a supply. In 1850, the Conference sent Rev. John Cumner to this charge, and through his efforts and the aid given by Salmon Brewster, a church building was contemplated and the plans for building were made.

Rev. Mr. Cumner appointed the following men as trustees of the church property: Salmon Brewster, Charles Stetson, George C. Lathrop, Warren Mower, Jacob Wheeler, Simeon Turner, and Nathan Morse. At the first meeting of the trustees held March 3, 1851, Salmon Brewster was chosen chairman, George Lathrop secretary and Simeon Turner treasurer; at this meeting of the trustees they voted to receive bids for building a church, until March 8th at one o'clock P.M.

At the next meeting of the board plans for the house were accepted and the bid of Mr. Charles Stetson to build the house for eight hundred and fifty dollars was accepted. At a later meeting of the trustees Nov. 29th, Charles Stetson was chosen to apprize the pews, subject to the approval of the trustees. On Jan. 1, 1852, the board voted to accept the house upon condition that it be finished according to contract. At one P.M. this same date, the sale of pews began. Seventeen pews were sold at this meeting and on Jan. 6, seven more were sold. The prices of the pews varied from fifteen to thirty dollars.

The exact date when the house was dedicated is not known, but it was in January of 1852 during the pastorate of Rev. Luther B. Knight. Mr. Knight's pastorate lasted for two years, from July 9, 1851, to June or July of 1853, and at this time there were six different classes, one at North Leeds, Quaker Ridge, South Leeds, Leeds Junction, in Greene, at West Leeds. But soon after, one of the classes was given up and its members were placed in one of the other classes.

Afterward the class at North Leeds joined the Wayne Circuit. By death and removals, one by one the classes have been abandoned. At the present a prayer-meeting is the only week-night service held.

In 1884, the society bought a parsonage and made of it a comfortable home for its pastors. There are about twenty acres of land in the parsonage lot and gives its ministers plenty of opportunity for out-door work in the summer.

Within a few years the church has been remodelled and beautified on the interior with paint, carpeting and new furnishings. These repairs were undertaken and accomplished through the efforts of Mr. Harry Cochrane, of Monmouth, who was then supplying this charge.

The society also assisted in building a very neat chapel at Keene's Corner, which was dedicated May 5, 1891. In this chapel the Methodists hold services once in two weeks. Services at the church on Quaker Ridge are also held once in two weeks, the pastor alternating between the two places in his Sunday services. The Sunday School, at present, is small in number but a good interest is manifested in the study of the Sunday School lessons. For a number of years Brother John F. Gray was Superintendent of the School and by his faithful efforts the school was kept in a flourishing condition. The society numbers at present only twenty-four members. Death and removals have decreased its numbers faster than additions have been made. Though the society is small, yet with the help of its friends, who are interested in sustaining religious services and have given liberally toward the support of the same, it has been able to give its pastors a comfortable support.

The following is the list of the names of its pastors who have served the church since 1849:

1849-50—Joseph Hawkes.
1850-51—John Cumner.
1851-52—Luther B. Knight.
1859-61—D. B. Holt.
1862-63—Levi Eldridge.
1863-64—William Stout.

1864-65—M. B. Cummings.
1865-66—W. Wyman.
1866-67—Jonathan Fairbanks.
1867-70— ———— Lufkin.
1870-73—S. M. Emerson.
1873-75—J. B. Fogg.
1875-76—Loring P. Gould.
1876-77—Nathan Andrews, —— Sanderson, J. B. Fogg.
1878-79—Nottage.
1879-80—McKenna.
1880-81—Greenwood Gordon.
1881-82—J. P. Cole.
1882-83— ———— Clifford.
1883-84—C. R. Dagget.
1885-86—J. P. Roberts.
1886-87—W. H. Congdon.
1888-90—Joseph Moulton.
1890-91—Isaac Beals.
1891-93—Charles D. Blaisdell.
1893-94—C. H. Williams.
1894-95—Powers, F. W. Smith.
1896-97—F. H. Billington, J. Buchanan.
1898-1901—F. H. Hall.

CHAPTER VIII.

UNIVERSALIST CHURCH.

From a very early period the preaching of Rev. Thomas Barnes had found sympathy in many households of Leeds. The earliest history of a Universalist organization is given in a manuscript in the handwriting of Israel Herrick, bearing date 1833, giving answers to questions asked in the Intelligencer of Sept. 28, relative to the state of Universalist societies in Kennebec and Somerset counties. He says:

"The first Universalist Society in Leeds was organized March 13, 1830, of sixty members. There usually attend meeting about 200 people. In the summer of 1832 the society hired preaching one-quarter of the time for six months. Rev. Thomas Dolloff preached, for which we paid him $24 in money, raised by subscription; we have no funds. Our society is scattered all over the town, and subscriptions fall on those near the meeting, besides our society generally is not of the wealthiest class, therefore our subscriptions are not in proportion to our numbers. The society has not much increased or diminished. Our prospects are as good as at any former period. We have had no difficulty in obtaining preaching in proportion to our means until the present season. We have no meeting-house, our meetings are well accommodated in the town-house. Our society is well united—a good degree of feeling existing among the members. We hold no meetings except on Sundays, have no Sunday-school nor Bible class. We have our regular yearly society meetings, besides intermediate meetings as occasion requires, but generally not fully attended. It is my opinion that the number that attends our meeting is larger than attends any other meeting in town except the Free Willers, which occasionally may be as large or larger than ours. I should think not far from one-half of the ratable polls were in favor of the doctrine of Universalism."

At this time some of the leading members were Israel Herrick, Levi Foss, John Francis, Caleb Carver, William Gott, Simeon Gould, Barnabas Davee, George Lathrop, Thomas W. Bridgham, Benjamin Millett, Alexander Jennings, Ebenezer Stinchfield, Samuel More, James Lindsay, John Carver, Solomon Lathrop, Samuel Jennings, Levi Dunham, Levi Caswell, Lemuel Sumner, James Stinchfield.

From this time we find no records until March 20, 1837, when a petition to George Lathrop, Esq., directing him to notify the petitioners to meet at the town-house, April 15, to organize the first Universalist Society of Leeds, was signed by Israel Herrick, Asa Rose, B. Millett, Jr., William P. Millett, O. J. Frost, Solomon Lathrop, Benjamin Millett, Thomas W. Bridgham, Franklin B. Leonard, Samuel More, Isaac Pratt, Eben Stinchfield, James K. Stinchfield, Isaac Boothby, John Carver, James Stinchfield, Jr., Aaron Dwinal, Barnabas Davee, Elias Lane, Robert Crumett. In 1836 the Baptist meeting-house had been jointly repaired by the Universalists and Baptists, and an agreement made whereby the Universalists were to occupy the house the fourth Sunday in each month. The society was duly organized, a constitution adopted, Israel Herrick elected clerk and assessors, etc., chosen.

It is most probable that the following were pew owners in the repaired church: Alexander Jennings, Aaron Dwinal, Samuel More, Solomon Lathrop two, Giddings Lane two, Eben Stinchfield, John D. Millett, Benjamin Millett, Jr., Israel Herrick, Lemuel Sumner, Ira Lamb, Isaac Pratt, Isaac Boothby, Robert Crumett.

Constitution.

We, the undersigned members of the First Universalist Society in Leeds agree to the following as the constitution of said society:

Art. 1st. The object of this society shall be the promotion of religion and morality amongst ourselves and our fellow-men.

Art. 2d. The annual meeting of this society shall be held on the Saturday next following the first Monday in April in each year for the choice of officers for said society and at such place and hour of the day as the assessors by legal warrant shall direct.

Art. 3d. The officers of this society shall consist of a moderator for the time being, a clerk, a board of assessors, a prudential committee, a treasurer and collector. All of these officers with the exception of the moderator, shall be elected to serve until the next annual meeting or until some others are chosen in their stead.

Art. 4th. A meeting of this society may be called at any time by the assessors if seven members shall in writing require them to do so.

Art. 5th. Seven members shall constitute a quorum for the transaction of business, but a smaller number may adjourn.

Art. 6th. Any person wishing to unite with us in the object of this society and believing in the truth of the sacred Scriptures and sustaining a good moral character may by being introduced or recommended by a member of regular standing be admitted a member of this society by a vote of the majority of the members present at any meeting of this society and subscribing to this constitution. And no member shall be excluded but by a majority of two-thirds present.

Art. 7th. No person of immoral habits shall ever be admitted to a membership in this society and it shall be a sufficient cause of admonition and ultimately of expulsion if any member shall contract such habits.

Art. 8th. Any article of this constitution, the first and seventh only excepted, may be altered at any annual meeting of this society by a vote of two-thirds of the members present.

And now commending ourselves, our families and our friends, with our brethren of the human race, to God, who is able to build us up in his most holy faith and prepare us for the purity and blessedness of his heavenly kingdom, we subscribe our names to this constitution and agree to abide by the same and by the rules and regulations of this society.

George Lathrop, Alexander Jennings, Eben Stinchfield, Caleb Wing, John D. Millett, Lemuel Sumner, George D. Lathrop, Israel Herrick, Benj. Millett, Isaac Pratt, Samuel More, Solomon Lathrop, Asa Rose, Aaron Dwinal, John Carver, Robert Crumett, Wm. P. Millett, Isaac Boothby, Barnabas Davee, Franklin B. Leonard, Giddings Lane, Ira Lamb.

In April, 1843, Giddings Lane, Israel Herrick, S. More were elected assessors, Samuel More, John D. Millett, Isaac Boothby a committee "to see whether the agreement entered into between the societies relative to the occupancy of the meeting house is binding." This was the commencement of a long and serious contest for the title of one-fourth of the house, culminating in a suit brought by the Baptist society against Perry Grant for malicious trespass in breaking open the meeting house for Universalist service. From the decision of the supreme court in favor of the Baptist ownership an appeal was taken.

The decision in favor of the plaintiffs was made in 1871 on the ground that under the act of incorporation of the Baptist society there could be no legal transfer of any of its property. In 1872 an elegant Universalist meeting-house containing fifty-two pews was built at a cost of $5,000, and Nov. 10, 1873, Isaiah B. Additon, Giddings Lane, Horace Herrick, B. Davee, R. Jennings, Charles S. Gordon, Lewis Churchill, H. L. Millett, Willard Lathrop, Rollins S. Loring, J. F. Jennings, L. H. Sumner and W. B. Sumner petitioned H. M. Brewster, Esq., for a warrant enabling the "Stockholders of the Leeds Centre Parish Church" to make an incorporation, which was effected November 18, when Giddings Lane was chosen clerk. He held that office until his death, when his son, G. W. Lane, succeeded him. Rev. Otis H. Johnson, of Jay, preached every fourth Sunday from 1869 to 1879 and part of the time every other Sunday. He was succeeded by Revs. Barnes, White, Cutler, Smith and Gould. At the present time meetings are held during the summer season only. There are a great many people in town who claim to be Universalists, but from lack of interest or other reasons do not attend meeting.

CHAPTER IX.

CHURCHES.

"The First Freewill Baptist Church" in town was organized at North Leeds, Feb. 11, 1829, by Elder Abizer Bridges. The original members were, Joshua Tupper, Warren Howard, Lucy Tupper, Mercy Dunham, Julia A. Stanley, Almira Turner, Martha Grant, Anna Additon, Deborah Bridges, Eliza Bridges. It belonged to Bowdoin Quarterly Meeting, and in 1836 had a membership of 75—the largest in its history. The Union Chapel was erected in that place on that date, one-half of which was owned by this society, one-fourth by the Methodist society and one-fourth by individuals of the Baptist and Campbellite (Christian) faith. From the church record we quote: "Dedicatory Exercises of Union Chapel, North Leeds, Convened at the Chapel on 16th day of November, 1836; 11 o'clock A.M.

"Introductory Prayer, by Rev. Daniel Hutchinson;
"Reading Scripture, by Elder Walter Foss;
"Dedicatory Prayer, by Elder Allen Barrows;
"Sermon, by Elder Daniel Hutchinson;
"Address to Society, by Elder Allen Barrows;
"Concluding Prayer, by Elder Walter Foss;

"Sacred Music, led and conducted by John Gould, Esq., in an able and devotional manner on the occasion."

Prior to the completion cf the Chapel the Free Baptists held their meetings in school and dwelling houses, but from this time their meetings were held in the house of the Lord every second Sabbath. From 75 members in that year, but 8 were on the rolls in 1891, yet the church was then recognized by the Quarterly Meeting. With the death of its deacon, Francis Davis Millett, which occurred in 1893, its identity was lost. Other deacons were Joshua Tupper, Warren Howard and George Gould. Those of Campbellite or Christian faith were not many; yet, for several years they held meetings in the chapel their allotted portion of the time. Rev. Greenwood C. Gordon was their pastor.

QUAKER SOCIETY.

In 1807, on Quaker Ridge in Leeds the Quaker Society erected a house of worship where they held meetings many years. In later years it was removed about one mile west,—

near their cemetery where it remained for a time, when it was again moved farther west to a place nearly opposite the dwelling of Stephen Welcome. Among the members and prominent supporters of this society were the Baileys, some of whom removed to Winthrop, whose children engaged in the manufacture of oil-cloth. Gradually the members decreased in number until the society lost its identity, and about 1869 the house was sold, torn down and carried away.

CHAPTER X.

SCHOOLS OF LEEDS.

In common with the early settlers of other New England towns, the people of Leeds, upon its first settlement, showed their interest in education by giving liberally of their means to establish a free public school system.

In 1801, upon the incorporation of the town, at the first town meeting, $200 was voted for the support of schools, and Joseph Day, Levi Bates, William Gilbert, John Jennings, Oliver Randall, and Obadiah Pettengill were chosen a committee to manage school matters.

In November of the same year it was voted to accept the division of the town into districts made by the selectmen and that each district draw its own money. In 1802 and 1803, $300 was voted for schools. In 1803, Elder Thomas Francis, Abiel Daly, and George Turner, Jr., were chosen to inspect schools and teachers.

From 1803 to 1860 when $1050 was raised for schools, the amount raised each year was increased as the means of the people increased and as the town gained in the number of its pupils. In 1868, 1870, and 1871, the maximum amount of $1200 was raised. At the present time (1901) $1,000 is voted by the town for common schools.

By a law passed in 1820, not less than 40 cents per each inhabitant in the town was required to be raised for school purposes. By another law passed in the same year, if a district received less than $35 as its share of the school funds, all of it might be expended for a school taught by a mistress but if more than $35 was received, two-thirds must be expended for a school taught by a master. Quite a different state of affairs from what exists at the beginning of the 20th century, when 99 per cent. of the teachers of the state are women and where in Leeds the past year but one male teacher was employed. In 1825, the law requiring the employment of male teachers was changed and it was left to the discretion of the district officers as to whether a master or a mistress should be employed.

In 1853, the amount required by law to be raised for schools was increased to fifty cents per inhabitant of the town. In 1854 it was increased to sixty cents per capita. In 1866, to seventy-five cents, and in 1868 to one dollar. In 1872, it was changed to eighty cents, as it remains at present.

It will be seen that one of the first things done by the town relative to schools, was the division of the town into districts. At first, nine districts were formed, but later as the population increased the number was changed to twelve, which was the number in 1893, when the districts were abolished by law of the state.

As the early settlers of Leeds, as of other New England towns, were pre-eminently a religious people, it is but natural that we should find the first teacher of a school in Leeds to be Elder Thomas Francis. Other early teachers were Elisha Sylvester, Parsons True, Benson Caswell and Lloyd Gould. Of a little later period we find the names of Barnabas Davēe, Stephen R. Deane, Seth Howard, J. C. Stinchfield, Joseph Gott, Henry Woodman, Rodolphus and Florius Jennings among the men as having taught many terms in town. Among the women who taught much were Mrs. Diana Wing Gilbert, Sallie Stinchfield, Mrs. Hannah Pollard and her sister, Kate Knapp.

Of the conditions existing at this time and the lack of nearly everything considered necessary for good teaching at present, a graphic description is given by the late Stephen R. Deane in the history of Leeds schools, given in the history of Androscoggin County and is as follows:—

"The acquisition of a common school education sixty years ago was often attended with difficulties of which scholars of the present age know nothing. Many districts had no school houses. I recollect attending school for a short time in three neighboring districts where the schools were kept in winter in a room in some dwelling house, and in summer sometimes in a shop, a corn house and in one instance on the big barn floor. The district in which I lived had no school house till several years after I ceased to be a scholar. The district lay on two roads nearly parallel to each other and about a mile apart, with no road within its limit to connect them, so the people could never agree upon a proper site for their house to stand. The school room was furnished with seats made of planks or slabs long enough to reach from end to end and from side to side of the room. The desk for writing was of like material, fastened to the walls (usually on three sides of the rooms) so that the scholars when writing were obliged to turn their backs to the teacher and face the wall, the window, and, too often, the darkness; for windows were neither large nor plenty, one or more corners of the room being too shady for the pupil to clearly discern the plummet lines under his copy. It was thought that for a boy to be able to perform all the hard problems in Kenney's arithmetic was about all he ever need to know of mathematics. Reading, writing and geography were to be studied but grammar was considered too effeminate and quite useless unless the boy aspired to become a teacher. Girls learned spelling, reading and grammar but arithmetic was regarded for them much as grammar was for boys.

"Ambitious mothers provided their daughters with a square of nice linen for the foundation of a sampler on which the letters of the alphabet, figures, her age, and other things (according to the fancy of her teacher and her skill) were to be wrought in needle work. There were but few who made teaching a business, and in general nothing beyond a common school education constituted their literary qualifications. The school fund was small and apportioned to the several districts according to the number of scholars in each."

The school-houses contained large fire places but a stove was unheard of. It was customary for green wood to be hauled to the school-house in large ox-sled loads, and there fitted for burning by the large boys. With this arrangement for heating, it was no surprising thing for the front row of pupils to be burning their faces while the back ones were nearly freezing.

Such a thing as a blackboard was unknown. To Mrs. Hannah Pollard belongs the honor of having and using the first one in town, while Francis Lathrop stands second, owning one which he used in the different schools where he taught.

The wages of the teachers seem very small compared with those received by the teachers of to-day. The women received fifty cents a week and their board, usually secured by boarding around. The mistress who got seventy-five cents a week was looked upon as receiving large wages. The men teachers were usually paid from $8 to $14 a month.

The teacher, master or mistress, to be successful had to have the ability to discipline and maintain order, sometimes by main strength. The schools numbered from sixty to eighty, with many of the pupils young men and women. In one school, that at West Leeds, eighty-five pupils were enrolled one term. That was rather more than one teacher or one school house could accommodate and those under twelve were sent to another house and furnished with a school mistress. In such schools it was no light task to keep order unless the teacher possessed unusual powers of mind or muscle.

In 1873, the legislature provided by law that any town sustaining a high school should receive from the state one-half of the amount actually expended for wages and board of teacher in such school to an amount not exceeding $500. If the town did not take advantage of this offer, any district might do so, provided that only two such schools should be maintained in one town.

In the year that this law was passed (1873) the town of Leeds took advantage of this offer by the state and raised the liberal sum of $400. With this sum, two schools of sixteen weeks each were held in different parts of the town that fall.

In 1879, the aid by the state to free high schools was temporarily withdrawn but in 1880 it was restored, though the maximum amount a town could receive was reduced from $500 to $250. Notwithstanding, a school of this nature was held nearly every year, either by vote of the town or by money raised in some district until 1897, when the law raising the grade and requiring all applicants for admission to be examined, had the effect of discontinuing the free high school in Leeds. The great help to the people of the town by the maintenance of these schools cannot be overestimated. The saving in expense to many families was great as their children attended school in their own town at slight expense instead of being sent out of town to academies or other schools at much greater cost. Then also a large part of the pupils were those who would have considered their education complete if the means of gaining a knowledge of the higher studies had not been placed at their own doors. There is no question but what the free high school law did much for the intellectual advancement of the town. Among some of the teachers of the first free high schools were John Hoffman, Forest L. Evans, ——— Lord, now city superintendent of schools in Portland, and Harrison Pratt, a native of Turner, and a teacher of unusual ability. Nearly all these early teachers were college graduates or undergraduates.

Some of the later teachers were James S. Norton, a normal graduate, and a very successful teacher both in methods of instruction and discipline.

To Miss Adelia J. Webber, who taught many terms of high and common school in town, many of our young men and women ascribe their thorough training in many things and their ambition to secure more of an education than the schools of the town could give. By them she is considered their benefactor in a large measure.

Miss Lettice B. Albee, of Bates College, also taught several successful terms of free high school in town.

In 1887, W. R. Pettengill, E. T. Clifford and E. E. Additon served the town as S. S. Committee. This was the last year in which a committee had entire charge of the schools of Leeds.

The following year a supervisor was chosen. The schools of the town made the usual advancement in 1888 and 1889, under the supervision of E. E. Additon.

In 1890, a radical departure from the established order of things was made by the election of Laura M. Sylvester, a graduate of Farmington Normal School and a successful teacher of experience, as supervisor. She was the first and so far the only woman to hold this office in Leeds. She served with credit to herself and town during the first year of her management of the schools that the free text book law went into effect. The furnishing of free text books was made compulsory upon the towns in 1890. Much good has resulted from this law to this town.

Miss Sylvester was succeeded by Frank H. Herrick as supervisor. He served during the years of 1892 and 1893. It was in the first year of his supervision that pupils who were regular in their attendance had their names printed in a Roll of Honor in the town reports. This new idea did much to secure the regular attendance of pupils.

In 1893, the town voted that the supervisor employ the teachers, which Mr. Herrick did to the satisfaction of the town.

The school this year, becoming very small in the Additon district, was closed and the pupils conveyed to West Leeds. The school has not been opened since.

It was in 1893 that the Androscoggin County Teachers' Association was formed. By invitation of W. W. Stetson, then Superintendent of Schools in Auburn, the supervisors of the towns in the county were asked to meet at the county buildings in Auburn, for the purpose of forming an association, having for its object the improvement of the schools of the county. There were present the superintendents of Lewiston and Auburn, the supervisor of Turner schools, J. H. Conant, and the supervisor of Leeds schools. The association was formed and plans made for three public meetings during the fall, two in Leeds and one in Turner. The first, held at Keen's Corner, was largely attended and very successful. Of the others, one was held at Leeds Center and one at North Turner.

In 1894, the law passed in 1893, to abolish school districts went into effect. This and the succeeding two years the schools were again under the management of E. E. Additon. Several terms of free high school were successfully held during this time. The school at North Turner Bridge was attended by so few pupils that it was closed by Mr. Additon and conveyance furnished to Gould's Corner. This arrangement has continued since.

The public educational meetings, begun during Mr. Herrick's term of office, were continued by Mr. Additon, two very successful meetings being held, at both of which W. W. Stetson, State Superintendent, was present. At the close of Mr. Additon's three years in office the schools were in a prosperous condition.

In 1897, W. H. Bishop, a teacher of ability and experience had charge of the schools as Superintendent.

The following year, 1898, W. E. Gould, M.D., assumed their management.

In 1899, F. H. Herrick was elected Superintendent, as also in 1900 and 1901.

In the spring of 1900, the S. S. Committee, A. L. Thomas, P. H. Deane and E. A. Russell, recommended that a course of study be adopted and the schools graded. As soon as possible a course of study was arranged and in the fall of 1900 went into effect. When the work of the eight grades into which the course is divided is completed, the pupils are fitted to enter a high school or academy. The present year, 1901, it is expected that a class of seven will graduate and receive diplomas as having completed the work of the primary and grammar grades. Already an improvement in the work of the schools is noted as a result of the adoption of the course. The change has received the hearty support of the citizens of Leeds.

A society, composed of teachers and those interested in the welfare of the schools was formed in the spring of 1900 and received the name of the Leeds Educational Club. Its meetings are held at the beginning, at the middle and at the close of each term of school. Subjects relating to school are discussed and original papers by the members presented.

A public educational meeting was held in the fall of 1899, on Quaker Ridge, in which the three towns of Leeds, Greene, and Turner participated. The superintendents and teachers of these towns were present and many citizens. An interesting program was given. W. W. Stetson, State Superintendent, was in attendance and gave valuable assistance.

School Improvement Leagues have been formed at North Leeds, which school has been named the Washington School, and at Quaker Ridge, which is called the Longfellow School. Books for the use of the schools have been procured, pictures to hang upon the walls and other improvements made.

The teachers in the different schools in the spring of 1901 are as follows:—

North Leeds, Washington School, Mrs. Kittie Russell.
Gould's Corner, Miss Addie F. Woodman.
Otis, Miss Lucy M. Foss.
West Leeds, Miss Marion T. Bishop.
Brick, Miss Mabel L. Dyer.
Curtis Corner, Miss Alice B. Lindsay.
Longfellow School, Miss Estella M. Johnson.
Keen's Corner, Miss Mable D. Lincoln.

CHAPTER XI.

PROFESSIONAL MEN.

Leeds has produced a goodly number of professional men; as many, perhaps, as most N. E. towns with no greater number of inhabitants. In the list are included a very few names of early settlers who were not born in the town, yet resided therein most of their lives. Most have been graduated from colleges in the State, some of whom we are uninformed as to place. Of medical men, the average of production has been one every four years; of lawyers, one every eight years; of ministers, one every four or five years. It will be observed that many more have been produced than required for home use; thus the legitimate claim is laid, that Leeds has furnished a surplus and is entitled to a seat of honor with towns in her class.

PHYSICIANS.

Bridgham, Thomas W.
Daly, Abial, first in the town.
Foss, Simeon.
Foss, Cordellus, graduate Bowdoin Medical College.
Gould, J. F., graduate Harvard Medical College.
Gould, E. T., graduate Bowdoin Medical College.
Gould, W. E., graduate Bowdoin Medical College.
Gould, Frank.
Howard, V. R., graduate Bowdoin Medical College.
Jennings, R. G., graduate Bowdoin Medical College.
Knapp, Cyrus, graduate Bowdoin Medical College, Class of 1825.
Loring, R. S., 45 years active practice in Leeds.
Millett, Asa.
Otis, Amos, graduate Bowdoin Medical College.
Parcher, Sewall, graduate Bowdoin Medical College.
Stinchfield, Thomas B., graduate Bowdoin Medical College.
Stinchfield, John K., graduate Bowdoin Medical College.
Stinchfield, Charles K., graduate Bowdoin Medical College.
Turner, George W.
Turner, Thomas.
Turner, John, graduate Bowdoin Medical College.
Turner, Benjamin, graduate Bowdoin Medical College.

LAWYERS AND JUDGES.

Boothby, Stephen, graduate Colby.
Bridgham, Thomas W., graduate Colby.
Gilmore, R. H., graduate Bowdoin.
Hutchins, C. K., graduate Bowdoin.
Jennings, Orville, graduate Bowdoin.
Knapp, Cyrus, Judge.
Lothrop, Jeremiah, graduate Bowdoin.
Lothrop, V. W., graduate Bowdoin.
Lindsey, John, graduate Bowdoin, Judge.
Otis, John, graduate Bowdoin, member of 31st Congress.
Stinchfield, S. D., graduate Bowdoin, Judge.
Stinchfield, A. G., graduate Bowdoin.
Stinchfield, O. O., graduate Amherst.

MINISTERS.

Boothby, Samuel, Baptist Minister.
Berry, Loren F., Congregational Minister.
Bishop—son of Welcome.
Carver, Elezer, Baptist Minister.
Carver, W. W., Baptist Minister.
Carver, F., Baptist Minister.
Francis, Thomas D., Baptist Minister, first in the town.
Foss, Walter, Baptist Minister.
Foss, Richard, Baptist Minister.
Foster, W. H., Methodist Minister, more than one-half century.
Gordon, G. C., Christian Minister.
Gould, L. P., Free Baptist Minister.
Howard, R. B., Congregational Minister.
Howard, L. L., Second Advent Minister.
Knapp, Aziel L., Minister.
Libby, Henry, Baptist Minister.
Millett, Joshua, Baptist Minister.
Millett, William, Baptist Minister.
Sylvester, Bradbury, Minister.
Wheeler, John, Second Advent Minister.
Wheeler, Asaph, Second Advent Minister.

OTHER PROFESSIONS.

Bates, George, Doctor of Dentistry.
Howard, Fletcher, Com. of Pharmacy.
Lothrop, Luther R., Civil Engineer.
Millett, Ozias, Civil Engineer.

In the hurried canvass made by Mr. Russell L. Gould, to whom is due the credit of obtaining the foregoing lists, omissions may have been made, yet better so than that no record should appear.

CHAPTER XII.

EXCERPTS FROM TOWN RECORDS—FIRST MEETING—FIRST OFFICERS, ETC.

The warrant for the first town meeting, that under which the town was organized, was issued by John Chandler, Esq., of Winthrop, and held at the house of Solomon Millett, April 6, 1801. Dr. Abiel Daily was chosen clerk and treasurer; John Whiting, Daniel Lothrop, Oliver Otis, selectmen and assessors; James Lindsey, collector; Levi Caswell, Stephen Welcome, John Jennings, Daniel Lothrop, Jr., fence viewers; Isaac Collier, Josiah Turner, Giddings Lane, Thomas Lindsey, tithing men; Josiah Turner, surveyor of boards; Isaac Collier, sealer of weights and measures; William Turner, viewer and sealer of brick moles; Abiel Daily, Benjamin Millett, Stephen Welcome, Cornelius Gilbert, Joseph Freeman, hog reeves; James Lane, pound-keeper; Robert Elms, William Gilbert, Samuel Jennings, William Pettengill, field drivers; Josiah Day, Joseph Day, William Gilbert, Samuel Jennings, Giddings Lane, Thomas Lindsey, highways; Joseph Day, Levi Bates, William Gilbert, John Jennings, Oliver Randall, Obadiah Pettingill, school committee. Voted to raise $700 for highways, and $200 for schools. Caleb Strong had 60 votes, and Elbridge Gerry 13 votes, for Governor. April 30, Isaac Collier and Obadiah Pettingill were added to the Board of Selectmen. June 1, voted to pay for recording the county roads laid out from Greene to Livermore and Monmouth. April 6, 1806, voted to raise $75 for town stock of powder, etc. May 11. 1807, voted that the selectmen petition the General Court to grant the petition for incorporating a canal from Androscoggin to Kennebec rivers. November 16, same year, voted to hold town meetings at the Baptist meeting-house. March 5, 1810, voted to raise $70, to procure military stores. May 7, voted that the selectmen be authorized to give a bounty of 25 cents to each person that shall present to them a crow killed in Leeds, at any time to the middle of July next. Nov. 5, voted to build a brick house to deposit the military stores in, to be completed by May first, 1811, and to put up the building of the house to the lowest bidder. Josiah Turner bid it off for $23. Dec. 20, 1810, voted to raise $130, to complete the stock of military stores and to defray other expenses. 1812. Nov. 2, voted to pay the detached militia men $5 per month, in case they are called into actual service. May 5,

1813, voted to pay the Baptist Society $8 for the use of the meeting-house to hold town meetings in. 1815, April 3, voted that the town treasurer pay to the officers commanding the militia companies in September last, 60 cents for each man in said companies who furnished themselves with three days' ammunition while in government service. May 8, voted to allow 60 cents to each commissioned officer and 20 cents to each soldier in the militia of the town who were called into service and not drafted at Pittston. May 20, 1816, on the question of separation of the District of Maine and its erection into a separate state, Leeds voted yes, 164; noes, 3. Sept. 20, 1819, Elder Thomas Francis chosen delegate to the constitutional convention in Portland, and December 6 it was unanimously voted to approve the constitution there adopted.

April 3, 1820, for the first Governor of Maine Hon. William King had 141 votes with 5 scattering. Sept. 9, 1822, voted to build a town house. Seth Fish bid off the building for $246. Voted that he come under bonds in the sum of $300 to finish the house by September next in a workmanlike manner. Sept. 8, 1823, the first meeting was held in the town house. In 1824, Daniel Foss, John Keen and Stephen Rackley were licensed to sell spirituous liquors. April 4, 1825, voted that Mr. Elias Lane build the pound according to the plan, for $30. March 7, 1831, voted to raise $400 for support of the poor. Voted to notify town meetings, in the future, by posting notices at the town house, at Oliver P. Frost's shop and at Stephen Welcome's store. In 1832, April 2, voted to notify town meetings in the future by posting notifications at Metcalf's store, at the Baptist meeting-house and at William Turner's store. Sept. 10, voted to build a stone bridge over the stream near Robert Gould's. (Westerly from and near North Leeds railroad station.) March 31, 1834, voted that Israel Herrick and Allen Freeman have gates on so much of the road as exists between the southeast corner of Samuel and Israel Herrick's orchard and Allen Freeman's corner, so called, during the pleasure of the town. In 1836, voted to build a good, new float bridge at or near where the old float bridge now is across Dead River. March 7, 1837, voted to raise $650, for support of the poor. April 1, 1839, the constable was directed to post up copies of the warrants for town meetings at Walter Foss's tavern, at Stephen Welcome's store, at Stephen Day's store and on the outside door of the town-house. Dec. 1, voted that Harvey Bates, Uriah Foss and Isaac Boothby, borrow $250 to pay the expenses of camp equipage, etc., furnished the soldiers drafted by order of the Legislature in 1839, and that they be remunerated (reimbursed?) from the town treasury.

In 1841, April 5, the town was divided into twelve school districts and the limits defined. March 8, 1843, resolved that the selectmen be instructed to use lawful means to suppress the sale of intoxicating drinks without a license in all places of the town. May 1, the constable was directed to notify town meetings by posting (copies of) the warrant at the Center Meeting-House, at Union Chapel, at Welcome's store, and at the school-house near Thomas Owen's. Dec. 9, the town line between Leeds and Monmouth was perambulated. 1846, Oct. 26, the much discussed bridge to succeed the float bridge across Dead River was let to Josiah Day, 2d, to build. Price $300 and old bridge. 1847, March 27, voted to raise $2,000 for highways, $450 for town expenses, $300 for bridge, $90 for making road to Monmouth line. 1848, April 25, East Livermore line perambulated. Sept. 11, voted to build a bridge near George Turner's. 1849, March 6, voted to build a hearse house and purchase hearse, harness, etc., for the town and to raise $100 for the purpose. 1851, March 4, the clerk was authorized to collect all the books, maps, charts and papers properly belonging to the town, and voted that, when any one takes out any of the above named, he shall be charged with the same; also, voted to repair the town house and that the selectmen shall erect guide-posts; also to petition the Legislature to define the boundaries of the town. April 7, voted to prosecute all violations of the law in the sale of intoxicating liquors. Feb. 9, 1852, voted to aid the Androscoggin Railroad to the extent of $15,000, 145 in favor, 106 against. March 10, voted that town meetings be notified by posting notices on all the meeting-houses in town except the Friends. 1853, March 7, raised $500 to pay town debts. 1854, March 7, voted $825 for schools, $800 for the poor, $250 for debts, $200 for expenses, $3,000 for highways. A new burying-ground in District No. 3 this year. In September cast 143 votes for Lewiston as county seat and 48 for Auburn. Oct. 2, John Gilmore, Issacher Lane and Isaac Boothby were chosen a committee to buy a town farm, which they did soon as Jan. 15, 1855, and it was voted that the committee who purchased the town farm procure all needed supplies for the poor, and February 10 William Robbins and wife were engaged to labor on and oversee the town farm and poor for $200 for the year. In April, 1857, voted to discontinue the bridge across Dead River near where Samuel Boothby formerly lived, and to rebuild the Foss and Stinchfield bridges. December 4, voted not to rebuild the buildings of the town farm, but instructed the selectmen to sell the farm and buy another whenever in either case they deemed it for the interest of the town to do so. [These buildings were burned November 25, 1857, and Mary Pease and Mary A. Bridgham lost their lives.] In 1860, Israel Washburn, Jr., had 171 votes for Governor and Ephraim K. Smart 120. In 1865, voted $1050 for schools, $500 for poor, $150 for repairing roads and bridges, $200 for expenses, $2,000 for town debt and interest.

$2,500 for highways. January 7, 1867, S. L. Howard chosen selectman in place Aaron Winslow, resigned. March 10, 1858, voted to raise $150 for guide-posts. May 4, voted $300 to repair town house. 1873, March 17, voted to raise $400 for the support of free high schools the ensuing year. 1874, March 9, voted that any corporation or individual investing not less than $3,000 in any manufacturing carried on by steam or water-power located at Leeds Center, shall be exempt from taxation for ten years. 1887, voted to abolish the liquor agency. 1879, Sept. 8, voted unanimously for biennial elections and sessions of the Legislature. 1880, March 8, voted Isaiah B. Additon to go before the Legislative committee on State valuation at such time as he may deem proper, to effect, if possible, a reduction of the valuation of the town. 1882, March 13, voted that the selectmen procure a hearse and provide a place to keep it. 1886, March 8, voted to exempt the Lewiston Monumental Works from taxation for six years if they will locate at West Leeds. 1887, March 14, voted to erect guide-boards at all points needed and repair old ones as required by law. 1890, March 10, the Superintending School Committee were instructed to expend the undrawn balance of the free high school appropriation of 1887 in the maintenance of a free high school in District No. 10 for not exceeding ten weeks from February 24. The appropriations were: For support of schools, $1,000; for support of poor, $600; for roads and bridges, $500; for labor and material on highways, $2,000; for school text-books, $300; for repair of farm buildings, $200; for miscellaneous purposes, $500. Sept. 8, the vote for Governor was: William P. Thompson, 98; Edwin C. Burleigh, 97; Isaac R. Clark, 11; Aaron Clark, 3. In 1891, the annual report shows a valuation of $302,369, of which $214,385 is resident real estate and $63,208 personal. The number of polls 271 at $2 each. The treasurer's account shows total receipts $4,676.99 and total expenditures $4,521.84, leaving an undrawn balance Feb. 20, 1891, of $155.15. Under the vote of May 7, 1810, to wit: "Voted that the selectmen be authorized to give a bounty of 25 cents each to each person that shall present to them a crow killed in Leeds at any time to the middle of July next," the records show that $7.90 was paid for dead crows, in conformity with that vote. The amount paid called for 31 3-5 dead crows. Query—Who killed the crow that was roosting on the town line, or presented to them one only 3-5 dead?

CHAPTER XIII.

LIST OF LEEDS TOWN OFFICERS.

Moderators.

1801-2, Isaac Collier.
1803, Oliver Otis.
1804-5-6, Capt. Seth Howard.
1807-8, Capt. Daniel Lothrop.
1809, Capt. Seth Howard.
1810-11, Capt. Daniel Lothrop.
1812, Oliver Otis.
1813, George Turner.
1814-15, Capt. Daniel Lothrop.
1816-17-18, Capt. Seth Howard.
1819-20, Capt. Daniel Lothrop.
1821-2, Stillman Howard.
1823, Capt. Daniel Lothrop.
1824, Levi Foss.
1825, Roland B. Howard.
1826-7, Stillman Howard.
1828, John Carver.
1829, Stillman Howard.
1830, Capt. Seth Howard.
1831, Levi Foss.
1832-3-4-5-6—Stillman Howard.
1837-8-9, Ensign Otis.
1840-1, Leavitt Lothrop.
1842-3-4-5, Uriah Foss.
1846, Walter Foss.
1847, Uriah Foss.
1848, Stillman Howard.
1849, Caleb Carver.
1850, Oscar D. Turner.
1851, Ozias Millett.
1852-3, Barnabus Davee.
1854-5, Issachar Lane.
1856-7, Uriah Foss.
1858, Oscar D. Turner.
1859, Barnabus Davee.
1860-1, Uriah Foss.

1862-3-4-5-6-7-8, Barnabus Davee.
1869, Oscar D. Turner.
1870, Barnabus Davee.
1871, Oscar D. Turner and B. Davee.
1872-3-4, B. Davee.
1875-6-7, Seth Howard.
1878-9-80, Rodolphus Jennings.
1881-2, Uriah Foss.
1883-4, R. Jennings.
1885-6-7-8, George Parcher.
1889-90-1-2, George Parcher.
1893-4-5-6-7, E. E. Additon.
1898-9, E. E. Additon.
1900, W. P. Foss.
1901, E. E. Additon.

Clerks.

1801 to 1803, Abial Daily.
1804, Isaac Collier.
1805, Abial Daily.
1806 to 1821, Thomas Davis Francis.
1822 to 1837, Thomas W. Bridgham.
1838 to 1841, Thomas D. Francis.
1842 to 1848, Barnabas Davee.
1849-1850, Friend D. Lord.
1851 to 1853, Franklin B. Leonard.
1854 to 1857, John Turner.
1858 to 1862, Gessius F. Jennings.
1863 to 1865, Davis Francis.
1866 to 1868, Joseph G. Gott.
1869 to 1878, John Turner.
1879, Charles H. Foster.
1880, William R. Pettingill.
1881-1882, Charles H. Foster.
1883, Gustavus W. Lane.
1884 to 1901, R. S. Loring.

Selectmen.

1801, John Whiting, Daniel Lothrop, Oliver Otis, Isaac Collier, Obadiah Pettingill.
1802, John Whiting, Uriah Foss, Isaac Collier.
1803-1804, Oliver Otis, John Whiting, Robert Gould.
1805, John Whiting, David Woodman, Uriah Foss.
1806, Uriah Foss, Isaac Collier, George Lothrop.
1807, George Lothrop, Isaac Collier, Robert Gould.

1808, Isaac George Lothrop, Capt. Othniel Pratt.
1809, Thomas D. Francis, John Whiting, Moses Stevens.
1810, Thomas D. Francis, John Whiting, George Lothrop.
1811, Thomas D. Francis, George Lothrop, Abial Daily.
1812-1813, Thomas D. Francis, Uriah Foss, Isaiah Beales.
1814, Thomas D. Francis, Uriah Foss, Martin Leonard.
1815, Thomas D. Francis, George Turner, Oliver Otis.
1816, Thomas D. Francis, Uriah Foss, Oliver Otis.
1817-18-19, Thomas D. Francis, Uriah Foss, George Lothrop.
1820-1821, Thomas D. Francis, Lewis Turner, Daniel Parcher.
1822, William Gould, Harvey Bates, John Francis.
1823-1824, Capt. John Francis, William Gould, Harvey Bates.
1825, Capt. John Francis, Harvey Bates, Solomon Lothrop.
1826, Capt. John Francis, Solomon Lothrop, Stephen Wellcome.
1827, Oliver Otis, Harvey Bates, Stephen Wellcome.
1828, Capt. John Francis, Solomon Lothrop, Levi Foss.
1829, Harvey Bates, Israel Herrick, Stillman Howard.
1820-1831, Harvey Bates, Levi Foss, Solomon Lothrop.
1832, Harvey Bates, Israel Herrick, John Gould.
1833-34-1835, Capt. John Francis, Stephen Rackley, Joshua S. Turner.
1836, Joshua S. Turner, Benjamin Francis, Issacher Lane.
1837, Harvey Bates, Benjamin Francis, Issacher Lane.
1838-1839, Harvey Bates, Uriah Foss, Isaac Boothby.
1849, John Gilmore, Uriah Foss, Isaac Boothby.
1841, John Gilmore, Reuel Foss, George K. Stinchfield.
1842, Josiah Day, 2d, Harvey Bates, Charles Knapp.
1843-1844, Leavitt Lothrop, Josiah Day, 2d, Benjamin Francis.
1845, Leavitt Lothrop, Benjamin Francis, Uriah Foss.
1846, Josiah Day, 2d, Uriah Foss, Thomas Owen.
1847, Uriah Foss, Thomas Owen, Isaac Boothby.
1848, Uriah Foss, Isaac Boothby, John Lane.
1849, Isaac Boothby, Peleg B. Caswell, Stillman L. Howard.
1850, Peleg B. Caswell, Stillman L. Howard, George K. Stinchfield.
1851, Stillman L. Howard, George K. Stinchfield, Davis F. Lothrop.
1852, Josiah Day, Cyrus Bates, Francis D. Millett.
1853-1854, Harvey Bates, S. L. Howard, Isaac True Boothby.
1855, S. L. Howard, Salmon Brewster, Uriah Foss.
1856-1857, Uriah Foss, Peleg B. Caswell, Isaiah B. Additon.
1858, P. B. Caswell, Isaac Boothby, Oscar D Turner.
1859-1860, I. B. Additon, O. D. Turner, Augustus Ramsdell.
1861, P. B. Caswell, Lloyd Gould, Samuel More.
1862, Benjamin Francis, Greenwood C. Gordon, Benj. Hodsdon.
1863, Benjamin Hodsdon, G. C. Gordon, Arza G. Lothrop.
1864, Seth Howard, Benjamin Turner, Henry F. Woodman.

1865, Stillman L. Howard, Uriah Foss, Davis Francis.
1866, S. L. Howard, Davis Francis, Benjamin Hodsdon.
1867, A. G. Lothrop, Freeman Andrews, Aaron Winslow.
1868, A. G. Lothrop, Benjamin Francis, Benjamin Hodsdon.
1869, A. G. Lothrop, Benjamin Francis, G. C. Gordon.
1870, I. B. Additon, G. F. Jennings, Thomas S. Carver.
1871 to 1878, I. B. Additon, T. S. Carver, A. J. Foss.
1879-1880, I. B. Additon, William B. Sumner, John F. Jennings.
1881-1882, I. B. Additon, W. B. Sumner, W. Henry Francis.
1883, I. B. Additon, J. F. Jennings, Joseph Moody.
1884-1885, Charles A. Lovejoy, J. F. Jennings, Joseph Moody.
1886-1887, C. A. Lovejoy, Henry F. Pettingill, Joseph Moody.
1888, C. A. Lovejoy, Cyrus B. Lane, George T. Bishop.
1889-1890, C. B. Lane, G. T. Bishop, G. A. Jennings.
1891, C. B. Lane, G. T. Bishop, George Parcher.
1892, C. B. Lane, G. T. Bishop, G. A. Jennings.
1893 to 1895, G. T. Bishop, E. V. Daly, G. T. Howe.
1896-1897, E. V. Daly W. P. Foss, S. Homer Deane.
1898-1899, George Parcher, Fred L. Additon, S. Homer Deane.
1900-1901, Fred L. Additon, S. Homer Deane, A. T. Barker.

Treasurers.

1801-2-3, Abiel Daily.
1804, Isaac Collier.
1805, Abiel Daily.
1806 to 1821, Thomas D. Francis.
1822 to 1829, Thomas W. Bridgham.
1830 to 1832, Stephen Rackley.
1833, Issacher Lane.
1834-5, Stillman Howard.
1836 to 1839, Stephen Rackley.
1840 to 1842, Issacher Lane.
1843 to 1849, Giddings Lane.
1850, Josiah Day.
1851 to 1855, John Gilmore.
1856 to 1862, Issacher Lane.
1863 to 1876, Benjamin Francis.
1877-1878, Davis Francis.
1879-1880, Seth Howard.
1881 to 1883, G. W. Lane.
1884-1885, Seth Howard.
1886-1887, Benjamin Turner.
1888, G. A. Jennings.
1889 to 1891, T. S. Carver.
1892, Seth Howard.
1893, C. B. Lane.

1894, Fred Perry.
1895, G. A. Jennings.
1896 to 1900, T. H. Boothby.
1901, D. P. True.

School Committee.

"The value of education was impressed upon the children of the first settlers by their first teacher, that wise man, Thomas D. Francis. The later families brought from their Massachusetts homes that reverence for learning so characteristic of the sons of the old Bay State."

April 6, 1801, the people of Littleborough gathered for the purpose of organizing a township, and when they went forth from that meeting they were citizens of Leeds. An important feature in the acts of those organizers was the granting of $200 for the support of schools. A committee was elected, whose duty it was to supervise the expenditure of that money and provide places in their respective sections of the town where the children could assemble for instruction. To them was the right given and the duty imposed of procuring the teachers. Not until 1824 are we able to learn from the records of the town, that a committee, vested with other powers and duties, were annually elected. It would appear, in the absence of proof, that instead of a committee of general supervision, the management of schools was vested in local agents elected from the various sections of the town where schools were wont to be taught. The members of the committee elected at the first meeting were: Joseph Day, Levi Bates, William Gilbert, John Jennings, Oliver Randell and Obadiah Pettingill. Nov. 7, 1803, Thomas D. Francis, Abiel Daily and George Turner, Jr., were chosen to inspect schools and teachers. Whether their official service continued until 1824, is a conundrum.

School Committee.

1824, Thomas W. Bridgham, John Francis, William Carver.
1825, Thomas W. Bridgham, John Francis, Ezekiel Bates.
1826, Thomas W. Bridgham, John Francis, Walter Foss.
1827, Thomas W. Bridgham, Walter Foss, Joshua Millett.
1828, Thomas W. Bridgham, Thomas D. Francis, Martin Leonard.
1829, Thomas W. Bridgham, Simeon Foss, John Francis.
1830-1, Thomas W. Bridgham, John Francis, Simeon Foss.
1832-3, Thomas W. Bridgham, Alanson B. Caswell, Barnabus Davee.
1834, Thomas W. Bridgham, Barnabus Davee, Sands Baily.

1835, Thomas W. Bridgham, John Francis, Walter Foss.
1836, Thomas W. Bridgham, Walter Foss, P. B. Caswell.
1837, Seth Millett, W. H. Foster, Franklin B. Leonard.
1838-9-40, Barnabus Davee, W. H. Foster, Seth Millett.
1841, Barnabus Davee, Stephen R. Deane, Samuel P. True.
1842, Stephen R. Deane, Samuel P. True, Benjamin Francis.
1843, S. R. Deane, S. P. True, Thaddeus F. More.
1844, Barnabus Davee, Isaiah B. Additon, Stillman L. Howard.
1845, S. P. True, Ozias Millett, Luther Thomas.
1846, O. Millett, Luther Thomas, Josiah Turner.
1847-8, Walter Foss, S. P. True, S. L. Howard.
1849, Ozias Millett, John Turner, P. B. Caswell.
1850, Ozias Millett, John Turner, I. B. Additon.
1851, Alden Barrows, Seth Howard, Ozias Millett.
1852-3, A. Barrows, Ozias Millett, Arza G. Lothrop.
1854, A. Barrows, Ozias Millett, Thomas W. Bridgham.
1855, Ozias Millett, T. W. Bridgham, I. B. Additon.
1856, T. W. Bridgham, I. B. Additon, Ozias Millett.
1857, I. B. Additon, Seth Howard, G. F. Jennings.
1858, Seth Howard, G. F. Jennings, Henry F. Woodman.
1859, G. F. Jennings, H. F. Woodman, Seth Howard.

Supervisors of Schools.

1860-1, George Parcher.
1862, Wallace R. Leadbetter.

School Committee.

1863, Wallace R. Leadbetter, Joseph G. Gott, Peter A. Bodge.
1864, J. G. Gott, Seth Howard, Rodolphus Jennings.
1865, Seth Howard, H. F. Woodman, J. G. Gott.
1866, J. G. Gott, Seth Howard, George Parcher.
1867-8, George Parcher, J. G. Gott, W. R. Leadbetter.
1869, no record.
1870, S. R. Deane (3 years term).
1871, J. G. Gott (3 years term).
1872, Rodolphus Jennings (3 years term).
1873, S. R. Deane (3 years term).
1874, William R. Pettingill (3 years term).
1875, R. Jennings (3 years term).
1876, S. R. Deane (3 years term).
1877, William R. Pettingill (3 years term).
1878, R. Jennings.

Supervisors.

1879-80, R. Jennings.
1881-2, G. W. Lane.

School Committee.

1883, G. W. Lane, G. W. Bates, J. C. Wing.
1884, George Parcher (3 years term).
1885, G. W. Bates (3 years term).
1886, J. C. Wing (3 years term).
1887, Wm. R. Pettingill, E. T. Clifford, E. E. Additon.

Supervisors.

1888-9, E. E. Additon.
1890-1, Laura Sylvester.
1892-3, F. H. Herrick.

School Committee.

1894, E. E. Additon, H. L. Grant. W. H. Bishop; E. E. Additon, Superintendent.
1895, P. L. Turner.
1896, E. E. Additon.
1897, W. H. Bishop.
1898, P. H. Deane, P. L. Turner, A. L. Thomas; W. E. Gould, Superintendent.
1899, P. H. Deane; H. H. Herrick, Superintendent.
1900, E. A. Russell; F. H. Herrick, Superintendent.
1901, A. L. Thomas; F. H. Herrick, Superintendent.

Constables and Collectors.

1801, James Lindsey.
1802, Othniel Pratt.
1803-4, Stephen Welcome.
1805, James Stanley.
1806, Phineas Foss.
1807, Levi Foss.
1808, James Stanley.
1809-10-11, Stephen Welcome.
1812, Joseph Bishop.
1813-14, Phineas Foss.
1815, George Lothrop.
1816, Stephen Welcome.
1817, Levi Foss.
1818, Levi Caswell.
1819-20-1-2, Levi Foss.
1823, Cyrus Foss.
1824, Caleb Carver.
1825-6-7-8-9, Cyrus Foss.
1830-1-2, Leavitt Lothrop.
1833, Nelson Gilbert.

1834, Uriah Foss.
1835, Peleg B. Caswell.
1836, Leavitt Lothrop.
1837, Stephen Day.
1838, P. B. Caswell.
1839, Joshua S. Turner.
1840, Phillips Turner.
1841, Giddings Lane.
1842, Phillips Turner.
1843-4-5, Issachar Lane.
1846-7-8-9-50-1, John D. Millett.
1852-3, John Y. Merrill.
1854-5-6, P. B. Caswell.
1857-8, Oscar D. Turner.
1859, Jason Woodman.
1860, Solomon L. Lothrop.
1861-2-3, Jason Woodman.
1864-5, O. D. Turner.
1866, Benjamin Francis.
1867, Ward B. Howard.
1868, Russell B. Hersey.
1869, Lewis P. Boothby.
1870, Melvin Berry.
1871, Jason Woodman.
1872-3-4, Chandler F. Cobb.
1875 to 1882, Lewis P. Boothby.
1883-4, Thomas H. Boothby.
1885-6-7, Lewis P. Boothby.
1888-9, Warren Carver.
1890 to 1897, Herbert L. Grant.
1898 to 1901, E. E. Additon.

Representatives to the Massachusetts Legislature.

Leeds was unrepresented until 1806. Its first representative was in attendance that year at the General Court.

1 Thomas Davis Francis, 1806;
2 Seth Howard, 1807;
3 Daniel Lothrop, Jr., 1808;
4 Daniel Lothrop, Jr., 1809;
5 Daniel Lothrop, Jr., 1810;
6 Daniel Lothrop, 1811;
7 Daniel Lothrop, 1812;
8 Daniel Lothrop, 1813;
9 Daniel Lothrop, 1814;
10 Martin Leonard, 1815;
11 Daniel Lothrop, 1816;

12   Daniel Lothrop, 1817;
13   Stillman Howard, 1820;
     Member of the Constitutional Convention Oct. 29:
14   Thomas D. Francis, 1819;
     Members of the Maine Legislature:
15   Thomas D. Francis, 1820;
16   Thomas D. Francis, 1821;
17   Thomas W. Bridgham, 1822;
18   Thomas W. Bridgham, 1823;
19   Thomas D. Francis, 1824;
20   Thomas D. Francis, 1825;
21   Thomas W. Bridgham, 1826;
22   Thomas W. Bridgham, 1827;
23   Stillman Howard, 1828;
24   Daniel Lothrop, 1829;
25   Stillman Howard, 1830;
26   John Francis, 1831;
27   John Francis, 1832;
28   Leavitt Lothrop, 1833;
29   Leavitt Lothrop, 1834;
30   Israel Herrick, 1835;
31   Israel Herrick, 1836;
32   Issacher Lane, 1837;
33   Solomon Lothrop, 1838;
34   Solomon Lothrop, 1839;
35   Joshua S. Turner, 1840;
36   John D. Millett, 1841;
37   Joshua S. Turner, 1842;
     Classification:
38   Barnabus Davee, 1845;
39   Thomas W. Bridgham, 1847;
40   Joseph Day, 2d, 1849;
41   Peleg B. Caswell, 1851;
42   Peleg B. Caswell, 1852;
     Androscoggin County:
43   Giddings Lane, 1854;
44   Thomas Owen, 1856;
45   Uriah Foss, 1858;
46   John Gilmore, 1860;
47   Davis Francis Lothrop, 1863;
47   Greenwood C. Gordon, 1866;
48   Wallace R. Leadbetter, 1868;
49   Joseph G. Gott, 1870;
50   Oscar D. Turner, 1872;
51   George Parcher, 1875;
52   Wallace R. Leadbetter, 1877;
53   Charles H. Lane, 1879;

Biennial sessions of Legislature:
54 Seth Howard, 1885;
55 Willard Lothrop, 1893;
56 Thomas H. Boothby, 1901.

Governor's Council.

Stillman Howard.
R. C. Boothby, b. and reared in Leeds.

Senators.
1 Thomas D. Francis,
2 Leavitt Lothrop,
3 George Parcher.

CHAPTER XIV.

MILITARY RECORD OF LEEDS.

This chapter, prepared to commemorate the people of Leeds who participated in the wars that gave to the country its independence, and since preserved its federal unity and national honor, is the result of a careful research of the Adjutant General's Reports, and contains as accurate an account of each soldier as can be drawn from those records made under the excitement and confusion of wars of such magnitude as those which have marked the milestones in our country's history. The solemnity of war and its attendant sufferings excludes a historian from including mirthful anecdote and embellishment.

War of the Revolution.

Many of the early settlers of Littleborough had been actively engaged in throwing off the "British Yoke."

Appended is a list of their names:

Major Daniel Lothrop,
Lieut. William Gilbert,
Thomas Stinchfield,
   (unattached service),
Thomas D. Francis,
Daniel Lane,
Joseph Knapp,
Increase Leadbetter,
William Lindsey,
Marshfield T. Paul,
Daniel Robbins,
Jirah Fish,
David Paul,
Stephen Foster,
Zadock Bishop,
Daniel Jones,
James Lindsey,
William Turner,
Nathaniel House,
———— Highland,
Cuff Chambers,
Simon Pero,
   Last three were negroes.

Lieut. Daniel Lothrop, 2d,
Lieut. Elisha Shaw,

Thomas Millett,
George Parcher,
Benjamin Woodman,
Francis George,
Andrew Cushman,
James Lamb,
Ebenezer Mason,
Abram Wickett,
Daniel Haines,
Oliver Randall,
Samuel Arnold,
Israel Royal,
Isaac Collins,
Aaron Brewster,
———— Phillips,

Prince D'Onset.

War of 1812.

Benjamin Woodman,
Charles Pratt,
Samuel Swift,
Allen Freeman,
Bennett Lamb,
William Mitchell,
A. Southard,
Walter Pratt,

Daniel Paul,
Joseph Freeman,
Levi Bates,
Eli Herrick,
Benjamin Higgins,
David Paul,
Nathaniel House, Jr.

Civil War.

Leeds has a war record unsurpassed by any town in the State, of its size. Some towns furnished more men, but no more in proportion to inhabitants and none better. Leeds' contribution was 161 men, headed by her "Christian Soldier," General Oliver Otis Howard, whose record alone is glory enough for one town; but, when we name the hero of every battle from Vera Cruz to the surrender of the City of Mexico, the same who led a regiment through the Civil War—Col. Warren L. Lothrop; and further present the names of Brevet Brigadier-General Charles Howard and the valiant young Lieutenant-Colonel of the First Maine Cavalry—Stephen Boothby, with the score of minor officers, and in all 161 men good and true, whose bravery, loyalty and fighting qualities they inherited from their Revolutionary ancestors, it is no illegitmate claim to make when it is asserted that, Leeds is the "Banner town in the State."

The citizens of the town, too aged or too young, or incapacitated, or ———, with liberality but less glory, perhaps, were loyal to the cause; paid their money cheerfully and generously for the defense of the "Stars and Stripes," and made ample provision for the families of their "Soldier Boys in Blue." At a special town meeting held on the 6th day of July, 1861, the selectmen, who were P. B. Caswell, Lloyd Gould and Samuel More, were authorized to draw orders on the treasurer for such sums of money as might be necessary for the support and comfort of the families of those who had gone into, or should subsequently go into the United States service in defense of "Old Glory." At the annual meeting in March, 1862, the selectmen, Benjamin Harris, Greenwood C. Gordon and Benjamin Hodsdon were made a committee to look after and properly furnish the families of the soldiers. At a special meeting held July 22, 1862, voted to pay each volunteer, when mustered into the United States service, $75. Aug. 26, voted to pay each volunteer under the last call of the President, $100, and each drafted man $50. Nov. 30, 1863, voted to pay each recruit, when mustered into the United States service $350. Voted to instruct the selectmen to designate some influential man to procure recruits to fill the town's quota.

Aug. 13, 1864, voted that the town furnish $300 for each man that enlists to fill the quota under the last call of the President. Dec. 26, voted to pay $400 as a bounty to each volunteer or drafted man to fill the quota. Voted that the town treasurer be authorized to procure the loan of the sum of $400 per man, and to make such papers as shall most effectually bind the town to the payment of the same.

At the annual meeting in March, 1865, voted to issue town bonds to the amount of the war debt.

Maine Regiments.

First Maine Infantry Regiment. Organized April 28, and mustered into United States service at Portland, Me., May 3, 1861. The field officers were: Col. Nathaniel J. Jackson, of Lewiston; Lieut.-Col. Albion Witham, of Portland; Major George G. Bailey, of Portland.
Term of enlistment three months.

Roster.
Leeds unrepresented.

Second Infantry Regiment. Rendezvoused at Bangor and left the State May 14, 1861. It was organized on Long Island, N. Y., May 28, 1861. Field officers: Col. Charles D. Jameson; Lieut.-Col. Charles W. Roberts; Maj. George Varney; all of Bangor.
Term of enlistment, two and three years.

Roster.
Albion Morris. Band.

Third Infantry Regiment. Went into camp at Augusta May 28, and was organized June 4, 1861. Field officers: Col. O. O. Howard, of Leeds; Lieut.-Col. Charles A. L. Sampson; Maj. Henry G. Staples.
Term of enlistment, three years.

Roster.
Oliver Otis Howard, Col., promoted Sept. 7, 1861, to Brigadier-General, later to Major-General.
Charles H. Howard, Drum Major, promoted to the staff of his brother, Gen. O. O. Howard, promoted to Brevet Brigadier-General.
Russell Carver, Co. A, wounded at Fair Oaks.
Page T. Francis, Co. A.

Jason Carver, Co. K, discharged Sept. 19, 1861.
Lloyd B. Caswell, Co. K, transferred to 17th Maine.
Francis George, Co. K.
John C. Keene, Capt. Co. K, killed at Gettysburg, July 2, 1863.
Levi R. Bates, Co. K, died in prison.
Henry S. Turner, Co. K, absent; wounded, July 2.
Benjamin Woodman, Co. K, died in service.
Elisha K. Mann, Corp. Co. K, promoted to Corp.; prisoner May 2, exchanged; transferred to 17th Maine.
Henry O. Fabyan, Co. K, died Oct. 30, 1862.
Walter W. Boothby, Co. K, killed Dec. 13, 1862.
Dexter W. Howard, Co. K, promoted to Sergeant, promoted to Captain, transferred to 17th Maine.
Joseph O. Sturtevant, Co. I, transferred to 17th Maine.

Fourth Infantry Regiment. Organized at Rockland, May 8, 1861. Mustered in United States service June 15, 1861. Field officers: Col. Hiram G. Berry, of Rockland; Lieut.-Col. Thomas H. Marshall, of Belfast; Maj. Frank S. Nickerson, of Searsport. Term of enlistment, three years.

Roster.

Leeds, unrepresented.

Fifth Infantry Regiment. Mustered into United States service June 24, 1861, at Portland. Field officers, Col. Mark H. Dunnell of Portland; Lieut.-Col. Edwin Hisley, of Limington; Maj. Samuel C. Hamilton, of Biddeford. Term of enlistment, three years.

Roster.

Jeremiah Day, E.
Charles H. Bodge, Corporal, E.

Sixth Infantry Regiment. Organized at Portland and mustered into United States service July 15, 1861. Field officers, Col. Abner Knowles, Lieut. Col. Hiram Burnham, Maj. Frank Pierce. Not represented.

Seventh Infantry Regiment. Organized August 21, 1861, with Edwin C. Mason, of Portland, Colonel; Selden Connor, of Fairfield, Lieut.-Col.; Thomas W. Hyde, of Bath, Major. These were three-years regiments. The Seventh returned to Augusta and those whose term of service had expired were mustered out Sept. 5, 1864, and the others consolidated with the Fifth and Sixth and constituted the First Veteran Infantry.

HISTORY OF LEEDS

Roster.

John B. Jennings, Co. K, killed May 4, 1863.
Marcellus F. Cushman, Co. K.
James W. Libby, Co. K, Sergeant.
Franklin Peare, Co. K.
Albert M. Rose, Co. K.
John Q. Robbins, Co. K, died Oct. 1862.
Wansbrow Turner, Co. K, died Nov. 24, 1861.

Eighth Infantry Regiment. Organized at Augusta, Sept. 7, 1861. Field officers were: Col. Lee Strickland, of Livermore; Lieut.-Col. John D. Rust, of Camden; Maj. Joseph S. Rice of Ellsworth.

Roster.
Leeds, unrepresented.

Ninth Infantry Regiment. Encamped at Augusta; mustered into United States service Sept. 22, 1861, and two days later started for the front. Col. Rishworth Rich, of Portland; Lieut.-Col. Colman Harding, of Gorham, and Sabine Emery, of Eastport, were the field officers. Term of enlistment, three years.

Roster.

John C. Gifford, Co. H.
Henry Hackins, Co. H.

Tenth Infantry Regiment. Encamped at Cape Elizabeth, and mustered into United States service Oct. 4, 1861. The field officers were: Col. George L. Beal, of Norway; Lieut.-Col. James S. Fillebrown, of Auburn; Maj. Charles Walker, of Portland.

Roster.
Leeds unrepresented.

Eleventh Infantry Regiment. Organized at Augusta Oct. 11, and mustered into the United States service Nov. 12. Field officers were: Col. John C. Caldwell, of East Machias; Lieut.-Col. Harris M. Plaisted, of Bangor; Maj. William M. Shaw, of Portland.

Roster.

Augustus S. George, F.
Otis B. George, F.
Enoch T. Fish, F.

Twelfth Infantry Regiment, mustered into United States service for three years, at Portland, Nov. 10, 1861. Its field officers were: Col. George F. Shepley, of Portland; Lieut.-Col. William K. Kimball, of Paris; Maj. David R. Hastings, of Lovell.

Roster.
Frank White, Co. K.

Thirteenth Infantry Regiment. Mustered into United States service at Augusta, Dec. 18, 1861. Field officers, Col. Neal Dow, of Portland; Lieut.-Col. Henry Rust, Jr., of Norway; Maj. Frank S. Hesselton, of Waterville.

Roster.
Leeds unrepresented.

Fourteenth Infantry Regiment. Organized in Augusta in Dec. 1861, to serve three years. Field officers were: Col. Frank S. Nickerson, of Searsport; Lieut.-Col. Elias Milliken, of Burnham; Maj. Thomas W. Porter, of Bangor.

Roster.
Daniel Brown, Co. H.

Roster Battalion and New Fourteenth Regiment.
James D. Towle, Co. F.
Jordan G. Carvill, 1st Lieutenant, Co. H.
Azel A. Burnham, Co. H.
James W. Libby, Captain, Co. K.
James Carver, Co. K.
Stephen W. Grant, Co. K.
George E. Gilbert, Co. K.
Lloyd A. Gilbert, Co. K.
David Morse, Co. K.
Herbert Hunton, Sergeant, Co. K.
John P. R. Sleeper, Co. K.

Fifteenth Infantry Regiment. Organized at Augusta in Dec., 1861, and mustered into United States service Jan. 23, 1862, for three years. Field officers were: Col. John McCluskey, of Houlton; Lieut.-Col. Isaac Dyer, of Skowhegan; Maj. Benjamin Hawes, of Ashland.

Roster.
Alonzo Impy, Co. D.

Sixteenth Infantry Regiment. Mustered into United States service at Augusta Aug. 14, 1862. The field officers were: Col. Asa W. Wildes; Lieut.-Col. Charles W. Tilden; Maj. Augustus B. Farnham. Term of enlistment, three years.

Roster.

Joseph G. Lamb, Corporal, Co. E, promoted to Sergeant.
Charles R. Berry, Co. E, died of wounds, Dec. 25, 1862.
John A. Burnham, Co. E.
Ebenezer Curtis, 2d, Co. E.
Francis George, Co. E.
George E. Hussey, Co. E.
Rollin F. Jennings, Co. E, transferred to Fifth Maine Battery.
George H. Peare, Co. E.
Samuel W. Pettingill, Co. E, transferred to V. R. C.
Granville Richmond, Co. E.
William W. Wheeler, Co. E.
Frank White, recruit.

Seventeenth Infantry Regiment. Mustered into United States service in Portland Aug. 18, 1862. Field officers were: Col. Thomas A. Roberts, of Portland; Lieut.-Col. Charles B. Merrill, of Portland; Maj. George W. West, of Fort Kent. Term of enlistment, three years.

Roster.

William Doyle, Co. K.
Dexter W. Howard, Co. C, promoted to Second Lieutenant, Co. E.
Dexter W. Howard, Co. E, joined as Lieutenant from Co. C.
Lloyd B. Caswell, Co. K, transferred from Third Maine, transferred to First Heavy Artillery.

Nineteenth Infantry Regiment. Organized at Bath, Aug. 25, 1862. Enlistment, three years. Field officers were: Col. Frederick D. Sewall, who had been on the staff of General Howard; Lieut.-Col. Francis E. Heath, who had been a captain in the Third Maine; Maj. Henry W. Cunningham, a former captain in the Fourth Maine.

Roster.

Thomas L. Bubier, Co. F, transferred to V. R. C.
Addison D. Gilbert, Co. F.
Calvin B. Keene, Co. F.

Twentieth Infantry Regiment. Organized at Portland, Aug. 29, 1862, to serve three years. Field officers were: Col. Adelbert Ames; Lieut.-Col. Joshua L. Chamberlain, Professor of Bowdoin College; Maj. Charles D. Gilmore, of Bangor.

Roster.

Winslow Turner, Co. C.

Twenty-First Infantry Regiment. Organized at Augusta in September and mustered into United States service, Oct. 14, 1862. This was a nine-months regiment. Field officers were: Col. Elijah D. Johnson, of Lewiston; Lieut.-Col. Nathan Stanley, of Vassalboro; Maj. Benjamin G. Merry, of Bath. Leeds unrepresented.

Twenty-Second Infantry Regiment. Another nine-months regiment was mustered into the United States service at Bangor, Oct. 18, 1862. Field officers were: Col. Simeon G. Jerrard, of Levant; Lieut.-Col. Alonzo G. Putnam, of Dover; Maj. ———. Leeds unrepresented.

Twenty-Third Infantry Regiment. This regiment was composed almost entirely of Androscoggin and Oxford men, and was mustered into the United States service at Portland, Sept. 29, 1862. Term of enlistment, nine months. Field officers were: Col. William Wirt Virgin, of Norway; Lieut.-Col. Enos T. Luce, of Auburn; Maj. Alfred B. Soule, of Lewiston.

Roster.

Charles H. Leadbetter, Sergeant, Co. I.
Oscar D. Turner, Sergeant, Co. I.
Albert Barker, Sergeant, Co. I.
Loring P. Gould, Corporal, Co. I.
Sewall Woodman, Corporal, Co. I.
Jason Carver, Wagoner, Co. I.
George T. Bishop, Corporal, Co. I.
Seth F. Burnham, Co. I, died March 8, 1863.
Milton W. Burnham, Co. I.
Joseph H. Burnham, Co. I.
Russell L. Gould, Co. I.
Daniel W. Hinkley, Co. I.
Charles T. Knights, Co. I.
Lorenzo Leadbetter, Co. I.
Frank J. Lindsey, Co. I.
Thomas J. Lindsey, Corporal, Co. I.
Rufus K. Peare, Co. I.

HISTORY OF LEEDS 293

Ireson B. Pettengill, Co. I, died March 21, 1863.
Elisha P. Ramsdell, Co. I, died Jan. 10, 1863.
John R. Smith, Co. I.
Joshua H. Sumner, Co. I.
James D. Towle, Co. I.
John E. Woodman, Co. I.

Twenty-Fourth and Twenty-Fifth Infantry Regiments. Nine-months regiments. The Twenty-Fourth was organized at Augusta, Oct. 16, 1862, and the Twenty-Fifth at Portland, Sept. 29, 1862. The Twenty-Sixth, Twenty-Seventh, Twenty-Eighth were also nine-months regiments. Leeds was not represented in any of them.

Twenty-Ninth Infantry Regiment. This was a veteran regiment, and most of its material went from Androscoggin County. In fact, the First, Tenth and Twenty-Ninth could with much justice have been styled one regiment. Many of the men saw service in all three regiments. Eight companies were organized in Augusta to serve three years. Companies A and B, then in service in Tennessee as part of the Tenth Maine Battalion, were transferred to complete the regimental organization, joining it at New Orleans, where the regiment arrived Feb. 16, 1864. Field officers were: Col. George L. Beale; Lieut.-Col. Chas. S. Emerson; Maj. William Knowlton.

Roster.

Henry T. Frost, Corporal, Co. A, John T. Salvador.
James H. Gardner, Co. A.
Henry Shea, Co. A.
Isaac T. Boothby, Co. C.

Thirtieth Infantry Regiment. Organized at Augusta in January, 1864. Term of enlistment, three years. Field officers were: Francis Fessenden, of Portland, Colonel; Thomas H. Hubbard, of Hallowell, Lieutenant-Colonel; Royal E. Whitman, of Turner, Major.

Roster.

Joseph M. Curtis, Co. A, killed April 9, 1864.
Willard J. Fish, Co. E.
Albert F. Gilmore, Co. G.
William O. Parlin, Co. G.
Page T. Francis, Co. I, transferred to V. R. C.

Thirty-First Infantry Regiment. This was a three-years regiment, organized in April, 1864. Col. Thomas Hight, of Augusta; Lieut.-Col. Stephen C. Talbot, of Machias; Maj. Daniel White.

Roster.

Caleb W. Battles, Co. B, from 32d.

Thirty-Second Infantry Regiment. Organized at Augusta, May 6, 1864. Mark F. Wentworth, of Kittery, was Colonel; John M. Brown, of Portland, Lieutenant-Colonel; Arthur Deering, of Richmond, Major.

Roster.

Caleb W. Battles, Co. B, transferred to 31st, Co. B.

First Veteran Volunteer Regiment. This was formed in Charlestown, Va., Aug. 21, 1864. Was made up of the Fifth, Sixth and Seventh Battalions.

Roster.

James W. Libby, Sergeant, Co. K.
Albert M. Rose, Corporal, Co. K.

First Infantry Battalion. This was organized at Augusta May 25, 1865, from four unassigned companies recruited for one year's service and originally designed for the Fourteenth regiment. It was commanded by Lieut.-Col. Calvin S. Brown.

Roster.

Erastus E. Gilbert, Co. B, died in service.

First Heavy Artillery (Eighteenth Infantry Regiment). Organized at Bangor and Augusta, Aug. 21, 1862, for three years.

Roster.

Elisha K. Mann, Sergeant, Co. C.
Warren Sturtevant, Co. G.
William Doyle, Co. K.

First Battalion Light Artillery. This name was given to an organization of seven batteries, mustered into the United States service at different times and places. First Battery at Portland, Dec. 18, 1861.

Roster.

William Morton, First Battery.

First Cavalry Regiment. This regiment of twelve companies was organized at Augusta, Nov. 5, 1861, for three years, and was made up from all parts of the state. The original field officers were: Col. John Goddard; Lieut.-Col. Thomas Hight; Majors Samuel H. Allen, David P. Stowell, Calvin S. Douty. Later, Stephen Boothby was Lieutenant Colonel.

Roster.

Roscoe G. Beals, Co. E.
Volney H. Foss, Co. G. promoted to First Sergeant, April, 1865.
Lucius C. Robbins, Co. G.
Leonard L. Rose, Corporal, Co. G.
Levi W. Wheeler, Co. G.
Seth G. Rose, Co. G.
J. S. Dow, Co. D.

First D. C. Cavalry Regiment. Eight hundred men, comprising eight companies, enlisted and organized at Augusta in March, 1864, to serve three years. This body was designed for special duty in the District of Columbia only, and was under the command of Col. L. C. Baker.

Roster.

Salmon C. Brewster, Co. K.

Second Cavalry Regiment. This was organized at Augusta, from Nov. 30, 1863, to Jan. 2, 1864. The field officers were: Col. Ephraim W. Woodman, of Wilton; Lieut.-Col. John F. Godfrey, of Bangor; Maj. Charles A. Miller, of Rockland.

Roster.

Lendall S. Caswell, Co. B.
E. Riley Bishop, Corporal, Co. I.
Charles T. Knight, Co. I, died Sept. 29, 1864.
David E. Trask, Co. M, died July 12, 1864.
Roscoe G. Lindsey, Co. I, died Sept. 8, 1864.

First Regiment Sharpshooters. This body of six companies was organized at Augusta to serve one and three years. Companies A and B left the state Nov. 12, 1864. Consolidated with the Twentieth Infantry Regiment.

Roster.

James W. Libby, Lieutenant, Co. E, promoted to Captain.
Albert M. Rose, Co. E, died Jan. 17, 1865.

Roster of unassigned companies of Infantry.

Orpheus M. Leonard, Twenty-Fifth.

Enlistments in the United States Navy.

Everett Lindsey,
Charles F. Lindsey,
Frank J. Lindsey,
Daniel McDaniels,
Doane S. Wing,
John Baptiste,
Timothy Connelly,
James A. Cronins,
Levi C. Sumner,
Clark R. Caswell,
James Cullen,
Charles E. Johnson.

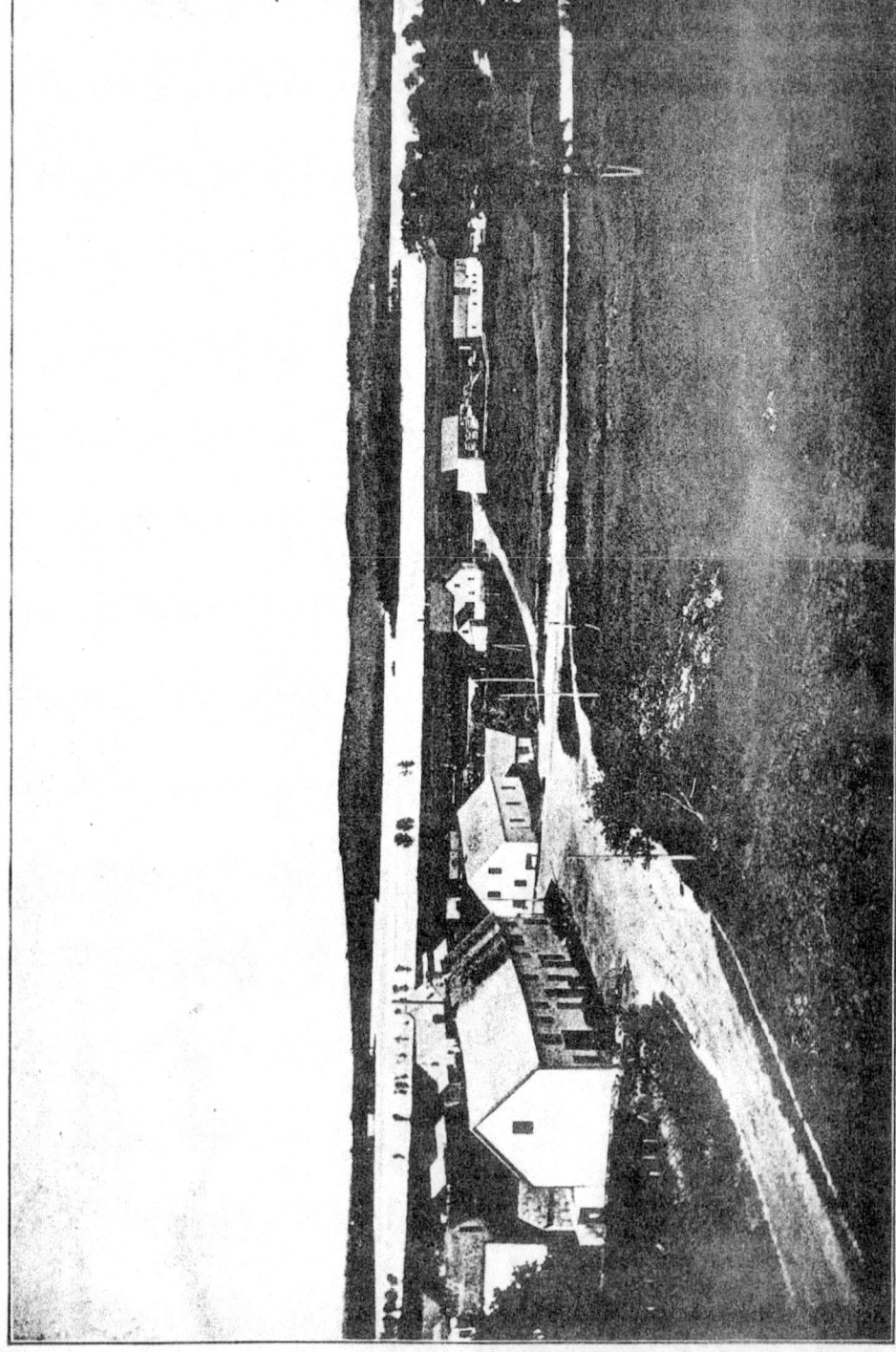

CHAPTER XV.

MAIL ROUTES—POST-OFFICES—POSTMASTERS.

In entering on a subject of such magnitude as the mail service of the United States, a volume much larger than this would contain but a small portion of it; and even the history of a single town, fully and minutely written, would occupy too much space for a work of this kind; and with a few important items noted, we pass to other subject matter. Shall we pause for a moment and ponder? Do we realize that those there are now living— the very few—whose memory goes back to the date of the establishment of the mail service by the United States? Previous to 1794, communication was an individual matter and transacted by the dispatch of private or special messengers. The primitive mail laws and regulations—good enough for their time, when the people were honest—were loosely constructed. Long routes,—extending through many towns,— usually requiring a week of travel to complete the trip, were established. The mails were carried by "post-riders" on horseback, in pouches or bags fastened in front and behind the saddle; the one for through mail matter, and the other for local use, receiving extra pay for the latter service. The mail matter sent or received by people whose residence was not situated on the line of route, was promiscuously taken or dumped in some store, shop or other place, and each person sorted from the pile what was directed to him or his house people. Farmington was incorporated in 1794, and a short time subsequent to that date a highway from that town was laid out on a direct line over the hills of Chesterville, Fayette, Wayne and Leeds to Greene, where it intersected another highway opened in 1793 from Augusta to Portland *via* Monmouth, Greene, Lewiston, Auburn, New Gloucester, etc. The Farmington road was laid on nearly a straight line from hill to hill where many of the people had settled to avoid destruction of crops by early frosts. Its course from Fayette Corner and beyond, lay over the easterly portion of Beech Hill in Fayette and Wayne, along the west shore of Androscoggin Lake to Lothrop's Corner; thence over Bates Hill or Quaker Ridge (following that bushed out in 1780) in Leeds, by Greene Upper Corner, and terminating near the meeting-house southwesterly of Greene railroad station. Not on account of the mail service were these highways constructed, but the convenience of travel and transportation of the necessaries of life; though later utilized for that purpose. The "post-riders" continued in the service until 1822, when, with the great growth in population and consequent increase of mail matter, carriages, drawn by two or more horses were required. These were replaced by passenger and mail coaches on the principal routes in 1826, and tri-weekly mails on these routes established. Passenger and mail coaches and stages were run throughout the country until they were replaced by steam-power, and only here and there a few lingering, dilapidated remnants of that once great system of travel remain.

The first post-office established in the limits of Androscoggin County was at Greene Corner, April 1, 1796; and the second, at Lewiston, July 15, 1799.

The first post-office in Leeds was on the line of the Farmington stage line at Lothrop's Corner, Aug. 27, 1822. Subjoined are the locations, names of postmasters and dates of their commissions:

Lothrop's Corner, or Leeds.

Solomon Lothrop,	Aug. 27, 1822
Giddings Lane, Jr.,	June 17, 1829.
Joseph Scammon,	April 19, 1830.
Stillman Howard,	March 10, 1834.
J. W. L. Mitchell,	Aug. 18, 1837.
Thomas W. Bridgham,	April 18, 1840.
Franklin B. Leonard,	July 10, 1841.
Issacher Lane,	July 19, 1845.
Isaac T. Boothby,	April 9, 1849.
Solomon T. Lothrop,	June 6, 1853.
Green C. More,	Oct. 7, 1864.
Charles H. Lane,	Jan. 28, 1868.
Albert Knight,	Jan. 30, 1880.
Willard Lothrop,	May 10, 1880.
Wallace L. Francis (Pres. P. M.),	Mar. 22, 1886.

North Leeds.

Walter Foss,	Jan. 28, 1826.
Reuel Foss,	March 5, 1842.
Thos. C. Foss,	Aug. 7, 1861.
Jason Woodman,	Dec. 20, 1871.
Louisa M. Woodman,	Dec. 10, 1880.
Charles A. Whitehouse,	Aug. 18, 1888.
Thomas C. Foss,	April 7, 1891.
Wallace C. Tribou,	Dec. 21, 1891.
Guy W. Foss,	July 15, 1895.
Vesta P. Foss (Pres. P. M.),	Jan. 19, 1901.

South Leeds.

Martin Leonard,	June 6, 1826.
Franklin B. Leonard,	Aug. 27, 1828.
Joshua S. Turner,	Dec. 5, 1838.
Oscar D. Turner,	July 27, 1840.
John Gilmore,	July 10, 1841.
Salmon A. Wing,	Aug. 16, 1843.
Armand T. Wing,	June 2, 1856.
William Wing,	March 10, 1863.
Sanford Gilbert,	May 19, 1863.
James L. Bates,	Jan. 2, 1865.
Duane S. Wing.	March 12, 1867.
Greenleaf Parker,	Jan. 18, 1876.
Lois V. Parker,	Aug. 3, 1887.
William Wing (Pres. P. M.),	Aug. 17, 1895.

West Leeds.

Jonas P. Lee,	April 10, 1828.
Perez S. Jennings,	Nov. 15, 1828.
Discontinued,	April 18, 1840.
Re-established.	
Gessius F. Jennings,	Feb. 24, 1866.
Stephen R. Deane,	April 28, 1868.
Gustavus A. Jennings,	May 2, 1883.
Roscoe E. Swain,	June 30, 1888.
Perry Grant,	July 28, 1893.
Howard E. Lincoln (Pres. P. M.),	Jan. 25, 1900.

East Leeds.

Stephen Day,	Aug. 5, 1840.
Discontinued,	Oct. 8, 1842.

Leeds Station.

George Beals,	April 15, 1850.
Changed to Leeds Junction	Mar. 15, 1859.
J. B. Brackett,	Dec. 3, 1883.
J. W. Ricker (Pres. P. M.),	May 8, 1891.

Curtis Corner.

Salmon Brewster,	Jan. 22, 1853.
Henry M. Brewster (Pres. P. M.),	Dec. 10, 1887.

CHAPTER XVI.

LADIES' AID SOCIETY.

As an important adjunct to the churches and church work in Leeds, the Ladies' Aid Society should receive special mention. Few societies of its size have accomplished more or better work during the past twelve years than the Ladies' Aid Society of Keen's Corner, Leeds; the originators of which were Mrs. Kate Quimby, Mrs. Vesta Bates and Mrs. Myra Boston. For the purpose of paying one hundred dollars of the indebtedness on the Methodist parsonage, the society was instituted on the 12th day of July, 1886. The remarkable short time required in discharging this debt and the success attending their first effort to improve the condition of the people in the vicinity, was seemingly a sufficient guarantee to warrant a permanent organization, and on July 14, 1890, under the laws of the State, the society was incorporated, with a membership of twelve, to wit: Rosa V. Hanscom, Mary A. Bishop, Millie E. Moody, Dora M. Nichols, Phebe A. Bates, Adellma C. Bates, Dorcas M. Parker, Annie F. Nichols, Edith W. Howe, Diana T. Gilbert, Adelia M. Libby and Serena E. Bates. As a result of their labors for the first year, $200 was in evidence, which was derived from suppers and entertainments given in the homes of several members. With this amount, which they placed as their donation at the head of a subscription paper, they solicited funds for the erection of a union chapel, promising its erection and completion before the beginning of the following winter. This paper was given a wide circulation not only in Leeds, but adjoining towns, but most of the money was obtained in the immediate vicinity in amounts varying from fifty cents to fifty dollars—each contributing their mite—supposed to be in keeping with their financial ability. The church lot was donated from the A. G. Bates farm. In due time the building was completed, and on May 20, 1891, eleven months and six days later than the date of incorporation, in this neat little structure the dedication exercises were held, participated in by ministers of various denominations. The expense of this little edifice, 45x30 feet, was about $1,500, of which sum $100 only remained unpaid with the dawning of dedication day. On this occasion no financial aid was solicited, and entertainment was liberally furnished to the many people who came from near and far to witness or participate in the exercises of the occasion. The remaining sum of $100 was soon forthcoming, and the little church stands there as a living memorial to the energy and honor of the ladies of Keen's Corner. In fact, as in name, this *is* a union chapel. In the summer months, Methodist and Universalist meetings are alternately held on Sundays, but in winter, while the Methodist meetings are continued every second Sunday, the Universalist meetings are discontinued. For the support of preachers, a certain amount is paid yearly, from the treasury of the "Ladies' Aid Society."

Success has crowned its every effort. The appreciation of their good work by the people may be inferred, from the proceeds of a fair held in the chapel March 19, 1891, which amounted to $204.39. Realizing the great value of church influence, and wishing to preserve in its beauty and purity this model little structure for the purpose for which it was made, and further realizing that everything good in life is not confined to churches, the society in continuing its labors, decided to erect a building in which to hold entertainments—so essential in all communities. In the spring of 1898, with sufficient means to warrant a beginning, by degrees, a two-story building with a basement for stabling horses has been erected and finished on the outside, and the inside is in readiness for masons who will be at work on the job with the coming of warm weather. The first floor is designed for a kitchen, dining-room and ticket office, and the second story a large hall where entertainments will be given. To the energy and unceasing labors of the society the public prosperity of the people in the vicinity is due. Great credit is awarded Mrs. Rosa V. Hanscom, president of the society, who has ably discharged the duties of that office eight years of the eleven it has existed. To her is conceded the praise of originating a major portion of the entertainments and successful financial engineering of the society. Not to the efforts of any one lady can be attributed the noble work accomplished by this society. She has been heartily and earnestly endorsed and aided by every member, whose unanimity and combined labor only, could have achieved so much. Theirs is a page of history sparkling with jewels, the luster of which will be seen from afar. A list of officers is here appended:

Rosa V. Hanscom,	President.
Edith W. Howe,	Vice-President.
Adelia M. Libby,	Treasurer.
Serena E. Bates,	Clerk.
Phebe A. Bates,	Collector and Asst. Clerk.

Their good work is still going on, and their unabated zeal and vigor is shining brighter and brighter as the days go by.

CHAPTER XVII.

SECRET SOCIETIES.

LEEDS GRANGE, P. OF H., NO. 99,

Was organized Feb. 1, 1875, by Deputy Robbins, with Davis Francis as Master and twenty-four (24) charter members, as follows:

Mr. and Mrs. Davis Francis,
Dr. and Mrs. R. S. Loring,
Mr. and Mrs. George Parcher,
Mr. and Mrs. A. Beals,
Mr. and Mrs. A. J. Lane,
Mr. and Mrs. G. A. Jennings,
Mr. and Mrs. B. C. Thomas,
Mr. and Mrs. W. B. Sumner,
Mr. and Mrs. A. J. Foss,
Mr. and Mrs. J. F. Jennings,
Mr. P. Lane,
Mr. G. B. Lane,
Mr. C. S. Knapp.

Seventeen members were initiated into the order between then and July 8, 1876, which is the date of the last meeting held till Jan. 1, 1885, when the Grange was reorganized by Fred A. Allen with George Parcher as Master.

In 1887, a hall 30x50 feet was built and in 1897, 20 feet more in length was added. The regular meetings are held on the second and fourth Saturdays of each month. Present membership, 151, with Phillip H. Deane, Master; Mrs. E. A. Russell, Lecturer; Abbie E. Deane, Secretary.

The following have served as officers:

Master, Davis Francis, two years.
    George Parcher, four years.
    A. F. Gifford, two years.
    Dr. R. S. Loring, two years.
    S. Homer Deane, three years.
    E. E. Additon, three years.
    Phillips H. Deane, three years.

Lecturer, George Parcher, two years.
    D. F. Lothrop, one year.
    A. T. Clifford, two years.
    Mrs. S. L. Herrick, two years.
    C. H. Foster, one year.

D. P. True, three years.
Rev. R. Scott, two years.
F. H. Herrick, three years.
F. L. Additon, two years.

Secretary, A. J. Foss, one year.
C. H. Foster, one year.
Dr. R. S. Loring, one year.
E. T. Clifford, two years.
S. Howard Deane, two years.
Abbie E. Deane, eleven years.

The Grange building now is a fine two-story structure, finished in hardwood, furnished with a nice set of furniture and a well filled library. The hall is now rented to the A. O. U. W. and the "Junior Order of American Mechanics" for holding their meetings. The Grange has taken first and second prizes for exhibits at the State Fair and has conducted fairs at home. It is the center for social intercourse and furnishes many public entertainments.

GEN. HOWARD LODGE, NO. 77, A. O. U. W.,

Was instituted at Leeds April 5, 1899, with the following officers and members:

E. A. Russell, P. M. W.;
W. H. Bishop, M. W.;
E. K. Merrill, F.;
A. L. Thomas, O.;
R. S. Higgins, Rec.;
H. E. Lincoln, Fin.;
W. H. Curtis, Receiver;
H. F. Gray, G.;
Daniel Maguire, I. W.;
A. P. Rose, O. W.;

And W. E. Gould, C. A. Bryant, George Dyer, W. C. Hosley, C. B. Brewster, F. E. Drake, E. E. Burgess, J. C. Wing, O. A. Wright, L. R. Bates, M. C. Howe, F. L. Morris, G. H. Anthony.

The present officers are:

A. L. Thomas, P. M. W.;
E. K. Merrill, M. W.;
O. A. Wright, F.;
R. L. Knapp, O.;
H. F. Gray, Rec.;
H. W. Lincoln, Fin.;
W. H. Curtis, Receiver;
G. H. Anthony, Guide;
J. M. Seymour, I. W.;
F. L. Morris, O. W.

CHAPEL HILL COUNCIL, NO. 43, J. O. U. A. M.

Was organized at Leeds, Jan. 8, 1900, with the following officers and members:

H. L. Grant,
John Rose,
W. H. Curtis,
R. D. Canwell,
J. C. Prescott,
W. L. Francis,
G. W. Lane,
Albert Rose,
Walter Hanscom,
C. C. Farmer,
J. F. Smith,
A. W. Hobbs,
Fred L. Wheeler,
Perley O. Maguire,
George Carpenter,
Fred S. Grant,
Will Rose.

Officers.

Councilor, W. H. Curtis;
Vice-Councilor, A. P. Rose;
Rec. Secretary, C. C. Farmer;
A. R. Secretary, W. L. Francis;
Fin. Secretary, F. S. Grant;
Treasurer, G. W. Lane;
Con., Arthur Hobbs;
W., George Carpenter;
I. S., J. C. Prescott;
O. S., John Rose;
C., Fred Smith;
P. S., H. L. Grant;
Trustees, W. L. Francis, W. H. Curtis, H. L. Grant.
Treasurer, W. L. Francis.

Since the order was organized it has increased in membership until it numbers 45 with a good financial standing.

MOUNTAIN VIEW LODGE, NO. 23, D. OF L.

Was instituted at Leeds, March 20, 1901, with the following officers and members:

Councilor, Mrs. Annie House;
Asso. Councilor, H. L. Grant;
Vice-Councilor, Mrs. Effie Grant;
Asso. Vice-Councilor, Fred S. Grant;
Jr. Ex. Councilor, Mrs. Addie Grant;
Jr. Ex. Asso. Councilor, W. H. Curtis;
Rec. Secretary, Gladys Francis;
Asst. R. Secretary, Herbert Wright;
Financial Secretary, Mrs. Effie Smith;
Treasurer, W. L. Francis;
Guide, Mrs. Emma Anthony;
Inside Guard, Arthur Grant;
Outside Guard, Bert Anthony.

Other members:

Charles A. Libby,
Grace Maguire,
Augusta W. Carver,
Walter House,
J. C. Prescott,
Dan Maguire,

Nedd Bishop,
Mrs. Nedd Bishop,
H. B. Curtis,
Gertrude Anthony,
Mrs. W. L. Francis,
J. F. Smith.

SONS OF TEMPERANCE.

But meager knowledge can be obtained in relation to this society further than the fact that, in 1845, an organization of a division of this Order was that year effected, and for a time had an existence in Leeds, but no records are available, and its history must ever remain unwritten.

TEMPERANCE WATCHMAN CLUB.

In the winter of 1851-2, at West Leeds, a club was organized, the chief object of which was to prevent the sale and use of intoxicating liquors, and to render aid to those addicted to the habit of drinking to excess, by inducing them to join the Order, in the meetings of which the evils of intemperance were earnestly discussed. Samuel P. True was Grand Master, and several men of prominence in the town, and even in the nation were members. Among them we notice the names of General O. O. Howard, Barnabus Davee, Gustavus A. Jennings, Melvin Berry, H. M. Brewster, Enoch Tupper, John Y. Merrill, Sylvanus C. Merrill, Nelson Rose, Calvin Rose and others. All enterprises have their ups and downs, and after a comparatively short life of usefulness, this had a down and never more an up.

I. O. G. T.

In 1887, a lodge of this Order was instituted in the south part of the town with twenty charter members. Following is a list of the officers at the date of institution:

Daniel S. Boston, L. D.; Henry M. Brewster, C. T.; Louisa Beals, V. T.; Moses G. Beal, Chaplain; Erwin M. Libby, Secretary. During the life of this lodge much good work was done, and over fifty names were enrolled on the records. The removal of many of the younger people so reduced the membership that, in 1897, after a life of ten years, a surrender of the charter was made.

CHAPTER XVIII.

ANDROSCOGGIN RAILROAD.

It may well be said, that to a few enterprising men of Leeds is due the credit of securing a charter and the building of this road. The charter was obtained August 10, 1848. Organization was soon effected with Giddings Lane, Ozias Millett and Ensign Otis on the board of directors. The soliciting of subscriptions of the stock was at once commenced with life and vigor, and the people of Leeds responded nobly. By a major vote (145 in favor, 106 against), in a meeting held February 9, 1852, the town loaned its credit in aid of the road to the amount of $15,000. To effect this enterprise it was necessary to pull every string to its full tension, and better men for the business could nowhere have been found. The writer was a little boy then, but in his memory is fresh the persuasive arguments of the solicitors. Through every man's door-yard, who lived in the valleys, and just under the brow of the hill, if his residence was on a high eminence, the road was sure to go. The valuation of every man's farm would thereby be increased 100 per cent. Money was needed to make the "mare go," and go she must, and go she did! With funds pledged sufficient to warrant construction, the grading of the road was begun in 1850, and in 1851 had been completed from Leeds Junction to Livermore Falls. In the spring of 1852, the laying of ties and rails was begun. A small locomotive and twelve platform cars were purchased, which constituted the company's rolling stock.

Josiah Littlefield, of Auburn, who later became the mechanical engineer of this road, a fearless and competent locomotive driver was secured, and to him was intrusted the whole charge of this supply and working train. With the iron laid a short distance out from the Junction, the rolling stock was put into use in supplying the crews with sleepers, rails and other material used in the construction of the road. Mr. Littlefield run his engine and the crew of train-workers with the assistance of Woodbury S. Knapp, of Leeds, who was fireman. The loaded cars were run up the track in advance of the engine which was also run backward. By this method the cars were run to the extreme end of the newly laid rails where they were unloaded and their contents left nearer the place of use than otherwise, as safety would not permit the engine to advance thus far. The opening of this road subjected the farmers along the line to lots of trouble as well as the train employees. Between pastures where stock was kept, and also beside fields of corn and grain, fences were, of necessity, taken down for the train to pass and repass on its mission of labor. This was a source of great annoyance to the train men and a greater one to the farmers. To Mr. Littlefield, who was obliged to stop and start his train at every fence crossing, this was especially annoying, and at times, he would leave them down when he was to soon return. When so left, the farmers, more or less angered, put them up. On one occasion, the writer readily recalls the fact (being a favorite of the fireman, though a little boy, accepted frequent invitations to ride on the engine), when the road was completed to near North Leeds, the train came up with a load, and was to make another trip that day. They had left the fence down between the field and pasture of Solomon Lothrop. As we descended the grade near the river, Mr. Littlefield said: "If Lothrop has put up his fence I shall not stop to take it down." When we rounded the little curve, we noticed that it was up all right. Littlefield reached out, pulled the throttle wide open, and we went into that fence a thirty clip. Rails flew in every direction and one, which was struck in the center by the guard went directly over the smokestack and landed on top of the second car. It was a sight to see the train men (who always rode on the first car near the tender) scamper for the hind end of the train, which pleased Mr. Littlefield much. The road was completed, with the exception of graveling, and opened to travel in November, 1852, when an invitation to the stockholders was issued for a free ride, which was very generally accepted and an enjoyable day passed by many who had never before been hauled by steam power.

A new purchase of rolling stock had just been made, and in all, consisted of one small engine, two passenger, one mail, six box and twelve platform cars. With no snow-plow and no snow fences, the mixed train made trips that winter when convenient, which was infrequent. Some witty son gave it the name of "Peanut Road," which attached to it for several years. In the summer of 1853, another locomotive was purchased and John Brooks, a little man, was procured to run it. This was employed most of that season and the following one in graveling the road, obtaining most of the material near where the Leeds Center railroad station is now situated and also near the dwelling of Samuel P. Libby southerly of Curtis Corner, both of which are in Leeds. Too poor to purchase a snow-plow, the company started in on its second winter—quite a severe one—and experienced many hardships. Dec. 29, 1853, fifteen inches of snow fell, and drifting badly, no trains were run Dec. 30, but late in the afternoon of the 31st one succeeded in reaching Livermore Falls. On February

23, 1854, snow commenced falling at 4 A.M., and continued all day. At ten o'clock A.M., a train started from the Junction, ran about three miles, got stuck in a drift, and the engine having nearly exhausted the supply of wood and water was unshackled from the cars, which were left in the snow, was run to Pettingill's crossing, where the tender received a new supply of water carried in pails from a brook ten or twelve rods distant, and a goodly amount of wood obtained, but instead of returning to the cars which contained two ladies and three gentlemen, the severity of cold, which had frozen the wet clothing of the carriers of the water, and the lateness of the hour decided the engineer to stop over night in the shelter of the woods where fuel and water was to be obtained, and an opportunity offered to move his engine back and forth to prevent it from freezing up and becoming a dead monster. The passengers remained in the cars two days and one night, supplied with food and fuel by the conductor and brakeman from the nearest farm houses. On the morning of the 24th, a crew of shovelers were at work, and at two o'clock P.M. the engine reached the enstalled cars, and after moving them out of their snowy beds to near the dwelling of Mr. Abram Wheeler, where the ladies were comfortably sheltered, started on its back track toward the Junction where it arrived, at last, at midnight. The following day, Feb. 25, this train again started out at noon, but got no farther than North Leeds, where the night was spent. Starting out at seven o'clock the following morning, Livermore Falls was reached about noon, where a rest was taken until March 1. From that time to the 18th, regular trips were made, but on that day the shortest one of the season is placed to its credit. Starting out at 11 A.M. it had proceeded less than a mile when a drift was encountered and a return to cover made. March 19, snowed all day and no train left its moorings. The following day a train left the Junction at noon after much shoveling had been done, and arrived at Livermore Falls at 5 P.M. March 24, two feet of snow fell and no trains were out that day. March 25, snow was deep on the track, and the train remained housed. The following day was blustering, as was also the succeeding one, and from then to April 1 the road was completely tied up; but in the afternoon of that day the shovelers made a trip possible, and about 2 P.M. a train was gotten through. From that time forth until the following winter, neither snow nor frost prevented the making of regular trips. On the 8th day of December, 1854, snow fell to the depth of eight inches, and clearing with the sunset, a strong northwest wind through the night filled all the cuts deep with hard-drifted snow. A train composed of two engines, a mail and baggage car, and a passenger car left Livermore Falls on time the next morning, and with great effort succeeded in reaching a cut through the side of a little round hill about 100 rods northerly of the station at Leeds Center, in which the train came to a sudden stop midway of the drift. Backing out with difficulty and running the train up the track to the bridge, a new start was made, and with all the speed possible they plunged into the drift a second time. They broke through it and in doing it the forward engine turned short to the left and the front end of the boiler was buried in the bank; while the other left the rails on the opposite side, toppled over on its side, and on the platform of the cab, which had broken from the tender, both Brooks and Knapp, engineer and fireman, rode out into the field uninjured. The draw or coupling rod broke behind the tender and left all the cars on the irons, uninjured. Josiah Littlefield was running the leading engine and slightly injured by being thrown against the end of the boiler, but so slight that he continued in the work of clearing up the wreck. This wreck was a strong incentive to procure a snow plow, and within a few days one was on the rails and a good engine to push it. An old engine called the "Old widow," was also procured, and transportation renewed. January 19, 1855, snow fell in quantity and the following day none but an engine and snow plow went over the road, starting from the Junction at noon, arriving at Livermore Falls at 10 P.M., and returning to the Junction that night. February 19, 1856, trains were again tied up on account of snow. January 9, 1857, train left the rails, though unattended with fatalities or personal injuries. Little snow fell the succeeding winter and travel but little impeded. December 21, 1858, completion of the road having been made to East Wilton, trains were that day put in operation to that village. On January 1, 1859, trains were housed where they remained until the afternoon of the 5th, when one started out from the Junction, drawn by two engines, and proceeding as far as Leeds Center, there, "thinking discretion the better part of valor," returned to winter quarters again. Soon after this train started on its return, Charles Garcelon came down the line with the "old widow" and no snow plow. In all probability a head on collision was averted by the lucky return of that train. No telegraphic wires had then been strung on this line, over which running orders were communicated. When the "old widow" arrived at the Junction, new life was infused into the two-engine train hands and starting anew at 10 P.M., a trip was made that night. Feb. 3, 1859, John Kauffer, engineer burned his mouth and throat so badly in blowing into a pet-cock which was frozen on his engine, that he lived but a few hours. The following day, the down train did not reach its destination until midnight, returning the next afternoon. Feb. 10, 1860, was a stormy and very blustering day. A train arrived at Curtis Corner at 2 P.M., destitute of wood and water, where both were supplied, the latter from a brook, distant about 20 rods, conveyed in a hogshead and drawn by oxen. The six passengers and train hands, with the exception of the engineer and fireman who stayed in the engine, were accommodated at the home of Salmon Brewster, where they remained until the afternoon of the following day when a start was made for the Junction, arriving there in safety and returning to Farmington that night. Similar experiences continued until the road was leased June 29, 1871, to the Maine Centrail Railroad Co. for a term of nine hundred and ninety-nine years, since which time, with the building of snow fences and other modern equipments the road has taken a place among those of high standard and good service. Let it ever be remembered, that to the enterprising citizens of Leeds is due the great advantage now being derived from the establishment of this great thoroughfare, which extends the entire length of the town, and along the shore of the most beautiful of the many sheets of water in New England.

CHAPTER XIX.

GLEANINGS.

Of necessity, the first settlers of new countries infested with wild animals were hunters and trappers. This was true of the pioneers of Leeds. Thomas Stinchfield was a daring and courageous hunter, and previous to his settlement here had hunted and trapped on the Androscoggin and its tributary waters even to the Rangeley Lakes, and knew all the country on either side of it from the Saco to the Kennebec rivers. Round Pond in the northerly part of the town of Livermore was early called Stinchfield Pond in honor of him. The name was given it by the Indians, and when the white settlers went in there, they adopted the Indian name and long retained it. As early as 1773, Thomas had camps there and on Dead River, and in fact, in many other localities. He won the friendship of the Indians by fair dealing and acts of kindness. He treated them justly and at the same time inspired them with confidence and fear. He trusted the resident Indians at all times and never lost a debt if the debtor lived. His wishes and advice were at all times and in all cases granted and accepted by them, and the lives of many white settlers were spared through his instrumentality. In the fall of 1782, a small white settlement had been made on the Sandy River where the village of New Sharon now stands. On a small, round hill just a little way north of Farmington Falls, an Indian wigwam village was planted. The red and white men both, were hunting and trapping on that river and the little brooks and streams that empty into it. Some of the white hunters stole game from the Indians' traps, repeatedly, and after due warning, still persisted in their robbery. In retaliation the Indians planned to massacre them. One of their number, more cautious of the consequences of such an act, came for "Father Thomas," arriving at his home after the sun set. After being refreshed, they set out for Farmington, guided only by spotted trees and their knowledge of the route, which was not a very desirable undertaking in the night time, with no light but that of torches of their make, arriving at the Indian village just as the morning light was breaking. The warriors were all absent, having gone to New Sharon under the cover of darkness to complete their arrangements for an attack when darkness should come again and the thieves all corralled. Tired from his night's tramp of twenty-five miles through the forest, Thomas accepted an invitation from the chief's squaw to rest on his couch of skins until the return of the warriors, who came in soon after the sun rose. When accosted by Thomas, their greetings were: "Ugh!" which he well knew meant persistent determination to wreak their vengeance on the thieves. Never before nor after, was his skill so taxed in managing the red man. It was a long time before he could persuade the chief to call his warriors around him and allow him to address them. After repeating the wrongs that had been done them, his determination to punish the guilty party, and showing them the injustice of taking the lives of the innocent men, women and children for the crimes of the guilty, he conceived the idea of making the thieves return to the Indians double the number of traps and skins taken, as many kettles as traps stolen, and 10 gallons of rum to celebrate their victory on. He then asked the chief to accompany him to New Sharon, and with twelve picked warriors they went there and he made his demand, with the additional proviso that, "if the thieves elected to pay the forfeit within twenty-four hours, and within as many hours thereafter leave that part of the country never to return, their lives would be spared them, otherwise their fate would be left to the merciful kindness of the people they had so grossly wronged." After assuring them that guards would be stationed to prevent their escape, he bade them good day. Before the day closed the skins, traps, kettles and rum were all delivered, and what otherwise would have ended in a tragedy, rid the settlement of thieves and the white and red men on Sandy River hunted and trapped together in peace.

The families of the early settlers were largely dependent for their meat on the moose, deer, caribou and bear with which the forest then abounded. On one occasion, Thomas Millett's store of meat was exhausted and he could not tell where he was to obtain a fresh supply. The March snow was deep on the ground, but with snow-shoes, dog and gun, Millett went to the house of Thomas Stinchfield, who knew the haunts of the meat animals of the woods, and sought his aid. Likewise equipped the two Thomases, accompanied by James Stinchfield, a lad 16 years old, who carried an ax, the two with two dogs, set out for a moose yard near where the buildings of the late William Boothby now stand. The snow was that deep, instead of ranging off to hunt for game, the dogs chose to follow in the snow-shoe tracks and occasionally to ride on the boy's shoes, which resulted in broken strings, the mending of which gave the men a lead of some distance ahead of him. The dogs had timely warning to not again repeat the trick, and their indifference was rewarded by an earnest reminder with the ax-handle. They at once decided to change the program and started out to break their own road. When a little way off, they set up a furious barking, though the lad gave them little attention, thinking that they were trying to redeem themselves with him,—barking at some small creature of no account, and started off to overtake the men. So persistently did they bark that he changed his course and on going to them found them digging in ice and snow at the base of a giant tree. The ice was an indication of the snow having been melted and frozen, and he at once knew the cause. A loud call from him, mingled with the baying of the dogs, soon brought back the men. His father took the ax and cutting away the ice soon came to a hole in the hollow tree. So earnest was Mr. Millett—less experienced then than later with the peculiarities of wild animals and having all confidence in his dog, requested that he be allowed to snuff in the hole of the tree, saying: "My dog can tell whether anything is there." Thus indulged, no later than the dog's head was well in the hole, a black glove with projecting hooks came down on it, and to prevent him from being drawn through the hole, Millett grabbed him by the hind legs and said: "I will have part of you." He succeeded in getting all of him except a little blood, but the skin from the top of his head was hanging down over his nose. After the ice was further cut away,—the hole sufficiently large, bruin committed the mistake of his life when he attempted to again view the outside world; for, when his clumsy body was midway in the hole, a well aimed blow of the poll of the ax prepared him for transportation. The snow being too deep and soft to haul him out on sleds, and to tie his legs together and carry him on a pole would sink their snow-shoes so deep that traveling would thus be made almost impossible, they removed his skin, cut him in quarters and with one each on their shoulders carried him to Stinchfield's in season for dinner. While eating, Benjamin, a son of Thomas Millett came in, having started out to meet his father. Taking each a quarter of the bear they departed for their home, which was where Herbert Millett now resides; while Stinchfield and his son James returned to the tree for the skin and the other quarter of the bear. In the place of moose meat they got that which was fully as welcome to them.

In the fall of 1781, the year following that of the settlement of Leeds, on an evening, Thomas Stinchfield was washing out his gun preparatory to a hunt the next day. His trusty dog, jumping up from the chimney-corner rushed to the door and gave tongue in unmistakable sounds of the near approach of some unwelcome guest. Just back of the house was, nearly ripe, a field of Indian corn. The door opened, into the corn went the dog and out of it went a bear so closely chased that he took refuge in a large tree on the edge of the clearing. After listening to the dog a minute Thomas said: "The dog has treed him," and taking a brand off the fire, which he handed to Thomas, Jr., a lad thirteen years of age, said: "You and Sarah (11 years) build a fire under the tree and keep him up there until I dry my gun out, and I will come out and shoot him." Where is the parent now who would send children of their ages on a like errand, and where are the children to be found who would unhesitatingly obey such a command?

On another occasion, Thomas Stinchfield, knowing where a bear and two cubs made their home, which was on the northerly end of Hedgehog Hill, took his son James with him to make them a visit, and if a favorable opportunity offered, to confiscate them. As a precaution, he took his gun along, but did not permit the dog to go. Approaching their haunt cautiously, they discovered the cubs near the den, enjoying a sun bath. They sprang forward and caught them, a much easier task than to hold and manage them afterward. Their screams soon brought the mother-bear to the scene of action, and such manifestations of temper are seldom witnessed as those displayed by her. She seemed anxious for them to know she had teeth, and even showed them without an invitation. Sometimes on end in fighting posture, not daring to strike for fear of injuring her own, round and round them she went uncomfortably near, first on the one side and then on the other, in front, but never behind (not allowable) and such growls and snarling as would put to shame the severer type of old maids. In this manner home was at last reached where the old bear was shot, having walked from her den and saved the labor of hauling or carrying her. In one way convenient, but never so pleasant or frequent as to become a fixed habit!

A moose yard was one winter made, near where the buildings of Robert Gould, at North Leeds, were later erected. Being in need of meat, Stinchfield, with Thomas, Jr., and James, his sons, started out for there with two sleds, an ax and gun. Knowing where and for what he was going, he took but three bullets with him. When they reached the yard, which contained a bull and two cow moose, it was decided to kill the bull. They came upon him broadside to them, standing with his head behind a large tree. The father, whose skill as a marksman was never in question, took aim for the vital spot and discharged his gun. The bull stood in his tracks apparently not even frighted to say nothing of being injured. Much surprised, he, no more so than the boys, who teasingly offered to make the next shot, again loaded without comment and gave the moose a second charge, and when the smoke cleared away the moose stood there still. "Boys, I don't understand it," he said. He again loaded and his last bullet was in the gun. He deliberately pulled the gun to his face and sent his last messenger of death mooseward, but with no better success than before—still the moose stood there. Shame mingled with a slight touch of anger, he handed the empty gun to a boy and taking the ax in hand said: "I will never go home and leave that moose standing there!" Approaching him in such a manner as to keep the tree in line between him and the moose's head, he reached it in safety and with ax raised jumped in front of the moose and dealt him a blow such as "Sampson" with that jaw-bone of the long-eared horse species must have wielded. Surprise again awaited him. The first shot killed the moose so quickly that his muscles became rigid, his limbs unbending and instead of falling, he leaned slightly against a tree on the opposite side from whence he was shot, which prevented him from falling. On examination, the three bullets had passed through his heart, and so near together, though making three holes, were nearly cut into one.

To become an expert in any life calling, experience and practice are necessary, without which none attain to perfection. In early days, the best instruments used in the various pursuits of life were, at best, but crude and awkward in their construction. When we consider that the fire-arms of our fathers were flint-locks and the uncertainty which attended their discharge, it is the more remarkable that a proficient gunner might then be found with whom the ablest of modern times, with their improved and newly invented rifles could but poorly contend in all the various places, on land and water, where guns were then so extensively used. That of "Father Thomas" was equally good with shot or ball and had a barrel 60 inches in length, which gave to the lead a greater velocity than that acquired from shorter guns in which the black, slow-burning powder of those days was but partially consumed. When old age had begun to dim his eye, the forests in the vicinity of home rid of their native wild animals—none having felled so many as he—long hunting tramps were abandoned. Loath to lay aside forever his trusty gun—a companion from youth—frequently did he request some grandson to paddle him down Dead River and along the shores of Androscoggin Lake where he could enjoy a season of pleasure shooting such fowl as frequented those waters. On one occasion the father of the writer, who often indulged the old gentleman, returning home from a trip of this kind, seeing a loon a distance away, called the old man's attention to it. "Do you want to see me shoot him?" he asked. "He is too far off—don't think you can." "I will try him!" He did try him and the loon made a quick dive. The old man reloaded and when the loon again came to the surface, he tried him a second time, but again the loon disappeared. "I must have hit him!" Nothing daunted, he proceeded to prepare another shot, the while looking for a return of that game fowl to the surface. The dives were numerous but short, and when an opportunity offered he tried him a third time, which proved fatal. On examination of the loon, one bullet cut the feathers on the top of his head, another on the side of his neck, while the third passed through his head.

In the late fall of 1773, Thomas and his older brother John, boated up the Androscoggin River to Rangeley Lakes, for the purpose of trapping and hunting, where they remained until the clearing of the ice in the spring. They built a camp and set up a line of traps, the circuitous distance of which they judged to be about fifteen miles. To obtain more game, they concluded to separate, build another camp and set up another line of traps. The distance between the camps was about ten miles. Game was plentiful and the work of tending the traps and caring for the skins together with fifteen miles travel each day, kept them busy; while their evenings were spent in gathering fuel and preparing food. Though but ten miles separated them when in camp, six weeks and more had passed without a meeting when, one evening, John appeared at the camp of Thomas and when they attempted to greet each other, surprise mingled with (what was until then a stranger to them) fear, was depicted in their faces; for neither could articulate audibly. In attempting to speak to his dog on that day, John discovered that he had nearly lost his speech, and at once started for the camp of his brother. Several days elapsed before their speech was fully recovered. From that time on they both occupied the same camp and readjusted their lines of traps.

The gun that Thomas used was his pride and the envy of the Indians. Their highest ambition was to become owners of it. The chief of the encampment of Roccomeco made fabulous offers for it, and at one time proffered the season's catch of fur of his village for it. This availed him nothing—it was not for sale while the owner was able to sight it. Despairing of obtaining it, the best gunners of that wigwam village, foremost among them the chief, purchased a lot of new guns and after good practice visited "Father Thomas" and challenged him to a shooting match. It was late afternoon on a cloudy, dark day, but a range was made on the cape—a six-inch ring with white border and center drawn, ready for action. To them Thomas said: "You are the challengers and may shoot all you like, but I shall shoot but twice." Then they decided to take two shots each, which would decide who was the victor. Thomas was to be the last of the 13 contestants to shoot. The Indians, by course, made their shots and good ones they were, ten of which were in or within the ring, and three in close proximity to the bull's eye. Confident of having won, the sachem said to Thomas, "Big shoot, no beat him white man!" When they gathered at the target to witness the effect of the white man's shot, the bull's eyesight had been hopelessly injured. Victory lost when so nearly won had its effect on the nervous systems of the Indians, and haste to achieve a victory the next time was more apparent than their accuracy of vision. Darkness was approaching and by the time Thomas' turn would come to shoot again, darkness would prevent him from plainly seeing the target. He suggested postponement until the morning, but hoping for the success of some of the first to shoot, and knowing their advantage, they persisted in shooting it off that night. Then said Thomas: "You may shoot when you like, but I shall wait for darkness to settle down and shoot then." The Indians, with the exception of the sachem, whose turn came next before Thomas', all chose to use the remaining daylight, but only four bullets were placed inside the ring and those near the circumference. Little later a candle and chalk were brought, the former was adjusted in front of the injured bull's eye, the latter rubbed on the two guns, and everything in order the chief made his shot, which was a good line exhibition, cutting off the candle about an inch below the center of the target. For once, the shores of the lake resounded with the whoops of the jubilant and cunning bucks, but to little purpose, for when the stub of the candle was relighted and readjusted with the blaze in front of the center of the target, unmoved by the noise which had died away in the distance, with nerves as steady as the eternal hills, Thomas deliberately brought his gun in line from his eye to the blaze of the candle and when it spoke forth, darkness prevailed on the face of the earth, and where were the Indians when the light went out?

On the low meadow, beside the lake, now owned by D. P. True, is a point on which rocks and bushes abound, and in the time of high water in spring and fall is an island. In early time, before the alluvial deposit attached it to the main land, it was named "Little Island," which name it has retained to the present. On this promontory, when the meadow is flowed, muskrats, driven from their haunts, there congregate in large numbers. In the latter part of the month of April, 1857, James Stinchfield, a son of Thomas, then a man nearly 84 years old—still retaining great vigor and his taste for hunting and trapping to which he had been accustomed thus far in life—betook himself, loaded with steel traps and a pocket of parsnips, to a boat on the shore near his house, and distant from the island near 100 rods. Although the ice yet remained in the lake, the rise of water left an open space between it and the shore, and open water covered the meadow. After launching the craft, he paddled to this island, and wishing to land on the lake side, opposite of where the rats had their places of abode, he made the attempt. The water was deep and the bushes too thickly set to admit the boat to pass through them to the land. He laid aside his paddle and going to the bow of the boat parted the bushes with his hands and holding on, attempted to pull the boat through them to the shore, but his strong pull was too much for the bush which suddenly broke, and consequently he went over the side of the boat, head foremost on his back, into the ice water. In making this backward dive, one of his feet became fastened between the side boards and a rave broken around on the inside of the boat's knees, and thus he was suspended, head downward and under water. For a young man to extricate himself from such a critical position would have been no easy task, and especially one of his avoirdupois (about 200 lbs.), but he freed himself, after a time, and climbing into the boat, paddled against a raw, cold, northeast wind to the shore. Having always been well and hardy, no particular precaution was taken more than a change of clothing and warmth by the fire, and pneumonia followed, from the effects of which he died, July 28, 1857.

River and lake waters offered like opportunities to the early settlers and the people of later time of becoming expert swimmers. Some there were, and some there are, who excel in the different works and amusements practiced by the human race. James Stinchfield was a man of great lung capacity and vitality and was thus enabled to hold his breath a long time. He became a celebrity as a long distance diver. From the Kennebec River came a man to visit the family of Daniel Lane. He was a diver of repute and not unboastful of his skill. He claimed to be boss of the Kennebec and could teach the boys of Leeds such water tricks as they had never known. The Lane boys and some of the men, even, not particularly pleased with his boasting, arranged a meeting at the river near where the bridges now span it, and invited James to witness the exhibition and also to test this man's ability in long diving. Everything in readiness, mid a large number of men and boys who were there gathered, they stripped for the contest. The agreement was, that the boaster should make his dive first and remain where he came up, treading water to keep himself in place. Among those who had gathered to witness the scene was one James Lindsey. (Those acquainted with the Lindsey people know their aptitude for fun and story-telling.) In apparent candor and soberness, he had just related the story that a monster sea turtle had been seen in the river but a few days previous, and that he caught and swallowed a sheep belonging to Increase Leadbetter while drinking from the river, and expressed his hope that the "critter" hadn't "come that way." This cooled the Kennebec man's ardor several degrees, but the dread of the fun that would be made at his expense if he backed out, was fully equal to his fear of the turtle, so he made his dive, which was a reasonably good one. Stinchfield, appreciating the force of Lindsey's story, made his dive, and after a time, passing where the man was yet treading water, rubbed his back against the man's feet, who, mistaking it for the turtle, squalled like a scared cat, and jumping as nearly out of the water as possible, made the shore as quickly as his trembling limbs would take him. His fright and defeat cost him a treat of all that gathered at the bar.

In early times, when military trainings were in order, Lothrop's Corner, being near the center of the town, was the place usually selected to parade and drill the people liable to do military duty; although Keene's Corner or Pine Plains sometimes enjoyed the honor. These were occasions when the people gathered in large numbers to witness the drill and the various amusements that were sure to follow. It is admitted that Leeds, in those days, was not, strictly, a temperance town. Most of the stores through the country dealt heavily in wet, West India goods, which were in good demand. Some events that transpired on those and other occasions, and especially the days of "muster," have been handed down and retained in the memory of those of the present generation. Practical jokes were not uncommon; and, to the natural wit and cunning of some of the people—quickened by the spirit—which was distributed in a pail and administered with a dipper, is due many original features of amusement. On one occasion, Mr. Samuel More, a positive, matter-of-fact gentleman and much-respected citizen, was the object selected to entertain the people. When the spirit moved with him, it was always in an antagonistic manner and he was ready to back up his argument by brute force. One Daniel Harvey, to whom the spirit added to his fund of native sport, engaged Mr. More in argument and a difference soon arose, which culminated in an agreement to fight. A condition was made to which they both positively agreed, which was: "When either one said 'enough,' the other should not strike another blow." They were both strong, resolute men, and to those who were not in the game, a hard battle was expected. They stripped for the fight. Harvey struck More a stunning blow and at the same time cried enough. More was a man of his word and kept it, but with poor grace.

On another occasion a foot-race from the town house to the store was a feature of the program. A large number of young men lined up to await the word, go! Levi Caswell, a man more than seventy years old, who never tempted the people who were light fingered by leaving his whip in his carriage, but always, on such occasions, carried it in his hand, asked the participants in the race if they were willing for him to start in behind and drive them. They readily assented and the word was given. After they were fairly under way the old man began to ply the lash, and before the store was reached he drove every one out of the road into the ditch. This is not offered to detract from the fleetness of the young men, but to show the agility of the old gentleman and his skill in the use of the whip.

In days of "ye olden time" an indispensable amusement was the wrestling match. Musters, trainings, raisings, huskings, town meetings, etc., were all occasions of which the last act was a test of the science and skill of the athletes. An imaginary line drawn across the town from east to west divided it into North and South, and a spirit of rivalry for the mastery existed. On these occasions a representative from each section would choose from his territory all that wished or would consent to participate in the contest. The non-participants as well were deeply interested in the success of their respective sides,—all the more so, as the defeated party was expected to stand a treat for the massive gathering. Among the experts of the North at collar and elbow were: John, Isaac and James Stinchfield, Jr., Walter Foss, Charles Knapp, Benjamin Francis, George and other Lothrop boys, several of the young Lanes and Jennings, Archibald and James Lindsey; while at the back-hug, where strength was a prominent feature, John Stinchfield, Thomas Graffam, several of the Leadbetter boys and others were among the chief contestants. But the former was the style most in use. In the Southern division the sons of Levi Caswell stood at the head and were ably seconded by the Curtises, Keenes, Sumners, Additons, Turners, Lindseys, Bishops, Pettingills, Bateses, etc. Although divided at home, when away at general musters, there was no North and South, but they all stood shoulder to shoulder like the noble sons of Leeds which they were. When the custom died out, Leeds contained several men whose backs had not been dirted for twenty years. It was very seldom that the best performers participated and the victories won were quite evenly divided between the two sections. Both the Caswell and Stinchfield boys were nautrally reserved and unassuming. Some of the former had lately returned from sea (I think,) and during their home stay it was planned by the mouth-pieces of both sections to have a general match and to arrange it so the boys of these families, who had never met in contest, would come together in the ring. It was on the occasion of a training when all liable to do military duty were expected to be present, and the place of meeting was Lothrop's Corner. After the drill was over, the two lines were drawn up facing each other and the contest begun at the lower end of the lines. The Caswell boys headed one line with the Curtis boys on their right next to them and others in their order. The Stinchfields headed the other line and Walter Foss, George Lothrop and Benjamin Francis on their left and others in their order. Gradually the lines shortened, but that of the North much the faster, until Benjamin Francis was sent in. He threw four. George Lothrop cut the number down three more. At this stage but four were remaining on the side of the North and six on the side of the South. Walter Foss was sent in and threw his man. His next antagonist was a Curtis and he threw him on his side, but in doing it broke his hold, which was decided to be an unfair throw. They tried it a second time and Curtis threw him. James Stinchfield was next sent in and Curtis and his brother were both thrown. The three Stinchfield brothers and three Caswell brothers remained. James was somewhat tired, for the two Curtis boys had not been thrown without taxing well his skill and efforts. It was known that John Stinchfield—much the larger and stronger of the three brothers—had a boil on his leg, and consented to enter the ring on condition that if the South threw all on his side he would wrestle once only, with anyone they might pick out. The odds were in favor of the Caswell brothers at this stage in the game. They were heavy, strong men and very agile. Isaac and James Stinchfield were not above medium size, but weighed well compared with their looks. Both sides dreaded the contest which was to be witnessed by an immense gathering, who stood speechless and anxious. James stood in the ring and awaited the coming of his new antagonist. It was evident from the first pass that Mr. Caswell intended to use his strength. He made several attempts to take an inside lock, when his supposed excess of muscle would do the rest. At last he succeeded in getting it, but to his surprise he came underneath. James immediately hopped on one foot back to his place in the line, where a seat was improvised at his request, and said to his brother Isaac, "I have hurt my leg and you better take my place." Two only on each side now remained. Isaac went in and took his injured brother's place and two fresh and anxious men came together. The first time Mr. Caswell took a foot from the ground he was almost instantly on his back. Getting up he said, "You did it fairly and easily, and I will consider it a personal favor if you will give me another chance to see how you did it." The answer was, "We will wait and let John and your brother try titles and if John don't oblige me to take his place I will accommodate you." After tearing up the ground a few minutes John landed his man. Then came the accommodation trial, which resulted like the first. The brother who had been thrown by John thought he saw how his brother was so easily thrown and asked for a chance to have it tried on him. But he also went down with little exertion and could not tell how. Their father, patting Isaac on the shoulder, said, "I did not bring my boys up to be thrown. If I was not so old I would try you."

CHAPTER XX.

MARRIAGE INTENTIONS, WITH DATE OF CERTIFICATE.

1801.

Obadiah Turner and Tabitha Dyer, July.
Thomas Lothrop and Cyntha Brett, September.
George Turner and Betsy B. Gilbert, September.
Alpheus Turner and Betsy Creech, November.
Edwin Baily and Ruth Bates of Greene, November.

1802.

Ahira Gilbert and Olive Gilbert, April.
James Stinchfield and Hannah Pettingill, June.
Levi Foss and Betsy Millett, September.
Daniel Lane and Ruth Pratt, October.
Jesse Torrey and Sally Morse, December.
Reuben Hanes and Jane Penley of Pejepscot, December.

1803.

Jira Fish, Jr., and Eunice Bumpus, September.
Hazerenan Draper and Hannah Pratt, September.
Abner Curtis and Lydia Turner, August.
Sylvanus Atkins and Susannah Mason, September.
Cyrus Sampson and Nabby Wing, September.
Joseph Turner and Deborah Gilbert, July.
William Day and Lucy Sampson, September.
John Row and Sally Stinchfield, October.
Thomas Southard and Anna Welcom, November.

1804.

Samuel Hanes and Priscilla Whitting, April.
John Leadbetter and Rachel Foss, July.
David Berry and Deborah Pratt, April 12.
Nathl. Gilbert and Sophia Stubbs, October.
Stephen Webster and Nancy Lowell, November.

1805.

Samuel Stubbs and Ruth Bates, April.
Benjamin Gilbert and Lydia Jones, September.
Benjamin Leadbetter and Jennie Collier, November.

1806.

Noah Frost and Sally Harmon, January.
David Atkins of Wayne and Margery Besse, March.
James Gilbert and Hannah Jacobs of Waterville, March.
Jabez Dagget and Mehitabal Drake, March.
Luther Cary of Livermore and Polly Lothrop, March.
Israel Millett and Betsy Harris of Greene, April.
Elijah Gilbert of Turner and Huldah Gilbert, June.
Samuel Leadbetter and Betsey Parcher of Saco, September.
Peter Comings of Greene and Sally Andrews, November.
Seth Burgess and Virtue Dicker of Monmouth, November.

1807.

Samuel Burgess of Livermore and Hannah Hammond, January.
Daniel Foss and Eunice Lane, February.
William Smith of Waterville and Rubey Streeter, April.
Henry Moss and Rebecca Bailey of Greene, February.
William A. Day and Betsey Jones, July.
Stillman Howard and Lydia Lothrop, September.
Amasa Dexter of Wayne and Patty Burgess, October.
Stephen Boothby and Susannah Buswell of Winthrop. November.
Ira Lothrop and Sally Leach, November.
Ebenezer Mason and Mercy P. Fish, December.

1808.

Massey Sylvester and Lyda Turner, March.
James McNeal and Nabby Hicks, July.
James Getchell of Waterville and Nancy Moss, April.
Constant Southard, Jr., of Fayette and Sally Hicks, May.
Cyrus Foss and Polly Lane, July.
Timothy Foster and Anne Moss, June.
Peter Lane and Grace Turner, June.
Abishai Washburn and Sally Sturdevant, July.
Capt. Daniel Lothrop and Lucy Gilbert, August.
Lewis Turner and Hannah P. Collier, July.
Henry Gilbert and Mehitabel Morse, July.
James Wing and Mary Richmond, October.
Samuel Jennings, Jr., and Phebe Morton, December.
John Wing of Wayne and Mary Burgess, October.
Daniel Lindsay and Jane Gilbert, October.
John Gould and Olive Andrews of Buxton, February.
George Foss and Anne Pettingill of Wayne, November.
John Foster and Priscilla Gilbert, October.

William Stinchfield and Sally Canwell, November.
Jonathan Gordon of Chesterville and Sarah Pettingill, November.

1809.

William Robinson of Lisbon and Keziah Andrews, January.
Caleb Wing and Joanna Gilbert, February.
Nathan Randell and Susanna Creach, March.
Warren Drake and Melinda Lothrop, April.
William Turner, Jr., and Hannah Tibbets, June.
Ebenezer Libby and Sally Foster, June.
Joseph Pettingill and Alice Allen of Greene, July 4.
Thomas Drinkwater of Livermore and Priscilla George, July.
William Brewster and Christiana Briggs of Greene, August.
Nathan Morse and Clarissa Sylvester of Greene, November.
Edwin Adams and Chloe Gilbert, August.
James Torry and Polly Joselin, August.
Joseph Freeman and Anne Judkins, October.
John Mower, Jr., of Greene and Mehitable Andrews, October.
Charles Grandison Gilbert and Martha Day, December.
John Francis and Patience Parcher, November.
Nathan Keith of Winslow and Harry Nesbit, November.
James Foss and Mary McKinney of Scarborough, November.
Thomas Labree and Judith Ham of Greene, December.
Micajah Dudley and Experience Wing, January.

1810.

Sylvanus Hammond, Jr., of Wayne and Betsey Curtis, January.
Arbida Briggs of Greene and Olive Brewster, January.
John Richards and Polly Thompson, March.
Naphtali Mason and Molly Jepson, February.
Stephen Hutchinson and Asenath Drew Gilbert, July.
Solomon Lothrop and Sarah Lothrop, July.
Samuel Brown and Sarah Cushman of Turner, June.
Zachariah Parcher and Persis Pratt, July.
Hirah House and Clarissa Streeter, November.
Simeon Gould and Abigail Stuart, August.
Jonathan Morse and Jane Libby of Saco, August.
Philip Libby and Christiana Howe, August.
Codding Drake and Sally Gilbert, November.
Joshua Davis of Winthrop and Betsey Jennings, November.
Amos Woodman and Mary Bradbury of Buxton, November.
Hazaranan Draper of Livermore and Mrs. Ruth Lane, December.
Joshua Lane and Mehitable Brett, December.

1811.

Zebulun Stinchfield and Sally Stuart, January.
Alexander Jennings and Mary Lindsay, January.
Moses Collier and Catherine Taylor, January.
Charles Knap and Catherine Lindsay, February.
Isaac Collier and Mrs. Susannah Dyer, April.
William Carver and Jane Smith, of Greene, September.
William Sprague, Jr., of Greene and Martha Brewster, April.
George Gordon of Wayne and Lydia Pettingill, July.
John Walker and Eliza Snellen of Greene, August.
Thomas Libby and Joanna Turner, November.
Richard Crockett and Polly Gilbert, November.

1812.

Peter Robinson and Maria Chambers, colored, January.
James Labree and Hannah Stetson of Greene, February.
Joseph Whitney and Betsey Meanes, March.
Joseph Knapp, Jr., and Deborah Cushman, March.
Josiah Brown of Wayne and Betsy Paul, April.
Abner Brown of Greene and Rachel Murray, May.
Philip Williams of Turner and Sally Jennings, June.
Heber Kimball and Olive Tupper, June.
Amos Murray and Mary Sampson of Greene, May.
Joseph Fellows of Winthrop and Mary Durell, June.
Simeon Gould and Betsey Leadbetter, June.
Epharaim Woodman of Wilton and Sally Otis, July.
John Additon and Hannah Robbins, September.
David Ridley and Polly Gould, September.
Sylvester Jones of Turner and Lydia Sampson, July.
Caleb Wing and Desire Turner, August.
Lebbeus Curtis and Betsey Tibbetts, November.

1813.

Allen House and Charity Hammond, of Wayne, February.
Reuel Pettingill and Lydia Briggs of Greene, March.
John Shepard Carey of Paris and Phebe Lane, March.
William Gould and Olive Gould, April.
John Thompson and Polly Ramsdell, June.
James Drew Gilbert of Turner and Rebecca Day, July.
Robert Sampson and Nancy Meanes, December.
James Lindsay and Lydia Lane.
Simeon Turner and Deborah Libby of Saco, November.
Cyrus Boothby and Charity Chubbock, December.

1814.

Alson Lothrop and Huldah Richmond of Winthrop, January.
Josiah Turner and Elmira Smith of Greene, January.
Zachariah Perry of Wayne and Ruby Smalley, February.
Daniel Cuff and Temperance Swift, March.
Luther Leadbetter and Jemima Lane, March.
Joshua Campbell of Livermore and Nancy Carver, March.
Amos Phillips and Patty Howard of Livermore, March.
John Gray of Paris and Solomon Berry, March.
Perez S. Jennings and Joanna Lane, June.
Ebenezer Harmon of Wayne and Janette Pettingill, December.
Arcadus Pettingill and Polly Tribou, November.
James Leadbetter and Fanny Otis, July.
Thaddeus Foss and Jedidah Norris of Wayne, August.
Aaron Morse and Polly Brewster, August.
William Manes and Hannah Day, November.
Dr. Thomas W. Brigham and Aurelia Howard, October.
Joseph Turner and Hannah Pettingill of Greene, October.
John Andrews and Polly Morse of Livermore, December.
Edward Doane of Hamden and Dorcas Gould, December.
James Taylor and Hannah Campbell of Livermore, December.
Nathaniel Richards and Jane Carle, December.
William Woodsum of Sumner and Rosannah Woodman, December.

1815.

Henry Austin and Hannah Lovejoy of Wayne, January.
Samuel Morse and Margaret Ayr of Buxton, February.
William Ramsdell and Anna Deane, March.
Howard Sylvester and Mehitable Wing, April.
William T. Gilbert and Anna Samson of Greene, October.
Robert Curtis of Greene and Deborah Curtis, April.
Samuel Gilbert and Anna Chase of Buckfield, April.
Bailey Gilbert and Sally B. Smart, April.
John Beals of Greene and Judith Jones, April.
David B. Creach and Betsey Ridley, April.
Josiah Curtis and Hannah Billington of Wayne, May.
Isaac Jones and Hannah Beals, August.
John Gould and Mrs. Ruth Powers of Buxton, September.
Jacob Bailey, Jr., and Lorana Nesbit, December.
John House and Nancy Perry of Wayne.

1816.

Zebulon Deane and Esther Millett of Turner, January.
Jerris Manwell and Phebe Bishop, April.
John Sturdivant of Wayne and Jerusha House, February.

Salmon Townsend of Turner and Deborah Samson, March.
Eleazer Carver, Jr., and Hannah Stinchfield, April.
Moses Collier and Hannah Turner, July.
David Morse and Hannah Day, April.
Nathanial Foy and Lydia Chute, September.
Alpheus Lane and Sally Foss, November.
Leavitt Lothrop and Betsy Lane, November.
Samuel Whitney and Salome Berry, November.
Thaddeus Foss and Jerusha Hanes, November.
John Ramsdell, Jr., and Mercy Rose, November.
Marcus Gilbert and Jane Samson of Greene, December.
John Mains and Abigail R. Day, July.

1817.

Thomas Lindsey and Olive Creach, March.
Josiah Gilbert and Bethany Day, March.
Zenas Vaughan of Livermore and Eunice Knapp, March.
Noah Blanchard of Freeman and Polly Knapp, March.
Henry Jennings and Hannah Lothrop, March.
John Perry of Wayne and Rhoda House, June.
William Walcott of New Sharon and Lydia Stetson, April.
Thomas Graffam and Lydia Bishop, May.
Ira Lamb and Polly Herrick, July.
John Keen of Greene and Polly Beals, December.
Eliab Alden of Greene and Eunice Collier, September.
Josiah Day and Mrs. Betsy Elms, November.

1818.

Stephen Foster, Jr., and Adeline Drake of Greene, April.
Jonas Harris and Mary Chambers, December.
William Mitchell and Abigail Morse of Turner, April.
Lewis Jennings and Nabby Foster, January.
Ichabod Carey, transient, and Persis Bishop, March.
Hannibal Farwell of Vassalborough and Alice Caswell, January.
Charles Bates and Betsy Merrill, February.
Solomon Davee of Hebron and Rachel Mason, March.
Stephen Boothby and Hepseba Tibbets of Wells, March.
Issachar Lane and Dorcas Lane, April.
John Jennings, Jr., and Hannah Carlton of Winthrop, May.
Samuel C. Hodgdon of Livermore and Betsey Lamb, April.
Stillman Harvey and Loria Prescott of Greene, April.
Gideon Owen and Amelia Hood of Turner, April.
Martin Mason and Mary Brown of Greene, April.
Daniel Burnham and Phebe Howe, July.
Jacob Chandler and Thankful Higgins, August.

Hazael Samson and Mary Wing, October.
Samuel Wood of Kingfield and Betsey Torrey, October.
Francis George, Jr., and Nancy Fish, August.
John Arno and Mrs. Miriam Hanes, August.
James Comings and Betsey Jack of Topsham, October.
Jeremiah Day and Polly Maines, October.
Ansel Lander of Kingfield and Bathsheba Cushman, November.

1819.

Enoch Tupper and Mehitable Robbins, November.
Isaac Bowley of New Sharon and Fanny Pratt, March.
Eliot Harper of Waldo and Lucy Pratt, March.
Caleb Carver and Bethiah Harvey, April.
Isaac Pettingill and Hannah Norris of Wayne.
William Robbins and Sally House, September.
Peter Colburn of Sumner and Rebecca Mason, October.
Joshua Ramsdell and Rebecca Thompson of Buckfield, November.

1820.

William Birt of Turner and Eunice Murray, March.
Zopher Deane and Deborah Robbins, January.
George Gordon of Wayne and Ruth Pettingill, January.
Charles Merrill of Turner and Elizabeth Freeman, January.
James Lamb, Jr., and Lillis Fish, March.
Nathaniel House, Jr., and Mary Parcher, March.
Joshua Tupper and Lucy Donham, May.
John Parcher and Matilda Pratt, July.
Joseph Gould, Jr., of Wayne and Hannah H. Libby, May.
James L. Bishop and Lois Whiting, November.
Jabez Leadbetter of Wayne and Lucretia Howard, November.
Oliver Cushman and Anice Lander, November.
John Melvin of Chesterville and Eunice Gould, November.
Caleb Carver and Augusta Copeland, November.
Warren L. Mitchell and Julia Gilbert, November.
Merrick Lamb and Eunice Washburn of Greene, December.
Edward Jones and Fanny Lane, December.
John Mason and Parmealia Soper of Chesterville, December.

1821.

Isaac Beals, Jr., and Lydia Briggs of Greene, January.
Thomas Additon and Anna Beals, January.
Joseph S. Dunham and Mercy Robbins, February.
Joseph Leavitt of Livermore and Judith Jones, March.
Levi Bates and Hannah Bailey, March.

Archibald Lindsey and Susanna Turner, November.
Ambrose Brown and Cynthia Phillips, June.
Zebulon Libby of Greene and Jane Turner, June.
Daniel Greene and Hannah Phelps of Buckfield, June.
Stephen Knapp and Sally Gott, August.
John Hatch and Sarah Pettingill of Lewiston, August.
Ira Sampson and Susan Gilbert, August.
Robert Lindsey and Vesta Merrill of Turner, August.
Samuel Maloon of Greene and Lucretia Wheeler, September.
Water Boothby and Betsey Ayer, October.
Israel Herrick and Abigail Lamb, February.
Jira Fish, Jr., and Mrs. Mary Mason, December.

1822.

Col. Walter Blaisdell of Lewiston and Ruby Additon, January.
William Elms and Loisania Shaw of Greene, February.
Isaac Mason and Eliza Donham of Hebron, February.
Abiel Bishop and Lydia Perry of Wayne, March.
Marshall Pratt of Greene and Martha Freeman, March.
Nathan Stetson and Abigail Pettingill, April.
Zebulon Stinchfield and Betsey Linscott of Chesterville.
Thomas Francis, Jr., and Alice Lothrop.
Thomas Haines and Lydia Howe, July.
Samuel Wing of Livermore and Lucinda George, June.
Stephen Rackley and Abigail Lane.
Andrew Cushman, Jr., and Sally King.
Simeon Foss and Betsey Livermore of Livermore.
Stephen Foy of Livermore and Elizabeth Bishop, August.
Edwin Turner and Anna Day, September.
Daniel Harvey and Mehitable Gott of Wayne, September.
John Lane and Vesta Phillips of Greene, March.
Robert Crummit and Mary Ann Foster, November.
Benjamin Berry and Abigail Lothrop, December.
Joseph Richmond of Greene and Anna Bailey, December.

1823.

Luther L. Howard and Rhoda Mitchell, March.
Daniel Foard and Jemima Bridgham of Winthrop, March.
Zachary Carey and Miriam Morse of Hebron, April.
Warren Studifant of Wayne and Charlotte Maines, May.
James Roberts and Elizabeth Chandler, December.
John Whiting, Jr., and Patience Bailey of Greene, July.
Charles Knapp and Hannah Lindsey, June.
John D. Millett and Axah Rose.
Levi Gilbert and Ruth Robbins, August.

Benjamin Beals of Dexter and Caroline Leonard, August.
Benjamin Ridley and Eliza Jenkins of Wayne, August.
David Lane and Lydia Brewster, November.
Zebulon Stinchfield and Keziah Freeman, September.
John Burnham and Elliance Richards, November.
Elijah Gott of Wayne and Polly Stinchfield, December.
Alvin Lane and Lucy Mitchell, December.
Jirah Fish and Joanna Irish of Turner, November.
Ansel Fish and Sarah Fish, December.
Salmon Brewster and Betsey Shaw of Greene, December.
John Drought of Livermore and Adeline Foss, December.
Marcus Gilbert and Miriam Coburn of Greene, December.

1824.

James Campbell of Livermore and Malinda George, March.
Harvey Bates and Nancy G. Rand of Monmouth, February.
Cyrus Bishop and Seviah Maxim of Wayne, March.
Martin Bates and Joanna Curtis, March.
Josiah Moulton and Olive Lane, March.
Almond Smith of Durham and Diana Turner, May.
Seth Fish, Jr., and Deborah Fish.
Oliver P. Frost and Esther M. Jennings, November.
Thomas Lothrop and Mrs. Mehitable Lane of Paris, September.
Nathaniel Walton of Wayne and Caroline Fish, September.
Charles Phillips of Greene and Olive Leonard, September.
Charles Bates and Hannah Lindsey, October.
Samuel B. Murray and Zebiah Deane, November.
William Gott, Jr., of Wayne and Ruth Gould, November.
Lewis Pettingill and Olive Fish, December.
David Higgins and Abigail Brown of Livermore, December.
Samuel Norris of Livermore and Lydia Higgins, December.
Jesse Lane and Charlotte Jones, December.
Isaac Jennings and Lucy Wentworth of Lisbon.
David Cary and Louisa Lothrop, December.
Seth Fish and Abigail Carver, December.

1825.

Asa Porter of Hamden and Dorcas Doane, January.
Levi Morrell of Sumner and Olive Woodman, March.
Eliphalet Loton Smart and Susan Robbins, March.
Joseph Bishop, Jr., and Jemima Norris of Wayne, April.
George Emery of Greene and Chloe Additon, November.
David House and Hannah B. Foster, April.
Asa Rose, Jr., and Tabitha Millet, October.
Simeon Foss and Sarah Ellen Norris, Wayne, July.

Thomas Owens and Betsey Bates, July.
Ezra Leadbetter and Sally Woodman, September.
Samuel Lothrop and Sally Records of Greene, October.
Samuel Elder of Buxton and Miranda Parcher, October.
Oren Whitman of Turner and Deborah C. Jennings, December.
John S. Carey and Aphia S. Bolster of Paris, November.
Zachariah Perry and Jane House, November.
Nelson Rose and Betsey Brown, November.
Salmon Elms and Jane Berry, November.
Luther Robbins and Susan A. Lothrop, December.

1826.

Luther Ramsdell and Achsah Pratt, March.
Jonathan Bartlett of Montville and Fanny Leadbetter, January.
Addison Martin of Guilford and Lydia Otis, January.
Luther Robbins and Susan A. Lothrop, December.
Allen Wing and Julia Ann Chandler of Monmouth, January.
Alvin Leavitt of Turner and Susan Deane, April.
Joshua P. Lamont of Bath and Betsey L. Mitchell, May.
Isaac Pratt and Abigail Parcher of Chesterville, April.
Elisha H. Sampson and Sylvia Gurney of Winthrop, September.
Sullivan Lothrop and Susan Bigelow of Bluefield, June.
Abial Bishop and Dorcas Lindsey, July.
Daniel Parcher and Clarissa Berry, July.
William Fish, Jr., and Lydia Reed, August.
Walter Foss and Dorcas Morrison of Wayne, August.
Benjamin Woodman and Joanna Leadbetter, August.
Amos Berry and Mary Curtis, August.
Morgan Brewster and Hannah Robinson of Greene, September.
Ammi Smith of Greene and Cyrene Bisbee, September.
Josiah Moulton and Lorinda Lane, September.
Henry A. Gilbert and Christinia Alden of Greene, October.
Jacob Sampson and Ruth Collins of Litchfield, October.
Ephraim Maxim of Wayne and Mrs. Susan Howard, November.
Stillman Moulton and Esther Foss, November.
Ephraim Foss and Harriet Townsend of Minot, December.

1827.

Abram Wheeler and Mahala Mitchell of Vienna, February.
Joseph Mitchell, Jr., and Hannah Robb of Bath, January.
Dodivah Harmond of Livermore and Phebe Harmond, February.

Hazel Rose of Greene and Betsey P. Turner, February.
Lincoln Curtis and Polly Perry, March.
Lorenzo Sylvester and Sarah Leavitt of Turner, March.
Ruel Foss and Polly Lothrop, June.
Joseph Metcalf of Hollis and Betsey Gould, October.
Ezekiel Bates and Sobrina Bates, May.
William Pettingill, Jr., and Eunice Day, May.
Ansel Turner and Lorana Francis, November.
Amasa W. Hall of Livermore and Jerusha Pratt, June.
Rufus Ramsdell and Olive Bailey of Greene, October.
Myrick Welch and Fanny Freeman, September.
Joshua House and Mrs. Lydia Bishop, November.
Ammi Woodman and Hannah Lane of Fayette, December.
David Wheeler, Jr., and Betsey Mitchell of Vienna.

1828.

James Keenan of Monmouth and Lovina Howe, March.
Charles Haws of Monmouth and Roxanna Turner, June.
Greenfield Rose of Greene and Roxanna Southard.
Rowland B. Howard and Eliza Otis, February.
Warren Howard and Mrs. Rhoda Howard, February.
William B. Davis and Weltha Dyer.
Davis Lane and Harriet Hayward of Readfield, April.
Benjamin Richmond of Greene and Mary Bailey, March.
Alpheus Lane of Wayne and Betsey Stinchfield.
Joseph Graves of Sebec and Anna Collier, May.
Joseph Frost and Mary Carver.
Joseph Mitchell and Hannah Foster of Topsham, May.
Joseph Scammon of Sangerville and Mrs. Esther Foss, June.
Jonas P. Lee and Anna Otis, July.
Neazer Dailey, Jr., of Livermore and Sally Pratt, July.
John Gould, 2d, and Mrs. Ann Foss.
Nathaniel Daggett and Desire Fish, September.
James Bishop and Jane Howe.
Jesse Wadsworth of Livermore and Phebe Additon, September.
George Gould and Hannah Lothrop.

1829.

Isaac D. Drake of Minot and Sally Woodman, January.
Columbus Jennings and Mary Sumner of Greene, January.
Dr. Cyrus Knapp of Winthrop and Susan C. Francis, January.
Ezra W. Fish and Sarah Mason, January.
Daniel Crossman of Greene and Mrs. Nancy Dennison, February.
Nelson Gilbert and Rebecca Sampson, April.

Isaiah Beals and Lucy Bailey, October.
Ezra Berry and Rachel Nichols, June.
John Higgins of Starks and Rachel Foss, June.
Archibald Leavitt of Turner and Polly Deane, May.
Azel Woodman and Sarah Ann Merrill of Minot, June.
David Sturtivant and Betsey Burnham.
Seth Fish and Rosilla Leadbetter.
Howard Lindsey and Caroline Lindsey, October.
Daniel Robbins, Jr., and Mercy Mason.
Calvin Fish and Cynthia Fish, November.
Amos Thoms, Jr., of Standish and Betsey Boothby, November.
Levi Dunham and Hannah Mitchell, December.
Lewis Soule and Mary Roberts of Wayne, December.
Amos Phillips and Naomi Brown, December.

1830.

Silas Coburn of Greene and Drusilla Caswell, January.
Salmon Cary and Ann Turner, March.
Isaac Boothby, Jr., and Jane Graves, April.
Benjamin Franklin Howard and Philena Gould.
Hirah Fish and Olive Leach, June.
Isaac Jennings and Lucy Stevens of Greene, June.
Eleazer Carver and Persis Lindsey, July.
Arunta Wheeler and Sally Berry of Vienna.
Edward Lucas of Dexter and Betsey Beals, October.
Job Caswell and Elvira Sprague of Greene.

1831.

Allen Freeman and Jane Leadbetter of Greene, February.
Seth Millett and Almira Foss.
Wheaton Bates and Lydia S. Bates, February.
Robert Elms and Mary Bailey of Greene, February.
Ebenezer Cobb of Livermore and Isabella Millett, March.
Samuel Boothby and Sally Leadbetter, April.
Isaac Leadbetter and Almira Sampson, April.
Ebenezer Wheeler and Agnes Beals of Scarborough.
John Stanley of Winthrop and Allura Foss.
Jacob Wheeler and Cordelia Day, June.
Francis George and Freelove Howe, July 4.
Spencer Trask and Hannah Carpenter.
William H. Jones of Bridgton and Mary Sampson, September.
Daniel Hinkley and Mehitable Sumner, September.
Alexander Day and Nancy Maloon, September.
Cyrus Leavitt, Jr., Turner and Saphrona Sylvester, September.

Jarvus Frizell of Wayne and Eunice Robbins.
Charles Gott of Wayne and Jane Foss, October.
Franklin B. Leonard and Almira Benson of Bridgewater, Mass., October.
Daniel Irish of Buckfield and Hannah Foster.
Sullivan Lothrop and Abigail V. Jennings.

1832.

Oscar D. Turner and Rosilla A. Howard, January.
Micajah Dunham and Salome Lincoln, February.
William Turner and Elvira Bradford of Turner, March.
Abiel D. Morton and Eliza B. Davis of Sidney, March.
Jeremiah Curtis and Christina Berry, March.
Daniel Randall of Fayette and Eliza Ann Burgess.
Charles Elms and Nancy Mower of Greene, March.
Dr. Horace A. Barrows and Irene Bearce of Hebron, March.
George W. George and Mary Ann Gilbert, March.
Uriah Foss and Mary Leadbetter, March.
Elliot S. Lamb and Julia Ann Stanley.
John A. True of Livermore and Martha Parcher, June.
George Lothrop and Mrs. Ruby Blaisdell, July.
Ansel Turner and Matilda Francis, August.
George Beals and Almira Luce of New Vineyard, September.
Peltiah Knapp and Mary Rann of Livermore, August.
Levi Key of Greene and Sally Morse, October.
Rufus Ramsdell and Hannah Draper of Livermore, December.
Samuel Erskine of Bristol and Mary Cushman, December.
John L. Hoit of Monmouth and Sarah K. Fales, December.
James Lamb and Olive Jennings, December.
Stillman L. Howard and Julia Ann Turner, March.

1833.

Sans Bailey and Nancy Mayhew of Foxcroft, January.
Marcus Caswell and Anna K. Sampson, February.
Seth Millett and Eliza Leadbetter, February.
Thomas Day of Westley and Sobrina Leathers.
William P. Millett and Charlotte Lamb, March.
James W. L. Mitchell and Rebecca D. Foster.
Samuel Francis and Sally True of Livermore.
Elias Lane and Mrs. Abi Brown, June.
Daniel L. Jones of Brighton and Semyntha Lane.
Anson Gott and Eunice Merrill of Livermore, July.
Welcome Beals of Turner and Octavia Gould, August.
Joseph Elms and Rebecca Leathers, August.

Joshua S. Turner and Betsey Lothrop, September.
John Fabian, Jr., and Julia M. Jackson, October.
Cypren S. Howe and Mary B. Graffam.
Giddings Lane and Cassandra Benson of Bridgewater, Mass., November.
George K. Stinchfield and Jane Libby, December.
Warren Foster and Arvilla Gilbert, December.
Alonzo Sylvester and Rhoda W. Caswell of Turner, December.
Ebenezer True of Turner and Olive Parcher, December.
Almond Curtis and Charlotte Mitchell, Vienna, December.
William Irish of Sumner and Aurelia Foster, February.

1834.

Ira Sampson and Patience Fish, February.
Calvin Briggs of Greene and Lydia Pettingill, March.
Wheaton Bates and Eleanor Elms, February.
Barnabas Howard, Jr., and Eunice Gould.
Jonathan Jewell of Bangor and Susan Lane, May.
Foster D. Wentworth and Aurelia Rose, June.
Phillips Turner and Mary L. Howard, July.
John Berry of Vienna and Rebecca Wheeler, September.
Isaac Stinchfield and Abigail Knapp, September.
Moses Harris of Greene and Joanna Coffin, September.
John Berry of Greene and Sarah Ramsdell, October.
Calvin Lane and Dulcena Lothrop, November.
William A. Gould and Mary Jane Elden of Buxton, October.
Charles Berry and Eunice Libby, November.
Caleb R. Sumner and Sophia Curtis, December.
Seth Rose and Caroline Rose, December.

1835.

Christopher G. Foss of Bangor and Olive Lothrop, January.
Moses Basford of Livermore and Lydia S. Lothrop, January.
George Lothrop and Huldah A. Gilmore, March.
Amos Thoms and Phebe Lamb of Standish, March.
George Harmon and Jedida Foss, May.
Peleg B. Caswell and Mary Q. Robbins of Greene, May.
Ebenezer Hodgdon of Turner and Mrs. Desire Daggett, August.
Jeremiah Mountford of Monmouth and Deborah Shaw.
William Boothby and Caroline Pinkham of Wayne.
Dodivah Ham of Monmouth and Ann H. Turner, October.
Abiah Day and Gracia L. Curtis, August.
Lewis P. True of Bangor and Jemima L. Foss, August.
Josiah Skillin of Albion and Orilla Sylvester.

Joshua Millett and Sophronia Howard of Bridgewater, Mass.
Alexander Erskine, Jr., of Bristol and Adaline Cushman, October.
Joseph Bates and Lovina Cannon.
Jonathan Thompson of Monmouth and Louisa C. Turner, October.
Cyrus B. Felch of Lisbon and Melvina J. Turner, November.
Freemon Coburn of Greene and Hannah T. Sumner, November.
William G. Turner and Ann C. Robb, November.
David H. Millett of Turner and Levana True, December.
Francis D. Millett and Elethere True, December.

1836.

Sanford Gilbert and Adeline Day, January.
Joshua Fabyens and Mary Ham of Monmouth, January.
Francis George and Tabitha Besse of Wayne, January.
Ralph Ames of Canton and Elizabeth Phelps, January.
Jethro Sprague of Phippsburg and Mrs. Hannah Leathers, February.
Veranus Lothrop and Esther Lane, March.
Benjamin R. Deane and Betsey Alden of Turner, August.
Francis L. Safford of Turner and Polly F. Millett, September.
Noah P. Durrell and Lieurana Rose.
James Clark of Wales and Irena Pettingill, December.
William C. Gordon and Diana Smith of Livermore, December.
Daniel B. Larrabee and Sophrona Larrabee of Parkman, November.
Benjamin Dunham and Lucinda Day, December.

1837.

Warren Fish and Irena Andrews of Turner, February.
Enoch Fish and Eliza Kimball of Turner, Feb. 12.
Dennis R. Gilbert and Mehitable Foster, April.
Reed B. Wheeler and Sally B. Parcher, April 8.
Amos Bishop and Eliza Ann Burgess, April.
Elisha D. Gould and Susan E. Gould, July 4.
Abner Burnham and Rhoda Holloway, July.
Alvin Foss and Cornelia B. Howard, July 30.
John L. Perry of Turner and Almedia Sampson, August.
Seth Rose, Jr., and Anna Brown, August.
Ebenezer Mason and Mrs. Hannah Norris of Livermore, Aug. 26.
Enos Brown and Clarissa Augusta Gilbert of Turner.

Joseph Turner and Mrs. Esther Scammon of Bloomfield, Oct. 23.
William Ham of Monmouth and Polly Turner, October.
Caleb S. Gilbert and Louisa Torsey of Winthrop, November.
Josiah Day, 2d, and Anna Ricker of Greene, November.
Job D. Shepherd of Fairfield and Ann Wing.
Seth Millett and Lucy S. Cobb, November.

1838.

William G. Turner and Mary S. Loring, Jan. 14.
William P. Millett and Augusta Rose, Jan. 14.
Henry A. Torsey of Winthrop and Judith B. Day, Feb. 3.
John Merrill of Durham and Rachel M. Morse, Jan. 21.
Orlando F. D. Blake of Monmouth and Mary Pettingill, Feb. 6.
David S. Hardy of Wilton and Susan B. Daggett, Feb. 5.
William Moulton and Mrs. Betsey Walker of Wilton, March 10.
David Basford and Elizabeth Coffin, March 19.
Ebenezer Mann, Jr., and Lucitta Keen of Greene, March 26.
Harrison Gould and Nancy Lane, March 26.
Edward T. Gilbert and Deborah Turner, April 2.
Leonard Foster and Rizilla A. Williams of Turner, April 18.
Samuel Leadbetter, Jr., and Calista Knapp, May 6.
Loring Foss and Jane Gott of Wayne, May 6.
Charles Gordon and Florinda Churchill of Monmouth, May 14.
Francis Millett and Sarah E. Noyes of Abington, Mass., June 24.
Horace Gould of Winthrop and Susan Lane, June 6.
Peltiah Libby and Betsey Carver, June 17.
Thomas Day and Mary P. Hilman, Aug. 29.
Jason Carver and Mary Libby, Sept. 2.
Charles Walton of Chesterville and Rosannah Leadbetter, Nov. 10.
Stephen W. Sylvester of Greene and Hannah Leadbetter, Nov. 14.
Isaac Plummer of Wales and Lois Freeman, Dec. 27.

1839.

James Stinchfield, Jr., and Clarissa S. Gould, Jan. 20.
John F. Gilmore and Betsy Cushman, Feb. 25.
Harrison Piper of Portland and Cynthia Turner, March 17.
Stephen Boothby and Hannah H. Page of Belgrade, March 18.
Rev. Wilson C. Rider and Catherine Millett, May 20.

John R. Yale and Almeda Owen, June 15.
John S. Loring and Lydia Turner, Aug. 18.
John Gould and Mrs. Charlotte Swift of Milton, Mass., Sept. 16.
Stephen Libby and Mary Ann Stinchfield, Sept. 29.
James L. House and Esther Lovejoy of Fayette, Sept. 21.
Leonard M. Fish and Catherine Gray of Embden, Dec. 14.
Eleazer Carver, 3d, and Sarah A. Gray of Embden. Dec. 14.
Matthias Hanscom of Monmouth and Florenia Keen, Dec. 16.
George W. George and Clarissa Leighton of Hartford, Dec. 14.
Isaac Cushman and Dorcas H. Loring of Pownal, Dec. 23.

1840.

Lloyd Gould and Lydia Arvilia Howard, Feb. 14.
Peter Lane, Jr., and Lucretia P. Howard, Jan. 28.
Barnabas Davee and Alice Stinchfield, Feb. 10.
George Curtis and Nancy E. Rowe of New Gloucester, Feb. 10.
Russell Lamb and Aphia Gould, March 2.
Ruggles Sylvester and Harriet N. Howard, March 2.
Lemuel H. Cumner and Olive C. Knapp, March 22.
William H. Foster and Harriet L. Curtis, March 21.
Solomon L. Lothrop and Hannah Turner, April 20.
Zenas Rogers of Hanover, Mass., and Ruth C. Sumner, Aug. 16.
Amasa H. Phillips and Susan Morse of Livermore, Sept. 12.
Jesse Mitchell and Alvira Knapp, Sept. 12.
Samuel Briggs of Minot and Drusilla L. Turner, Aug. 27.
Greenwood C. Gordon and Hannah Stinchfield, Sept. 4.
James B. Willey and Clarissa Lamb, Sept. 23.
William Carver, Jr., and Celia Cobb of Turner, Sept. 26.
James Jones of Turner and Almedia Owen, Oct. 24.
Beniah Taylor of Farmington and Sarah Foss, Dec. 20.

1841.

Elbridge G. Rose of Greene and Almedia Jane Brown, Jan. 18.
Obadiah Millett and Eliza Safford of Turner, March 1.
Nathan Timberlake of Livermore and Adelia Millett, March 15.
Josiah Moulton and Sarah Brown of Mercer, May 1.
Daniel Foss and Nancy F. Moulton of Wayne, May 10.
Bradbury Sylvester and Lydia A. Bean of Wayne, June 23.
Ebenezer Cushman of Paris and Celia Sampson, Aug. 13.
Loren Parcher and Hannah G. Hunton of Livermore, July 25.
Wilson Gilbert and Catharine Day, Nov. 1.

Uriah Libby and Betsey Hallowell, Nov. 25.
Samuel P. True and Ruth Carver. Nov. 26.
John S. Loring and Joanna Wing, Nov. 30.

1842.

George Whitney and Phœbe Jennings, Jan. 1.
Melvin Berry and Amanda F. Turner, March 7.
Levi Foss and Emeline Leadbetter, April 9.
Elias L. Lothrop and Jane L. Morse, April 24.
Alson Lothrop of Jay and Orissa Lothrop, June 12.
Zopher D. Ramsdell and Almeda Alden, July 3.
James Coffin, Jr., and Nancy Bradford of Farmington, Aug. 7.
Warren Mower of Greene and Louisa Jane Gilmore, Sept. 4.
James G. Lindsey and Ann Graffam, Sept. 11.
Stephen Safford of Turner and Lydia Millett, Sept. 25.
Charles Gott and Annie Wood of Norridgewock, Oct. 9.
Reuben H. Webster and Rozilla H. Morse, Oct. 16.
David L. Page of Belgrade and Aurelia Parcher, Oct. 16.
Samuel Boothby of Livermore and Fanny G. Foss, Oct. 23.
Egbert Griswold and Eliza H. Wentworth of Webster, Oct. 30.
John Keen of Turner and Lydia P. L. Mitchell, Nov. 9.
Peltiah Gould, Jr., and Rossa H. Leadbetter of Wayne, Nov. 20.
Washington Hanscome of Monmouth and Betsey E. Day, Nov. 29.
John Dunham of Wales and Sarah Arno, Dec. 5.
John N. Gilbert and Silence H. Keen, Dec. 12.
Arvida B. Pettingill and Alvira Ann Sumner, Dec. 18.

1843.

Alpheus Foss and Abigail J. Hall of Boston, Mass., Jan. 22.
Alvin Lane and Mrs. Hannah L. Dunham, Jan. 29.
Nathaniel Moulton of New Bedford, Mass., and Elvira J. Deane, March 19.
Alanson W. Daggett and Ruth B. Taylor, March 19.
Elbridge G. Knowlton of Nobleborough and Mary Ann Carver, April 8.
Joseph R. Gilbert and Mary Ann Crummett, April 30.
Rev. Samuel H. Leighton and Fidelia Williams of Easton, Mass., April 30.
Samuel Fuller, Jr., of Livermore and Louisa Carver, April 23.
Melvin H. Carver and Phebe C. Drake of Lowell, Mass., June 4.
Thaddeus R. Foss of Winthrop and Clarissa J. Sturtivant, June 4.

John Pettingill and Maria Arno, June 25.
Ebenezer Stinchfield, Jr., and Hannah Lincoln, Aug. 27.
Niah Hinkley of Lisbon and Clarissa Day, Oct. 21.
Aranda Gilbert and Diana T. Wing, Nov. 12.
Thomas S. Carver and Elizabeth Nichols, Nov. 25.
John Millett and Mrs. Betsey Daily of Livermore, Dec. 31.
Atwood B. Bumpus of Hebron and Betsey F. Millett, Dec. 13.

1844.

Archibald L. Knapp and Jane White of Dixfield, Feb. 20.
Loring Foster and Ellen Crummett of Lowell, Mass., April 9.
Ormand T. Wing and Octavia Ann Brewster, April 13.
Stephen R. Deane and Alvira Pratt, April 28.
Phillips Pettingill and Mrs. Joan Harris, May 18.
Joseph Frost and Florentine Rose, June 9.
William H. Hallowell and Eliza Ann Fish, July 21.
Major John Carver and Mrs. Martha Smith, July 21.
Daniel Moulton of Chesterville and Mary Day, Aug. 11.
Jonathan Sturgis of Vassalboro and Mrs. Polly Foss, Aug. 11.
John Coffin and Lois Townsend of Auburn, Sept. 3.
Joseph R. Curtis and Louisa J. Sumner, Sept. 15.

1845.

Cyrenus Pettingill and Amy Bates, Jan. 10.
Daniel Moulton and Mary Day, March 31.
Jason Pettingill and Lucetta Gordon of Wayne, March 31.
Aruna Beals and Mary Coffin, April 20.
Benjamin Grant, Jr., and Columbia Phillips, April 20.
Jeremiah Day, Jr., and Betsey Libby, June 15.
Nathan Coffin and Aureiia Gott of Wayne, Sept. 14.
Moses Marshall of Fayette and Hannah Amanda Foster, Sept. 29.
Bemis Lamb and Eunice F. Lane, Oct. 19.
Asa Libby and Joanna D. Fish, Nov. 16.
Charles B. Collier and Clara Mitchell, Nov. 16.
Oliver Fabyan and Susan Tucker of North Conway, N. H., Nov. 25.
Leonard Quimby of Turner and Dorcas L. Turner, Dec. 7.
Samuel M. Parcher and Ann B. Day, Dec. 21.
Charles A. Thomes and Abigail C. Mitchell of Lowell, Mass., Dec. 28.
Amos Thomes and Rosalinda Sylvester, Dec. 28.

1846.

George W. Treat of Canton and Bethia Carver, Jan. 24.
Joseph M. Niles of Lisbon and Nancy Trask, Feb. 1.
James Peare of Turner and Betsey F. Cole, Feb. 15.

Gustavus Gilbert and Hannah L. Ballou of Turner, March 8.
Levi C. Littlefield of Turner and Sarah H. Grant, April 5.
Josiah Day, Esq., and Mrs. Judith Dwinal, May 12.
Leonard Rose and Mrs. Eliza Turner, May 16.
Morgan Brewster, Jr., and Susan Robinson of Greene, Sept. 20.
Samuel Crummett and Mrs. Melinda Jordan of Monmouth, Sept. 27.
Isaac Howe and Roxanna Fish, Oct. 4.
James D. Gilbert, Jr., of Turner and Adeline Curtis, Nov. 11.
Luther B. Gilbert of Greene and Penelope Rose, Nov. 1.
William G. Knapp and Cynthia Ripley, Nov. 8.
Josiah F. Bradbury of Auburn and Mrs. Druzilla L. Berry, Nov. 22.
Davis F. Lothrop and Caroline S. Morse, Nov. 22.

1847.

Benjamin R. Woodsom and Pamelia W. Leadbetter, Jan. 17.
Isaac S. Daly of Livermore and Augusta Carver, Jan. 17.
Daniel Crossman, Jr., of Greene and Harriet Amanda Gilbert, Feb. 7.
Greenlief N. Keen and Angeline Andrews of Minot, March 8.
Samuel Richards and Parutha Henderson, April 4.
Nicholar Loring and Phebe Millett, April 4.
Joseph Ellms and Ann Griffith of Livermore, April 23.
Jonas H. Torsey of Winthrop and Druzilla Gilbert, May 2.
Everett H. Bridgham and Sally Ann Worthing of China, July 2.
Ormand Carey and Almira Jane Jennings, August 1.
Perez Loring and Nancy Barton of Poland, Aug. 8.
James M. Moulton of Wayne and Novella Lindsey, Aug. 22.
Stephen W. Grant and Columbia Fish, Sept. 19.
John H. Otis and Helen M. Worthing of China, Sept. 26.
Harrison Gould and Sarah Stinchfield, Oct. 11.
Oliver P. Frost and Susan Stevens of Greene, Oct. 17.
Asa Knapp and Mrs. Sarah Thompson of Kingfield, Nov. 28.
Charles Peare of Turner and Martha E. Grant, Dec. 5.

1848.

Davis Francis and Rosamond Lane, Jan. 3.
Augustus L. Foss and Caroline E. Lothrop, Jan. 16.
Alphonso P. Richmond of Turner and Roxanna Owen, Feb. 14.
Russell Carver and Elsie Ann Banks of Saco, Feb. 26.
Samuel Hanson of Mount Vernon and Harriet A. Bates, April 2.

Thomas S. Harlow of Canton and Jannett Carver, May 7.
Charles Jones of Livermore and Elizabeth M. Jones, May 21.
Calvin Campbell of Jay and Jane Carver, May 21.
Andrew Mason of Augusta and Hannah A. More, June 11.
Eliab Sturtevant of Charlestown, Mass., and Lorania Parcher, June 29.
Samuel P. Torsey of Winthrop and Clarissa A. C. Morse, Aug. 19.
Lloyd Carver and Sarah Edgcombe of Livermore, Oct. 1.
Isaac T. Boothby and Louisa M. Spear of Standish, Oct. 9.
Daniel A. Lane of Manchester, Conn., and Pamelia Jennings, Oct. 9.
Joshua Lothrop and Mary Jane Campbell, Nov. 5.
Elbridge Francis of Turner and Cynthia D. Millett, Dec. 31.
Samuel J. Bonney of Winthrop and Allura L. Larrabee, Dec. 31.
Joshua H. Sumner and Clorinda Ann Maloon, Dec. 31.

1849.

Jason P. Fogg of Monmouth and Hannah J. Libby, April 22.
Silas Fish and Susan D. Millett, May 19.
William B. Curtis, 2d, and Augusta W. Sumner, June 19.
Job C. Dennen of Greene and Martha J. Brewster, July 1.
Oakes A. Jennings and Martha M. Stetson of Nobleboro, Aug. 12.
John R. Libby of Monmouth and Evaline Keene, Aug. 19.
Samuel M. Parcher of Winthrop and Clarissa Day, Sept. 30.
Seth Howard and Amanda Additon, Oct. 28.
Ansel Curtis and Minerva L. White, Nov. 11.
Caleb H. Rose and Mary A. Page, Nov. 11.

1850.

Phineas Neal of Fayette and Amanda A. Carver, Feb. 17.
Lewis Churchill and Ruth Pettingill, Feb. 17.
John Packard, Jr., of Dover and Elizabeth Knapp, March 3.
Joshua Elder of Lewiston and Araminta Pettingill, Feb. 24.
Cyrus Alden of Auburn and Mrs. Charlotte Lane, March 10.
Abner P. Campbell of Bowdoinham and Olive S. Curtis, March 12.
Nemiah B. Bicknell of Boston, Mass., and Sarah Millett, April 15.
Lucius Andrews of Livermore and Sarah Moulton, April 21.
Ward H. Jennings and Almira Parcher, May 5.
Leonard C. Lothrop and Sarah L. Judkins of Fayette, April 28.
Henry C. Millett and Olive B. Rose, May 5.

Hartley Gray of Embden and Lovina Fish, July 21.
Charles Owen and Martha A. Adams of Litchfield, Aug. 12.
Azel Burnham and Rosannah Sturtevant, Aug. 12.
Benjamin F. Lane and Harriet Herrick, entered Sept. 8.
Gustavus A. Jennings and Elvira A. Jennings, Sept. 28.
Josiah L. F. Grant and Rebecca Rose, Sept. 29.
John H. Hanscom and Marinda J. Gilbert, Dec. 22.

1851.

John Keene, Jr., and Orrilla J. Ellms, Feb. 17.
Benjamin F. Howard and Fannie C. Gould, March 16.
Orison Leadbetter and Lucy L. Dunham, March 23.
Charles Towle of Gardiner and Eliza Carver, March 23.
Edmond S. Deane of Buckfield and Hannah S. Brown, March 23.
Valentine R. Bridgham and Mehitable C. Josselyn, March 23.
John F. Gray of Greene and Zilpha A. Rose, May 6.
Abner Curtis, Jr., and Mary H. Curtis, June 9.
William Frost and Elizabeth Lothrop, Aug. 3.
Granville Richmond and Eliza E. Owen, Sept. 21.
Joseph P. Johnson of Monmouth and Aurelia A. Stetson, Sept. 28.
Charles Brown of Carroll and Lydia Turner, Oct. 5.
Lorenzo P. Stetson of Greene and Lucy S. Bates, Nov. 2.
Nelson Rose and Emeline B. Proctor of Canton, Nov. 23.

1852.

Emery Foss of Wayne and Sarah E. Foss, Feb. 15.
George Bishop and Susan Lowell of Monmouth, Feb. 29.
Charles C. Sylvester and Hannah Sylvester, March 14.
Orson Lane and Susan E. Boothby, March 21.
Francis D. Millett and Lucina Phillips of Auburn, March 28.
Isaiah B. Additon and Eliza A. Jennings, April 25.
Jeremiah Sylvester and Rachel Brown, entered April 25.
Freedom W. Gould and Adelia Perley of Livermore, May 15.
Benjamin Turner and Harriet H. Lane, entered June 5.
Horace Herrick and Sophronia L. Palmer, entered June 24.
George B. Greenwood of Monmouth and Sarah F. Gould, entered Aug. 28.
Albert W. Sumner and Lucy A. Robbins, entered Sept. 13.
Arza G. Lothrop and Martha J. Ramsdell, entered Oct. 10.
Jessie R. Hall of Brunswick and Judith L. Gilbert, entered Nov. 1.
Jonathan Moulton of Wayne and Lucy M. Foss, entered Dec. 4.
Sylvanus Hammon of Greene and Sophrona Beals, entered Dec. 31.

1853.

John Lewis of Paris and Penelope Rose, entered March 27.
Isaac Cushman and Angeline Harvey of Winthrop, entered March 28.
Dana Goff of Auburn and Orintha H. Foss, entered June 3.
Melville C. Mower of Greene and Hannah L. Jennings, entered May 28.
Samuel P. True and Susan W. Stinchfield, entered June 29.
David S. Wilson of Hillsboro, N. H. and Laverna C. Thomas, entered Aug. 29.
Aruna B. Beals and Nancy E. Ridley of Jay, entered Aug. 30.
John D. Millett and Augusta Millett, entered Sept. 17.
Judson A. Lane and Ann H. Foss, entered Sept. 18.
Amos H. Woodward of Lowell, Mass., and Eunice F. Foss, entered Oct. 2.
Granville C. Carver and Margaret S. Moses of Standish, entered Oct. 8.
Ebenezer Stinchfield and Diodama Larrabee, entered Oct. 8.

1854.

William C. Lincoln and Mahala Bishop, Feb. 4.
Josiah C. Hammon of Greene and Ann M. Howe, Feb. 14.
Gilman Moulton and Mrs. Jane Carey, March 21.
James B. Walker of Turner and Prudence Dillingham, March 18.
Benjamin Swain of Wayne and Hannah W. Stinchfield, April 20.
Rev. Joseph Crehore of Bath and Ellen L. Mitchell, May 17.
Sumner Bailey of Turner and Sophrona Sylvester, June 5.
Calvin M. Rose and Annorille Proctor of Canton, July 18.
Charles S. Knapp and Vesta A. Sole, Oct. 2.
Charles W. Prescott of Monmouth and Elmira Mountford, Oct. 25.
Charles H. Lane and Sarah Turner, Nov. 12.
Patrick Maney and Mary Powers, Nov. 17.
John Turner and Elizabeth B. Manwell, Nov. 22.
Thomas C. Foss and Elizabeth L. Cobb, Dec. 12.

1855.

Leonard G. Sampson and Martha J. Hodgdon, Jan. 9.
Charles White and Adeline Bradford of Turner, Feb. 24.
Samuel Leadbetter and Mrs. Aurelia Bridgham, March 18.
Andrew J. Hinkley of Monmouth and Mary A. Newton, April 13.
Zopher Deane and Susannah Burnham, May 4.
Rowland A. Gilmore and Cynthia L. Lothrop, May 12.

Robert F. Wheeler and Rhoda E. Beals, July 28.
Isaiah Gifford of Albion and Cynthia W. Turner, Aug. 6.
Nathaniel Harris of Greene and Lydia Jane Curtis, Aug. 19.
Isaac A. Strout of Wales and Betsey A. Rose, Sept. 10.
Isaiah B. Keen and Eliza Jane Skillings of Strong, Sept. 23.
Sylvanus C. Merrill and Rosina Manwell, Oct. 14.
John Carver, 2d, and Mary Ann Packard, Oct. 19.
Isaac Ridley and Marva Keen of Palmyra, Oct. 20.
John Y. Merrill and Nancy Manwell, Oct. 28.
William H. Huskins and Sarah T. Pearl of Mt. Vernon, Dec. 19.
Charles C. Lane and Mary J. Lothrop, Dec. 24.
James Carver and Mary Fish, Dec. 31.

1856.

Roscoe G. Lindsey and Eliza Ann Berry, Jan. 16.
Sewall Stinchfield and Hannah E. Raymond of Wayne, Jan. 22.
William Wing and Francis A. Bates, Jan. 22.
Josiah Turner and Hannah E. Dunham, March 1.
David Grant and Tabitha R. Mitchell, March 26.
Amasa Wheeler and Rosine Harris, May 13.
Moses H. Mitchell (of Letter E) and Jane P. Knapp, June 3.
Horatio L. Williams and Betsey Boothby, June 4.
Benjamin Pearson of Abington, Mass., and Mary L. Hutchins, Sept. 5.
Sewall A. Allen of Greene and Lovisa Additon, Sept. 20.
Sturges N. Jennings and Martha A. Turner, Sept. 21.
John P. Hodsdon of Jay and Laura A. Curtis, Nov. 16.
Cylenus H. Bates and Mary H. Sturtevant of Monmouth, Dec. 17.
John C. Hammon of Livermore and Mary Bates, Dec. 28.

1857.

Benjamin F. Lewis of Paris and Nancy G. Rose, Jan. 14.
Jabez B. Gould of Monmouth and Olive E. Bates, April 20.
Rollin F. Jennings and Harriet S. Frost, April 22.
Rodolphus Jennings and Lenora M. Hosley, April 30.
John F. Jennings and Eliza A. Additon, April 30.
Ebenezer Stinchfield and Clarissa Judkins of East Livermore, May 26.
John Burnham, Jr., and Hannah Sturtevant, certified July 16.
Oren S. Bates and Tiley Lindsey, certified Aug. 15.
Salmon Brewster and Mrs. Laverna C. Gilmore of Wayne, certified Aug. 30.
Job C. Dennen and Harriet L. Berry, certified Sept. 19.

Russell S. Linscott of Boston, Mass., and Dorcas Ellen Foss, Oct. 25.
James A. Berry of Fayette and B. Jane Wheeler, Dec. 19.

1858.

Stephen Jones of Turner and Mrs. Celia Cushman, Feb. 1.
Thomas J. Additon and Rozilla Smart of Parkman, May 30.
John H. Johnson of Monmouth and Deborah J. Maloon June 5.
Oliver S. Gilbert and Lucia H. Turner, June 14.
John H. Bates and Jane B. Cook, June 17.
William A. Burnham and Lucinda A. Sturtevant, June 17.
John C. Keene and Josephine Gilbert, Sept. 12.
Edwin S. French of Turner and Lydia W. Leonard, Sept. 18.
George B. Lane and Viola A. Ramsdell, Oct. 24.
David E. Trask and Mary J. Bishop, Nov. 3.
Chessman Curtis and Prudence E. R. Gooch, Nov. 6.
John Burnham and Sarah Magna, Nov. 13.
Isaac H. Bean of Norridgewock and Rebecca Wheeler, Dec. 20.
William H. Francis and Ziporah Perley of Livermore, Dec. 25.

1859.

Adoniram J. Foss and Theressa M. Howard, Jan. 24.
Thornton Lyford of Boston and Emily Woodman, Jan. 31.
Barnabas Davee and Hannah L. Knapp, Feb. 16.
David R. Berry and Rhoda A. Knapp, Feb. 27.
Franklin S. Francis and Charlotte Millett, March 2.
Stephen R. Deane and Victoria H. Turner, April 2.
Ensign Otis and Laura B. Howard, April 30.
Abisha Sturtevant and Phebe Bates.
Robert S. Thomas of Greene and Helen A. Ballou, July 27.
Henry M. Brewster and Angela Bishop, Aug. 27.
Aaron Mower of Greene and Anna A. Rackley, Sept. 15.
George Burnham and Sophrona Sturtevant of Wayne, Sept. 7.
Amos Stetson of Wayne and Priscilla H. Smith, Sept. 17.
William J. Warren of Boston and Anna C. Turner, Sept. 24.
Wesley D. Wheeler and Dora H. Wardwell of Greene, Oct. 25.
Jeremiah P. H. Sullivan of Winthrop and Esther A. Carver, Nov. 4.
Orson Lane and Viora G. Boothby of Lewiston, Dec. 17.
Giddings L. Foss of Farmington and Cordelia Gould, Dec. 31.

1860.

Willard Lothrop and Emeline L. Boothby, Jan. 10.
John Beals and Mary H. Wilber of East Livermore, Jan. 26.
Alanson Rose of Greene and Mary G. Rose, Feb. 3.
Cyrus H. Tobin and Elizabeth A. Wigglesworth, Feb. 10.
Joel Fairbanks of Monmouth and Mrs. Achsa Ramsdell, Feb. 13.
Albion K. P. Mower of Turner and Vanelia E. Sylvester, March 10.
John C. Prescott of Wayne and Ellen Ellms, May 4.
Nathan Bishop and Lucy D. Skillings, May 5.
Elisha P. Ramsdell and Lucy C. Mitchell of Greene, May 6.
Amos B. Bishop and Almira A. Wheeler, May 22.
Gessius F. Jennings and Orra M. Foss, May 24.
John O. Beals and Ellen J. Howe, May 30.
John O. Palmer and Abigail R. Lane, June 2.
Rowland B. Howard and Mary Ellen Patten of Bath, Aug. 14.
Perry Grant and Caroline R. Millett, Oct. 15.
George E. Fogg of Greene and Octavia E. Maloon, Dec. 21.
Charles W. Stuart of Belgrade and Miranda Parcher, Dec. 22.

1861.

Llewellyn J. Gould and Mary Jane Millett, Jan. 5.
Earl F. Caswell and Augusta M. Young of Belgrade, Jan. 21.
George T. Smith of Windham and Orissa D. Lamb, Feb. 2.
Seth Fish and Tirzah Ann Carver, Feb. 19.
Lucius Smith of Readfield and Nancy Tobin, March 3.
Joshua Weymouth of Webster and Orissa A. Bates, March 16.
George H. Peare and Ann E. Blackstone of Turner, April 23.
L. Mellen Sylvester and Saphila C. Metcalf of Hope, Aug. 10.
Reuben Beals of Greene and Octavia F. Wheeler, Oct. 19.
Daniel W. Stevens of Winthrop and Matilda Bates, Nov. 15.
Rufus K. Peare and Hannah C. Maxim of Wayne, Dec. 8.
Joseph G. Gott and Rose E. Stinchfield, Dec. 28.

1862.

Ward B. Howard and Hannah L. Howard, Jan. 2.
William H. Fuller and Polly C. Keen, Jan. 15.
James N. Atwood of Livermore and Mary E. Knight, Feb. 22.
Benjamin F. Trask and Tabitha A. Millett, March 6.
William Luce Beals of Wales and Elvira Wheeler, March 28.
Wheaton Bates and Mrs. Jane Moore of Lewiston, May 9.
William W. Edgecomb of Livermore and Rufina A. Carver, May 23.
John H. Trask and Mary E. Brown of Livermore, May 31.
Chessman D. Gould and Sarah E. Gardner, July 12.

Rufus Trask and Mary J. Burnham, Aug. 16.
Roscoe V. Shaw of Greene and Emma Deane, Aug. 24.
Amos P. Grant and Almira J. Libby, Sept. 20.

1863.

Patrick Murray and Margaret O'Conners of Lewiston.
Gustavus W. Lane and Helen M. Snow of North Bridgewater, Mass., Feb. 17.
David B. Beals and Lydia A. Howe, Feb. 28.
Alexander Mank and Roxanna Bishop, April 4.
Eli Berry of Wayne and Esther A. Lane, April 5.
Augustus B. Caswell of Greene and Ann N. Mann, May 30.
Jeremiah T. Burnham and Carrie M. Hodgdon, Aug. 2.
Hiram H. Gilman of Hallowell and Sarah J. Wheeler, Aug. 18.
William B. Canwell of Franklin Pl't'n and Ellura Bishop, Sept. 12.
John F. Jennings and Emeline Foster, Sept. 19.
Milton W. Burnham and Betsey M. Farrington of Fayette, Sept. 29.
John R. Mitchell and Rozillah Berry of Wayne, Nov. 28.
Joseph M. Curtis and Sarah Jane Hodsdon, Dec. 4.
Charles Woodman and Jerusha Ann Hagden of Madison, Dec. 25.
John F. Lewis and Eliza A. Verrill of Auburn, Dec. 30.

1864.

Wm. M. Sawyer of Stoughton, Mass., and Betsey C. Bates, Jan. 10.
James W. Libby and Octavia J. Berry, Jan. 19.
Wm. B. Sumner and Julia A. Lindsey, Jan. 24.
James E. Bates and Augusta L. Wheeler, Feb. 8.
Stephen W. Grant and Mary A. Smith of Veazie, March 31.
Thomas W Mower of Greene and Laura E. Blue, April 9.
Cyrus Bishop and Fiducy A. Wellington of Livermore, June 4.
John C. Stinchfield and Catherine H. Graves of Wayne, July 3.
Albert Mann and Polly Fuller, Aug. 14.
Henry T. Frost and Clementine J. Chandler of Winthrop, Aug. 10.
Wm. E. Elder of Lewiston and Lydia Pettingill, Sept. 3.
Augustus B. Jones of Lewiston and Vesta C. Wing, Dec. 30.
William H. Foss of Wayne and Viora A. Carver, Dec. 31.

1865.

Levi Owen and Amanda T. Curtis, Jan. 8.
John E. Woodman and Laura Whitamore of Fayette, Jan. 18.
Cyrus B. Lane and Lydia A. Lothrop, Jan. 25.
William Stout and Lucretia A. Robinson of Webster, Feb. 1.
Jerome Ridley of Wayne and Clara Knowlton, Feb. 3.
Cyrenus Berry of Wayne and Maria P. Abbott, Feb. 10.
Asa Libby and Adeline Skillings, Feb. 19.
Jason M. Ridley of Wayne and Abbie L. Stinchfield, March 12.
Davis Francis and Mrs. Julia Ann Fernald, April 23.
William H. Erskins of Wayne and Lucretia Pettingill, June 1.
Lucius Clark Robbins and Sally S. Train of Philadelphia, June 21.
Ebenezer Curtis and Cordelia Briggs, July 21.
William P. Pettingill of Monmouth and Hannah Owen, July 31.
Henry A. Brown and Susan Jane Towle, Oct. 5.
Ebenezer Wheeler and Marcia Pullen of Monmouth, Oct. 26.
Jonathan Lovewell of Livermore and Eliza P. Gould, Nov. 12.
Salmon C. Brewster and Henrietta Libby, Dec. 23.
Lucius C. Dunham and Marcia E. Andrews, Dec. 26.

1866.

Duane S. Wing and Clara C. Howard, Jan. 5.
Thomas B. Norris of East Livermore and Mary E. Cobb, Jan. 29.
Thomas S. Rose of Greene and Hortencia W. Rose, Feb. 20.
Everett Lindsey and Mary Jane Howard, March 11.
Albert L. Additon of Greene and Florence A. Turner, May 1.
George E. Minot of Belgrade and Effie C. Parcher, June 5.
William Bodge and Josephine S. Tenny of Raymond, June 25.
Asa I. Soule of Phillips and Prudence A. Briggs, June 23.
Charles F. Lindsey and Mrs. Mary J. Trask, July 13.
James H. Libby of Turner and Orrah A. Millett, Aug. 2.
Rodelphus H. Gilmore of Iowa and Rose E. Deane, Aug. 8.
S. B. Harmon of Lewiston and Mrs. Lydia W. French, Aug. 11.
Orin E. Bates and Anna Waymouth of Webster, Aug. 23.

1867.

Joseph H. Burnham and Rozillah Abbott, Jan. 4.
Arcadius Pettingill and Lois J. Norris of Wayne, Jan. 12.
John Abbott and Lucretia D. Gould of Wayne, Jan. 13.
J. L. B. Farrington of Wilton and Orrah A. Boothby, Feb. 19.

HISTORY OF LEEDS 351

Clabon Carter and Mary Fager, Feb. 22.
Dexter W. True of Livermore and Celestia A. Hosley, May 1.
Wallace R. Leadbetter and Irene E. Nichols of Monmouth, May 10.
Frank M. Higgins and Flora L. Lothrop, Sept. 10.
George E. Wardwell of Greene and Elacta D. Gilbert, June 6.
Martin Maxim and Amanda Adams of Lewiston, June 21.
Aaron Hartt of Brookline and Helen M. Libby, July 14.
Benjamin P. Winslow and Emily F. Quimby of Greene, Sept. 7.
Stephen D. Knapp and Lizzie B. More of Livermore, Oct. 29.
L. H. Foss and Clara O. Woodford, Nov. 9.
Warren L. Lothrop and Abbie F. Knowles of Corinna, Nov. 23.
Granville Richmond and Isabell W. Jones of Turner, Dec. 10.
Charles D. White and Clara E. Palmer, Dec. 24.
Thomas H. Boothby and Sarah C. Libby, December.

1868.

Hezekiah S. Gordon and Phebe J. Gordon, January.
William R. Pettingill and Fannie P. Libby, Aug. 15.
David Trask and Rosannah Hanscom.
Marcellus F. Cushman and Frances M. Pettingill, Aug. 20.
Samuel Walker of Litchfield and Mrs. Martha A. Owen, Sept. 12.
Moses Fogg and Lizzie D. Williamson of Greene, Sept. 13.
Charles A. Wing of Franklin and Sarah E. Burnham, Nov. 20.
C. W. Battles and Mira B. Knapp, Nov. 16.
Lorenzo Leadbetter and Jennie O. Hall of Turner, Nov. 22.
Francis E. Howe of Greene and Elenor C. Pettingill, Dec. 24.

1869.

John F. Keith and Sarah F. Hill, Feb. 2.
Augustus S. George and Huldah J. Sprague, Jan. 29.
Frank G. Foss and Vesta T. Foss, Jan. 31.
Thomas J. Hallowell and Eliza A. Libby, Feb. 26.
Russell L. Gould and Ada S. Greenwood, Mar. 14.
Almon L. Ray and Eliza J. George, Oct. 6.
Everett Lindsay and Mrs. Eliza A. Lindsay of Monmouth, Oct. 20.
Rufus F. Burnham and Mrs. Rosialla Burnham, Nov. 2.
George Parcher and Carrie W. Norton, Nov. 17.
Benjamin H. Boynton of Rumford and Emma E. Libby, Nov. 22.
Alonzo Davis of Gorham and Carrie A. Foster, Nov. 28.

Hiram Q. Hammond and Rose S. Frost, Dec. 2.
Charles W. Libby and Phœbe C. Levitt, Dec. 2.
George T. Bishop and Julia H. Byrom of Phillips, Dec. 23.

1870.

Robert Burell and Mrs. Fannie Swinton of Auburn, Jan. 21.
Almon L. Ray and Eliza J. George, Jan. 25.
John Coleman and Sarah R. Soper, April 11.
Solomon Dyer and Julia A. Trufant, April 23.
Levi Bates and Maria E. Cook, April 30.
George H. Douglass of Gorham and Hattie A. Foster, May 5.
Ebenezer Stinchfield and Almira Berry, May 13.
Amos F. Thomes and Mary E. Soper, June 19.
Philo C. Gilbert and Mary C. Ellenwood of Lowell, Nov. 20.
Henry A. Libby and Carrie E. Boynton of Rumford, Dec. 5.
Jeremiah F. Burnham and Abby P. Taylor, Dec. 17.
A. House, Jr., Monmouth, and Mrs. Zipporah C. Gordon, Dec. 27.
Benjamin Gilbert and Amanda F. Wagner, Dec. 29.

1871.

Charles R. Libby and Emma R. Day of Monmouth, Jan. 12.
D. H. Dearborn of Moumouth and Lucy Robbins, March 8.
George E. Gilbert and Amanda J. Chase of Buckfield, April 5.
Franklin J. Lindsay and Huldah L. Richmond of Livermore, April 11.
Melvin Berry and Kate M. Foss, April 15.
John A. Wheeler and Helen L. Gilbert of Winthrop, April 29.
Horatio Bradford of Paris and Laura M. Larrabee, May 2.
William R. Millett and Viora H. Gordon, May 30.
Thomas J. Harrington and Jane A. Burnham, August 1.
George W. Wing and Sarah F. Harrington of Livermore, Sept. 2.
Herbert L. Millett and Lydia A. Gordon, Sept. 2.
George E. Watts and Hattie A. Work, Sept. 14.
Charles L. Thomas of Greene and Mary Deane, Oct. 5.
Columbus P. Hosley and Bessie A. Bodge, Oct. 15.
Henry B. Greenleaf and Lourana Maguire, Oct. 24.
Henry F. Pettingill and Adelia M. Gordon of Vienna, Nov. 21.

1872.

Lorenzo Leadbetter and Hattie A. Foster of Wayne, Jan. 21.
Stephen Knapp and Mrs. Abbie E. Marden, Feb. 20.
Charles Wentworth and Mrs. Eunice Magner, May 14.
George Tarr of Brunswick and Flora E. Hallowell, Aug. 20.
Lendall S. Caswell and Thressa H. Parsons, Sept. 3.

HISTORY OF LEEDS 353

Louville W. Gould and Mary E. Gray, Sept. 14.
Thomas W. Curtis of Gardiner and Mary Ann Day, Nov. 14.
Lewis L. Lindsay and Flora C. Curtis, Nov. 18.
James McClusky and Anna L. Libby, Dec. 22.
George E. Carver and Augusta A. Sprague, Dec. 24.
Charles R. Besse of Vienna and Lydia J. Boothby, Dec. 25.
Chandler F. Cobb and Ella Gordon, Dec. 31.

1873.

E. M. S. Abbott and Helen S. Weston of Readfield, Jan. 2.
Amos H. Bishop and Mrs. Thompson of Strong, Feb. 20.
John L. Plummer of Monmouth and Victoria Wheeler, Mar 4.
Sewall W. Stinchfield and Jennie S. Teague of Mt. Vernon, May 9.
Horace H. Burbank and Fannie M. Sprague, May 22.
John E. Carver and Jennie L. Richards, May 25.
S. C. Merrill and Addie E. Rose, June 4.
Frank E. Gould and Sarah L. Peare, June 28.
Thomas I. Jepson and Columbia H. Berry, Aug. 6.
Herbert L. Grant and Addie N. Smith, Nov. 21.
Edgar Rose and Adelia Rounds of Auburn, Dec. 5.

1874.

Minot Williams of Bowdoin and Lucy E. Rowe, March 25.
Henry M. Beals and Anvalette Caswell of Auburn, April 4.
John W. Beckler and Mary F. Ham of Wales, April 30.
James S. Wing and Ellen F. Hallowell, May 15.
S. P. Libby and Emma L. Norris of Wayne, May 25.
Davis P. True and Bessie R. Stinchfield of Auburn, May 31.
Roscoe P. Wheeler and Sarah S. Bodge, August 28.
Lewis S. Wheeler and Rosemand Waterhouse of Poland, August 29.
William H. Wing and Lilla E. Hallowell, Sept. 20.
David Sturtevant and Betsey A. Burnham, Sept. 20.
John Dumley and Ellen Lynch, Oct. 23.
Frank H. Hussey and Annie L. Morrill of Etna, Nov. 24.
Walter P. Foss and Hattie F. Cox of Farmingdale, Dec. 23.
Horace F. Alden of Turner and Esta B. Hussey, Dec. 30.

1875.

Isaac C. Libby and Albina L. Fogg, Feb. 11.
Wallace W. Mower of Greene and Lizzie J. Pettingill, March 15.
John A. Burnham and Lucretia D. Taylor, March 16.

Peltiah F. Libby and Mrs. Mary Ann Knowlton, May 5.
Warren Carver and Hannah E. Mower, July 9.
Charles S. Moody and Millie E. Shorey of Monmouth, Dec. 24.

1876.

Elisha Sampson and Sarah A. Keith, March 20.
William D. Bornemon and Ella E. Libby, April 28.
George Caswell of Monmouth and Nancy J. Libby, June 13.
Henry F. Woodman and Mary F. Whitemore, July 16.
Frank E. Andrews of Winthrop and Lizzie D. Turner, Sept. 22.
John J. McKarthy of Lewiston and Mrs. Nora Powers, Oct. 26.
Lafayette C. Wing and Luella Burnham, Nov. 29.

1877.

Edwin W. Morris and Nancy E. Vose of Winthrop, Jan. 10.
Wesley Welch of Wayne and Arobine Churchill, April 21.
Frederick H. Knight and Lenora L. Prince, May 16
David P. Freeman and Edith Rose, August 4.
David Sturtevant and Mrs. Elmira Folsom, August 11.
Joseph A. Trask and Addie J. Holt of Augusta, August 22.
John A. Beales of Brunswick and Clara D. Coolidge, Sept. 7.
A. J. Nash of Greene and Inez Rose, Oct. 6.
Alonzo House of Wayne and Nellie Fuller, Nov. 13.
Mellen J. Hanscom and Rosa V. Gilbert, Nov. 21.

1878.

Cyrus B. Howe of Greene and Rosilla Bishop, March 13.
Alvin D. Morris and Mary A. Richards of Salem, April 15.
Willis A. Knapp and Julia A. Carver, June 14.
George T. Howe and Mrs. Edith W. Church, July 2.
William A. Bowers and Nellie L. Fabyan, Sept. 6.
Charles H. Richmond of Fayette and Clara A. Jennings, Sept. 21.
Willis G. Magner and Eva E. Borneman, Sept. 28.
Charles K. Leadbetter and Ella F. Stinchfield, Sept. 29.
James W. Lindsay and Ida Atkins, Nov. 24.
Lewis J. Pollard of Auburn and Hannah L. Davee, Nov. 17.

1879.

Otis K. Prescott of Monmouth and Elvira J. Pettingill, Feb. 10.
William Churchell and Emily B. Armstrong, March 7.
Abial D. Knapp and Ella C. Millett, April 2.

Fred A. Parker and Lois V. Gilbert of Lewiston, May 3.
Alvah D. Ames and M. Etta Spofford of Greene, June 6.
Joseph Torrey of Lewiston and Flora E. Maguire, July 6.
Oliver A. Johnson of Wayne and Minnie A. Foss, July 7.
Charles M. Pettingill of Monmouth and Etta E. Beals, August 23.
Lewis M. Larrabee and Angelia Bryant, Oct. 15.
Franklin E. Carver of Canton and Etta L. Sprague, Nov. 24.
George J. Potter of Monmouth and Jennie L. Rose, Dec. 8.
Daniel P. Hall of Monmouth and Lucilla D. Day, Dec. 9.
George S. Buck of Hopkinton, Mass., and Mary J. Libby, Dec. 17.

1880.

John H. Bates and Serena E. Sumner, Jan. 16.
Lot Howard and Ella T. Millett, May 3.
Martin V. Burgess and Albina V. Burnham, May 18.
Frank Parker of Lewiston and Laura Etta Nichols, April 29.
Frank H. Gooch of Yarmouth and Letitia E. Curtis, May 15.
T. C. Libby and Mrs. Esther L. Lothrop, June 5.
Uriah F. Libby and Lucy Ann Sumner, July 24.
John R. Millett and Mrs. Orinza Potter, Nov. 17.
Walter Hutchinson of Turner and Ada M. Gilbert, Dec. 16.

1881.

Willard F. Maguire and Mary L. Knapp, Jan. 31.
Joseph L. Taylor and Mrs. Lucretia D. Burnham, Feb. 24.
George D. Whittier of Chesterville and Minnie J. Morris, Feb. 28.
Frank E. Pettingill and Edith M. Coffin, April 28.
Charles H. Berry and Julia A. Griswold, June 7.
Manly M. Coffin and Emily A. Pettingill, June 17.
A. F. Tinkham of Augusta and Jennie M. Brewster, Aug. 11.
Leander M. Howard and Clara E. Boothby, Sept. 30.
George E. Merrill and Mary E. Burnham, Oct. 29.
Gustavus W. Burnham and Vesta E. Wing, Nov. 17.

1882.

William H. Thomas of Greene and Luetta M. Additon, Feb. 13.
Fred W. Walton and Emma F. Remick of Wayne, May 13.

1883.

Lewis M. Larrabee and Lillian W. Keith, Jan. 25.
Benjamin Lord of Peru and Mrs. Mary J. Trask, Feb. 15.
Charles S. Parker and Isabelle E. Rose, Feb. 22.

J. Henry Moore of Winthrop and Oleva E. Sumner, March 24.
Junius C. Wing and Mary E. Hamond, April 18.
William C. Taylor and Judith Burnham, April 23.
John E. Gordon and Nellie A. Briggs, April 30.
Dole B. Wiley of Greene and Elvira E. Deane, Sept. 5.
Gustavus W. Lane and Susan E. Lothrop, Sept. 8.
Henry F. Woodman and Martha Deane, Sept. 15.
Richard Clemonds and Mercy I. Canwell, Dec. 15.
Herbert W. Bates and Clara E. Beals of Greene, Dec. 20.
Orin E. Curtis and Ermina A. Pettingill, Dec. 22.

1884.

Joel E. Taylor and Caroline R. Burnham, Jan. 15.
Frank Wadsworth of Monmouth and Iva S. Caswell, March 1.
John H. Parker of Greene and Mary J. House, March 22.
George C. Coolidge and Mrs. Viora A. Foss, March 29.
Thomas C. Foss and Abby J. Cox of Farmingdale, March 31.
Leander Patten of Greene and Nancy E. Caswell, April 19.
Hiram F. Kincade of East Livermore and Mary F. Wing, May 17.
Jeremiah Donnally and Annie Foss of Farmington, July 26.
Daniel Maguire and Allura Carver, August 23.
Charles L. Bates and Clara A. Bates, Sept. 12.
Abial F. Deane and Julia A. Woodman, Nov. 17.
George L. Beals of Greene and Alena M. Wing, Nov. 22.
Bert Merrill and Clara R. Cary of Turner, Nov. 26.
Ralph L. Knapp and Nettie M. Lindsay, Dec. 19.
Fred C. Foss and Eugenia E. Jennings, May 12.
Asa G. Gordon and Melintha G. Pettingill, Dec. 29.

1885.

Thomas S. Carver and Elnora Y. Parsons, April 16.
Wills Libby of Auburn and Cora E. House, July 4.
Albertus Nichols and Annie F. Taylor of Freeman, Sept. 19.
Joseph E. Maxim of Wayne and Susan J. Burnham, Oct. 3.
Augustus S. Tuck of Fayette and Mrs. Vesta W. Jones, Dec. 24.

1886.

Fred C. Jackson of Auburn and Flora A. Leavitt, Jan. 16.
Elwin E. Additon and Mary A. Thomas of Greene, Feb. 4.
Hartland F. Gray of Monmouth and Lovina E. Morris, March 5.
Fred A. Perry and Ellen E. Smith, March 5.
Benjamin M. Norton and Laura E. Parker, March 13.

Leonard F. Addison of Roxbury, Mass., and Rosa E. Grant, April 25.
Austin H. Wing and Betsey A. Burnham, May 10.
Eugene Kincade of Livermore and Betsy M. Wing, June 11.
E. H. Wagner of Monmouth and Edith Currier, Nov. 2.
Andrew L. Johnson of Livermore and Lillian Trask, Dec. 31.

1887.

Lucian F. Berry and Mrs. M. Anna Coburn, April 10.
Jason Carver and Mrs. Augusta W. Curtis, April 16.
J. F. Burnham and Lena B. Hallowell, Nov. 5.
James F. Burnham and Lucy A. Wing, July 8.
John H. Burnham and Lizzie A. Merrill, August 11.
Truman M. Shaw of Greene and Annie S. Additon, Sept. 9.
Joseph F. Moody and Louise S. Bragdon of Monmouth, Sept. 13.
William H. Morris and Ella C. Millett, Sept. 17.
C. A. Whitehouse and Mary L. Woodman, Sept. 28.
A. C. B. Keene and Vesta A. Gilmore of Turner, Oct. 1.
Charles M. Fish and Hannah E. Ridley of Wayne, Oct. 20.
Josiah F. Burnham and Betsey Hollowell, Nov. 5.
Fred N. Howard and Alura F. Abbott of Deering, Nov. 7.
Daniel E. Haynes and Lenora M. Hallowell, Jan. 22.

1888.

Albion H. Hodsdon of Turner and Hattie M. Brewster, Nov. 14.
William J. Wing of Peru and Ida M. Burnham, Feb. 18.
Anson G. Knapp and Alice M. Dascomb, August 24.
Fred L. Additon and Lenora J. Howe, August 31.
Clarence F. Greeley and Ella A. Lovell, Sept. 9.
Daniel Maguire and Grace Anthony, Sept. 9.
John M. Turner, M.D., of Gardiner and Olive M. Lothrop, Sept. 26.
Chester C. Farmer and Cassie B. Lane, Oct. 22.
Stillman N. Dixon of Clinton and Alice M. Carver, Nov. 11.
Victor A. Rose and Etta M. Gill, Dec. 21.

1889.

Forest Morris and Emma Brown, March 4.
N. P. Gould and Mae G. Pease of Fayette, March 25.
Joshua H. Sumner and Mrs. Asenath C. Martin of Monmouth, Dec. 31.
Harry N. Gould and Mary E. Roach, June 22.
Alexander Ramsay and Etta G. Burnham, July 2.
Seth F. Carver and Effie M. Rose, July 13.

Edward L. Grant and Myra M. Carver, August 18.
Francis A. Wing and Augusta R. Burnham, Oct. 14.
John R. Newcomb and Lizzie B. Burnham, August 31.
Freeland Q. Wing and Nellie F. McCulla, Sept. 6.
Fred A. Wade and Grace L. Libby of Exeter, Nov. 15.

1890.

Stephen L. Mayo of St. Albans and Betsey B. Rose, Jan. 6.
Frank H. Hussey and Sarah A. Purington of Jay, Feb. 16.
Elmer E. Burgess and Lulie L. Libby, April 13.
George L. Delano of Monmouth and Bertha H. Watson, April 26.
Alton L. Thomas and Annie E. Lincoln, May 9.
John A. Gordon and Adelia C. Hartt, May 22.
W. S. Gilmore of Turner and Sadie M. Keene, May 23.
Fred W. Adams of Auburn and Nellie M. Sprague, Nov. 5.
Herbert S. Wadsworth of Wales and Ella M. Ridley, June 14.
Irving R. Canwell and Ella F. Hinkley, July 3.
Lenord L. Rose and Mrs. Emma Jordon, Dec. 29.

1891.

Albion Brewster and Lilla N. Beal of Monmouth, Jan. 28.
Jeremiah H. Sullivan and Hannah A. Bates, March 9.
Frank E. Pettingill and Georgia A. Beal of Monmouth, March 7.
Oscar W. Merrill and Lula L. Edgecomb, April 1.
Peter L. Turner and Adelaide C. Abbott of Medway, Mass., July 24.
Ralph L. Knapp and Eva J. Carville of Lewiston, Oct. 9.
Almond N. Gordon of Mt. Vernon and Eva J. Maxim, Oct. 29.
Junius C. Wing and Dora L. Howard, Nov. 24.

1892.

Chas. A. Austin and Carrie May Clinton Keene, March 5.
Wm. H. Wing and Emma M. Place, Lewiston, April 17.
Eli Edgecomb and Eva May Fickett, Auburn, April 30.
Geo. H. Knowles and Mrs. Albina V. Burgess, May 7.
Perry Grant and Mrs. Genie Morgan, Auburn, May 13.
Alfred A. Mower, Greene, and Jennie M. Bates, August 6.
Arthur C. Leadbetter, Wayne, and Grace H. Turner, Sept. 20.
Fred E. Burnham and Eva Maxim, Oct. 9.
Loretus A. Strout, Wales, and Nettie Beal, Oct. 17.
Loring L. Churchell and Mira H. Gulliver, Readfield, Oct. 30.
George Calley, Poland, and Kate Hayes, Nov. 7.

Thomas H. Boothby and Estella Stinchfield, Nov. 23.
Warren L. Smith and Georgie A. Walton, Nov. 26.
Benjamin F. Burgess and Mary L. Mitchell, Lisbon, Dec. 31.

1893.

Benjamin R. Ramsdell and Susie G. Wood, Westford, Mass., May 1.
Isaiah Henry Mann and Esther Augusta Rose, Greene, May 21.
Albert Bryant and Flora E. Lovewell, Livermore, June 24.
James C. Gordon and Sarah E. Swift, East Livermore, July 4.
Perley Wing and Georgianna P. Wing, July 20.
Ernest W. Russell, Lewiston, and Caroline H. Sumner, August 29.
George E. Wills, Auburn, and Sophia B. Sumner, August 29.
Sanford Adams, Monmouth, and E. Gertrude Pettengill, Sept. 14.
Wm. H. Howard, Manchester, and Georgia E. Farrington, Sept. 30.
Philip Long, Chelsea, and Mrs. Francina J. Latio, Dec. 23.
Edson Waite, Livermore, and Bertha A. Grant, Dec. 24.
Bertus E. Wight and Luta M. Dyer, Dec. 30.

1894.

Joseph L. Grant and Lizzie Mabel More, Lewiston, Feb. 23.
Ernest A. Russell and Kittie Lane, March 18.
Ray L. Harvey and Eva B. Lothrop, Auburn, April 5.
James I. Simpson and Lucretia D. Taylor, April 5.
William H. Roach and Sadie Jane Hadley, July 7.
Andrew S. Clark and Nettie May Peare, July 12.
Fred S. Grant and Effie A. Cooper, Roxbury, July 21.
Frank H. Herrick and Lucy M. Sylvester, Turner, August 15.
Chas. H. Lane and Mrs. Nellie M. Wright, Greene, Oct. 20.
William A. Jennings and Hannah A. Adams, Greene, Nov. 26.
Denis Carter, East Livermore, and May A. Knapp, Dec. 27.

1895.

John L. Raymond, Wayne, and Mrs. Ada J. Trask, Jan. 21.
Benjamin K. Alden, Greene, and Mrs. Etta B. Dudley, Jan. 10.
Charles B. Brewster and Lizzie L. Boothby, March 1.
Carroll G. Parker, Greene, and Blanche M. Pinkham, Aug. 17.
James S. Magner and Mrs. Ella F. Pearce, Nov. 24.
John F. Gilmore and Vesta E. Hammond, Greene, Dec. 18.

1896.

Israel H. Herrick and Alice Hanson, Biddeford, Jan. 15.
Charles H. Lord and Lillie Gooldrup, Feb. 25.
Rodger E. Dalton and Mrs. Addie F. Lymes, Livermore, March 21.
Ernest E. Jordan, Turner, and Emma A. Carver, March 25.
Thomas H. Nevens, Portland, and Sadie E. Lane, May 22.
Fred A. Sedgley and Susan J. Wyman, June 6.
Roland M. Maxim and Sarah E. Burnham, July 12.
John C. Houghton and Harriet A. White, Aug. 26.
John T. Collins and Lina Hobbs, Oct. 27.
Melville G. Libby and Glennie Bishop, Dec. 28.
Ora Allen Knox and Blanch M. Wing, Nov. 26.
Howard Elliott Lincoln and Gertrude E. Howie, Whitneyville, Dec. 1.
Carrol Albion Bryant and Rosilla P. House, Dec. 23.
Stephen A. Taylor and Mrs. Lizzie A. Taylor, Dec. 12.

1897.

Herbert W. Ryder and Lucy M. Adams, Greene, Feb. 27.
Thurston S. Heald and Helen May Curtis, Monmouth, May 16.
John H. Neal and E. Alice Sanborn, June 26.
Tafuest Knowles and Ella M. Williams, Sept. 1.
Frank G. Davis, Readfield, and Annie H. Foss, Sept. 23.
Lafayette A. Cochran, Oakland, and Lucinda D. Burnham, Oct. 28.
Percy L. Fogg, Greene, and Bessie B. Bates, Nov. 20.
Lucius L. Gould, East Livermore, and Mrs. Emily B. Churchill, Dec. 9.
Paul Smith Palmer, Stockbridge, and Lena Howard Foss, May 24.
Arthur W. Hobbs and Mabel H. Alden, Dec. 22.

1898.

George W. Maguire and Celia M. Maguire, Augusta, Jan. 10.
Richard Wing and Bertha Maxim, Jan. 22.
Herbert A. Wing and Mrs. Albina V. Knowles, May 31.
Allen H. Sprague and Grace M. Sleeper Litchfield, June 5.
Fred A. Howard and Mrs. Evelyn Merritt, Lewiston, June 14.
Augustus E. Campbell and Alice B. Hamilton, July 2.
Frank Hosea Hall and Eveline Francelia Kelly, Stoneham, Mass., July 1.
George H. Anthony and Gertrude M. Graham, Oct. 2.
Frank L. Carver and Abbie House, Oct. 23.
George F. Cooper and Mrs. Florence A. Nason, Lewiston, Dec. 14.

1899.

Ned R. Bishop and Myrtle M. Grant, Jan. 30.
Alfred S. Wing and Carrie M. Higgins, Feb. 5.
Fred D. Brackett and Mrs. Mertie J. Clemens, Feb. 25.
George H. Wing and Celia May Wing, March 20.
Elwood Richards and Hattie M. Wing, March 25.
Walter B. House and Annie E. Nichols, March 30.
C. H. Brown and Emogene Cushman, May 14.
W. R. Carville, Lewiston, and Fannie Maguire, July 8.
Milton W. Burnham and Vilina J. Anderson, Aug. 15.
Marshal S. Sawtelle and Patea M. Emery, Industry, June 26.
Charles M. Kenny and Lucy C. Hutchins, Oct. 6.
Arthur W. Fish and Grace M. Maguire, Oct. 26.
Nathan D. Merrill, Turner, and Mildred B. Francis, Oct. 27.
Joseph Henley and Kate A. Roach, Nov. 19.
Charles Carpenter (Poland) and Hattie M. Beckler, Dec. 18.
Alton G. Millett and Winifred Pettengill, Dec. 28.

1900.

C. Warren Barker and May Emma McClusky, March 26.
Victor Bernier and Cora E. Murry, June 10.
S. A. Richardson, Greene, and Edith Howe, June 28.
John G. Daggett, Wayne, and Mrs. Ella Knapp, July 14.
Tracy L. Barker, Lewiston, and Annie B. Davis, Aug. 4.
Clinton L. Bodge and Mrs. Lizzie R. Homes, Westbrook, Aug. 9.
Leon Mortimer Norton and Alice Clyde Nichols, Sept. 20.
Lemuel Gile (Wales) and Annie Dascomb, Oct. 13.
Albert P. Rose and Florence M. Libby, Oct. 30.
James B. Neal and Mary C. Edgecomb, Nov. 20.

1901.

Allie J. Howard and Delia Daggett, Jan. 14.

It will be observed that changes have been made in the spelling of names since their first appearance on the records of the town: Morse for Moss, Knapp for Knap, Thompson for Tomson, Sampson for Samson, etc., etc.

CHAPTER XXI.

GENEALOGY.

ADDITON, ELWIN E.

Children:

NAME.	BIRTH.		DEATH.	
Louise M.,	July,	1891.		
Marion L.,	Mar.,	1894.		
Orland H.,	Apr.,	1896.		
Vina A.,	Aug.,	1899.		

Parentage:

Elwin E. Additon,	Aug.,	1864.		
Mary A. Thomas,	June,	1865.		

Paternal Grand:

Thomas J. Additon,	Aug.,	1832,	Mar.,	1897.
Rozilla Smart,	Mar.,	1832.		

Maternal Grand:

Charles L. Thomas,	Oct.,	1831.		
Hannah M. Maxwell,	Feb.,	1838,	Nov.,	1867.

ADDITON, FRED L.

Children:

Orville J.,	Aug.,	1889.
Ernest F.,	Apr.,	1891.
Leslie F.,	June,	1893.
Ivan B.,	Nov.,	1894.
Clayton E.,	Aug.,	1896.
Edna,	Mar.,	1898.
Florus J.,	Dec.,	1899.

Parentage:

Fred L. Additon,	Jan.,	1864.
Leonora I. Howe,	Dec.,	1871.

Paternal Grand:

Isaiah B. Additon,	Nov.,	1823,	July,	1894.
Eliza A. Jennings,	Oct.,	1831.		

Maternal Grand:

NAME.	BIRTH.	DEATH.
Francis E. Howe,	Feb., 1843.	
Eleanor C. Pettingill,	May, 1845,	Aug., 1895.

BATES, JAMES E.

Children:
Willis,	May 18, 1865.	
Nancy E.,	Nov. 8, 1866.	
Mary A.,	Sept. 4, 1870,	Jan. 13, 1873.
Lester R.,	Feb. 8, 1874.	

Parentage:
James E. Bates,	Jan. 20, 1832.
Augusta L. Wheeler,	Feb. 28, 1831.

Paternal Grand:
Hervey Bates,	June 10, 1789,	May 10, 1877.
Nancy G. Rand, of Monmouth,	Apr., 1799,	Dec. 12, 1856.

Maternal Grand:
Aruna Wheeler,	Apr. 25, 1808,	Feb. 19, 1874.
Sally Berry, of Vienna,	Apr. 14, 1808,	Feb. 27, 1880.

BATES, AVERSON G.

Children:
Clara Adelma,	June, 1863.	
Alverda Ellsworth,	June, 1861,	Aug., 1862.
Roy Averson,	Oct., 1875.	

Parentage:
Averson Green Bates,	May, 1835.
Phœbe Anne Day,	June, 1834.

Paternal Grand:
Cyrus Bates,	June, 1800,	Mar., 1860.
Sophia Keay,	Feb., 1802,	Apr., 1859.

Maternal Grand:
Randall Day,	Mar., 1806,	Apr., 1879.
Phœbe Shaw,	Dec., 1809,	May, 1882.

BEALS, THOMAS A.

Children:
Luretta E.,	Feb. 6, 1857.	
Lenora A.,	Feb. 24, 1861,	Mar. 15, 1862.

Parentage:

NAME.	BIRTH.	DEATH.
Thomas A. Beals,	Jan. 15, 1828.	
Mary E. Lewis,	May 10, 1836.	

Paternal Grand:

Isaac Beals, Jr.,	June 11, 1792,	June 17, 1885.
Lydia Briggs,	Nov. 1, 1796,	Feb. 26, 1875.

Maternal Grand:

William Lewis,	Oct. 20, 1810,	May 9, 1876.
Elizabeth Boyd,	Sept. 22, 1816,	Aug. 5, 1885.

BEAL, MOSES G.

Children:

Jarvis T.,	Nov. 25, 1845.	
Arvilla J.,	May 23, 1847.	
Georgianna,	Apr. 6, 1850.	Apr. 10, 1850.
Herbert M.,	Jan. 28, 1854.	
Francisco G.,	Mar. 12, 1856.	
Stephen S.,	Sept. 18, 1857.	
Ella L.,	Jan. 9, 1863.	
Fred,	Nov. 27, 1862.	Aug. 13, 1882.
Georgia A.,	Oct. 13, 1864.	
Ortez,	Feb. 9, 1866.	
Nettie,	Sept. 1, 1869.	
Lilla M.,	Feb. 15, 1871.	
Moses E.,	Oct. 10, 1873.	Oct. 18, 1866.

Parentage:

Moses G. Beal,	Nov. 11, 1821,	Feb. 15, 1890.
Sarah Ames,	July 2, 1826,	Aug. 13, 1861.
Lovina Pickens,	Apr. 23, 1840.	

Paternal Grand:
Stephen Beal,
Charlotte Gould,

Maternal Grand:
Daniel Ames,
Mary Dingley,

Elisha Pickens,	Jan. 13, 1799,	Aug. 13, 1864.
Meroah Hathaway,	June 1, 1805,	Nov. 25, 1874.

BECKLER, GEORGE W.

Children:

Kimball G.,	Dec. 3, 1861.
Hattie M.,	July 21, 1866.
Bert H.,	Oct. 27, 1876.

Parentage:

NAME.	BIRTH.	DEATH.
George W. Beckler,	May 27, 1834.	
Esther M. Fuller,	Jan. 27, 1840.	

Paternal Grand:

Phillip C. Beckler.	Nov. 22, 1796,	Sept. 25, 1870.
Fanny Otis,	Apr. 25, 1803,	May 9, 1840.

Maternal Grand:

Kimball Prince Fuller,	June 30, 1795,	Oct. 19, 1866.
Miranda Carman,	Aug. 17, 1804,	Jan. 2, 1887.

BISHOP, W. SCOTT.

Children:

Clifton D.,	May,	1873.
Glenn C.,	June,	1875.
Nedd R.,	Dec.,	1879.
Laura E.,	Jan.,	1886.

Parentage:

W. S. Bishop,	June,	1848.
E. E. Rackley,	March,	1851.

Paternal Grand:
Amos H. Bishop,
Eliza A. Burgess.

Maternal Grand:
Jason Rackley,
Nancy West.

BREWSTER, HENRY M.

Children:

Hattie Myrtle,	Oct.,	1863.
Maria Betsey,	Apr.,	1867.
Charles Bishop,	Nov.,	1871.
Carrol Henry,	July,	1882.

Parentage:
Henry M. Brewster.
Angelia Bishop,   Sept. 23, 1838.

Paternal Grand:
Salmon Brewster.
Betsey Shaw.

Maternal Grand:

Abial D. Bishop,	Jan. 1, 1800,	May 9, 1877.
Dorcas Lindsey,	June 15, 1802,	June 15, 1877.

BRIDGHAM, DR. THOMAS W.

Children:

NAME.	BIRTH.	DEATH.
Everett,	Oct. 28, 1815,	Sept. 2, 1818.
Amanda,	Apr. 16, 1817,	Sept. 28, 1842.
Lloyd Howard,	Oct. 12, 1818,	Sept. 16, 1826.
Everett Howard,	Mar. 16, 1821.	
Thomas Wats,	Feb. 22, 1823.	
Mary Ann,	July 19, 1824,	Nov. 25, 1857.
Eliza,	July 16, 1827,	Sept., 1828.
Lloyd H.,	Dec. 24, 1829,	Aug. 26, 1875.
Voluntine R.,	Feb. 16, 1832.	
Ora L.,	Oct. 17, 1833,	Mar. 13, 1842.
William A.,	Aug. 23, 1837.	

Parentage:
Thomas W. Bridgham.
Aurelia Howard.

Maternal Grand:
Seth Howard,
Desire Bailey.

BURNHAM, M. MILTON.

Child:
E. M.,   Oct. 5, 1864.

Parentage:
Milton M. Burnham,   Feb. 22, 1844.
Maria B. Farrington,   May 16, 1848.

CAMPBELL, HORACE L.

Child:
Lena E.,   Aug. 6, 1882.

Parentage:
Horace L. Campbell,   May 2, 1849.
Maria S. Carr,   Apr. 5, 1847.

Paternal Grand:
Calvin Campbell,   June 14, 1824,   July 1, 1892.
Jane Carver,   May 14, 1822.

Maternal Grand:
Amos Carr,   Jan. 19, 1812.
Charlotte Rogers,   Feb. 20, 1817,   June 3, 1890.

CARVER, EVERETT.

Children:

NAME.	BIRTH.	DEATH.
Julia Augusta,	July, 1850,	Nov., 1892.
Everett Lowell,	Dec., 1852.	
Wallace Elwood,	June, 1863.	

Parentage:

Everett Carver,	July, 1821,	Nov., 1881.
Julia Ann Baldwin,	Mar. 4, 1826.	

Paternal Grand:

Caleb Carver,	June, 1800.	
Augusta Copeland.		

Paternal Great-Grand:

Eleazer Carver.
Nancy Jones.

Maternal Grand:

Robert Baldwin,	Oct. 10, 1785,	Apr. 29, 1863.
Ruth Riggs,	1785,	Feb. 12, 1857.

CARVER, JAMES.

Children:

Eunice Ellen,	Apr., 1857.	
Seth,	July, 1859.	
Abbie,	Oct., 1861,	Dec., 1863.
Abbie,	Aug., 1864.	
Lura,	Dec., 1865,	Jan., 1885.
Mary Alice,	Oct., 1868.	
Frank Leslie,	Nov., 1870.	
Myra May,	Sept., 1872.	
Emma Arvilla,	May, 1879.	

Parentage:

James Carver,	Mar., 1833.	
Mary Fish,	Apr., 1837.	

Paternal Grand:

Eleazer Carver, Jr.,	Apr., 1788,	Dec., 1856.
Hannah Stinchfield,	Dec., 1794,	Jan., 1872.

Maternal Grand:

Seth Fish,	Mar., 1783,	Oct., 1859.
Abigail Carver,	Aug., 1803,	Feb., 1860.

CARVER, JOHN E.

Children:

NAME.	BIRTH.	DEATH.
Blanche M.,	Mar., 1874.	
George R.,	May, 1876,	Mar., 1881.
Mabel M.,	Nov., 1878.	
Bessie J.,	Nov., 1881.	
Nettie R.,	May, 1886.	
Georgie A.,	July, 1893,	

Parentage:
John E. Carver.

Paternal Grand:
Jason Carver.
Mary Libby.

Paternal Great-Grand:
Eleazer Carver.
Hannah Stinchfield.

Maternal Grand:
Solomon Libby.
Dorcas Foss.

CARVER, J. E.

Children:

M. Blanche,	Mar. 8, 1874.	
George R.,	May 10, 1876,	Mar. 27, 1881.
Mabel,	Nov. 3, 1878.	
J. Bessie,	Nov. 27, 1881.	
Nettie R.,	May 10, 1886.	
Georgie,	July 30, 1893.	

Parentage:

John Edd. Carver,	July 28, 1851.
Jennie D. Richards,	June 7, 1852.

Paternal Grand:

Jason Carver,	Apr., 1819.	Dec., 1893.
Mary Libby,	Nov., 1820,	May, 1881.

Maternal Grand:

Freedom Richards,	Dec., 1818,	May, 1898.
Sarah Brown,	Jan., 1822,	July, 1889.

COFFIN, NATHAN W.

Children:

Manley M.,	July 6, 1850.	
Edith M.,	Jan. 2, 1858,	May 27, 1885.

Parentage:

NAME.	BIRTH.	DEATH.
Nathan W. Coffin,	Nov. 2, 1819.	
Aurelia Gott,	Jan. 15, 1821,	Feb. 16, 1885.

CURTIS, WILLIAM B.

Children:
William H.,	Mar. 19, 1855.	
Henry B.,	Jan. 5, 1858.	

Parentage:
William B. Curtis,	May 26, 1818,	Mar. 27, 1879.
Augusta W. Sumner,	Dec. 6, 1823.	

Paternal Grand:
Ebenezer Curtis,	June 23, 1775,	Aug. 22, 1868.
Esther Randall,	Dec. 12, 1785,	Mar. 9, 1865.

Maternal Grand:
Houghton Sumner,	Mar. 30, 1783,	Aug. 28, 1862.
Mary Rogers,	June 20, 1782,	May 10, 1865.

Ebenezer Curtis came to Leeds about the year 1824 and settled on the place now owned by Mrs. A. W. Carver about one mile west from Curtis Corner. He was the oldest member of the family of Curtis consisting of six brothers and one sister which came from Hanover, Mass. and all settled near Curtis Corner.

CURTIS, EBENEZER.

Parentage:
Eben Curtis,	Apr. 21, 1836.	
Cordelia Briggs,	May 14, 1836.	

Paternal Grand:
Jeremiah Curtis,	June 26, 1806,	Aug. 11, 1880.
Christina Berry,	Jan., 1811,	Jan. 5, 1848.

Maternal Grand:
Calvin Briggs,	Aug. 6, 1806,	Dec. 27, 1887.
Lydia Pettingill,	Dec. 14, 1813,	Apr. 3, 1890.

CURTIS, ORIN EDSON.

Children:
Ada Mina,	May,	1885.
Walter Edson,	June,	1887.
Archie Merwin,	Dec.,	1894.

Parentage:

NAME.	BIRTH.	DEATH.
Orin Edson Curtis,	Aug., 1857.	
Ermina Ella Pettengill,	Nov., 1862.	

Paternal Grand:

Abner Curtis,	Dec., 1825,	Feb., 1876.
Mary House,	July, 1832.	

Maternal Grand:

Cyrenus Pettengill,	Mar., 1820.	
Amy A. Bates,	Jan., 1826.	

CUSHMAN, ANDREW.

Children:

Deborah,	Oct. 12, 1788.
William,	May 5, 1790.
Andrew,	Mar. 15, 1793.
Bathsheba,	Feb. 23, 1794.
Olive,	Apr. 18, 1796.
Oliver,	July 9, 1798.
Hannah,	Jan. 8, 1800.
Isaac,	July 17, 1801.
Mary,	Sept. 25, 1803.
Seth.	Apr. 25, 1807.
Adeline,	June 11, 1809.
John,	May 19, 1812.
Betsey,	June 11, 1814.

Parentage:

Andrew Cushman,	Jan. 6, 1761,	Feb. 6, 1844.
Bathsheba Jennings,	1767,	May 12, 1842.

Paternal Grand:

Isaiah Cushman,	Feb. 2, 1730.
Sarah Ring,	Sept. 2, 1737.

Sarah Ring, daughter of Andrew Ring and Zeruiah Standish, was a great-granddaughter of the famous Miles Standish.

DAVIS, ALONZO.

Child:

Annie Belle (adopted),	Oct., 1878.

Parentage:
Alonzo Davis.
Orrie A. Foster.

HISTORY OF LEEDS 371

Paternal Grand:

NAME.	BIRTH.	DEATH.

Benj. Davis, of Gorham.
Dorcas Mason, of Gorham

Paternal Great-Grand:
Timothy Foster.
Nancy Morse.

Maternal Grand:
William Henry Foster.
Harriet Lowe Curtis.

Maternal Great-Grand:
William Curtis.
Olive Stubbs.

Occupy the Foster farm originally owned by Timothy Foster, whose father was the first white male child born in the town of Winthrop. The family of Timothy Foster consisted of twelve children of whom five are now living: William Henry, aged 88 years, residence Livermore Falls, Methodist clergyman. Ward Locke, aged 77, manufacturer of shoes at North Easton, Mass., for many years. A soldier in War of Rebellion now living in Stoneham, Mass. Charles Robert, aged 75, farmer, also a soldier in War of Rebellion, now an inmate of the Massachusetts State Home for Soldiers at Chelsea. Everett Foster, aged 63; engineer on M. C. R. R., residence West Farmington, Me. Emeline, aged 68, wife of John F. Jennings of this town.

DUNHAM, BENJAMIN.

Children:
Hannah E.,	Jan.,	1838.		
Lucius C.,	Aug.,	1840.		

Parentage:
Benjamin Dunham, Jr.,	Mar.,	1807,	Jan.,	1863.
Lucinda Day,	Oct.,	1809,	Apr.,	1892.

Paternal Grand:
Benjamin Dunham,	Jan.,	1767,	Dec.,	1850.
Sibil Dudley,	Mar.,	1782,	Nov.,	1808.

Maternal Grand:
William A. Day.
Betsey Jones.

DYER, SOLOMON.

Children:

NAME.	BIRTH.	DEATH.
George,	Nov., 1870.	
Mrs. B. E. Wight,	Sept., 1873.	
Mabel L.,	Nov., 1878.	

Parentage:

Solomon Dyer,	Feb., 1844.	
Julia Trufant,	April, 1847.	

Paternal Grand:

Daniel Dyer,	Dec., 1816.	
Lois ———,	May, 1818.	

Maternal Grand:

Joseph Trufant,	June, 1819.	
Sivinah Trufant,	Dec., 1816.	

EDGECOMBE, AUBREY W.

Children:

Mae C.,	Aug., 1881.	
S. Etta,	Mar., 1886.	

Parentage:

Aubrey W. Edgecombe,	Mar., 1849.	
Annie W. Foss,	Nov., 1850.	

Paternal Grand:

Benjamin Edgecombe,	Jan., 1824,	Aug., 1899.
Rossie L. Foss,	June, 1826.	

Maternal Grand:

Cyrus W. Foss,	Aug., 1816,	Feb., 1890.
Kate B. Swanson,	Jan., 1828,	Dec., 1883.

NAME.	WHEN AND WHERE BORN.	DEATH.
Uriah Foss,	Saco, Mar. 6, 1760,	June 16, 1824.
Sarah Goodridge,	Saco, Aug. 24, 1759,	Jan. 28, 1831.

Children:

Levi,	Leeds, Apr. 10, 1782,	Nov. 23, 1831.
Cyrus,	Leeds, June 21, 1785,	Oct. 16, 1836.
Daniel,	Leeds, June 21, 1785,	Apr. 14, 1827.
Rachel,	Leeds, Mar. 19, 1788,	July 9, 1819.
Ephraim,	Leeds, Sept. 6, 1791,	Aug. 15, 1877.
Thaddeus,	Leeds, June 13, 1793,	May 10, 1819.
Simeon,	Leeds, July 5, 1795,	July 12, 1865.
Sally,	Leeds, Mar. 25, 1797,	Aug. 25, 1826.
Walter,	Leeds, May 18, 1799,	Apr. 13, 1875.
Ruel,	Leeds, Feb. 24, 1802,	Jan. 21, 1877.

Foss, Walter.

Walter Foss, b. in Leeds May 18, 1799; d. in Leeds April 12, 1875.

Dorcas S. Morrison, b. in Wayne Aug. 10, 1806; d. in Leeds April 29, 1882.

Children:

Lucy M., b. in Leeds Jan. 14, 1827; d. in Wayne Jan. 3, 1894.
John M., b. in Leeds Dec. 29, 1827; d. in Leeds Jan. 3, 1875.
Thomas C., b. in Leeds March 18, 1829; d. in Leeds Nov. 22 1891.
Sarah E., b. in Leeds Sept. 19, 1830; d. in Wayne Feb. 4, 1864.
Adoniram J., b. in Leeds Jan. 30, 1832.
Ann H., b. in Leeds Aug. 18, 1833.
James M., b. in Leeds Aug. 4, 1835; d. in New York City Nov. 4, 1864.
Dorcas E., b. in Leeds Dec. 14, 1836; d. in Boston Dec. 21, 1859.
Laura M., b. in Leeds May 22, 1839; d. in Leeds Feb. 25, 1852.
Rachel E., b. in Leeds Dec. 6, 1840; d. in Leeds Jan. 28, 1853.
Catherine, b. in Leeds June 6, 1842; d. in Leeds Sept. 10, 1874.
Walter P., b. in Leeds Jan. 6, 1844.
Vesta P., b. in Leeds Jan. 18, 1846.
Charles W., b. in Leeds Oct. 11, 1847; d. in California, Aug. 31, 1868.
Varnum R., b. in Leeds April 10, 1850; d. in Leeds Aug. 19, 1854.

Moulton, Jonathan.

Jonathan Moulton, b. in Hartford, April 22, 1823; d. in Wayne Nov. 7, 1887.

Lucy M. Foss, b. in Leeds Jan. 14, 1827; d. in Wayne Jan. 3, 1894.

Children:

Sumner C., b. in Wayne Oct. 1, 1853; d. in Wayne Oct. 1, 1876.
James M., b. in Wayne Sept. 26, 1859.

Foss, Thomas C.

Thomas C. Foss, b. in Leeds March 18, 1829; d. in Leeds Nov. 22, 1891.

Elizabeth Cobb, b. in Leeds July 13, 1835; d. in Leeds Aug. 6, 1882.

Children:

V. Richardson, b. in Leeds Jan. 3, 1857; d. in Portland Mar. 3, 1896.
Isabella, b. in Leeds Aug. 1, 1862.
Grace, b. in Leeds May 21, 1871.

Preston W., b. in Leeds Sept. 1, 1865; d. in Leeds Aug. 23, 1869.
Catherine M., b. in Leeds Oct. 5, 1874.
Thomas C., b. in Leeds May 26, 1878.

Second Marriage:

Thomas C. Foss, b. in Leeds March 18, 1829; d. in Leeds Nov. 22, 1891.
Abby J. Cox, Gardiner; d. in Leeds Oct. 25, 1891.
No children.

Foss, Emery.

Emery Foss, b. in Wayne April 10, 1823; d. in Wayne Sept. 11, 1872.
Sarah E. Foss, b. in Leeds Sept. 19, 1830; d. in Wayne Feb. 4, 1864.

Children:

John M., b. Jan. 20, 1854.
Walter E., b. July 29, 1860.

Foss, Adoniram Judson.

Children:

Lena H.,	Mar. 1, 1867.	
Lucy M.,	Sept. 15, 1878.	

Parentage:

Adoniram Judson Foss,	Jan. 30, 1832.	
Maria Theresa Howard,	May 24, 1835,	Jan. 18, 1897.

Paternal Grand:

Walter Foss,	May 18, 1799,	Apr. 14, 1875.
Dorcas S. Morrison,	Aug. 10, 1806,	Apr. 29, 1882.

Maternal Grand:

Benjamin Franklin Howard,	June 4, 1806,	Dec. 30, 1882.
Philena Gould,	1809,	Apr. 12, 1845.

Lane, Adoniram J.

Adoniram J. Lane, b. in Leeds July 18, 1830.
Ann H. Foss, b. in Leeds Aug. 18, 1833.

Children:

Ada A., b. in Leeds May 23, 1855; d. in Leeds Nov. 8, 1873.
Fremont, b. in Leeds Jan. 21, 1857; d. in Leeds June 30, 1863.
Willie E., b. in Leeds Aug. 11, 1860; d. in Brewer May 29, 1899.
Sadie E., b. in Leeds May 28, 1864.

Scott W., b. in Leeds Sept. 13, 1865.
Allie, b. in Leeds July 4, 1873; d. in Leeds Sept. 6, 1874.
Issa, b. in Leeds Sept. 7, 1877.

LINSCOTT, RUSSELL.

Russell Linscott, b. in Nashua, N. H., Jan. 22, 1835; d. in Oakland, Cal., Aug. 30, 1887.

Dorcas E. Foss, b. in Leeds Dec. 14, 1836; d. in Boston, Dec. 21, 1859.

Children:
Walter, b. in Boston; d. in Dorchester, Mass.
Hattie E., b. in Boston, Dec. 14, 1859.

BERRY, MELVIN.

Melvin Berry, b. 1815; d. in Leeds May 10, 1888.
Catherine M. Foss, b. in Leeds June 6, 1842; d. in Leeds Sept. 10, 1874.

FOSS, WALTER PAYSON.

Child:
George Morrison, Feb. 16, 1881.

Parentage:
Walter Payson Foss.
Harriet F. Cox.

Paternal Grand:
Rev. Walter Foss.
Dorcas S. Morrison.

Maternal Grand:
George T. Cox.
Abby Sargent.

Frank G. Foss, b. in Leeds Jan. 3, 1842.
Vesta P. Foss, b. in Leeds Jan. 18, 1846.
Children:
Alvin W., b. in Leeds June 3, 1871; d. in Leeds Dec. 3, 1872.
Guy W., b. in Leeds June 12, 1874; d. in Leeds Jan. 3, 1901.
Annie H., b. in Leeds Oct. 3, 1876.
Oliver J., b. in Leeds Oct. 13, 1882.
F. Maynard, b. in Leeds June 29, 1890.

FOSS, FRANK GUSTAVUS.

Children:

NAME.	BIRTH.		DEATH.	
Alvin Wilson,	June,	1871.	Jan.,	1873.
Guy Wilson,	June,	1874,	Jan.,	1901.
Annie Howard,	Oct.,	1876.		
Oliver Johnson,	Oct.,	1882.		
Frank Maynard,	June,	1890.		

Parentage:

Frank A. Foss,	Jan.,	1842.
Vesta T. Foss,	Jan.,	1846.

Paternal Grand:

Alvin Foss,	Nov.,	1816,	Oct.,	1869.
Cornelia B. Howard,	Mar.,	1820.		

Maternal Grand:

Walter Foss,	May,	1799,	Apr.,	1875.
Dorcas S. Morrison,	Aug.,	1806,	Apr.,	1882.

FRANCIS, REV. THOMAS D.

Children:

Thomas,	Jan. 26, 1785,	Jan. 27, 1869.
John,	Dec. 2, 1787,	Sept. 23, 1864.
Mark,	Oct. 7, 1789,	Oct. 2, 1864.
Davis,	Apr. 9, 1791,	Mar. 19, 1830.
Esther,	June 6, 1793,	Dec. 22, 1813.
Eunice, twin,	Dec. 9, 1794,	Dec. 18, 1862.
Lois, twin,	Dec. 9, 1794,	Dec. 12, 1794.
Matilda,	Oct. 9, 1796.	
Betsy,	Oct. 10, 1798,	Aug. 24, 1816.
Polly,	July 28, 1800,	Mar. 15, 1813.
Susan Collier,	Aug. 9, 1802.	
Benjamin,	Oct. 31, 1804,	June 3, 1884.
Samuel,	Aug. 23, 1806,	Feb. 11, 1889.
Lorania,	June 13, 1808,	Sept. 30, 1831.

Parentage:

Rev. Thomas Davis Francis,	Nov. 23, 1764,	May 9, 1836.
Eunice Millett,	Sept. 23, 1764,	Dec. 24, 1852.

Maternal Grand:

Thomas Millett,	Oct. 2, 1737,	1823.
Eunice Parsons,		

FRANCIS, THOMAS, ESQ.

Children:

Davies,	Nov. 2, 1823,	May 29, 1883.
Mary H.,	Apr. 1, 1833,	July 25, 1893.

Parentage:

NAME.	BIRTH.	DEATH.
Thomas Francis, Esq.,	Jan. 26, 1785,	Jan. 29, 1869.
Alice Lothrop,	Apr. 4, 1795,	1880.

Paternal Grand:

Thomas D. Francis,	Nov. 23, 1764,	May 9, 1836.
Eunice Millett,	Sept. 23, 1764,	Dec. 24, 1852.

Maternal Grand:

Daniel Lothrop, Jr.,	Mar. 28, 1767.	
Sally Whiting.		

FRANCIS, CAPT. JOHN.

Children:

Sewall,	Sept. 18, 1811,	Aug. 22, 1814.
Esther,	June 26, 1815.	
Orissa,	May 20, 1828.	

Parentage:

Capt. John Francis,	Dec. 9, 1787,	Sept. 23, 1864.
Patience Parcher.		

Paternal Grand:

Thomas D. Francis,	Nov. 23, 1764,	May 9, 1836.
Eunice Millett,	Sept. 23, 1764,	Dec. 24, 1852.

FRANCIS, SAMUEL L.

Children by first wife:

Susan Maria,	Mar. 5, 1834,	Jan. 29, 1837.
William Henry,	Jan. 12, 1836.	

Children by second wife:

Page Lane,	Feb. 12, 1843.
John Adams,	Jan. 10, 1850.

Parentage:

Samuel L. Francis,	Aug. 23, 1806,	Feb. 11, 1889.
Naomi P. True.	Feb. 11, 1815,	Oct. 12, 1881.
Sally Storrs True, first wife,	Jan. 25, 1806,	Feb. 3, 1837.

Paternal Grand:

Thomas Davis Francis,	Nov. 23, 1764,	May 9, 1836.
Eunice Millett,	Sept. 23, 1764,	Dec. 24, 1852.

Maternal Grand:

Joshua Morse True,	May 13, 1770,	Feb. 5, 1846.
Lucy Page,	Apr. 15, 1771,	Feb. 26, 1829.

FRANCIS, DAVIS.

Children:

NAME.	BIRTH.	DEATH.
Wallace L.,	May 12, 1850.	
Frederick D.,	May 11, 1852,	Sept. 23, 1859.
B. Franklin,	Dec. 9, 1854,	Apr. 12, 1880.
Thomas Edwin,	Mar. 18, 1857,	Sept. 18, 1874.
Fremont Davis,	Aug. 23, 1863,	Feb. 16, 1864.
Rosa Lena,	Apr. 14, 1861,	Nov. 30, 1891.
Fred E., second wife's child,	Oct. 7, 1874.	

Parentage:

Davis Francis,	Nov. 2, 1823,	May 29, 1883.
Rosamond Lane,	Mar. 28, 1827,	Dec. 24, 1863.
Second, Julia Ann Fernald,	Jan. 12, 1835,	Fall, 1876.

Paternal Grand:

Thomas Francis, Esq.,	Jan. 26, 1785,	Jan. 29, 1869.
Alice Lothrop,	Apr. 4, 1795,	1880.

Maternal Grand:

Issacher Lane,	May 2, 1798,	Dec. 23, 1891.
Dorcas Lane,	July 19, 1798,	Nov. 22, 1884.

FRANCIS, WILLIAM HENRY.

Children:

Samuel P., twin,	Oct. 23, 1859.
Ulmer P., twin,	Oct. 23, 1859.
Augustus S.,	Nov. 17, 1864.
Louise H.,	Nov. 15, 1874.
Millie B.,	June 7, 1880.

Parentage:

William Henry Francis,	Jan. 12, 1836.
Zipporah L. Perley,	Sept. 8, 1835.

Paternal Grand:

Samuel L. Francis,	Aug. 23, 1806,	Feb. 11, 1889.
Naomi P. True,	Feb. 11, 1815,	Oct. 12, 1881.

Maternal Grand:

Ulmer Perley,	Sept. 4, 1808,	Aug. 23, 1888.
Louise H. Merrill,	Apr. 10, 1810,	Nov. 25, 1899.

FRANCIS, WALLACE L.

Children:

Gard Rosamond,	Feb. 29, 1880.
Gladys Hester,	Jan. 5, 1883.

Parentage:

NAME.	BIRTH.	DEATH.
Wallace L. Francis,	May 12, 1850.	
Georgia A. Francis,	June 8, 1859.	

Paternal Grand:

Davies Francis,	Nov. 2, 1823,	May 29, 1883.
Rosamond Lane,	Mar. 28, 1827,	Dec. 24, 1863.

Maternal Grand:

John G. Francis,	Oct. 10, 1826,	Jan. 23, 1893.
Hester A. Haskell,	Feb. 10, 1823,	Oct. 28, 1900.

FROST, JOSEPH.

Children:
William,
Nathan Newell,

Parentage:
Joseph Frost,
First, Mary Carver.

Paternal Grand:
Dominicus Frost,
—— Abbott.

Maternal Grand:
Eleazer Carver.

Second Marriage:
Joseph Frost married second, Florentine Rose.
William Frost married Elizabeth Lothrop.

FROST, OLIVER P.

Children:

Orintha J.,	June, 1826,	Sept. 11, 1899.
Oliver P.,	Dec., 1827.	
Deborah W.,	Oct. 30, 1829.	
Bartlett C.,	Mar. 31, 1832.	
Esther A.,	Jan. 8, 1835.	
Evander D.,	Nov., 1836.	Nov., 1846.
Harriet S.		

Parentage:
Oliver P. Frost.
Esther May Jennings.

Paternal Grand:
Dominicus Frost.
———— Abbott.

Maternal Grand:
John Jennings.
Sally Mourton.

FULLER, KIMBALL PRINCE.

Children:

NAME.	BIRTH.	DEATH.
William H.,	Dec. 24, 1829,	May 18, 1863.
Miranda,	Dec. 25, 1831,	Apr. 22, 1853.
Caroline R.,	Mar. 20, 1835,	Mar. 26, 1855.
Esther M.,	Sept. 8, 1837,	Aug. 15, 1840.
Esther M.,	Jan. 27, 1840.	
Kimball P.,	May 17, 1842,	Aug. 22, 1861.
Josephine W.,	Apr. 2, 1844.	

Parentage:

Kimball Prince Fuller,	June 30, 1795,	Oct. 19, 1866.
Miranda Carman,	Aug. 17, 1804,	Jan. 2, 1887.

Paternal Grand:
Jesse Fuller,
Ruth Prince.

Maternal Grand:
Thomas Carman.
Elinor Gardner.

GILMORE, ROLAND A.

Children:

John F.,	Mar. 30, 1856.
Lizzie J.,	Apr. 1, 1859.

Parentage:

Roland A. Gilmore,	Oct. 26, 1827.
Cynthia L. Lothrop,	Nov. 14, 1837.

Paternal Grand:

John Gilmore,	Nov. 1, 1790,	Sept. 14, 1864.
Huldah Alger,	May 1, 1794,	July 16, 1870.

Maternal Grand:

Thomas Lothrop,	1812,	Sept. 24, 1888.
Jane Bartlett,	Nov. 16, 1814,	Jan. 12, 1899.

GORDON, GREENWOOD C.

Children:

NAME.	BIRTH.		DEATH.	
Hezekiah S.,	Dec.,	1842,		
John A.,	June,	1846,		
Henry G.,	Apr.,	1848,		
Viola H.,	Oct.,	1851,	Feb.,	1896.

Parentage:

Greenwood C. Gordon,	Feb.,	1815,		
Hannah Stinchfield,	Dec.,	1814.		

Paternal Grand:

Jonathan Gordon,	Feb.,	1786,	Jan.,	1876.
Sarah Pettingill,	May,	1788,	Dec.,	1880.

Maternal Grand:

James Stinchfield,	Aug.,	1773,	July,	1857.
Hannah Pettingill,	Feb.,	1786,	June,	1871.

GORDON, JOHN A.

Child:

John H.,	July,	1894.

Parentage:

John A. Gordon,	June,	1846,
Adelia C. Hartt,	May,	1860.

Paternal Grand:

Greenwood C. Gordon,	Feb.,	1815.
Hannah Stinchfield,	Dec.,	1814.

Maternal Grand:

Samuel Hartt,	May,	1828.	Mar.,	1897.
Mary A. Hayes,	Feb.,	1825.		

GORDON, CHARLES WALLACE.

Children:

Evelyn Blanche,	April,	1886.		
Lillian Frances,	Jan.,	1889.		
Harold Wallace,	Dec.,	1889.		
Florence May,	July,	1892,	Apr.,	1893.

Parentage:

Charles Wallace Gordon,	Jan.,	1849.
Annie F. Burrell,	Feb.,	1861.

Paternal Grand:

Charles Smith Gordon,	July,	1812,	July,	1883.
Florinda Wing Churchill,	Oct.,	1817,	May,	1886.

Maternal Grand:

NAME.	BIRTH.		DEATH.	
Alvin Richardson Burrell,	Mar.,	1830.		
Lorana Frances Burrell,	May,	1834.		

GOULD, RUSSELL L.

Children:

Willis Elden,	Apr.,	1870.		
John Carlos,	Apr.,	1875,	June,	1875.
Alice May,	July,	1879.		
Moses Greenwood,	Dec.,	1881.		

Parentage:

Russell L. Gould,	Dec.,	1842.
Ada Serena Greenwood,	Mar.,	1850.

Paternal Grand:

Elisha D. Gould,	Oct.,	1812,	Mar.,	1897.
Susan Elden Gould,	Aug.,	1816,	Oct.,	1883.

Maternal Grand:

Moses Greenwood,	Mar.,	1806,	Mar.,	1887.
Serena Deane Willis,	June,	1808,	Jan.,	1851.

GOULD, FRANK E.

Children:

Maude V.,	May,	1874.
Earl L.,	Oct.,	1877.

Parentage:

Frank E. Gould,	Mar.,	1848.
Sarah L. Peare,	Jan.,	1854.

Paternal Grand:

Elisha D. Gould,	Oct.,	1812,	Mar.,	1897.
Susan E. Gould,	Aug.,	1816,	Oct.,	1883.

Maternal Grand:

Moses B. Peare,	Apr.,	1818,	June,	1887.
Phebe Grant,	July,	1816.		

GOULD, NATHANIEL P.

Child:

Bernice A.,	May,	1890.

Parentage:

Nathaniel P. Gould,	Nov.,	1863.
Mae G. Pease,	July,	1865.

Paternal Grand:

NAME.	BIRTH.		DEATH.	
Freedom W. Gould,	Nov.,	1830.		
Adelia Perley,	Mar.,	1830,	Feb.,	1892.

Maternal Grand:

Augustus Pease,	Mar.,	1840.		
Fannie F. Blaisdell,	July,	1840,	Sept.,	1869.

GRANT, JOSIAH L.

Child:

Herbert Leroy,	Jan.,	1852.

Parentage:

Josiah L. Grant,	1827.
Rebecca Rose,	1834.

Paternal Grand:
Benjamin Grant.
Martha Peare.

Maternal Grand:
Harvey Rose.
Phebe Peare.

GRANT, AMOS P.

Children:

Harry A.,	May,	1863.		
Edward L.,	Apr.,	1865,	Dec.,	1898.
Rose E.,	Apr.,	1868.		
Joseph L.,	Apr.,	1871.		
Bertha A.,	Nov.,	1875.		
Arthur W.,	Mar.,	1881.		
Linwood S.,	Jan.,	1886.		

Parentage:

Amos P. Grant,	Mar,	1842.
Elmira J. Libby,	July,	1842.

Paternal Grand:

Benjamin H. Grant,	Feb.,	1792,	Dec.,	1876.
Martha Peare,	July,	1797,	Aug.,	1894.

Maternal Grand:

Uriah F. Libby,	Apr.,	1817,	Aug.,	1894.
Betsey E. Hallowell,	July,	1819,	Aug.,	1894.

GRANT, EDWARD L.

Children:

NAME.	BIRTH.		DEATH.	
Alton,	Aug.,	1890.		
Della,	Dec.,	1891.		
Edward L.,	Aug.,	1896.		
Parentage:				
Edward L. Grant,	Apr.,	1865,	Dec.	1898.
Myra M. Carver,	Sept.,	1872.		
Paternal Grand:				
Amos P. Grant,	Mar.,	1842.		
Elmira F. Libby,	July,	1842.		
Maternal Grand:				
James Carver,	Mar.,	1834.		
Mary Fisk,	July,	1837.		

HANSCOM, MELLEN J.

Arthur S.,	Aug.,	1880.		
Selden L.,	Nov.,	1881.		
Henry B.,	Apr.,	1884.		
Florence L.,	Dec.,	1888.		
Eva M.,	Jan.,	1893.		
Ora L.,	Oct.,	1895.	Mar.,	1896.
Parentage:				
Mellen J. Hanscom,	Nov.,	1853.		
Rosa V. Gilbert,	Feb.,	1855.		
Paternal Grand:				
Matthias Hanscom,	Jan.,	1812.	Feb.,	1887.
Florene Keen,	Dec.,	1818,	June,	1872.
Maternal Grand:				
Aranda Gilbert,	Feb.,	1818,	Sept.,	1876.
Diana T. Wing,	Aug.,	1818,	July,	1899.

HARVEY, SILAS.

Children:

Ray L.,	Dec.,	1869.
Wilbert N.,	Jan.,	1872.
Parentage:		
Silas Harvey,	Mar.,	1837.
Cora Cushman,	Nov.,	1843.

HISTORY OF LEEDS 385

Paternal Grand:
| NAME. | BIRTH. | DEATH. |

John Harvey.
Sophia Norris.

Maternal Grand:
Isaac Cushman,		June,	1801.	Dec.,	1882.
Dorcas Loring,		May,	1808.	May,	1850.

HERRICK, FRANK H.

Child:
Laura Margaret,		Apr. 15, 1899.

Parentage:
Frank H. Herrick,	Aug. 22, 1856,
Lucy M. Sylvester,	Apr. 26, 1867.

Paternal Grand:
Horace Herrick,		Dec. 1, 1826,	Nov. 9, 1890.
Sophronia L. Palmer,	May 23, 1834,	Mar. 26, 1901.

Maternal Grand:
Lorenzo Mellen Sylvester,	Oct. 1, 1834.
Saphila C. Metcalf,		Dec. 9, 1839.
Margaret M. Herrick, sister of
  Horace Herrick,		Nov. 6, 1822.
Lottie A. Herrick, sister of
  Frank H. Herrick,		Sept. 3, 1868.

HOBBS, ARTHUR W.

Child:
Dora B.,		Dec.,	1899.

Parentage:
Arthur W. Hobbs,	May,	1872.
Mabel H. Alden,		Aug.,	1877.

Paternal Grand:
Josiah W. Hobbs,	Feb.,	1847.
Dora L. Bryant,		April,	1849.	Jan.,	1873.

Maternal Grand:
Horace F. Alden,	Nov.,	1842.	Aug.,	1880.
Esther B. Hussey,	Feb.,	1845,	July,	1897.

Hosley, Columbus P.

Children:

NAME.	BIRTH.	DEATH.
William C.,	Sept., 1872.	
Freddie L.,	Feb., 1876.	July 30, 1877.
Linwood P.,	Nov., 1882.	
Charles G.,	Apr., 1885.	

Parentage:

Columbus P. Hosley,	May, 1847.	
Bessie A. Bodge,	Jan., 1847.	

Paternal Grand:

Columbus C. Hosley,	Apr., 1802.	Oct. 6, 1885.
Abigail Griffith,	Feb., 1805.	July 20, 1886.

Maternal Grand:

Andrew Bodge,	Jan., 1810.	Oct. 31, 1899.
Sally Manson,	Jan., 1811.	May 30, 1894.

Howards in Direct Line from the Plymouth Colony

John Howard[1], Bridgewater, Mass.
Maj. Jonathan[2], Bridgewater, Mass.
Seth[3], Bridgewater, Mass.
Jesse[4], Bridgewater, Mass.

Capt. Seth[5] settled in Leeds in 1802. Married Nov. 21, 1782,	Nov. 5, 1762,	Jan. 5, 1844.
Desire Bailey,	Jan. 23, 1762,	Dec. 28, 1829.

Children:

Stillman[6],	May 20, 1785,	Feb. 16, 1861.
Everett,	Nov. 22, 1785,	Nov. 23, 1820.
Ward,	Dec. 18, 1789,	July 19, 1855.
Seth,	Aug. 9, 1792,	Feb. 12, 1847.
Rowland Bailey,	July 29, 1795,	Apr. 30, 1840.
Aurelia,	June 28, 1797.	
Lucretia,	Feb. 2, 1800,	Dec. 28, 1884.
Valantine Rathburn,	Apr. 11, 1803,	1828.
Benjamin Franklin,	June 4, 1806,	Dec. 30, 1882.

Stillman Howard[6],	May 20, 1785,	Feb. 16, 1861.
Lydia Lothrop,	May 5, 1789,	Apr. 6, 1872.

Married Sept. 27, 1807.

Children:

Lloyd Everett,	Aug. 8, 1808,	Oct. 9, 1810.
Stillman Lothrop[7],	Mar. 10, 1810,	Nov. 9, 1890.
Rozilia Augusta,	Jan. 30, 1812,	Oct. 4, 1859.

NAME.	BIRTH.	DEATH.
Mary Louisa,	May 14, 1816,	Aug. 17, 1856.
Lydia Arvilla,	Mar. 25, 1818,	Nov. 9, 1848.
Lucretia Phillips,	Sept. 19, 1820,	Dec. 23, 1844.

Seth Howard[7].
Amanda Additon.   June 6, 1828.

Children:
Elsie Amanda,	May 17, 1851.	
Florilla, twin,	Oct. 5, 1853.	
Fletcher, twin,	Oct. 5, 1853.	
Lydia Ann,	June 18, 1857.	
Seth Adelbert,	June 6, 1859.	
Dora Lovisa,	July 29, 1863.	
Lucretia Lane.	Aug. 22, 1866.	

Elsie A. Howard.
Herbert W. Lincoln.
   Married Apr. 11, 1869.

Children:
Annie Elsie,	July 21, 1870.	
Howard Elliot,	Dec. 16, 1877.	
Mabel Dora,	Nov. 12, 1879.	

Florilla Howard.
Jas. C. Pike.
   Married Nov. 18, 1877.

Children:
Frank Howard,	Jan. 4, 1879.	
Cora Mary,	Oct. 15, 1881.	
Edna Amanda,	Dec. 19, 1883.	

Fletcher Howard[8].
Nancy Percy Pike.
   Married July 21, 1883.

Lydia Ann Howard.
Charles S. Pike.
   Married Sept. 13, 1882.

Seth Adelbert Howard[8].
Stella Tryon.
   Married Sept. 27, 1883.

Children:
George,	July 28, 1884.	
Seth,	Feb. 15, 1886.	

Dora Lovisa Howard.
Junius C. Wing.
  Married Nov. 24, 1891.

  Children:

NAME.	BIRTH.	DEATH.
Beulah Amanda,	Mar. 4, 1893.	
Arland Junius,	Mar. 3, 1897.	
Stella Ardelia,	Aug. 21, 1900.	

HOWARD, ROWLAND B.

Rowland Bailey Howard,   July 29, 1795,   Apr. 30, 1840.
Eliza Otis,

  Children:
Oliver Otis,   Nov.,   1830.
Rowland Bailey.
Charles Henry.

HOWARD, LOT.

  Child:
Francis Davis Millett,   Feb.,   1891.

  Parentage:
Lot Howard,   Feb. 24, 1861.
Ella T. Millett,   Aug. 6, 1853.

  Paternal Grand:
Luther Loomis Howard,   Mar.,   1826.
Sarah P. Hussey,   Jan. 5, 1822.

  Maternal Grand:
Francis Davis Millett,   Oct. 1, 1811,   Dec. 28, 1893.
Lusina Phillips,   Jan. 9, 1819.

HUSSEY, GEORGE G.

  Children:
John Q.,	Dec.,	1832.		
Calvin C.,	Dec.,	1835.		
Maurice S.,	Sept.,	1838.		
George G., Jr.,	Aug.,	1841,	Oct. 28, 1862.	
Esta B.,	Feb.,	1845,	July 17, 1897.	
Frank H.,	Aug.,	1848.		

  Parentage:
| George G. Hussey, | June, | 1809, | June, | 1888. |
| Jemima Coburn. | June, | 1810, | Dec., | 1893. |

Paternal Grand:
Nathanal Hussey.
Hannah Lovejoy.

Maternal Grand:
Jesse Coburn.
Nancy Tarr.

KEMP, JOHN H.

Children:

NAME.	BIRTH.		DEATH.	
Etta G.,	Jan.,	1880.		
Blanche E.,	June,	1882,		
Blaine,	Aug.,	1884,	Aug.,	1884.
Maria W.,	Aug.,	1887.		
Lottie May,	Dec.,	1893.		
Henry Washington,	Nov.,	1898.		

Parentage:
John H. Kemp,   June,   1855.
Maggie L. Stewart.

Paternal Grand:
George Washington Kemp.
Maria A. Kemp.

Maternal Grand:
George Stewart,   1828.
Eliza Stewart,   1831.

KENNEY, GEORGE MONROE.

Children:

Charles Monroe,	Jan.,	1876.
Willard Lorenzo,	Oct.,	1877.
Clarabella Mae,	July,	1882.

Parentage:

George Monroe Kenney,	June,	1849.
Eliza Ann Jones,	Nov.,	1848.

Paternal Grand:

Willard Kenney,	Aug.,	1803.	June,	1879.
Polly Cummings Staples,	Mar.,	1818,	May,	1887.

Maternal Grand:

Lorenzo Jones,	Dec.,	1806,	Dec.,	1862.
Arabella Rawson Newman,	May,	1819,	July,	1889.

KNAPP, CHARLES.

Children:

NAME.	BIRTH.	DEATH.
Azel,	May 20, 1811,	Aug. 10, 1844.
Simeon H.,	Oct. 11, 1812,	July 27, 1823.
Abigail L.,	Mar. 3, 1814,	Oct. 7, 1884.
Colista,	May 15, 1816,	Jan. 23, 1872.
Hannah L.,	Mar. 17, 1818.	
Archibald L.,	Aug. 7, 1819,	May 8, 1897.
Charles Sewall, twin,	Aug. 15, 1821,	Jan. 5, 1892.
Catharine, twin,	Aug. 15, 1821,	May 15, 1823.
Catharine L., child of Hannah,	Aug. 31, 1825.	

Parentage:

Charles Knapp,	July 2, 1788,	Sept. 26, 1875.
Catharine Lindsey,	Apr. 15, 1787,	Mar. 27, 1823.
Second, Hannah Lindsey,	Jan. 17, 1783,	Apr. 13, 1874.

Paternal Grand:

Joseph Knapp, Jr.,		Aug. 7, 1840.
Eunice Carver,		Apr., 1845.

Maternal Grand:

William Lindsey,	June 16, 1747,	Mar. 21, 1831.
Hannah,	Nov. 6, 1752,	May 7, 1831.

KNAPP, ARCHIBALD L.

Children:

Flavilla Ruby,	Jan. 30, 1845.	
Rose Emma,	Mar. 8, 1847.	
James White,	May 1, 1848,	June 8, 1848.
Charles Burton,	May 4, 1850.	
Bradford Archibald,	Mar. 9, 1857.	
Jennie White,	Oct. 26, 1861.	

Parentage:

Archibald L. Knapp,	Aug. 7, 1819,	May 8, 1897.
Jane White,	Feb. 5, 1820,	Dec. 6, 1891.

Paternal Grand:

Charles Knapp,	July 2, 1788,	Sept. 26, 1875.
Catherine Lindsey,	Apr. 15, 1787,	Mar. 27, 1823.

Maternal Grand:

James White,	July 31, 1780,	June 15, 1834.
Nancy Kenney,	Nov. 15, 1780,	July 31, 1860.

KNAPP, STEPHEN D.

Children:

NAME.	BIRTH.	DEATH.
Frank M.,	July, 1868.	
Willie B.,	Aug., 1870.	
Charlie R.,	June, 1874.	
Rollie D.,	June, 1886.	

Parentage:

S. D. Knapp,	Nov., 1839.	
Lizzie B. Moore,	Mar., 1850.	

Paternal Grand:

Stephen Knapp,	Sept., 1800,	1892.
Sarah Gott,	Oct., 1798,	1870.

Maternal Grand:

Abner Moore,	June, 1810,	1879.
Eliza Moore,	Jan., 1819.	

KNAPP, ABIAL D.

Children:

George D.,	May 28, 1880.
Clyde P.,	Oct. 11, 1884.

Parentage:

Abial D. Knapp,	May 10, 1829,	Feb. 20, 1897.
Ella C. Millett,	Nov. 29, 1852.	

Paternal Grand:

Peltiah Knapp,	Mar., 1800,	Mar., 1881.
Abigail Norris,	Apr., 1797,	1831.

Maternal Grand:

Seth Millett,	Sept. 10, 1805,	Mar. 29, 1879.
Lucy Millett,	July 24, 1812,	Jan. 26, 1899.

Abial D. Knapp and Ella C. Millett were married in Leeds April 5, 1879, living in Leeds until Mr. Knapp's death, having two sons. George D. Knapp at the time of his father's death was at work in Massachusetts as station agent. Clyde Knapp was attending school at the time of his father's death.

KNAPP, WOODBURY S.

Child:

Willis A.,	Jan., 1856.

Parentage:

Woodbury S. Knapp,	May, 1831,	Sept., 1897.
Rachael B. Greenwood,	July, 1837.	

Paternal Grand:

NAME.	BIRTH.		DEATH.	
Pelatiah Knapp,	Mar.,	1800.		
Abigail Norris,	Apr.,	1797,	Oct.,	1831.

Maternal Grand:

Moses Greenwood,	Mar.,	1806,	Mar.,	1887.
Susan Dean Willis,	June,	1808,	Jan.,	1851.
Second, Mehitable Chute,	May,	1801,	Apr.,	1887.

KNAPP, WILLIS A.

Child:
Maud L.,   Sept.,   1881.

Parentage:

Willis A. Knapp,	Jan.,	1856.		
Julia A. Carver,	July,	1850,	Nov.,	1892.
Second, Mabel W. Brown,	Apr.,	1873.		

Paternal Grand:

Woodbury S. Knapp,	May,	1831,	Sept.,	1897.
Rachael B. Greenwood,	July,	1837.		

Maternal Grand:

Everett Carver,	July,	1821,	Nov.,	1881.
Julia A. Baldwin,	Mar.,	1826.		

Maternal Great-Grand:
Caleb Carver,   June,   1800.

LANE, GEORGE BAILEY.

Children:

John,	Sept. 5, 1859,	Sept. 5, 1883.
Justin Palmer,	Dec. 12, 1865,	Feb. 16, 1885.
Kittie,	Feb. 27, 1875.	

Parentage:

Geo. Bailey Lane,	Feb. 16, 1833.
Viola Ann Ramsdell,	May 1, 1839.

Paternal Grand:

John Lane,	Aug. 31, 1796,	May 12, 1863.
Vesta Phillips.	Aug. 20, 1800,	Feb. 23, 1890.

Maternal Grand:

Luther Ramsdell,	Sept. 3, 1799,	Jan. 26, 1852.
Achsah Pratt,	Jan. 24, 1808,	Jan. 22, 1878.

LANE, ADONIRAM JUDSON.

Children:

NAME.	BIRTH.		DEATH.	
Ada A.,	May,	1855,	Nov.,	1873.
Fremont,	Jan.,	1857,	June,	1863.
Willie E.,	Aug.,	1860,	May,	1899.
Sadie E.,	May,	1864.		
Winfield S.,	Sept.,	1865.		
Allie,	July,	1873,	Sept.,	1874.
Issachar,	Sept.,	1877.		

Parentage:
Adoniram Judson Lane.
Ann Hazeltine Foss.

Paternal Grand:
Issachar Lane.
Dorcas Lane.

Maternal Grand:
Rev. Walter Foss.
Dorcas S. Morrison.

LARRABEE, DANIEL BRIGGS.

Children:

Arthur G.,	Oct.,	1839,	Mar.,	1898.
Three boys, died in infancy.				
Charles W.,	Mar.,	1843,	Jan.,	1888.
Emily,		1847,		1853.
Lewis M.,	Aug.,	1851.		

Parentage:

Daniel Briggs Larrabee,	Nov.,	1806,	Nov.,	1890.
Saffronia Larrabee,	Jan.,	1811,	April,	1883.

Paternal Grand:
Samuel Larrabee,
Ruth Moore,

LARRABEE, LEWIS M.

Lewis M. Larrabee,	Aug.,	1851.
Lillian W. Keith,	Dec.,	1861.

Children:

Catharine S.,	Nov.,	1883.		
Arvilla S.,	Feb.,	1885.		
Lewis Winn,	Aug.,	1886.		
Frances,	June,	1892.		
Ella A.,	Sept.,	1893,	Sept.,	1894.

LIBBY, LORIN F.

Children:

NAME.	BIRTH.	DEATH.
Cora May Belle,	Nov. 19, 1868.	
Lulu Lyden,	Dec. 30, 1872.	
Lorin Percival,	Apr. 11, 1877.	
Charles A.,	Jan. 19, 1872,	Mar. 2, 1872.
Edward Pearl,	Dec. 18, 1886.	

Parentage:
Lorin F. Libby,	Jan. 18, 1847.	
Flora A. Drake,	Apr. 30, 1852.	

Paternal Grand:
Asa L. Libby,	Sept. 22, 1820.	
Joan D. Fish,	Nov. 28, 1825.	

Maternal Grand:
Daniel Drake,	1831.	
Rosilla Gilbert,	May 7, 1832.	

LIBBY, SAMUEL P.

Children:

	BIRTH	DEATH
Horace J.,	Sept. 26, 1875.	
Olive Mabel,	Apr. 3, 1879.	
Charles Norris,	Apr. 1, 1881.	
Connie E.,	Feb. 23, 1884.	
Willie H.,	Apr. 14, 1886.	

Parentage:
Samuel P. Libby,	Dec. 13, 1843.	
Emma L. Norris,	July 20, 1856.	

Paternal Grand:
Pelatiah F. Libby,	May 9, 1815,	Mar. 17, 1887.
Betsey Carver,	Nov. 8, 1816,	July 15, 1872.

Maternal Grand:
Charles Norris,	July 10, 1827,	June 1, 1895.
Olive A. Maxim,	Feb. 13, 1832.	

LINDSEY, WILLIAM.

Children:

	BIRTH	DEATH
John,	Mar. 19, 1775,	Feb. 1, 1834.
Polly,	Mar. 21, 1777,	June 9, 1819.
Abigail,	Jan. 26, 1779,	July 23, 1813.
Azel,	Jan. 6, 1781,	July 23, 1802.
Hannah,	June 17, 1783,	Apr. 13, 1874.
Lucy,	Aug. 30, 1785,	Apr. 8, 1816.
Catharine,	Apr. 15, 1787,	Mar. 27, 1823.

NAME.	BIRTH.	DEATH.
James,	May 20, 1789,	Feb. 8, 1870.
William,	Aug. 26, 1791,	Mar. 31, 1810.
Betsey,	July 24, 1793,	July 30, 1746.
Archibald,	May 22, 1795,	Nov. 15, 1870.

Parentage:

William Lindsey,	June 16, 1747,	Mar. 21, 1831.
Hannah ———,	Nov. 6, 1752,	May 7, 1831.

LINDSEY, HOWARD.

Children:

Roland,	Apr. 6, 1830,	Aug. 6, 1855.
Everett,	May 20, 1831.	
Roscoe Green,	Feb. 5, 1833,	Sept. 9, 1864.
Rossa Jane,	Sept. 8, 1834.	
Frederic Shaw,	Sept. 29, 1837,	Nov., 1875.
Julia Ann,	Oct. 6, 1839.	
Thomas Jennings,	Mar. 12, 1844.	
George Albert,	Dec. 17, 1845,	Feb. 9, 1893.
Lewis Leavitt,	Dec. 8, 1847.	
Robert, Jr.,	Nov. 27, 1851.	

Parentage:

Howard Lindsey,	Jan. 25, 1800,	Jan. 21, 1880.
Caroline Lindsay Lindsey,	May 1, 1810,	Dec. 15, 1895.

Paternal Grand:

Thomas Lindsey,	1756,	Dec. 25, 1802.
Thankful Bailey,	1765	Sept. 4, 1847.

Maternal Grand:
Daniel Lindsey.
Jane Gilbert.

Thomas Lindsey, father, settled on Bishop Hill in 1797, was drowned in Androscoggin Pond Dec. 25, 1802. James Lindsey, maternal grand., was a Revolutionary soldier. Of the above eight sons of Howard and Caroline Lindsey, four were soldiers in the Union army during the Rebellion (1861-1865), Everett L., Roscoe L. (who died at Barrancas, Florida), Frederic S. and Thomas L.

LINDSAY, DANIEL.

Children:

William H.,	Feb. 1 1809,	Oct. 18, 1850.
Caroline,	May 1, 1810,	Dec. 15, 1895.
James,	Oct. 19, 1811,	Mar. 7, 1894.

NAME.	BIRTH.	DEATH.
Charles F.,	Dec. 13, 1813,	
Julia A.,	Aug. 25, 1815,	Nov. 28, 1858.
Silas A.,	Dec. 30, 1817,	Oct. 9, 1845.
Betsey,	Oct. 16, 1819,	Oct. 28, 1873.
Alvin H.,	Nov. 13, 1821,	Apr. 20, 1896.
Josephine B.,	Aug. 14, 1823,	Mar. 18, 1901.
Clarinda F.,	July 14, 1825.	
Everett H.,	Sept. 3, 1827,	1830.
Wallace B.,	May 2, 1830,	Mar. 27, 1861.
Daniel W.,	Aug. 5, 1832,	

Parentage:

Daniel Lindsay,	Feb. 11, 1784,	May 27, 1863.
Jane (Gilbert) Lindsay,	June 29, 1791,	Apr. 17, 1867.

Paternal Grand:

James Lindsay,	July 22, 1755,	Jan. 19, 1849.
Phebe (Pettengill) Lindsay,	Oct. 25, 1755,	Oct. 13, 1843.

Maternal Grand:

Capt. William Gilbert,	1756,	May 25, 1816.
Betsey (Bailey) Gilbert,	1760,	Aug. 11, 1834.

LINDSEY, LEWIS L.

Children:

Arthur L.,	July 15, 1874.	
Bertha M.,	Nov. 30, 1875.	
Alice B.,	June 3, 1880.	
Annie L.,	April 10, 1885.	
Harry C.,	Nov. 6, 1892.	

Parentage:

Lewis L. Lindsay,	Dec. 8, 1847.
Flora E. (Curtis) Lindsay,	June 2, 1852.

Paternal Grand:

Howard Lindsay,	Jan. 25, 1800,	Jan. 21, 1880.
Caroline Lindsay,	May 1, 1810,	Dec. 15, 1895.

Maternal Grand:

Abner Curtis,	Dec. 28, 1825,	Feb. 11, 1876.
Mary H. Curtis,	July 31, 1832.	

LOTHROPS FROM DANIEL THE FIRST LOTHROP IN LEEDS.

Daniel Lothrop,	Dec. 10, 1745,	1837.
Mary Turner, third wife,		

Children:

Polly,	Oct. 29, 1787,	1881.
Lyda,	May 5, 1789,	Apr. 6, 1872.

NAME.	BIRTH.	DEATH.
Alson,	Feb. 7, 1792.	
Jonah,	July 23, 1795,	Aug. 23, 1795.
Rhoda,	April 29, 1799.	
Capt. Daniel Lothrop, Jr.,	Mar. 28, 1767.	
Sarah Whiting,		July 8, 1807.

Children:

Ira,	Nov. 2, 1787.	
Malinda,	Mar. 29, 1789.	
Sarah Whiting,	July 25, 1791.	
Hannah,	Aug. 26, 1793.	
Alice,	April 4, 1795.	
Daniel, 3d,	May 11, 1797,	Jan. 8, 1821.
Eaton Whiting,	Apr. 12, 1801.	
George Howard,	Apr. 22, 1803.	
Willard,	Dec. 10, 1805.	
Lucy Gilbert, second wife,		

Children:

Lucy,	May 9, 1811.	
Dulcenia,	Apr. 11, 1813.	
Augustus Washington,	June 23, 1815.	
William G.,	Apr. 11, 1817.	
Orman Franklin,	Dec. 10, 1818.	
Daniel 3d,	Apr. 20, 1821.	
Jane,	Oct. 20, 1822.	
Emily,	Jan. 9, 1827.	
Mary Francis,	Feb. 23, 1825.	
George Lothrop,	June 13, 1765,	Mar. 4, 1839.
Polly Thayer,		Oct. 25, 1831.

Children:

Solomon,	Feb. 26, 1788,	Aug. 12, 1873.
Levit,	May 19, 1793.	
Hannah,	Mar. 19, 1800.	
Jeremiah,	Oct. 29, 1802,	Sept. 25, 1874.
Polly,	Dec. 17, 1804.	
Thomas Lothrop.		
Cynthia Brett,		Sept. 4, 1823.

Children:

Louisa,	Dec. 9, 1802.	
Osbert,	Oct. 11, 1804.	
Ebenezer,	Sept. 10, 1807,	Dec. 2, 1851.
Cynthia,	Nov. 9, 1809.	
Thomas, Jr.,	Oct. 26, 1811.	

NAME.	BIRTH.	DEATH.
Lydia Susan,	Aug. 18, 1815.	
Rufus Daniel,	July 28, 1817.	
Leonard Carey,	Apr. 15, 1821.	
Aseneth L.,	Sept. 10, 1826,	Nov., 1829.
Mehitable, second wife,		Sept. 4, 1852.
Joshua,	Dec. 22, 1827.	

Sullivan Lothrop.
Polly Haines,   Apr.,   1823.

Children:

Ruthy,	Mar. 22, 1799,	July 7, 1823.
Willis,	Jan. 26, 1801.	
Sullivan, Jr.,	Oct. 15, 1802.	
Hannah Seavey,	Aug. 30, 1804.	
Olive,	July 7, 1806,	Feb. 15, 1889.
Veranus,	Apr. 9, 1808.	
Achsa,	Jan. 10, 1810.	
Polly Haines,	Apr. 8, 1812,	June 29, 1823.
Fittzelon,	Jan. 19, 1815,	Dec. 6, 1815.
Arza Gilmore,	Feb. 20, 1821.	

Mrs. Abigail Jennings, 2d wife.
Daniel.
Mary Ann.
Abbie.

Alson Lothrop.
Huldah Richmond.

Children:

Alson, Jr.,	Jan. 15, 1815.
Drusilla Augusta,	Mar. 29, 1816.
Leonard Richmond,	Apr. 22, 1817.
Daniel,	Jan. 10, 1820.

George D. Lothrop,
Hulda Gilmore,   Nov. 30, 1862.

Children:

Mary Francis,	Dec 3, 1837.
Helen Augusta,	July, 1841.

Solomon Lothrop.
Sarah W. Lothrop.

Children:

George Daniel,	Aug. 24, 1811.
Betsey,	Dec. 13, 1813.
Solomon Leavitt,	June 10, 1817.
Orissa,	Dec. 30, 1819.
Willard,	June 18, 1828.

NAME.	BIRTH.	DEATH.
Leavitt Lothrop,		Apr. 17, 1849.
Betsey Lane.		

Children:

NAME.	BIRTH.	DEATH.
Elias Lane,	Nov. 19, 1817.	
Davis Francis,	Sept. 11, 1820.	
Warren Lane,	July 5, 1823.	
Caroline Elizabeth,	Oct. 17, 1825.	
Mary Jane,	July 12, 1833.	
Solomon L. Lothrop,		Feb. 8, 1874.
Hannah Turner.		

Children:

NAME.	BIRTH.	DEATH.
Lewis Leavitt,	Oct. 21, 1840,	Feb. 4, 1842.
William Henry,	May 17, 1842.	
Lydia Albina,	Aug. 3, 1844.	

Willard Lothrop.
Emeline L. Boothby.

Children:

NAME.	BIRTH.	DEATH.
Susan,	Jan. 11, 1861.	
Frank Burton,	July 1862.	
Sarah Clyde,	Aug. 6. 1879.	

NAME.	BIRTH.	DEATH.
Davis F. Lothrop.		
Caroline S. Morse,		Feb. 16, 1901.

Children:

NAME.	BIRTH.	DEATH.
Flora Lovisa,	Sept. 1, 1847.	
Adonia,	Mar. 26, 1849,	Sept. 9, 1852.
Eugene,	Oct. 6, 1851,	Aug. 30, 1852.
Elias.	July 7, 1853.	
Seville,	Jan. 10, 1855,	Jan. 16, 1856.
Irvin Scott,	Feb. 22, 1856.	
Olive Morse,	May 5, 1858.	
Ralph,	Nov. 24, 1860.	
Elias L. Lothrop,		Sept. 30, 1852.
Jane Morse.		

Children:

NAME.	BIRTH.	DEATH.
Leavitt,	June 10, 1848.	
Mary Morse,	Dec. 3, 1849.	
Veranus Lothrop,	Apr. 9, 1808,	Dec. 23, 1861.
Esther Lane.		

Children:

NAME.	BIRTH.	DEATH.
Warren Lane,	July 21, 1847.	
Aubrey Giddings,	Apr. 10, 1854.	

NAME.	BIRTH.	DEATH.
Arza G. Lothrop,	Feb. 20, 1821.	
Martha J. Ramsdell,	Mar. 8, 1827,	July 20, 1892.

Children:

Luther Ramsdell,	Nov. 24, 1853.	
Veranus Willis,	Jan. 24, 1863.	

Turners.

Josiah Turner.
Lydia.

Children:

Cyntha, born in Bridgewater,	Feb. 15, 1779.	
Joseph, born in Bridgewater,	Mar. 19, 1781.	
George, born in Bridgewater,	Jan. 2, 1783,	Oct. 2, 1862.
Lewis, born in Bridgewater,	Nov. 15, 1784.	
Lydia, born in Bridgewater,	Oct. 16, 1786.	
Josiah, Jr., born in Leeds,	Jan. 1, 1789.	
Desire, born in Leeds,	Mar. 31, 1791.	
Benjamin,	Apr. 6, 1793.	
Hannah,	July 10, 1797.	
Diana,	Oct. 18, 1799.	

William Turner.   Mar. 2, 1829.
Joanna.

Children:

Obadiah,	Mar. 11, 1783.	
Lydia,	Nov. 28, 1784.	
William, Jr.,	Aug. 12, 1786.	
Gracy,	Nov. 4, 1788.	
Simeon,	June 22, 1791.	
Joanna,	Mar. 17, 1794.	
James,	Feb. 18, 1796,	Apr. 13, 1812.
Jane,	Apr. 19, 1798.	
David,	Feb. 1, 1801,	Feb. 3, 1801.
Edwin,	Aug. 27, 1802.	

George Turner.,	June 2, 1783,	Oct. 2, 1862.
Betsey Gilbert,		Apr. 8, 1854.

Children:

Cynthia,	Dec. 10, 1801,	July 19, 1803.
Betsey Palmer,	Oct. 2, 1803.	
Cyntha,	Mar. 31, 1805.	
Sobrina,	Oct. 3, 1807.	
George Washington,	Mar. 6, 1810.	
Lydia,	Jan. 21, 1812.	

HISTORY OF LEEDS 401

NAME.	BIRTH.	DEATH.
Deborah,	May 2, 1814,	Sept. 3, 1815.
Josiah,	May 25, 1816.	
Hannah,	Oct. 11, 1818.	
William,	Feb. 27, 1821.	
John,	Aug. 10, 1823.	
Sarah,	Nov. 13, 1826.	
Benjamin,	July 8, 1828.	
Martha Ann,	Mar. 25, 1832.	
Joseph Turner,		Apr. 30, 1860.
Deborah Gilbert,		Apr. 24, 1814.
Children:		
Eunice,	July 25, 1803.	
Phillips,	Aug. 8, 1805.	
Joseph, Jr.,	Nov. 5, 1807,	May 13, 1854.
Julia Ann,	Oct. 13, 1809,	Mar. 7, 1901.
Joanna,	Feb. 26, 1812,	Mar. 8, 1835.
William Gilbert,	Apr. 21, 1814.	

Hannah Pettingill, second wife.

Children:		
John,	Oct. 14, 1816,	Mar. 1 1817.
Jane Robinson,	Aug. 7, 1824.	
Josiah,	Oct. 11, 1829.	
Cynthia Welcome,	Sept. 15, 1826.	
Mrs. Esther Scammon, 3d wife,		Sept. 29, 1855.
Lewis Turner.		Aug. 19, 1866.
Hannah Collier.		
Children:		
Oscar Dunreath,	May 29, 1809.	
Joshua Shaw,	July 13, 1811.	
Francis Orman,	Mar. 24, 1813,	July 30, 1818.
Lucius Clark,	Dec. 15, 1816.	
Amanda Fitzelen,	Oct. 20, 1822.	
Charles Osburn,	Jan. 25, 1826.	
Oscar D. Turner,		Mar. 15, 1882.
Rozilla Howard,		Oct. 7, 1859.
Children:		
Lucia,	June 10, 1834.	
Florence Augusta.	Oct. 4, 1848.	

Joshua S. Turner.
Betsey Lothrop.

Children:

NAME.	BIRTH.	DEATH.
Ermina Jane,	Aug. 6, 1834.	
Emmie Clark,	Jan. 13, 1837.	
Francis Orman,	Apr. 16, 1839.	

Phillips Turner.   Mar. 3, 1844.
Mary L. Howard.   Aug. 17, 1856.

Children:

Victoria Helen,	Mar. 3, 1838.	
Herbert Phillips,	Nov. 3, 1842,	Feb. 2, 1846.

William G. Turner.
Mary S. Loring,   Jan. 23, 1886.

Children:

Stephen Welcome,	Dec. 6, 1838.	
Ann Clark,	Jan. 24, 1840.	
Henry Sewall,	Feb. 13, 1841.	
Cynthia Welcome,	Dec. 16, 1842.	
Samuel Loring,	July 19, 1844.	
Mary Thomas,	Feb. 6, 1847,	Mar. 5, 1850.
William P.,		Mar., 1862.
Hannah E.,		Mar., 1862.
Jacabina,		Mar., 1862.

Last three died with diphtheria.

Josiah Turner, son of Joseph
  Hannah Dunham.

Children:

Lizzie Dunham,	July 10, 1857.	
Ernest Linwood,	Jan. 22, 1865.	
Alice Gertrude,	May 4, 1869,	June 25, 1884.

John Turner.
Elizabeth B. Manwell,   Aug. 31, 1886.

Children:

John Manwell,	Aug. 12, 1856,	Dec. 24, 1899.
Marion Elizabeth,	Oct. 28, 1860.	
Benjamin Manwell,	Mar. 14, 1864,	Oct., 1900.
Lelia Annah,	Aug. 12, 1866,	1899.

Dr. John M. Turner.   Dec. 24, 1899.
Olive M. Lothrop.

Child:
Florence E.,   June 11, 1891.

Benjamin Turner.
Harriet H. Lane.
   Children:

NAME.	BIRTH.	DEATH.
George Henry,	June 2, 1855.	
Peter Lane,	Sept. 15, 1857,	
Grace Haywood,	Mar. 10, 1863.	

Obadiah Turner.
Tabitha ———.   June 20, 1840.
   Children:

Susannah,	Nov. 14, 1803.	
Anna,	Jan. 23, 1806.	
Ansel,	Feb. 2, 1808,	Mar., 1875.

William and Sarah Turner.
   Children:

Kate Ina,	May 15, 1859.
Fred Otis,	May 13, 1861.
Charles Clark,	Nov. 8, 1865.

Ansel Turner.
Lorania Francis, first wife,   Sept. 2, 1831.
Matilda Francis, second wife,
   Child:
Thomas Francis,   Apr. 26, 1833,   Dec. 26, 1876.

Sumners.

Houghton Sumner,   Aug. 29, 1862.
Mary Rogers,   May 10, 1865.
   Children:

Mary Houghton,	Sept, 22. 1806.	
Hannah Rogers,	May 4, 1808.	
Albert,	Mar. 30, 1811.	
Caleb R.,	Oct. 15, 1812,	Jan. 19, 1858.
Rachel,	Feb. 14, 1816,	Apr. 19, 1816.
Ruth Curtis,	Oct. 18, 1817.	
Alvira A.,	Oct. 11, 1820.	
Augusta W.,	Dec. 16, 1823.	

Caleb R. Sumner.
Sophia Curtis,   Jan. 27, 1889.
   Children:

William Benson,	June 4, 1835.
Levi Curtis,	Feb. 27, 1847.
Albert Winzer,	Jan. 4, 1852.

NAME.	BIRTH.	DEATH.
Lemuel Sumner,		Aug. 21, 1858.
Mehitable ———.		
Children:		
Nancy,	Apr. 13, 1812.	
Samuel Houghton,	Feb. 9, 1816,	Jan. 29, 1895.
Albert Winsor,	Nov. 9, 1822.	
Lemuel H. Sumner.		
Olive Knapp.		
Children:		
Almina Jane,	Feb. 28, 1841,	July 14, 1885.
Mary Ellen,	July 31, 1843.	
Lucille La Roy,	Oct. 7, 1847,	Aug. 30, 1849.
Ezra Ramsdell,	Oct. 6, 1850,	Aug. 10, 1873.
Oleva Estelle,	Feb. 13, 1856.	
Albert W. Sumner,		May 15, 1871.
Lucy Ann Robbins,		Nov. 23, 1876.
Children:		
Lucy Ann,	Aug. 28, 1854,	Apr. 20, 1883.
Charles Albert,	Aug. 18, 1856.	
Nancy Mehitable,	Mar. 5, 1860,	Nov. 26, 1885.
Edward Windsor,	Aug. 24, 1866.	
Ellen Frances,	Dec. 10, 1869.	

OTIS, ENSIGN.

NAME.	BIRTH.	DEATH.
Ensign Otis,		Sept. 17, 1872.
Martha, first wife,		Aug. 18, 1858.
Child:		
John Harrison,	Oct. 28, 1824,	. 1900.
Laura Howard, second wife.		
Child:		
Ensign, Jr.,	June 11, 1863,	Dec. 21, 1879.

BAILEY, JACOB.

NAME.	BIRTH.	DEATH.
Jacob Bailey,		Dec. 15, 1857.
Sarah ———,		July 29, 1839.
Children:		
Sarah,	Mar. 11, 1791.	
Jacob,	May 1, 1792.	
Ezekiel,	Sept. 12, 1793.	
Martin,	Feb. 19, 1795.	
Hannah,	Apr. 12, 1796.	

NAME.	BIRTH.	DEATH.
Ruth,	June 21, 1797.	
David,	Feb. 24, 1799.	
Anna,	Aug. 24, 1800.	
Mary,	Mar. 4, 1802.	
Lucy,	Aug. 5, 1803.	
Sands,	May 17, 1806.	
Esther,	June 2, 1809.	Mar. 10, 1832.

OTIS, OLIVER.

Oliver Otis,		Sept. 28, 1844.
Betsy Stinchfield.		

Children:

Fanny,	May 11, 1793.	
Ensign,	Apr. 11, 1795.	
Sally,	Apr. 28, 1797.	
Lydia,	June 24, 1799.	
John,	Aug. 3, 1801.	
Eliza,	Dec. 10, 1804.	
Amos,	Sept. 19, 1813.	Aug., 1844.
Martha Jane,	Sept. 30, 1821.	

LOTHROP, WILLARD.

Children:

Susan Emily,	Jan. 1861.	
Frank Burton,	July 1862.	
Sara Clyde,	Aug. 1879.	

Parentage:

Willard Lothrop,	June 18, 1828.	
Emeline Boothby,	Feb. 1842.	

Paternal Grand:

Solomon Lothrop,	Feb. 1788,	Aug., 1873.
Sarah Whiting Lothrop.		

Paternal Great-Grand:

George Lothrop,	June 1765,	Mar., 1839.
Polly Thayer.		

Paternal Great-Great-Grand:

Daniel Lothrop,	Dec. 10, 1745.	
Hannah Howard.		

Maternal Grand:

Rev. Samuel Boothby,	Apr. 17, 1808.	July 9, 1884.
Sarah Leadbetter,	Sept. 1811.	

MANN, I. HENRY.

Parentage:

NAME.	BIRTH.		DEATH.	
Albert H. Mann,	Nov.	1833.		
Polly C. Keene,	July	1828,	Jan.,	1894.
Paternal Grand:				
Ebenezer Mann,	Oct.	1788,	May,	1884.
Alma Josselyn,	Nov.	1793,	Feb.,	1883.
Maternal Grand:				
Abiathar Keene,			Dec.,	1870.
Sarah M. Coburn,			July,	1884.

Ebenezer Mann was born in Pembroke, Mass., in 1788, and came to Leeds in 1818.

MERRILL, SYLVANUS COBB

Children:

Louisa Elizabeth,	Jan.	1857,	Aug.,	1882.
Zalinda Ann,	June	1862.		
Burt,	April	1864.		
Maude Eveline,	June	1872.		
Rosina,	March	1874.		
Freeman,	Nov.	1876.		
Irving,	June,	1879.		
Nellie,	April,	1884.		

Parentage:

S. C. Merrill,	Oct.	1826.		
First, Rosina Manwell,			Oct.,	1865.
Second, Eliza A. Rose,	April,	1854.		
Paternal Grand:				
Charles Merrill,	April,	1798,	June,	1837.
Elizabeth Wing Freeman,	Aug.,	1801,	July,	1846.
Maternal Grand:				
Jarius Manwell.				
Phœbe Bishop,			July,	1882.

Eliza A. Rose, born in Abington, Mass.

MERRILL, EDWIN K.

Children:
Carl S.,   June 4, 1883.
Belva L.,   Sept. 25, 1884.
Percy W.,   April 5, 1886.
Lester M.,   Apr. 18, 1894.

	NAME.	BIRTH.	DEATH.
Parentage:	Edwin K. Merrill,	Nov. 20, 1859.	
	Carrie W. Thomas,	Feb. 12, 1861.	
Paternal Grand:	John Y. Merrill,	Oct. 19, 1823,	Nov. 1, 1898.
	Nancy S. Manwell,	Jan. 22, 1827,	June 17, 1860.
Maternal Grand:	William Thomas,	July 21, 1831.	
	Louisa C. Woodbury,	April 1, 1838.	

MILLETT, HERBERT L.

Child:
Alton Gordon,   June 1872.

Parentage:
Herbert L. Millett.
Lydia A. Gordon.

Paternal Grand:
Benjamin Millett.
Eliza G. Lincoln.

Maternal Grand:
Charles S. Gordon.
Florinda Churchill.

MOODY, CHARLES S.

	BIRTH		DEATH	
Child: Bertha L.,	Aug.	1877.		
Parentage:				
Charles S. Moody,	April,	1848.		
Millie E. Shorey,	Feb.,	1849.		
Paternal Grand:				
William Moody,	Feb.,	1808,	June,	1884.
Eliza Weymouth,	Jan.,	1812,	July,	1880.
Maternal Grand:				
Ivory Shorey,	July,	1808,	Oct.,	1884.
Elmira B. Thompson,	Aug.,	1816,	June,	1886.

NORTON, BENJAMIN M.

Children:
Leon M.,   May, 1870.
Grace M.,   Nov., 1873.
Ethel E.,   Jan., 1887.

NAME.	BIRTH.		DEATH.	
Carrie A.,	Jan.,	1889.		
Vaella,	Aug.,	1893.		

Parentage:
Benjamin M. Norton,	Feb.,	1848.		
Laura E. Nichols,	Mar.,	1858.		

Paternal Grand:
Benjamin C. Norton,	Jan.,	1819,	Feb.,	1890.
Sarah J. Nichols,	Dec.,	1824,	Mar.,	1856.

Maternal Grand:
Charles E. Nichols.	Feb.,	1831.		
Dora M. Bubier,	July,	1825,	Nov.,	1898.

PARKER, FRED A.

Children:
Lindley Gilbert,	Feb.,	1880.		
Baby,	July,	1885,	July,	1885.
Percy Russell,	Mar.,	1888.		
Syline,	Sept.,	1891.		
Gladys,	Dec.,	1893.		
Stanley Bradbury,	Sept.,	1895.		

Parentage:
Fred Augustine Parker,	Aug.,	1855.
Lois Viola Gilbert,	Aug.,	1852.

Paternal Grand:
Greenlief Parker,	Sept.,	1819,	July,	1887.
Frances Stoddard,	Dec.,	1818,	June,	1894.

Maternal Grand:
Avanda Gilbert,	Feb.,	1818.	Sept.,	1876.
Diana Wing,	Aug.,	1818,	July,	1899.

PETTINGILL, CYRENIUS.

Children:
Henry F.,	Apr. 10, 1846.	
Emily A.,	Sept. 14, 1850,	Nov. 27, 1855.
Emily A.,	Aug. 28, 1860.	
Ermina E.,	Nov. 28, 1862.	

Parentage:
Cyrenius Pettengill,	Mar. 27, 1820.
Amy A. Bates,	Jan. 15, 1826.

Paternal Grand:

NAME.	BIRTH.	DEATH.
Reuel Pettengill,	Sept. 17, 1792,	Oct. 23, 1862.
Lydia Briggs,	Feb. 14, 1794,	Dec. 21, 1873.

Maternal Grand:

Hervey Bates,	June 10, 1789,	May 9, 1877.
Nancy G. Rand,	Apr., 1799,	Dec. 12, 1856.

PETTENGILL, HENRY F.

Children:

Winifred,	Feb. 26, 1874.
Carl S.,	May 14, 1876.
Ethel G.,	Aug. 29, 1878.
Irving H.,	July 3, 1880.
Clarence B.,	Jan. 13, 1884.

Parentage:

Henry F. Pettengill,	Apr. 20, 1846.
Adelia M. Gordon,	Dec. 13, 1846.

Paternal Grand:

Cyrenius Pettengill,	Mar. 26, 1820.
Amy A. Bates,	Jan. 15, 1826.

Maternal Grand:

Sewall B. Gordon,	June 19, 1817,	Dec. 27, 1892.
Asenath Gordon,	Nov. 25, 1820.	

PETTENGILL, FRANK E.

Children:

Lena May,	Apr. 21, 1882.
Aubrey E.,	May 18, 1885.

Parentage:

Frank E. Pettengill,	July 5, 1861.	
Edith M. Coffin,	Jan. 2, 1858,	May 27, 1885.

Paternal Grand:

Arvida B. Pettengill,	June 27, 1818.	
Elvira A. Sumner,	Oct. 11, 1819,	Nov. 16, 1899.

Maternal Grand:

Nathan W. Coffin,	Nov. 2, 1819.	
Aurelia Gott,	Jan. 15, 1821,	Feb., 1885.

Frank E. Pettengill and Georgia A. Beal, married March 8, 1891.

ROSE, EUGENE.

Children:

NAME.	BIRTH.	DEATH.
Edna Jennie,	Apr. 5, 1892.	
Infant,	Jan. 12, 1894,	Jan. 22, 1894.
Flora Gladys,	Mar. 29, 1895.	
Guy Eugene,	June 4, 1898.	

Parentage:
Eugene Rose, Apr. 23, 1869.
M. Blanche Carver, Mar. 8, 1874.

Paternal Grand:
Caleb Rose, July 5, 1829.
Mary Ann Page, Nov. 4, 1833.

Maternal Grand:
John Edd. Carver, July 30, 1852.
Jennie D. Richards, June 7, 1851.

RIDLEY, EDWIN J.

Children:
Jennie M., Aug., 1886.
Edwin H., Sept., 1891.
Sadie Bertha, June, 1896.

Parentage:
Edwin J. Ridley, Apr., 1852.
Sarah A. Stetson, Jan., 1851.

Paternal Grand:
Alexander Ridley, 1825.
Rachel J. Additon, May, 1833.

Maternal Grand:
Caleb Stetson, Feb., 1815.
Hannah York, Mar., 1819.

RUSSELL, ERNEST ALONZO.

Child:
Eula Lane, Feb. 3, 1896.

Parentage:
Ernest Alonzo Russell, Feb. 17, 1872.
Kittie Lane, Feb. 27, 1875.

Paternal Grand:
Alonzo Proctor Russell, Feb. 12, 1843.
Mary Ann Goddard Richardson, Mar. 5, 1846.

Maternal Grand:

NAME.	BIRTH.	DEATH.
George Bailey Lane,	Feb. 16, 1833.	
Viola Ann Ramsdell,	May 1, 1839.	

SPRAGUE, ORRIN S.

Children:

Nellie M., b. in Leeds,	Jan. 2, 1873.	
Allen H., b. in Leeds,	Aug. 11, 1875.	
Maud M., b. in Leeds,	May 7, 1878.	
Mattie S., b. in Leeds,	Sept. 3, 1888.	

Parentage:
Orrin S. Sprague, b. St. Albans, Aug. 13, 1845.
Happie W. Kelley, b. in Unity, Jan. 10, 1848.

Paternal Grand:

Jason Sprague, b. in Greene,	June 6, 1820,	June 3, 1877.
Sophronia Bangs, b. in Wales,	Dec. 28, 1821,	July 1, 1854.

Maternal Grand:

Burnham Kelley, b. in Unity,	Oct. 20, 1806,	Oct. 15, 1862.
Martha Stone, b. in Gorham,	Apr. 10, 1809,	Oct. 5, 1892.

Married in Lewiston, Oct. 21, 1871, by Rev. Mr. Burgess. Have lived on the Morgan Brewster place, South Leeds, 26 years.

STINCHFIELD, THOMAS.

Children:

Thomas, b. in New Gloucester,	Sept. 8, 1768,	1798.
Sarah, b. in New Gloucester,	July 10, 1770,	1848.
James, b. in New Gloucester,	Aug. 10, 1773,	July 28, 1857.
Martha (called Pattie), b. in New Gloucester,	Nov. 28, 1774,	1850.
Samuel, b. in New Gloucester,	Nov. 6, 1777,	May 20, 1826.
John, b. in New Gloucester,	Sept. 13, 1779.	
Rebecca (first white child b. in Leeds),	Dec. 11, 1780,	Mar., 1869.

By second wife:

Hannah,	Dec. 4, 1793,	Jan., 1872.

Parentage:

Thomas[2] Stinchfield, b. in Gloucester, Mass.,	Dec. 29, 1746,	Oct. 25, 1837.
Sarah True,	May 6, 1744,	Nov. 18, 1791.
Hannah Lindsey,		

Paternal Grand:

NAME.	BIRTH.	DEATH.
John¹ Stinchfield, b. in Leeds, Eng.,	Oct. 12, 1715,	Jan. 3, 1783.
Elizabeth Burns, b. North of Ireland,	Dec. 21, 1713,	Aug. 19, 1795.

Maternal Grand:
Dea. Benjamin True, of Turner.

STINCHFIELD, ROGERS M. W.

Children:

Betsey, b. in New Gloucester,	Apr. 14, 1774.	
Abigail, b. in New Gloucester,	Mar. 18, 1776,	Mar. 27, 1852.
Susanna, b. in New Gloucester,	Sept. 2, 1778.	
Capt. Rogers (first white male child born in Leeds),	Feb. 9, 1781,	May 31, 1662.
Zebulon,	July 2, 1783,	Mar. 25, 1836.
Sarah,	May 27, 1785.	
William,	Nov. 14, 1787,	Oct. 24, 1850.
Ezra,	Feb. 22, 1790,	June 17, 1851.
Solomon,	Mar. 13, 1792,	Aug. 14, 1869.
Ezekiel,	Apr. 17, 1795,	1852.
Benjamin,	June 29, 1798.	

Parentage:

Rogers Stinchfield, b. in Gloucester, Mass.,	Oct. 13, 1752,	May 2, 1827.
Sarah Babson, b. in Gloucester, Mass.,	May 9, 1757,	Feb. 10, 1822.

Paternal Grand:

John Stinchfield, b. in Leeds, Eng.,	Oct. 12, 1715,	Jan. 3, 1783.
Elizabeth Burns,	Dec. 21, 1713,	Aug. 19, 1795.

STINCHFIELD, JAMES.

Children:

John,	Dec. 16, 1802,	Nov. 2, 1871.
Isaac,	May 5, 1804,	Jan. 9, 1878.
Mary, called Polly,	Dec. 9, 1805,	May 25, 1890.
James,	Sept. 9, 1807,	Dec. 21, 1887.
Elvira,	June 29, 1809,	Apr. 18, 1842.
Joel,	Mar. 4, 1811,	Sept. 12, 1888.
Thomas,	Dec. 6, 1812,	Sept. 1, 1863.
Hannah,	Dec. 25, 1814.	
Abigail,	Oct. 16, 1817,	Nov. 27, 1897.

NAME.	BIRTH.	DEATH.
Aramenta,	Aug. 24, 1819,	Aug. 9, 1862.
Sewall,	Mar. 29, 1822.	
Allen,	Apr. 8, 1825.	
Eliza A.,	Nov. 29, 1830,	July 3, 1831.

All born in Leeds.

Parentage:

	In New Gloucester.	In Leeds.
James[3] Stinchfield,	Aug. 10, 1773,	July 28, 1857.
	In Bridgewater.	In Leeds.
Hannah Pettingill,	Feb. 14, 1786,	June 19, 1871.

Paternal Grand:

	In Gloucester, Mass.	In Leeds.
Thomas[2] Stinchfield,	Dec. 29, 1746,	Oct. 25, 1837.
		In Leeds.
Sarah True,	May 6, 1744,	Nov. 18, 1791.

Maternal Grand:

	In Bridgewater, Mass.	In Leeds.
William Pettingill,	Nov. 29, 1759,	Nov. 16, 1846.
	In Bridgewater, Mass.	In Leeds.
Lydia Cobb,	Nov. 3, 1761,	Dec. 3, 1853.

STINCHFIELD, CAPT. SAMUEL.

Children:

George K.,	Apr. 2, 1806,	Dec. 4, 1881.
James K.,	July 9, 1808,	Mar. 28, 1838.
Mary A.,	May 15, 1810.	
Samuel,	Feb. 1, 1812,	July 7, 1834.
Thomas B., M.D.,	Jan. 9, 1814,	Jan. 9, 1862.
Adelia,	Jan. 6, 1816.	
John K., M.D.,	July 6, 1818,	July 11, 1883.
Stephen D., Attorney, Judge,	May 15, 1820.	
Anson Gancello, Atty.-at-Law,	Sept. 7, 1822.	

Parentage:

Capt. Samuel[3] Stinchfield,	Nov. 6, 1777,	May 20, 1826.
Mary King,	Dec. 9, 1780,	Jan. 21, 1858.

Paternal Grand:

Thomas Stinchfield,	Dec. 29, 1746,	Oct. 25, 1837.
Sarah True,	May 6, 1744,	Nov. 18, 1791.

STINCHFIELD, ISAAC.

Children:

Isaac, Jr.,	Oct. 29, 1836,	Sept. 8, 1860.
Thomas Jefferson,	Apr. 6, 1838,	May 24, 1867.
Charles Knapp,	Feb. 26, 1840,	Apr. 1, 1875.

NAME.	BIRTH.	DEATH.
John Clark,	Nov. 3, 1843.	
Rose Ellen,	Dec. 6, 1845.	
Abbie Lovina,	Jan. 3, 1848.	
Sewall Wallace,	May 10, 1850,	Feb. 22, 1899.
George Swain,	Nov. 25, 1852,	Nov. 14, 1877.
Ella Frances,	Nov. 1, 1856,	June, 1889.

Parentage:

Isaac Stinchfield,	May 5, 1804,	Jan. 9, 1878.
Abigail Lindsey Knapp,	Mar. 3, 1814,	Oct. 6, 1884.

Paternal Grand:

James Stinchfield,	Aug. 10, 1773,	July 28, 1857.
Hannah Pettingill,	Feb. 14, 1786,	June 19, 1871.

Maternal Grand:

Charles Knapp,	July 2, 1783,	Sept. 26, 1875.
Catharine Lindsey.		
Second, Hannah Lindsey.		

STINCHFIELD, EBENEZER.

Children:

Susan,	Sept. 2, 1810,	Jan., 1879.
Seth,	Aug. 30, 1812.	
Sarah,	May 12, 1815,	Jan. 10, 1901.
Woodbury A.,	July 2, 1817,	1881.
Ebenezer,	Nov. 22, 1820,	Jan. 22, 1849.

Parentage:

Ebenezer Stinchfield,	Feb. 7, 1787,	Jan. 23, 1878.
Mary Woodbury,	Sept. 25, 1786,	Oct. 31, 1852.
Second, Diadama Larrabee.		
Third, Clara Judkins.		
Fourth, Almira Berry.		

Paternal Grand:

John Stinchfield,	Nov. 4, 1762,	Nov. 15, 1835.
Mary Lake,	Sept. 30, 1767,	Sept. 30, 1852.

SUMNER, HOUGHTON.

Children:

Mary H.,	Sept. 22, 1806.	
Hannah R.,	May 4, 1808.	
Albert,	Mar. 30, 1811.	
*Caleb R.,	Oct. 15, 1812,	Jan. 19, 1858.
Rachel,	Feb. 14, 1816,	Apr. 19, 1816.
Ruth C.,	Oct. 18, 1817.	
Alvira A.,		

Parentage:

NAME.	BIRTH.	DEATH.
Houghton Sumner,		Aug., 1862.
Mary ———,		May, 1865.

Children of Caleb R. Sumner and Sophia (Curtis) Sumner: William Benson, b. June, 1835; Levi Curtis, b. Feb. 27, 1847; d. in navy Sept., 1864; Albert Winzer, b. Jan. 4, 1852; Edwin A., b. Oct. 20, 1853.

SUMNER, LEMUEL H.

Children:

Almina J.,	Feb. 24, 1841,	July 15, 1885.
Mary E.,	July 31, 1843.	
Lucille L.,	Oct. 7, 1847,	Sept. 30, 1849.
Ezra R.,	Oct. 6, 1850,	Aug. 10, 1873.
Estelle O.,	Feb. 13, 1856.	

Parentage:

Lemuel H. Sumner,	Feb. 9, 1866,	Jan. 29, 1895.
Olive C. Knapp,	Feb. 17, 1815.	

Paternal Grand:

Lemuel Sumner,	Dec., 1781,	Aug., 1858.
Mehitable Ludden,	Nov., 1786,	Sept., 1870.

Maternal Grand:

Joseph Knapp, Jr.,	Oct., 1790,	Oct., 1831.
Deborah Cushman,	Sept., 1788,	Sept., 1868.

Lemuel H. Sumner and Olive C. Knapp were married April 19, 1840. Lemuel H. Sumner was fatally hurt by an accident Jan. 18, 1895; died Jan. 29, 1895.

SUMNER, JOSHUA HOUGHTON.

Children:

Martin W.,	Nov. 5, 1850,	Dec. 6, 1850.
Serena E.,	Dec. 11, 1851.	
Viola A.,	Nov. 16, 1854,	Apr. 14, 1872.
Mary E.,	Feb. 21, 1857,	Mar. 25, 1885.
Russell H.,	Feb. 3, 1859,	July 8, 1864.
Rogers C.,	Nov. 28, 1861.	
Josephine S.,	Sept. 4, 1865.	
Levi E.,	Oct. 7, 1871,	Oct. 21, 1871.

Parentage:

Joshua Houghton Sumner,	July 6, 1826.	
Clorinda Ann Maloon,	Dec. 20, 1823,	Feb. 20, 1887.

Paternal Grand:		
NAME.	BIRTH.	DEATH.
Houghton Sumner,	Mar. 30, 1783,	Aug. 28, 1862.
Mary Rogers,	June 20, 1782,	May 10, 1865.

Maternal Grand:
| Simon Maloon, | Nov. 3, 1795, | Jan. 11, 1873. |
| Sally Drake, | Jan. 6, 1797, | Feb. 26, 1865. |

Thomas, Benjamin C.

Child:
Alton L., April, 1868.

Parentage:
| Benjamin C. Thomas, | Feb., | 1844. |
| Susan L. Rounds, | Jan., | 1849. |

Paternal Grand:
| William Thomas, | Jan., | 1815. |
| Sarah ———, | June, | 1816. |

Maternal Grand:
| Leonard Rounds, | | 1827. |
| Betsey Rounds, | | 1832. |

Thomas, Alton L.

Child:
Fletcher A., April, 1896.

Parentage:
| Alton L. Thomas, | April, | 1868. |
| Annie E. Lincoln, | July, | 1870. |

Paternal Grand:
| Benjamin C. Thomas, | Feb., | 1844. |
| Susan L. Rounds, | Jan., | 1849. |

Maternal Grand:
| Herbert W. Lincoln, | Jan., | 1848. |
| Elisa A. Howard, | May, | 1851. |

Turner, Peter L.

Children:
Harriett Grace,	Sept. 22, 1895.
Benjamin Abbott,	Mar. 14, 1898.
Roy Stanley,	Apr. 3, 1900.

Parentage:
| Peter L. Turner, | Sept. 15, 1857. |
| Adelaide C. Abbott, | Nov. 17, 1864. |

Paternal Grand:

NAME.	BIRTH.	DEATH.
Benjamin Turner,	July 8, 1828,	Oct. 18, 1896.
Harriett H. Lane,	Oct. 16, 1832,	Jan. 7, 1892.

Maternal Grand:

Albert Abbott,	1838,	Dec. 20, 1874.
Harriett Farrington,	Feb. 11, 1842,	Mar. 21, 1898.

WADE, FRED ADELBERT.

Child:
Ola Mabel,   May,   1892.

Parentage:
Fred Adelbert Wade.
Grace Linda Libbey.

Paternal Grand:
Samuel Wade.
Harriet Newell Parsons.

Maternal Grand:
Albert L. Libbey.
Clara A. Libbey.

Samuel Wade and Harriet Newell Parsons had four children, born as follows:

Albert T.,	Sept.,	1844,	June,	1884.
Nancy P.,	May,	1846,	Sept.,	1870.
Helen D.,	Mar.,	1854,	Feb.,	1857.
Fred A.,	Dec.,	1858.		

WING, BACHELDER.

Bachelder Wing,	Feb. 12, 1763.	
Mary Tribou,	Aug. 25, 1764.	

Children:

Nabby,	Aug. 29, 1781.	
Hannah,	Mar. 26, 1783.	
Caleb,	Apr. 2, 1785,	Mar. 2, 1854.
James,	June 18, 1787.	
Experience,	Oct. 5, 1789.	
Allen,	Mar. 14, 1792.	
Mary,	May 9, 1794.	
Mehitable,	Sept. 15, 1796.	
Sands,	Feb. 8, 1799.	
Phebe,	Mar. 12, 1801.	
Almira,	Aug. 17, 1803.	
William,	Sept. 15, 1805.	

27

WING, CALEB.

NAME.	BIRTH.	DEATH.
Caleb Wing.	Apr. 2, 1785,	Mar. 2, 1854.
Joanna Gilbert,		Nov. 5, 1811.

Child:

Adna,	Feb. 17, 1810,	July 5, 1864.
Desire Turner, second wife,	Mar. 31, 1791,	July 20, 1874.

Children:

Salmon Alden,	July 15, 1813,	Mar. 13, 1901.
Joanna,	Oct. 22, 1815,	July 1, 1890.
Diana,	Aug. 24, 1818,	July 14, 1899.
Ormand Turner,	June 15, 1821.	
Hiram C.	Dec. 14, 1824,	Apr. 25, 1832.
Stephen D.,	Sept. 10, 1826,	Mar. 25, 1851.
William,	Jan. 13, 1829.	

WING, JAMES.

James Wing.		Oct. 24, 1857.
Mary ———.		

Children:

Almira,	Dec. 10, 1809.	
Hannah,	Nov. 23, 1811.	
Anna,	Dec. 22, 1813.	
Loring,	July 14, 1814.	
Henry,	July 5, 1818.	
Allen,	Jan. 11, 1821,	Nov. 1827.
Cyrus S.,	Mar. 6, 1823.	
Chandler,	Feb. 6, 1825,	Apr. 17, 1830.
Mary Richmond,	Apr. 14, 1827.	

WING, SALMON A.

Salmon A. Wing,	July 15, 1813,	Mar. 13, 1901.
Ardelia Coffin,	May 6, 1820,	Mar. 18, 1890.

Children:

Duane Snyder,	Nov. 18, 1842.
Vesta Coffin,	Apr. 12, 1846.
Elsie Howard,	Feb. 6, 1848.
Junius Carlos,	June 19, 1860.
Stephen Arland,	Oct. 10, 1865.

WING, ORMAND T.

Ormand T. Wing,	June 15, 1821.
Octavia Brewster.	

HISTORY OF LEEDS 419

Children:

NAME.	BIRTH.	DEATH.
Orville D.,	Apr. 21, 1848.	
Clara A.,	Apr. 19, 1850,	Feb. 29, 1852.
Ellen M.,	Mar. 14, 1854,	Feb. 27, 1852.
Fred B.,	Sept. 4, 1857.	

WING, WILLIAM.

Children:
Roswell S.,   Feb. 20, 1857.
Alena M.,   Apr. 25, 1865.

Parentage:
William Wing,   Jan. 13, 1827.
Frances A. Bates,   Jan. 16, 1836.

Paternal Grand:
Caleb Wing,   Apr. 2, 1785,   Mar. 2, 1854.
Desire Turner,   Mar. 31, 1791,   July 20, 1874.

Maternal Grand:
Martin Bates,   1800,   Nov. 5, 1861.
Joanna Curtis,   1803,   Dec. 18, 1849.

APPENDIX I: Additional Families of Leeds, Maine
by David C. Young
(See p. 427 for List of Works.)

CHAMBERS

Cuff Chambers born in Dover, MA, d 8 June 1818 at Leeds, ME, bur in Riverside Cem, Leeds, ME, res Dover, Andover, Amherst, MA & Littleboro (Leeds/Greene), ME, servant of Samuel BLANCHARD of Dover, MA & Rev soldier. He settled in Littleboro Plt before 1810. [census records] He married 16 Sept 1762 at Andover MA, Betsey ____, who d 26 Jan 1839 ae 94y in Leeds, ME. "Although not recorded morally certain had one son Thaddeus Chambers" [MSA]. On 19 Mar 1849, Elizabeth Roberts, a widow ae 62 (Born abt 1787) & the only surviving child of Cuff & Bette Chambers, applied for the pension which was due her mother of the service of her father in the Rev. The claim was allowed. It stated that the Cuff & Bette Chambers had several children. Only Elizabeth is named in the claim. In 1849, Lydia Gannon, res of Brunswick, Cumberland Co, stated she was the dau/o Elizabeth Roberts, who resided with her. Children of Cuff Chambers:
   2 Thaddeus, q.v.
   3? Mary, q.v.
   4 Elizabeth m James Roberts (see Roberts)

2

Thaddeus Chambers most likely s/o Cuff Chambers. Thaddeus Chambers m Huldah Wood d/o Simeon Pero Wood. They moved to Wilton, ME, before 1820. Children:
   Rhoda Benson b 29 Oct 1804 at Leeds, ME
   Phillip b 19 Mar 1806 [MSA]

3?

Mary CHAMBERS res Leeds, ME, a black, married Joseph/Jonas Harris, int 19 Mar 1814.
   Children: Lucy Wood Chambers 1 Dec 1805 [MSA]

DUNSWICK/DUNCAT/DUNCIE/DUSWICK/D'ONSET

Prince DUNSWICK/DUNCAT/DUNCIE/DUSWICK/D'ONSET born 1751 in Africa, d 1838 in Leeds, ME, the head of the household of four blacks in Littleboro, (Leeds/Greene) Lincoln Co, ME, in 1790. By 1800, he was living in Kennebec Co with his wife. According to pension records he was stolen from Africa when he was ae 8. In 1810, in Leeds, ME, and in 1820, was living in Greene, ME.

By 1830, he was in Greene, ME, with wife plus one female under 10 yrs & one female ae 24 - 36. In 1803, Prince Dunswick received a quit claim deed from Josiah Little for land in Leeds, ME [Kennebec Deeds, Book 12 p 581]. In 1807, Prince was living in Leeds and sold land in Leeds, ME, to Simeon Pero-wood, a black man [Kennnebec Co Deeds 15-206]. He was a resident of Hanover, MA, in 1780, when he took his master's name (Bailey) to enter military service [Fisher's *Soldiers, Sailors, & Patriots of Revolutionary War Maine*]. He married 10 Oct 1780, at Hanover, MA, Hannah Venifon/Benson (Wood) b 1765, d/o Simeon & Rhoda (Benson) Perowood/Wood. [Q] **What is Q?? [Fisher]. He left the Quaker church in 1818 & she left in 1843 [Kennebec Probate records of Simeon Wood/Perowood]. There was a Hannah Dunswick ae 85 living in Brunswick ME in 1850 with a Thankful Chambers ae 35; they appear to be living in the Richard Garrison/Gassison household. The following were her heirs:

Thankful b 1815, m ____ Chambers
Hannah m John Roberts of Bath, ME
Huldah m Rufus Hill of Brunswick ME
[Brunswick Census 1850] [Records from Barry Tracy, New
    Sharon, ME, 1990] [Cumberland County Deeds 175-32]
[Cumberland Co Deeds 274-468]

FOYE

Hosea Foye d circa 1835, probate records called him a "collard man" [sic] late of Augusta, ME. He was a successful black businessman/barber late of Boston, MA, & Augusta/Hallowell, ME; left widow Mary Foye. Hosea Foye of Boston, MA, yeoman, sold to Robert Lewis & Henry Nichols, yeomen, both of Augusta, land in Augusta, ME, in 1829 [Deed 65-549]. His widow later m(2) Sampson

Freeman of Waterville, ME [Kennebec Co probate record of Sampson Freeman & H Foye].

2

Levi FOYE b 1800, a black man, s/o Hosea & Mary (____) Foye. He was by occ' a "victuller," m int 6 Sep 1835, Durinda Moody b circa 1810, died 25 Apr 1886 ae 75. Children:
- Jane W b 7 July 1836 m Emerson Peters [Stakeman's *ME Black Pop*]
- John Henry b 8 Sept 1843, d 27 Mar 1853 in Augusta ae 9y [*Morning Star* 10 Aug 1853]
- Julia Ann b 17 Nov 1837
- Levi G b 11 Sept 1839
- Mary Ann C b 6 Dec 1845 m Parker Gardiner of Augusta ME
- Susan b 14 Oct 1841.
- also listed in family of 1850 census Sarah Williams b 1830 female black. [MSA] [US Census records]

FREEMAN

Caesar FREEMAN of Bowdoin, ME, in 1790, eight non-white persons living in his family. It was more likely than not they lived near what has been known as Caesar's Pond in Bowdoin.
  Children (we are guessing):
- Adams b 1782 to 1799 m Nancy ____ d 9 Jan 1882 ae 85y, who was white
- Anthony b 25 Mar 1788 at Bowdoinham, ME, m 16 Dec 1813 Rachel Lee b 4 Apr 1788 of Bath/Brunswick ME, moved to Newcastle, ME
- Ephraim b 1801, m Priscilla ____ res Brunswick, ME
- Margaret b 1787
- Jane m 20 Apr 1798, Charles Boaz of North Yarmouth, ME
- Henry b 1797 m Phyllis Stewart
- John b abt 1780 moved to Newcastle, ME.

[N.B. The above children might have been all or partly the children of Sampson Freeman, perhaps a brother or no relation at all to Caesar Freeman.] (from D. Hall, *Notes on Non-white families of Maine, 1990*.)

Sampson FREEMAN died 28 Mar 1843 Waterville, ME, bur in Monument Park, Waterville, ME, [MSA grave index] (maybe) brother of Caesar Freeman. Sampson [black man] res in Bowdoin 1790; Thompsonboro/Lisbon/ Webster 1800; Greene 1810; Peru, ME, 1820: & lived on High St., Peru, ME, in 1821; & Waterville 1840. In 1806, deeded land in Greene, ME, from Josiah Little, Lot # 232 containing 70 acres [Deed 9-513]. After his marriage to Mary Foye, the widow of Hosea Foye, he moved to Waterville, ME. In 1836, res in Waterville, ME. He enlisted 1 Feb 1777 at Salem, MA [MSA]. Sampson was a member of the Baptist Church and was expelled from membership on 23 June 1827, for being "intemperate". His probate record states he left two daughters, one in Bangor, ME, & the other in or near Boston, MA, but no widow. [see Kennebec Co Probate rec. F-6 & *The History of Peru 1789-1911* by Hollis Turner, printed by Maine Farmer Pub., Augusta, n.d.] Sampson & Catherine Freeman had four children:
  Peggy
  Jane
  Rhody b 1806
  Jefferson b 1809

Peter FREEMAN was born 18 May 1778 in MA [MSA microfilm #204, Births and Deaths, Vol. I, p 236, Greene ME] a blackman, d 19 Mar 1858 ae 90 [*sic*, should be ae 80, or he was b in 1768] at Greene ME [obit, *Morning Star*, 23 June 1858] [1850 Census of Greene, ME.] Married Leah ____ b 8 Nov 1784 (1781?), d 30 Mar 1833 at Greene, ME, ae 52y [*sic*], [*Morning Star*, obit, 18 Jul 1833]; m(2) Sally (Dole) b ??, d 29 Oct 1841 at Greene [*Morning Star*, obit, 20 Jul 1842]; m(3) by Elder Jairus Fuller on 11 Dec 1845 Mrs Prudence Lee Freeman who died 8 Aug 1862 of erysipelas ae 64y at Greene, ME. This family was Freewill Baptist [church records MHS], lived in Bowdoin (1790), Thompsonboro/ Lisbon/ Webster (1800), and Greene (1810-1850). [Census records] [*VR Greene, ME*, p 236] [Lapham, *VR Hallowell* printed] Children:
  Hannah b Dec 1800, d 20 Sep 1804
  James b 10 Feb 1802, d 28 Aug 1802
  Sarah Ann b 7 Dec 1803
  Issabella McDaniel b 25 Feb 1808 married Joseph Matthews of Greene ME
  Chandler Bradford b 29 Mar 1809, d 1832
  Samuel Bradley b 22 Sep 1810, d 17 Dec 1835

Loisa Jane b 28 May 1814, d 11 Dec 1836
Elivra Griffin b 16 Sep 1817, d 28 Mar 1838
Alonzo Greely b 16 Sep 1819, d 18 Apr 1832
Aaron Osgood b 18 Sep 1821, d 28 Mar 1832
Oscar Fitzalan b 1 Mar 1824
Sarah b circa 1834
George b 1836.

Betsy FREEMAN m 6 Apr 1808 Daniel W. Lewis both of Greene, ME; "black people" [MSA].

Elizabeth Freeman d 21 Aug 1803 "black woman," Greene, ME. [*VR Greene, ME*]

James FREEMAN of Brunswick, ME, m Louisa P ____. They bought land from Hannah Dunswick of Greene, ME, w/o Prince Dunswick, land by the head of New Meadows River, in 1830. [Cumberland Co Deed 175-32]

John FREEMAN m 21 Aug 1806, Eda Griffin at Greene ME. [married by Benjamin Merrill, Justice of the Peace, *VR Greene ME*]

____ Nathan - Born ??, d ??, s/o ?? Nathan or "Black Nathan" was a colored man who was reported to have lived in Greene ME in 1805. He had title to land called the "Nathan lot." [*Lewiston Weekly Journal*, 14 Oct 1880]

ROBERTS

James Roberts married 23 Dec 1823, Elizabeth Chambers who was b abt 1787 in Livermore, (the southeast corner, which later became part of Leeds) in 1802. She was the d/o Cuff & Betty Chambers. Children:
   Lydia m Mr Gannon, moved to Brunswick, ME.

WOOD

Simeon Wood (alias Pero) dc 1814, [*American Advocate & Kennebec Advertiser* issue 3 Sep 1814] bur Mann Cem, So Leeds, ME, Revol soldier, Census of 1810, Leeds, ME, lists 3 blacks. Simeon Wood (alias Simeon Pero) (b 17 Jan 1744) might have been the son of

Margaret Peters & Nip "Negro" [see *VR Hanover, MA*]. Simeon Wood, "a negro servant of John Hardin of Abington, MA, m int 29 Sep 1764, Rhoda Vinson/Benson?, "a free negro woman" [p 419 *Bridgewater, MA, VR*] [Kennebec Co Probate P-10]. Children:
  2 Simeon was living in Leeds, ME, in 1811
  3 Hannah m Prince Dunsick of Greene, ME
  4 Huldah m Thaddeus Chambers of Leeds, ME [Kennebec Co Deeds 23-247] [Deed Kennebec Co, ME, 18-316]

2

Simeon WOOD Jr s/o Simeon Pero Wood. Simeon Wood Jr m int 28 June 1801, m cert 26 Nov 1801, Temperance Poconutt/Poconut. [VR Leeds at MHS] The 1810 Census of Leeds, ME, counted 5 blacks in his household. Children:
  Jacob b 9 June 1803
  Sophronia b 3 Jan 1807
  Browman b 9 May 1809
  Huldah b 9 Dec 1810
  Lewen b 20 Apr 1815

List of Works

AHS = Androscoggin Historical Society Files
BRYANT, Albert Scott. *Cemeteries of Leeds, Maine*. Unpublished, at AHS, no date
CARVER, Mr. & Mrs. Fred E. *Gravestone Inscriptions from Cemeteries in the Town of Leeds, Maine*. Unpublished, 1967, at AHS
DAVIS, Amos, *Lot Plan for the Town of Leeds, Maine*, (1800?)
ELDERS, Janus G. *Notes on Leeds Maine Families*, Notebook at AHS
FISHER, Carleton E. *Soldiers, Sailors, & Patriots of Revolutionary War Maine*. Louisville, KY: The National Society of Sons of the American Revolution, 1982.
HALL, Douglas A., *Genealogical References on Black Families in Maine, Notes on Maine Families with Afro-American Heritage* unpublished, no date.
LAPHAM, William Berry. *Hallowell Vital Records*. Maine Historical Series II. Vol 6-9 1890's
Leeds Town Records
MSA = Maine State Archives
Q = Quaker Records (see Whiting, below)
STAKEMAN, *Maine's Black Population*, Bowdoin College, Brunswick, ME: 1985? unpublished.
TRACY, Barry. *Records on Maine Black Families*. New Sharon, ME, unpublished, 1990
TURNER, Hollis. *The History of Peru 1789-1911*. Augusta ME: Maine Farmer Publisher [n.d.]
WHITING, Mabel Stewart. *Leeds Monthy Meeting of Friends 1813-1872 (Lewiston, Leeds, Litchfield, Winthrop & Wilton)*. Patience Stanly DAR typescript, no date

Brunswick, Maine, Census 1850
Leeds Baptist Church Records 1804-1874. Photocopies at AHS
Cumberland Co., Maine, Deeds
Greene Baptist Church Records at Maine Historical Society
Lewiston Weekly Journal 1880
Morning Star, Dover, NH, 1853
Vital Records of Greene, ME, p. 236, original records at the town office, not published.

APPENDIX II: Schedules of Settlers on Townships in Pegyscot (Pejepscot) Patent: Littleboro (Leeds). Original at MHS.

P = Land held by the Pejepscot Proprietors
PND = no deed
Date = when settled
The number in the two right columns is the number of acres owned or claimed.

	Date	P	PND
ANDREWS Ephraim	1781		26
ANDREWS Ephraim	1785		100
ANDREWS Abraham	1791		100
ADDITON Thomas	1787		51
BISHOP Joseph	1789		100
BISHOP Welcom	1783		100
BURGESS Seth	1791		
BATES Levi	1782	80	
BAILEY Jacob	1782	50	
BREWESTER Morgan	1781		200
BERRY Ames	1791		200
BERRY Joshua	1791		100
BUTLER John	1793		100
BURNAM Abner	1792		100
BROWN John	1782		159
BISHOP Zadock	1783		200
CURTIS William	1791		120
CARLE Benjamin	1792		100
CURTIS Ebenezer	1791		150
CURTIS William Jr	1793		150
CROCKER Abel	1783		120
COLLIER Isaac & Asa	1783		130
CRAWFORD Andrew	1791		77
CROSWELL Job	1791		50
CUSHMAN Andrew	1787		100
DRAKE Oliver	1781		130
DAY Josiah	1791		107
DAY Joseph	1791		200

Name	Year		Amount
DANSISK Prince	1786		100
DAY Jacob	1792		85
ELMS Robert	1791		150
FREEMAN Stephen	1779		60
FISH Benjamin	1779		94
FISH Jonathan	1786		100
FOSTER Stephen	1782		140
FISH Jira	1783		120
FARROW Gershom	1788		75
GILBERT William	1781	205	
GILBERT William	1784		310
GILBERT Samuel	1786		75
GILBERT Hensey	1783		75
HOWE Nathaniel	1788		100
JENNINGS Nathaniel	1785		
JONES Edward	1783		75
LANE Daniel	1781		100
LANE Elias	1790		
LOTHROP Daniel Jr	1783		100
LANE Gideon	1783		100
LANE James	1783		100
LANE Daniel Jr	1782		100
LANE Peter	1785		100
LINDSAY Thomas	1783		150
LINDSAY James	1789		120
LOTHROP Daniel	1782		100
LOTHROP Samuel	1789		100
MILLETT Solomon	1781		200
MITCHELL Joseph	1783		150
OWENS Nathaniel	1788		59
OTIS Oliver	1781		7
PARKER Asa	1779		40
PETTINGILL William	1788		140
PETTINGILL Obadiah	1793		150
ROBBINS Daniel	1783		80
RANDALL Oliver	1783		100
STINCHFIELD Rger	1779	215	
STINCHFIELD Thomas	1779	150	
SHAW Elisha	1787		150
STRONG Samuel	1798		100

SYLVESTER Hawey	1791		300
STANDLEY James	1794		100
SAMSON James	1783		80
SAMSON Beriah	1782		130
SAMSON Beriah	1790		50
TURNER William	1788		200
TURNER Josiah	1783		100
TURNER George	1789		100
WHITING John	1782	50	
WOOD Simeon Jr	1786	100	
WITHAM Peter	1790		150
WING Batchelor	1786		100
WHITNEY John	1783	80	
WHITING John	1790		100
WOOD Simeon	1793		100

Lot Plan for the Town of Leeds, Maine, by Amos Davis, early 1800s. Courtesy of the Androscoggin Historical Society.

HISTORY OF LEEDS 431

APPENDIX III

Settlers in Leeds, Kennebec Co., Maine (now part of Androscoggin Co, est. 1854) copied by Janus G. Elder from Pejepscot Claim papers (1800?), Androscoggin Historical Society

(See Amos Davis' Lot Plan for Leeds, ME)

name of Settler	Lot #	acres	value
GILBERT Hersey	1	9	$ 14.06
GILBERT Samuel	2	72	110.88
SAMPSON Michael	3	100	152.00
JENNINGS Nathaniel 94 rods in length on Westerly end of Lot #30 to make up his 100 acres as per plan exhibited	7 &	100	147.20
BUTLER John	32	100	124.80
GILBERT William	34	100	99.60
WELCOME Stephen	74	100	132.00
DUNHAM Benjamin	73	100	132.80
JONES Edward	72	100	132.80
SAMPSON Beriah	41	100	166.00
SAMPSON Beriah Jr	40	100	180.80
SAMPSON Leah	39	100	132.80
MITCHELL Joseph	37	100	196.00
DRAKE Oliver	36	100	166.00
CROOKER Joseph	35	37	62.25

The above nine lots adjoining each & twenty-five acres out of Lot #87. the North west quarter of said lot on which Joseph Mitchell now lives, to be conveyed to the above named nine settlers to be held by them according to their present possessions, each settler paying the sum against his name.

OWEN Nathaniel	38	61	87.11
DUNNIRICK Prince	42	100	142.40
GILBERT Benjamin	43	100	106.80

TURNER George	45	100	190.40
CUSHMAN Andrew	49	100	73.60
ROBBINS Daniel	65	100	96.00
NASH Ebeneser	66	100	135.60
FISH Jonathan	67	100	142.40
TURNER Jonah	76	100	128.00
WING Balchelder	77	100	106.80
ADDINGTON Thomas	78	100	117.60
BREWSTER Morgan	83	100	118.40
MILLETT Solomon	84	100	148.00
COLLIER Isaac	82	100	128.00
MITCHELL Thomas	89	100	147.20
LOTHROP Thomas	93	100	103.20
LANE James & Daniel	94	100	160.00
LANE J & Geddys	95	100	160.00
FISH Benjamin	96	100	128.00
OTIS Oliver (to be conveyed according to their possession)			
	97	100	113.60
BOOTHBY Isaac	64	100	113.60
BOOTHBY Isaac, Asa PARKER & Roger STINCHFIELD			
westerly left of Lot	108	50	44.40
FISH Jiva	109	100	81.60
RANDALL Oliver	111	100	128.00
BURNHAM Abner	112	100	95.20
LANE Elias	114	100	156.80
ANDROS Abner	115	100	166.40
ANDROS Ephraim part of 118 & part of 87 & 119 according to the plan exhibited		100	137.60
BATES Levi part of according to the plan exhibited	119	37	38.18
WHITNEY John & Jacob BAILEY			
	120	100	88.20
STRONG Samuel & Lane STUBBS agreeable to their possessions			
	124	72	89.85
DAY Josiah	129	100	166.40
CASWELL Levi	130	100	171.20
CASWELL John	131	100	180.80
ELMS Robert	158	100	135.60

Name	Lot	Acres	Value
BERRY Amos	132	100	166.40
BERRY Joshua	133	100	124.80
DAY Joseph	134	100	124.80
CURTIS Ebenezer	136	100	146.40

PETTENGILL Nere - Southerly half of Stephen FOSTER, a gore joining the pond containing 60 acres & 40 acres on lot #144 as exhibited by the plan.

Name	Lot	Acres	Value
	140 & 141	100	95.20
		100	73.60
LOTHROP Daniel	145	100	154.00
LOTHROP Sullivan	146	100	117.60
HOW David	169	100	95.20
LOTHROP Daniel Jr &	187	100	121.20
BISHOP Welcome	147	100	161.60
BISHOP Joseph	148	100	135.60
HOUSE Nathaniel	149	100	121.20
TURNER William	150	100	121.20
LOTHROP George	151	100	152.00
CURTIS William	154	100	166.40
GILBERT Nathaniel	156	100	124.60
MORSE David	159	100	59.20
MORSE Joshua	162	100	128.40
CRAFFORD Andrew	163	100	85.60
HAMMOND Paul	173	100	83.20
PETTENGILL William	175	100	128.40
LINDSEY Thankful	176	100	161.60
BISHOP Zadock	177	100	166.00
TURNER Alpheus	179	100	156.80
LINDSEY Jaines	180	100	156.80

HISTORY OF LEEDS 435

INDEX OF PEOPLE, PLACES AND SUBJECTS

This index covers pages 1-419 except for the lists of town officers on pages 275-284. On pages 244-247 only the surnames were included.

ABBOTT, Adelaide C 358 416 Albert 417 Alma 196 Alura F 357 E M S 353 John 350 Maria P 350 Miss 379 380 Rozillah 350
ABORIGINES 9 Abenakis 10 13 Abinakis nation 16 Algonkin 14 Algonkins 9 Anasagunticooks 10 12 13 Caghnawga Indians 13 Canibas 10 Canibas tribe 11 Cocheco 11 Etchemins 10 Huron-Iroquois 10 Indian cemetery 15 Mohawk 13 slavery 11 Sokokis 10 12 Wawenocks 10 11
ADAMS, Amanda 351 Ann 151 Capt 151 Edwin 325 Emma Gertrude (Pettingill) 155 Fred W 358 Hannah A 359 Hannah M 83 Lucy M 360 Martha A 344 Mary 240 Samuel 83 Sanford 155 359
ADDISON, Leonard F 357
ADDITON, Albert 180 Albert L 350 Amanda 172 180 343 387 Ann 81 Anna 261 Anna (Beals) 172 Annie S 173 357 Bethiah 172 Chester J 173 Chloe 172 331 Clayton E 173 David 172 E E 171 266 267 302 Edna 173 Eliza A 83 172 346 Eliza A (Jennings) 172 Eliza Ann (Jennings) 81 Elwin E 172-174 356 Ernest F 173 Everett 172 F L 75 303 family 172 362 Flora L 172 173 Florence (Turner) 180 Florus J 173 Forest O 173 Fred 171

ADDITON (Cont.) Fred L 81 172 173 357 Henrietta S 173 Hulda 172 I B 86 Isaiah B 81 172 259 274 344 Isaiah Beals 172 Ivan B 173 John 172 326 Joseph 172 Juliette J 172 Lenora I (Howe) 173 Leslie F 173 Loren J 172 Lorette 172 Louise M 174 Lovisa 172 346 Lucy A (Benner) 173 Luetta M 173 355 Marion L 174 Mary A (Thomas) 174 Orland H 174 Orville I 8 172 173 Orville J 173 Otis 172 Phebe 172 333 Rachel J 410 Razzilla (Smart) 173 Ruby 172 330 Thomas 6 81 83 172 174 244 329 Thomas J 172 174 347 Thomas Jefferson 173 Thomas Jr 172 180 Vina A 174
ALABAMA, 176
ALBEE, Lettice B 266
ALDEN, Almeda 340 Almenda 218 Benjamin 76 Benjamin K 359 Betsey 337 Christina 76 332 Cyrus 343 Eliab 328 Horace F 353 385 John 218 Mabel H 360 385 Mary A 218 219 Priscilla (Mullen) 218
ALGER, Huldah 380
ALLEN, Abigail 143 Alice 325 Dr 181 Eliza Shepherdson 228 Fannie 23 Fred A 302 Fred Hovey Rev 49 John Rev 254 Lovisa (Additon) 172 S A Dr Mrs 172 Samuel H 295 Sewall A 346

AMES, Adelbert 292 Alvah D 355
Daniel 364 Oliver 29 Ralph 337
Sarah 364 Thomas 175
ANDERSON, Vilina J 361
ANDREWS, Angeline 342 Ephraim
6 244 Frank E 354 Irena 337
Irene 117 Joseph 327 Keziah 325
Lucius 343 Marica E 350
Mehitable 325 Nathan 256 Olive
324 Sally 220 324
ANDROSCOGGIN RAILROAD,
Pettingill's Crossing 308 "Old
Widow" 309 "Peanut Road" 307
ANTHONY, Bert 304 Emma 304 G
H 303 George H 360 Gertrude
305 Grace 357 Lydia F (Curtis)
159
ANTIGUA ISLAND, 45
ARCHIBALD, Mr 320
ARDDATON, family 172
ARIZONA, 185
ARKANSAS, Little Rock 80-82
Washington, Hempstead Co 81
82
ARMSTRONG, Emily B 354
ARNO, Maria 156 341 Sarah 340
ARNOLD, Samuel 285
AROOSTOOK WAR (1839) 272
Capt Giddings Lane's Military
112
ATKINS, David 324 Ida 354
Sylvanus 323
ATWOOD, Abbie A 41 Clara A 215
Hezekiah 215 James N 348
Nancy 215
AUSTIN, Charles A 358 Clarinda F
(Lindsey) 128 Frank 78 Henry
327 Ransom B 128
AVERY, Abigail 64
AYER, Betsey 210 330 Margaret
327
BABCOCK, Catherine 125
BABSON, Eunice 44 Sarah 18 412
BAILEY, 24 Anna 330 Betsey 74

BAILEY (Cont.)
396 C C 87 Desire 129 175 186
366 386 Edward 7 family 262
404 George G 287 Giles Rev 142
Hannah 221 329 Jacob 6 Jacob Jr
327 Jonathan 129 175 Lucia A
(Turner) 87 Lucy 334 Mary 333
334 Olive 333 Patience 330
Rebecca 324 Sans 335 Sophronia
(Sylvester) 114 Sumner 114 345
Thankful 129 130 395
BAILY, Edwin 323
BAISY, Betsey 135
BAKER, L C 295
BALDWIN, Julia A 238 392 Julia
Ann 367 Robert 367
BALLOU, Hannah 79 Hannah L 342
Helen A 347
BALSTER, Aphia S 332
BANGS, Sophronia 411 Wales 411
BANKS, Elsie Ann 342
BAPTIST, Good Brethren 92
Meeting House 271 Society 272
BAPTISTE, John 296
BARKER, A Mr 97 Albert 292 C
Warren 361 John L 361
BARNES, Rev 260 Thomas 257
BARROWS, Allen 252 Allen Elder
261 Horace A Dr 335
BARRY, Joshua 6
BARTLETT, Fannie (Otis)
(Leadbetter) 163 Jane 380
Jonathan 163 332
BARTON, Nancy 342
BASFORD, David 338 Moses 336
BATES, A G 169 A G 300 Adeline
159 Adellma C 300 Amy 221
341 Amy A 154 221 370 408 409
Augusta L (Wheeler) 221 Bessie
B 360 Betsey 221 222 Betsey C
349 Carrie W (Thomas) 224
Charles 130 221 248 328 331
Charles H 159 Charles L 356
Clara A 356 Cylenus H 346

BATES (Cont.)
   Cyrenius H 221 Doubty 221
   Ezekiel 221 222 244 333 family
   221 363 Frances A 159 171 419
   159 Francis A 346 George 221
   Hannah A 358 Hannah (Bailey)
   221 Hannah (Lindsey) 130 221
   Harriet A 342 Harvey 221 272
   331 Helen 159 Herbert W 356
   Hervey 409 Huldah 221 James
   159 221 James E 221 349 Jane
   221 Jason 222 Jennie M 358
   Joan (Curtis) 222 Joanna 159
   Joanna (Curtis) 159 John 6 222
   John H 347 355 John Henry 222
   John O 159 Joseph 337 L R 303
   Levi 6 147 221 222 263 271 279
   286 329 352 Levi R 288 Lloyd
   221 Lucy S 344 Lydia 221 222
   Lydia S 334 Lydia (Bates) 222
   Lydia (Sylvester) 221 Martin
   159 222 331 419 Mary 159 346
   Mary A (Sturtevant) 221 Mary E
   221 Matilda 348 Nancy G
   (Rand) 221 Olive E 346 Oren D
   130 Oren S 346 Orin E 350
   Orissa A 348 Orlando 159 Orren
   221 Phebe 347 Phebe A 300 301
   Polly 221 Polly (Perry) 221
   Roswell 159 Ruth 323 Sabrina
   222 Sabrina (Bates) 222 Serena
   E 300 301 Sibyl 222 Silas 159
   221 Sobrina 333 Solomon 221
   222 Tiley Merrill (Lindsey) 130
   Tylia (Lindsey) 221 Vesta 300
   Wheaton 222 334 336 348
   William 221
BATTLES, Abbie 137 C W 351
   Caleb 137 Caleb W 294
   Elizabeth (Knapp) (Kenney) 137
   Winfield 137
BEAL, family 364 George L Col 289
   Georgia 154 Georgia A 358 409
   Lilla 149 Lilla N 358 Moses G

BEAL (Cont.)
   149 305 Nettie 358
BEALES, John A 354
BEALS, A 302 Agnes 334 Alfred
   159 Anna 172 180 329 Aruna
   341 Aruna B 345 Benjamin 331
   Betsey 334 Clara E 356 David B
   349 Etta E 355 family 363
   George 335 George L 293 356
   Hannah 327 Henry M 353 Isaac
   256 Isaac Jr 329 Isaiah 334 John
   244 252 327 348 John O 348
   Louisa 305 Polly 328 Reuben
   348 Rhoda E 346 Roscoe G 295
   Sarah (Curtis) 159 Sophrona 344
   Welcome 335 William Luce 348
BEAN, Isaac H 347 Lydia 113 Lydia
   A 339
BEANY, Amos 6
BEARCE, Irene 335
BECKLER, family 364 George 169
   Hattie M 361 John W 353
BELDEN, C L 195 Melissa Almira
   (Howard) 195
BENJAMIN, John M Hon 143
BENNER, Lucy A 173
BENSON, Almira 335 Cassandra 53
   336 Cyrus Dr 53 Joseph 157
   Mary (Curtis) 157
BERNIER, Victor 361
BERRY, Almira 41 352 414 Amos
   158 332 Ann R (Knapp) 137
   Benjamin 330 Catharine M
   (Foss) 103 Charles 336 Charles
   E 138 Charles H 355 Charles R
   291 Christina 158 335 369 Clara
   220 Clarissa 332 Columbia H
   353 Cyrenus 350 David 91 137
   323 David R 347 Druzilla L Mrs
   342 Edith 138 Eli 349 Eli N Mrs
   54 Eliza 137 Eliza Ann 131 346
   Esther (Foss) 54 Ezra 152 244
   334 family 375 Fannie S 138
   Harriet L 346 Hiram G 288

BERRY (Cont.)
  James A 347 Jane 332 John 219
  336 Lucian F 357 Mary (Curtis)
  158 Melvin 103 305 340 352
  Miss 52 Octavia J 349 Rozillah
  349 Sally 334 363 Salome 328
  Sarah (Ramsdell) 219 Solomon
  327 surname 24 Willis R 138
BERRY's, George company 89
BESSE, Charles R 353 Margery 324
  Reuben 21 Ruth 150 Tabitha 337
BICKNELL, Nehemiah B 49
  Nemiah B 343 Sarah (Millet) 49
BIGELOW, Susan 332
BILLINGS, Rachel 52
BILLINGTON, F H 256 Hannah 162
  327
BIRT, William 329
BISBEE, Cyrene 332
BISHOP, Abial 66 128 133 332 365
  Abial D 149 Abiel 330 Abigail
  (Avery) 64 Adeline 66 Alice M
  67 Aluria 66 Amos 66 337 Amos
  B 348 Amos Bradford 66 Amos
  H 66 353 Angela 149 347
  Angelia 66 365 Anna L 67
  Bertha 66 Betsey (Lindsey) 65
  127 Bridget 64 Charles 66 Clara
  I 67 Clifton D 67 Cyrus 331 349
  65 Demas 65 Dorcas (Lindsey)
  66 133 149 E Riley 295 Edward
  2nd 63 Edward 63 Elimina
  (Wheeler) 66 Eliza (Burgess) 66
  Elizabeth 66 330 Elizabeth
  (Hale) 64 Ella (Smith) 67 Ellen
  W 67 Ellouisa 67 Ellura 349
  Elvira (Rackley) 67 Emery 67
  Emery B 67 Emily E 67 Emily
  (Lothrop) 67 Emma L 67 Erastus
  66 family 63 365 Florrie M 68
  Francina J 66 Frank P 67 George
  65-67 344 George R 67 George
  T 66 67 292 352 Georgia L 67
  Glen Cora 67 Glennie 360 Gould

BISHOP (Cont.)
  64 Hannah 63 Hannah (Morey)
  65 Harriet 66 Harriet E (Tobin)
  65 Henry H 66 Horace W 67
  Isabelle (Farnham) 65 James 65
  127 333 James L 329 James Rev
  65 Jane (Turner) 66 Jemima
  (Norris) 66 Jennie W 67 Jesse 65
  Job 127 Jonathan 64 Jonathan G
  65 Joseph 65-67 Joseph Jr 331
  Joseph P 67 Judith (Gilbert) 77
  Julia 66 Julia (Byron) 68 Julia
  (Jackson) 66 Julia (True) 65
  Laura E 67 Lucy (Chisolm) Mrs
  65 Lucy (Maxim) 65 Lucy
  (Skillings) 67 Luvernia 66 Lydia
  65 168 328 Lydia Mrs 333
  Mahala 66 234 345 Margaret W
  (Clark) 65 Marion T 68 268
  Mary 64-66 128 Mary A 300
  Mary H 65 Mary J 347 Mary
  (Rawson) 64 Mary (Thompson)
  66 Myrtle (Grant) 67 Naaman 65
  Nathan 65-67 348 Nathan N 66
  Ned R 361 Nedd 305 Nedd R 67
  Octavia 66 Patience (Titus) 64
  65 Persia 127 Persis 328 Phebe
  66 127 327 Phoebe 406 Reginald
  S 67 Rosilla 67 354 Roxanna
  349 Roxanna L 66 Samuel T 65
  Sarah (Wildes) 64 Savilla Ann
  65 Squier 65 Squire 64 65 Susan
  (Lowell) 67 Sylvia 66 Thomas
  127 W H 267 303 Walter 66 67
  Welcome 65 127 Weston H 68
  Winfield Scott 67 Zadoc 2 142
  Zadock 24 64-67 244 285
BLACK, 326 Josiah 241 Juliet P 81
  Olive (Woodman) (Chase) 241
BLACKBOARD, 265
BLACKSTONE, Ann E 348
BLAIR, Frank Col 73
BLAISDELL, Charles D 256 Fannie
  F 383 Ruby 335 Walter Col 330

BLAKE, Minnie A (Curtis) (Harris)
161 Orlando 155 Orlando F D
338 Samuel 161
BLANCHARD, Catharine 137
Elizabeth 137 Joseph K 137
Lucretia 137 Mary Ann 137
Noah 137 328 Polly (Knapp) 137
BLUE, Carrie May 198 Laura E 349
BODGE, Andrew 386 Bessie A 352
386 Charles H 288 Clinton L
361 Mary 18 Sarah S 353
William 350
BOND, John 201 Mary 201
BONNEY, Samuel J 343
BOOTH, Thomas 43
BOOTHBY, Abigail 209 211 Anna
(Foss) 209 Augusta R 312 Bessie
M 312 Betsey 210 312 334 346
Betsey (Ayer) 210 Bradford 195
Brice 208 Caroline (Pinkham)
211 Carrie 171 Carrie H 216
Charity (Chubbuck) 211 Charles
D 312 Charles E 206 Charles R
312 Clara 195 Clara A (Atwood)
215 Clara E 355 Col 214 Cyrus
211 312 326 Cyrus H 312 Elias
P 215 Emeline 405 Emeline L
348 399 53 Emma L 216 70
Estella M (Stinchfield) 40
Estella S (Stinchfield) 312
Eugene Humphrey 217 family
205 Frank M 312 Hannah 210
312 Hannah (Churchill) (Page)
209 Hannah (Foss) 90 91 208
Hannah (Page) 209 Heloise
Helena 217 Henry 207 208
Hepsabeth (Tibbetts) 209
Horatio R 312 Ida K (Simons)
217 Isaac 91 149 208 210 258
259 272 273 312 Isaac Jr 334
Isaac Sr 90 210 Isaac T 293 312
343 Jane (Graves) 210 John Rev
209 Jonathan 207 Joseph 207
208 Julia A (Coffin) 215 Lewis P

BOOTHBY (Cont.)
216 Lizzie L 312 359 Lois A
(Hersey) 216 Louisa M (Spear)
312 Lydia 209 Lydia J 312 353
Lydia (Came) 207 Mabel
(Wilds) 312 Marietta 216 217
Mary (Jennings) 210 Mr 92
Orissa 216 Orrah A 216 350
Rafina A 312 Rosewell Eugene
217 Roswell C 215 217 Sally
(Leadbetter) 211 Samuel 207
209 213 273 334 340 Samuel
Drydon 217 Samuel Rev 54 60
70 207 211 405 Sarah H 216
Sarah S 312 Sarah (Leadbetter)
70 Stephen 209 211 244 286 295
324 328 338 Stephen Col 213
Susan E 213 344 Susan (Buzzell)
209 Susanna (McLellan) 208
Susannah 54 Thomas 207 208
Thomas H 149 351 359 40
Thomas Henry 312 Vesta Julia
217 Viora 54 Viora G 215 347
Walter 210 312 Walter W 288
312 Water 330 William 150 209
211 216 312 336
BORNEMAN, Eva E 354 William D
354
BOSTON, Daniel S 305 Myra 300
BOSWORTH, Sarah 161
BOURNE, Judge 207
BOWERS, Abbie (Gilbert) 78
Charles 78 William A 354
BOWLEY, Isaac 329
BOYD, Elizabeth 364
BOYNTON, Benjamin H 351 Carrie
E 352
BRACKETT, Fred D 361
BRADBURY, Josiah F 342 Mary
325
BRADFORD, Adeline 345 Clara 160
Elvira 335 Horatio 352 Martha
(True) 228 Miss 107 Nancy 340
Simeon 228 Wait 228

BRADSTREET, Alice 100
BRAGDON, Louise S 357 Martha 99
BRAGG, John 202 Mary 202
BRALEY Fannie (Plimpton) 100 W A 100
BRETT, Cyntha 323 397 Mehitable 325
BREWSTER, Aaron 285 Albion 149 358 Angela (Bishop) 149 Arvida (Briggs) 148 Betsey (Shaw) 148 Bryant M 148 C B 303 Carrol H 149 Charles B 149 312 359 Charles H 149 Christina (Briggs) 147 Clark S 37 family 365 George 149 H M 259 312 305 Hannah 148 Hannah (Robinson) 148 Hattie M 149 357 Henrietta B (Libby) 37 149 Henry M 148 250 305 347 Jennie M 149 355 Laverna C (Gilmore) 148 Lilla (Beal) 149 Lizzie L (Boothby) 312 Lizzie (Boothby) 149 Luvernia (Bishop) (Gilmore) 66 Lydia 148 331 54 Lyman (Wheeler) 148 Maria B 149 Martha 148 326 Martha J 343 Martha (Stetson) 147 Mary 148 Morgan 6 24 147 244 332 411 Morgan Jr 148 342 Octavia 171 341 Octavia 418 Octavia Ann 148 Olive 325 Olive (Morgan) 147 Oliver 148 Orin Wheeler 148 Polly 327 S 149 Salmon 148 250 254 310 331 346 Salmon C 149 295 350 Solomon 66 W H 250 William 147 325 William Elder 147
BRIDGES, Abizer Elder 261 Deborah 261 Eliza 261
BRIDGHAM, Aurelia Mrs 345 Aurelia (Howard) 176 Everett H 342 family 366 George 244 Jemima 330 Mary A 273 Thomas

BRIDGHAM (Cont.) Dr 28 Thomas W 257 258 Thomas W Dr 176 269 Valentine R 344
BRIGGS, Abiatha 85 Arbida 148 325 Calvin 153 336 369 Christiana 325 Christina 147 Cordelia 153 158 350 369 Eunice (Turner) 85 Francis V 153 Lydia 153 326 329 364 409 Nellie A 356 Prudence A 153 350 Samuel 339
BRIGHAM, Thomas Dr 28 Thomas W Dr 327
BRITISH NAVY IMPRESSED, 115
BROOKS, Melinda L 178 Mr 309
BROWN, Abi Mrs 335 Abigail 331 Abner 326 Almedia Jane 339 Ambrose 330 Anna 337 Betsey 332 Betsey A 152 C H 361 Calvin S Col 294 Charles 344 Daniel 290 E 124 Emma 357 Emma L (Bishop) 67 Emogene (Cushman) 124 Enos 337 Flora M (Jennings) 81 95 Hannah 112 Hannah S 344 Hannah (Boothby) 312 Henry A 312 350 J Eugene 81 95 John 239 John M 294 Josiah 326 Leo J 95 Mabel W 392 Martha 128 Mary 328 Mary E 152 348 Mary (Woodman) 239 Mr 244 Naomi 334 Rachel 113 344 Samuel 325 Sarah 339 368 W H 67 Zilda J 95
BROWNSON, S S 252
BRYANT, Albert 359 Angelia 355 C A 303 Carrol Albion 360 Dora L 385 Eliza A 159 J B 252 Olive 241 Sally 241
BUBIER, Dora M 408 Thomas L 291
BUCHANAN, J 256
BUCK, George S 355 37 Mary Jane (Libby) 37

BUCKLEY, Ralph 79 Rozilla
  (Gilbert) 79
BUMPUS, A Francis 160 Atwood B
  49 341 Betsey (Millett) 49 Clare
  160 Eunice 323 Harold 160
  Hester A 160 Lydia J (Day) 160
  Mabel L (Perham) 160 Martin K
  160 Mr 244 Nora B 160 Raleigh
  160
BUNKER, Love 44
BURBANK, Horace H 353
BURELL, Robert 352
BURGESS, Albina V Mrs 358
  Benjamin F 359 E E 303 Eliza
  365 66 Eliza Ann 335 337 Elmer
  E 358 John 65 Martin V 355
  Mary 324 Patty 324 Rev 411
  Samuel 324 Savilla Ann
  (Bishop) 65 Seth 324
BURGOYNE, General 117-119
BURLEIGH Edwin C 274
BURNHAM, Abner 232 Abner 337
  Abner Jr 232 Abner Sr 232
  Albina V 355 Augusta R 358
  Azel 232 344 Azel A 290 Betsey
  334 Betsey A 353 357 Caroline
  R 356 Daniel 232 328 Etta G
  357 family 232 366 Fred E 358
  George 347 Gustavus W 355
  Hiram Col 288 Ida M 357 J F
  150 J F 357 Jane A 352 Jeremiah
  F 352 Jeremiah T 349 John 232
  331 347 John A 291 353 John H
  357 John Jr 346 Joseph H 292
  350 Josiah F 357 Judith 356
  Lizzie B 358 Lucinda D 360
  Lucretia D Mrs 355 Luella 354
  Mary E 355 Mary J 349 Milton
  W 292 349 361 Mr 244 Rosialla
  Mrs 351 Rufus F 351 Russell L
  292 Sarah E 351 360 Seth F 292
  Susan J 356 Susannah 345
  William A 347
BURNS, Elizabeth 17 412 Mrs 96

BURRELL, Alvin Richardson 382
  Annie F 381 Lorana Frances 382
BURRILL, Annie 230
BUSWELL, Susannah 324
BUTTERFIELD, Desire 167
BUZZELL, Susan 209
BYROM, Julia H 352
BYRON, Julia 68
CAIT, Abigail 44 John 44
CALDERWOOD, Miss 107
CALDWELL, John C Col 289
CALIFORNIA, 30 34 36 53 72 73 94
  102 104 108 116 137 138 145
  152 159 161 163 164 193 219
  236 373 Butte County 162
  Collegeville 51 97 Colusa 94 Los
  Angeles 205 Nevada City 104
  Oakland 103 106 San Francisco
  72 164 188 San Jose 94 96
  Sonora 152 Stockton 226 Valejo
  97
CALLEY, George 358
CAME, Lydia 207
CAMPBELL, Abner P 343 Augustus
  E 360 Bellie 237 Callie P 237
  Calvin 237 343 Eldon R 237
  Emma J 237 family 366 Hannah
  327 Horace L 237 Horatio 237
  James 110 331 Jane (Carver)
  237 John 110 John L 237 Joshua
  237 Malinda (George) 110 Mary
  Jane 343 Nancy J 237 Nancy
  (Carver) 237 Reuben 14 Rose
  237 Rosina 237
CANADA, 76 240 Halifax Nova
  Scotia 208 45 Liverpool Nova
  Scotia 45 Montreal Quebec 67
  New Brunswick 105 108 129
  230 Newfoundland 45 Nova
  Scotia 207 Quebec 117
CANNON, Lovina 337
CANWELL, Aluria (Bishop) 66
  Irving R 358 Mercy I 356 R D
  304 Sally 325 Sarah 23 William

CANWELL (Cont.)
  66 William B 349
CAREY, Ichabod 328 Jane Mrs 345
  John S 332 John Shepard 326
  Ormand 342 Zachary 330
CARLE, Jane 327
CARLL, Benjamin 244 Hannah 89
CARLTON, Hannah 83 328
CARMAN, Miranda 365 380
  Thomas 380
CARPENTER, Charles 361 George
  304 Hannah 334
CARR, Amos 366 Maria S 366 Mary
  (Mitchell) 199
CARTER, Clabon 351 Denis 359
  Olivia M (Stinchfield) 38
  Richard E Esq 38
CARTIER, 9
CARVER, 24 A W 369 Abigail 233
  235 237 238 331 367 Alice 27
  236 237 Alice M 357 Allura 235
  356 Amanda A 343 Annie 235
  Arvilla 236 Arvilla A 27 236
  Augusta 238 342 Augusta W 305
  Augusta (Copeland) 237 Aurora
  238 B Franklin 237 Bertha
  (Harvey) 237 Bethia 341 Bethiah
  237 Betsey 27 235 237 338 394
  Caleb 235 237 257 329 392
  Chandler 235 Copeland 238
  Cordelia 238 Eleazer 251 334
  379 Eleazer Jr 328 Elezer 27 109
  128 235 237 Elezer Rev 235
  Eliza 237 344 Elizabeth
  (Nichols) 236 Elizer Jr 125
  Emily 237 Emma A 360 Esther
  237 Esther A 347 Eunice 134
  390 Eunice (Knapp) 235 Everett
  100 238 392 Everett L 237
  Everett Lowell 238 family 235
  367 368 Frank L 360 Franklin E
  355 George 237 George E 353
  Granville 238 Granville C 345
  Hannah 27 236 Hannah

CARVER (Cont.)
  (Stinchfield) 125 235 Harriet
  237 Henry 236 I S 4 Isaac S 22
  236 27 James 27 236 238 290
  346 384 Jane 237 343 366 Jane
  (Smith) 235 Jannett 343 Jason
  27 235 236 288 292 338 357
  Jennett 237 Jennett (Treat) 237
  John 27 235-237 257-259 329
  John 2d 346 John E 236 353
  John Edd 410 John Major 229
  341 Julia A 354 392 Julia A
  (Baldwin) 238 Julia Augusta 238
  Lloyd 238 343 Louisa 238 340
  Lowell 238 M Blanche 410
  Martha (Smith) 237 Mary 27
  235 237 238 333 379 Mary A
  235 Mary Ann 27 236 340 Mary
  (Fish) 236 238 Mary (Libby) 236
  Mary (Taylor) 236 Melvin 237
  Melvin H 340 Mr 244 Myra M
  358 384 Nancy 27 235-238 327
  Nancy (Jones) 235 Nora (Parson)
  236 Persis (Lindsey) 128 Rufina
  A 348 Ruphina 236 Russell 238
  287 342 Ruth 229 237 340 Seth
  F 357 Thirza A 236 Thomas S 27
  235 236 341 356 Tirzah Ann 348
  Ursola 235 Ursula 238 235 Viora
  236 Viora A 349 Wallace
  Elwood 238 Warren 236 354
  William 109 235 326 William Jr
  339 William Mrs 235
CARVILL, Jordan G 290
CARVILLE, Eva J 358 W R 361
CARY, Clara A (Day) 161 Clara R
  356 Clara Richardson 224
  Daniel 161 David 331 John Esq
  240 John S 50 Luther 74 324 Mr
  244 Pheba (Lane) 108 Phebe S
  (Lane) 50 Polly (Lothrop) 74
  Ralph 161 Salmon 334 Seth 248
  Shephard 91 Zachary 248 249
CASE, Isaac 251

CASWELL, 24 Alanson B 167 Alice 166 328 Alice (Clark) 166 Annie L (Richards) 167 Anvalette 353 Augusta M (Young) 167 Augustus B 166 349 Benson 264 Chandler 167 Clark R 167 296 Cyrus M 166 Drusilla 334 Druzilla 166 167 Earl 167 Earl F 348 Elmina (Stinchfield) 167 Elvira F (Emerton) 167 Elvira (Sprague) 166 family 166 Frederick L 167 George 354 Harry R 167 Iva S 356 Jason 167 Job 166 334 John Q 167 Juliette 167 Lendall 167 Lendall S 167 295 352 Levi 166 257 271 320 Levi G 167 Levi Jr 166 Lloyd B 167 288 291 Marcus 335 Mary A 167 Mary H 167 Mary Q (Robbins) 167 Mr 244 Nancy E 167 356 P B 286 Peleg B 167 336 Rhoda 113 Rhoda W 336 Sarah J 167 Theresa H (Parson) 167 W Benson 167

CENSUS, 1860, UNITED STATES AGENT, 173

CHAMBERLAIN, Joshua L 292 Mary 151 Mr 249

CHAMBERS, Cuff 285 Maria 326 Mary 328 Mr 244

CHANDLER, Clementine J 349 Cora 102 E B 102 Edith 195 Elizabeth 330 Jacob 328 John 21 271 John Esq 8 Julis Ann 332

CHAPIN, Joel P 252 F A 96 Rena May (Foss) 96

CHAPMAN, John 43 Joyce 43

CHASE, Amanda J 352 Anna 327 Joseph 241 Olive (Woodman) 241

CHESSMAN, Harriet M 41

CHILDS, Daniel Dr 228 Doctor 162 Xoa 228

CHISOLM, Lucy Mrs 65

CHOATE, Alice Frances 106 Arthur Henry 106 Frances Ellen (Linscott) 106 Harry Wingate 106 Henry A 106

CHUBBOCK, Charity 109 326

CHUBBUCK, Charity 211

CHURCH, Benjamin Major 13 Edith W 354 Mehitable S 99

CHURCHELL, Loring L 358 William 354

CHURCHILL, Arobine 354 Emily B Mrs 360 Florinda 230 338 407 Florinda Wing 381 Lewis 155 Lewis 259 343 Ruth (Pettingill) 155

CHUTE, Lydia 328 Mehitable 234 392

CIVIL WAR, 48 53 59 66 68 72 81 82 86 94 103 117 122 126 145 146 158 219 232 236 243 286 371 395 415 1st Maine Heavy Artillery 291 294 1st Maine Infantry 287 294 1st Maine Light Artillery 82 1st Maine Regiment Sharpshooters 295 1st Veteran Volunteer Regiment 294 1st Missouri Light Artillery 73 1st Maine Cavalry 95 213 295 1st Battalion Light Artillery 294 1st District of Columbia Cavalry 295 2nd Vermont Vol 182 2nd Maine Infantry 94 287 2nd Maine Cavalry 131 164 295 3d Maine Infantry 110 165 182 189 193 312 287 291 4th Maine Vol 182 291 5th Virginia Regiment 218 4th Wisconsin Regiment 152 5th Maine Regiment 123 182 5th Maine Battery 291 6th Maine Battery 131 7th Maine Infantry 288 7th Maine Regiment 122 8th Maine Infantry 164 289 9th Maine Infantry 289 10th Maine Battalion 293

CIVIL WAR (Cont.)
    11th Maine Infantry 111 289 290
    12th Maine 290 13th Maine
    Infantry 290 14th Maine Infantry
    290 15th Maine Infantry 290
    16th Maine Infantry 291 155
    17th Maine Infantry 291 193
    19th Maine Infantry 291 20th
    Maine Infantry 292 21st Maine
    Infantry 292 22nd Maine Infantry
    292 23d Maine Volunteers 154
    132 292 24th Maine Infantry 293
    25th Maine Infantry 293 26th
    Maine Infantry 293 27th Maine
    Infantry 293 28th Maine Infantry
    293 29th Maine Infantry 293
    30th Maine Infantry 293 31st
    Maine 294 32rd Maine Infantry
    294 44th Massachusetts 103
    59th Reg Co I 103 Adairsville
    183 Allatoona Pass 184
    Antietam 122 183 189 Army of
    the Cumberland 183 Army of
    Tennessee 183 Atlanta 183
    Bentonville 184 Broad 184 Bull
    Run 94 122 182 183 189
    Cassville 183 Cedar Mountain
    131 Chancellorsville 183 189
    Cold Harbor 130 Columbia 184
    Congaree 184 CSA 38 Dalton
    183 Edisto 184 Ezra Church 183
    189 183 Fair Oaks 189 287 Fort
    McAllister 184 Fort Fisher 131
    Franklin 218 Fredericksburg 82
    155 166 183 189 312 Gardern's
    Corner 184 Gettysburg 82 123
    166 183 188 189 288 Golden
    Farm 122 Griswoldville 184
    Guyandot 218 Hall's Second
    Maine Battery 82 James River
    122 Jonesboro 183 Kenesaw
    Mountain 183 Kingston 183
    Knoxville 183 Lookout Valley
    183 189 Lovejoy Station 184 183

CIVIL WAR (Cont.)
    Maine Regiments 287 Malvern
    Hill 122 Marye Heights 183
    Mechanicsville 122
    Milledgeville 184 Missionary
    Ridge 189 Muddy Creek 183
    New Hope Church 183 Ogeechee
    River 184 Orangeburg 184
    Peachtree Creek 183 Petersburg
    218 Pickett's Mill 183
    Pocotaligo 184 Potomac 82
    Prisoner by Morgan's Army 177
    Rappahannock 182 Resaca battle
    183 Richmond 122 Roster
    Battalion & New Fourteenth
    Regiment 290 Salkehatchie 184
    Saluda 184 Savage Station 122
    Savannah 189 184 Shepardstown
    213 Ship *Ino* 123 Smyrna Camp
    Ground 183 Soldier 117 The
    Wilderness 82 Union Army 47
    149 United States Navy 296
    Unites States War Vessel
    Monadnock 131 Vera Cruz 286
    Veteran Reserve Corps 155 War
    of Rebellion 182 Warwick Creek
    122 Western Division of Army
    165 Williamsburg 122
    Winchester 218
CLARK, Aaron 274 Alice 166
    Andrew S 359 Caroline
    Wilhelmina (Linscott)
    (Patterson) 106 Daniel Rev 99
    Henry D 106 Irena (Pettingill)
    156 Isaac R 274 James 156 337
    John Wesley 99 Josephine B
    (Foss) 99 Margaret W 65 Mary
    (Knight) 99 Miss 107
CLEMENS, Mertie J Mrs 361
CLEMONDS, Richard 356
CLIFFORD, A T 302 E T 266 303
    Rev 256
CLOYCE, Sarah 64
CLUB, Elks BPO Lodge #65 132

CLUB (Cont.)
    May-Flower Colony 132 Mt
    Sinai RAC 132 Pilgrim Fathers
    132 Subordinate Lodge of Good
    Templars 149
CNOEP, John 133
COBB, Celia 339 Chandler F 230
    353 Eben 47 Ebenezer 334
    Eleanor 156 Elizabeth 101 373
    Elizabeth L 345 Isabella (Millet)
    47 Lucy S 338 Lydia 25 153 156
    413 Mary E 350 Mary Ella
    (Gordon) 230
COBURN, Ann 86 Druzilla
    (Caswell) 167 Freemon 337
    Jemima 388 Jesse 389 M Anna
    Mrs 357 Marian 78 Miriam 331
    Sarah M 406 Silas 167 334
COCHRANE, Harry 225 Harry H 32
    33 Ida L (Gott) 32 Lafayette A
    360 Lorena 32
COFFIN, Ardelia 170 Ardelia 418
    Aurelia (Gott) 136 Betsey 215
    Edith 136 Edith M 154 355 409
    Elizabeth 338 Emily A
    (Pettingill) 154 family 368
    James Jr 340 Joanna 336 John
    341 Julia A 215 Manley 136
    Manley M 154 355 Mary 341
    Nathan 136 341 Nathan W Paul
    Rev 75 Warren 215
COLBURN, Peter 329
COLBY, E Clarence 100 Fred 100
    Hattie (Martin) 100
COLE, Betsey F 341 J P 256
COLEMAN, John 352
COLLIER, 24 Anna 333 Charles B
    198 341 Clara M (Mitchell) 198
    Eunice 328 Hannah 85 401
    Hannah P 324 Hannah (Turner)
    85 Isaac 6 271 326 Jennie 323
    Miss 107 Moses 85 326 328 Mr
    244
COLLINS, Isaac 285 John T 360

COLLINS (Cont.)
    Ruth 332
COLORADO, 49 55 96 226 Cripple
    Creek 188 Denver 39 165
    Watson, Pitkin Co 96
COLORED, 326
COMINGS, James 329 Peter 324
CONANT, Charles E 41 Edith H
    (Stinchfield) 41 J H 267
CONFEDERATE STATES OF
    AMERICA, 82
CONGDON, W H 256
CONNECTICUT, Bolton 83
    Danbury 134 Fairfield 134
    Fairfield Co 134 Greenwich 134
    Hartford 120 373 Lebanon 147
    Manchester 343 New Haven 134
    Norwalk 134 Putnam 171 216
    Stamford 134
CONNELLY, Timothy 296
CONNOR, Seldon 288
CONTINENTAL, Army 48 Money
    69
COOK, Jane B 347 Maria E 352
COOLIDGE, Clara 234 Clara D 354
    George 234 George C 356 Lillie
    234 Lovice J (Greenwood) 234
    Oberon 234 Rutellius 234 Tillie
    234 Willis 234
COOPER, Effie A 359 George F 360
COPELAND, Augusta 237 329 367
CORSE, General 184
COUSENS, (Sarah) Miss 100
COX, Abby J 102 356 373 George T
    375 Harriet F 375 Hattie F 103
    353
CRAIG, James 21
CREACH, David B 327 Olive 128
    129 328 Susanna 325 Betsy 323
CREHORE, Joseph Rev 345
CREKORE, Ellen (Mitchell) 198
    Joseph Rev 198
CROCKETT, Alice A 131 Clara M
    (Mitchell) (Collier) 198 Polly

CROCKETT (Cont.)
  (Gilbert) 77 Richard 326 77
CRONINS, James A 296
CROSBY, Mary F 191
CROSSMAN, Daniel 333 Daniel Jr
  342 Joseph 84 Margaret (Turner)
  84 Nancy (Gilbert) 77
CROWNINSHIELD, Richard 56
CRUMETT, Robert 248 258 259
CRUMMETT, Ann (Foster) 146
  Charles 146 Ellen 341 Hannah
  (Foster) (Irish) 146 Mary A 77
  Mary Ann 340 Robert 146
  Samuel 342
CRUMMIT, Mr 244 Robert 330 258
CUFF, Daniel 327
CULLEN, James 296
CUMMINGS, Annie 226 M B 256
CUMNER, John 255 John Rev 254
  Lemuel H 339
CUNNINGHAM, Henry W 291
CURRIER, Edith 357
CURTIS, Abel 157 Abner 132 158
  159 323 396 Abner Jr 158 161
  344 Abner Sr 159 Ada C 161
  Addie 162 Adeline 159 161 162
  342 Albina L 161 Almon 159
  Almon Capt 160 Almond 336
  Amanda M (Millet) 49 Amanda
  T 158 350 Amy A 158 Ann 158
  Ansel 159 161 343 Archie 161
  Augusta W Mrs 357 Augusta
  (Sumner) 158 Benjamin 157
  Berry R Esq 157 Betsey 158 325
  Charity 158 162 Charles 158
  Charlotte (Mitchell) 159
  Chesman 162 Chessman 347
  Christina 158 Christina (Berry)
  158 Clementine 161 Cordelia
  (Briggs) 158 Cynthia 158
  Cynthia (Stetson) 158 Deborah
  158 162 327 Deborah (Curtis)
  157 162 E Alfred 159 Ebenezar
  350 Ebenezer 158 291 Edward B

CURTIS (Cont.)
  159 Eliza A (Bryant) 159 Erin H
  159 Ermima E (Pettingill) 154
  Estella 161 Esther (Randall) 158
  family 157 369 Flora C 353
  Flora E 132 161 396 Florentine
  161 George 158 339 George T
  Esq 157 Gracia 159 160 Gracia
  L 336 H B 305 Hannah 158
  Hannah (Billington) 162 Harriet
  158 Harriet L 145 339 Harriet
  Lowe 371 Helen May 360 Henry
  158 Hiram 49 Horace P 159
  Irven 161 James 159 Jeremiah
  158 335 Joan 222 Joanna 159
  331 419 Joel 157 John 157
  Joseph 157 Joseph M 293 349
  Joseph R 341 Joseph R Capt 158
  Josiah 158 162 327 L Albina 161
  Laura 162 Laura A 346 Lebbeus
  162 326 Ledru R 159 Letitia 162
  Letitia E 355 Libbeus 158
  Lincoln 158 162 333 Louisa 159
  Louisa (Sumner) 158 Lucretia
  (Smith) 159 Lydia 159 Lydia F
  159 Lydia J 159 161 Lydia Jane
  346 Lydia (Turner) 159 Margaret
  (Pratt) 157 Marion 161 Martha
  (Mane) 157 Mary 157 158 332
  Mary H 132 158 344 396 Mary
  H (Curtis) 158 161 Millard 161
  Mina (Pettingill) 161 Minerva
  (White) 161 Mr 244 O E 154
  Obed 159 Olive 158 Olive S 343
  Olive (Stubbs) 158 Oren 159
  Oren E 161 Oren J 161 Orin E
  356 Prudence (Goch) 162
  Rachael 157 Reuben D 159
  Richard Esq 157 Roa 158 Robert
  162 327 Sarah 162 Sarah A 159
  Sarah (Bosworth) 161 Sophia
  158 336 403 415 Stephen 157
  Sylvanus (Hammond) 162
  Thomas 157 Thomas W 353

CURTIS (Cont.)
  W H 303 304 Walter 161 Walter
  P 159 Washington 158 Willard
  M 161 William 157-159 371
  William 3rd 157 William B 158
  William B 2d 343 William D
  159 William H 158 159 William
  Jr 157 William Mrs 236 William
  the 4th 157 William the 5th 157
CUSHING, Jane (Gilbert) 78 Mary
  51 William 78
CUSHMAN, Adaline 337 Andrew Jr
  330 Andrew 6 24 117 122 248
  285 Angeline (Harvey) 122
  Angie 124 Angie D 122
  Bathsheba 117 329 Bathsheba
  (Jennings) 117 121 248 Betsy
  338 Celia Mrs 347 Cora 384
  Corilla F 123 Corrilla F 122
  Deborah 136 326 415 Dorcas H
  (Loring) 122 Ebenezer 339
  Emogene 122 361 family 122
  370 Flavilla 124 Flavilla A 122
  Isaac 117 123 339 345 385 John
  B 122 124 Levi 117 Marcellus F
  122 156 289 Marcellus F 351
  Mary 335 Matilda F (Pettingill)
  156 Matilda (Pettingill) 123 Mr
  244 Oliver 329 Ray L 123
  Robinston F 123 Sarah 325
  Thirza S 122 123 Wilbert N 123
CUTLER Rev 260
D'AILLEBOUT, Mr 13
D'ONSET, Prince 285
DAGGATT, Alanson W 340
DAGGET, Jabez 324
DAGGETT, C R 256 Della 361
  Desire Mrs 336 Desire (Fish)
  117 Fred 117 Jabez 75 Lloyd 117
  Mr 244 Nathaniel 117 333
  Pamelia (Wing) 117 Susan B
  338 Warren 117
DAILEY, Abiel 6 Neazer Jr 333
DAILY, 24 Abiel 271 279 Abiel Dr

DAILY (Cont.)
  70 271 Betsey 341 Elizabeth
  (True) 227 Mr 244 Nathaniel
  227
DAKOTA, 139
DALTON, Rodger E 360
DALY, Abial Dr 269 Abiel 263 E V
  85 171 Isaac S 342
DAMON, Betsey (Curtis) 158
  Hannah (Curtis) 158 John 158
DASCOM, Alice 137 Anna A 137
  George W 137 Lucinda (Knapp)
  137 T A 137
DASCOMB, A 93 Alice M 357
  Annie 361
DAVEE, Alice (Stinchfield) 126 B
  259 Barnabas 139 249 257-259
  264 339 347 Barnabus 305
  Barnabus Mrs 126 Hannah L 354
  Hannah L (Knapp) 139 Solomon
  328
DAVIS, Abigail (Stinchfield) 23
  Alonzo 145 351 (Amos) 202
  Annie B 361 Annie Howard
  (Foss) 104 Eliza B 335 family
  370 Frank G 104 360 Hattie F
  195 Jacob 66 Joshua 325 Martha
  163 Mrs 127 Muriel 104 Octavia
  J (Bishop) 66 Orrie A (Foster)
  141 145 Shubel 23 William B
  333
DAVY, Humphrey 42
DAY, A G 160 Abiah 336 Abigail R
  328 Ada Louise 160 Adaline 79
  337 Alexander 334 Almira A 47
  Almon C 160 Almon D 160 Ann
  B 341 Anna 330 Bethany 328
  Betsey E 340 Catherine 339
  Charles A 160 Clara A 160 Clara
  Addie 160 Clara (Bradford) 160
  Clarissa 341 343 Cordelia 334
  Elsie A 160 Emma R 352 Eunice
  155 333 Gracia (Curtis) 160
  Hannah 327 328 Henry F 160

DAY (Cont.)
Hester A 160 Jacob 7 77
Jeremiah 288 329 Jeremiah Jr
341 Joseph 77 263 271 279
Joseph H 77 Josiah 249 271 328
Josiah 2d 338 Josiah Esq 342
Judith B 338 Lovinia Josephine
(Gilbert) 77 Lucilla D 355
Lucinda 337 371 Lydia J 160
Martha 325 77 Mary 341 Mary
Ann 353 Mr 244 Nellie A 160
Phoebe Anne 363 Randall 363
Rebecca 326 Rebecca (Gilbert)
77 Ruth (Gilbert) 77 Stephen
249 272 Thomas 335 338
Wallace 160 Wallace E 160
Weston B 160 William 323
William A 324 371 William S
160 Winifred G (Francis) 160
DEAN, Sarah 175
DEANE, Abbie E 196 302 303 Abial
196 243 Abial F 356 Abiel 196
Anna 196 218 327 Augustine V
169 Benjamin R 197 337
Benjamin Rackley 196 brothers
14 115 Carrie May (Blue) 198
Cyrus 196 Edmond S 344 Elvira
E 356 Elvira J 196 340 Elvira
(Pratt) 196 Emma 349 Esther
(Millett) 196 family 86 196
Henry Homer 196 John 196 Julia
Ann (Woodman) 243 Maria 194
Martha 242 356 Mary 352 Mary
(Rackley) 196 Mr 169 244 P H
268 Percy Harold 197 Phillip H
197 302 Phillips Herbert 197
Polly 334 Rose E 350 Rose Ellen
165 196 S Homer 197 302 S
Howard 197 303 Stephen Homer
197 Stephen R 85 249 264 341
347 Stephen Rackley 196 Steven
R 180 Stillman Howard 197
Susan 196 332 Truman 26
Victoria H (Turner) 85 196

DEANE (Cont.)
Victoria Helen (Turner) 180
Volney A 196 197 Walter 196
Wealthy 196 Zebiah 196
331Zebiah (Field) 196 Zebulon
196 197 327 Zopher 196 329
345
DEARBORN, D H 352 General 64
DEERING, Arthur 294 family 207
DELANO, George L 358
DELAWARE, 119
DeMANTEL, Mr 13
DENNEN, Job C 148 343 346
Martha (Brewster) 148
DENNETT, David 151 Sally (Gould)
151
DENNISON, Nancy Mrs 333
DEXTER, Amasa 324 Carrie May
117 Francis Deacon 117 Henry
137 Sarah 116 117 Sarah
(Knapp) 137 Winfred 117
DICKER, Virtue 324
DICKINSON, A R 34 Eliza Ann
(Stinchfield) 34
DILLINGHAM, Prudence 345
DINGLEY, Carrie 88 Mary 364
DISTRICT of COLUMBIA,
Georgetown 154 Washington
167 187 217
DIXON, Stillman N 357
DOANE, Dorcas 331 E H 252
Edward 327
DOLLOFF, Thomas Rev 257
DOLLY, Frances 35
DONALLY, Anna (Foss) 95
DONHAM, Eliza 330 Hannah E 86
DONNALLY, Jeremiah 356
DOUGLASS, Abbie A 128 Betsey
(Lindsey) 128 Carrie 128
Charles 128 Daniel W 128 Ellen
128 Forest 128 Frank 128
George H 352 Henry 128
Herbert 128 Isabelle 128 James
128 Jefferson 128 John 128

DOUGLASS (Cont.)
  John L 128 Josephine B
  (Lindsey) 128 Julia A 128 Olive
  J 128 Wallace B 128 William
  128
DOUTY, Calvin S 295
DOW, J S 295 Neal 209 Neal Col
  290
DOYLE, William 291 294
DRAKE, Adeline 144 328 Codding
  76 325 Daniel 394 F E 303
  family 76 Flora A 394 Isaac D
  333 Mehitabal 324 Mr 244
  Phebe C 340 Sally 416 Sally
  (Turner) 76 surname 24 Warren
  325
DRAPER, Hannah 219 Hannah 335
  Hazaranan 325 323 Mr 244
DRINKWATER, Mr 244 Priscilla
  (George) 110 Thomas 110 325
DROUGHT, John 331
DROUT, Almira (Foss) 93 Elizabeth
  93 John 93
DUCKWORTH, Evelyn P
  (Stinchfield) 34 George L 34
DUDLEY, Etta B Mrs 359
  Experience (Wing) 170 Micajah
  144 325 Sibil 371 Susan (Foster)
  144
DUMLEY, John 353
DUNBAR, Melatiah 175 Roa
  (Curtis) 158 Seth 158
DUNHAM, Benjamin 169 337
  Family 371 Hannah 402 Hannah
  E 346 Hannah L Mrs 340
  Hannah Mrs 54 Hannah (Wing)
  169 John 340 Joseph S 329 Levi
  257 334 Lucius C 350 Lucy L
  344 Matilda 128 Mercy 261
  Micajah 233 335 Mr 244 Salome
  (Lincoln) 233 surname 24
DUNNELL, Mark H 213 288
DUNTON, W C 112
DURELL, Mary 326

DURKESHIRE, Miss 108
DURRELL, Noah P 337
DURRILL, Dorcas (Gould) 151
  Nathaniel 151
DWINAL, Aaron 258 259 Capt 176
  Judith 342
DYER, Cynthia 49 family 372
  George 303 Isaac 290 Luta M
  359 Mabel L 268 Solomon
  352 Susannah Mrs 326 Tabitha
  323 Weltha 333
EDDGECOMB, Mary Cardiff 99
EDGCOMBE, Sarah 343
EDGECOM, Ruphina (Carver) 236
EDGECOMB, Annie W (Foss) 98
  Aubrey Mrs 98 Aubrey Wilson
  98 Benjamin 90 Benjamin Capt
  98 Benjamin Jr 98 Dr 95 Eli 358
  99 Eva Mae (Fickett) 99 Lula L
  358 Mary C 361 Phineas Capt 90
  Sarah Etta 99 Sarah (Foss) 90 98
  William W 348
EDGECOMBE, Family 372
EDGECOME, Aubry 150
EDGERTON, Ophelia 37
EDISON, Miss 235
EDSON, Mary 153
EIRIKR, family 199
ELDEN, Mary Jane 336 Ruth 151
  152 Samuel 220
ELDER, Araminta (Pettingill) 155
  156 Joshua 156 244 343 Lydia
  (Pettingill) 155 Samuel 332
  William E 155 349
ELDRIDGE, Levi 255 Tamson 23
ELLENWOOD, Mary C 352
ELLIOTT, Gertrude E 82
ELLMS, Ellen 348 Joseph 342
  Orrila J 344
ELMS, Betsy Mrs 328 Charles 335
  Eleanor 222 336 Joseph 335
  Robert 244 271 334 Salmon 332
  William 330
EMERSON, Charles S 293 S M 256

EMERTON, Elvira F 167
EMERY, George 331 Sabine 289
EMMONS, Francina J (Bishop) 66
ENDICOTT, Gov 43 44 Mary 202
ENERY, Patea M 361
ENGLAND, 43 69 79 133 153 172
　Apledore, Kent 157 Battle of
　Worcester 229 Beaumauar Park
　201 Chard 196 Chertsey,
　Surreyshire 43 Chertsey 43
　Christian Malford 238 Corsham,
　a village in Wiltshire 238 County
　of Kent 157 County of Sussex
　157 Great Strettan, Leicester Co
　200 Hampshire 240 Houghton
　200 Leeds 1 17 412 Leicester
　200 201 Leominster 43
　Lincolnshire 206 London 55 201
　Norfolk 133 Redwood 43 Staples
　Inn (Holborn) 43 Southhampton
　238 Sussex Co 134 Tenterden
　157
ENGLISH, Anglo-Saxon 133 Naval
　practice frigate *Milford* 80
EPES, Thomas 6
ERSKINE, Alexander Jr 337 Lucetta
　(Pettingill) 155 Robert 22
　Samuel 335 William H 155 350
ESTES, Cyrus 170 Phebe (Wing)
　170
EVANS, Forest L 266
EVELITH, Abigail (Cait) 44 Mary
　44
EYRICK, John 200 Nicholas 200
　Thomas 199 200
EYRYK, Agnes 200 Henry 200
　Joanna 200 John 200 Robert 200
　William Sir 200
FABIAN, John Jr 336
FABYAN, Henry O 288 Nellie L
　354
FABYENS, Joshua 337
FAGER, Mary 351
FAIRBANKS, Joel 348 John 137

FAIRBANKS (Cont.)
　Jonathan 256 Sarah (Knapp)
　(Dexter) 137
FAIRFIELD, Enos 142
FALES, Sarah K 335
FAREWELL, Alanson 166 Alice
　(Caswell) 166 Chandler 166
　Hannibal 166
FARLEY, Charles H 171 Cyrus H
　171 Elizabeth 171 Elsie Howard
　(Wing) 171 Florence 171 Henry
　G 171 Phillip H 171
FARMER, C C 53 304 Cassandra B
　(Lane) 53 Cassie B (Lane) 70
　Chester C 357
FARNHAM, Augustus B 291
　Isabelle 65
FARR, Bertha Estella 161 Henry H
　161 Marion (Curtis) 161
FARRAR, Daniel S 129 Naomi
　(Lindsey) 129 Olive B 129
　William A 129
FARRINGTON, Betsey M 349
　Georgia E 359 Harriett 417 J L B
　350 James Rev 216 John L B
　216 Maria 366 Melinda F 216
　Orrah A (Boothby) 216 Susan F
　216
FARWELL, Hannibal 328
FAYAN, Oliver 341
FELCH, Cyrus B 337 Samuel 244
FELLOWS, Joseph 326
FENDERSON, Elizabeth 164
FENWICK, Benedict Bishop 11
FERNALD, Julia Ann 378 Julia Ann
　Mrs 350 Julia Ann (True) 59
FESSENDEN, Francis 293
　Remember 80
FICKETT, Eva Mae 99 Eva May 358
　Loring Curtis 99 Martha
　(Bragdon) 99
FIELD, Mary 239 Zebiah 196
FILLBROWN, James S 289
FINK, Flavilla A (Cushman) 124

FINK (Cont.)
  Robert O 124
FIRST THINGS, Blacksmith 248
  Christian (male) Child born in
  Winthrop ME 140 142 Female
  Supervisor of Leeds Schools 115
  Grist-mill 248 Man child born in
  Newbury MA 239 Merchant 248
  Mill & Mill-dam in Wayne ME
  168 Minister 251 Postmaster 70
  Sawmill 248 Tanner 248 White
  Child born in Leeds 27 90 227
  411 White Male born in Leeds
  126 412 White Male child born
  in Winthrop 371
FISH - see MORRIS 238
FISH, Abigail 238 Abigail (Carver)
  233 238 Ansel 331 Arthur W
  361 Arvilla 117 Austin A 117
  Calvin 334 Capt 92 Caroline 116
  331 Caroline W 117 Charles 238
  Charles M 357 Columbia 233
  238 342 Deborah 331 Desire 116
  117 333 Eliza Ann 341 Eliza M
  117 Eliza (Kimball) 117 Elmira
  117 Enoch 116 117 337 Enoch Jr
  117 Enoch T 289 Ezra W 333
  family 231 Grace 116 Hannah
  (Ridley) 238 Hira 238 Hirah 231
  334 Irene (Andrews) 117 Jira Jr
  323 330 Jirah 24 57 231 285 331
  Jirah Jr 244 Joan D 394 Joanna
  D 341 Jonathan 6 Leonard M
  339 Lillis 329 Lovina 238 344
  Lydia (Reed) 116 Lyllis 238
  Major 235 Mary 116 236 238
  346 367 Mehitable (Tupper) 115
  Mercy P 324 Miss 233 Nancy
  110 Octavia 117 Olive 116 331
  Olive R 117 Patience 116 117
  336 Rosilla (Leadbetter) 116
  Roxanna 342 Sally 238 Samuel
  238 Sarah 331 Sarah J 117 Seth
  109 116 231 233 238 272 331

FISH (Cont.)
  334 348 367 Seth Jr 331 Seth
  Mrs 236 Silas 238 343 Thirza A
  (Carver) 236 238 Warren 116
  117 337 Willard 238 Willard J
  293 William 115 William H 117
  William Jr 116 332 (illegible) 7
FISK, Mary 384
FLAX BUSINESS, 75
FLETCHER, John 108 Rachael
  (Leadbetter) 108
FLORIDA, 219 Barrancas 66 131
  395 Tallahassee 73
FOARD, Daniel 330
FOGG, Albina L 353 George E 348 J
  B 256 Jason P 343 Moses 351
  Percy L 360
FOLSOM Elmira Mrs 354
FORD Mr 245
FORD - see FOARD 330
FOSS, A J 165 171 175 186 190 302
  303 A J Mrs 176 Abby J (Cox)
  102 Abigail Jane (Hall) 98
  Abigail (Hill) 89 Adeline 94 331
  Adoniram J 347 Adoniram
  Judson 102 104 Allura 27 105
  334 Almira 93 100 334 Alpheus
  340 Alpheus L 98 Alpheus Lane
  97 Alvin 27 105 192 194 337
  Alvin Wilson 104 Ann 192 194
  Ann H 54 102 104 345 374 Ann
  Hazeltine 393 Ann Mrs 333
  Anna 95 209 Annie 356 Annie H
  360 Annie Howard 104 Annie W
  98 372 Anourille C 98 Anourille
  Coolidge 97 Arthur C 94 Asa 34
  90 Augustus 73 Augustus L 93
  96 97 342 Benjamin 90 Betsey
  (Millett) 49 93 Brothers 92
  Caroline E (Lothrop) 73 Caroline
  (Lothrop) 96 Carrie F Barker 97
  Catharine M 103 Catherine M
  375 Catherine 102 Catherine B
  (Swanson) 98 Charles 96

HISTORY OF LEEDS

FOSS (Cont.)
Charles Wilson 104 Charlott (Towle) 98 Christopher G 336 Christopher Gore 97 Clara (Woodford) 96 Columbia 100 Cora (Chandler) 102 Cordelia (Gould) 94 Cordellus 95 Cordellus Dr 269 Cornelia B (Howard) 192 Cyrus 90 93 99 324 Cyrus Capt Esq 97 Cyrus W 98 372 Cyrus Wilson 97 Daniel 90 93 97-99 272 324 339 Dorcas 368 Dorcas E 103 375 Dorcas Ellen 347 Dorcas S (Morrison) 101 104 Edith (Chandler) 195 Eliakim 90 Eliza 27 Eliza W 105 106 Elizabeth 102 Elizabeth (Cobb) 101 Elizabeth (Foss) 102 Elizabeth (Smith?) 90 Elmer E 95 Emeline (Leadbetter) 96 Emery 102 344 Emma 51 97 Ephraim 332 Ephraim D 99 Ephraim W 93 99 Esther 54 93 332 Esther Mrs 333 Ethel 95 Eugenia F (Jennings) 194 Eunice 93 96 Eunice F 345 Eunice (Lane) 99 family 27 89 373 374 376 Fannie (Rafter) 96 Fanny G 340 Fernando C 94 Fernando Capt 62 Flora M (Jennings) 95 Florida 104 73 Florilla 100 Frances 100 Francis G 192 194 Frank 73 97 Frank G 103 195 351 Frank G Mrs 104 Frank Maynard 104 Fred C 192 194 356 George 90 324 George M 103 Georgie Baker 96 Gidding L 94 Giddings L 347 Giddings Lane 97 Grace 102 Guy 250 Guy W 104 Hannah 90 91 105 208 Hannah (Carll) 89 Harriet 105 27 Harriet (Townsend) 99 Hartland 95 Harty 95 Hattie F (Cox) 103 Howard C 95

FOSS (Cont.)
Isabella 102 James 89 90 325 James M 103 Jane 136 335 Jane (Gott) 106 136 Jedida 336 Jedidah 93 96 Jemima L 336 Jemima Lane 97 Jennie 97 Jerusha (Hanes) 100 John 90 102 105 John M 101 Joseph 89 Josephine B 99 Josephine Bonaparte 97 Kate M 352 L H 351 Laura M 103 Laura (Rowe) 105 Lemuel 90 Lena H 102 Lena Howard 360 Leroy 96 Levi 49 89 90 93 97 257 323 340 Levi Esq 93 Levi F 94 Levi Jr 93 96 Lizzie 97 Loring 27 105 106 136 338 Lucy 62 Lucy M 101 102 268 344 373 Marcena 100 Maria (Deane) 194 Martha Jane (Shaw) 98 Mary 90 Mary Jane 97 99 Mary (Leadbetter) 81 94 108 Mehitable S (Church) 99 Minnie A 192 194 355 Mr 93 245 Nancy (Moulton) 98 Nathan 90 Olive (Lothrop) 97 Olive (Smith) 90 Oliver Johnson 104 Orintha H 345 Orinthia 73 Orissa 100 Orra M 348 Pelatiah 89 Phineas 24 90 105 107 Phineas Capt 27 91 92 105 Phineus (Jr) 27 Polly Mrs 341 Polly (Lothrop) 73 104 Preston 102 Preston E 192 194 Rachael 93 96 99 107 Rachael E 103 Rachel 93 323 334 Rachel (Milliken) 90 Rebecca (Stinchfield) 27 90 105 Rena May 96 Rodney 73 104 Rosalinda L 98 Rosalinda Lane 97 Rose 40 Rossie L 373 Ruel 73 93 93 104 333 Sally 328 Samuel 90 Sarah 53 89 90 93 96 98 100 339 Sarah E 344 Sarah E (Foss) 102 Sarah (Goodrich) 90 Sarah (Goodridge) 93 105

FOSS (Cont.)
  Sarah (Norris) 100 Simeon 93
  249 330 331 Simeon Dr 100 269
  Stillman 94 T C 102 T Clarkson
  249 Thaddeus 93 100 327 328
  Thaddeus R 340 Thaddeus W 98
  Thaddeus Warsaw 97 Theresa
  (Howard) 102 Thomas C 101
  102 345 356 Uriah 24 81 90 93-
  95 103 105 108 272 335 V
  Richardson 102 Varnum R 104
  Vesta 104 Vesta P Mrs 250
  Vesta P (Foss) 103 194 Vesta T
  351 Viora A Mrs 356 Volney H
  95 295 Walter 89 93 100 194
  272 320 321 332 Walter E 102
  Walter Elder 252 261 Walter Jr
  89 Walter P 353 Walter Payson
  91 101 103 104 Walter Rev 54
  104 106 393 Warren Howard
  192 194 Warren L 97 William
  96 William H 349
FOSTER, Abigail 146 Abigail
  (Allen) 143 Adaline 144 Adeline
  (Drake) 144 Alice 60 Alice I 145
  Alonzo 145 Amanda 144 145
  Amelia 145 Ann 144 146 Aurelia
  336 Billy 143 C H 249 C H 302
  303 Carrie A 351 Charles
  Freemont 146 Charles Henry 145
  Charles Robert 145 371 Charles
  Warren 131 Clarissa 144
  Columbus 144 Daniel 143 144
  David Jr 144 Diadama (Johnson)
  141 Eliphalet 143 Elizabeth 143
  Emeline 83 145 145 349 Eunice
  144 Everett 145 146 371 family
  140 Frank L 146 Freeman 144
  Hannah 143 146 333 335
  Hannah Amanda 341 Hannah B
  331 Harriet 144 Harriet L
  (Curtis) 145 Harriet (Curtis) 158
  Hattie 226 Hattie A 145 352
  Henry Ward 146 Ichabod 144

FOSTER (Cont.)
  Isaac 144 James 144 Jane 113
  Jerusha (Wadsworth) 144 John
  77 143 144 324 John Winthrop
  144 Joseph 333 Lavina 144
  Leonard 145 338 Loring 341
  Lydia 145 Maria L 126 Martha R
  145 Mary Ann 330 Mary J
  (Morse) 146 Mehitable 337
  Melissa 144 Millicent (Howe)
  144 Molly 143 Moses 144 Mr
  142 245 N Emma 145 Nabby
  328 Nancy (Morse) 144 145
  Nathan 144 Oliver 143 144 Orra
  A 144 141 145 370 Otis 143
  Phoebe 144 Preston 144 Priscilla
  (Gilbert) 77 144 Rebecca D 335
  Rossa Jane (Lindsey) 131 Sadie
  E (Pratt) 146 Sally 146 325 Sally
  (Streeter) 141 144 Sarah 36 37
  252 Sarah (Stevens) 146 Sibler
  143 144 Sibler (Freeman) 140
  143 Sibyl 144 Stephen 6 140 143
  144 285 Stephen Jr 144 328
  Stuart 143 144 Stuart Jr 144
  Susan 143 144 Tabbie 146
  Thomas 143 Timothy 21 83 144
  145 158 324 371 Timothy Capt
  140 141 Timothy H 145 Timothy
  Jr 143 144 W H 226 W H Rev
  158 Wadsworth 144 Ward L 145
  Ward L Capt 145 William H 339
  William Henry 145 371 William
  Henry Rev 145
FOY, Elizabeth (Bishop) 66
  Nathaniel 328 Stephen 330 Steve
  66
FRANCIS, Ada A (Sarner) 62 Alice
  (Foster) 60 Alice (Lothrop) 58
  Augustus S 62 B Franklin 59
  Benjamin 58 61 320 321 Betsey
  58 61 Betty (Johnson) 63 Davis
  54 58 59 61 302 342 350
  Elbridge 343 Elder 252 Esther

FRANCIS (Cont.)
  58 61 Esther (Francis) 60 Eunice
  58 61 Eunice (Millett) 57 46
  family 55 376-378 Frank 63
  Franklin 63 Franklin S 347 Fred
  E 59 60 Frederick 59 Fremont
  Davis 59 Gard Rosamond 59
  Georgia A (Francis) 59 Gladys
  304 Gladys Hester 59 Grace 63
  Herbert Henry 63 Hester A
  (Haskell) 59 John 46 58 60 257
  325 John Adams 62 63 John G
  59 Julia Ann (True) Fernald 59
  Lois 58 61 Lorana 333 Lorania
  58 63 Louise 63 Louise H 62 63
  Lucy (Foss) 62 Mark 58 60
  Martha/Patty 57 Mary 59 61
  Mary H 60 Matilda 58 61 335
  Mellie Bursely 63 Mildred B
  361 Millis B 62 Mr 245 Naomi
  O (True) 62 Nellie (Leadbetter)
  62 Orissa Helen 60 Page T 287
  293 Page True 62 63 Patience
  (Parcher) 60 Percy W 63 Polly
  58 Rosa Lena 59 Rosamond
  (Lane) 54 59 Roy P 63 Ruth 63
  Samuel 335 46 58 Samuel L 62
  Samuel P 1 107 125 62 Samuel
  P Mrs 94 Sarah S (True) 62
  Sewall 60 Susan 135 Susan C
  333 Susan Maria 62 Susanna C
  58 61 Thomas 6 24 46 Thomas D
  24 25 251 279 285 Thomas D
  Rev 109 135 253 Thomas Davis
  55 Thomas Davis Rev 24
  Thomas Edwin 59 Thomas Elder
  263 264 272 Thomas Jr 57 58 60
  330 Thomas Rev 25 46 251
  Thomas D Elder 1 Ulmer P 34
  62 W Henry 57 61 190 W L 249
  250 304 W L Mrs 305 Wallace L
  59 60 William H 347 William
  Henry 62 Winifred G 160
  Zipporah L (Perly) 62

FREE WILLERS, 257
FREEDMEN'S BUREAU, 185 189
FREEMAN, Allen 26 272 286 334
  Barzilla 26 David P 354
  Elizabeth 26 329 Elizabeth W
  223 Ezra 26 family 26 Fannie 26
  Fanny 333 Isaac 26 57 203 223
  251 252 Joseph 271 286 325
  Keziah 23 26 331 Lois 338 Lois
  L 26 Lydia 26 Martha 26 330
  Martha (Stinchfield) 26 223
  Martha/Patty (Francis) 57 Mr
  245 Rosilla 26 Samuel 26 Sarah
  True 26 Sibler 140 143 Stephen
  23 Susanna (Stinchfield) 23
FREEWILL BAPTIST, 261
FRENCH, Edwin S 347 Esther 153
  Georgina (Gould) 152 Lydia W
  Mrs 350 Walter A 152
FRIZELL, Jarvus 335
FROST, family 232 379 Harriet 82
  Harriet S 346 Henry Elder 209
  Henry T 293 349 Joseph 232 238
  341 Mary (Carver) 238 Mr 245
  Noah 324 O J 258 Oliver P 82
  232 248 272 331 342 Rose S 352
  William 344
FULLER, Esther 365 Family 380
  Frances 41 Job 21 Nellie 354
  Polly 349 Samuel Jr 340 William
  H 348
FULTON, Elder 252
GARCELON, Alonzo Dr 82 Charles
  309
GARDNER, Elinor 380 Hezekiah S
  230 James H 293 Lizzie 152
  Phebe Jane (Gorden) 230 Sarah
  E 348
GARFIELD, President 190
GATES, Augusta E 128 General 118
  119
GEORGE, Amanda (Hundon) 111
  Annie A 111 112 Augustus S
  110 111 289 351 Charity 109

GEORGE (Cont.)
  Charity (Chubbock) 109 Charles
  L 110 112 Clarissa (Leighton)
  110 Cyrus 110 112 Donald D
  112 Eliza J 351 352 Eliza Jane
  110 112 Ernest 111 family 14 19
  24 25 48 109 110 285 288 291
  334 337 Francis Jr 110 329
  George W 335 339 George
  Washington 110 112 Georgie
  (Todd) 112 Henry 110 112
  Hulda J (Sprague) 111 Ida (Ray)
  111 Lewis W 111 Loren 110 111
  Lucinda 110 330 Malinda 110
  331 Mary Ann (Gilbert) 110
  Mira 111 Mr 245 Nancy (Fish)
  110 Otis B 110 111 289 Priscilla
  110 325 Sally 48 110 Volney
  110 112
GEORGIA, 81 173 176 Macon 226
  Savannah 184
GERMANY, Saxony Province 133
GERRY, Elbridge 271
GETCHELL, Elizabeth 78 Jas 324
GIDDINGS, Aubrey 399
GIFFORD, A F 302 Cynthia
  (Turner) 86 Isaiah 86 346 John C
  289
GILBERT, Abbie 78 171 Ada M 355
  Adaline (Day) 79 Addison D 291
  Adeline (Curtis) 161 Ahira 77 79
  323 Albion 79 Alden 76 Alfred
  77 Alvira 77 Ann C 161 Ann
  (Whitney) 77 Annie 76 Annie
  (Sampson) 78 Aranda 78 171
  225 341 384 Asenath Drew 325
  Augusta 337 Avanda 408 Bailey
  327 Benjamin 77 79 323 352
  Benjn 7 Betsey 70 75 76 85 400
  Betsey Alden 76 Betsey (Bailey)
  74 Betsy B 323 Caleb S 77 338
  Caroline 79 Carrie L (Sweeny)
  78 Catherine (Day) 79 Chandler
  77 Charles 77 Charles Grandison

GILBERT (Cont.)
  325 Chloe 325 Christina (Alden)
  76 Cornelius 6 76 79 271
  Deborah 78 79 85 323 401
  Deborah (Turner) 79 86 Dennis
  77 Dennis R 337 Diana T 300
  Diana T (Wing) 78 225 Diana
  Wing 264 Diana (Wing) 171
  Drusilla 77 342 Earl 78 Earl S
  78 Edward 79 86 Edward T 338
  Elacta D 351 Elijah 75 324
  Elijah Jr 78 Elizabeth (Getchell)
  78 Ella 79 Ellerson 86 Elvetta
  Delilah 77 Emma Amelia 77
  Emma F 161 Erastus E 294
  Everett 77 family 74 George E
  290 352 George Elliot 77
  Gustavus 79 342 Hannah 79
  Hannah (Ballou) 79 Harriet
  Amanda 342 Heircy 7 Helen L
  352 Henry 324 Henry A 76 332
  Hersey 75 76 Hersey Jr 77
  Huldah 77 78 324 Irvilla 77
  James 324 James C 77 James D
  161 James D Jr 342 James Drew
  326 James Henry 76 James
  Nelson 77 Jane 78 127 130 324
  395 396 Jane (Sampson) 78
  Jedson 77-79 Jerome B 77
  Joanna 78 79 170 325 418 John
  N 340 Joseph R 77 340
  Josephine 347 Josiah 328 Joseph
  Ransom 77 Judith 77 Judith L
  344 Julia 76 198 329 Lafayette
  78 Leonard 79 Levi 75 77 330
  Levi J 77 Lewis Irvin 77 Lloyd A
  290 Lois 78 171 Lois V 355 Lois
  Viola 408 Louisa (Torsey) 77
  Lovinia Josephine 77 Lucia
  (Turner) 79 Lucilla Alice 77
  Lucinda 77 Lucy 73 324 397
  Luther B 342 Lydia 79 Lydia
  (Jones) 79 Mabel 78 Marcellus
  77 Marcus 77 78 328 331

GILBERT (Cont.)
   Marian 78 Marian (Coburn) 78
   Marinda J 344 Martha Almedia
   77 Martha (Day) 77 Mary A
   (Crummett) 77 Mary Ann 79 110
   335 Mehitable (Morse) 77 Mr
   245 Nancy 77 Nathaniel 75 77
   323 Nelson 79 333 Olive 323
   Olive (Gilbert) 77 79 Oliver 79
   Oliver S 347 Otis Hayford 76
   Philo 79 Philo C 352 Polly 77
   326 Priscilla 77 144 324 Proctor
   78 Ransellear 79 Rebecca 77
   Rebecca (Sampson) 79 Rhoda 77
   Rollin 78 171 Rosa 78 171 Rosa
   V 225 354 384 Rosilla 394
   Roswell C 161 Rozilla 79 Ruth
   77 Sally 77 325 Samuel 7 327
   Sanford 79 337 Spirren 77 Susan
   76 330 Tertia 76 Vantile 86
   Wallace 86 Walter Guy 78
   Warren Foster 77 Wealthy 77
   William 7 24 76 263 271 279
   William Capt 74 75 77 William
   Jr 76 William Lieut 285 William
   S 77 78 William T 78 327
   Wilson 79 339
GILE, Lemuel 361 Etta M 357
GILMAN, Elizabeth (Woodman) 240
   Hiram H 349 Jonathan 240
GILMORE, Albert F 293 Arza 148
   66 Charles D 292 Eliza (Otis)
   (Howard) 165 Family 380
   Hannah (Lothrop) 69 Hulda 70
   397 Huldah A 336 John 74 273
   John Col 69 165 196 198 John F
   338 359 Joshua 69 Laverna C
   148 Laverna C Mrs 346 Louisa
   Jane 340 Luvernia (Bishop) 66 R
   H 196 Rodelphus H 165 350
   Rose Ellen (Deane) 165 196
   Rowland A 345 Rowland Mrs 74
   Vesta A 357 W S 358
GILPATRICK, Abbie 128

GLIDDEN, Mary 229
GOCH, Prudence 162
GODDARD, John Col 295
GODFREY, John F 295
GOFF, Dana 73 104 345 Orintha
   (Foss) 73 104
GOOCH, Frank H 355 Prudence E R
   347
GOODRICH, Sarah 90
GOODRIDGE, Mary 239 Mehetable
   (Woodman) 239 Phillip 239
   Sarah 93 105
GOOLDRUP, Lillie 360
GORDEN, Adelia C (Hartt) 230
   Charles Smith 230 Florinda
   (Churchill) 230 Greenwood C
   230 Hannah (Stinchfield) 230
   Hezekiah S 230 John Allen 230
   Phebe Jane 230
GORDON, Addie M 154 Adelia C
   (Hartt) 35 Adelia M 352 409
   Alexander 229 Almond N 358
   Annie (Burrill) 230 Asa G 156
   230 356 Asenath 409 Carrie E
   (Peaslee) 35 Carrie (Peaslee)
   230 Charles 35 338 Charles S
   259 407 Charles Wallace 230
   Costello D 35 Daniel 229 Diana
   (Smith) 230 Elizabeth
   (Harriman) 229 Elizabeth
   (Smith) 229 Ella 353 Ellery W
   35 family 35 229 381 Fannie 47
   G C Rev 127 George 153 154
   168 326 329 Greenwood 256
   Greenwood C 35 58 69 125 261
   286 339 Hannah Viola 230
   Hannah (Stinchfield) 35 Henry G
   35 230 Hezekiah S 35 351 Ira D
   35 Irving 35 Ithiel 229 James C
   230 359 Jeremiah 230 John A
   358 John Allen 35 John E 356
   John H 35 Jonathan 153 229 325
   Jonathan Glidden 230 Joseph
   Pettingill 230 Josephine E 35

HISTORY OF LEEDS

GORDON (Cont.)
Josiah 229 Leland H 35 Lucetta 156 341 Lydia 123 Lydia A 352 407 Lydia Ann 230 Lydia (Pettingill) 153 Mary Ella 230 Mary Jane 230 Mary (Glidden) 229 Mary (Lyssom) 229 Melintha G (Pettingill) 156 230 Oliver Cobb 230 Phebe J 351 Phebe Jane (Gordon) 35 Ruth (Pettingill) 154 Sarah Ann 230 Sarah E (Swift) 230 Sarah (Pettingill) 153 229 Sewall B 409 Susanna 229 Thomas 229 Viola H 35 352 Wallace 129 William C 337 William Crosby 229 Zipporah C Mrs 352

GOTT, Alfrida 136 Annie (Wood) 136 Anson 136 335 Aurelia 136 341 369 409 Charles 136 335 340 Charles S 136 Elijah 33 34 136 331 Eliza 136 Elvira 136 Elvira S 33 Gardiner G 136 George H 136 Harrison 136 Howard C 136 Ida L 32 Ida Lorena 32 Jane 136 338 Jane (Foss) 136 Jared 136 Jennie M 136 John M 136 John W 136 Joseph 136 264 Joseph G 32 348 Louisa 136 Malinda 136 Mary 136 Mary Ann 33 62 136 Matilda 136 Mehitable 136 330 Polly (Stinchfield) 33 136 Rhoda (Knapp) 106 136 137 Rose Ellen (Stinchfield) 32 Ruth (Gould) 32 136 242 Sally 330 Sarah 136 137 391 Susan 135 136 William 32 106 136 137 242 257 William Jr 331 William Jr (IV) 136 William (3rd) 136 Winifred A 32

GOULD, 24 Abigail 151 Ada (Greenwood) 152 Adelia (Perley) 151 Alice May 152 234 Ann (Adams) 151 Annie 150

GOULD (Cont.)
Annie (Parcher) 150 Aphia 339 Asa 150 Betsey 150 333 Betsey A (Brown) 152 Betsey (Leadbetter) 107 108 150 Blanche 152 Brothers 92 C D 235 Calvin 150 Carl 152 Caroline 150 Charles 151 152 Charlotte 151 364 Chessman 151 Chessman Capt 152 Chessman D 151 152 235 348 Clarissa 34 Clarissa S 338 Clark 152 Columbia Arvilla 180 Cordelia 94 150 347 Cyrus 151 Dorcas 150 151 327 E T 269 Effie 151 Eli 150 Elias 151 Elisha 151 Elisha D 151 337 Elisha T 151 152 Eliza P 350 Elizabeth 108 150 Ernest 152 Eunice 150 151 192 336 family 150 382 Fannie 151 Fannie C 344 Fannie H 151 Frank 108 150 152 269 Frank E 151 152 353 Freedom 109 150 Freedom W 151 344 George 73 103 150 236 261 333 George B 151 152 Georgina 152 Gertrude 152 Granville 151 Gustavus 151 Hamilton 150 151 Hannah (Lothrop) 73 Harrison 36 40 94 150 338 342 Harry 152 Harry N 357 Hepsibeth 151 Horace 338 Ingraham 150 Irenia 151 Isaac 150 Ivory 151 J F 269 Jabez 150 Jabez B 346 Jacob 151 Jeremiah 150 John 91 150-152 324 327 339 John 2d 333 John C 152 234 John Esq 261 Joseph 150 151 252 Joseph F 152 Joseph Jr 150 329 Lawrence 152 Leonard 151 Levi 151 Lizzie (Gardner) 152 Llewellyn 111 Llewellyn J 348 Lloyd 108 180 264 286 339 Loring 152 Loring B 151 Loring P 256 292 Loring P Rev 152

GOULD (Cont.)
  Louville W 353 Lucius L 360
  Lucretia D 350 Luther 151
  Luville 36 40 Lydia Arvilla
  (Howard) 180 Mary E (Brown)
  152 Mary (Chamberlain) 151
  Mary (Gray) 36 Maud 152
  Merritt 152 Miriam 151 Morris
  151 Moses 151 Moses G 152
  234 Moses Jr 151 Mr 245 N P
  73 357 Nathaniel P 151 Octavia
  151 335 Olive 150 326 Oren 150
  Orville 73 Patience 135 150 151
  Pelatiah 150 151 Peletiah 91
  Philena 150 176 334 374 Phoebe
  47 150 Polly 326 Rev 260 Robert
  40 92 93 98 140 150 220 272
  314 Rufus 34 150 Russel L 234
  Russell 150-152 351 Russell S
  137 138 Ruth 32 136 150 151
  242 331 Ruth (Besse) 150 Ruth
  (Elden) 151 152 S Ada
  (Greenwood) 152 234 Sally 150
  151 Samuel 150-152 Sarah 36
  151 234 Sarah F 344 Sarah L
  (Peare) 152 Sarah (Stinchfield)
  36 40 Simeon 107 108 150-152
  257 325 326 Stewart 150 Susan
  151 152 Susan E 337 Susan
  (Gould) 151 Theodore 151
  Thomas 151 W E 269 303 W E
  Dr 267 Welcome B 150-152
  William 150 151 326 William A
  336 Willis E 152 E 234 Willis E
  Dr 152
GRAFFAM, Ann 128 340 Lydia
  (Bishop) 65 168 Mr 232 245
  Thomas 65 168 320 328
GRAHAM, Gertrude M 360
GRANGE, Patron Of Husbandry,
  173 Leeds 174
GRANT, Addie 304 Addie (Smith)
  233 Amos 232 233 Amos P 349
  Arthur 304 Benjamin 232

GRANT (Cont.)
  Benjamin Jr 341 Bertha A 359
  Caroline (Millett) 233 Charles
  233 Clara I (Bishop) 67
  Columbia (Fish) 233 David 346
  Edward L 358 Effie 304 Ellen
  165 F S 304 family 232 383 384
  Flora 233 Fred 233 Fred S 304
  359 General 184 H L 304
  Herbert 233 Herbert L 353
  James 67 Joseph L 359 Joshua
  233 Josiah 232 233 Josiah L F
  344 Martha 232 233 261 Martha
  E 342 Mr 245 Myrtle 67 233
  Myrtle M 361 Perry 232 233 249
  250 259 348 358 Phoebe 382
  Rebecca (Rose) 233 Rosa E 357
  Sarah 232 233 Sarah H 342
  Stephen 232 233 Stephen W 290
  342 349
GRAVES, Catherine H 31 349
  Charles 31 Charles O 53 Helen
  G 188 Jane 210 Jane 334 Joseph
  333 Mr 245 Paulina (Ridley) 31
GRAY, Aramantha P (Stinchfield)
  36 Augusta Ann 36 Capt 187
  Catherine 339 Elizabeth 35
  Grace (Howard) 187 H F 303
  Hartland F 356 Hartley 238 344
  John 327 John F 255 344 Lovina
  (Fish) 238 Mary 36 Mary E 353
  Olive 240 Simon P 36
GREELEY, Clarence F 357 Horace
  63 107
GREEN, Arthur S 161 Bertha
  Estella (Farr) 161
GREENAWAY, John 43 Ursula 43
GREENBACK MOVEMENT, 114
GREENE, Daniel 330
GREENLEAF, Henry B 352
GREENWOOD, Ada 152 Ada S 351
  Ada Serena 382 Asenath (Hill)
  234 Clara C 234 family 234
  George B 234 344

GREENWOOD (Cont.)
George Bradford 234 Lovice
Jane 234 Mehitable (Chute) 234
Moses 234 382 392 Nellie 234
Rachael 135 Rachael B 234 391
392 S Ada 152 234 Sarah
(Gould) 234 Serena Deane
(Willis) 234
GRIFFITH, Abigail 386 Ann 342
GRISWOLD, Egbert 340 Julia A 355
GULLIVER, Mira H 358
GURNEY, Elder 252 Sylvia 332
HACKINS, Henry 289
HADEN, Jerusha A 242
HADLEY, Sadie Jane 359
HAGDEN, Jerusha Ann 349
HAINES, Daniel 285 Mr 245 Polly 397 Thomas 330
HALE, Asenath (Lane) 51 108 David Dr 51
HALE, Doctor 108 Elizabeth 64 Fessenden 51 Flora 51 Mary 51 Nathan 64
HALL, Abigail J 340 Abigail Jane 98 Amasa W 333 Daniel P 355 F H 256 Frank Hosea 360 Jennie O 351 Jesse R 79 Jessie R 344 Judith (Gilbert) 79
HALLOWELL, Betsey 340 Betsey E 383 Ellen F 353 Flora E 352 Lenora M 357 Lilla E 353 Thomas J 351 William H 341
HAM, Dodivah 336 Judith 325 Mary 337 Mary F 353 William 338
HAMILTON, Alice B 360 E D 70 Ermina (Turner) 70 Sam'l C 288
HAMMON Charity 326 Ebenezer 154 Hannah 324 Hiram Q 352 Jennette (Pettingill) 154 John 221 John C 346 Josiah C 345 Lydia (Gilbert) 79 Mary E 171 Mary E (Bates) 221 Mary Emma 154 Miss 55 Sylvanus 162 344 Vesta E 359

HAMOND, Mary E 356
HANCOCK's, Company Capt 90
HANDY, Ebenezer 21
HANES, Jerusha 100 Jerusha 328 Miss 150 Nancy 329 Reuben 323 Samuel 323
HANNOND, Sylvanus Jr 325
HANSCOM, Arthur S 225 Eva M 225 family 224 384 Florence L 225 Florence (Keen) 224 Henry B 225 John H 344 Matthias 224 339 Mellen J 78 225 354 Ora L 225 Rosa V 300 301 Rosa V Mrs 171 Rosa V (Gilbert) 225 Rosa (Gilbert) 78 Rosannah 351 Selden L 225 Walter 304 Washington 340
HANSON, Alice 360 Alice G 205 Samuel 342
HAPSGOOD, Sarah 168
HARDING, Colman 289 Hannah 40
HARDY, David S 338
HARLOW, Jennett (Carver) 237 Thomas 237 Thomas S 343
HARMON, Ebenezer 327 George 96 336 Jedidah (Foss) 96 Mr 11 Mr 245 S B 350 Sally 324
HARMOND, Dodivah 332 Phebe 332
HARPER, Eliot 329
HARRIMAN, Elizabeth 229
HARRINGTON, Adelaide C 88 89 Albert Abbott 88 89 Harriet 88 89 Sarah F 352 Thomas J 352
HARRIS, Benjamin 286 Betty 324 Joan Mrs 341 Joanna 156 Jonas 328 Lawrence J 20 Lydia J (Curtis) 161 Minnie A 161 Moses 336 Nathaniel 161 Nathaniel 346 Rosine 346
HARRISON, Mehitable (Gott) 136
HART, Mary 312
HARTT, Aaron 351 Aaron Rev 37 Adelia C 35 230 358 381

HARTT (Cont.)
  Clara 37 Helen H (Libby) 37
  Samuel 381
HARVEY, Angeline 122 Angeline
  345 Bertha 237 Bethiah 329
  Corilla F (Cushman) 123 Daniel
  319 330 family 384 General 182
  Ray L 359 Silas 123 Stillman
  328
HASKELL, Elsie A (Day) 160
  Hester 379 Hester A 59 Jerusha
  (Hanes) (Foss) 100 Job 100
  Robert 160
HASLEY, Leonora M 83
HASTINGS, David R 290
HATCH, John 330
HATHAWAY, Meroah 364
HAWES, Benjamin 290
HAWKES, Joseph 254 Joseph 255
HAWS, Charles 333
HAYES, Kate 358 Mary A 381
HAYNES, Daniel E 357
HAYWARD, Harriet 333 Lydia 202
  Mary 190 Miss 54 Martha 175
  Thomas 175
HAZARD, Olive B (Woodman) 164
  Samuel L 164
HEALD, Thurston S 360 Susan Ann
  38 W J E Capt 38
HEATH, Francis E 291 Miss 95
HENDERSON, Parutha 342
HENLEY, Joseph 361
HENRY, the Eighth 42 133 Sixth 42
HERRICK, 24 Abigail 203 Abigail
  Jr 203 Abigail K 204 Abigail
  (House) 203 Abigail (Kilham)
  202 Abigail (Lamb) 203 Alice G
  (Hanson) 205 Benjamin 201 202
  Betsey 203 Betsey R 204
  Clarissa 203 Edith 202 Editha
  202 Editha (Laskin) 201 Eli 203
  286 Elizabeth 201 203 Ephraim
  201 F H 267 303 family 199 385
  Frank E 204 Frank H 115 204

HERRICK (Cont.)
  267 359 Harriet 203 344 Hattie
  A 204 Henry 201 Horace 203
  204 259 344 Israel 259 330
  Israel H 204 205 360 Isreal 202
  203 257 258 272 J R 252 Joan
  (May) 201 John 200-202 Joseph
  201-203 Laura Margaret 205
  Loring 204 205 Lottie A 204 205
  Lucy M (Sylvester) 115 204
  Lydia (Hayward) 202 Margaret
  203 Margaret M 204 Mary 203
  Mary A 23 Mary (Bragg) 202
  Mary (Endicott) 202 Mary
  (March) 202 Mr 245 267 Polly
  203 328 Robert 200 S L 302
  Samuel 203 Sarah (Leach) 202
  Sophronia Lyford (Palmer) 204
  Thomas 201 William 201
  Zacharie 201
HERSEY, Harriet 216 Lois A 216
  Samuel 216
HERVE, Francis E 156
HESSELTON, Frank S 290
HEYRICK, John 200 Mary (Bond)
  201
HICKS, Abiagil 25 Abraham 25
  Annie 25 Elbridge 25 family 25
  Franklin 25 Hannah 25 Mr 245
  Nabby 324 Sally 324 Samuel 25
  Sarah 25 Sarah (Stinchfield) 25
  Sullivan 25 Thomas S 25
  Zephaniah 25 25
HIGGINS, Almira 96 Benjamin 286
  Carrie M 361 David 331 Flora L
  (Lothrop) 72 Frank 72 Frank M
  351 Holmes B 96 John 96 334
  Lydia 331 R S 303 Rachael
  (Foss) 96 Richard 6 Ruggles 72
  Thankful 328 Wilbur T 96
HIGGINSON, Rev 202
HIGHLAND, Mr 285
HIGHT, Thomas 295 Thomas Col
  294

HISTORY OF LEEDS 461

HILDRETH, Paul 20
HILL, Abigail 89 Asenath 234 B I 73 Benjamin J Capt 104 Florida (Foss) 104 73 Jeremiah Capt 240 Sarah F 351
HILL'S COMPANY, Jeremiah Capt 90
HILMAN, Mary P 338
HILTON, Hannah 239
HINDS, Hiram 98 Nancy (Moulton) (Foss) 98
HINKLEY, Andrew J 345 Daniel 248 334 Daniel W 292 Ella F 358 Niah 341
HISCOCK, Sarah 164
HISLEY, Edwin 288
HISTORY, an unwritten 167
HOBBS, A W 304 Arthur 304 Arthur W 360 family 385 Lina 360
HODGDON, Carrie M 349 Charles 117 Desire (Fish) (Daggett) 117 Eben 117 Ebenezer 336 Martha J 345 Martha Jane 117 Matilda 117 Samuel C 328
HODSDON, Abion H 149 Albion H 357 Benjamin 286 Hattie M (Brewster) 149 John P 162 346 Laura (Curtis) 162 Sarah Jane 349 H H 178 John 266 Lillian 178
HOIT, John L 335
HOLLOWAY, Rhoda 337
HOLLOWELL, Betsey 357
HOLMES, Elizabeth 48
HOLMES, Myra 47
HOLT, Addie J 354 D B 255
HOMES, Lizzie R Mrs 361
HOOD, Amelia 328
HOOPER, J H 197
HOSLEY, Celestia A 351 Columbus P 352 Family 386 Lenora M 346 W C 303
HOUGHTON, John C 360

HOUSE, A Jr 352 Abbie 360 Abigail 203 Allen 326 Alonzo 354 Annie 304 Cora E 356 David 331 Hirah 325 James L 339 Jane 332 Jerusha 327 John 327 Joshua 333 Mary 370 Mary J 356 Mr 245 Nathaniel 285 Nathaniel Jr 6 286 329 Rhoda 328 Rosilla P 360 Sally 329 Walter 305 Walter B 361
HOUSTON, General 38
HOWARD, 24 Abigail 175 Alfrida (Gott) 136 Allie J 361 Alma (Abbott) 196 Almina Augusta 192 193 Amanda (Additon) 172 180 Anna 191 Anna (Beals) 180 Arthur Day 190 Aurelia 175 327 366 Barker Brooks 178 Barnabas 175 Barnabas 57 Barnabas Jr 135 336 Barnabus 190 191 Barnabus Jr 191 192 Benjamin F 344 Benjamin Franklin 151 175 176 334 374 Bessie 187 Betsey (Stinchfield) 186 Betty 175 Bradford 191 Burt Foster 190 C H Gen 176 Calvin 175 Caroline A 191 Caroline A (Howard) 191 Charles 188 286 Charles H 186 189 287 Charles H General 165 Chauncey Otis 187 Clara 170 Clara Cornelia 192 194 Clara (Boothby) 195 Cordelia 176 Coridon 176 Cornelia 191 376 Cornelia B 192 337 Daniel 191 Daniel H 177 David 189 David Patten 188 Desire (Bailey) 129 175 186 Dexter W 288 291 Dexter Waterman 192 193 Direct Line from Plymouth Colony 386 Donald Charles 190 Dora L 171 358 Dora Lovisa 180 181 Dorothy 189 Ebenezer 175 Elathear True (Millet) 47 Elisa A 416 Eliza (Otis) 165 186

HOWARD (Cont.)
Elizabeth 175 Elizabeth Ann (Waite) 187 Ella 189 Ella Marilla 193 195 Ella T (Millet) 49 Ella True (Millett) 195 Ella (Patten) 187 Elsie Amanda 180 Emma Dunton 178 Emma (Maxwell) 177 Ephraim 175 Esther 195 Everett 175 176 family 175 386 388 Fannie (Gould) 151 Fletcher 180 181 Florilla 180 181 Francis Davis Millett 50 195 Franis Gilman 188 Franklin 102 Fred A 360 Fred N 193 195 357 Gen 176 184 291 George 181 Grace E 187 Guy 187 Guy Col 187 Hannah 69 405 Hannah L 348 Hannah L (Howard) 177 Hannah Lane 192 Hannah Lane (Howard) 194 Harriet 113 Harriet N 339 Harriett Newall 191 192 Harry Stinson 187 Hattie F (Davis) 195 Helen G (Graves) 188 Henrietta 177 31 Henry 175 Henry H 194 Henry Harrison 192 Homer 196 Howland 177 Howland Maxwell 178 James 175 James Waite 187 Jason 191 Jesse 175 Jesse Capt 175 John 175 187 Jonathan 175 Joshua 175 Julia 177 Julia A (Turner) 194 Julia Ann (Turner) 177 86 Julia Etta 178 Katherine 190 Katie Julia 177 Kezia 175 Laura 163 404 Laura B 347 Laura Jane 191 192 Lawrence Riggs 190 Leander M 193 195 355 Lillian (Hoffman) 178 Lizzie 177 217 Lizzie Emma 194 Lizzie T 193 195 Lizzie (Kirtz) 177 Lloyd 175 Lot 47 49 193 195 355 Lucius 177 Lucius Stillman 178 Lucretia 107 175 Lucretia

HOWARD (Cont.)
Lane 180 Lucretia P 55 176 339 Lucretia Phillips 180 Lucy M 219 Lucy Mitchell 192 193 Luretia 329 Luretia L 181 Luther L 330 49 Luther Loomis 191 195 Luther Loomis 3rd 193 Luther Loomis Jr 191 192 195 Lydia A 176 Lydia Ann 180 181 Lydia Arvilia 339 180 Lydia (Lothrop) 55 74 85 175 Marcellus 176 Maria Theresa 374 Marilla Mark 192 193 Martha (Hayward) 175 Mary 175 Mary D 192 Mary Dunbar 191 Mary F (Crosby) 191 Mary Jane 131 192 350 Mary L 85 176 196 336 402 Mary Louisa 180 Mary (Ames) 175 Matilda (Ostland) 195 Melatiah (Dunbar) 175 Melinda L (Brooks) 178 Melissa Almira 193 195 Melvin 191 192 Melvin Clark 192 193 195 Melvin David 195 Minnie Stillman 177 Mr 245 Nancy P (Pike) 181 Nina Foster 190 O O 176 188 189 305 O O Col 287 O O Gen 102 Oliver Otis 186 287 Oliver Otis General 165 286 Oliver Otis Jr 188 Oren G 192 194 Orren 217 Otis 136 Otis McGaw 190 Patty 327 Pelatiah 175 Perez 175 Philena (Gould) 176 R B Rev 176 Rhoda B (Mitchell) 191 192 Rhoda B (Mitchell) (Howard) 191 Rhoda Mrs 333 Roland 196 Roland B 176 Roland Bailey 175 186 187 Roland Bailey Rev 165 Roland Jr 186 Rosilla A 335 Rowland B 333 348 Rowland S 189 Rozilia A 176 Rozilla 401 S L 274 S L Esq 25 Sarah 175 Sarah F 195 Sarah Florence 193 Sarah P (Hussey) 192 Sarah P (Hussey)

HOWARD (Cont.)
  195 Sarah (Dean) 74 87 175
  Seth 165 175 176 181 248 264
  343 366 Seth Adelbert 180 181
  Seth Capt 102 129 175 177 182
  186 190 Seth Hon 180 181 Seth
  Mrs 172 Stella (Tyron) 181
  Sewall 191 192 Sewall P 192
  194 Sophie 195 Sophronia 337
  Stillman 55 74 85 175 177 197
  248 324 179 Stillman Lothrop
  Esq 31 86 176 177 178 194 335
  Susan Mrs 332 Susanna 175
  Theresa 102 176 Theressa M
  347 Uncle 130 V R Dr 269
  Valentine R 176 Valentine
  Rathburn 175 Vesta P (Foss) 194
  Vivian Luther 195 Ward 175 176
  Ward B 177 194 348 Ward
  Benton 177 Ward Ray 178
  Warren 177 191 261 333 Warren
  Deacon 131 219 William H 359
HOWE, Ann M 345 Charles 168
  Christiana 325 Christina 168
  Cyprian 168 Cyrus 67 168 Cyrus
  B 354 David 168 Edith 168 361
  Edith W 300 301 Edith
  (Hutchins) 168 Eleanor
  (Pettengill) 173 Eleanor (Turner)
  168 Ella Marilla (Howard) 195
  Ellen J 348 Eugene L 195 Eunice
  168 family 168 Frances 168
  Francis E 173 351 363 Freelove
  334 George 77 168 George T 65
  168 354 Icabod 168 21 Isaac 342
  Jane 168 333 Jonathan 22 168
  Lenora I 173 Lenora J 357
  Leonora 362 Lewis 168 Lovina
  168 Lovina 333 Lydia 168 330
  Lydia A 349 M C 303 Marcellus
  168 Mary (Graffam) 168
  Millicent 144 168 Mina I 195
  Moses 168 Mr 245 Phebe 328
  Rosilla (Bishop) 67 Sarah 168

HOWE (Cont.)
  Sarah (Hapsgood) 168 Stephen
  168 Susanna 168 William O 195
HOWIE, Gertrude E 181 360
HUBBARD, Thomas H 293
HUDSON, Emily F (Martin) 164
  Henry 164 James 164 Micajah
  164
HUNDON, Amanda 111
HUNTER, Annie 88
HUNTON, Hannah G 339 Herbert
  290 Wellington 102
HUNTOON, Hannah 220
HUSKINS, William H 346
HUSSEY, Esta B 353 Esther B 385
  Family 388 Frank H 353 358
  George E 291 Sarah P 192 195
  388
HUTCHINS, C K Professor 30
  Charles K Capt 126 Edith
  (Walton) 168 James 168 Lucy C
  361 Mary L 346
HUTCHINSON, Daniel 252 Daniel
  Rev 261 Stephen 325 Walter 355
HYDE, Thomas W 288
ILLINOIS, 52 130 173 Cardova 173
  Chicago 97 113 155 190 Des
  Plaines 98 Galesburg 181
  Glencoe 190 Princeton 187 188
IMPY Alonzo 290
INDIANA, Fort Wayne 97 Richmond
  166
INDIAN, Chiricaua Apaches 185
  Roccomeco 316 Servant John 64
  Village 311 Seminole 182
  Sheepeaters 185
INDIAN WARS, 1720 Fort Mary
  240 In 1690 Anticosti 240 Piute
  & Bannock 185
INGERSOLL, Joanna 153 Richard
  153
INTERNAL REVENUE
  COLLECTOR WHISKEY
  TAXES, 177

IOWA, 52 82 196 350 Des Moies
181 Marion 23 126 Mason City
82 Onawa 181 Waltham 161
IRELAND, 17 208 Magwater 207
North of 125
IRISH, Daniel 146 Daniel 335
Hannah (Foster) 146 Joanna 331
William 336
ISLAND MARTINIQUE, 126
ITALY, Rome 187 188
JACK, Betsey 329
JACKSON, Colonel 121 Fred C 356
Julia 66 Julia M 336 Nathaniel J
Capt 287 Stonewall 183
JACOB, Hannah 324
JACOBS, I S 95 Mary 81 Mary
Virginia 95
JAMESON, Charles D 287
JENKINS, Eliza 209 Eliza 331
Hamilton 209 Lydia (Boothby)
209 Mr 245
JENNINGS, Abigail Mrs Abigail
Mrs 397 Abigail V 335 Abigail
(Foster) 146 Alexander 82 84 89
129 257 258 259 326 Alexander
Jr 83 Almira Jane 342 Augusta E
83 Bathsheba 80 117 121 248
370 Betsey 82 325 Chester 81
Clara A 354 Columbus 81 82 83
333 Cresos 82 Daniel M 83
David 82 Deborah 80 Deborah C
332 82 Deborah (Newcomb) 80
Eliza A 51 172 344 362 Eliza A
(Additon) 83 172 Eliza Ann 80
81 Elmer E 81 Elvira 83 Elvira
A 344 Elvira A (Jennings) 81
Emeline (Foster) 145 371
Emeline (Foster) 83 Esther 80
Esther M 82 331 Esther M 82
Esther May 379 Eugenia E 356
Eugenia F 194 family 79 Flora
M 81 95 Florius 264 Frank N 83
Franklin N 82 Fred M 83 G A
302 G F 95 Gertrude 145

JENNINGS (Cont.)
Gertrude E (Elliott) 82 Gertrude
M 83 Gessius 80 Gessius F 51
81 348 Gustavus A 51 80 81 305
344 Hannah 80 Hannah L 345
Hannah M (Adams) 83 Hannah
(Carlton) 83 Harold W 83
Harriet (Frost) 82 Henry 328
Howard L 83 Howard S 83 Isaac
331 334 J F 259 J F 302 J F Mrs
172 Joanna (Lane) 108 172
Joanna (Lane) 51 80 John 6 24
79 80 82 115 248 263 271 279
380 John B 289 John F 83 176
346 349 371 John Frank 145
John Jr 80 82 83 328 Julia E
(Maine) 83 Juliet P (Black) 81
Lavinia 83 Leonora L 83
Leonora M (Hasley) 83 Lewis
146 328 Martha Ann (Turner) 89
Mary 210 Mary H (Sumner) 81
83 Mary L 83 Mary Virginia
(Jacobs) 95 Mary (Jacobs) 81
Mary (Jr) 83 Mary (Lindsey) 129
83 Mira (Parcher) 220 Mr 245
320 Mrs 94 Nathaniel 24 80
Oakes A 343 Octavia Orville 82
Olive 335 Olive (Tupper) 115 80
Orrah M Mrs 108 Orrah M
(Foss) 81 95 Orville 51 80 81
Pamelia 83 343 Perez 108 Perez
S 51 80 172 327 Phebe W 82
Phoebe 340 Polly 80 R 259 R G
Dr 269 Remember (Fessenden)
80 Rhodolphus 249 Robert 82
Rodolphus 83 248 264 346
Rollin F 81 82 291 346 Roscoe
G 51 81 82 Ruhama 79 Sally 326
Samuel 24 80 115 257 271
Samuel Jr 80 83 324 Sarah 80 82
83 Sarah (Morton) 82 Sturges N
82 83 89 346 Thomas 83
Thomas L 83 Ward H 220 343
William 80 William A 83 359

JENNINGS (Cont.)
　　William Sir 79
JEPSON, Eli 197 Molly 325 Thomas I 353
JERRARD, Simeon G Col 292
JERRY, John 96 Sarah Jane (Taylor) 96
JEWELL, Alfred 76 Betsey Alden (Gilbert) 76 Jonathan 336
JOHNSON, Abigail S 126 Andrew L 357 Betty 63 Charles E 296 Elijah D Col 292 Estella M 268 John H 347 Joseph E 184 Joseph P 344 Minnie A (Foss) 194 Mr 135 O A 194 Oliver A 355 Otis H Rev 259 Owen 194 Susan (Knapp) (Knight) 135 William 141
JONES, Augustus 171 Augustus B 349 Betsey 324 371 Charles 343 Charlotte 54 331 Daniel 285 Daniel Capt 52 Daniel L 335 Edward 329 Eliza Ann 389 Elizabeth M 343 G W 113 Isaac 327 Isabell W 351 James 339 John B 171 Judith 327 329 Judith (Lane) 52 Lorenzo 389 Louis A 171 Lydia 323 Lydia 79 Mr 245 Nancy 235 367 Orilla (Sylvester) (Skillings) 113 Ralph D 171 Stephen 347 Sylvester 326 Vesta Coffin (Wing) 170 Vesta W Mrs 356 William H 334
JORDAN, Ernest E 360 Melinda Mrs 342
JORDON, Emma Mrs 358
JOSELIN, Polly 325
JOSSELYN, Alma 406 Mehitable C 344
JUDKINS, Anne 325 Clara 414 Clarissa 346 Sarah L 343
JUNKINS, Clara 41
JUSTICE OF THE PEACE, 93 97 100 149 176 216 220 221

KAUFFER, John 309
KEARNY, Fort 73
KEAY, Sophia 363
KEEN, Florence 224 Florene 384 Florenia 339 Greenlief N 342 Isaiah B 346 John 77 272 328 340 Lucitta 338 Marva 346 Miss 77 Polly C 348 Silence H 340
KEENAN, James 333
KEENE, A CB 357 Abiathar 406 Calvin B 291 Carrie May Clinton 358 Evaline 343 Jerusha 23 John 249 John C 288 347 John Jr 344 Polly C 406 Sadie M 358
KEITH, John F 351 Lillian W 393 Nathan 325 Sarah A 354
KELLEY, Burnham 411 Happie W 411 Lydia 40
KELLY, Eveline Francelia 360
KEMP, Family 389
KEMPTON, Alice I (Foster) 145 Lyman 145
KENNEY, Charles 137 David 137 Elizabeth (Knapp) 137 family 389 Nancy 390
KENNISTON, Jennie (Foss) 97
KENNY, Charles M 361
KENT, John 239 Sarah (Woodman) 239
KENTUCKY, 177 60 Lebanon 177
KEY, Levi 335
KILBRETH, Annie (Gilbert) 76 Joseph 76
KILHAM, Abigail 202
KIMBALL, Eliza 117 337 Heber 326 Mr 245 William K 290
KINCADE, Eugene 357 Hiram F 356
KING, A Ella (Ramsdell) 219 B 219 Egbert 206 Mary 26 413 Sally 330 William 272
KIRTZ, Lizzie 177
KNAP, Charles 326

KNAP - see KNAPP 361
KNAPP, 24 Abial 135 151 Abial D
135 354 Abigail 336 Abigail L
29 138 139 Abigail Lindsey 414
Abigail (Norris) 135 Alma A 137
Almira 137 Alvira 339 Ann 134
Ann R 137 Anson G 357 Anson
G Ward 135 Arch L 139
Archibald L 138 341 Asa 135
137 138 342 Azel 138 139
Bartley 140 Bashaby 134 135
136 Betsey 135 Betsey (Baisy)
135 Bradford 139 C S 302 Caleb
134 Calista 338 Catherine 138
Catherine L 125 138 140
Catherine (Lindsay) 29 126
Catherine (Lindsey) 138 Celia
(Pullen) 137 Charles 29 30 108
126 135-140 320 330 414
Charles B Capt 126 Charles R
137 Charles S 345 Charles
Sewall 138 140 Charles Uncle
138 Colista 108 139 Colista May
138 Cynthia (Ripley) 137 Cyrus
135 Cyrus B Judge 136 Cyrus Dr
61 135 269 333 Deborah
(Cushman) 136 Delphinia 137
Dorothea 135 151 Earl 137
Edward 137 Eleanor 134 Elijah
134 135 137 151 Eliza 134 Eliza
(Berry) 137 Elizabeth 134 137
343 Ella 137 Ella (Millett) 135
Elvira 199 Eunice 135 137 235
251 328 Eunice (Carver) 134
family 133 390 Flavilla 139
Frank M 137 George Henry 135
Hannah 134 138 Hannah L 139
347 Hannah (Lindsey) 126 138
Hattie 137 Henry 137 Herbert
137 Ina 137 Irena 136 Isabella
137 Isabelle 137 James 134 Jane
135 136 151 Jane P 346 Jane
(Spear) 136 Jane (White) 139
Jared 34 135 136 151 Jennie 139

KNAPP (Cont.)
John 133-137 Jonathan 134
Joseph 46 61 126 134-136 285
Joseph Jr 134 135 235 326 415
Joseph Sr 135 136 192 Joshua
134 Judith 134 Kate 264 Levi
136 Lillian 137 Lizzie B (Moore)
137 Louvisa 136 Lucinda 137
Lucretia 135 138 Lucy (Lindsey)
126 136 Lydia 134 Margie 137
Martha (Wing) 137 Mary 134
136 137 140 Mary Ann 135
Mary J 137 Mary L 355 Matilda
134 135 138 46 May A 359 Mira
B 351 Miranda Ellen 135 Moses
134 Mr 245 309 Nathan 134
Nicholas 134 Olive 404 Olive C
339 415 Owen 136 Patience
(Gould) 135 151 Pelatiah 135
151 Peltiah 335 Polly 137 135
328 R L 303 Rachael 136
Rachael B (Greenwood) 234
Rachael (Greenwood) 135 140
Ralph L 356 358 Rhoda 106
134-137 151 Rhoda A 347
Richard 137 Roger 134 Roger de
133 Rollie D 137 Rose Emma
139 Rossa 137 Ruth 134 135 138
Sarah 134 Sarah F 137 Sarah
(Gott) 136 137 Sarah
(Thompson) 137 Simeon 126
135 136 139 Simeon Jr 136
Statira 136 Stella 137 Stephen
135-137 330 352 Stephen D 137
351 Susan 135 Susan Ellen 137
Susan (Francis) 135 Susan (Gott)
135 136 Susan (Packard) 134
Susanna C (Francis) 61 Timothy
134 Unity 134 Vesta A (Soule)
140 W S 234 Ward 135 151 Wm
134-137 Wm G 137 342 Wm Jr
134 Willie B 137 Willis 135 234
Willis A 354 Woodbury S 135
306 Ziba 61 134 135 Ziba Jr 135

KNIGHT, Charles T 295 Fred H 150
    Frederick H 354 Luther B 255
    Luther B Rev 255 Mary E 348
    Mr 135 Susan (Knapp) 135
KNIGHTS, Charles T 292
KNOPP, John 133
KNOWLES, Abbie F 351 Abner 288
    Albina V Mrs 360 George H 358
    Tafuest 360
KNOWLTON, Carrie Denning 63
    Clara 236 350 Elbridge 236
    Elbridge G 340 Harry Hale 63
    John 63 Louise H (Francis) 63
    Mary Ann Mrs 354 Mary Ann
    (Carver) 236 William Maj 293
KNOX, Ora Allen 360
LABREE, James 326 Thomas 325
LADD, Grace Adelia 132
LAFITAU, 9
LAIN, Jamey 6
LAKE, Mary 414
LAMB, 24 Abigail 203 330 Bemis
    341 Bennett 286 Betsey 328
    Charlotte 335 Clarissa 339 Eli H
    129 Elliot S 335 Frederic 129 Ira
    203 248 258 328 James 248 285
    335 James Jr 329 Joseph G 291
    Leonie 129 Mary (Herrick) 203
    Merrick 329 Mr 245 Nancy
    (Lindsey) 129 Orissa D 348
    Phebe 336 Russell 339
LAMONT, Betsey L (Mitchell) 199
    Joshua P 199 332 Mary 198
LAND, G W 4
LANDER, Anice 329 Ansel 329
LANE, A J 163 302 54 A J Mrs 104
    Abbie (Perkins) 52 Abigail
    Rackley 51 Abigail 108 330
    Abigail R 348 Abigail
    (Leadbetter) 50 107 108 Ada 54
    Ada A 102 Adoniram Judson 54
    102 Alden 52 108 Allie 54 103
    Almira 54 Alonzo 54 Alpheus 52
    53 100 126 328 333 Alvin 52 54

LAMB (Cont.)
    213 331 340 Ann H (Foss) 54
    102 Asenath 108 Avis 52
    Benjamin 52 Benjamin F 55 344
    Betsey 71 328 399 Betsey
    (Stinchfield) 53 Calvin 52 54
    336 Cassandra B 53 Cassandra
    Benson 217 Cassandra (Benson)
    53 Cassie B 70 357 Catherine
    (Pingray) 54 Charles 52 60 73 88
    Charles C 34 Charles Cary 51
    Charles H 55 249 345 359
    Charlotte Mrs 343 Charlotte
    (Jones) 54 Clara 54 194
    Columbus 52 108 Cypren 336
    Cyrus B 249 350 Cyrus Benson
    53 Cyrus E 70 Daniel 6 24 50 54
    285 318 323 Daniel A 343
    Daniel Capt 240 Daniel Jr 6 52
    David 52 54 148 331 Davis 54
    333 Dorcas 52 59 328 378
    Dorcas (Lane) 54 Dulcina
    (Lothrop) 54 Ebenezer 54 Elias 6
    50 52 71 198 248 258 272 335
    Eliphalet 52 54 Eliphalet Gilman
    50 Eliphalet Jr 54 Eliza 108
    Eliza 52 Elizabeth 51 52
    Elizabeth (Stinchfield) 126 Ellen
    52 Emery 54 Emma (Foss) 51
    Erastus 54 Esther 52 54 337 399
    Esther A 349 Eunice 50 52 324
    99 Eunice F 341 Eunice (Verrill)
    50 Family 50 374 393 Fannie 52
    Fanny 329 Francina 52 Francis
    54 Franklin 52 54 Freemont 54
    102 G B 71 250 259 302 304
    George B 219 347 George Bailey
    411 Giddings 50 52 97 164 217
    251 252 258 259 271 306
    Giddings Jr 52 53 Giddings Sr
    54 Giddins 6 Grace (Turner) 52
    Gustavus W 53 217 250 349 356
    Hannah 108 333 Hannah
    (Dunham) Mrs 54 Harriet 52

LAMB (Cont.)
 Harriet H 88 344 403 Harriett H
 417 Helen 53 Helen M (Snow)
 53 Henry K 52 Isaacher 59 Issa
 54 Issachar 52 54 103 273 328
 378 James 50 52 53 80 107 108
 182 271 Jemima 52 54 107 251
 327 Jemima (Norris) 52 54 97
 Jesse 52 54 331 Joanna 51 52 80
 108 172 327 John 51 108 219
 330 John Frank 51 Josephine 52
 Joshua 50 52 249 325 Judith 50
 52 Judith (Verrill) 52 Judson A
 345 Justin 219 Justin 51 Justin
 Palmer 51 Kittie 51 219 359 410
 Lizzie (Howard) 217 Lois 50 52
 Lois (Verrill) 52 Lorinda 50 332
 Louisa 148 Louisa (Wyman) 52
 108 Lucretia P (Howard) 55
 Lucretia Phillips (Howard) 180
 Lucy M 217 Lucy (Mitchell) 54
 213 Lydia 50 52 126 326 Lydia
 A (Lothrop) 53 Lydia Albina
 (Lothrop) 70 Lydia (Brewster)
 54 148 Lydia (Trask) 54 Mary
 50 52 97 Mary J (Palmer) 55
 Mary Jane (Lothrop) 51 73 Mary
 (Lawrence) 52 71 Mary
 (Rackley) 52 108 Mehitable Mrs
 331 Mehitable (Brett) 52 Millie
 M (Wright) 55 Mr 245 254 320
 Mrs (Berry) 52 Nancy 50 52 338
 Neva 73 Neva C 51 Olive 50 54
 331 Orsan 54 Orson 213 215 217
 344 347 Otis 53 P 302 Palmer 51
 Peter 50 52 55 6 88 89 180 248
 324 Peter Jr 339 Pheba 108
 Phebe 50 326 Polly 52 97 324
 Rachel (Billings) 52 Rosabel 52
 Rosamond 54 59 342 378 379
 Roscoe 53 Ruth Mrs 325 Ruth
 (Pratt) 50 Sadie E 54 360
 Samuel 50 52 54 Sarah 53 100
 Sarah E 103 Sarah (Foss) 53 100

LAMB (Cont.)
 Sarah (Nye) 52 Sarah (Turner)
 55 88 Scott W 54 103 Semyntha
 52 335 Sewall 53 100 Shepherd
 108 Stephen B 217 Susan 336
 338 Susan E 217 Susan E
 (Boothby) 213 Susan E (Lothrop)
 53 217 Susan Scott 54 Susannah
 52 Susannah (Boothby) 54 Susie
 E (Lothrop) 71 Vesta (Phillips)
 51 108 Viola A (Ramsdell) 219
 Viola Ann (Ramsdell) 51 Viora
 G 217 Viora G (Boothby) 215
 Viora (Boothby) 54 Virginia 53
 Waldo 53 Warren 52 54 Willie E
 54 103
LARRABEE, Allura L 343 Daniel B
 337 Diadama 41 414 Diodama
 345 Elvira Jr 129 Elvira
 (Lindsey) 129 Eveline Jr 129
 Eveline (Lindsey) 129 Everett B
 129 family 393 Freeman H 129
 Henry 129 John A 129 Laura M
 352 Lewis M 355 Lovina 129
 Lucia 129 Melvin 129 Moses
 129 Sophrona 337
LASKIN, Editha 201 Hugh 201
LATHROP, Francis 265 George 257
 259 George C 254 George D 259
 George Esq 258 Solomon 257
 Solomon 258 Solomon 259
 Willard 259
LATIO, Francina J 359
LAWRENCE, Mary 52 71 Nellie A
 (Day) 160 Walter 160
LAWTON, J W 252
LAWYERS & JUDGES, 270
LEACH, Olive 334 Richard 202
 Sally 324 Sarah 202
LEADBETER, Charles Frederic 34
 family 33 Grace (Turner) 34
 Shirley Francis 33 Verner Fay 33
LEADBETTER, Abigail 107 Abigail
 50 Alva 99 Alvah 108 Anita 226

LEADBETTER (Cont.)
Annie (Cummings) 226 Arthur 226 Arthur C 358 Arthur C 89 Arthur Clark 34 Asaph 99 108 Aurelia B 108 Benjamin 107 108 323 Betsey 107 150 211 326 Betsey (Parcher) 107 226 Catherine (Babcock) 125 Charles 139 Charles H 108 226 292 Charles K 33 354 Colista (Knapp) 108 139 Delphina 108 Eliza 99 108 335 Eliza (Shaw) 226 Ella Frances (Stinchfield) 33 Emeline 96 108 340 Ezra 107 108 241 332 family 33 34 107 Fannie (Otis) 107 163 Fanny 332 Flora 226 Freddie Clark 34 Grace Haywood (Turner) 89 Hannah 107 125 338 Hattie A (Foster) 145 Hattie (Foster) 226 Henry B 108 Herbert 139 Horace 108 139 226 Increase 24 50 62 107 125 176 226 241 242 285 318 Irene (Nichols) 226 Isaac 334 Jabez 107 108 176 329 James 107 163 327 Jane 334 Jemima (Lane) 107 Jesse 226 Joanna 107 332 Joanna (Woodman) 241 John 107 108 323 99 L Clark 62 Laura M 108 Lorenzo 108 145 226 292 351 352 Lucius 139 Lucius Clark 33 89 108 Lucretia (Howard) 107 176 177 Luicia J 108 Luther 107 327 Mary 81 94 108 139 335 Mary Ann (Gott) 33 62 Mr 177 246 320 Nellie 62 Nellie Ann 34 Nelson H 108 Orisa 108 Orison 344 Orson 108 Pamelia 108 Pamelia W 342 Rachael 108 Rachael Jr 99 Rachael (Foss) 99 107 Rena May 33 Rhodephus H 108 Rodelphus 177 Rosa 108 Rosannah 338 Roscoe 139

LEADBETTER (Cont.)
Rosilla 116 334 Sally 107 108 211 334 Sally (Woodman) 107 241 Samuel 91 107 108 139 176 211 226 324 345 Samuel Jr 108 338 Sarah 70 405 Thomas 107 108 Valencia Lorenzo 226 Wallace 108 Wallace R 226 Wallace R 351 Warren 99 108

LEATHERS, Hannah Mrs 337 Rebecca 335 Sobrina 335

LEAVITT, Alvin 332 Archibald 334 Cyrus 113 Cyrus Jr 334 Flora A 356 Joseph 329 Sarah 113 333 Sophronia (Sylvester) 113

LEE, Ann F (Otis) 165 General 152 Jesse 251 Jesse Rev 254 Jonas P 165 249 333 Samuel Perry Capt 165 Sarah 165 Silas Dr 165

LEEDS, Addition district 31 Addition Neighborhood 75 Bates Hill 130 248 297 Bishop Hill 2 3 27 67 95 125 142 Bog Brook 4 Boothby Hill 312 Boothby's Hill 208 Brewster farm 158 Carrying Place 141 Coffin's Mills 198 Crummett place 55 Curtis Corner 4 148 149 158 162 221 236 249 250 369 Day place 79 Dead River bridges 5 Dead River Cemetery 27 Dr Lorings Corner 249 Dwinold house 99 Fish Hill 231 Foss' Corner 104 Foster place 116 Friends Burial Ground 78 Gould's Corner 267 Hedgehog Hill 26 314 Joshua Turner place 75 Keen's Corner 77 100 224 225 249 255 267 300 301 Keen's Mills 148 198 Leeds Center 4 Leeds Crossing 4 Lincoln Hill 233 Lothrop Cemetery 26 Lothrop's Corner 60 92 166 231 233 297 Morrison's Heights 27

LEEDS (Cont.)
    North Leeds 4 Old brick Powder
    House 79 Otis Hill 109 Phillips
    Turner place 75 76 Pine Plains
    232 Quaker Ridge 2 4 78 79 85
    92 130 148 169-172 192 198 221
    222 234 248 250 254 255 268
    297 Richmond Hill 169 Ridge
    Road 233 Robert Gould
    Cemetery 27 110 South Leeds
    Cemetery 75 78 Stinchfield cape
    141 Stinchfield neighborhood
    135 Strickland's Ferry 4 Sunny
    Shore Farm 197 The Cape 3
    Welcome Hill 75 78 West Leeds
    4 White's Mill 57
LEIGHTON, Clarissa 110 Clarissa
    339 S S 252 Samuel H Rev 340
LEITH, Lillian W 355
LeMOYNE, Mr 13
LEONARD, Caroline 331 Franklin B
    258 259 335 Lydia W 347 Olive
    331 Orpheus M 296
LEVITT, Phoebe C 352
LEWIS, Abbie 129 Benjamin F 346
    John 345 John F 349 Mary E 364
    William 364
LEWISTON MONUMENTAL
    WORKS, 274
LIBBEY, Albert L 417 Clara A 417
    Grace Linda 417
LIBBY, Adelia M 300 Adelia M 301
    Almira J 349 Anna L 353 Asa
    341 Asa 350 Betsey 341 Betsey
    (Carver) 236 Charles A 305
    Charles F 37 Charles R 352
    Charles W 352 Clara (Hartt) 37
    Deborah 326 Eben 36 37 236
    312 Ebenezer 146 325 Ebenezer
    A 37 Eliza 351 Ella E 354
    Elmira F 384 Elmira J 383
    Emma E 351 Erwin M 305
    Eunice 336 family 394 Fannie P
    155 351 Florence M 361

LIBBY (Cont.)
    Glen Cora (Bishop) 67 Grace L
    358 Hannah H 329 Hannah J 343
    Helen H 37 Helen M 351
    Henrietta 149 350 Henrietta B
    37 Henry A 252 352 Isaac C 353
    James H 350 James W 289 294
    295 349 James W Captain 290
    Jane 36 72 146 325 John 146
    John R 343 Lulie L 358 Mary
    236 338 368 Mary Ann
    (Stinchfield) 37 Mary J 355
    Mary Jane 37 Mary (Hart) 312
    Melville G 360 Melvin 67 Miss
    233 Mr 246 Nancy J 354
    Pelatiah 236 338 Peltiah F 354
    Philip 325 S P 353 Sally (Foster)
    36 37 146 Samuel P 307 Sarah
    312 Sarah C 351 Sarah
    (Stinchfield) 126 Solomon 368
    Stephen 37 146 339 T C 355
    Thomas 326 Tilloston 146 312
    Uriah 340 383 Uriah F 355 Wills
    356 Zebulon 330
LINCOLN, Abraham 233 Annie E
    180 358 416 Charles D 234 Eliza
    G 407 Ellis L 234 Elsie A
    (Howard) 180 family 233
    Gertrude 234 Gertrude E
    (Howie) 181 H E 303 H W 249
    303 Hannah 233 341 Hannah 41
    Harry 234 Herbert W 180 387
    416 Howard E 181 Howard
    Elliot 180 360 I D 112 Irving D
    234 Mabel Dora 180 Mable D
    268 Mahala (Bishop) 66 234 Mr
    246 Norris K 234 Rufus 233
    Salome 233 335 William C 66
    234 345
LINCSOTT, Dorcas E (Foss) 106
LINDSAY - see LINDSEY,
    LINSEY, LINDSY, LINSAY
LINDSAY, Alice B 268 Catherine
    29 326 Daniel 324 Eliza A Mrs

HISTORY OF LEEDS

LINDSAY (Cont.)
351 Everett 351 Franklin J 352
James 257 James W 354 Lewis L
353 Mary 326 Nettie M 356
Thomas 6

LINDSEY, Abbie (Gilpatrick) 128
Abbie (Lewis) 129 Abigail 126
Alice A (Crockett) 131 Alice B
133 161 Alvin 129 Alvin H 127
128 Ann 127 Ann (Graffam) 128
Anna Ann 128 Annie Etta
(Smallidge) 133 Annie L 133
161 Archibald 126 330
Archibald Col 127 Arthur L 132
161 Augusta E (Gates) 128 Azel
126 B B 67 Bertha M 133 161
Berton B 129 Betsey 65 126-128
Caroline 127 133 334 Caroline
(Lindsey) 128 130 395 Catharine
390 126 138 Catherine 414 Celia
129 Charles 66 Charles F 128
128 296 350 Charles Frederic
127 131 Clara J 131 Clarinda F
127 128 Converse LOwell 130
Daisy 129 Daniel 76 127 128
130 Daniel Webster 127 128
Dorcas 66 133 149 332 365
Edward 129 Elisha G 128 Eliza
Ann (Berry) 131 Eliza Ann
(Berry) (Lindsey) 131 Eliza
(Muzzy) 128 Elizabeth (Turner)
84 125 127 Elvira 129 Emeline
129 Ernest 128 Evelyn F 129
Everett 131 296 350 Everett H
128 Everett Howard 127 family
76 124 394 Flora E (Curtis) 132
161 Forest 130 Frank J 292
Franklin Jennings 130 Frederic
Shaw 131 130 George Albert
130-132 George S 128 Grace
Adelia (Ladd) 132 Hannah 27
125 126 130 138 221 330 331
390 411 414 Hannah
(Leadbetter) 125 Hannah

LINDSEY (Cont.)
(Turner) 84 125 Harry C 133
161 Howard 125 128 130 133
334 Howard E 131 Hulda L
(Richmond) 130 Ira 130 Ira L
130 James 124-129 271 285 318
320 James 84 James G 128 340
James Greenleaf 127 James W
128 Jane (Gilbert) 127 130 Jane
(Turner) 76 Jennie 128 Jennie W
(Bishop) 67 Joanna (Merrill) 130
John 126 John Capt 126
Josephine A 131 Josephine B
127 128 Julia A 349 Julia Ann
127 128 130 132 Levi 130 Lewis
L 125 161 Lewis Leavitt 130 132
Lorinda B 128 Lucy 126 136
Lydia (Lane) 126 Maria L
(Nutting) 131 Maria Theresa 130
Martha E 128 Martha (Brown)
128 Mary 23 83 127 129 Mary E
128 Mary Elizabeth (Culver) 132
Mary Howard 131 Mary Jane
(Howard) 131 Mary (Bishop)
128 Mary (Bishop) (Trask) 66
Matilda (Dunham) 128 Miranda
129 Mr 246 Nancy 129 Naomi
129 Novella 342 Olive (Creach)
128 129 Orrin H 129 Orrin L
129 Persis 128 334 Phebe
(Pettingill) 127 128 Polly 126
Robert 130 133 330 Roland 130
131 Roland B 131 Roland
Everett 130 Roscoe E 131
Roscoe G 295 346 Roscoe
Greene 130 131 Roscoe Jr 131
Rose Jane 128 130 131 Ruth 129
Silas 128 Silas Augustus 127
Silas D 128 Silvia 130 Sophronia
(Stevens) 128 Susanna (Turner)
127 Thankful (Bailey) 129 130
Thomas 27 84 124 125 128-130
271 328 Thomas J 292 Thomas
Jennings 130 132 Thomas Jr 125

LINDSEY (Cont.)
  Tiley 346 Tiley Merrill 130
  Tylia 221 Vesta (Merrill) 130
  Violia C 129 Wallace B 127 128
  William 125-127 138 285 390
  William H 128 William Henry
    127
LINDSY, Everett 193 Mary Jane
    (Howard) 193
LINSAY, James 326
LINSCOTT, Betsey 330 Calvin W
  106 Caroline Wilhelmina 106
  Dorcas E (Foss) 103 Edwin W Jr
  106 Edwin Wingate 106 Eliza W
  (Foss) 106 Elizabeth 106
  Elizabeth (Razin) 106 Family
  375 Frances Ellen 106 Harriet
  Eliza 106 Hattie E 103 106
  Jennie Augusta 106 Russell S
  103 347 Russell Street 106
  Samuel C 106 Walter 103
  Walter E 106 Wingate 106
LINSEY, James 24 William 24
LIST OF TOWN OFFICES, Clerks
  276 Constables & Collectors 281
  282 Moderators 275 School
  Committee 279-281 Selectmen
  276-278 Treasures 278 279
LITTLE, Edward Esq 13 Moses 75
  Moses Col 74
LITTLEFIELD, Josiah 306 Josiah
  309 Levi C 342 Mr 307
LIVERMORE, Betsey 330 Elijah
  Deacon 92 235
LONG, Philip 359
LONGFELLOW, Elizabeth 240 poet
  240 Stephen 240 William 240
LORD, Benjamin 355 Charles H 360
  Mr 266
LORING, Dorcas 385 Dorcas H 122
  339 Dr 249 Joanna (Wing) 171
  John D 86 John S 339 340 Lydia
  (Turner) 86 Mary S 86 338 402
  Nicholar 342 Perez 342 R S 302

LORING (Cont.)
  R S Dr 112 182 248 302 303
  Rollins S 259
LOTHROP, A G 219 Abigail 330
  Abigail (Foster) (Jennings) 146
  Adonia 72 Alice 58 330 377 378
  Alson 70 74 327 340 Alson Jr 70
  Alson Jr 74 Azra G 344 Betsey
  336 Betsey 401 Betsey 70 Betsey
  (Lane) 71 Caroline E 342
  Caroline E 73 Caroline Elizabeth
  71 Caroline S (Morse) 72 Clyde
  71 Cynthia 380 Cynthia L 345 D
  F 302 Daniel Daniel 7 58 69 76
  175 251 271 Daniel 2d Lieut 285
  Daniel Capt 70 73 324 Daniel
  Col 69 73 74 Daniel Jr 7 24 69
  271 377 Daniel Major 285 Davis
  F 50 71 72 87 342 Davis Francis
  71 74 Dolly (Whiting) 58
  Dulcena 336 Dulcina 54 Elias 72
  Elias L 71 340 Elias Lane 71
  Elizabeth 344 379 Elizabeth
  (Lane) 51 Elmina 129 Emeline L
  (Boothby) 53 Emily 67 Emma L
  217 Emma L (Boothby) 70 216
  Ester L Mrs 355 Eugene 72 Eva
  B 359 family 69 76 396 405
  Flora L 72 351 Flora Louvisa 72
  Frank B 71 217 Frederic 129
  George 7 69 70 74 320 321 335
  336 George Daniel 70 Georgia F
  (Noyes) 70 Hannah 69 70 328
  333 Hannah (Howard) 69
  Hannah (Turner) 53 70 87 Harry
  129 Helen Augusta 70 Hulda
  (Gilmore) 70 Huldah
  (Richmond) 74 Ira 324 Irvin 72
  Jane (Morse) 71 Jeremiah 70
  Jonah 70 Joshua 343 Leavitt 328
  Leavitt 51 Leavitt 70 71 Leavitt
  Col 3 96 Leonard C 343 Lewis
  70 Louisa 331 Lucile (Piazia) 72
  Lucy (Gilbert) 73 Lucy (Turner)

LOTHROP (Cont.)
76 Lydia 55 70 74 85 175 179 324 386 Lydia A 350 Lydia A 53 Lydia Albina 70 Lydia S 336 Lydia (Willis) 69 Marinda (Lindsey) 129 Mark 69 Martha J (Ramsdell) 219 Mary Francis 70 Mary J 346 Mary Jane 51 71 Mary Morse 71 Mary (Turner) 69 74 Melinda 325 Mr 246 Olive 97 Olive M 72 87 357 402 Oliver 336 Orissa 70 340 Orissa (Lothrop) 70 74 Polly 70 74 104 324 333 Polly (Thayer) 70 Ralph 72 Rhoda 70 74 Rhoda (Willis) 69 Sally 216 Samuel 69 73 332 Samuel Jr 69 Sarah 71 325 Sarah Clyde 217 Sarah W (Lothrop) 70 Sarah Whiting 405 Sarah (Whiting) 70 73 Serville 72 Solomon 70 74 122 216 249 307 325 Solomon L 53 70 87 249 339 Solomon L Mrs 74 Solomon Leavitt 70 Stillman H 129 Sullivan 7 69 73 146 332 335 Susan A 332 Susan A 332 Susan E 53 217 356 Susie E 70 71 Thomas 69 73 74 323 331 380 Veranus 337 Warren L 351 Warren L Col 73 286 Warren Lane 71 Willard 70 74 348 William 53 216 217 William Henry 70

LOUISBURG, the capture of 89

LOUISIANA, 37 72 New Orleans 164 293

LOVE, J W Professor 124 Thirza (Cushman) 124

LOVEJOY, Arthur 234 Benjamin 65 Charles A 234 Clara C (Greenwood) 234 Esther 339 Hannah 327 389 Mary H (Bishop) 65 Minnie 234

LOVELL, Charles 106 Ella A 357

LOVEWELL, Flora E 359 John 12 Jonathan 350

LOWELL, Nancy 323 Susan 67 344

LOWLE, Benjamin 239 Ruth (Woodman) 239

LUCAS, Edward 334

LUCE, Almira 335 Enos T 292

LUDDEN, Mehitable 415 Mr 233 Sarah (Grant) 233

LUFKIN, Rev 256

LYFORD, Emily (Woodman) 242 243 Marion 243 Thornton 242 347

LYMES, Addie F Mrs 360

LYNCH Ellen 353

LYSSOM, Mary 229

MACOMBER, Eleanor (Turner) 84 Jacob 84

MAGNA, Sarah 347

MAGNER, Eunice Mrs 352 James S 359 Willis G 354

MAGOWN, Mr 246

MAGUIRE, Celia M 360 Dan 305 Daniel 303 356 357 Fannie 361 Flora E 355 George W 360 Grace 305 Grace M 361 Lourana 352 Perley O 304 Willard F 355

MARYLAND, Baltimore 39 53 217 Frederick 213 Lock 21, on the Potomac (near Georgetown, DC) 154 Point Lookout 213

MAINE, Julia E 83

MAINE, 219 Addison 77 Albion 336 346 Andover 114 Anson 75 137 Aroostook Co 211 Ashland 290 Athens 40 Auburn 1 13 20 40 49 59 71 73 95 100 104 111 114 116 154 160 163 166 178 197 224 267 273 289 292 306 341-345 349 352-354 356 358 359 Auburn (then Bakerstown) 227 297 Augusta 32 56 61 67 92 98 99 122 136 141 161 187 193 226 287-291 293-295 297 343 354

MAINE (Cont.)
 355 360 Bakerstown (see Auburn) 297 Bancroft 40 Bangor 25 39 56 72 87 95 98 131 139 187 189 190 243 287 289 290 292 294 295 336 Baring 47 Barker's Mills, Lewiston 36 202 Bath 49 91 100 105 151 197-199 222 288 291 292 332 345 348 Battle Brook 12 Beech Hill in Fayette 297 Belfast 100 106 112 163 191 Belgrade 167 209 220 338 340 348 350 Biddeford 89 205 240 288 312 360 Bingham 167 Black Point 208 Bloomfield 338 Bluefield 332 Bowdoin 151 353 Bowdoinham 114 115 343 Bradford 74 Brettun's Mills 197 Bridgton 180 334 335 Bristol 335 337 Brownville 88 Brunswick 55 64 68 78 111 168 199 344 352 354 Brunswick Falls 13 Bryant's Pond 160 Buckfield 75 113 160 327 329 330 335 344 352 Buckfield (see Bluefield) 332 Bucksport 23 Burnham 290 Buxton 164 239 240 241 324 325 327 332 336 Camden 82 107 289 Canton 13 66 71 137 237 337 341 343-345 355 Cape Elizabeth 289 Carroll, Penobscot Co 54 67 73 74 76 127-129 204 344 Castine 24 25 56 Chandlerville (after 1841 Detroit) 170 Charlestown 48 Chelsea 193 359 Cherryfield 48 Chesterville 106 167 229 230 297 329 330 332 338 341 355 China 170 176 342 Clinton 357 Columbia Falls 67 Corinna 351 Corinth 164 Curtis Corner 222 Damariscotta 236 Danforth, Washington Co 40 312 Danville 23 52 229 Danville Jct 94

MAINE (Cont.)
 Danville (see Pejepscot) 40 Dead River 192 Deering 357 Dexter 331 334 Dixfield 87 139 341 Dover 292 343 Durham 331 338 East Livermore 1 35 36 41 63 100 135 139 145 152 154 180 215-217 221 230 242 273 346 348 350 356 359 360 East Livermore Mills 59 E Machias 289 East Monmouth 64 226 East Readfield 145 East Wilton 309 East Winthrop 169 170 Easton 128 Eastport 209 289 Ellsworth 289 Embden, Somerset Co 211 339 344 Etna 353 Exeter 358 Fairfield 288 338 Falmouth 11 56 92 109 135 Farmingdale 353 356 Farmington 29 49 68 81 94 95 108 124 135 139 146 167 187-189 243 297 311 339 340 347 356 Farmington Falls 311 Fayette 52 66 115 116 136 145 216 297 324 333 335 339 341 343 347 349 350 354 356 357 Lovejoy Cemetery in Fayette 116 Fayette Mills 110 Forks of the Road 170 Fort Kent 291 Fort Richmond 11 Foxcroft 335 Franklin 351 Franklin Pl't'n 349 Freeman 137 138 328 356 Freeport 112 147 Fryeburg 12 Gardiner 67 72 87 88 103 344 353 357 374 Glenburn 108 139 Gorham 229 289 351 352 411 Gray 18 56 109 135 Greene 1 7 8 21 23 25 26 51 55 56 59 71 76 79 83 87 111-113 115 136 137 147 148 153 156 159 162 166 167 173 180 196 203 204 219 222 255 268 271 297 323-330 332 333 335-340 342 344-352 355 356 359 360 411 Greene Corner 297 Greenwood 66

MAINE (Cont.)
Guilford 164 165 332 Hallowell 39 52 71 78 99 147 148 165 166 170 182 192 193 195 235 237 293 349 Hallowell Granite Quarries 39 Hamden 327 331 Hartford 110 137 339 Hebron 49 160 328 330 335 341 Hollis 333 Hope, Knox Co 114 348 Houlton 163 290 Industry 361 Jay 13 35 74 259 340 343 345 346 358 Kennebec Arsenal 182 Kent's Hill 68 179 189 197 243 Kingfield 35 75 136 137 138 151 329 342 Kittery 207 208 294 LaGrange 127 144 Lee 128 129 Leeds 369 Leeds Juction, Greene 255 Letter E 346 Levant 292 Lewiston 20 21 30 40 56 68 77 78 80 82 87 96 100 106 107 111 112 114 124 152 155 156 159 163 168 171 173 178 180 202 205 211 213 215-217 273 292 297 330 343 347-350 351 354 355 358-361 411 Lewiston Falls 20 Lexington 117 Limerick 72 Limington 241 288 Lincoln 99 128 Lisbon 71 100 148 151 325 331 337 341 359 Litchfield 97 100 332 344 351 360 Littleboro' 1 6 24 50 57 58 69 80 90 105 109 125 135 140 147 163 166 198 231 251 254 279 Livermore 1 7 8 21 47 57 62 83 96-99 102 107 110 113 114 136 137 145 151 160 162 164 170 215 219 220 228 235-237 241 271 289 324 325 327 328-337 339-344 346-352 357 359 360 Livermore Falls 13 35 101 136 145 194 197 216 226 306-309 371 72 Livermore Grant 91 92 Lovell 290 Lubec 166 Machias 165 294 Madison 349 Madrid 199

MAINE (Cont.)
Manchester 76 170 359 Mercer 136 339 Milford 164 Milo 23 53 97 127 198 235 Minot 99 166 332-334 339 342 Monmouth 1 2 7 8 32 35 59 63 64 67 115 122 141 153-155 161 170 179 180 197 198 219 221 222 224 254 255 271 273 297 324 331-333 335-340 342-348 350-359 363 Montville 163 332 Mount Vernon 32 192 342 346 353 358 Mt Desert 133 "New Boston" 1 New Glocester 4 17 18 20-25 41 44 45 50 56 57 66 109 162 186 222 227 231 297 339 411-413 New Meadows 64 65 New Portland 138 145 New Sandwich 46 80 139 145 311 312 328 329 New Vineyard 146 335 Nobleboro' 340 343 Norlands 96 Norridgewock 11 131 340 347 Norris Island 15 North Auburn 111 North Greene 170 171 North Leeds 27 32 62 80 81 92 96 104 106 108 135 137 140 150-152 167 219 249 North Leeds- Robert Gould Cemetery 93 North Monmouth 53 65 66 131 North Monmouth Moody Stream 64 North Turner 267 North Turner Bridge 233 236 241 North Wayne 117 North Yarmouth 44 67 121 122 227 Norway 102 289 290 292 Number 6, Penobscot Co 76 Oakland 32 111 360 Oldtown 11 94 129 199 Palmyra 47 110 346 Paris 98 290 326 327 331 332 339 345 346 352 Parkman 77 85 147 173 337 347 Parsonsfield 208 Pejepscot 41 Pejepscot Claim 1 Pejepscot Falls 13 Pejepscot (Danville) 40 323 Pemaquid 11 Penobscot 11

MAINE (Cont.)
  Peperellboro' 89 90 93 97 99
105 Peru 65 241 355 357
Phillips 99 100 350 352 Phipps
Canada 13 Phippsburg 337
Poland 78 225 342 353 358 361
Poland Springs 155 Pond Town
21 64 Portion of Leeds annexed
to Wayne 150 Portland 21 29 39
41 55 70 87 88 92 96 97 100-102
106 155 164 166 170 171 178
194 196 213 225 240 266 272
287-294 297 338 360 373
Pownal 339 Presque Isle 131
Rangeley 145 Raymond 350
Readfield 2 38 173 254 333 348
353 358 360 Richmond 294
Robbinston 23 Roccomeco 13
Roccomeco House, Livermore
Falls 52 Rockland 288 295 Rome
193 Roxbury 359 Rumford 351
352 Rumford Falls 155 Sabattus
112 Saco 12 27 36 89 90 107
109 123 135 150 151 209 211
220 241 324-326 342 372 Saco
Valley 209 Salem 354
Sangerville 65 333 Scarborough
89 90 207 208 224 325 334
Searsport 162 288 290 Sebec
333 Sidney 222 335 Skowhegan
51 114 290 Solon 116 South
Harpswell 243 South Leeds 170
171 196 252 411 South
Monmouth 149 St Albans 47 358
411 Standish 210 312 334 336
343 345 Starks 96 334
Stickland's Ferry 92
Stinchfield's Point 15 Strong 346
353 Sumner 87 117 160 161 329
331 336 Sylvester township 227
Thirty Mile River 14 Togus 111
Topsham 329 333 Turner 1 18
21 22 41 47 63 75 76 78 113 114
130 134 136 137 147 159 160

MAINE (Cont.)
162 163 171 196 198 218 220
222 224 227 229 266-268 293
324-343 345 347 348 350 351
353 355-359 361 412 Unity 411
Upper Stillwater 128 Vane 7
Vassalboro' 71 79 86 115 166
230 233 292 328 341 Veazie 93
349 Vienna 154 159 332-334
336 352 353 363 Waldo 329
Wales 1 124 224 337 338 340
346 348 353 358 361 411
Waterville 123 145 155 167 205
290 324 Wayne 1 7 21-23 30-34
36 38 40 41 46-48 53 54 63 65
66 80 90 92 96 98-101 106 111-
113 115-117 135-137 150 151
154 156 162 168 176 178 179
181 194 209-211 223 224 227
229 230 234 236 241 251 255
297 324 326-332 337 338 340-
342 344 346-350 352-357 359
373 374 Beech Hill in Wayne 22
30 100 Craig Bridge in Wayne
92 Mills in Wayne 107 Pocaset
House in Wayne 31 Village in
Wayne 28 William Wing farm in
Wayne 116 Webster 148 340 348
350 Weeks Mills, New Sharon
96 Wells 207-209 328 Wesley 23
see also Westley 335 West
Farmington 146 371 West Leeds
115 122 144 177 196 198 203
229 238 249 265 267 West Paris
66 West Peru 65 West Poland
193 Westbrook 11 361 Westley
335 Weston 128 White-Oak
Island 15 Whitneyville 360
Wilton 137 151 164 166 216 234
295 326 338 350 Windham 18
348 Winslow 325 Winter Harbor
240 Winthrop 21 22 30 33 36 56
61 63 64 66 67 76 82-84 105 107
111 121-123 135 140-144 168

MAINE (Cont.)
  177 197 205 209 221 249 262
  271 324-328 330 332-334 338
  340 342-343 345 347-349 352
  354 356 Winthrop Cemetery 142
  Winthrop Towle Academy 30
  Yarmouth 355 York 43 157
MAINES, Charlotte 330 Polly 329
MAINS, John 328
MALOON, Clorinda Ann 343 415
  Deborah J 347 Nancy 334
  Octavia E 348 Samuel 330
  Simon 252 416
MANE, Martha 157
MANES, William 327
MANEY, Patrick 345
MANK, Aleck 66 Alexander 349
  Roxanna L (Bishop) 66
MANLEY, David 84 Joanna
  (Turner) 84 John Capt 45
MANN, Albert 349 Ann N 349
  Ebenezer Jr 338 Elisha K 288
  294 family 406 Henry 359
MANSON, Sally 386
MANTER, A W 250 A W Mrs 250
MANUEL, Jarius 66 Phebe 66
  Phebe (Bishop) 66
MANWELL, Elizabeth B 87 345 402
  Jarius 406 Jerris 327 Nancy 346
  Nancy S 223 407 Rosina 224 346
  406
MARCH, George Capt 202 Mary
  widow 202
MARDEN, Abbie E Mrs 352
MARSHALL, Moses 341 Thomas H
  288
MARSTON, Allie 40 Hester A
  (Bumpus) 160
MARTIN, Addison 164 332 Addison
  Jr 164 Almira (Foss) 100
  Asenath C Mrs 357 Charles Mrs
  236 Emily F 164 Hannah
  (Carver) 236 Hattie 100 J D 100
  Louisa (Brooks) 164 Lydia 164

MARTIN (Cont.)
  Lydia P (Otis) 164 Martha 165
  Oliver 164
MASON, Andrew 343 Dorcas 371
  Eben 248 Ebenezer 285 324 337
  Edwin C 288 Gorham 371 H I
  161 Isaac 330 John 328 329
  Mary Mrs 330 Mercy 334 Mr
  246 Naphtali 325 Nora B
  (Bumpus) 161 Rachel 328
  Rebecca 329 Sarah 333
  Susannah 323
MASSACHUSETTS, 76 79 145 218
  219 221 230 Abington 79 153
  161 218 338 346 406 Andover
  239 240 Arlington 115
  Attleboro' 140 143 Bedford 86
  Beverly 63 201 202 Biddeford
  89 Billerica 171 Blandford 220
  Boston 11 30 31 39 48 49 70 72
  77 95 103 106 111 117 119 134
  157 162 164 167 168 170 178
  194 217 229 242 243 312 340
  343 347 373 375 Boxford 202
  203 Bradford 205 Bridgewater
  25 26 41 53 69 84 124-127 129
  134 135 138 175 176 179 182
  186 190 229 233 235 335-337
  400 413 Brighton 55 Brockton
  53 156 192 194 217 234
  Brookfield 43 Brookline 351
  Cambridge 168 202 Campello 41
  Canton 221 Cape Ann 43 Cape
  Cod 46 Cape-Ann-Syde of Bass
  River 201 Charlestown 203 220
  343 Chelsea 146 371 Cherry
  Hill, Salem 202 Danbury 134
  Dorchester 43 106 375 Duxbury
  172 174 East Abington 78 East
  Boston 60 220 East Bridgewater
  47 48 Easton 84 134 227 340
  Eastport 219 Everett 95 100
  Forest Hill Cemetery, Forest Hill
  106 Fort George 90 Framingham

MASSACHUSETTS (Cont.)
181 Gage's Ferry, Methuen 202
Gloucester 17 43-46 50 220 227
411-413 Great Barrington 115
Groton 132 Hanover 74 75 147
157 158 162 166 167 203 222
224 339 369 Hanson, Plymouth
Co 218 Hingham 158 Hopkinton
355 Jamaica Plains 195 Kettle
Cove 44 Lawrence 113 114 131-
133 Lowell 40 55 98 137 146
159 197 312 340 341 345 Lower
Beverly 201 Lynn 197 Malden
165 Marblehead 202 229
Marlboro 168 Mattapoisett 47
Medway 358 Melrose 166
Middleboro' 49 Milford 230
Milton 161 339 Mt Auburn 164
Naumkeag 201 New Bedford
196 197 340 Newbury 153 202
238-240 Newbury Falls 240
Newton 39 134 234 Newtonville
51 North Abington 224 North
Bridgewater 153 349 Peabody
198 Pembroke 406 Pittsfield 115
Plymouth 41 86 172 209
Plymouth Co 47 Plympton 117
119 121 Rehoboth 64 Rochester
41 Rockport 188 Rowley 239
Roxbury 134 157 357 359 Salem
63 153 201 202 Salisbury 222
227 Sandwich, Cape Cod,
Barnstable Co 80 83 115 117
169 Scituate 74 112 113 134 157
158 162 166 186 191 221 234
Sewall's Point 119 South
Abington 49 South Boston 65
152 South Braintree 34 194 195
South Framingham 78 South
Weymouth 41 Spencer 134
Squaw-Betty 29 Stockbridge 114
115 360 Stoneham 360 371
Stoughton 349 Swansea 64 65
Taunton 48 109 134 196

MASSACHUSETTS (Cont.)
Topsfield 202 240 Vineyard
Haven 166 Waltham 94
Watertown 134 149 Wenham
202 West Bridgewater 47-49 69
84 175 191 West Medford 178
Westfield 195 Westford 359
Weymouth 84 152 Wilmington
154 Worcester 130 197
Wrentham 156
MATHER, Cotton 63
MAVERICK, Adolphus 43
MAXIM, Bertha 360 Ephraim 332
Eva 358 Eva J 358 Hannah C
348 Joseph E 356 Martin 351 V
136 Matilda (Gott) 136 Olive A
394 Roland 136 Roland M 360
Seviah 331 Lucy 65
MAXWELL, Emma 177 Hannah 174
Hannah M 362
MAY, Esther (Tupper) 116 Joan 201
John Col 116 Judge Hon 80
Richard 201 Seth 116
MAYHEW, Nancy 335
MAYO, Stephen L 358
McALLISTER, Florence O 194
George E 194 Henrietta W 194
Irene H 194 Lizzie Emma
(Howard) 194
McCLUSKEY, John Col 290
McCLUSKY, James 353 May Emma
361
McCULLA, Nellie F 358
McDANIEL, Mary (Woodman) 241
Shirley W 241
McDANIELS, Daniel 296
McDOWELL, Mr 182
McKARTHY, John J 354
McKENNA, Rev 256
McKENNEY, Emily E (Bishop) 67
George 67
McKENNY, Mary 98
McKINNEY, Mary 325
McLELLAN, Brice 208 Susanna 208

McLELLAN (Cont.)
　family 208
McNEAL, James 324
McPHERSON, General 183
MEADE, Gen 183
MEANES, Nancy 326
MEANS, Betsey 326
MERRICK, Maria (Otis) 165 Mr 165
MERRILL, Allen Freeman 223 Ann 156 Belva L 224 Bert 356 Bethia 222 Betsey 222 Betsy 328 Burt 224 Carl S 224 Charles 222 223 329 Charles B 291 Charles S 40 Clara Richardson (Cary) 224 Cora Evelyn 224 Cynthia 223 Daniel Deacon 227 E K 303 Edwin K 223 Eliza Adelaide (Rose) 224 Elizabeth W (Freeman) 223 Eunice 335 family 222 406 Fanny 223 Freeman 223 224 George Bates 223 George E 355 Irving 224 Isaac Joseph 223 224 Jabez 223 Jabez Jr 223 Jane (Young) 222 Joanna 130 Job 223 338 John Maurice 224 John Y 224 305 346 John Young 223 Joseph 222 Joseph 3rd 222 Joseph Jr 222 Joseph T 223 Lester M 224 Levi 223 Lizzie A 357 Louisa Elizabeth 224 223 Louise H 378 62 Lydia (White) 224 Millie Bursely (Francis) 63 Miss 221 Nancy S (Manwell) 223 Nathan 63 Nathan D 361 Nellie 224 Olive Whitman 223 Orilla D (Stinchfield) 40 Oscar W 358 Percy W 224 Perley L 63 Rhoda 227 Rosina 224 Rosina (Manwell) 224 Ruth 223 S C 353 Sarah Ann 334 Seriah 223 Stella 223 Sylvanus C 224 305 346 Sylvanus Cobb 223 224

MERRILL (Cont.)
　Vesta 130 330 Zelinda Ann 224
MERRITT, Evelyn Mrs 360
MERROW, Miss 104
MERRY, Benjamin G 292
MESERVEY, Clement 240
　Elizabeth (Woodman) (Gilman) 240
METCALF, Joseph 333 Saphila C 114 348 385 store 272
METCHELL, William 198
MEXICAN WAR, 128 73
MEXICO, City of Mexico 73 286 Vera Cruz 73
MICHIGAN, 108 Battle Creek 195 Detroit 221 Lapeer 220 Laper 82
MIDDLESEX, Hayes 42 Hayes Court, 42
MIGHILL, Sarah 239
MILET, John 42
MILLAIS, Everett 42
MILLER, Charles A Major 295
MILLET, Aaron 46 47 Abigail (Cait) (Evelith) 44 Adelia 46 Almira A (Day) 47 Amanda M 48 Benjamin 45 46 49 Betsey 46 48 49 Catherine 48 49 Charles Holmes 47 Charles Sumner 47 Cynthia (Dyer) 49 Deliverance (Rich) 46 49 Elathear (True) 47 Elethea (True) 49 Eliza A 48 Eliza (Safford) 47 Elizabeth (Holmes) 48 Ella C 48 Ella T 49 Elmira 48 Eunice 46 Eunice (Babson) 44 Eunice (Parsons) 44 46 57 family 41 Francis Davis 42 46 47 49 Francis G 48 49 George Lewis 48 Henry 42 Herbert 49 57 60 Isabella 46 James O 49 Jean Francois 42 John 42 44 46 48 John R 48 Joseph C 48 Joshua 48 Joshua Howard 48 Josiah Byram 47 Love (Bunker) 44 Lucina (Phillips) 49 Lucy A

MILLET (Cont.)
  48 Lydia 46 47 Mary (Evelith)
  44 Mary (Greenaway) 43
  Matilda 48 Mitilda (Knapp) 46
  Myra (Holmes) 47 Nathaniel 44
  Obadiah 46 47 Ozias 48 Parsons
  46 Phooebe (Gould) 47 Polly 48
  Polly Francis 46 Sally (George)
  48 Sarah 48 49 Sarah (Noyes) 49
  Seth 48 Solomon 6 46 47
  Sophronia 48 Tabitha 331
  Thomas 7 41 43 44 46 47 57 60
  Thomas Lieut 44 Warren L 48
  William Parsons 45 William R
  48 Zebulon P 49 Zebulon
  Parsons 46
MILLETT Adelia 339 Alton G 154
  361 Asa 47 269 Augusta 345 B
  Jr 258 Benjamin 249 257-259
  271 313 Benjamin Jr 258 Betsey
  93 Betsey F 341 Betsy 323
  Caroline 233 Caroline R 348
  Catherine 338 Charlotte 347
  Cynthia D 343 David H 229 337
  Davis F 229 Elethea (True) 229
  Eliza (Leadbetter) 108 Ella 135
  Ella C 354 357 391 Ella T 355
  388 Ella True 195 Esther 196
  327 Eunice 24 377 family 35 407
  Francis 338 Francis D 195 337
  344 Francis Davis 261 388
  Grace 43 H L 259 Hannah Viola
  (Gordon) 230 Henry C 343
  Herbert L 230 352 Isabella 334
  Israel 324 John 110 233 341
  John D 258 259 330 345 John R
  355 Joshua 337 Lavinia (True)
  229 Lucy 391 Lydia 340 Lydia
  Ann (Gordon) 230 Mary Jane
  348 Matilda 251 Matilda
  (Knapp) 135 Mr 246 Obadiah
  339 Orrah A 350 Ozias 306
  Phebe 342 Polly F 337 Sally
  (George) 110 Sarah 343 Seth

MILLET (Cont.)
  108 109 334 335 338 391
  Solomon 271 Susan 238 Susan D
  343 Tabitha A 348 Thomas 24
  25 93 135 252 285 312 313
  Viola H (Gordon) 35 William A
  35 William P 258 259 335 338
  William R 35 352 William R
  Rev 230 Winfred (Pettingill) 154
  Zebulon 252
MILLIKEN, Elias 290 Mr 102
  Rachel 90
MILLIONAIRE, 94
MILLS, Joseph Major 228 Mary
  (True) 228
MINISTERS, 270 Baptist 100 Free
  Baptist 152 Free Will Baptist
  111 Methodist Conference 100
  145
MINNESOTA, 23 60 67 128
  Hutchinson 96 Minneapolis 83
  167 St Paul 63 219 Stillwater
  153
MINOT, Effie C (Parcher) 220
  George E 220 350
MISSION FOR THE INDIANS
  DAKOTA, 190
MISSISSIPPI, 164 176 Raymond 164
  Vernon, Madison Co 164
  Vicksburg 164 Water Valley 96
MITCHELL, Abigail C 341 Abigail
  (Morse) 198 Benjamin 199
  Betsey 333 Betsey L 199 332
  Charlotte 159 336 Clara 76 341
  Clara M 198 Ellen 76 198 Ellen
  L 345 Elvira (Knapp) 199 family
  198 Hannah 334 Henry 76 198 J
  Warren L 198 James W L 335
  James Warren Lamont 198
  Jeseph Jr 332 Jesse 199 339
  John R 349 Joseph 6 198 333
  Julia (Gilbert) 198 Julia (Turner)
  76 Lucy 33 54 213 Lucy C 348
  Lydia P L 340 Mahala 332 Mary

MITCHELL (Cont.)
  199 Mary L 359 Mary (Lamont)
  198 Mary (Mitchell) 199 Moses
  H 346 Mr 246 Rhoda 330 Rhoda
  B 191 192 Tabitha R 346
  Thomas 198 248 Thomas Jr 199
  Warren 76 198 Warren L 329
  William 198 286 328
MISSOURI, 126 139 St Louis 73 82
MONROE, Benjamin 158 Mary
  (Curtis) 158
MONTANA, 63 116
MOODY, Charles S 354 Dorothy
  239 family 407 Joseph F 357
  Millie E 300
MOORE, Abner 391 Eliza 391
  Florenda 156 J Henry 356 Jane
  Mrs 348 Lizzie B 137 391 Ruth
  393
MORE, G C 249 Hannah A 343
  Lizzie B 351 Lizzie Mabel 359 S
  259 Samuel 248 257-259 286
  319 Thaddeus 249
MOREY, Hannah 65
MORGAN, Genie 358 Oliver 147
MORRELL, Levi 331
MORRILL, Annie L 353 Levi 241
  Olive (Woodman) 241
MORRIS, Albion 287 Alvin D 354
  Edwin W 354 F L 303 Forest
  357 Lovina E 356 Minnie J 355
  Silas 238 Susan (Millett) 238
  William H 357
MORRISON, Dorcas 332 Dorcas S
  101 104 373-376 393
MORSE, Aaron 148 Aaron 327
  Abigail 198 328 Betsey (Knapp)
  (Redding) 135 Caroline M 113
  Caroline S 72 342 399 Clarissa
  A C 343 David 290 David 328
  Jane 399 71 Jane L 340 Jane
  (Libby) 72 Jonathan 325 72
  Mary 399 Mary J 146 Mary
  (Brewster) 148 Mehitabel 324

MORSE (Cont.)
  Mehitable 77 Miriam 330 Mr
  135 Nancy 144 145 371 Nathan
  254 Nathan 325 Polly 327
  Rachel M 338 Sally 323 Samuel
  327 Silas 249 Susan 339 Theresa
  Mrs 156
MORSE - see MOSS 361
MORTON, Abiel D 335 Alonzo D
  77 Lucilla Alice (Gilbert) 77
  Phebe 324 Sarah 82 William 294
MOSES, Margaret S 345
MOSS, Anne 324 Henry 324 Nancy
  324
MOSS - see MORSE 361
MOULTON, Daniel 341 Daniel 341
  Elvira J (Deane) 196 Estella A
  101 Esther (Foss) 93 Family 373
  Gilman 91 345 James 98 James
  M 40 101 342 Jonathan 101 344
  Jonathan E 101 Joseph 256
  Josiah 331 332 339 Lucy M
  (Foss) 101 Mary (McKenny) 98
  Mr 11 246 Nancy F 339 Nancy L
  101 Nathaniel 340 Nathaniel P
  196 Sarah 343 Sarah
  (Stinchfield) 40 101 Stillman
  332 93 Sumner C 101 William
  338
MOUNTFORD, Elmira 345
  Jeremiah 336
MOURTON, Sally 380
MOWER, Aaron 347 Albion K P
  348 Alfred A 358 Delora
  (Sylvester) 114 Hannah E 354
  Harrison G O 114 J Elizabeth
  (Pettingill) 156 John Jr 325
  Melville C 345 Nancy 335
  Thomas W 349 Wallace W 156
  353 Warren 254 340
MULBERRY ORCHARD, 203
MULLEN, Priscilla 218
MURPHY, Catherine M 98
MURRAY, Amos 326 Eunice 329

MURRAY (Cont.)
   Mr 246 Patrick 349 Rachel 326
   Samuel B 331
MURRY, Cora E 361
MUZZY, Eliza 128
MYLETT, Henry 43 John 42 John 43
MYLLET Joyce (Chapman) 43
NASH, A J 354 Florence A 360
NEAL, Arvilla (Carver) 236 James B 99 361 John H 360 Mary Cardiff (Edgecomb) 99 Phineas 343 Phineus 236
NEBRASKA, 124 243 Fremont 124 Graford 63 Fort Kearney 73 Omaha 124 176
NEGROES, 285
NESBIT, Harry ? (Harriet?) 325 Lorana 327
NEVENS, Thomas H 360
NEW HAMPSHIRE, 52 180 199 218 219 230 Auburn 97 Bartlett 155 Berlin 205 NH Deerfield 229 Dover Neck 44 Durham 44 Exeter 229 Farmington 160 Hillsboro' 345 Keene 234 Littleton 161 Manchester 73 Nashua 96 103 106 108 Nashua 171 375 New Ipswich 21 168 North Conway 341 Randolph 2 Rye 134 Somersworth 169
NEW JERSEY, 119 East Orange 188 Elizabethtown 45 Passaic River 120
NEW MEXICO, 185
NEW YORK, 55 87 167 176 187 188 218 219 228 Albany 13 118 177 Bellevue Hospital College 30 Brooklyn 106 216 217 Elmira 38 39 Farmersville 228 Geneva 39 Hudson 228 Huntington Long Island 54 Long Island 287 McDougal Hospital 103 New York 26 30 79 106 130 217 373

NEW YORK (Cont.)
   Niagara 117 Peekskill 134
   Prattsville 170 Rochester 61 136
   Rome 37 147 Saratoga 118 119
   Saratoga Springs 155
   Schenectady 13 Syracuse 95
   Ticonderoga 89 117 118 Troy 187 Villenora 228 Watervliet arsenal 182 West Point 182 187 189 White Plains 120
NEWCOMB, Deborah 80 John R 358
NEWMAN, Arabella Rawson 389
NEWSPAPER, Chicago Advance 188 190 Democratic Press 39 Farm, Field & Fireside 190 Intelligencer 257 Lewiston Evening Journal 178 National Tribune 190
NEWTON, Mary A 345 Mr 246
NICHOLS Albertus 356 Alice Clyde 361 Annie E 361 Annie F 300 Charles E 408 Dora M 300 Elizabeth 236 341 Irene 226 Irene E 351 Laura E 408 Laura Etta 355 Rachel 334
NICKERSON, Frank S 288 Frank S Col 290
NILES, Augusta W (Pettingill) 154 Frank 154 Joseph M 341
NORCROSS, family 52 Lydia (Lane) 52
NORRIS, Abigail 135 391 392 Beulah P 116 Emma L 353 394 Emma (Turner) 70 Hannah 154 329 337 James 70 Jane 156 Jedidah 327 Jemima 52 66 97 331 Lois A (Pettingill) 156 Lois J 350 Rocellus C 156 Samuel 331 Sarah 100 Sarah Ellen 331 Sophia 385 Thomas B 350
NORTH CAROLINA, 45 Newbern 103
NORTH OF IRELAND, 124 412

NORTON, Benjamin M 356 Carrie W 220 351 family 407 James S 266 Leon Mortimer 361
NOTTAGE, Rev 256
NOYES, Georgia F 70 Helen Augusta (Lothrop) 70 Sarah 49 Sarah E 338 W S 70 W W 70 William E 252
NUTTING, Maria L 131
NYE, Sarah 52
O'CONNERS, Margaret 349
OHIO, 150 219 Cincinnati 178 219 Maineville 99
OREGON, 51 Pendleton 73 Portland 36 187
OSTLAND, Matilda 195
OTIS, 24 Amos 163 Amos Dr 166 269 Ann F 163 Ann F 165 Anna 333 Betsey (Stinchfield) 23 162 166 Eliza 163 165 186 333 388 Elizabeth 165 Ellen (Grant) 165 Ensign 163 306 347 family 162 404 405 Fannie 107 163 Fanny 327 365 Frances 165 Frances (Vaughn) 165 Harrison G 163 Harrison Gray 162 James 162 John 163 165 John H 342 John Jr 165 Laura D (Woodbury) 166 Laura (Howard) 163 Lydia 332 Lydia P 163 164 Maria 165 Martha J 163 Martha Jane 166 Martha (Davis) 163 Mary 165 Mr 246 Oliver 6 23 102 162 163 166 186 190 271 Sally 326 Samuel 165 Sarah B 163 164 Vaughn 165 Welleon O 165
OUTHOUSE, Evelyn H 156
OWEN, Almeda 339 Almedia 339 Amanda T (Curtis) 158 Betsey (Bates) 222 Charles 344 Eliza E 344 Gideon 328 Hannah 350 Levi 158 350 Martha A Mrs 351 Mr 246 Nathaniel 6 Roxanna 342 Thomas 222 273

OWENS, Thomas 332
OWING, Mr 246
PACKARD, Florence Grace 161 Harold Winwood 161 James B 161 James Roy 161 John Jr 343 Mary Ann 346 Minnie A (Harris) 161 Susan 134 Thomas 170 Winfield Forest 161
PAGE, Aurelia (Parcher) 220 David L 220 340 Hannah H 338 Hannah Mrs 209 Hannah (Churchill) 209 Lucy 377 62 Mary A 343 Mary Ann 410
PAINE, Henry W Hon 39
PALMER, Abigail 113 Abigail Rackley (Lane) 51 Clara E 351 family 51 George 51 Irving O 51 James Capt 55 John O 348 51 Justin A 51 Lottie L 51 Marie I 51 Marjorie C 51 Mary J 55 Mary (Cushing) 51 Paul Smith 360 Rosie E 51 Sophronia 385 Sophronia L 344 Sophronia Lyford 204
PANLEY, James S 6
PARCHER, Abigail 332 Almira 343 Annie 150 Aurelia 220 Aurelia 340 Betsey 107 Betsey 324 Carrie W (Norton) 220 Clara May 220 Clara (Berry) 220 Daniel 91 220 332 Effie C 220 350 Elias 220 Eunice (Gould) 151 family 220 Fred N 220 George 151 220 302 351 George Elder 151 Hannah (Huntoon) 220 John 329 Loraine 220 343 Loren 339 Loring 220 Martha 220 335 Mary 329 Mira 220 Miranda 220 332 348 Miranda (Elden) 220 Mr 246 Olive 220 336 Patience 60 325 377 Sally B 337 Sally (Andrews) 220 Samuel M 341 343 Sewall Dr 269 Sewall F Dr 220 Zachariah 325

PARKER, Carroll G 359 Charles S 355 David C 164 David S 164 Dorcas M 300 Elisie F 164 Flora M 164 Frank 355 Fred A 78 355 George 285 Gladys 78 Herbert 15 John H 356 Laura E 356 Lillie L 164 Lindley 78 Lizzie O 164 Lois (Gilbert) 78 Lydia (Martin) 164 Mabel H 164 Percy 78 Stanley 78 Sylvie 78

PARLIN, William O 293

PARRIS, Samuel 64

PARSON, Theresa H 167

PARSONS, Elnora Y 356 Eunice 44 46 376 Eunice 57 Harriet Newell 417 Nora 236 Sarah 18 Thomas 46 Thressa H 352

PATTEN, David Capt 187 Ella 187 Leader 167 Leander 356 Lorey 167 Mary Ellen 348 Nancy E (Caswell) 167

PATTERSON, Caroline Wilhelmina (Linscott) 106 Frank W 106

PAUL, 24 Betsy 326 Daniel 286 David 285 286 Marshfield 18 20 23 25 57 190 227 Marshfield T 285 Mr 246 Sarah 18 Sarah (True) 90 105 227

PEABODY, Betsey (Knapp) 138 Nathan 138

PEARCE, Ella F Mrs 359

PEARE, Charles 233 Charles 342 Franklin 289 George H 291 348 James 341 Martha 383 Martha (Grant) 233 Moses B 382 Nettie May 359 Phebe 383 Rufus K 292 Rufus K 348 Sarah L 152 353 382

PEARL, Sarah T 346

PEARSON, Benjamin 346

PEASE, Augustus 383 Mae G 357 382 Mary 273

PEASLEE, Carrie 230 Carrie E 35

PENLEY Jane 323

PENNELL, Dwight Richard 106 Frances Cornelia 106 Jennie Augusta (Linscott) 106 Maude Robie 106 William D 106

PENNSYLVANIA, Philadelphia 98 119 165 167 217 236 350 Valley Forge 119

PERHAM, Mabel L 160

PERKINS, Abbie 52 Miss 108 William 43

PERLEY, Adelia 151 344 382 Eliza A 51 Eliza (Lane) 108 51 John 51 Nathaniel 108 51 Peleg 51 Samuel F 51 Ulmer 378 Ziporah 347 Zipporah L 378

PERLY, Esquire Ulmer 62 Grandfather 62 Louise H (Merrill) 62 Zipporah L 62

PERO, Simon 285

PERRY, Fred A 356 John 328 John L 337 Lydia 330 Mr 246 Nancy 327 Polly 221 333 Zachariah 327 332

PETTENGILL, Amy A (Bates) 221 Cyrenius 221 David 20 Eleanor 173 Hannah 29 Ireson B 293 Obadiah 263 William 271

PETTINGILL, Abigail 330 Addie M (Gordon) 154 Alice (Allen) 153 Alpheus Tribou 156 Amy A (Bates) 154 Ann P 156 Ann (Merrill) 156 Anna (Woodman) 240 Anne 324 Araminta 155 343 Arcadius 156 350 Arcadius Jr 156 Arcadus 327 Arvida B 154 340 Aubrey E 154 Augusta W 154 Benjamin 156 240 Carl S 154 Charles M 355 Clara Eunice 155 Clara May 155 Clarence 154 Cyrenius 154 341 370 Daniel 153 E Gertrude 359 Edith M (Coffin) 154 Eleanor C 156 363 Eleanor (Cobb) 156 Elenor C 351 Elvira A (Sumner) 154

PETTINGILL (Cont.)
Elvira J 154 354 Emily A 154 355 Emma Gertrude 155 Ermina A 356 Ermina E 154 Ermina Ella 370 Esther (French) 153 Ethel G 154 Eunice (Day) 155 Evelyn H (Outhouse) 156 family 153 408 Fannie Lovisa 155 Fannie P (Libby) 155 Florenda (Mrs Moore) 156 Francis E (Herve) 156 Frank E 154 Frank E 355 358 Fred Russell 155 George B 156 Georgia (Beal) 154 Grace Vernon 155 Hannah 25 26 85 153 323 401 413 414 Hannah (Norris) 154 Henry 61 Henry F 154 352 Irena 156 Irene 337 Irison B 154 Irving 154 Isaac 154 329 J Elizabeth 156 James Garfield 155 Jane (Norris) 156 Janette 327 Jason 156 341 Jason Deacon 123 Jennette 154 Jessie (Robinson) 155 Joanna (Harris) 156 Joanna (Ingersoll) 153 John 156 341 Joseph 153 Joseph 325 Lecetta 155 Lena M 154 Lewis 116 331 Lizzie J 353 Lois A 156 Lucetta 155 Lucetta (Gordon) 156 Lucretia 350 Lydia 84 153 155 326 336 349 369 Lydia (Briggs) 153 Lydia (Cobb) 153 156 Lydia (Gordon) 123 Lydia (Phillips) 153 Maria 156 Maria (Arno) 156 Mary 154 155 338 Mary (Edson) 153 Mary (Stickley) 153 Matilda F 156 Matilla 123 Melintha G 156 230 356 Mina 161 Mr 246 Obadeah 6 24 127 153 156 271 279 Obadiah Jr 156 Olive (Fish) 116 Orlando (Blake) 155 Phebe 127 128 156 396 Phillips 156 341 Polly H (Tribou) 156 Reuel 153 326 Reuel Jr 153 Richard 153

PETTINGILL (Cont.)
Ruth 154 155 329 343 Ruth Eugenia 155 Samuel 153 Samuel Henry 155 Samuel W 155 Samuel W 291 Sarah 153 229 325 330 381 Sarah C 156 Sarah Rudy 155 Sarah (Poor) 153 Sewall 154 Theresa (Mrs Morse) 156 W R 266 Wilbert H 156 William 6 24 127 153 154 413 William H 156 William Jr 155 333 William P 350 William R 25 155 351 William Sr 155 156 William Tillotson 155 Winifred 154 361
PHELEPS, Elizabeth 337 Hannah 330
PHILIPPINES, 187
PHILLIPS, Amasa H 339 Amos 327 334 Charles 331 Columbia 341 Cynthia 330 Hiram 76 Julia (Gilbert) 76 Julia (Gilbert) (Phillips) 76 Lucina 47 49 344 388 Lydia 153 Lydia (Staples) 49 Miss 232 233 Mr 246 285 Otis 49 Ruel 76 Sam'l 7 8 Vesta 51 108 330 392
PHILPOT, John 157
PHINNEY's Battalion Edmund Col 90
PIAZIA, Lucile 72
PICKENS, Elisha 364 Lovina 364
PIERCE, Frank Major 288
PIKE, Charles S 181 Charles S 387 Cora May 181 Edna Amanda 181 Florilla (Howard) 181 Frank Howard 181 James C 181 Jas C 387 Lydia Ann (Howard) 181 Nancy Mercy 387 Nancy P 181 Peleg F Hon 181
PINGRAY, Catherine 54
PINKHAM, Anna L (Bishop) 67 Blanche M 359 Caroline 211 336 Fred 67 Isaac 211

PIPER, Cynthia (Turner) 87
Harrison 87 338 Mr 246
PIRATES, 151
PLACE, Emma M 358
PLAISTED, Grace Vernon
(Pettingill) 155 Harris M 289
John 155
PLIMPTON, Alice (Bradstreet) 100
Fannie 100 George D 100 Geo
Elias 100 Orissa (Foss) 100
PLUMMER, Benjamin 240 Isaac
338 John L 353 Sarah
(Woodman) 240
POLLARD, Hannah 265 Hannah L
33 Hannah L (Knapp) (Davee)
139 Hannah Mrs 264 Lewis J
139 354 Silvia (Lindsey) 130
POMPILLY, Samuel Capt 228 Sarah
(True) 228
POOR, Sarah 153
PORTER, Asa 331 Elizabeth 138
Lucretia 138 Mary Ann 138
Matherine 138 Rufus J H 138
Ruth (Knapp) 138 Thomas W
Maj 290
POTTER, Elder 251 George J 355
Orinza Mrs 355
POWERS, John E 88 Marion
Elizabeth (Turner) 88 Mary 345
Nora Mrs 354 Rev 256 Ruth Mrs
327 William L 88
PRATT, 24 246 Achsa 219 Achsah
51 332 392 Alvira 341 Charles
286 Deborah 323 Elvira 196
Fanny 329 Hannah 323 Harrison
266 Isaac 91 258 259 332
Jerusha 333 Lucy 329 Margaret
157 Marshall 330 Matilda 329
Persis 325 Ruth 323 50 Sadie E
146 Sally 333 Walter 286
PRESCOTT, Charles W 345 E K
154 Elvira J (Pettingill) 154 J C
304 305 John C 348 Loria 328
Otis K 354

PRINCE, Lenora L 354 Ruth 380
PROCTOR, Annorille 345 Emeline
B 344
PROFESSIONAL MEN, 270
PROHIBITORY LAWS, 223
PULLEN, Celia 137 Marcia 350
Matilda (Knapp) 138 Stephen
138
PURINGTON, Sarah A 358
PUTNAM, Alonzo G 292
QUAKER FRIENDS, 261 273
QUEEN ELIZABETH, 201
QUIMBY, Emily F 351 Kate 300
Leonard 341
RACKLEY, Abigail (Lane) 51 108
Anna A 347 E E 365 Elvira 67
Jason 52 108 196 365 Mr 246
Stephen 51 108 272 330
RAFTER, Fannie 96
RAMSAY, Alexander 357
RAMSDELL, A Ella 219 A Ella 219
Achsa Mrs 348 Achsa (Pratt)
219 Achsah (Pratt) 51 Almeda
(Alden) 218 Anna (Deane) 218
Augustus 218 219 B Roswell
218 Benjamin R 359 E A Gov
218 Edward 218 Elisha 219
Elisha P 219 293 348 Ezra 111
Ezra B 193 219 Gersham 219
Gersham Jr 218 Hannah
(Draper) 219 Howard 193 Irena
W 219 John 218 John Jr 328
Joshua 218 219 329 Lucy M
(Howard) 219 Lucy (Mitchell)
193 Luther 193 218 219 332 392
400 Luther 51 Marilla 193
Martha J 219 219 344 400 Mary
A (Alden) 218 219 Mary M 219
Melvina 218 Melvina J 219
Mildred 193 Mr 112 246 Polly
218 219 326 Roswell 218 219
Rufus 218 219 333 Sarah 218
219 336 Susie G (Wood) 218
Viola 219 Viola Ann 51 392 411

RAMSDELL (Cont.)
 Violia A 347 William 218 327
 Zophar D 218 340
RAND, Eleazer 6 Nancy G 221 331
 363 409 R D 149 250
RANDALL, Abigail Miss 76 Daniel
 335 Esther 158 369 Mr 246
 Nathan 249 Oliver 263 271 285
RANDALL, Fort l 73
RANDELL, Nathan 325 Oliver 279
 Oliver 6
RANN, Mary 335
RASLE, Father Sebastian 11 & 12
RAWSON, Mary 64
RAY, Almon L 351 Almon L 352
 Almond 112 Eliza Jane (George)
 112 Lorania Mrs 148
RAYMOND, Hannah 36 Hannah E
 346 John L 359 William 21
RAZIN, Elizabeth 106
REBEL ARMY, 82
REBELLION OF 1861, 81 82
RECORDS, Sally 332
REDDING, Betsey (Knapp) 135
REDMAN, 9
REED, Lydia 116 Lydia 332
REMICK, Emma F 355
REPRESENTATIVES, Maine
 Legislature 283 Massachusetts
 Legislature 282-283
REVOLUTIONARY WAR, 45 56 69
 74 89 90 105 107 109 117 125
 134 147 151 153 172 175 221
 240 241 395 Army 115 109
 Bagaduce in 1779 141 Battle of
 Lexington 143 Beeman's Height
 118 Bunker Hill 202 Fort Mella
 118 Habbleton 118 King's Ferry
 120 Lake Champlain 118 Mount
 Defiance 118 Provincial Army at
 Cambridge MA 143 Provincial
 Congress 168 Querman's
 Overslough 119 Soldier 52 142
 285 Stillwater 118

REVOLUTIONARY WAR (Cont.)
 Stony Point 120 West Point 120
 121
REYNOLDS, Gen 183
RHODE ISLAND, 120 Providence
 190 198
RICE, Eveline B 39 Joseph S 289
RICH, Deliverance 46 49 Rishworth
 Col 289
RICHARD, Nathaniel 327
RICHARDS, Annie L 167 Elliance
 331 Elwood 361 Freedom 368
 Jennie D 368 410 Jennie L 353
 John 325 Mary A 354 Mr 246
 Samuel 342
RICHARDSON, Mary Ann Goddard
 410 O 252 S A 361
RICHMOND, Alphonso P 342
 Benjamin 333 Charles H 354
 Granville 291 344 351 Hulda L
 130 Huldah 74 327 397 Huldah
 L 352 Joseph 330 Mary 324
 Mary Reliance 74 Mr 246
 Nathan 74 Rhoda (Lothrop) 74
RICKER, Anna 338
RIDER, Wilson C 252 Wilson C Rev
 338
RIDLEY, Abbie Lovina (Stinchfield)
 32 Benjamin 209 331 Betsey 327
 Charles Adelbert 32 Clara
 (Knowlton) 236 David 326 Eliza
 (Jenkins) 209 Ella M 358 family
 410 H J 30 Hannah 238 Hannah
 E 357 Isaac 346 Jason M 32 350
 Jerome 236 350 Nancy E 345
 Paulina 31
RIDLON, Mary 65
RIGGS, Ruth 367
RING, Andrew 370 Sarah 370
RIPLEY, Cynthia 137 342
ROACH, Kate A 361 Mary E 357
 William H 359
ROBB, Ann C 337 Anna Clark 86
 Hannah 332

ROBBINS, Daniel 24 251 285
  Daniel Jr 334 Deborah 329
  Deputy 302 Edw'd H 7 8 Eunice
  335 Hannah 326 John Q 122 289
  Lucius C 295 Lucius Clark 350
  Lucy 352 Lucy A 344 Lucy Ann
  404 Luther 332 Mary Q 167 336
  Mehitable 329 Mercy 329 Mr
  246 Ruth 330 Susan 331
  William 273 329
ROBERTS, Charles W 287 J P 256
  James 330 Julia (Bishop) 66
  Loring 66 Mary 334 Thomas A
  291
ROBINS, Daniel 7
ROBINSON, Hannah 148 332 Jessie
  155 Lucretia A 350 Peter 326
  Susan 342 William 325
ROGERS, Charlotte 366 Mary 234
  369 403 416 Zenas 339
ROLLINS, Moses Elder 209
ROME, Elisha 129 Minnie 129 Ruth
  (Lindsey) 129 Tena 129
ROSE, A P 303 A P 304 Addie E
  353 Alanson 348 Albert 304
  Albert M 289 294 295 Albert P
  361 Asa 258 259 Asa Jr 331
  Augusta 338 Aurelia 336 Axah
  330 Betsey A 346 Betsey B 358
  Betsey P (Turner) 87 Caleb H
  343 Calvin 305 Calvin M 345
  Caroline 336 Edgar 353 Edith
  354 Effie M 357 Elbridge G 339
  Eliza A 406 Eliza Adelaide 224
  Esther Augusta 359 family 409
  Florentine 341 379 Greenfield
  333 Harvey 383 Hazel 87 333
  Hortencia W 350 Inez 354
  Isabelle E 355 Jennie L 355 John
  304 Leonard 342 Leonard L 295
  358 Lieurana 337 Mary G 348
  Mercy 328 Mr 246 Nancy G 346
  Nelson 305 332 344 Olive B 343
  Penelope 342 345 Rebecca 233

ROSE (Cont.)
  344 383 Seth 336 Seth G 295
  Seth Jr 337 Thomas S 350 Victor
  A 357 Will 304 Zilpha A 344
ROUNDS, Adelia 353 Betsey 416
  Leonard 416 Susan L 416
ROW, John 323
ROWE, John 23 Laura 105 Lucy E
  353 Mary (Lane) 52 Mr 246
  Nancy E 339 Sarah (Stinchfield)
  23 Stephen 52
ROYAL, Adams 163 Israel 285
RUSSEL, Eurania T (Stinchfield) 40
RUSSELL, A P 112 A P 218 Almira
  40 E A 219 268 302 303 Edward
  40 Ernest A 359 Ernest A 51
  Ernest W 359 Eula 219 51
  family 410 Kittie 268 Kittie
  (Lane) 51 219 Martha R (Foster)
  145
RUST, Henry Jr 290 John D 289
RYDER, Catherine (Millet) 49
  Herbert W 360 Wilson C Rev 49
  Wilson Clarkson 49
SABATTIS, Indian Chief 19
SAFFORD, Eliza 339 Eliza 47
  Francis L 337 Stephen 340
SAINT CLAIR, Gen 117 118
SAINT EUSTASIA, 45
SALSTANSALL, Mr 134
SALVADOR, John T 293
SAMPSON, 24 Ada 117 Almedia
  337 Almira 334 Anna K 335
  Annie 78 Celia 339 Charles A L
  287 Cyrus 169 248 249 323
  Elisha 354 Elisha H 332 Hazel
  170 Ira 76 77 117 330 336 Jacob
  332 James 251 Jane 78 John 117
  Julia 77 Laura 77 Leonard G 117
  345 Lucy 323 Lydia 326 Mary
  326 334 Mary (Wing) 170 Mr
  246 Nabby (Wing) 169 Patience
  (Fish) 117 Rebecca 79 333
  Robert 326 Susan (Gilbert) 76

SAMPSON (Cont.)
  William 77
SAMSON, Anna 327 Beriah 6
  Beriah Jr 6 Deborah 328 Hazael
  329 James 6 Jane 328 Micah 7
  Zoar 6
SAMSON - see SAMPSON 361
SANBORN, Abram 39 E Alice 360
SANDERSON, Dr 206 Rev 256
SANDS, James 151
SARGEANT, Abby 375
SARGENT, Elders 252 Sarah (Lee) 165
SARNER, Ada A 62
SAWTELLE, Marshal S 361
SAWYER, William M 349
SAXTON, Gen 189
SCAMMON, Esther Mrs 338 401
  Esther Mrs 85 Joseph 333 widow 99
SCHOOLS, Bangor Seminary 189
  Bates College 99 117 152 155
  181 216 266 Bowdoin Medical
  College 269 Bowdoin College 30
  39 135 152 189 292 Coburn
  Classical Institute 123 205 Colby
  College 167 205 Edward Little
  High 99 225 Edward Little
  Institute 178 Free text book law
  267 Harvard Medical College
  269 Hebron Academy 117 Kent's
  Hill 117 Leland & Gray
  Seminary 99 Lewiston Academy
  114 Lewiston High 225
  Litchfield Seminary 213 Maine
  State College 167 Maine
  Wesleyan Seminary 39 68 Maine
  State Seminary 30 Maine
  Wesleyan Seminary & Female
  College 243 Monmouth
  Academy 39 178 186 226 312
  Northwestern University 190
  State Normal, Farmington 68 87
  114 115 124 154 178 205 217

SCHOOLS (Cont.)
  242 266 Straight University in
  New Orleans 190 Theological
  Institute 155 Toogaloo
  University in Mississippi 190
  Topsham Academy 189
  Waterville College 213 Wendell
  Institute, Farmington ME 146
  Westbrook Seminary 225 173
  Yarmouth Academy 187 189
SCOTLAND, 208 229
SCOTT, R Rev 303 Robert 249
  Robert 252 Winfield Gen 73
SCRIBNER, Estella 40
SEASON OF 1816 "COLD
  SEASON", 190-191
SEAVY Miss 220
SECOND, Physician in Leeds 176
  Teacher of Greene 113
SECRET SOCIETIES, Chapel Hill
  Council #43 JOUAM 304 Delta
  Upsilon Fraternity 205 Gen
  Howard Lodge #77 AOUW 303
  Grange P of H #99 302 IOGT
  305 Junior Order of American
  Mechanics 303 Masonic 216
  Free & Accepted Masons Tuscan
  Lodge 132 Free & Accepted
  Mason 32nd degree 127 Free &
  Accepted Masons Asylum Lodge
  151 Free Mason Oriental Star
  Lodge 101 Mountain View
  Lodge #23 D of L 304 Sons of
  Temperance 305 Temperance
  Watchman Club 305
SEDGLEY, Fred A 360
SEGAR, William Sir 157
SEWALL, Annie 240 Frederick D
  291 Henry 240 Samuel Judge 240
SEYMOUR, J M 303 Mr 85
SHAPEIRO, Georgia L (Bishop) 67
  Morris 67
SHAW, Ada 137 Annie S (Additon)

SHAW (Cont.)
  173 Betsey 148 331 365 Deborah 336 Elisha Lieut 285 Eliza 226 Jacob 137 Loisania 330 Martha Jane 98 Mary J (Knapp) 137 Phoebe 363 Roscoe V 349 T M Mrs 173 Truman M 357 William M Major 289 Zebedee 148
SHEA, Henry 293
SHEPHERD, Job D 338
SHEPLEY, George F 290
SHERMAN, Gen 183 152 Mr 184
SHIP, Black Prince 56 James 238 Lion 157 Mayflower 147 218 Milford 80 Monadnock 170
SHOREY, Ivory 407 Millie E 354 407
SILK WORMS, 203
SIMONS, Ida K 217
SIMPSON, Albert 145 James I 359 N Emma (Foster) 145
SKILLIN, Josiah 336
SKILLINGS, Adeline 350 Eliza Jane 346 Josiah 113 Lucy 67 Lucy D 348 Orilla (Sylvester) 113
SLAVES, 38
SLEEPER, Grace M 360 H S Dr 31 John P R 290 Minnie Etta (Stinchfield) 31
SLOCUM, Mr 184
SMALL POX, 119
SMALLEY, Ruby 327
SMALLIDGE, Annie Etta 133
SMART, Eliphalet Loton 331 Ephraim K 273 Razzilla 173 Rozilla 347 362 Sally B 327
SMITH, Addie 233 Addie N 353 Almira 85 Almond 331 85 Ammi 332 C H Col 213 Catherine 240 Diana 337 Diana (Turner) 85 Dianna 230 Effie 304 Elisha 235 Elizabeth 229 Ella 67 Ellen E 356 Elmira 327 F W 256 Fred 304 George Esq 38 George T

SMITH (Cont.)
  348 Glovina 38 J F 304 305 Jane 235 326 John R 293 Lucius 348 Lucretia 159 Martha Mrs 237 341 Mary A 349 Miss 87 Mrs 233 Olive 90 Priscilla H 347 Rev 260 Warren L 359 William 324
SNELLEN, Eliza 326
SNOW, Elbert 33 Elvira S (Gott) 33 Helen M 349 53 John P 33 Murietta Edora 33
SNYDER, Abram 252
SOLE, Vesta A 345
SOPER, Mary E 352 Parmealia 329 Sarah R 352
SOULE, Alfred B 292 Asa I 350 Lewis 334 Vesta A 140
SOUTH AMERICA, 236 Cartagena 195
SOUTH CAROLINA, Beaufort Island 184
SOUTH DAKOTA, Iroquois 161
SOUTH WALES, Hay, Breconshire Co 55 56
SOUTHARD, A 286 Constant Jr 324 Mr 246 Roxanna 333 Thomas 323
SPANISH-AMERICAN WAR, 186 Philippines 188
SPEAR, Almira Mrs 54 Jane 136 Louisa M 312 343
SPOFFORD, M Etta 355
SPRAGUE, Allen H 360 Augusta A 353 Elvira 166 334 Etta L 355 family 411 Fannie M 353 Hulda J 111 Huldah J 351 Jethro 337 Martha (Brewster) 148 Nellie M 358 Orin 148 William 148 William Jr 326
SPRINGER Keziah H (Stinchfield) 40 Melville S 40
STANDISH, Miles 370 Miles Capt 175 Zeruiah 370
STANFORD, Fred 217 Frederick B

STANFORD (Cont.)
  216 Harold B 217 Louise A 217
  Sarah 217 Sarah H (Boothby)
  216
STANLEY, Allura (Foss) 105 Grace
  (Tupper) 116 James 116 John
  105 John 334 Julia A 261 Julia
  Ann 335 Mr 246 Nathan 292
STANTON, Mr 184
STAPLES, Abigail 228 Alma 129
  Celia (Lindsey) 129 Charles 129
  Ellouisa (Bishop) 67 Frank B
  129 Henry G Major 287 Joseph
  W 129 Lydia 49 Myra B 129
  Polly Cummings 389 R H 67
  Roland H 129 Rose E 129 Willis
  T 129
STARBIRD, Mira (George) 111 Rev
  111
STARR, Robert 252
STATE MILITIA, 237 238 242
STENCHFIELD, Rogers 7
STETSON, Amos 347 Aurelia A 344
  Caleb 410 Charles 254 Cynthia
  158 Deborah 222 Hannah 326
  Isaiah Capt 120 Lorenzo P 344
  Lydia 328 Martha 147 Martha M
  343 Mr 246 Nathan 330 Sarah A
  410 W W 267 268
STEVEN, Hannah (Brewster) 148
STEVENS, Abel 116 Abel Jr 116
  Anna 144 Aran 144 Calvin 225
  Daniel W 348 Eliphalet 144
  Elizabeth 239 Emily 116
  Ephraim 144 Ephraim Jr 144
  Grace (Fish) 116 Hannah 144
  Harriet 116 Hiram 116 John 116
  John Capt 239 Joshua 144 Lucy
  334 Sarah 146 Sibler (Foster)
  144 Sophronia 128 Susan 342
  Sybil 144 Thomas 144
STEWART, Eliza 389 George 389
  Maggie L 389 Miss 150 Sarah
  23

STICKLEY, Mary 153
STINCHFIELD, Abbie A (Atwood)
  41 Abbie Lovina 32 Abbie L 350
  Abigail S (Johnson) 126 Abigail
  L (Knapp) 29 139 Abigail 26 22
  23 Adelia 38 26 Alice S 126
  Alice 339 Allen Howard 178
  Allen Howard 31 Allen 36 26
  Allie (Marston) 40 Alluva H 35
  Almira (Russell) 40 Almira
  (Berry) 41 Almira C 35 Amaziah
  P 40 Ann Eliza 35 Annette 40
  Anson G 26 Anson Gancello 39
  Aramantha P 26 36 Armenta 26
  Azel 126 Bartley K 37 Benjamin
  22 23 Bessie R 229 353 Betsey
  22 23 53 162 166 186 333 405
  Brothers 92 Catherine 126
  Charles Knapp 30 Charles 35
  Charles K Dr 269 Christiana B
  35 Clara (Judkins) 41 Clarissa
  (Gould) 34 Desire (Butterfield)
  167 Diadama (Larrabee) 41 Dora
  M 34 Eben P 40 Eben A W 41
  Eben 40 41 105 258 259
  Ebenezer Jr 341 Ebenezer 229
  233 234 257 345 346 352 Edith
  Helen 41 Edith H 41 Edward
  Everett 39 Eliza Ann 34 Eliza J
  35 Eliza 26 Elizabeth (Gray) 35
  Elizabeth 17 18 126 Ella Frances
  33 Ella F 354 Elmina 167 Elmira
  26 35 Emma J 35 Estella S 312
  Estella (Scribner) 40 Estella M
  40 Estella 359 Eurania T 40
  Eveline B (Rice) 39 Evelyn 34
  Ezekiel 22 23 Ezra 22 F
  Carabelle 35 Ezra 126 family
  411 family 17 Father Thomas 91
  Florence Mabel 41 Florence E
  35 Frances (Fuller) 41 Frances
  (Dolly) 35 Fred E 35 Frederic W
  40 Gancello 38 Gancello S 37
  George Swain 33 George K 36

STINCHFIELD (Cont.)
336 George 26 George Barclay
38 George H 37 Glovina (Smith)
38 Guy C 33 Hannah (Pettingill)
153 Hannah 26 35 328 230 339
367 368 381 Hannah E 35
Hannah Jr 27 125 Hannah W
345 Hannah (Harding) 40
Hannah (Lincoln) 41 233
Hannah (Lindsey) 27 125
Hannah (Pettingill) 25 26
Hannah (Raymond) 36 Harriet M
(Chessman) 41 Henrietta
(Howard) 178 Henry W 34
Horace W 40 Isaac 26 29 30 33
139 320 336 J C 178 264 James
18 25 29 153 227 229 312 317
318 James Sr 26 James 26 29
257 James K 37 James K 26
James 34 40 321 323 James H
34 James Jr 237 258 320 338
James K 258 Jane (Libby) 36
Jennie S (Teague) 32 Jeremiah
167 Jerusha (Keene) 23 Joel 26
35 John 1 17 26 27 29 227 316
320 321 John Allen 35 John
Barry 38 John C 349 John Clark
31 John K 26 John K Dr 38 269
John R 126 Keziah H 40 Levi G
34 Lewis D 41 Lewis Delmar
234 Lizzie 34 Llewellyn A 40
Lucinda 35 Lydia (Cobb) 25
Lydia (Kelley) 40 Maria L
(Foster) 126 Martha 223 227
Martha/Patty 26 Mary Ann 26 37
339 Mary K 39 Mary V 38 Mary
(King) 26 Mary (Lindsey) 126
Mary (Woodbury) 40 41 229
Mary/Polly 26 Minnie Etta 31
Mr 247 246 Nancy Maria 36 old
homestead 236 Olivia Morton 38
Ophelia (Edgerton) 37 Orilla D
40 Polly (Lindsey) 126 Polly 33
136 331 Rebecca 27 90 227

STINCHFIELD (Cont.)
Roger Capt 23 53 126 Roger 1
18 22 23 24 31 57 162 190 231
Rose (Foss) 40 Rose Ellen 32
Rose E 348 Rufus B 40 Sallie
264 Sally 323 Samuel B 36 37
Samuel Capt 229 26 Samuel 37
227 261 Sarah 23 25 40 227 314
342 Sarah B 126 Sarah Jane 36
Sarah Paul (True) 27 Sarah
(Canwell) 23 Sarah (True) (Paul)
90 105 227 Sarah 22 101 Seth 40
101 229 312 Sewall W 353
Sewall Wallace 32 Sewall
Warren 36 Sewall 26 36 346
Solomon 23 22 Stephen Decateur
39 Stephen D 26 Susan W 345
Susan Ann (Heard) 38 Susan 40
Susanna W 229 Susanna 23 22
Tamson (Eldridge) 23 Thirza M
40 Thomas 1 4 18 20 24-29 32
35 56 57 90 92 105 109 125 227
231 248 285 311-313 316 317
Thomas B 26 Thomas B Dr 269
Thomas Bartley Dr 38 Thomas
Jefferson 30 Thomas Jr 314
Thomas S 35 William 17 18 22
23 126 325 Willington 40
Woodbury A 40 41 Zebulon 22
23 326 331 330
STODDARD, Frances 408
STONE, Martha 411
STOUT, William 255 350
STOWELL, David P 295
STREET, Clarissa 325
STREETER, Rubey 324 Sally 141
144
STRICKLAND, C H 166 Frances
164 Lee 289 Martha Jane (Otis)
166
STRONG, Caleb 8 271 Samuel 6
STROUT, Isaac A 346 Loretus A
358
STUART, Abigail 325 Charles W

STUART (Cont.)
 220 348 Miranda (Parcher) 220
 Sally 326
STUBBS, Mr 247 Olive 158 371
 Samuel 323 Sophia 323
STUDLEY, Arthur Irving 224 Arthur
 W 224 Ethel Louise 224 Zelinda
 Ann (Merrill) 224
STURGIS, Jonathan 341
STURTEVANT, Abisha 347
 Clarissa J 340 David 334 353
 354 Eliab 220 343 Hannah 346
 John 327 Joseph O 288 Loraine
 (Parcher) 220 Lucinda A 347
 Mary A 221 Mary H 346 Mr 247
 Noah 249 Rosannah 344 Sally
 324 Sophrona 347 Warren 294
 330
SULLIVAN, General 120 Jeremiah
 H 358 Jeremiah P H 347
SUMNER, Albert W 234 Albert W
 344 Alvira Ann 340 Augusta W
 234 369 Caleb 158 Caleb R 234
 336 Caroline H 359 Caroline
 Howard 132 Elvira A 154 234
 409 family 234 414 General 182
 Hannah T 234 337 Houghton 83
 234 369 Joshua H 293 343 357
 Julia Ann (Lindsey) 132 L H 259
 Lemuel 257-259 Lemuel Mrs
 136 Levi C 234 296 Louisa 158
 Louisa J 234 341 Lucy Ann 355
 Mary 333 Mary H 234 Mary H
 81 Mary H 83 Mary (Rogers)
 234 Mehitable 334 Mr 247
 Oleva E 356 Rachael D 234
 Robert Lindsey 132 Ruth C 234
 339 Serena E 355 Sophia B 359
 Sophia Benson 132 Sophia
 (Curtis) 158 W B 259 302
 William B 349 William B Enson
 132
SUMNERS, family 403
SWAIN, Benjamin 234 345

SWAIN (Cont.)
 R E 4 248 249
SWANSON, Andre 98 Catherine B
 98 Catherine M (Murphy) 98
 Kate B 372
SWEDEN, Stockholm 62
SWEENY, Carrie L 78
SWIFT, Charlotte Mrs 339 Mr 247
 Nellie M 243 Sam'l 286 Sarah E
 230 Sarah E 359 Temperance 327
SWINTON, Fannie Mrs 352
SWISS CONSUL AT NEW
 ORLEANS, 72
SYLVESTER, Abigail (Palmer) 113
 Alonzo 113 Arthur M 114 Arthur
 Mellen 114 Bradbury 113 339
 Caroline M (Morse) 113 Charles
 113 Charles C 344 Clarissa 325
 Delora 114 Elisha 113 264
 family 112 Hannah 344 Hannah
 (Brown) 112 113 Hannah
 (Sylvester) 113 Harriet (Howard)
 113 Harriett Newall (Howard)
 192 Harvey 112 113 Harvey Jr
 113 Henry Cole 114 Howard 170
 327 Iva (Taylor) 113 Jane
 (Foster) 113 Jeremiah 113 344 L
 Mellen 348 Laura M 115 266
 Laura Metcalf 114 Lorenzo 113
 114 333 Lorenzo Mellen 114 385
 Lucy M 204 359 385 Lucy
 Metcalf 114 Lydia 221 Lydia
 (Bean) 113 Lydia (Turner) 85
 Macy 203 Masey 85 Massey 324
 Mehitable (Wing) 170 Miss 267
 Mr 247 Orilla 336 Rachel
 (Brown) 113 Rhoda (Caswell)
 113 Rosalinda 113 341 Ruggles
 113 192 339 Saphila C (Metcalf)
 114 Saphrona 334 Sarah
 (Leavitt) 113 Sewall 113
 Sophrona 345 Sophronia 113 114
 Stephen W 338 Vanelia E 348
TALBOT, J F 165 Sarah (Lee)

TALBOT (Cont.)
    (Sargent) 165 Stephen C 294
TANNERY, 248
TARBOX, Elizabeth Mrs 240
TARR, George 352 Nancy 389
TAYLOR, Abby P 352 Annie F 356
    Beniah 339 Beniah 96 Catherine
    326 Iva 113 James 327 James M
    96 Joel E 356 Joseph L 355
    Lizzie A Mrs 360 Lucretia D 353
    359 Mary 236 Orrin B 248 Ruth
    B 340 Sarah (Foss) 96 Stephen
    A 360 William C 356
TEAGUE, Jennie S 32 353
TEMPLE, Miss 82
TENNESSEE, 189 293 Jackson 81
TENNEY, Daniel 239 Elizabeth
    (Woodman) 239
TENNY, Josephine S 350
TEXAS, 165 Chapel Hill 38 Egypt,
    Wharton Co 38 Rutherville
    College 39 San Jacinto 38
THAYER, Mr 247 Polly 70 397 405
THOMAS, A L 268 A L 303 Alton L
    180 358 Amos Jr 334 Annie E
    (Lincoln) 180 B C 302 Carrie
    164 Carrie W 224 407 Charles L
    174 352 362 family 416 Father
    15 Fletcher A 180 Gen 183
    Hannah (Maxwell) 174 Luetta M
    (Additon) 173 Mary A 174 356
    362 Robert S 347 W H Dr Mrs
    173 William 407 William H 355
THOMES, Amos 113 Amos F 352
    Rosalinda (Sylvester) 113
THOMPSON, Elimira B 407 John
    138 219 326 Jonathan 337
    Lucretia (Knapp) 138 Mary 66
    Mr 247 Mrs 353 Polly 325 Polly
    (Ramsdell) 219 Rebecca 329
    Sarah 137 Sarah Mrs 342
    William P 274
THOMS, Amos 336 Laverna C 345
THURSTON, Dorothy (Woodman)

THURSTON (Cont.)
    239 John 239 Parson 142
TIBBETS, Hannah 325 Hepsabeth
    209 Hepseba 328
TIBBETTS, Betsey 326
TILDEN, Charles W 291
TILTON, Elder 252
TIMBERLAKE, Nathan 339
TINKHAM, A F 355 Frank A 149
    Jennie M (Brewster) 149
TITUS, Patience 64
TOBIN, Cyrus H 348 Harriet E 65
    Nancy 348
TODD, Georgie 112
TOMES, Amos 341 Charles A 341
TOMSON - see THOMPSON 361
TOOTHAKER, Abram 78 Marian
    (Gilbert) 78
TORREY, Betsey 329 Jesse 323
    Joseph 355 James 325
TORSEY, Drusilla (Gilbert) 77
    Henry A 338 Holman H 77 Jonas
    H 342 Louisa 77 338 Samuel P
    343
TOWLE, Charles 237 Charles 344
    Charlotte 98 Eliza (Carver) 237
    James D 290 James D 293 Susan
    Jane 350
TOWNSEND, Harriet 332 Harriet
    99 Lois 341 Salmon 328
TRAIN, Sally S 350
TRANSIENT, 328
TRASK, Ada J Mrs 359 B F 135
    Benjamin F 348 David 351 66
    David E 295 347 John H 348
    Joseph A 354 Lillian 357 Lydia
    54 Mary J Mrs 350 355 Mary
    (Bishop) 66 Mr 247 Nancy 341
    Rufus 349 Speencer 334
TREAT, George W 341 Jennett 237
TRIBOU, Mary 417 Polly 327 Polly
    H 156 W C 249
TRUE, Abigail (Staples) 228
    Benjamin 227 49 Benjamin

HISTORY OF LEEDS

TRUE (Cont.)
    Deacon 18 222 227 412
    Benjamin Jr 228 229 Bessie R
    (Stinchfield) 229 Betsey 228
    Betsey R (Stinchfield) 40 D P 14
    19 40 237 303 Daniel 97 Davis P
    26 109 229 353 Dexter W 351
    Eben 220 Ebenezer 336 Elathear
    47 Elethea 49 228 229 Elethere
    337 Eliza Shepherdson (Allen)
    228 Elizabeth 227 Emma Sarah
    97 family 227 Giles 228 Henry
    227 Jabez 227 228 Jane 228
    Jemima L (Foss) 97 John A 220
    335 Joshua M 62 Joshua Morse
    377 Julia 65 Julia Ann 59
    Lavania 228 229 Levaba 337
    Lewis P 336 Lewis Page 97 Lucy
    (Page) 62 Martha 228 Martha
    (Parcher) 220 Mary 228 Naomi P
    62 377 378 Olive (Parcher) 220
    Parsons 264 Rhoda 228 Rhoha
    (Merrill) 227 Ruth (Carver) 229
    237 Sally 335 Sally Storrs 377
    Sally (West) 97 Samuel P 237
    305 340 345 Samuel P 36 40
    Samuel Parsons 228 Sarah 18 90
    105 227 228 411 413 Sarah Paul
    27 Sarah S 62 Susan
    (Stinchfield) 40 Xoa (Childs)
    228
TRUFANT, Joseph 372 Julia 372
    Julia A 352 Sivinah 372
TRYON, Stella 387
TUCK, A S 170 171 Augustus S 356
TUCKER, Susan 341
TUPPER, Enoch 305 329 Esther 116
    Grace 116 Joshua 261 Joshua
    261 Lucy 261 Mehitable 115 Mr
    80 115 247 326
TURNER CENTER DAIRY
    ASSOCIATION, 197
TURNER CENTER FACTORY, 197
TURNER, Adelaide C (Harrington)

TURNER (Cont.)
    88 Alice Gertrude 87 Almira 261
    Almira (Smith) 85b Alpheus 323
    84 Amanda F 340 Amanda
    Fitzelen 85 Ann 334 Ann H 336
    Ann (Coburn) 86 Anna C 347
    Anna Clark 86 Anna Clark
    (Robb) 86 Annie (Hunter) 88
    Ansel 61 63 333 335 Benjamin
    76 84 85 88 344 Benjamin
    Abbott 89 Benjamin Dr 269
    Benjamin M Dr 88 Benjamin 87
    Betsey 76 Betsey P 87 333
    Betsey Palmer 85 Betsey
    (Gilbert) 70 76 85 Betsey
    (Lothrop) 70 Carrie (Dingley) 88
    Charles Clark 87 Charles Osburn
    85 Cynthia 76 84-87 338 Cynthia
    W 85 346 Cynthia Welcome 86
    Deborah 79 85-87 338 Deborah
    (Gilbert) 78 85 Desire 84 85 170
    326 418 419 Diana 84 85 331
    Dorcas L 341 Drusilla L 339
    Edwin 330 Eleanor 84 168
    Eleanor (Whitman) 84 125 Eliza
    Mrs 342 Elizabeth 125 127
    Elizabeth 84 Elizabeth B
    (Manwell) 87 Ernest Linwood 87
    Esther Mrs (Scammon) 85
    Eunice 78 85 family 84 400
    Flora E 72 Florence 180
    Florence A 350 Florence E 88
    Francis A 70 Francis Orman 85
    Fred Otis 87 George 7 70 76 84
    85 125 273 323 George Esq 87
    George Henry 88 George Henry
    Jr 88 George Jr 263 George Jr
    279 George W 87 George W Dr
    269 George Washington 85
    Grace 34 52 55 324 Grace H 358
    Grace Haywood 89 Hannah 53
    70 76 84 85 87 125 328 339 399
    Hannah E 86 Hannah E
    (Donham) 86 Hannah (Collier)

TURNER (Cont.)
85 Hannah (Pettingill) 85 Harriet Grace 89 Harriet H (Lane) 88 Henry S 288 Henry Sewall 86 Herbert 180 Herbert Phillips 85 Isaiah 84 Jacabina 86 Jane 66 76 84 330 Jane R 85 86 Jenny 84 Joanna 78 84-86 251 326 John 76 84-87 345 John Dr 269 John M Dr 357 John M Dr 72 John 87 John Robbins 84 Joseph 78 84-86 177 323 338 Joseph Jr 78 85 Joshua S 336 Joshua Shaw 85 Josiah 6 24 69 76 84-87 271 327 346 Josiah Jr 84 85 Julia 76 78 Julia A 194 Julia Ann 85 86 177 335 Kate Ina 87 Lelia Annah 87 88 Lewis 84 85 324 Lizzie D 354 Lizzie Donham 87 Lorania (Francis) 61 63 Louisa C 337 Lucia 79 Lucia A 87 Lucia H 347 Lucius Clark 85 Lucy 76 Lydia 76 84-87 159 323 324 339 344 Lydia (Pettingill) 84 Margaret 84 Marion Elizabeth 87 88 Martha 76 Martha A 346 Martha Ann 85 Martha Ann 89 Mary 69 74 84 396 Mary L (Howard) 85 196 Mary Louisa (Howard) 180 Mary S (Loring) 86 Mary Thomas 86 Matilda (Francis) 61 Melvina J 337 Miss 99 Mr 247 Obadiah 323 Olive M (Lothrop) 72 87 Oscar D 292 335 Oscar Dunreath 85 Peter L 358 Peter L 88 Phillips 78 85 86 180 196 336 Polly 338 Roxanna 333 Roy Stanley 89 Sally 76 Samuel Loring 86 Sarah 55 76 85 87 88 345 Simeon 254 326 Sobrina 76 85 Sobrina 87 Stephen Welcome 86 Susanna 127 330 Thomas 84 Thomas Dr 269 Thomas Francis Dr 61

TURNER (Cont.)
Victoria H 85 196 347 Victoria Helen 85 180 Wansbrow 122 289 Washington 76 William 6 24 69 84 85 87 125 159 249 271 272 285 335 William G 337 338 78 85 86 William Jr 325 76 William P 86 Winslow 292
TUTIS, Patience 65
TYM, Angie D (Cushman) 124 Franklin 124
TYRON, Stella 181
VARNEY, George Major 287
VARNUM, Asa 20
VAUGHAN, Zenas 328
VAUGHN, Eunice (Knapp) 137 Frances 165 Zenas 137
VERRILL, Eliza A 349 Eunice 50 Judith 52 Lois 52
VERMONT, Bennington 118 Burlington 187 Island Pond 148 Plymouth 234 St Johnsbury 66 Townsend 99 Woodstock 235 Woodstock 237
VIRGIN, William Wirt 292
VIRGINIA, 53 164 Alexandria 243 Beaver Dam Station 213 Charlestown 294 Norfolk 78
VOSE, Abbie E 36 Abigail C (Stinchfield) 35 Charles Allen 36 family 35-36 James Sewall 36 John W 35 John W Jr 36 Miney E 36 Nancy E 354
VOSE's Regiment Col, 90
VOSMUS, Edwin W 40 Mary Augusta (Stinchfield) 40
WADE, family 417 Fred A 358
WADSWORTH, Frank 356 Herbert S 358 Jerusha 144 Jesse 333
WAGNER, Amanda F 352 E H 357
WAITE, Edson 359 Elizabeth Ann 187
WALCOTT, William 328 General 184

WALDO's REGIMENT COL, 89
WALKER, Annie A (George) 112
  Betsey Mrs 338 Charles Major
  289 Elizabeth (Stinchfield) 18
  Fred 112 James B 345 John 326
  John Deacon 18 Owen McKinley
  112 Samuel 351
WALLS, Eurania T (Stinchfield)
  (Russel) 40 Nathan 40
WALTON, Beulah P (Norris) 116
  Caroline (Fish) 116 Charles 338
  Charles H 116 Edith 168 Fred W
  116 355 George W 116 Georgie
  A 359 Herbert N 116 Jeremiah D
  116 Lucy A 116 Martha M 116
  Nathaniel 116 Nathaniel 331
  Sarah E (Dexter) 116 117
WAR, King George's 89 Nez Perce
  185
WAR OF 1812, 46 58 71 78 211 218
  232 248 286 Capt N Pettingill's
  Co 97 Lt-Col Ellis Sweet's Reg't
  97 Quebec 203
WAR OF THE REBELLION, 170
  Battle of Fort Fisher 170
WARDWELL, Dora H 347 George E
  351
WARREN, William J 347
WASHBURN, Abishai 324 Elihu
  165 Eunice 329 Israel Jr 273
WASHINGTON, 219 226 General
  69 119 120 121 General's aids
  119
WATER SHED, Dead River 2 Thirty
  Mile River 2
WATERHOUSE, Rosemand 353
WATSON, Bertha H 358 Flora 74,
  Fred Odlin 74, Henry 74, John
  74, Mary Reliance (Richmond)
  74, Odlin 74, Thomas 74
WATTS, George E 352
WAYMOUTH, Anna 350
WAYNE, General 120
WEBBER, Adelia J 266

WEBSTER, Mr 247 Reuben H 340,
  Stephen 323
WEEKS, Esther 240
WELCH, Helen 243 Myrick 333
  Wesley 354
WELCOME, Anna 323 Cynthia
  (Turner) 84 Mr 247 Stephen 84
  86 248 249 262 271 272
WELLCOME, Stephen 6
WELLINGTON, Fiducy A 349
WENDELL, Mr 247
WENTWORTH, Charles 352 Eliza
  H 340 Foster D 336 Lucy 331
  Mark F 294
WEST, George W 291 Nancy 365
  Sally 97
WEST INDIES, 30
WEST VIRIGINA, 219 Cereda 218
WESTON, Helen S 353
WEYMOUTH, Eliza 407 Joshua 348
WHEELER, Abram 308 332 Almira
  A 348 Amasa 346 Aruna 363
  Arunta 334 Augusta L 221 349
  363 B Jane 347 David Jr 333 E E
  248 Ebenezer 334 350 Elmina 66
  Elvira 348 Fred L 304 Jacob 254
  334 James 240 Joel 252 John A
  352 Levi W 295 Lewis S 353
  Lucretia 330 Lyman 148 Mary
  (Woodman) 240 Octavia F
  Rebecca 336 347 Reed B 337
  Robert F 346 Roscoe P 353
  Sarah J 349 Victoria 353 Wesley
  D 347 William W 291
WHITAMORE, Laura 350
WHITE, C H 231 C H 5 Charles 345
  Charles D 351 Daniel Major 294
  Frank 290 291 Harriet A 360
  James 390 Jane 139 341 390
  Lydia 224 Minerva 161 Minerva
  L 343 Nehemiah 157 Rachael
  (Curtis) 157 Rev 260
WHITEHOUSE, C A 357 C H 250
  Charles A 242 Mary Lousia

WHITEHOUSE (Cont.)
  (Woodman) 242 Ruby 242 Ruth
  Lousia 242
WHITEMORE, Mary F 354
WHITING, 24 Cynthia (Curtis) 158
  Dolly 58 John 271 John Jr 330
  Lois 329 Sally 377 Sarah 70 73
  397 William 158
WHITMAN, Abiah 84 Eleanor 125
  Eleanor 84 Oren 332 Royal E
  293
WHITNEY, Ann 77 George 340
  Joseph 326 Luella 243 Samuel
  328
WHITTEMORE, Frank E 242 Laura
  Ann 243
WHITTIER, George D 355 Mr 11
WHITTING, Priscilla 323
WICKETT, Abram 285
WICOMB, Mehetable 239
WIGGLESWORTH, Elizabeth A 348
WIGHT, Bertus E 359 Mrs B E
  (DYER) 372
WILBER, Mary H 348
WILDES, Asa W 291 Sarah 64
WILDS, Mabel 312
WILEY, Dole B 356
WILLEY, James B 339
WILLIAM THE CONQUEROR, 42
WILLIAMS, Betsey (Boothby) 312 C
  H 256 Dr 55 Ella M 360 Fidelia
  340 Horatio 312 Horatio L 346
  Minot 353 Philip 326 Rizilla A
  338
WILLIAMSON, Lizzie D 351
WILLIS, Lydia 69 Rhoda 69 Serena
  Deane 234 382 Susan Dean 392
  Thomas 69 Veranus 400
WILLS, George E 359
WILSON, David S 345
WINDSHIP, Mehitable 18
WING, Abigail (Gilbert) 78 Adna 78
  Adna 170 Alena M 171 356
  Alfred S 170 Alfred S 361 Alfred

WING (Cont.)
  194 Allen 170 Allen 332 Allen
  169 Almira 169 Alpheus 228
  Ann 338 Ardelia 216 Ardelia
  (Coffin) 170 Arland J 171 181
  Austin H 357 Bachelder 169
  Bachler 6 Benjamin Jr 228 Betsy
  M 357 Beulah A 181 171 Blanch
  M 360 Caleb 78 85 169 170 259
  325 326 Carrie H (Boothby) 216
  Carrie (Boothby) 171 Celia May
  361 Charles A 351 Charles Dr
  136 Clara Cornelia (Howard)
  194 Clara (Howard) 170 Clara A
  171 Desire (Turner) 85 Desire
  (Turner) 170 Diana T 384 Diana
  384 408 Diana T 78 341 Diana
  170 171 Diana T 225 Doane S
  296 Dora Lovisa (Howard) 181
  Dora L (Howard) 171 Duane
  Snyder 170 Duane S 194 350
  Ellen M 171 Elsie 194 Elsie
  Howard 170 171 Elsie H 170
  Experience 169 170 325 F B 148
  family 417 169 Fannie (Bates)
  222 Frances A (Bates) 171
  Francis A 358 Fred B 171
  Freeland Q 358 George W 352
  George H 361 Georgianna P 359
  Hannah 169 Harold 171 Hattie
  M 361 Herbert A 360 Hiram C
  170 171 J C 303 James 169 324
  James S 353 Joanna 170 171 340
  Joanna (Gilbert) 170 John 324
  Junius C 154 171 Junius C 181
  356 358 388 Junius Carlos 170
  Lafayette C 354 Lucinda
  (George) 110 Lucy A 357
  Martha 137 Mary 169 170 329
  Mary (Gott) 136 Mary Emma
  (Hammond) 154 Mary F 356
  Mehitable 169 170 327 Mr 247
  Nabby 169 323 O D 148 250
  Obed 228 Obed Sr 228 Octavia

WING (Cont.)
(Brewster) 171 Octavia Ann
(Brewster) 148 Ormand T 148
170 171 341 Orville D 171
Pamelia 117 Perley 359 Phebe
169 170 Rhoda (True) 228
Richard 360 Roswell S 171
Salmon 216 Salmon A 170
Samuel 110 330 Sands 169 170
Stella A 171 181 Stephen 216
Stephen A 171 Stephen Arland
170 Stephen D 170 171 Thomas
136 Thomas 22 Vesta C 349
Vesta Coffin 170 Vesta E 355
William 169-171 222 346
William H 353 358 William J
357 Willis 170
WING, Lewis H, G.A.R. Post 111
WINGATE, Frederic 182 James 163
Jonathan 163 Laura Ann (Otis)
163 Mary 163 Mr 163
WINSLOW, Aaron 274 Benjn P 351
WINTHROP, Mr 134
WISCONSIN, 102 140 152 219
Fond-du-lac 26 36 37 39
Watertown 37
WITCH-CRAFT TRIALS, 63 64
WITHAM, Albion 287 Mr 247
WOOD, Annie 136 340, Melvina J
(Ramsdell) 219 Mr 247 R E 219
Samuel 329 Simon Jr 6 Susie G
218 Susie G 359
WOODBURY, Laura D 166 Louisa
C 407 Mary 40 41 229 414
WOODFORD, Clara 96 Clara O 351
WOODMAN, Abbie 52 Adda
Florence 242 Addie F 268
Almarilla 242 Ammi 52 108 333
Amos 241 325 Anna 240 Annie
(Sewall) 240 Archelaus 238 Azel
334 Benjamin 92 107 108 239
240 241 285 286 288 332
Benjamin Capt 242 Benjamin Jr
108 243 Carrie (Thomas) 164

WOODMAN (Cont.)
Catherine (Smith) 240 Charles
108 242 349 Charles Aubry 52
Clark 52 David 7 239 240 Deane
242 Dorothy 239 Dorothy
(Moody) 239 Edward 108 238
239 Edward Kent 243 Elizabeth
239 240 Elizabeth (Fenderson)
164 Elizabeth (Longfellow) 240
Elizabeth (Stevens) 239 Ellen 52
Emily 108 242 347 Ephraim 164
241 326 Ephraim W 164 295
Esther (Weeks) 240 family 52
238 Frances (Strickland) 164
Frank E (Whittemore) 242 Frank
N 243 Frank Newell 243 Gladys
243 Hannah 52 Hannah (Hilton)
239 Hannah (Lane) 52 108
Helen (Welch) 243 Henry 108
242 250 264 Henry F 354 356
Henry Frost 242 Ivey 164 Jason
108 242 250 Jerusha A (Haden)
242 Joanna 238 Joanna
(Leadbetter) 107 108 John 108
239 240 241 John E 293 350
John Elmore 243 Jonathan 239
240 Joseph 240 Joshua 239 240
Joshua 241 Julia 108 Julia A 356
Kenneth Elmore 243 Laura 52
Laura Ann (Whittemore) 243
Louisa M (Gott) 242 Luella
(Whitney) 243 Martha (Deane)
242 Mary 239 Mary 240 241
Mary L 357 Mary Lousia 242
Mary (Adams) 240 Mary (Field)
239 Mary (Goodridge) 239
Mehetable 239 Mehetable
(Wicomb) 239 Moses 241 Mr 24
247 Nathan 240 241 Nellie M
(Swift) 243 Olive 241 331 Olive
B 164 Olive (Bryant) 241 Olive
(Gray) 240 Oliver Otis 164
Pamelia 241 Rosanna 241
Rosannah 327 Ruth 239 Sally

WOODMAN (Cont.)
  107 241 332 333 Sally (Bryant) 241 Samuel 241 Sarah 239 240 Sarah (Hiscock) 164 Sarah (Mighill) 239 Sarah B (Otis) 164 Sewall 108 241 243 292 Shuball 241 Stephen 240 Susan 241
WOODS, Charles R 184
WOODSOM, Benjamin R 342
WOODSUM, Rosanna (Woodman) 241 Sumner 327 William 327 William Elder 241
WOODWARD, Amos 96 Amos H 345 Eunice (Foss) 96
WORK, Hattie A 352
WORTHING, Helen M 342 Sally Ann 342
WRIGHT, A S 177 Herbert 304 Millie M Mrs 55 Nellie M Mrs 359 O A 303
WYER, Josiah 235
WYMAN, Louisa 52 Lovisa 108 Susan J 360 W 256
YALE, John R 339
YORK, Hannah 410
YOUNG, Augusta M 167 348 Jane 222 Job 147
YOUNGLOVE, Mr 43

www.ingramcontent.com/pod-product-compliance
Lightning Source LLC
Chambersburg PA
CBHW071429300426
44114CB00013B/1371